ALMANAC
OF THE
Christian
Church

AN
ALMANAC
OF THE
Christian
Church

WILLIAM D. BLAKE

BETHANY HOUSE PUBLISHERS
MINNEAPOLIS, MINNESOTA 55438
A Division of Bethany Fellowship, Inc.

Copyright © 1987
William Blake
All Rights Reserved

Published by Bethany House Publishers
A Division of Bethany Fellowship, Inc.
6820 Auto Club Road, Minneapolis, Minnesota 55438

Printed in the United States of America

Library of Congress Cataloging-in-Publication Data

Blake, William, 1946–
    An almanac of the Christian church.

    Includes index.
    1. Chronology, Ecclesiastical.   I. Title.
CE81.B53 1987   270'.02'02   87-32643
ISBN 0-87123-897-7

Dedication

For Cyndi, Andrew, Erin, Adam
—Four special people who have taught me
that God is the giver of many good gifts.

WILLIAM D. BLAKE received a B.A. from Asbury College in Christian Education, an M.A. from Wheaton College in Theological Studies, and is pursuing a Ph.D. at St. Louis University. Having served several churches as the Director of Christian Education, he also began a series of articles called "A Calendar of Christian Days" which first appeared in *Eternity* magazine throughout 1984. The success of this series and his rich theological background led to the writing of this book. His family includes three children, and he and his wife make their home near St. Louis, Missouri.

Foreword

It is entirely possible that someone will pick this book up and say, "What use is *An Almanac of the Christian Church*? Who really cares what happened on such and such a day years ago, or even recently?"

The Christian Church has always opposed this ignorance of its past. Why? I think I can answer that question from my own experience in reading this book.

First, I found this almanac to be a stimulus to praise. As I read of Augustine, John Chrysostom, Bernard of Clairvaux, Luther, Calvin and many others, I was reminded of the influence that so many believers have had throughout history. But this book is much more than a mere reminder, it is a call to praise for the example and testimony that God's people have left.

Second, in an age that is highly existential and antihistorical, these pages confronted me with a continuity that gives meaning to the present. For example, to read that on Jan. 1, Basil the Great died in 379, or to be told that Aimee Semple McPherson opened the doors of her famous Angelus Temple in Los Angeles in 1923, is to put my own era into perspective and connect it with former workers in God's vineyard.

Finally, reading this book gave me a sense of the communion of the saints, reminding me that I am not alone in this world. I join with the lives, the voices and the acts of ten thousands and more who have gone before me to praise Christ and to work for his kingdom.

Therefore, reading *An Almanac of the Christian Church* is no dry exercise in historical facts, but a powerful and prayerful encounter with a tradition, a people and a communion. William Blake has done the church a marvelous service by making this contribution to our spiritual lives.

Robert Webber
Wheaton College

Preface

How well do we understand the beginnings of our church? Who were its founders? How did our denomination get its name? Why is our theological tradition "the right one"? What about those religious communities across the street, or on the other side of town? Do members of other churches also go to heaven? Do they also have a spiritual heritage of which to be proud, a theological tradition worth knowing something about?

Modern church members are often unaware of the historical forces that served in shaping our individual denominational traditions. Much ink was spilled—and not a little blood!—that we might clothe the body of our Christian beliefs with a well-tailored theological wardrobe—each garment an interweaving of confession, tradition and liturgy.

As a Protestant, I am concerned by my limited understanding of early Catholic tradition. Sadly, many denominational seminaries in their theological history courses have little to say about the great advances in Christendom achieved prior to the Reformation. Yet we would all agree God did not wait 15 centuries after His Son's resurrection to activate His mission to the Gentiles. God instituted our Christian era in the days of the New Testament—if not before. The church that Jesus founded has existed longer than a mere five centuries. It goes back at least 2,000 years!

We who would seriously follow the Christ of the New Testament cannot grow in our faith and remain in a social vacuum for long. Sooner or later, we who claim to be Christ's must bring to Scripture the questions and contexts of our daily experience—whether in the home, the community, our place of recreation, the school, office, factory or marketplace.

The answer to life's deepest questions begins with our comprehension of biblical truth. But it often takes deeper root when we acquaint ourselves with Christian heroes of earlier generations. God's people, in all ages and cultures, have fleshed out deep insights into God's will through their many different achievements; and we should learn of these if we would better understand the purposes of God. As beloved missionary-martyr Jim Elliot wrote in his journal:

> Noted again the importance of biography and history in learning God's ways. (11/17/1949)

When we thus acquaint ourselves with the "record" of God's will as it has been wrought through the lives of earlier saints, personal questions arising within our own Christian experience begin to find workable answers. As English nonconformist clergyman J. C. Philpot advised, in writing to a friend:

> Many children of God who are sound in the truth, though they

cannot explain their own views, can understand them when they are put forth by others. (12/3/1860)

Then why an "almanac"? Why divide up Christian history in so artificial a manner? Because an almanac entertains as it informs. An almanac is a compendium filled with little-known curiosities, mixed together with more helpful and needed information. For many, an almanac is an unpretentious delight to read—whether scanning, selectively choosing, or extensively absorbing its contents.

Unfortunately for the book trade, busy readers today require information that may be accessed (or set aside) for various lengths of time. J. C. Philpot, in another letter, sets down an apt description of popular reading material:

It may be taken up and laid down at vacant moments without, as in systematic writings, losing the thread . . . . (9/11/1854)

This demand is also well-served by the "almanac." Undiluted history can become oppressively time-consuming and, to some, quite boring. But bite-sized, historical anecdotes beg from the reader only a moment, while at the same time offering the serious student insights into the more important workings of that almanac's particular field of concentration.

In the pages that follow, several thousand date-documented "Christian moments" have been set forth in easy-to-read historical vignettes. Included are the lives of hundreds of the church's earliest theologians and pastors, missionaries and hymnwriters, evangelists and Bible scholars, denominational and religious leaders. Read of the early persecutions of the church, the Crusades, the ecumenical councils, famous missionary campaigns and their ensuing revivals and reforms. Discover little-known details regarding some of the more recent translations of the Scriptures. Share the intimate thoughts of such pioneers in the faith as Martin Luther, John Calvin, John Wesley, George Whitefield, John Newton, David Brainerd and others. Follow also the prayers, the correspondence and the journals of more recent interpreters of the Christian faith: Dietrich Bonhoeffer, Peter Marshall, Jim Elliot, Dag Hammarskjold, C. S. Lewis, Francis Schaeffer and more.

These assorted capsules of Christian history are designed to delight the curious and encourage the serious to quest after spiritual excellence. For the young believer, who seeks role models through whom to define and clarify his own unique vision, herein are contained a hundred examples of life callings that led to Christian destiny—people whose memory God has preserved down to our present generation.

And what of the more mature disciples who dare believe that other churches may also "have it right"? For them, these pages offer abundant records of the great good (and some bad) achieved by God's people within the many Christian traditions. Here is a sourcebook of theological origins spanning the past 20 centuries—a multifaceted portrait of how Adam's twice-born race fulfilled that petition in the Lord's Prayer that entreats:

Thy Kingdom come, thy will be done in earth. . . .

Does *An Almanac of the Christian Church* have something to say to you? Turn to your own date of birth and test it for yourself. Do the lives and events recorded on that date affirm, rebuke or otherwise widen the horizons of your own Christian faith? Then read on.

As time permits, investigate some other important calendar dates in your life. But however you start, begin adding a new dimension to your faith by acquainting yourself with "the biography of the Bride"—the history of God's redeemed people. Discover some of the famous firsts and lasts, leasts and mosts—the beginnings and the endings of those persons and events associated with this most sacred of all human eras.

William D. Blake
St. Louis, Missouri
August 10, 1987

January

January 1

379 Death of Basil the Great (b.329), early Eastern church father. He was known as the Prelate among the three "Cappadocian Fathers," the other two being his brother, Gregory of Nyssa, and his lifelong friend, Gregory Nanzianzus. Basil lived an ascetic life doing works of benevolence, opposing Arianism, and writing books in defense of the deity of Christ and the Holy Spirit.

1484 Birth of Ulrich Zwingli, Swiss reformer, at Wildhaus, Switzerland. As a parish priest in Zurich, he left the Roman Catholic Church in 1525 after news of his secret marriage in 1522 was made public. He helped translate the Scriptures into German-Swiss and was instrumental in spreading the Reformation to German and Italian cantons in Switzerland.

1701 This date became Jan. 12 in the Swiss Canton of Basel when it adopted the Gregorian calendar (created by Pope Gregory XIII in 1582) to replace the older, more inaccurate Julian calendar (created by Julius Caesar in 46 B.C.).

1784 In colonial America, the Methodist movement within the Anglican Church officially seceded, forming a new Protestant denomination: the Methodist Episcopal Church.

1819 Birth of Philip Schaff, American church historian, at Chur, Switzerland. Coming to America in 1843, he became an outstanding leader in the German Reformed Church. Out of his immense literary output, perhaps his two most famous works are his eight-volume *History of the Christian Church* (1858–92) and his three-volume *The Creeds of Christendom* (1877).

1865 Birth of James Rowe, American hymnwriter, in Devonshire, England. Coming to America in 1890, he devoted most of his adult life to literary pursuits, writing songs and editing music journals. He is best remembered as the author of the hymns "Love Lifted Me" and "I Would Be Like Jesus."

1871 The Church of Ireland was officially disestablished. Owing its origin to St. Patrick, the church very early retained her independence from Rome. Between 1200 and 1500, as the influence and authority of English government grew stronger, the Irish church became more and more dependent upon the state. It underwent its own reformation but a general spiritual decline during the early 19th century led to the 1869 Act of Disestablishment, which went into effect two years later.

1887 Birth of Vincent Taylor, British New Testament scholar and Methodist clergyman. He started his first pastorate in 1909, and in 1930 moved into education, thereafter associating with such schools as the University of Leeds, London University, and the University of Wales. He authored many scholarly works, specializing in the Gospels.

1907 American Congregational missionary Howard A. Walter, while teaching English at Waseda University in Tokyo, Japan, penned the words to the hymn, "I Would Be True, for There Are Those Who Trust Me."

1918 This date became Jan. 14 in Finland, Russian-held Poland, and western Russia when those governments adopted the Gregorian calendar.

1919 Death of Lewis Hartsough (b.1828), American Methodist clergyman who wrote both words and music for "I am Coming, Lord." He served churches in New York, Utah, Wyoming, Iowa, and the Dakotas. He also wrote a number of hymns and hymn tunes for a published collection of hymns called *The Revivalist*, a work which went into 11 editions.

1923 Evangelist Aimee Semple McPherson opened the famous 5,000-seat Angelus Temple in Los Angeles. Today, the Angelus Temple is the headquarters of the International Church of the Foursquare Gospel, the church body Mrs. McPherson incorporated in 1927 and served as president until her death in 1944.

1937 Death of J. Gresham Machen (b.1881), American Presbyterian scholar and apologist. After teaching New Testament at Princeton Seminary 1906–29, he founded Westminster Theological Seminary, serving as president and professor of New Testament 1929–37. In 1936 Machen and 16 other clergy and laymen founded the Orthodox Presbyterian Church, with Machen chosen as the first Moderator. An active scholar and writer, Machen never married. His most enduring writings include: *New Testament Greek for Beginners* (1923), *What Is Faith?* (1925), and *The Virgin Birth of Christ* (1930, 1932).

1955 English scholar and Christian apologist C.S. Lewis, after nearly 30 years of teaching at Magdalen College, Oxford University, assumed the newly created professor's chair of medieval and Renaissance English at Cambridge University.

1975 The World Literature Crusade moved into its present headquarters at Chatsworth, California. Founded in Prince Albert, Saskatchewan, Canada, in 1886, this evangelical, interdenominational mission agency presently works in nearly 50 countries, distributing Bibles, planting churches and supporting evangelistic efforts of nationals.

1977 Jacqueline Means, wife of an Indiana truck driver and mother of four, became the first woman in the U.S. to be ordained a priest in the Episcopal Church.

January 2

1744 David Brainerd, colonial missionary to the New England Indians, commented in his journal: "We are a long time in learning that all our strength and salvation is in God."

1792 Death of Edward Perronet (b.1726), Swiss-born English clergyman and poet. A close friend of John and Charles Wesley at one time, Perronet spent much of his life attacking abuses within the Church of England. Today he is remembered best as author of the hymn of praise "All Hail the Power of Jesus' Name."

1828 Birth of Jeremiah E. Rankin, American Congregational clergyman, in Thornton, New Hampshire. Ordained in 1855, he served pastorates in five different states. He became president of Howard University in Washington, D.C., in 1889. He is best remembered as author of the hymns "Tell It to Jesus" and "God Be with You Till We Meet Again."

1878 Death of Edward Caswall (b.1814), an English clergyman who left the Anglican Church in 1847 to become a Roman Catholic. He published many hymns during his lifetime, but few were used outside the Roman Catholic Church because of their doctrinal content. Among Protestants, however, he is remembered as the English translator of two popular hymns: "Jesus, the Very Thought of Thee" and "When Morning Gilds the Skies."

1914 Birth of Rachel Saint, American missionary, in Jenkintown, Pennsylvania. A member of Wycliffe Bible Translators, Rachel was responsible for the conversion of Dayuma, the first Auca Indian converted to Christ. Rachel's brother, Nate Saint, was among five American missionaries martyred by the Auca Indians of Ecuador in 1956.

1921 Calvary Episcopal Church in Pittsburgh, Pennsylvania, sponsored the first religious program in the U.S. to be broadcast by radio. It was aired over Pittsburgh radio station KDKA.

1924 Death of Sabine Baring-Gould (b.1834), an Anglican clergyman with extraordinarily wide-ranging interests and literary achievements. He wrote many books on history, biography, poetry and fiction. He is best remembered as the author of two popular hymns: "Onward, Christian Soldiers" and "Now the Day Is Over."

1945 Death of Vedanayakum Samuel Azariah (b.1874), the first Indian bishop of the Anglican Church in India. Ordained a deacon in 1909, Azariah was consecrated a bishop in 1912. A small diocese was created for him at Dornakal, India, with 6 clergy and 8,000 Christians. When the Anglican Church in India became an independent denomination, Azariah's diocese had grown to the size of her mother church, with over 100,000 Christians! He served as bishop for 33 years, leaving behind a Christian community of 400,000.

1968 Swiss Reformed theologian Karl Barth declared in a letter: "In the Church of Jesus Christ there can and should be no non-theologians."

January 3

1521 At age 38, German reformer Martin Luther was excommunicated by Pope Leo X from the Roman Catholic Church for challenging many of the church's doctrines and abuses. Luther soon after went into hiding for eight months at the Wartburg Castle, where he began his famous translation of the Bible into German.

1828 The parents of Dwight L. Moody, Edwin Moody and Betsy Holton, both of Northfield, Massachusetts, married. Dwight Lyman was born Feb. 5, 1837, their sixth child. Edwin died in 1841, leaving behind nine children—seven boys and two girls. D.L. Moody left home in 1854 to work in a shoe store owned by his mother's brother in Boston. His Sunday-school teacher, Edward Kimball, led him to Christ there the following year, on April 21, 1855. Moody went on to become the most successful American evangelist of his day. His mother Betsy became a Christian at the age of 70.

1830   Birth of Alexander Ewing, Scottish veteran of the Crimean War. He studied music at the University of Heidelberg in Germany during his earlier years and is remembered primarily for only one piece of music he composed: the hymn tune EWING, to which we sing "Jerusalem, the Golden."

1840   Birth of Father Damien (Joseph de Veuster), Roman Catholic missionary to Hawaii, at Tremelo, Belgium. A member of the Picpus Fathers religious order, Fr. Damien volunteered in 1873 to work with the lepers on the island of Molokai. He contracted the fatal disease in 1883 and died in 1889.

1884   Birth of E. Stanley Jones, Methodist missionary, in Clarksville, Maryland. He first went to India after his ordination in 1907. In 1928 he became a Methodist bishop, but resigned his position soon after so that he might return to Far Eastern Missions. A prolific devotional writer, his best-known works include *The Christ of the Indian Road* (1925) and *Abundant Living* (1936).

1918   Death of Annie Sherwood Hawks (b.1835), American Baptist hymnwriter. Encouraged in youth by her pastor, hymn-compiler Robert Lowry, she penned more than 400 hymns in her lifetime. Perhaps her most enduring hymn is one for which Lowry himself composed the melody: "I Need Thee Every Hour."

1930   American Congregational missionary to the Philipines Frank C. Laubach noted in a letter: "I have done nothing but open windows—God has done all the rest."

1958   Death of Blanche Kerr Brock (b.1888), American sacred music artist. Blanche and her husband, Virgil P. Brock, worked together for years in evangelism and hymnwriting. Two of Virgil's hymns that Blanche set to music are still popular: "He's a Wonderful Savior to Me" and "Beyond the Sunset."

1984   Death of Dr. Jacob Gartenhaus (b.1896), founder and first president of the International Board of Jewish Missions, Inc. Founded in 1949 in Atlanta, Georgia, I.B.J.M. is an evangelical, interdenominational organization ministering to Jews in the U.S. and nearly a dozen countries overseas. Headquartered in Chattanooga, Tennessee, since 1971, I.B.J.M. engages primarily in radio broadcasting, church planting and literature distribution.

January 4

1528   Ferdinand of Austria, younger brother of Holy Roman Emperor Charles V, became the first secular ruler to issue a mandate forbidding the Anabaptist religious movement.

1581   Birth of Archbishop James Ussher, Anglican primate, in Dublin, Ireland. He is remembered chiefly today for his book, *Annals of the Old and New Testaments* (1654), which first set forth the teaching that Adam's race was created only 6,000 years ago. Many Bible students still adhere to Ussher's conclusions. His biblical chronology has been incorporated in many editions of the Bible.

1745   Birth of Johann Jacob Griesbach, New Testament scholar, at Butzbach, Germany. One of the earliest pioneers in textual (or lower) criticism, Griesbach's two-volume critical edition of the Greek New Testament (1775–77) laid the foundation for all later scholarly work on the original Greek text.

1821 Death of Mother Elizabeth Bayley Seton (b.1774), founder of the American Sisters of Charity, a Roman Catholic religious order, and first American-born Roman Catholic saint. Beginning in 1809, Mrs. Seton helped lay the foundation for the present system of Catholic parochial schools in the U.S. In 1975, she was canonized by Pope Paul VI.

1947 Presbyterian clergyman the Reverend Peter Marshall (*A Man Called Peter*) was officially elected Chaplain of the U.S. Senate. Serving until his untimely death on Jan. 25, 1949, he was the 54th chaplain chosen in the Senate's history and the first Presbyterian appointed since 1879.

1953 *The Catholic Hour* aired for the first time, over NBC television. This long-running series (aired through Aug. 1970) was produced by NBC in cooperation with the National Council of Catholic Men.

January 5

1527 Felix Manz (b.ca.1498), Swiss Anabaptist reformer, was drowned in the Limmat River by Swiss religious authorities as punishment for his belief and practice of "rebaptizing." Manz thus became the first Protestant in history to be martyred at the hands of Protestants.

1782 Birth of Robert Morrison, first Protestant missionary to China, in Northumberland, England. In 1807 the London Missionary Society ordained and sent Morrison to Canton where he concentrated on literary work. He completed a translation of the entire Bible in Chinese by 1823.

1877 Birth of Henry Sloane Coffin, American Presbyterian educator, in New York City. Coffin was both a clergyman and a professor of practical theology at Union Theological Seminary, New York City; but he is perhaps best remembered today as the English translator of the hymn of petition "O Come, O Come, Emmanuel."

1906 Birth of Kathleen Kenyon, the British archeologist who supervised a major excavation of ancient Jericho. She was the first to use radioactive carbon dating on artifacts from the site.

1910 Death of Timothy R. Matthews (b.1826), English clergyman who composed the hymn tune MARGARET, to which we sing "Thou Didst Leave Thy Throne." He composed more than 100 hymn tunes during his lifetime.

1949 U.S. Senate Chaplain Peter Marshall, less than three weeks before his death at age 47, prayed: "Our Father in heaven, give us the long view of our work and our world. Help us to see that it is better to fail in a cause that will ultimately succeed than to succeed in a cause that will ultimately fail."

1964 Pope Paul VI, during an unprecedented pilgrimage by air to the Holy Land, met with Greek Ecumenical Patriarch Athenagoras I in Jerusalem. This was the first such meeting between leaders of the Roman Catholic and Greek Orthodox churches in over 500 years.

1972 In Britain, the Congregational Church in England and Wales and the Presbyterian Church of England voted to merge. The new church was named the United Reformed Church.

1982 A federal judge in Arkansas struck down a state law requiring the teaching of the biblical theory of creation, ruling that the teaching of creation science violated the constitutional requirement of the separation of state and organized religion.

January 6

1412 Birth of Joan of Arc, French heroine, in Domremy. At age 16, claiming to be guided by divine voices, she led the French to victory over the English at Orleans during the Hundred Years War. The English later captured her and burned her at the stake for heresy at age 19. Exonerated of all charges in 1456, she was canonized in 1920 by Pope Benedict XV.

1740 Birth of John Fawcett, Baptist clergyman and educator, in Yorkshire, England. Ordained in 1763, he held several pastorates before founding Rawdon College. Fawcett penned many sermons, essays and over 150 hymns. Two of these hymns are often sung at the end of religious services: "Blest Be the Tie That Binds" and "Lord, Dismiss Us with Thy Blessing."

1754 John Wesley, founder of Methodism, commented in his journal: "I began writing *Notes on the New Testament*, a work which I should scarcely ever have attempted had I not been so ill as to be unable to travel or preach, and yet well enough to be able to read and write."

1850 Famed English Baptist preacher, Charles Haddon Spurgeon, at the age of 16, was converted to Christ. Spurgeon had walked into a Methodist chapel to warm himself during a snowstorm. Less than 15 people were present, and even the minister did not appear. A layman preached on the text in Isaiah 45:22: "Look unto me, and be ye saved. . . ." Spurgeon did, and his life touched off a new era of evangelism in London.

1884 Death of Gregor Johann Mendel (b.1822), Austrian-born (modern Czechoslovakia) Roman Catholic monk whose botanic experiments in the monastery garden were published in 1866 but ignored by botanists until 1900. Mendel's laws of genetics have become the basis of the modern theory of heredity.

1887 Birth of Virgil P. Brock, American music evangelist. He and his wife Blanche were known as "The Singing Brocks," one of the outstanding hymnwriting teams of the first half of this century. Two of their most enduring Gospel songs are "Beyond the Sunset" and "He's a Wonderful Savior to Me."

1896 Birth of Vergilius T.A. Ferm, American Lutheran theologian, in Sioux City, Iowa. As professor of philosophy for many years at the College of Wooster in Ohio, Ferm authored and edited many important works on religion. One work still in print today is *The Encyclopedia of Religion* (1945), which he edited.

1934 The Rev. Peter Deyneka founded the Slavic Gospel Association, in Chicago. Headquartered today in Wheaton, Illinois, the S.G.A. is an interdenominational mission agency engaged primarily in radio broadcasting, evangelism and Bible production and distribution to nations in Europe, and Central and South America.

1966 Harold Robert Perry, age 49, became the auxiliary Bishop of the Roman Catholic Archdiocese of New Orleans. Consecrated at New Orleans' St. Louis Basilica, Perry was only the second black since 1875 to be elevated to a bishopric in the U.S.

January 7

1584 This date became Jan. 17 when Bohemia (Austria) and the rest of Germany adopted the Gregorian calendar (created by Pope Gregory XIII in 1582) to replace the older, more inaccurate Julian calendar (created by Julius Caesar in 46 B.C.).

1597 This date became Jan. 17 in the Swiss canton of Appenzell, when the Gregorian calendar was adopted to replace the Julian calendar.

1715 Death of Francois Fenelon (b. 1651), French theologian and mystic. As a Roman Catholic priest, he served as a friend of mystic Madame Guyon as well as court tutor to the young Duke of Burgundy, the grandson of Louis XIV. Though loyal to his church, his involvement with the mystic and Jansenist controversies eventually brought him censure by Pope Innocent XII.

1829 Birth of Frederick Whitfield, Anglican clergyman and author of the hymn "Oh, How I Love Jesus," in Shropshire, England. During his lifetime he published about 30 volumes of prose.

1832 Birth of Thomas DeWitt Talmage, American Presbyterian clergyman, near Bound Brook, New Jersey. One-time chaplain in the Union Army, he later became a famous lecturer and syndicated religious writer both in America and Europe. He was once editor of *The Christian Herald.*

1844 Birth of St. Bernadette Soubirous, the French peasant girl who, at age 14, had several visions of the Virgin Mary in a cave near the Gave River close to her birthplace in Lourdes. The site of her visions became an important center for pilgrimages, and many have claimed healing in the waters of the grotto at Lourdes.

1856 Famed English preacher Charles H. Spurgeon, age 22, married Susannah Thompson, one of the parishioners at the church where he was pastoring: New Park Street Baptist Chapel, Southwark, London.

1858 Birth of Henry W. Frost, American missionary pioneer. Dr. Frost was responsible for establishing an American headquarters for the China Inland Mission. Founded 1865 in Great Britain by missionary J. Hudson Taylor, C.I.M. relocated its offices to America in 1901, changed its official title to the Overseas Missionary Fellowship (O.M.F.) in 1965, and has been headquartered in Robesonia, Pennsylvania, since 1974.

1868 William B. Bradbury (b. 1816), the composer of the hymn tune for "Jesus Loves Me" (CHINA), died after publishing 59 collections of sacred and secular music. His most enduring hymn tunes include BRADBURY ("Savior, Like a Shepherd Lead Us"), WOODWORTH ("Just As I Am"), YARBROUGH ("Take My Life, and Let It Be"), and the hymn melodies to "He Leadeth Me," "The Solid Rock" and "Sweet Hour of Prayer."

1918 Death of Julius Wellhausen (b.1844), German theologian and biblical scholar. He is best known for his elaboration of the Graf-Wellhausen theory which states that the final form of the Pentateuch was arranged sometime after 587 B.C., and that different parts were written by different authors at different times, rather than solely by Moses.

1921 Death of Alexander Whyte (b.1836), Scottish clergyman. Starting in 1909, he was minister of the largest and most influential congregation of the Free Church of Scotland, as well as professor of New Testament Literature at New College, Edinburgh. He was a respected preacher and author of a number of devotional books.

1934 Billy Sunday, baseball player-turned-evangelist, began a two-week revival service at the age of 70 in Calvary Baptist Church in New York City. Born in 1862, Sunday played National League baseball between 1883–1891. Converted to Christ in 1886, Sunday left the game in 1891, became an evangelist of the Gospel in 1893, and preached to thousands from then until his death in 1935.

January 8

1198 Italian cardinal Lotario di Segni was elected the church's 175th pope, taking the name Innocent III. Pope Celestine III, Innocent's uncle, had died (b. 1106) the same day. Under Innocent III, the medieval papacy reached the peak of its authority and influence because his guiding doctrine submitted earthly rulers to the rule of the church. His career climaxed in the Fourth Lateran Council (1215), which he called.

1792 Birth of Lowell Mason, American sacred music composer, in Medfield, Massachusetts. He spent his life stimulating religious community life by organizing church choirs and fostering congregational singing. During his lifetime he published more than 40 collections of music, and wrote or arranged more than 1,000 hymn tunes. The most enduring of his sacred melodies include BETHANY ("Nearer My God, to Thee"), DENNIS ("Blest Be the Tie That Binds"), HAMBURG ("When I Survey the Wondrous Cross"), OLIVET ("My Faith Looks Up to Thee"), UXBRIDGE ("Be Present at Our Table, Lord") and the melody to "Work, for the Night Is Coming."

1849 During the Italian Revolution of 1848–49, a popular uprising in the Papal States deprived Pope Pius IX of his temporal powers and forced him to flee to Gaeta on the Italian Coast.

1866 C.F.W. Walther, founder of the Missouri Synod of the Lutheran church, observed in a letter: "If a person were to receive whatever he wishes in temporal things, he would still not have peace, but his wishes would only grow that much larger. The joy of the world is like drinking salt water—the more you drink, the thirstier you get."

1881 Birth of Clovis G. Chappell, American Methodist clergyman, in Flatwoods, Tennessee. He became a popular speaker during the first half of this century and filled Methodist pulpits in six different southern Methodist conferences. He also published several devotional collections on various topics under the title *Sermons on. . . .*

1945 Death of Henry W. Frost (b.1858), American missionary pioneer who was responsible for establishing the American headquarters for the China Inland Mission. Founded in 1865 in Great Britain by missionary J. Hudson Taylor, C.I.M. transferred its offices to America in 1901, changed its official title to Overseas Missionary Fellowship (O.M.F.) in 1965, and has been headquartered in Robesonia, Pennsylvania, since 1974.

1945 The New Tribes Mission held its first training session at its California Boot Camp. Founded 1942 in Los Angeles by Paul W. Fleming, N.T.M. is a fundamentalist, interdenominational mission society involved in Bible translation, church planting, and the production and distribution of Christian literature in 18 countries around the world.

1956 Jim Elliot and four other American missionaries were martyred by the Auca Indians in Ecuador. Jim Elliot, Peter Fleming, Edward McCully, Nate Saint and Roger Youderian were attempting to evangelize the Auca under the Plymouth Brethren and Missionary Aviation Fellowship. Elliot's widow Elisabeth, later published the story of their missionary work and martyrdom in her book *Through Gates of Splendor* (1957).

1979 Francis Schaeffer, American Presbyterian apologist for the Christian faith, noted in a letter: "A Christian is a person who has the possibility of innumerable new starts."

January 9

1569 St. Philip of Moscow, primate of the Russian Orthodox Church, was murdered by Czar Ivan IV ("Ivan the Terrible").

1777 Francis Asbury, pioneer Methodist bishop asserted in his journal: "My soul lives constantly as in the presence of God, and enjoys much of His divine favor. His love is better than life!"

1836 The first Roman Catholic college to be founded in the deep South, Spring Hill College, was established in Spring Hill, Arkansas.

1924 Death of British Armenian scholar Frederick C. Conybeare (b. 1856). After seven years at Oxford University (1881–1887), he resigned his chair to devote himself to research in the Armenian language. Due to the religious nature of the many manuscripts he studied, he later became interested in church history and in textual criticism, and how they both related to the Septuagint (the Greek Old Testament) and the New Testament.

1970 The Church of Jesus Christ of Latter-day Saints (The Mormons), after 140 years of unofficial discrimination against blacks within the church, issued an official letter stating their position on race relations within the church: ". . . Joseph Smith and all succeeding presidents of the church have taught that Negroes, while spirit children of a common father, and the progeny of our earthly parents Adam and Eve, were not yet to receive the priesthood, for reasons which we believe are known to God, but which He has not made fully known to man." (See also June 8, 1978.)

January 10

1514 The first section of the Complutensian Polyglot, the first multi-language Bible, was printed at Alcala (Complutum in Latin), Spain, under the direction of Arnold Guillen de Brocar. Begun in 1502 by Cardinal Francisco Ximenes, Archbishop of Toledo, the complete translation was published in six volumes when it was finished in 1517.

1760 John Newton, Anglican hymnwriter, commanded in a letter: "Take this for your motto; wear it in your heart; keep it in your eye: the cross of Christ is the tree of life and the tree of knowledge combined. Like a tree by the highwayside, it affords its shade to every passenger without distinction."

1858 Frances Ridley Havergal, English devotional poet and hymnwriter, while visiting in Germany at age 21, wrote the words to her first popular hymn "I Gave My Life for Thee."

1867 Birth of William P. Merrill, author of the hymn of invitation "Rise Up, O Men of God," in Orange, New Jersey. He was an American Presbyterian clergyman and author of a number of books and hymns.

1896 Death of Allen W. Chatfield (b.1808), Anglican clergyman. He spent the last 50 years of his life as Vicar of Much-Marcle, in Herefordshire, England. Today he is remembered as translator of the hymn of meditation "Lord Jesus, Think on Me."

1947 Peter Marshall, U.S. Senate chaplain, prayed: "May we resolve, God helping us, to be part of the answer, and not part of the problem."

1951 Jim Elliot remarked in his journal: "For youth there is a special wretchedness, for then the powers within conflict bluntly with the powers about. Restraint is most galling; release most desired. To compensate for these, unusual strength is a premium for youth; acuteness and retentive powers are more real in youth; victory sweetest in youth. In Solomonic wisdom I would rejoice in youth, yet remember my Creator."

January 11

1523 German reformer Martin Luther explained in a letter: "It is un-Christian, even unnatural, to derive benefit and protection from the community and not also to share in the common burden and expense; to let other people work but to harvest the fruit of their labors."

1777 Anglican hymnwriter John Newton disclosed in a letter: "A soul may be in as thriving a state when thirsting, seeking and mourning after the Lord as when actually rejoicing in Him; as much in earnest when fighting in the valley as when singing upon the mount; nay, dark seasons afford the surest and strongest manifestations of the power of faith."

1791 William White founded the First Day Society in Philadelphia, Pennsylvania. This marked the beginning of the American Missionary Fellowship, which was chartered in 1817. Today, this evangelical and interdenominational organization is headquartered in Villanova, Pennsylvania, and works primarily in the U.S. in missionary training and evangelism.

1817 Death of Yale president Timothy Dwight (b.1752). A native of Massachusetts and grandson of Jonathan Edwards, Dwight served as the eighth president of Yale College from 1795 until his death. He is remembered today as author of the hymn of testimony "I Love Thy Kingdom, Lord."

1843 Death of Francis Scott Key (b.1779), Maryland-born son of a Continental Army officer. Although usually touted as the author of America's national anthem, Key was also a devoted member of the Protestant Episcopal Church, and taught Bible classes in and around Washington, D.C. He was also among the organizers of the Domestic and Foreign Missionary Society, founded in 1820.

1877 Death of Charles W. Everest (b. 1814), American Roman Catholic priest. He was Rector of Hamden, Connecticut, from 1842–73. Today, however, he is better remembered as the author of the hymn of invitation "Take Up Thy Cross."

January 12

1167 Death of Aelred (a.k.a. Ailred, Ethelred) (b.1109), abbot of the Cistercian abbey of Rievaulx in Yorkshire, England. During his lifetime he was acquainted with both King David of Scotland and the Saxon ruler Edward the Confessor. He wrote a number of treatises on the Christian faith from a mystical viewpoint, and thus came to be known as "the English St. Bernard."

1584 This date became Jan. 22 in the Swiss cantons of Fribourg, Lucern, Schwyz, Solothurn, Unterwalden, Uri and Zug when they adopted the Gregorian calendar (created by Pope Gregory XIII in 1582, to replace the older, inaccurate Julian calendar created by Julius Caesar in 46 B.C.).

1730 Death of Johann Christoph Schwedler (b.1672), Silesian clergyman. Of more than 500 hymns he wrote during his lifetime, the one which still remains popular is "Ask Ye What Great Thing I Know."

1779 Francis Asbury, pioneer Methodist missionary, recorded in his journal: "If the Lord is pleased to work, who or what can hinder?"

1825 B.F. Westcott, British New Testament scholar, was born near Birmingham, England. Having held pastorates from 1850, he was appointed in 1870 to the chair of Regius Professor of Divinity at Cambridge. In 1881 he and F.J.A. Hort co-edited their famous critical text of the Greek New Testament, which is the basis for many current translations and critical editions of the New Testament.

1839 Scottish clergyman Robert Murray McCheyne observed in a letter: "It is not the tempest, nor the earthquake, nor the fire, but the still small voice of the Spirit that carries on the glorious work of saving souls."

1871 Death of Henry Alford (b.1810), English Bible scholar. His greatest literary contribution to critical biblical scholarship was *The Expositor's Greek Testament* (1849–61), which he edited. He is also remembered as author of the thanksgiving hymn "Come, Ye Thankful People, Come."

January 13

1501 The world's first hymnbook to be printed in a vernacular language was published in Prague. It contained 89 hymns in the Czech language, and was published by Severin for the Hussites of Bohemia. The name of the hymnal is no longer known, since the only surviving copy lacks the title page.

1559 Death of Menno Simons (b.1496), early Dutch Anabaptist leader. Though educated for the Roman Catholic priesthood, the martyrdom of his brother, a Munsterite Anabaptist, brought Menno to join the Anabaptists. Though he did not found the Mennonites, he played such a vital role in their early history that since 1550 they have borne his name.

1635 Birth of Philip Jacob Spener, founder of German pietism, in Alsace. While preaching in Frankfurt, he also held semiweekly Bible studies (known as *Collegia Pietatis*) in his home. The name came to be associated with his followers, who were eventually called Pietists.

1691 Death of George Fox (b.1624), founder of the Society of Friends (the Quakers). His associations early in life with both Puritan and Anabaptist circles caused Fox to leave the Anglican Church at age 23 and become a wandering preacher. He stressed the Holy Spirit's dwelling in the human heart, and every individual's direct communion with God. Fox founded the Quaker movement in 1660 at age 36.

1836 Alexander Whyte was born in Forfarshire, Scotland. A Free Church of Scotland clergyman, in 1909 he became minister of the largest and most influential congregation of his denomination and New Testament professor at New College, Edinburgh. His aggressiveness at "weeding out" the lazy among both ministers and students earned him the title "the last of the Puritans."

1909 Death of Josiah K. Alwood (b.1828), author of both the words and the music to the popular Gospel song "The Unclouded Day." An American United Brethren in Christ clergyman, he spent many years in the North Ohio Conference as a circuit rider and later as presiding elder. Alwood was returning home one clear moonlit night around 1890 when he penned the words and melody to the song.

1935 Death of Eleanor H. Hull (b.1860), founder of the Irish Text Society. Today her name endures for having arranged the English versification of the Irish hymn "Be Thou My Vision."

1936 American Baptist clergyman B.B. McKinney wrote the words and the tune to "Wherever He Leads, I'll Go," a few days before the opening of a Sunday school convention in Alabama.

1974 A Gallup poll on religious worship showed that fewer Protestants and Roman Catholics were attending weekly services than ten years earlier, but that attendance at Jewish services had increased over the same period.

January 14

1529 Spanish reformer Juan de Valdes (c. 1500–41) published his famous *Dialogue on Christian Doctrine*. Its emphasis on faith and religious feeling, as well as disregard of ecclesiastical authority, paved the way in Spain for Protestant ideas. But the treatise was condemned by the Spanish Inquisition, and Valdes himself was forced to flee from Spain, never to return again. His followers, called "Valdesians," included the names of Peter Martyr Vermigli and Bernardino Ochino.

1811 Birth of Rowland H. Prichard, composer of HYFRYDOL ("Jesus! What a Friend of Sinners!"). A Welsh musician and laborer of humble rank, he lived near his native Bala, North Wales, most of his life. A well-known amateur musician, he published a number of hymn tunes during his lifetime, but the most famous is HYFRYDOL ("Good Cheer" in Gaelic), written when he was less than 20 years old.

1875 Birth of Albert Schweitzer, theologian and missionary, in Alsace. Following publication of his classic theological work *The Quest of the Historical Jesus* (1906), he began the study of medicine. In 1913 he founded a hospital at Lambarene, Gabon (modern French Equatorial Africa), and served there for the next 52 years as a medical missionary.

1876 Death of Edmund Sears (b.1810), author of "It Came upon a Midnight Clear" and an American clergyman. Although a Unitarian, he once admitted that "I believe and preach the divinity of Christ." He authored a number of deeply spiritual books during his life, but is solely remembered for his famous Christmas carol.

1892 Birth of Martin Niemoller, German Lutheran pastor, in Westphalia. At the beginning of Nazi rule, he helped organize the Confessing Church in Germany. From 1937 to 1945, he was held prisoner in Nazi concentration camps for his opposition to Adolf Hitler.

1893 Pope Leo XIII appointed Archbishop Francesco Satolli as the Vatican's first Apostolic Delegate to the U.S. (Apostolic delegates represent the papacy in the country in which they reside, insuring that laws of the church are observed correctly. They also communicate special instructions from the pope, grant papal dispensations and absolutions, within the limits of their office.)

1972 Francis Schaeffer, Christian apologist, noted in a letter: "I have come to the conclusion that none of us in our generation feels as guilty about sin as we should or as our forefathers did."

1983 Death of Lillian Dickson (b.1901), founder of The Mustard Seed, Inc. Incorporated in Glendale, California, in 1954, The Mustard Seed is an interdenominational mission agency of evangelical Presbyterian tradition. Working primarily in Taiwan, Indonesia, and Papua New Guinea, The Mustard Seed engages in relief aid, public health and Christian education.

January 15

1841 Birth of Charles A. Briggs, American clergyman and theologian, in New York City. He was an outstanding scholar in Hebrew and its cognate languages at Union Theological Seminary (New York City). Two of his most enduring contributions to biblical scholarship, which he helped edit, were the *International Critical Commentary* (ICC) Series and the *Brown, Driver, & Briggs Hebrew-English Lexicon*.

1844 The University of Notre Dame was chartered under Roman Catholic auspices in Notre Dame, Indiana.

1852 Mt. Sinai Hospital was incorporated by Sampson Simson and eight associates in New York City. It was the first Jewish hospital in the U.S.

1863 Birth of Frederick George Kenyon, British archeologist and philologist, in London. Closely associated with the British Museum throughout his professional life, he devoted himself to discovering biblical parallels in ancient Greek papyrii, making them intelligible to laymen, and convincing laymen that science does not disprove the Bible. Perhaps his most reprinted work has been *Our Bible and the Ancient Manuscripts* (1895, rev. 1939).

1873 Founder of the Missouri Synod of the Lutheran church, C.F.W. Walther, warned in a letter: "Inactivity is the beginning of all vice."

1896 Birth of Dr. Jacob Gartenhaus, founder and first president of the International Board of Jewish Missions, in Austria. Gartenhaus founded I.B.J.M. in 1948 in Atlanta, Georgia. Today, this evangelical, interdenominational mission ministers to Jews both in the U.S. and in nearly a dozen countries overseas. Headquartered in Chattanooga, Tennessee, since 1971, I.B.J.M. engages primarily in radio broadcasting, church planting and literature distribution.

1898 Birth of Frank S. Mead, renowned American authority on the historical and contemporary church. His most reprinted (and updated) work has been the *Handbook of Denominations in the United States* (1951), now in its eighth edition (1985).

1915 Death of Mary Slessor (b.1848), Scottish missionary to West Africa. Converted under Presbyterian influence in her teens, Mary first sailed to Nigeria in 1876, and worked continuously with tribal peoples until her death nearly 40 years later. She possessed an uncanny insight into the African mind, and worked to eliminate witchcraft, drunkenness, twin-killing and other cruel customs among the Ibo people.

1951 Death of Harry A. Ironside (b.1878), American clergyman. Converted at age 14, he began a preaching ministry soon after, associating at various periods in his life with the Salvation Army and Plymouth Brethren. He pastored at Moody Memorial Church in Chicago from 1930–48 (his only pastorate). He also authored more than 60 works, many of which are commentaries on books of the Bible.

1951 The U.S. Supreme Court struck down a New York City ordinance requiring a police permit for street preachers. The court determined that the ordinance violated the First Amendment, which guarantees freedom of speech and religion.

January 16

1545 Death of Georg Spalatin (b. 1484), German reformer and friend of Martin Luther. Luther wrote him more than 400 letters. His life in the court allowed him to give the secular government a better understanding of Luther's ideas.

1561 French reformer John Calvin admonished in a letter: "Let every one go whither he shall be called, even if he should not have a single follower. Even if the whole world should be blind and ungrateful, and that it should seem to you that all your pains had been laid out in vain, let it satisfy you that God and the angels approve of your conduct."

1604 At the Hampton Court Conference, Oxford divine John Rainolds presented to King James I the motion ". . . that there might bee a newe translation of the Bible." Approved the next day, Rainolds' motion led ultimately to the 1611 publication of the King James (authorized) version of the Bible.

1740 English revivalist George Whitefield commented in a letter: "If I see a man who loves the Lord Jesus in sincerity, I am not very solicitous to what cultural communion he belongs. The Kingdom of God, I think, does not consist in any such thing."

1786 The Virginia Legislature adopted the Ordinance of Religious Freedom, which guaranteed that no man would be forced to attend or support any church, nor belong to any religious organization. This mandate eventually became the model for the First Amendment to the U.S. Constitution.

1867 C.F.W. Walther, founder of the Missouri Synod of the Lutheran Church, observed in a letter: "He shapes our poor lives so that when they are past, they are not like flowers that wither, the places of which no one recognizes, but they leave behind in the future of the Kingdom of God signs of powerful results which reach into eternity."

1876 Death of Edmund Sears (b.1810), American clergyman, and author of the Christmas hymn, "It Came upon a Midnight Clear." Though ordained in the Unitarian Church, Sears wrote many books revealing a personal spiritual depth.

1919 The Prohibition (18th) Amendment became a part of the U.S. Constitution after it was ratified by Nebraska.

January 17

356 Death of St. Antony (b.ca.251), "founder of Christian monasticism." His parents died when he was 18, and he literally became a hermit in an attempt to follow the Scriptures. He drank only water; ate only bread, salt and dates; and slept on a pallet of straw. He sought solitude as an escape from even the monks who sought his counsel. At age 105, he died. Another early church father, Athanasius, wrote his biography.

1377 The Papal See was moved back to Rome by Pope Gregory XI, after having been located in Avignon, France, for 72 years. Thus ended what church historians have since called Roman Catholicism's "Babylonian Captivity." (The See had been moved by the French pope Clement V from Rome to southern France in 1305 to escape the political turmoil which was then raging in Italy.)

1463 Birth of Frederick III (Frederick the Wise), Elector of Saxony and Martin Luther's secular prince, near Leipzig, Germany. It was Frederick's sense of justice that led him to protect Luther during his persecution. While protecting Luther, Frederick became more sympathetic with his doctrines.

1484 Birth of Georg Spalatin, German reformer, at Spalt, Germany. His association with Luther at Wittenburg left a profound spiritual influence on him.

His position in Frederick the Wise's court gave Luther and the Reformation much support. Spalatin was one of the leading figures in the formulation of the Schmalkaldic Articles in 1537.

1604 At the Hampton Court Conference, called by England's King James I, the motion was carried ". . . that a translation be made of the whole Bible, as consonant as can be to the original Hebrew and Greek. . . , to be used in all Churches of England in time of divine service."

1745 Colonial American missionary to the New England Indians David Brainerd recorded in his journal: "Oh, how comfortable and sweet it is, to feel the assistance of divine grace in the performance of the duties which God has enjoined on us!"

1932. Death of Charles Gore (b.1853), Anglican bishop. As leader of the Anglo-Catholic (or liberal) party of the English Church, Gore wrote many books on theology and creed, as well as on biblical criticism.

1963 The Baptist World Mission was incorporated in Chicago, Illinois. This independent and fundamentalist organization of Baptist tradition is engaged primarily in evangelism, church planting and education in 17 countries.

1968 Death of Bob Jones, Sr. (b.1883), the militant fundamentalist evangelist who, in 1924, founded the school known as Bob Jones University.

January 18

1562 The Council of Trent, the Roman Catholic council called to deal with the monumental problems caused by the Reformation and with renewal in the Roman church, reconvened after a suspension of ten years.

1793 Birth of William H. Havergal, English clergyman and father of hymnwriter Frances Ridley Havergal. The elder Havergal composed many tunes for his daughter's religious verses, but is remembered today for the hymn tune EVAN, to which we sing "Oh, For a Faith That Will Not Shrink."

1806 Death of William Shrubsole (b.1760), English church chorister and organist. He was a close friend of Edward Perronet, for whose hymn, "All Hail the Power of Jesus' Name," he wrote MILES LANE, the hymn tune for which he is best remembered.

1815 Birth of L.F.K. Tischendorf, German Bible and textual scholar, at Langenfeld, Saxony. He discovered one of the oldest known (and most valuable) manuscripts of the Greek Bible at a Sinai monastery in 1844. The manuscript was called the Codex Sinaiticus and dates to the 4th century.

1846 Taylor University was established in Fort Wayne, Indiana, under Methodist sponsorship.

1875 Death of Joseph P. Webster (b. 1819), American musician and religious composer who wrote the melody for the Gospel favorite "In the Sweet By and By." In his lifetime, he is said to have composed over 1,000 works.

1895 Birth of Paul H. Vieth, American pioneer in Christian education, in Warrenton, Missouri. He was a Congregational Church member, but he taught religious education at Duke and Yale universities. Two of his many books were *How to Teach in the Church School* (1935) and *The Church and Christian Education* (1947).

1917 Death of Andrew Murray (b.1828), South African Dutch Reformed minister. He spent most of his life in Christian social and educational ministries. His books and sermons stress the deeper spiritual life and introduced the Keswick spirit into South Africa.

1917 Death of Louisa M.R. Stead (b.ca.1850), South American-born missionary to Southern Rhodesia. Though she is little-remembered for her mission work, her name is preserved as author of the hymn "'Tis So Sweet to Trust in Jesus."

January 19

1563 The Heidelberg Catechism, written by Peter Ursinus and Caspar Olevianus, was published in the Palatinate (the district in southwest Germany where the Holy Roman Emperor resided). Comprising a balanced statement of Calvinist tradition, it was soon after accepted by nearly all of the Reformed churches in Europe.

1568 Death of Miles Coverdale (b.1488), publisher of the first printed English Bible. He completed the translation of the Old Testament which William Tyndale had left unfinished at his death. Although Tyndale had openly criticized Henry VIII, Coverdale dedicated his 1535 edition of the Bible to him.

1804 Anglican missionary to Persia Henry Martyn asserted in his journal: "To be made fit for the work of a missionary I resigned the comforts of a married life when they were dear to me, and that was a severe struggle. Now again will I put forth the hand of faith, though the struggle will be far more severe."

1836 Birth of Henry L. Gilmour, Irish-born American Methodist chorister, in Londonderry. He spent the last 35 years of his life in active service to the Wenonah Methodist Church in New Jersey, which was founded in his home. The author and composer of many Gospel songs, Gilmour is perhaps best remembered as the author of "The Haven of Rest."

1889 The America Salvation Army split, with one faction renouncing allegiance to General William Booth. Ballington and Maud Booth, General Booth's son and daughter-in-law, led the splinter group. In 1896, they incorporated as the Volunteers of America, a religious welfare organization that is still active in social service in principal American cities.

January 20

1637 The Rev. John Wheelwright of Boston lent his support to Anne Hutchinson and her religious teachings in a sermon. Hutchinson advocated grace over works as well as the need for personal revelation. As a result of Wheelwright's sermon, he was convicted of contempt and sedition.

1669 Birth of Susannah Annesley (Wesley), mother of John and Charles Wesley, in London. Her father was a nonconformist clergyman; but Susannah renounced Nonconformity early in life and gave her allegiance to the Church of England. Born the 25th child in her family, she married Samuel Wesley in

1689 and bore him 19 children, the last 2 being John and Charles Wesley. Susannah Wesley was a remarkable preacher's daughter, preacher's wife and preacher's mother.

1758 English founder of Methodism, John Wesley, confessed in a letter: "I cannot think of you, without thinking of God. Others often lead me to Him, as it were, going round about. You bring me straight into His presence."

1813 Birth of Samuel P. Tregelles, English Bible scholar, in Falmouth, England. Though of Quaker parentage, Tregelles associated with the Plymouth Brethren. From the age of 25, he devoted his life to the study of the Scriptures. His most famous writings include *The Englishman's Greek and Hebrew Concordances* (1857–72), as well as his English translation of Gesenius' *Hebrew and Chaldee Lexicon*(1847).

1879 Birth of Albert Simpson Reitz, American Baptist minister, in Lyons, Kansas. The son of a Methodist minister, he spent his life in evangelism and in the pastorate for the Baptists. He published over 100 hymns during his lifetime, and is remembered for the words and music he wrote for the hymn of petition, "Teach Me to Pray, Lord."

1918 All church property was confiscated, and all religious instruction in the schools was abolished in Russia following the Bolshevik Revolution.

January 21

1525 The first Anabaptist baptismal service took place in Zurich, Switzerland, when Conrad Grebel (re-)baptized George Blaurock.

1549 British Parliament passed the Act of Uniformity, which required the universal use of the Book of Common Prayer (later called the First Prayer Book of Edward).

1738 English revivalist George Whitefield declared in his journal: "I desire to have no greater portion than the prayers of the poor."

1772 Francis Asbury, colonial Methodist bishop, pointed out in his journal, "Though a stranger in a strange land, God has taken care of me."

1797 Birth of Edward Mote, British cabinetmaker and hymnwriter, in Southwark, England. In 1852, Mote became a Baptist minister, and during his remaining 22 years of life wrote over 100 hymns. Of these, he is best remembered as author of "My Hope Is Built On Nothing Less" (a.k.a. "The Solid Rock").

1849 Birth of Julia Harriette Johnston, American hymnwriter, in Salineville, Ohio. At age six, she moved with her family to Peoria, Illinois, where she spent the rest of her life. A devoted and active member of the First Presbyterian Church of Peoria, she wrote many primary Sunday school materials and authored about 500 hymns. Her best known work is "Marvelous Grace of Our Loving Lord" (a.k.a. "Grace Greater Than Our Sin").

1870 Birth of William M. Runyan, American Methodist clergyman and music editor, in Marion, New York. Ordained to the pastorate at age 21, Runyan later quit because of his increasing deafness. He devoted himself to the music fields of teaching, composing and editing and is remembered for composing the hymn "Great Is Thy Faithfulness."

1887 Birth of Alfred H. Ackley, American Presbyterian pastor and hymn composer, in Spring Hill, Pennsylvania. Throughout his ministry he maintained a keen interest in writing hymns and hymn tunes. He is best remembered as the author and composer of "He Lives."

1980 American Presbyterian apologist for the faith, Francis Schaeffer, two years after being diagnosed with lymphoma, wrote in a letter: "I do believe God can either heal with medicine or without, and more often with a combination of the two. I am so glad that in my theology there is no tension between using the best medicine possible at my point in history, and knowing that God can work directly into my body."

January 22

1522 German reformer Martin Luther concluded in a letter: "Love cares for the problems of others as if they were one's own."

1843 Birth of Friedrich Wilhelm Blaśs, German philologist and grammarian. His 1896 *Grammatik des Neutestamentlichen Griechish* (*Grammar of New Testament Greek*, 1896 English translation) was foundational to the study of the New Testament Greek. A revision of the text is still used today.

1855 Birth of Carrie Ellis Breck, American Presbyterian homemaker, in Vermont. She wrote many devotional poems, three of which we sing as Gospel songs: "Nailed to the Cross," "Help Somebody Today" and "Face to Face with Christ My Savior."

1876 Death of John B. Dykes (b. 1823), English clergyman. Revealing a musical talent as early as age ten, he became a prolific composer of hymn tunes, writing nearly 300 during his lifetime. Those which still endure today include DOMINUS REGIT ME ("The King of Love My Shepherd Is"), LUX BENIGNA ("Lead, Kindly Light"), NICAEA ("Holy, Holy, Holy"), ST. AGNES ("Jesus, The Very Thought of Thee"), and VOX DILECTI ("I Heard the Voice of Jesus Say").

1882 The Fifth Street Presbyterian Church of Troy, New York, became the first church in America to be lit by electric lights after they were invented by Thomas Edison in 1879.

1913 Death of John Julian (b.1839), English musicologist and editor of the monumental (and still reprinted) *Dictionary of Hymnology* (1892, 1907). Julian devoted his life to musical research, and was awarded a doctor of divinity degree both in England and in America in 1894 at the age of 55.

1922 Death of Pope Benedict XV (b.1854). Born Giacomo della Chiesa, in Genoa, Italy, he had been elected to follow Pope Pius X in the papal office in 1914.

1947 U.S. Senate Chaplain Peter Marshall prayed: "Deliver us, O Lord, from the foolishness of impatience. Let us not be in such a hurry as to run on without Thee. We know that it takes a lifetime to make a tree; we know that fruit does not ripen in an afternoon; and Thou Thyself didst take a week to make the universe."

1963 Swiss Reformed theologian Karl Barth assured in a letter: "In Jesus Christ, God and man, and man and man, are already at peace—not as enemies but as true companions. In Him salvation is already present and at work."

1973 The U.S. Supreme Court handed down a decision on the *Roe* v. *Wade* case. The court decided that a state could not make any law which would restrict a woman's right to have an abortion before the fetus is viable (after the sixth month).

January 23

1755 Anglican clergyman John Fletcher was saved. While coming under strong Methodist influence in his early life, Fletcher nevertheless stayed in the Anglican Church. During the Calvinistic controversy in the English church, Fletcher became the chief defender of evangelical Arminianism. One of his best-written works is his *Checks to Antinomianism* (1771–75).

1789 Georgetown College was founded by Father John Carroll in Washington, D.C.—the first Roman Catholic college in America.

1858 Death of John Wyeth (b. 1770), printer and newspaper editor. In addition to editing the Federalist newspaper in Harrisburg, Pennsylvania, for 35 years, Wyeth also wrote and published sacred music. We remember him for composing the hymn tune NETTLETON, to which we sing "Come, Thou Fount of Every Blessing."

1875 Death of Charles Kingsley (b.1819), English socialist and Christian novelist. As professor of modern history at Cambridge, Kingsley sought to reform education and sanitation.

1893 Death of Phillips Brooks (b.1835), American Episcopal clergyman. In 1869 he began a 22-year pastorate at Trinity Church, Boston, and became recognized as one of America's most outstanding preachers. He also wrote the hymn "O Little Town of Bethlehem."

1915 Death of Anna B. Warner (b.1820), the American hymnwriter who created the song "Jesus Loves Me." She also penned a number of novels and two collections of verse during her lifetime.

1935 British expositor Arthur W. Pink commented in a letter: "Growth in grace is like the growth of a cow's tail—the more it truly grows, the closer to the ground it is brought."

1943 The New Tribes Mission was incorporated in Los Angeles, California, by Paul W. Fleming. Today, this interdenominational missionary agency is headquartered in Sanford, Florida. Working in 18 countries overseas, N.T.M. engages primarily in Bible translation, church planting, missionary training, literature production and aviation.

1950 Israel proclaimed Jerusalem as its capital city. Under British rule, Israel gained its independence in May of 1948. Soon after, she was attacked by invaders from four surrounding Arab nations. A 1949 U.N. armistice agreement guaranteed Israel possession of her ancient lands.

January 24

1573 Birth of John Donne, English poet and divine, in London. At age 21 he abandoned Roman Catholicism for the Anglican Church. He was ordained to the priesthood at age 42 and is known as one of the most remarkable poet-preachers of the 17th century. His most memorable work was *Devotions upon Emergent Occasions* (1623–24), which contains his most quoted line: "No man is an island, entire of itself. . . . Any man's death diminishes me, because I am involved in Mankind."

1738 Exactly four months before his life-changing conversion at Aldersgate, John Wesley cried out in his journal: "I went to America to convert the Indians. But oh! who shall convert me? I have a fair summer religion; I can talk well; nay, and believe myself, while no danger is near. But let death look me in the face, and my spirit is troubled. Nor can I say, 'To die is gain!' "

1818 Birth of John Mason Neale, Anglican clergyman, in London. As a student of the liturgies and practices of the early church, Neale was one of the first to translate ancient Greek and Latin hymns into English. Some of his translations that we sing today include the hymns "All Glory, Laud, and Honor," "The Day of Resurrection," "Good Christian Men, Rejoice," "Jerusalem the Golden," and "O Come, O Come, Emmanuel."

1827 Birth of John Albert Broadus, American Baptist scholar, in Virginia. He served as New Testament professor, and later president, of Southern Baptist Theological Seminary in Louisville, Kentucky (1859–95). He was also member of the International Lesson Committee (1878–95).

1918 Birth of Oral Roberts, American evangelist, in Ada, Oklahoma. He began his evangelistic work in 1936–41. In 1947, he began a multi-media worldwide evangelistic ministry through radio, television, and literature. In 1963, he founded Oral Roberts University, in Tulsa, Oklahoma, and has since served as president.

1975 Dr. F. Donald Coggan became the 101st Archbishop of Canterbury (Primate of Anglicanism), at Canterbury Cathedral in London. A representative from the Vatican, Johannes Cardinal Willebrands, was also present, the first Vatican representative to attend this Anglican ceremony since the Reformation.

January 25

1530 The Confession of Augsburg was published: a summary of the evangelical (i.e. Lutheran) faith presented to Emperor Charles V of Spain. The German translation by Jonas in 1532 helped to make this the principal confession of the Lutheran Church from that time on.

1825 Birth of Edward H. Bickersteth, Anglican clergyman, in Islington, England. During his lifetime he published several collections of verse and hymns. Of these works, one which still endures today is his hymn "Peace, Perfect Peace."

1861 C.F.W. Walther, founder of the Missouri Synod of the Lutheran Church, insisted in a letter: "Only the concept of the church as a fellowship, assembled in the Spirit, of those who are born again and renewed, corresponds to the nature of living Christianity, whereas the mechanical concept of the church as a fellowship of the orthodox, whether converted or unconverted, will necessarily lead to a dead Christianity."

1863 Birth of Rufus M. Jones, American Quaker philosopher and educator, at South China, Maine. He was the first editor of the *American Friend* magazine (1894–1912), and one of the organizers of the Five Years Meetings of Friends. He also helped found the American Friends Service Committee (1917), serving as its chairman for 20 years. He believed in a mystical relation with Christ which could be lived out practically in the modern world.

1887 Death of Rowland Prichard (b. 1811), Welsh hymn writer. At the age of 20, he composed the hymn tune HYFRYDOL, to which we sing Wilbur Chapman's "Jesus! What a Friend of Sinners!"

1944 Miss Florence Time-Oi Lee of Macao became the first woman in the Anglican Church to be ordained a priest. At Shie Hing in Kwangtung Province, China, Bishop R.O. Hall of the Diocese of Hong Kong and South China ordained Miss Lee because the war had brought a critical shortage of ordained male Anglican priests.

1949 Death of Peter Marshall (b.1902), Presbyterian clergyman and Chaplain to the U.S. Senate (1947–49). Even though he died at an early age, his name soon became a household word through the publication of his biography, *A Man Called Peter* (1951), by his widow, Catherine Marshall.

1959 At St. Paul's Outside the Walls, Pope John XXIII first announced his intention to summon the Vatican II Ecumenical Council. Held in four sessions in St. Peter's Basilica, the first session (Oct. 11–Dec. 8, 1962) was opened by Pope John himself. Pope Paul VI convened the other three sessions (1963, 1964 and 1965). A total of 2,860 priests from nearly every country participated.

January 26

1564 The decrees and definitions of the Council of Trent were confirmed by Pope Pius IV in the papal encyclical *Benedictus Deus*.

1779 Pioneer American Methodist Bishop Francis Asbury declared in his journal: "We should so work as if we were to be saved by our works; and so rely on Jesus Christ, as if we did no works."

1844 Birth of Albert L. Peace, church organist, at Huddersfield, England. Peace was one of the most prominent Scottish organists of his day and was popular as a recitalist. He composed many cantatas, organ pieces, hymn tunes and musical collections for the Church of Scotland. Today he is best remembered for his hymn tune ST. MARGARET, to which we commonly sing the haunting hymn of repose "O Love That Wilt Not Let Me Go."

1905 Birth of Maria von Trapp, musical Austrian baroness, in Vienna, Austria. She left the convent while in her 30s to marry Baron von Trapp. The family escaped to Switzerland during the Nazi occupation and toured the world from 1938 to 1956. Maria's life during her last months as a nun was immortalized by Julie Andrews in the 1965 film version of the Rodgers and Hammerstein musical "The Sound of Music."

1930 Pioneer linguistic educator Frank C. Laubach, while serving as a Congregational missionary to the Philippines, asserted in a letter: "I am disgusted with the pettiness and futility of my unled self. If the way out is not more perfect slavery to God, then what is the way out?"

1948 Senate Chaplain Peter Marshall prayed: "We need Thy help to do something about the world's true problems—the problem of greed, which is often called profit; the problem of license, disguising itself as liberty; the problem of materialism, the hook of which is baited with security."

1958 The religious program, *Our Goodly Heritage*, was last broadcast, over CBS television. Having debuted five years earlier (Nov. 16, 1952), this Sunday morning Bible study program was hosted by William Rush Baer of New York University.

1967 Swiss Reformed theologian Karl Barth declared in a letter: "What God has done is well done."

1971 Food for the Hungry was incorporated in Glendale, California. Founded by Larry Ward, this interdenominational, evangelical mission supplies relief internationally for disaster victims. Headquartered today in Scottsdale, Arizona, F.F.H. also works with community development and self-help projects, and serves as an information service for other missions.

1973 Death of E. Stanley Jones (b.1884), American Methodist missionary to India. Ordained in 1907, he afterward became a missionary-evangelist, working with the upper castes of India. He instituted Christian *ashrams* (Hindi for *"retreat"*) in 1917 as a new way of reaching India for the Gospel. Primarily a devotional writer, Jones authored 29 books, 2 of which are still popular: *The Christ of the Indian Road* (1925), and *Abundant Living* (1942).

January 27

1756 Birth of Wolfgang Amadeus Mozart, extraordinary Austrian composer, at Salzburg. A musical prodigy from age four, he remained a lifelong member of the Roman Catholic Church. Prolonged overwork undermined his health and led to his premature death at 36. But he left some 600 music compositions. The church especially prizes the hymn tunes ARIEL ("O Could I Speak the Matchless Worth") and ELLESDIE ("Jesus, I My Cross Have Taken").

1839 Birth of John Julian, English musicologist, in Cornwall, England. Having devoted his life to musical research, he was awarded a doctor of divinity degree both in England and America in 1894, at age 55. His undoubted masterwork is the monumental *Dictionary of Hymnology* (1892), which was updated and reissued in 1957.

1860 Birth of "Uncle" Buddy Robinson, illustrious illiterate American evangelist.

1972 The white and black United Methodist conferences in South Carolina—separated since the Civil War—voted in their respective meetings in Columbia to adopt a plan of union.

1972 Death of Mahalia Jackson (b.1911), black American religious vocalist. Her style demonstrated a close link between the religious and secular roots of jazz.

January 28

1077 King Henry IV was un-excommunicated by Pope Gregory VII after pleading barefoot for three days in the snow. At the Synod of Worms the year before, bishops backed by Henry had deposed Gregory. In return, Gregory declared both the rebellious bishops and Henry excommunicated from the church. Robbed of papal support, Henry faced fresh German revolts. Therefore, humbling himself before Gregory at Canossa, Italy, was more likely a political decision than a spiritual gesture.

1581 Scotland's King James VI (who in 1603 became England's King James I, of King James Bible fame) signed the second Scottish Confession of Faith.

1814 Birth of Frederick W. Faber, English clergyman, in Yorkshire, England. Ordained an Anglican priest, he became an ardent follower of the Oxford Movement, and in 1846 converted to the Roman Catholic faith. Faber wrote over 150 hymns during his lifetime. Two remain popular today: "Faith of Our Fathers" and "There's a Wideness in God's Mercy."

1822 Birth of William D. Longstaff, English philanthropist and son of a wealthy shipowner, in Sunderland, England. The author of the hymn "Take Time to Be Holy," he was a close acquaintance of Dwight L. Moody and Ira Sankey.

1834 Birth of Sabine Baring-Gould, Anglican clergyman and writer, in Exeter, England. A man of diversified interests, he wrote many books on such varied subjects as history, biography, poetry, and fiction. He was also a pioneer in the collection of folk songs. His name endures as the author of two popular hymns: "Onward, Christian Soldiers" and "Now the Day Is Over."

1856 Birth of Reuben A. Torrey, American Congregational evangelist, in Hoboken, New Jersey. He served as the second president of Moody Bible Institute (1889–1908), later as Dean of the Bible Institute of Los Angeles, now called Biola University (1912–24). A popular conference speaker, Torrey authored more than 40 books on devotional subjects.

1896 Death of Joseph Barnby (b.1838), English church chorister. He wrote 246 hymns during his lifetime, all of which were published in one volume after his death. Three hymn-tunes still in popular use are: LAUDES DOMINI ("When Morning Gilds the Skies"), MERRIAL ("Now the Day Is Over") and ST. ANDREW ("We Give Thee but Thine Own").

1947 A copy of the *Bay Psalm Book* was purchased for $150,000 in an auction at Parke-Bernet Galleries in New York City. At that time, it was the highest price ever paid for one book. The *Bay Psalm Book*, originally published in 1640, is the earliest known English-language book to be printed in the British American colonies. Its original title was *The Whole Book of Psalmes Faithfully Translated into English Metre.*

January 29

1336 Pope Benedict XII issued the bull *Benedictus Deus*, which decided the dispute regarding the Beatific Vision.

1499 Birth of Katherine von Bora, the German ex-nun who became Martin Luther's wife. They married in 1525—he was 41, she, 26. During their 21–year marriage, she bore him 3 sons and 3 daughters. "Kate" survived her husband by 6 years: he died in 1546, she in 1552.

1685   The Edict of Nantes was revoked by Louis XIV, thus forcing a half million Huguenots (French Protestants) to flee their country. As a result, the mercantile economy was severely damaged, and criticism of absolute government in France began. (The edict was originally signed by Henry IV of France in 1598, after he became a Catholic, in order to stop the French Wars of Religion. It gave religious freedom to French non-Catholics.)

1688   Birth of Emmanuel Swedenborg, Swedish mystic and scientist, in Stockholm, Sweden. He claimed to have had the first of several divine revelations of the deep secrets of the universe at age 55. Swedenborg recorded these "revelations" over the next 30 years. In 1787, 15 years after his death, his followers formed the New Jerusalem Church in London. The movement still survives, but has never grown appreciably in size or influence.

1739   Death of Thomas Shepherd (b.1665), nonconformist English clergyman. Originally ordained in the Anglican Church, he severed his connections in 1694 to pastor small independent congregations. Shepherd's name is remembered as the author of the popular hymn of resolve "Must Jesus Bear the Cross Alone?"

1850   Birth of Rufus H. McDaniel, American Christian Church clergyman, in Brown County, Ohio. During his several pastorates, he is credited with having written more than 100 hymns. One of his hymns, "Since Jesus Came into My Heart," is still popular.

1866   English church worker Katherine Hankey penned the words to the Gospel song "Tell Me the Old, Old Story."

1880   Death of Frederick Oakeley (b. 1802), one of the Tractarian authors during the Oxford Movement in England. After the conversion of John Henry Newman to the Roman Catholic Church in 1845, Oakeley soon followed. Oakeley's fame rests primarily on his translation of the Latin hymn "*Adeste Fidelis*," which we sing as the Christmas carol "O Come, All Ye Faithful."

1904   Death of George Minor (b.1845), American Baptist sacred music publisher. One of his most enduring hymn tunes is HARVEST, to which we sing the hymn of missionary joy "Bringing in the Sheaves."

1930   Pioneer linguistic educator Frank C. Laubach, while serving as a Congregational missionary to the Philippines, commented in a letter: "I feel simply carried along each hour, doing my part in a plan which is far beyond myself. This sense of cooperation with God in little things is what so astonishes me; God takes cares of all the rest."

1957   The University of Chicago Press published the first edition of its English translation of Walter Bauer's New Testament Greek Lexicon (*A Greek-English Lexicon of the New Testament and Other Early Christian Literature*). Under the co-editors William F. Arndt and F. Wilbur Gingrich, the translation project had taken eight years.

January 30

435 Rome recognized the expanding Vandal territories in northwest Africa (in the area of modern Tunis) as *"federati"* in an attempt to appease their military forces and postpone, if only temporarily, their invasion of Italy. The invasion was successfully postponed for about 20 years.

1831 Birth of Alexander B. Bruce, Free Church of Scotland theologian. His reputation as a Bible scholar was recognized early in his life, and after the death of Patrick Fairbairn in 1875, Bruce filled the chair of apologetics and New Testament exegesis in the Free Church Hall in Glasgow. From 1875–99, Bruce published most of his scholarly writings.

1867 The American branch of the Evangelical Alliance was organized at the Bible House, in New York City, with William E. Dodge elected president.

1869 Death of Charlotte A. Barnard (b.1830), English student of music. During her brief 39-year lifetime, she published over 100 ballads. She is best remembered for composing the music for the hymn "Give of Your Best to the Master."

1912 Birth of Francis Schaeffer, American Presbyterian apologist for Protestant fundamentalism, in Germantown, Pennsylvania. After pastoring churches in Pennsylvania and Missouri, he and his wife Edith moved to Europe to serve as missionaries with the Independent Board for Presbyterian Missions. In 1948 he developed an evangelistic ministry based in Lausanne, Switzerland, to despairing intellectuals. In 1955 the Schaeffers began a new, independent work that led to the 1958 founding of the L'Abri Fellowship. From 1958 through Schaeffer's death in 1984, L'Abri served as a religious oasis where searching students could come and talk through their most troubling questions about God.

January 31

1538 French reformer John Calvin expressed his hope in a letter: "I pray the Lord to keep you in His holy protection, and so to direct you that you may not go astray in that slippery path whereon you are, until He shall have manifested to you His complete deliverance."

1752 The profession ceremony for Sister St. Martha Turpin was held at Ursuline Convent in New Orleans, Louisiana. She was the first American-born woman to become a nun in the Roman Catholic Church.

1797 Birth of Franz Schubert, Austrian composer, in a suburb of Vienna, Austria. A child prodigy on the violin, piano and organ, Schubert had written some of his most celebrated music by age 17. At his death he left more than 1200 compositions, including much sacred music.

1843 The young Church of Scotland minister Robert Murray McCheyne asked in a letter: "Is not a Christian's darkest hour calmer than the world's brightest?"

1892 Death of Charles Haddon Spurgeon (b.1834), English Baptist preacher. Soon after his conversion, at age 16, Spurgeon began preaching. At times his audiences numbered 10,000. He pastored the Metropolitan Tabernacle in London from 1861 until his death. His 49-volume *Metropolitan Pulpit* was not only his largest work, but one of the largest 19th-century works still in print.

1915 Birth of Thomas Merton, Roman Catholic Trappist monk, in Prades, France. At 26, Merton left behind a successful career as a theology professor and entered the Abbey of Gethsemani in Kentucky. He continued to write, however, and is perhaps best remembered for his spiritual autobiography *The Seven Storey Mountain* (1948).

1944 The European Evangelistic Crusade was incorporated in Buffalo, New York. Changing its name to Global Outreach Mission in 1971, this interdenominational mission agency works in over a dozen countries primarily in evangelism, radio broadcasting, literature distribution and support of Christian nationals.

1949 American missionary and Auca Indian martyr Jim Elliot maintained in his journal: "One does not surrender a life in an instant—that which is lifelong can only be surrendered in a lifetime."

1952 Worldwide Evangelization for Christ International moved to its present headquarters in Fort Washington, Pennsylvania. Founded 1913 by A.W. Ruscoe, in Seattle, Washington, under the name Worldwide Evangelization Crusade, the name was changed in 1984. W.E.C. International is an interdenominational and evangelical mission agency that works in 26 countries. The organization is engaged primarily in evangelism, Bible translation, church planting, theological education and medical assistance.

1955 Death of John R. Mott (b.1865), Methodist layman and founder of the Student Christian Movement. Between 1888–1931, when the organization was strongly evangelistic, Mott served as an executive with the Y.M.C.A.

1968 Living Bibles International was incorporated, in Wheaton, Illinois, by founder and first director Kenneth N. Taylor. Headquartered today in nearby Naperville, Illinois, this interdenominational, evangelical mission organization translates and supplies copies of the Living Bible to nearly 50 countries worldwide, distributing them primarily through national workers.

February

February 1

1650 Death of Rene Descartes (b.1596), French scientist and philosopher. Descartes, beginning with radical skepticism, attempted to prove through deductive reasoning the existence of the world and God.

1750 Anglican hymnwriter John Newton (author of "Amazing Grace") married Mary Catlett. They were married 40 years before she died on Dec. 15, 1790. Newton outlived her by 17 years, dying on Dec. 21, 1807.

1791 English founder of Methodism John Wesley admitted in a letter: "Probably I should not be able to do so much did not many of you assist me by your prayers."

1803 Anglican missionary to India and Persia, Henry Martyn, recorded this prayer in his journal: "Oh, that I may learn my utter helplessness without Thee, and so by deep humiliation be qualified for greater usefulness."

1831 Birth of Henry McNeal Turner, black American Methodist clergyman, in Newberry Court House, South Carolina. In 1863 Turner became the first black chaplain to be commissioned in the U.S. Army. He also served as bishop of the African Methodist Episcopal Church in 1880.

1845 Baylor University was founded in Independence, Texas, under Baptist sponsorship. First known as the Texas Baptist Educational Society, it was moved to Waco in 1866 where it consolidated with Waco University and adopted the present name of Baylor.

1891 Death of Edward H. Plumptre (b.1821), Church of England clergyman and theologian who wrote the hymn "Rejoice, Ye Pure in Heart."

1909 Birth of George Beverly Shea, song evangelist, in Ontario, Canada. Since the late 1940s, Shea has served as the featured vocalist with the Billy Graham Evangelistic Association, and has sung for Billy Graham's crusades around the world. In 1956 Shea was awarded an honorary doctorate from Houghton College in recognition of his many years of unflagging zeal and Christian music ministry.

1963 The Lutheran Free Church (an American denomination with Norwegian roots) merged with the American Lutheran Church. The resulting group had a total membership of nearly 2.5 million. A conservative minority of Lutheran Free churches did not choose to merge and formed the Association of Free Lutheran Congregations.

February 2

1594 Death of Giovanni P. Palestrina (b.1525), Italian choirmaster. At the age of 19 he became organist and choirmaster in his native city of Palestrina, Italy. He moved to Rome seven years later and spent the rest of his professional life there. His compositions include 100 masses and some 200 other music arrangements, including the hymn tune VICTORY, to which we sing "The Strife Is O'er, the Battle Done."

1779 Pioneer American Methodist Bishop Francis Asbury assured in his journal: "God is gracious beyond the power of language to describe."

1784 Death of Henry Alline (b.1748), colonial American Free Will Baptist evangelist. During the time of America's break with England, Alline's emotional preaching fostered the growth of the "New Light" movement within New England Congregational and Baptist churches. Alline's theology and piety were greatly influenced by English divine William Law.

1832 Twenty-three-year-old Baptist seminary student Samuel Francis Smith penned the words to the American patriotic hymn "My Country, 'Tis of Thee."

1881 The first Young People's Society of Christian Endeavor (the forerunner of the modern church "youth fellowship") was organized at Portland, Maine, by Rev. F.E. Clark of the Williston Congregational Church.

1882 The Roman Catholic Church permitted the organization of the Knights of Columbus, bowing to an increasing national interest in fraternal groups.

1891 Birth of Frederick C. Grant, American Episcopal theologian, in Beloit, Wisconsin. After serving five parishes, Grant later taught at Western Theological Seminary in Evanston, Illinois, and at Union Theological Seminary in New York City.

1895 Death of A.J. Gordon (b.1836), American Baptist clergyman. Once a close friend of Dwight L. Moody, Gordon is remembered as the composer of the hymns "In Tenderness He Sought Me" and "My Jesus, I Love Thee."

1918 This date became Feb. 15, in Estonia, Latvia, and Lithuania when they adopted the Gregorian calendar (created by Pope Gregory XIII in 1582), to replace the older, inaccurate Julian calendar (created by Julius Caesar in 46 B.C.).

1924 Birth of Rev. Jack McAlister, founder and first president of World Literature Crusade. This interdenominational mission agency was founded in 1946 in Canada. In 1975 its headquarters moved to Chatsworth, California. W.L.C. is engaged in Bible and literature distribution, evangelism and church planting in 43 countries worldwide.

1944 German Lutheran theologian and Nazi martyr Dietrich Bonhoeffer lamented in a letter from prison: "There is a kind of weakness that Christianity does not hold with, but which people insist on claiming as Christian, and then sling mud at it."

February 3

1518 Silence was imposed on the Augustinian monks in the Roman Catholic Church by Pope Leo X.

1744 Colonial missionary to the American Indians David Brainerd explained in a tract: "God designs that those whom He sanctifies in part here, and intends for immortal glory, shall tarry awhile in this present evil world, that their own experience of temptations may teach them how great the deliverance is, which God has wrought for them."

1786 Birth of Heinrich Friedrich Wilhelm Gesenius, German biblical scholar, at Nordhausen, Hanover. He spent his life concentrating on problems of Semitic philology, becoming the outstanding Hebrew scholar of his generation. His chief work was *Hebraisches und Chaldaisches Handworterbuch* (1810–12, the English translation *Hebrew and Chaldee Lexicon* is still in print), which became the basis of the later biblical Hebrew lexicon known commonly as *Brown, Driver, and Briggs* (1906), often reprinted.

1809 Birth of Felix Mendelssohn, German composer, at Hamburg. His compositions were light and easily understood, noted for their gracefulness, sweet melody and delicate details. In 1835 he wrote the oratorio *St. Paul*, and in 1846 he produced *Elijah*—considered by many to be one of the greatest oratorios of the 19th century, second only to Handel's *Messiah*.

1832 Birth of William H. Doane, Baptist hymnwriter, in Preston, Connecticut. He composed more than 2,200 melodies during his lifetime. He successfully collaborated with Fanny Crosby, for whose religious texts Doane frequently created hymn tunes. His most famous tunes include EVERY DAY AND HOUR ("Savior, More Than Life to Me"), I AM THINE ("I Am Thine, O Lord"), "More Love to Thee," "Near the Cross," "Pass Me Not," PRECIOUS NAME ("Take the Name of Jesus with You"), RESCUE ("Rescue the Perishing") and the words and tune for "To God Be the Glory."

1842 Birth of Sidney Lanier, Confederate poet, in Macon, Georgia. Weak in health from Civil War imprisonments, he nevertheless published 24 volumes. Ten of these were poetic verse. Today he is remembered as the author of the hymn "Into the Woods My Master Went."

1864 Independent congregations of Methodist, Presbyterian, Congregational and United Brethren churches met in Columbus, Ohio, to organize and found an association called The Christian Union. Although it avoided creeds, this association of churches was basically evangelical in theology and congregational in church polity. The member congregations were found mostly in Ohio, Indiana and Missouri.

1888 Birth of Blanche Kerr Brock, who with her husband, Virgil, formed one of the best-loved Gospel hymnwriting and singing teams in America in the early part of the 20th century, and were known as "the singing Brocks."

1943 The Allied troopship Dorchester was torpedoed and sunk. Four chaplains selflessly helped men to safety and ministered to the dying as the ship sank. Their bravery is honored in "Four Chaplains Day."

February 4

1441 The encyclical *Cantante Domino* was issued by Pope Eugene IV. It was a proclamation by the Council of Florence that the Roman Catholic Church's biblical canon contained both the 66 protocanonical and 12 deuterocanonical ("apocryphal") books, identical to the lists drawn up at the Councils of Hippo (A.D. 393) and Carthage (A.D. 397 and 419).

1810   The Cumberland Presbytery was organized in Dickson County, Tennessee. As an outgrowth of the great revival of 1800, several Presbyterian congregations rejected the fatalism conveyed by the Westminster Confession of Faith. Led by their founders, the pastors Finis Ewing, Samuel King and Samuel McAdow, these congregations departed from the American Presbyterian Church to form the Cumberland Presbytery. In 1983 the church numbered about 88,000 members, located primarily in 11 southern states.

1856   Birth of Robert Dick Wilson, American Presbyterian philologist, in Indiana, Pennsylvania. He devoted his life to the study and teaching of biblical languages and literature. He taught at Western, Princeton and Westminster theological seminaries. His many technical writings included *Elements of Syriac Grammar* (1890), *Hebrew Syntax* (1902), and *Hebrew Grammar for Beginners* (1907).

1873   Birth of George Bennard, American Methodist evangelist, in Youngstown, Ohio. During his lifetime he wrote more than 300 Gospel songs, but he is remembered today primarily for authoring one of the church's most beloved hymns: "The Old Rugged Cross."

1874   English poet and devotional writer Frances Ridley Havergal penned the lines to the hymn of personal commitment "Take My Life, and Let It Be."

1883   Birth of George K.A. Bell, Anglican clergyman, at Hayling Island, England. Consecrated Bishop of Chichester in 1929, it was Bell who was elected the first chairman of the Central Committee when the World Council of Churches was formed in 1948 at Amsterdam.

1906   Birth of Dietrich Bonhoeffer, Lutheran theologian, in Breslau, Germany. He took a leading part in the preparation of the Barmen Declaration of 1934, which opposed the Nazification of the German Confessing Church. His resistance activities brought about his arrest by the Gestapo in 1943 as well as his execution for treason two years later. His name endures through his books, especially *The Cost of Discipleship* (1948) and *Letters and Papers from Prison* (1953,1971).

1944   Death of Cleland B. McAfee (b.1886), American Presbyterian clergyman and theologian. He taught systematic theology for 18 years at McCormick Seminary in Chicago (1912–30), but he is better remembered as the author and composer of the hymn "There Is a Place of Quiet Rest."

1950   American missionary and Auca Indian martyr Jim Elliot resolved in his journal: "I may no longer depend on pleasant impulses to bring me before the Lord. I must rather respond to principles I know to be right, whether I feel them to be enjoyable or not."

February 5

1631   Roger Williams, colonial American clergyman, first arrived in New England, landing at Boston. Called to serve in the Salem and Plymouth churches, Williams soon began questioning the legality of the Massachusetts Bay Colony charter in religious matters. He was banished to Rhode Island five years later for his controversial views on church-state separation. At Providence, he established the first Baptist church in America.

1682 This date became Feb. 16, in Alsace (part of France at that time) when the Gregorian calendar was adopted.

1705 Death of Philip Jacob Spener (b.1635), German Lutheran Pietist leader. His religious upbringing caused him to set up weekly sessions in his home where pastors and laymen could meet together for Bible study and prayer. His most famous writing is no doubt the 1675 tract *Pia Desideria* (*Pious Desires*), in which he set forth the essence of the doctrines of Pietism. His emphasis on the new birth and exemplary Christian living helped revitalize German Lutheranism.

1736 John and Charles Wesley, the two English brothers who helped pioneer the Methodist movement, first arrived in America at Savannah, Georgia. While yet students at Oxford University, they had been invited by Georgia's governor Oglethorpe to come to America as missionaries to the Indians.

1837 Birth of Dwight L. Moody, American evangelist, at Northfield, Massachusetts. At age 18, he gave his life to Jesus Christ through the testimony of his Sunday-school teacher, Edward Kimball. Five years later he left his job in his uncle's shoe repair shop to devote his life to Christian evangelism and education.

1887 The Chicago Evangelization Society was founded by evangelist Dwight L. Moody and English-born educator Emma Dryer. This educational organization eventually grew to become the Moody Bible Institute.

1898 Death of William F. Moulton (b.1835), English Bible scholar. One of the leading Greek scholars of his day, he translated Winer's *Grammar of New Testament Greek* (1870) and, together with A.S. Geden, compiled *A Concordance to the New Testament Greek* (1897), which is still in print.

1918 Following the Bolshevik Revolution, the Russian Orthodox Church was formally separated from the state in Russia.

1928 Birth of Martin E. Marty, church history professor at the University of Chicago and popular religious lecturer. He is well known as a weekly columnist for *Christian Century* magazine.

1944 German Lutheran theologian and Nazi martyr Dietrich Bonhoeffer observed in a letter from prison: "Much that worries us beforehand can afterwards, quite unexpectedly, have a happy and simple solution. Worries just don't matter. Things really are in a better hand than ours."

February 6

679 Death of Amandus (b.ca.584), founder of Belgian monasticism. During his 95 years, he founded 8 abbeys, 5 in the southern Netherlands.

1612 Birth of Antoine Arnauld, French theologian, in Paris. The 20th child of a French lawyer, Arnauld is generally considered the foremost follower of the French Jansenist movement and a key figure in the struggle between the

Jansenists and Jesuits for the control of the Roman Catholic Church in France.

1812 Adoniram Judson, along with four other men (Hall, Newell, Nott, Rice) and their wives, was ordained a missionary by the Congregational Church in Salem, Massachusetts. Judson and his wife, Ann, had married the day before.

1839 Scottish clergyman Robert Murray McCheyne assured in a letter: "Even in the wildest storms the sky is not all dark; and so in the darkest dealings of God with His children, there are always some bright tokens for good."

1910 Death of Harriett E. P. Buell (b.1834), American Methodist devotional writer. She was a regular contributor to the *Northern Christian Advocate*, out of Syracuse, New York, for nearly 50 years; but she is better remembered as author of the hymn "I'm a Child of the King."

1922 Italian cardinal Achille Ratti was elected the 258th Pontiff of the Roman Catholic Church, following the death of Pope Benedict XV on Jan. 22, 1922. Ratti served the church as Pope Pius XI for the next 17 years, until his death in 1939 at the age of 82.

1931 American pioneer in linguistic education Frank C. Laubach, while serving as a Congregational missionary to the Philippines, pointed out in a letter: "There is a deep peace that grows out of illness and loneliness and a sense of failure. God cannot get close when everything is delightful. He seems to need these darker hours, these empty-hearted hours, to mean the most to people."

1952 American missionary and Auca Indian martyr Jim Elliot assured in his journal: "Christianity, disruptive in nature, has nonetheless integrating powers for the individual in the culture, though both he and it may expect revolution."

February 7

1478 Birth of Sir Thomas More, British Roman Catholic humanist, in London. As Lord Chancellor to Henry VIII, he was suspected of infidelity to the throne for his excessive papal loyalty, which revealed itself in his refusal to annul Henry's marriage to Catherine of Aragon. In 1535 he was beheaded for treason. In 1886 More was beatified by Pope Leo XIII for his heroic allegiance to the Roman Catholic faith.

1528 Bern, the strongest canton (state) in southern Switzerland in its day, officially embraced the Protestant faith of Ulrich Zwingli, Oecolampadius and other Swiss reformers.

1832 Birth of Hannah Whitall Smith, American Quaker evangelist and author, in Philadelphia. With a tendency toward deep religious introspection, she and her husband were exposed to the Wesleyan-based "holiness" movement in 1865 and soon began preaching the "higher life" message, taking it even to England in 1873. In 1875 she published her most popular book, *The Christian's Secret of a Happy Life* (which is still in print in several languages), a guide to practicing a complete personal surrender to God's will.

1869 Connecticut Congregational clergyman, Dr. Samuel Wolcott, upon returning home from a Y.M.C.A. evangelistic service in Ohio, penned the words to the missionary hymn "Christ for the World We Sing." The hymn was first published in W. H. Doane's *Songs of Devotion* (1870).

1903 Birth of Dr. Donald P. Shidler. From 1952 to 1967 he was President of Gospel Missionary Union. Founded in 1892 in Topeka, Kansas, G.M.U. has been headquartered since 1978 in Kansas City, Missouri. This interdenominational organization utilizes evangelism, Bible translation, radio ministry and leadership training in 20 countries.

1947 U.S. Senate Chaplain Peter Marshall prayed: "We want to do right, and to be right; so start us in the right way, for Thou knowest that we are very hard to turn."

February 8

1587 Mary Queen of Scots was beheaded at Fotheringhay Castle in England. The daughter of James V, she became queen when six days old. She was raised a Catholic in France, while England became more and more anti-Roman Catholic. Returning to Scotland at age 19 (1561), domestic scandals removed her from the throne six years later (1567). Political intrigue aimed at returning her to the English throne led to her execution.

1693 The College of William and Mary was founded in Williamsburg, Virginia, under Anglican auspices, for the purpose of educating Anglican clergymen. It is the second oldest (after Harvard) institution of higher learning in America.

1744 Colonial American missionary to the New England Indians David Brainerd lamented in his journal: "I find that both mind and body are quickly tired with intenseness and fervour in the things of God. Oh that I could be as incessant as angels in devotion and spiritual fervour."

1851 Death of James Alexander Haldane (b.1768), Scottish evangelist. In 1797 he founded the Society for Propagating the Gospel at Home, after discovering that the Church of Scotland was as little interested in home missions as in foreign missions. In 1799 he became the first Congregational minister in Scotland. He pastored in Edinburgh for nearly 50 years.

1865 Birth of Lewis Edgar Jones, American Y.M.C.A. director, in Yates City, Illinois. For Jones, hymnwriting was only a hobby, but we continue to sing the hymn he authored and composed: "There Is Power in the Blood."

1878 Birth of Martin Buber, Jewish religious philosopher, in Vienna, Austria. Much influenced by the mystical aspects of Soren Kierkegaard's existentialism, Buber's writings stressed that kind of encounter between God and man. His most famous work, *I and Thou* (1937, 1958), seeks to demonstrate how God cannot be exhaustively described merely as an object ("It") outside ourselves. Rather, God may only be adequately addressed as a person ("Thou").

1936 Death of James H. Fillmore (b.1849), American clergyman in the Christian Church. In addition to pastoring, Fillmore also operated a successful sacred music firm, composing a great deal of the music he published. He is still remembered for the hymn tune RESOLUTION ("I am Resolved No Longer to Linger").

1950 American missionary and Auca Indian martyr Jim Elliot warned in his journal: "Sin in a Christian makes God seem distant, deaf. In the body, sin saps animation, as cancer. In the soul, sin stifles the affections, as corrosion. In the spirit, sin solidifies the attitudes, as a callous."

February 9

1791 English founder of Methodism John Wesley advised in a letter: "Do a little at a time, that you may do the more."

1819 Birth of William True Sleeper, New England Congregational clergyman and author of the hymns "Jesus, I Come" ("Out of my bondage, sorrow, and night...") and "Ye Must Be Born Again," in Danbury, New Hampshire.

1839 Scottish clergyman Robert Murray McCheyne declared in a letter: "In spiritual things, this world is all wintertime so long as the Saviour is away."

1912 Death of Andrew Martin Fairbairn (b.1838), English Congregational theologian. While at St. Paul's Congregational Church in Aberdeen, Scotland (1872–77), he won great fame as a preacher and as a lecturer in philosophy and theology. In 1886 he established a Congregational college at Oxford, called Mansfield, which he served as principal until his retirement in 1909.

1914 Birth of Bruce M. Metzger, American Presbyterian New Testament scholar, at Middletown, Pennsylvania. Since he began teaching at Princeton University in 1938, he has become a leading authority of the critical text of the Greek New Testament, as well as a leading evangelical spokesman within higher education.

1930 American pioneer in linguistic education Frank C. Laubach, while serving as a Congregational missionary to the Philippines, acknowledged in a letter: "The sense of being led by an unseen hand which takes mine, while another hand reaches ahead and prepares the way, grows upon me daily."

1931 Birth of Jack Van Impe, American fundamentalist evangelist, in Freeport, Michigan. The son of Belgian immigrants, Van Impe has grown to become a world-renowned Gospel evangelist. He has memorized nearly the entire Bible.

1948 U.S. Senate Chaplain Peter Marshall prayed: "We are tempted to despair of our world. Remind us, O Lord, that Thou hast been facing the same thing in all the world since time began."

February 10

1546 German reformer Martin Luther commanded in a letter: "Pray, and let God worry."

1791 Birth of Henry H. Milman, Anglican churchman and scholar, in London. Though he published several famous scholarly works in his day, we remember him as the author of the hymn "Ride On! Ride On in Majesty."

1819 Birth of Richard S. Willis, American Catholic music critic, in Boston. He published several collections of hymns during his lifetime, composed the popular hymn tune CAROL ("It Came upon the Midnight Clear") and arranged CRUSADERS' HYMN ("Fairest Lord Jesus").

1870 The first chapter of the Y.W.C.A. was established in America, in New York City. Two separate organizations founded in Britain in 1855 united in 1877 to form the present Y.W.C.A. The first Y.W.C.A. World Committee met in London in 1894, followed by the first World Conference in 1898.

1899 The Church of England first authorized use of the 1881 English Revised Version of the Bible (known also as the E.R.V. or R.V.) in the Anglican liturgy and worship.

1912 Death of Tullius C. O'Kane (b.1830), American educator and music publisher. Late in life, O'Kane published several collections of his own sacred melodies. One of his hymn tunes popular today is O'KANE, to which we sing "On Jordan's Stormy Banks I Stand."

1929 Famed English Baptist preacher and devotional writer F.B. Meyer, preached his last sermon, in Wesley Chapel in London. He soon entered a nursing home where his health failed rapidly. He died on March 28, 1929.

1939 Death of Pope Pius XI (b.1857), 258th Pontiff of the Roman Catholic Church. Born Achille Ratti near Monza, Italy, Ratti was made a cardinal in 1921. Less than a year later, on Feb. 6, 1922, Ratti was elected to the papacy following the death of Benedict XV in January.

1947 U.S. Senate Chaplain Peter Marshall prayed: "Save Thy servants from the tyranny of the nonessential. Give them the courage to say 'No' to everything that makes it more difficult to say 'Yes' to Thee."

1969 The World Home Bible League moved to its present headquarters in South Holland, Michigan. Founded in 1938 in Chicago, this interdenominational agency is involved in Christian literature production and distribution of the Scriptures in over 70 countries.

February 11

1717 Birth of William Williams, evangelist and author of "Guide Me, O Thou Great Jehovah," at Cefn-y-coed, Wales. His evangelical ideas led him to leave the established church, thereafter becoming an exceedingly popular preacher within the Welsh Calvinistic Methodist Church. He wrote 900 hymns during his lifetime.

1779 English founder of Methodism, John Wesley, reported in a letter: "Chance has no share in the government of the world. The Lord reigns, and disposes all things, strongly and sweetly, for the good of them that love Him."

1826 Birth of Alexander MacLaren, English Baptist preacher, in Glasgow, Scotland. As pastor of the Union Chapel on Oxford Road, Manchester from 1858–1903, he became a profound Bible expositor. His sermons drew vast congregations, who gave him his reputation as "Prince of expository preachers."

1836 Birth of Washington Gladden, American advocate of a "social Gospel," in Pottsgrove, Pennsylvania. He pastored Congregational churches between 1860 and 1914 in New York, Massachusetts and Ohio. A pioneer in applying the teachings of Christ to various social problems, Gladden is also remembered as author of the hymn "O Master, Let Me Walk with Thee."

1858 Fourteen-year-old French peasant girl Bernadette Soubirous (St. Bernadette) experienced her first vision of the Virgin Mary ("Our Lady of Lourdes") in a grotto, or river cave, by the River Gave. Between this date and July 16, Bernadette experienced 18 such visions.

1871 Birth of Hugh T. Kerr, Canadian-born American Presbyterian clergyman, in Elora, Ontario. Kerr became one of the very first radio preachers in America, airing programs between 1922 and 1942. He also published more than 20 books, including several collections of children's sermon stories.

1888 Death of James G. Small (b.1817), pastor in the Free Church of Scotland. Small was greatly interested in hymnology during his lifetime, and is still remembered as the author of "I've Found a Friend, Oh, Such a Friend."

1895 Birth of Paul B. Peterson, founder and early president of Eurovision. Peterson incorporated this interdenominational mission organization in 1927 in Chicago. Headquartered today in Pasadena, California, Eurovision supports the work of Christian nationals in nearly a dozen European countries by supplying literature and relief, as well as shortwave radio broadcasts.

1903 Birth of Lillian Gartenhaus, in Toronto, Canada. In July 1949, she and her husband, Dr. Jacob Gartenhaus, founded the International Board of Jewish Missions, in Atlanta, Georgia. Headquartered today in Chattanooga, Tennessee, the I.B.J.M. is an evangelical mission agency ministering to Jews in both the U.S. and overseas.

1929 Vatican City was created as an independent, sovereign state within Rome, Italy.

1948 U.S. Senate chaplain Peter Marshall prayed: "We ask Thee not for tasks more suited to our strength, but for strength more suited to our tasks."

February 12

1663 Birth of Cotton Mather, colonial American theologian, in Boston. The commonly recognized leader of the conservative Puritans of his day, Mather sought to maintain a theocratic rule, which was on the decline among the New England clergy. In 1692 he involved himself in the Salem witch trials, going so far as to advocate prosecution of witches. He wrote over 400 books and treatises.

1737 Death of Benjamin Schmolck (b.1672), German Lutheran clergyman. Credited with authoring over 900 hymns, his hymn "My Jesus, As Thou Wilt" is still being sung.

1741 English revivalist George Whitefield stated in a letter: "I want to leap my seventy years, and fly away to God."

1797 Franz Haydn's tune AUSTRIAN HYMN, originally composed for the national anthem of Austria, was first performed for the Emperor Francis II's fifth birthday. We sing "Glorious Things of Thee Are Spoken" to his tune.

1807 Anglican missionary to India and Persia, Henry Martyn, acknowledged in his journal: "Amazing patience, He bears with this faithless foolish heart, and suffers me to come, laden with sins, to receive new pardon, new grace, every day! Why does not such love make me hate sin that grieves Him and hides me from His sight?"

1834 Death of Friedrich Schleiermacher (b.1768), German theologian and philosopher. Schleiermacher made religion a matter of the will, defining it as feeling an absolute dependence upon God. His most important work was his 1799 publication *On Religion: Speeches to Its Cultured Despisers*.

1877 Death of Henry W. Baker (b.1821), English vicar and editor of the standard hymnal of the Anglican Church, *Hymns Ancient and Modern* (1861). Subsequent hymnal compilers owe him credit for the marriages of many texts and tunes which first appeared together in this compilation. Baker composed the hymn tune STEPHANOS ("Art Thou Weary, Art Thou Troubled?") and authored the hymn "The King of Love My Shepherd Is."

1915 Death of Fanny Crosby (b.1820), the famed Gospel songwriter who lost her sight at the age of six weeks. In 1858 she married Alexander Van Alstyne, a blind musician and teacher at the New York Institution for the Blind where she both attended and taught. She began writing texts for Gospel songs during the 1860s. She died at age 95 after composing more than 8,000 texts. Some of her most enduring hymns include: "Blessed Assurance," "Rescue the Perishing," "He Hideth My Soul," "Close to Thee" and "Saved by Grace."

1952 The Roman Catholic religious program *Life Is Worth Living* debuted on Dumont television. Hosted by Bishop Fulton J. Sheen and televised Tuesday nights 8:00–8:30 p.m. EST, it became the longest-running religious TV series of its era, lasting until Feb. 8, 1957.

1962 Swiss Reformed theologian Karl Barth concluded in a letter: "The day will come one day when we shall no longer speak of Roman Catholic and Protestant Christians but simply of Evangelical Christians forming one body and one people."

1971 Death of Nelson Glueck (b.1900), American Jewish archeologist. Associated with the American School of Oriental Research in Jerusalem in various capacities between 1927–47, Glueck succeeded in examining and dating more than 1,500 lower Palestinian and trans-Jordanian sites, including the ancient town of Ezion-geber. Perhaps his most important discovery was King Solomon's copper mines (1933–46).

February 13

1728 Death of Cotton Mather (b.1663), colonial American Puritan theologian. The eldest son of Increase Mather, he published over 400 works, the bulk of them after 1692. The theology he defended in later years indicates that he began to move away from orthodox Calvinism.

1826 The American Temperance Society was founded in Boston. Originally called the American Society for the Promotion of Temperance, its founders comprised an all-male group of clergy and laity. (The first organization in the U.S. to advocate the prohibition of alcoholic beverages had been founded 18 years earlier in Saratoga County, New York.)

1827 Birth of Susan McGroarty, Roman Catholic religious educator, in County Donegal, Ireland. Emigrating to the U.S. at age four, she was educated at the convent school of the Sisters of Notre Dame de Namur, a Belgian-based religious order which she eventually joined. In 1860 she became the first American superior of the order. During her period of leadership, she founded 14 new convents, a novitiate and an orphanage. In 1897 four years before her death, she helped establish Trinity College in Washington, D.C.

1849 Otterbein College was chartered in Westerville, Ohio, under the United Brethren.

1940 Death of Rufus H. McDaniel (b.1850), American clergyman in the Christian Church. Ordained at age 23, he served many churches in the Christian Church, chiefly in southern Ohio. Credited with having written over 100 hymns during his lifetime, we remember him chiefly as the author of "Since Jesus Came Into My Heart."

1951 Death of Lloyd C. Douglas (b.1877), American clergyman and novelist. He served various Congregational pastorates from 1903–33. In 1929 he published his first religious novel, *Magnificent Obsession*. His religious bestsellers have also included *The Robe* (1942) and *The Big Fisherman* (1948).

1984 Death of Roland Bainton (b.1894), American Congregational historian. His expertise was Reformation scholarship. Perhaps his most important work was the 1950 biography *Here I Stand: A Life of Martin Luther*.

February 14

1488 Holy Roman Emperor Frederick III established the Great Swabian League—a confederation of 22 German cities in the Duchy of Swabia (parts of modern-day Baden, Wurttemberg, Bavaria and Switzerland). Seeking to protect and defend its lands from oppression and military violence by their land-owning nobility, the confederation lasted until 1534, when it was dissolved because of political and religious conflicts arising from the Reformation. Until that time, the Great Swabian League had succeeded in maintaining internal order.

1760 Birth of Richard Allen, black American church leader, in Philadelphia, Pennsylvania. Converted at 17, Allen soon joined the Methodist Church. After purchasing his freedom, he was ordained in 1784 as an itinerant preacher. In 1816 Allen was ordained an elder, and he and others organized a black Methodist denomination, the African Methodist Episcopal (later A.M.E. Zion) Church. Chosen by the new denomination as its first bishop (1816–31), Allen became the first black Methodist bishop in America.

1843 Birth of Jesse Lyman Hurlbut, Methodist clergyman, in New York City. After holding pastorates in New Jersey and New York between 1865–79, he was appointed to the Methodist Sunday School Union, working with them from 1879–1900. He wrote thirty books on Bible study, Bible history and Sunday school work. One of his most popular works was *Story of Jesus* (1915).

1884 Birth of Luther B. Bridgers, southern American Methodist pastor and evangelist, in Margaretsville, North Carolina. He is better remembered as author and composer of the hymn "He Keeps Me Singing" (a.k.a. "Jesus, Jesus, Jesus, Sweetest Name I Know" or "There's Within My Heart a Melody").

1892 Birth of Robert H. Pfeiffer, American Methodist biblical scholar, in Bologna, Italy. He directed archeological excavations at Nuzi between 1928–29, edited the *Journal of Biblical Literature* from 1943–47 and served as president of the Society of Biblical Literature in 1950. Considered a liberal scholar by many fundamentalists of his day, Pfeiffer's major contributions were in the fields of Old Testament and Assyriology.

1913 Birth of James A. Pike, controversial American Episcopal bishop, in Oklahoma City, Oklahoma. Ordained into the Episcopal priesthood in 1944, Pike became a noted champion of civil rights and social reform. After his son's suicide in 1966, he resigned his bishop's office and began deep investigations into Spiritualism. He died in the Judean wilderness of Palestine in 1969 while on a personal pilgrimage.

1914 Birth of Ira F. Stanphill, American song evangelist, in Bellview, New Mexico. Converted at age 12, Stanphill immediately began preparing himself for the ministry. He served Assembly of God pastorates in Florida, Pennsylvania and Texas. As a singing evangelist, he has preached throughout the U.S. and in 40 other nations. He is best known today for the hymn "Room at the Cross," which he wrote in 1946. The hymn has been used by the nationally-aired radio broadcast *Revival Time* as its closing theme for many years.

1949 Chaim Weizmann was elected the first president of modern Israel. Born in 1874, Weizmann was trained in chemistry but became involved in the Zionist movement while still a student. During World War I, he was instrumental in influencing the British government to proclaim the Balfour Declaration, endorsing the establishment of a Jewish national homeland in Palestine. Working at reducing Arab resistance to the implementation of the Balfour Declaration between 1921 and 1945 in various leadership capacities, Weizmann saw the establishment of modern Israel in 1948.

1952 Death of Francis H. Rowley (b.1854), American Baptist clergyman and humanitarian. The Rowley School of Humanities at Oglethorpe University in Atlanta was named in his honor. He is more widely remembered as author of the hymn "I Will Sing the Wondrous Story."

February 15

1386 King Jagiello of Lithuania was baptized into the Christian faith—thus, in effect, Christianizing all of Lithuania, the last remaining heathen nation on the European continent. This event marks the completion of the evangelization of Europe in the expansion of the early church, a task which began the night the Apostle Paul received the vision of a Macedonian (European) calling to him, "Come over into Macedonia, and help us" (Acts 16:9).

1497 Birth of Philip Melanchthon, German humanist and reformer, at Bretten. In 1518 he began a long personal association with Martin Luther. Melanchthon attended the 1519 Leipzig Disputation between Luther and Eck, nevertheless he was of a more peaceful nature. Called the "formulating genius of the Reformation," Melanchthon composed the Augsburg Confession. After Luther's death in 1546, Melanchthon became the acknowledged leader of the German Reformation.

1730 Death of Thomas Bray (b.1656), Anglican clergyman. Born in Shropshire, England, Bray was sent to America in 1699 to organize the Anglican Church in Maryland, after which he returned to London the following year. Having become interested in mission work among the New England Indians, Bray became one of the founders of the Society for the Propagation of the Gospel, in 1701. In 1698 he had founded the Society for Promoting Christian Knowledge (S.P.C.K.). These were England's two oldest missionary societies.

1762 Anglican clergyman and hymnwriter John Newton assured in a letter: "We serve a gracious Master who knows how to overrule even our mistakes to His glory and our own advantage."

1860 Wheaton College (Illinois) was chartered in Wheaton, Illinois, under Methodist sponsorship. The following year the school passed to Congregational control, and is presently independent.

1861 Birth of Alfred North Whitehead, British philosopher and clergyman, at Ramsgate, Kent. Emmigrating to America in 1924, he taught at Harvard until his retirement in 1938. Whitehead constructed a philosophical system kindred to Platonism, known as the "philosophy of organism." Its theology conceived God as receiving enrichment from the world processes, and in turn synthesizing human events into the most meaningful whole they are capable of forming. In collaboration with his pupil Bertrand Russell, Whitehead published his monumental *Principia Mathematica* in 1910–13.

1867 Birth of Charles W. Douglas, author of the hymn tune ST. DUNSTAN'S, to which we sing the hymn "He Who Would Valiant Be."

1930 Death of Franklin L. Sheppard (b.1852), a dedicated church layman of the Episcopal Church and later of the Presbyterian church in the northeastern U.S. Interested in music all his life, he served on the editorial committee of the 1911 edition of the *Presbyterian Hymnal*. He composed the hymn tune TERRA BEATA, to which "This Is My Father's World" is sung.

1932 Birth of W. Elmo Mercer, popular American arranger of Christian Gospel music.

1986 Living Bibles International moved to its present headquarters in Naperville, Illinois, from nearby Wheaton, Illinois. Founded in 1968 by the editor of *The Living Bible*, Kenneth N. Taylor, L.B.I. is an interdenominational service agency engaged primarily in Bible translation, printing and distribution through Christian nationals within 45 countries.

February 16

1607 A Mother Goose nursery rhyme was born when neighborhood children serenaded Archdeacon John Sprat of St. David's Church in London. The archdeacon was known for his small appetite compared with that of his robust wife. (People often tried to invite him to a meal without asking his wife.) Thus children sing today: "Jack Sprat could eat no fat; his wife could eat no lean; and so betwixt them both, you see, they licked the platter clean."

1741 English revivalist George Whitefield admonished in a letter: "Use the world, but let it be as though you used it not."

1801 The African Methodist Episcopal Zion (A.M.E.Z.) Church was officially incorporated as a Protestant denomination, distinctly separate from its parent, the Methodist Episcopal Church. The founders of the black denomination first met to organize the prototype denomination of the A.M.E.Z. Church in 1796; and they constructed the first frame church the following year. The church held its first national conference in June 1821. Today, there are slightly over one million members in the A.M.E.Z. Church.

1865 English clergyman Sabine Baring-Gould first published the popular hymn "Now the Day Is Over," in *The Church Times*. The hymn was based on the text of Prov. 3:24: "When thou liest down, thou shalt not be afraid: yea, thou shalt lie down, and thy sleep shall be sweet."

1872 Death of Henry F. Chorley (b.1808), self-educated English music journalist who worked as the music editor of the London *Athenaeum* for 35 years. He authored the hymn "God the Omnipotent!"

1911 "Rise Up, O Men of God," by William P. Merrill, was first published in the Presbyterian periodical *The Continent*. Merrill wrote the hymn that same year while aboard a steamer on Lake Michigan, heading back to his home in Chicago.

February 17

1741 English revivalist George Whitefield admonished in a letter: "Be content with no degree of sanctification. Be always crying out, 'Lord, let me know more of myself and of thee.' "

1760 This date became Feb. 28 in Lorraine (in northeastern France) when it adopted the Gregorian calendar (created by Pope Gregory XIII in 1582), to replace the older, inaccurate Julian calendar (created by Julius Caesar in 46 B.C.).

1816 Birth of Edward Hopper, American Presbyterian clergyman, in New York City. He spent all but 11 years of his ministry at pastorates within his native city. He is remembered as author of the hymn "Jesus, Savior, Pilot Me."

1841 Birth of Alfred Plummer, Anglican theologian and church historian, at Heworth, Durhamshire, England. Plummer authored several definitive works on early church history, as well as contributing several volumes to the *Cambridge Bible for Colleges*, the *International Critical Commentary* and the *Pulpit Commentary* series.

1888 Birth of Ronald A. Knox, Roman Catholic scholar, at Kibworth, England. Raised an Anglican, Knox converted to Catholicism at the age of 29. Ordained a priest in 1919, he served as the Catholic chaplain at Oxford from 1926–39, after which he devoted himself to translating the Bible into English. He completed the New Testament in 1945, and the Old Testament in 1949.

1889 William Ashley ("Billy") Sunday, baseball player-turned-evangelist, made his first appearance in Chicago as an evangelist. Strongly fundamentalist in his theology, Sunday preached for temperance in drinking and against scientific evolution. Over 100 million people are said to have heard him preach before he died in 1935.

1898 Death of Frances E. Willard (b.1839), American educator and temperance reformer. She was appointed Dean of Northwestern Women's College in 1871, but left the post three years later when her interest turned to the anti-saloon crusade then sweeping the country. Convinced that prohibition and women's suffrage went hand-in-hand, she became a strong supporter of the Prohibition Party and served as President of the Women's Christian Temperance Union (W.C.T.U.) from 1879 until her death. Passage of the 18th and 19th Amendments to the U.S. Constitution are partially a result of her work.

1903 Death of Joseph Parry (b.1841), Welsh-born music scholar and composer. He taught music at both the Welsh University College at Aberystwyth (1873–79) and the University College, Cardiff (1888–1903). He wrote many volumes of music, but is remembered chiefly for a single hymn tune: ABERYSTWYTH, to which we sing "Jesus, Lover of My Soul."

1906 Birth of Paul S. Minear, American Congregational theologian, at Mount Pleasant, Iowa. He taught religion and New Testament studies at the Hawaii School of Religion (1933–34), Garrett Biblical Institute (1933–44), and Andover-Newton Theological Seminary (1944–56), and Yale Divinity School (1956–71).

1921 Death of B.B. Warfield (b.1851), American Presbyterian theologian and educator. Between 1887–1921, Warfield taught theology at Princeton Seminary and served twice as its president (1902–03, 1913–14). An enthusiastic Calvinist, Warfield belonged to the Fundamentalist side of the Modernist controversy, which polarized American denominations during the first part of the 20th century. Holding a high regard for the Westminster Confession of Faith, Warfield believed in original sin, predestination, limited atonement and biblical inerrancy.

1952 Birth of William Patrick ("Pat") Terry, contemporary Christian songwriter and music artist. His Pat Terry Group recorded several popular Christian songs, including "Home Where I Belong," "I Can't Wait" and "Meet Me Here."

February 18

1546 Death of German reformer Martin Luther (b.1483), who nailed 95 theses for discussion on the Wittenberg Castle church door on Oct. 31, 1517, the effective symbol of the beginning of the Protestant Reformation in Europe.

1562 Religious wars in France between the Huguenots (French Protestants) and the Roman Catholics (lasting until 1598) forced a band of Huguenot colonists to leave France for religious refuge in Florida.

1564 Death of Michelangelo Buonarroti (b.1475), Italian Renaissance artist and one of the greatest artists of Western history. A genius in nearly every medium of art he attempted, he worked under the patronage of Popes Julius II, Leo X, Clement VIII and Paul III. Perhaps his most popular works are the frescoes in the Sistine Chapel, which took nearly a dozen years to complete (1508–12, 1535–41).

1571 A group of Spanish Jesuits in the Chesapeake Bay area were murdered by the Indians they came to convert. Having arrived six months earlier, these missionaries were led by Fray Batista Segura. The massacre (which had begun five days earlier) ultimately led to the withdrawal of all Jesuits from Florida as well.

1678 John Bunyan's *Pilgrim's Progress* was first published, in England. A Puritan, Bunyan was imprisoned frequently between 1660 and 1672 for preaching without a license. It was during these sequestered times that Bunyan collected the ideas which enabled him to produce this masterpiece of Christian literature.

1753 This day became March 1 in Sweden when that nation adopted the Gregorian calendar to replace the older, inaccurate Julian calendar.

1781 Birth of Henry Martyn, Anglican missionary to India and Persia, in Cornwall, England. Martyn first sailed to India in 1805 as a chaplain for the East India Company. His outstanding linguistic gifts eventually led him into one of his greatest tasks: the translation of the New Testament into Hindustani. By Feb. 1812, he had also completed translations of the New Testaments in Arabic and Persian. He died in October of that same year, at the young age of 31, while on a ship taking him back to England.

1867 The Augusta Institute was founded in Georgia, in the basement of the Springfield Baptist Church of Augusta. Established as a college for black students, it moved to Atlanta in 1879, changing its name to the Atlanta Baptist Seminary. In 1913 it became Morehouse College.

1874 Death of William Sandys (b.1792), English lawyer and composer of "The First Noel." Admitted to the bar at age 22, Sandys maintained a successful legal practice until his retirement in 1873. His name is known in the church for pioneering popular interest in Christmas carols.

1946 American Roman Catholic Archbishop Francis Joseph Spellman was made a cardinal under the pontificate of Pius XII.

February 19

1568 Death of Miles Coverdale (b.1488), translator and publisher of the first complete Bible to be printed in English (1535). Coverdale was also editor of the Great Bible (1539), thus responsible for the publication of England's first two "authorized versions" of the Scriptures. Due to the vacillation of the British monarchy between Catholic and Protestant allegiance, Coverdale spent much of his life outside his native England to escape persecution for heresy.

1682 This day became March 1 in Strassburg, Germany when that city adopted the Gregorian calendar to replace the older inaccurate Julian calendar.

1700 This day became March 1 in Denmark and Norway when those nations adopted the Gregorian calendar.

1812 New England Congregational missionary Adoniram Judson and his wife set sail from Salem, Massachusetts, to Calcutta, India, for the first time. Bombay had been selected as the first mission center of the newly formed American Board of Commissioners for Foreign Missions, although Judson eventually devoted his missionary labors to the people of Rangoon, in Burma.

1849 Death of Bernard Barton (b.1784), England's "Quaker Poet." From 1810 until his death, he served as a clerk in the Woodbridge, Suffolk, local bank, enjoying the friendship of Charles Lamb, Byron and Shelley during this period. From 1812 to 1845 he published about ten books of verse, from which we get the hymn "Walk in the Light!"

1869 Death of Elizabeth Clephane (b.1830), Scottish poetess. Raised an orphan, her frail body was often in poor health. Yet she dedicated her limited resources to benefit the poor in her community. She wrote fewer than a dozen hymns, all of which were published posthumously. Two of these hymns endure: "Beneath the Cross of Jesus" and "The Ninety and Nine."

1907 Birth of Rev. E.V. Steele, a Canadian who founded the World Missions Fellowship in 1946. This interdenominational agency is headquartered in Grants Pass, Oregon, and is engaged in evangelism, camping and leadership programs in India, Austria, Ireland, Brazil and Japan.

February 20

1494 Birth of Johann Agricola, German Protestant reformer, in Eisleben. He studied under Martin Luther at Wittenberg and served as Luther's recording secretary at the Leipzig Disputation (1519). In 1527 a falling out with Philip Melanchthon over the place of the law in Christian experience led Agricola to break with Luther completely. After 1540 he devoted most of his energies to translating his theology into political policies.

1743 Colonial American missionary to the New England Indians David Brainerd cautioned in his journal: "Selfish religion loves Christ for his benefits, but not for himself."

1950 American missionary and Auca Indian martyr Jim Elliot warned in his journal: "One may know God's work for his soul without understanding it all. He that grasps God intellectually grips Him coolly. Let the heart be warm at all costs to the head in the getting of Christianity."

1960 Death of Rev. William M. Strong (b.1877), founder of the Gospel Mission of South America (1923). Incorporated in 1940 in the U.S., G.M.S.A. is presently headquartered at Ft. Lauderdale, Florida. This interdenominational sending agency of Baptist tradition is involved in evangelism, broadcasting, Bible correspondence courses, literature, camps and theological education. Its primary works are in Argentina, Chile and Uruguay.

1960 Death of Sir Charles Leonard Woolley (b.1880), British archeologist. Spending more than 40 years of his life in archeological research, his achievements in the field include the excavation of Ur of the Chaldees between 1922–34. He is also known for discovering the Sumerian civilization. A writer whose literary skills captured popular interest in archeology, one of Woolley's best written works was *Ur of the Chaldees* (1929).

1976 Death of Kathryn Kuhlman (b.1907), popular American radio/TV evangelist and faith-healer. Born in Concordia, Missouri, Kuhlman was ordained by the Evangelical Church Alliance, but later joined the American Baptist Convention. Her preaching emphasized the healing power of the Holy Spirit.

Her organization was also devoted to drug rehabilitation and the education of blind children.

February 21

1109 Death of Anselm of Canterbury (b.1033), Italian-born Catholic priest and theologian. In theological literature, Anselm is best remembered for his 1099 religious classic *Cur Deus Homo* (*Why God Became Man*). He has been called the most original thinker in the Roman Catholic Church since St. Augustine. He made faith the foremost tenet of philosophy, as seen in his oft-quoted statement: "I believe, that I may understand."

1142 Death of Peter Abelard (b.1079), French philosopher and theologian. He is remembered by laymen for his love affair with one of his female students, Heloise (ca.1098). Theologically, he challenged earlier church traditions by teaching that Christ's death demonstrated God's love, but was not vicarious. Strong opposition led by Bernard of Clairvaux led to Abelard's excommunication two years before his death. He spent his last days at the monastery of Cluny writing his *Confession* and *Apology*.

1173 Under Pope Alexander III (1159–81), the Roman Catholic Church canonized Thomas Becket, the Archbishop (1162–70) of Canterbury, England, who was martyred by King Henry II three years earlier.

1795 Freedom of worship was established in France under the constitution that came out of the French Revolution of 1789.

1801 Birth of John Henry Newman, British Anglican-turned-Catholic, in London. Research behind his 1833 publication *Arians of the Fourth Century* led him to doubt the authenticity of the Church of England. He was joined by Keble, Froud and Pusey after 1839, who spearheaded the Oxford Movement, created to address laxity within the Anglican Church. In 1843 Newman resigned his Anglican post and was received into the Roman Catholic Church in 1845. In 1879 he was elevated to the office of cardinal.

1945 Death of Eric Liddell (b.1902), Scottish Olympic champion and missionary to China. While a student at Edinburgh, Liddell became the best known athlete Scotland had produced. In 1925 he joined the staff of the Anglo-Chinese Christian College in Tientsin, China (his birthplace). In 1942 he became a prisoner of the Japanese. His death from a brain tumor occurred just before he would have been released from his captors.

1954 The religious program *Hour of Decision* was aired for the last time on ABC television. Hosted by Billy Graham, one of the first evangelists to utilize television, this 15-minute program first aired two and a half years earlier, on Sept 30, 1951. It played messages Graham had delivered during his many crusades throughout the world.

February 22

1076 At a Roman synod, Pope Gregory VII excommunicated Holy Roman Emperor Henry IV, suspended him from using royal powers and released his subjects from allegiance to him. Henry had been interfering with the church's right to choose and install clerics.

1805 Birth of Sarah Flower Adams, English religious writer, in Harlow, Essex. Her literary talents generated both verse and prose, even a catechism for children. Her one writing that still endures is the hymn "Nearer, My God, to Thee."

1819 Birth of James Russell Lowell, American poet and author of the hymn "Once to Every Man and Nation."

1840 Birth of Milton S. Terry, American Methodist clergyman and educator, at Coeymans, New York. After serving several pastorates in the New York area, Terry was appointed professor of Hebrew, Old Testament exegesis, and Christian doctrine at the Garrett Bible Institute in Evanston, Illinois. Perhaps his most famous writing is *Biblical Hermeneutics*, which is still in print.

1874 Dr. Thomas DeWitt Talmage's reconstructed Brooklyn Tabernacle was dedicated in New York City. The original church building had been erected by his American Presbyterian congregation in 1870, with a seating capacity of 4,000. This structure and its two successors were destroyed by fire in 1872, 1889, and 1894.

1901 O.M.S. International was founded by Charles and Lettie Cowman, who arrived in Japan to help establish a Bible training institute. Today, the O.M.S. headquarters is in Greenwood, Indiana. This interdenominational mission organization of Wesleyan tradition engages in evangelism, church planting, radio/TV broadcasting, and the support of national churches in over a dozen countries.

1906 Birth of Betty Stam, American missionary martyr. She met her husband John Stam (b.1907) while they were students at Moody Bible Institute. Betty went to China in 1931 under the China Inland Mission, followed by John in 1932. They married in 1933 and were sent to Tsingteh. In 1934 they were both martyred (beheaded) by the Chinese Communists. The public response to their deaths brought in resources and new volunteers for missions.

1980 American Presbyterian apologist for the Christian faith, Francis A. Schaeffer, explained in a letter: "None of us are normal, even after we are Christians—if we mean by that being perfect. What is possible, however, is for us to live in the fullness of life in the circle of who we are, constantly pressing on the border lines to try to take further steps."

February 23

155 Martyrdom of Polycarp, early church Father and Bishop of Smyrna. A disciple of the Apostle John, Polycarp was placed under Roman arrest at the age of 86 and burned at the stake for refusing to deny his Christian faith.

1662 Death of Johann Cruger (b.1598), chief musician at the Lutheran Cathedral of St. Nicholas, in Berlin, from 1622 until his death. His chief contributions to hymnody were the chorale melodies he composed as settings for some of the great Lutheran hymns of his day. His *Praxis Pietatis Melica*, which passed through 44 editions between 1644–1736, was the most outstanding collection of hymns to be published in the 17th century. One of his hymn tunes still endures: NUN DANKET, to which we sing "Now Thank We All Our God."

1685   Birth of George Frederick (Georg Friedrich) Handel, German music composer, at Halle. In 1741, at the age of 56, he composed his musical masterpiece: the immortal oratorio *Messiah*. Handel spent the last six years of his life in total blindness.

1744   Colonial American missionary to the New England Indians David Brainerd commented in his journal: "There is a God in heaven who over-rules all things for the best; and this is the comfort of my soul."

1775   Anglican clergyman and hymnwriter John Newton assured in a letter: "How great and honorable is the privilege of a true believer! That he has neither wisdom nor strength in himself is no disadvantage, for he is connected with infinite wisdom and almighty power."

1813   Birth of Franz Delitzsch, Lutheran Old Testament scholar, at Leipzig, Germany. Teaching principally at the universities of Rostock (1846–50), Erlangen (1850–67), and Leipzig (1867–90), Delitzsch's greatest contribution to biblical studies is the Old Testament commentary series he collaborated on with J.F.K. Keil, published in 1861 and still in print.

1816   Birth of John E. Bode, Anglican clergyman, in London. His writings were chiefly collections of original ballads and poems. He is remembered as author of the hymn "O Jesus, I Have Promised."

1834   Scottish clergyman Robert Murray McCheyne recorded in his diary: "Rose early to seek God and found Him whom my soul loveth. Who would not rise early to meet such company?"

1904   Pope Pius X issued the Apostolic Letter *Scripturae Sacrae*, which empowered the Pontifical Biblical Commission to confer college degrees in scriptural studies within the Roman Catholic Church.

1961   The National Council of Churches endorsed artificial contraception as an aid to family planning.

1965   Retired Swiss Reformed theologian Karl Barth asserted in a letter: "Each may and must follow his own path and have his own style of thought and speech."

February 24

303   The first official Roman edict for the persecution of Christians was published by Roman Emperor Galerius Valerius Maximianus.

1500   Birth of Holy Roman Emperor Charles V, at Ghent in Flanders. Reigning from 1519–56, he was the European ruler who officially pronounced Martin Luther an outlaw and heretic.

1509   Pope Julius II issued a papal bull condemning the practice of dueling.

1582   A commission working under Pope Gregory XIII at the papal Villa Mondragone completed its reform of the old Julian calendar. Adopting the new Gregorian calendar involved dropping ten days (Oct 5–14, 1582) and an adjustment of the rule for counting leap years. The new calendar was adopted immediately by Catholic states in Europe; by Protestant and orthodox governments as late as 1918.

1633 Death of George Herbert (b.1593), English religious poet. A student of another famous English divine, John Donne, the sense of devotion in Herbert's poetry is much more subdued. While his fame rests largely on his poems ("The Temple," "Sacred Poems," et al.), Herbert was also passionately fond of music, and authored the hymn "The God of Love My Shepherd Is."

1782 Early American Methodist Bishop Francis Asbury conceded in his journal: "I find my greatest trials to arise from 'taking thought': it is by this Satan tries to come in; it is my constitutional weakness to be gloomy and dejected; the work of God puts life into me."

1886 Death of Samuel Wolcott (b.1813), American Congregational clergyman and missionary. Starting at age 56, Wolcott wrote more than 200 hymns. His best-remembered hymn is probably the missionary hymn he wrote on Feb. 7, 1869: "Christ for the World We Sing."

1930 Famed American clergyman and Bible expositor, Harry A. Ironside, was issued a unanimous call to become pastor at the Moody Memorial Bible Church, in Chicago. Ironside accepted the call, and pastored at Moody from 1930–48. Better known for his evangelistic, radio and writing ministries, this was Ironside's only pastorate.

1967 Retired Swiss Reformed theologian Karl Barth, the year before his death, assured in a letter: "The statement that God is dead comes from Nietzsche and has recently been trumpeted abroad by some German and American theologians. But the good Lord has not died of this; He who dwells in the heaven laughs at them."

February 25

1570 Pope Pius V excommunicated and "deposed" Protestant Queen Elizabeth I, declaring her to be a usurper to the throne of England. It was the last such sentence to be made against a reigning monarch by any pope.

1738 English revivalist George Whitefield commented in a letter: "God, I find, has a people everywhere; Christ has a flock, though but a little flock, in all places."

1796 Death of Samuel Seabury (b.1729), first bishop of the Protestant Episcopal Church in America. Born in Groton, Connecticut, Seabury went to Edinburgh to study medicine. In England, he was ordained an Anglican priest in 1753, returning to America the next year as a missionary for the Church of England. Following the American Revolution, Seabury and three other American bishops collaborated on a new constitution that made the American Protestant Episcopal Church (the Episcopalians) independent and autonomous from England.

1852 Death of Thomas Moore (b.1779), British Roman Catholic writer. During his lifetime, his social graces made him a favorite in London. However, we remember him as author of the hymn "Come, Ye Disconsolate."

1862 Death of Andrew Reed (b.1787), English Congregational clergyman. His gift for writing sacred music is memorialized in the hymn "Holy Ghost, with Light Divine," which he authored.

1902 Birth of Oscar Cullmann, New Testament scholar, at Strasbourg, Germany. He is best known for his views of "Heilsgeschichte" or "salvation history," which sees the biblical story as the unfolding of the divine purpose in the salvation of humankind. Two of his publications are *Christ and Time* (1946) and *Christology of the New Testament* (1959).

1940 Death of Mary Mills Patrick (b.1850), American missionary to Turkey, Greece and Armenia. In 1871 she was sent by the American Board of Commissioners for Foreign Missions to teach in an eastern Turkey mission school. In 1875 she was transferred, and began teaching at the Constantinople Women's College. Her leadership kept the school open through the Balkan Wars, the Turkish Revolution and World War I. She retired as president of the school in 1924, and wrote a history of the college in 1934.

February 26

1732 The only Roman Catholic church built and maintained in the American colonies before the American Revolutionary War celebrated its first mass. (In other American colonies, such as Maryland, Catholics were forced to practice their rituals in private homes.)

1807 Birth of Johann Karl Friedrich Keil, German Lutheran Bible scholar. Influenced by Hengstenberg, Keil was a vigorously conservative theologian, rejecting rationalistic views of Scripture. His Old Testament Bible Commentary, written in collaboration with Franz Delitzsch, first appeared in print 1861 and is still in print.

1835 An edict was issued by Ranavalona I, Queen of Madagascar, forbidding the newly established Christian faith. The church in Madagascar had earlier been planted by Welsh missionary David Jones, who had returned home because of failing health in 1831 after spending 13 years in the field. In spite of the persecution that followed the queen's edict, the Malagasy church grew tremendously. In 1837 Jones returned to Mauritius and the church there grew from 20 to over 7,000 members.

1840 Church of Scotland clergyman Robert Murray McCheyne reminded in a letter: "Our soul should be a mirror of Christ; we should reflect every feature: for every grace in Christ there should be a counterpart in us."

1846 Birth of George C. Stebbins, American Baptist music evangelist, in Orleans County, New York. For 25 years he was associated with D.L. Moody; later he assisted Ira Sankey in compiling several editions of the *Gospel Hymns* series. He composed over 1,500 Gospel song tunes. Many of these are still popular: STEBBINS ("Jesus Is Tenderly Calling Thee Home"), FRIEND ("I've Found a Friend, Oh, Such a Friend"), HOLINESS ("Take Time to Be Holy") and POLLARD ("Have Thine Own Way, Lord").

1897 Birth of Dr. Basil W. Miller, founder and first president of World-Wide Missions. Miller originally incorporated his missions organization in Altadena, California, under the name Basil Miller Foundation. The name was changed to World-Wide Missions in 1959. Today, W.W.M. is headquartered in Pasadena, and works in over 30 countries. This interdenominational agency engages primarily in supporting national workers and churches, relief aid and medicine on mission fields where needed.

1914   Death of Samuel R. Driver (b.1846), English Old Testament scholar. Connected with Oxford University all his professional life, he succeeded E.B. Pusey in the Regius chair of Hebrew in 1883 until his death. His famous literary contributions include membership on the Old Testament Committee of the 1885 English Revised Version of the Bible, also the *Hebrew and English Lexicon of the Old Testament* (1906, but still in print), which he coauthored with F. Brown and C.A. Briggs.

1932   Birth of Johnny Cash, born-again American country and western songwriter and vocalist, in Kingsland, Arkansas. In 1968 he married June Carter, formerly of the Carter Family and the Carter Sisters country music groups. Cash underwent a spiritual conversion about this same time.

February 27

280   Birth of Constantine the Great, the first Roman emperor to be converted to the Christian faith (ca.312), thereby making the early church (politically and otherwise) "Roman" Catholic.

1807   Birth of Henry Wadsworth Longfellow, American poet, in Portland, Maine. Remembered more popularly for such writings as *The Song of Hiawatha* (1855) and *The Courtship of Miles Standish* (1858), the tragic death of his second wife in a fire turned Longfellow's writing to more spiritual topics. One of his greatest works was an English translation of Dante's *Divine Comedy*. But Longfellow is regarded among churchgoers for the Christmas hymn he penned in 1864: "I Heard the Bells on Christmas Day."

1838   Birth of William J. Kirkpatrick, American Methodist music composer, in Duncannon, Pennsylvania. He edited his first collection of hymns at age 21. We still use several of his hymn tunes, including JESUS SAVES ("We Have Heard the Joyful Sound"), KIRKPATRICK ("He Hideth My Soul"), REDEEMED ("Redeemed, How I Love to Proclaim It"), TRUST IN JESUS ("'Tis So Sweet to Trust in Jesus") and both words and music to "Lord, I'm Coming Home."

1839   Church of Scotland clergyman Robert Murray McCheyne lamented in a letter: "Most of God's people are contented to be saved from the hell that is without. They are not so anxious to be saved from the hell that is within."

1843   Birth of Joseph Yates Peek, American Methodist layman, in Brooklyn, New York. Peek worked as a carpenter, farmer, druggist's clerk, Civil War soldier, florist and lay preacher. But his name endures today as composer of the hymn tune PEEK ("I Would Be True").

1849   William Jewell College was chartered in Liberty, Missouri, under Baptist sponsorship.

1871   Birth of Lewis Sperry Chafer, American Presbyterian educator, in Rock Creek, Ohio. In 1924 Chafer founded Dallas Theological Seminary, serving there as president and professor of theology until his death in 1952. Chafer's eight-volume *Systematic Theology* (1947) is one of the most detailed analyses of dispensational premillenial Protestant theology available today.

1938 English Bible expositor Arthur W. Pink challenged in a letter: "Slackness and carelessness are inexcusable in a child of God. He should ever present a model and example of conscientiousness, painstaking care, and exactness."

1963 Death of C. Harold Lowden (b.1883), American Evangelical and Reformed (now United Church of Christ) sacred music artist. He worked over 60 years in various branches of sacred music, serving as music editor for the Reformed Church Board, teaching music at the Bible Institute of Pennsylvania, and serving 28 years as minister of music at the Linden Baptist Church of Camden, New Jersey. He composed a number of hymn tunes during his lifetime, two of which are still in use: GENEVA ("God Who Touchest Earth with Beauty") and LIVING ("Living for Jesus a Life That Is True").

February 28

1638 The castle of Hara, on the island of Amakusa, Japan, held by 30,000 Christian troops under Masada Shiro, was captured after hard fighting by 125,000 troops of the Shogun Yoshimune. The defenders set fire to the castle and all perished either in the flames or by the sword. From then until 1873 (235 years later), Christianity was banned in Japan under penalty of death.

1759 Pope Clement XIII granted permission for the Bible to be translated into all the languages of the Roman Catholic states.

1784 English founder of Methodism John Wesley formally chartered the movement thereafter known as Wesleyan Methodism.

1815 Birth of Karl Heinrich Graf, German Protestant Old Testament critic, at Muhlhausen, in Alsace. While yet a student, Graf embraced the theory of a post-exilic Pentateuch, eventually passing it on to its most articulate proponent, Julius Wellhausen. The theory has since come to be called the "JEDP Hypothesis" or the "Graf-Wellhausen Theory" and claims that the final form of Genesis-Deuteronomy was not published until after the time of Judah's exile in Babylon (after 500 B.C.).

1857 Birth of Alfred Loisy, French Roman Catholic theologian, in Marne. After 1904 Loisy became the most prominent representative of modern biblical criticism within his church, costing him excommunication in 1908. He discarded his clerical garb and taught history of religions at the College de France, 1909–1930.

1865 Birth of Sir Wilfred Grenfell, medical missionary to Labrador, in Cheshire, England. Converted to the Christian faith at one of Dwight Moody's evangelistic services in 1885, he began his famous 42-year-long work as a missionary and physician among the fisherfolk in Labrador and Newfoundland in 1892.

1873 The Society of Mary was officially sanctioned by Pope Pius IX. This Roman Catholic religious order, founded in 1816, seeks to unite the work of education with missions.

1875 Death of Jean Claude Marie Colin who founded the Roman Catholic religious order the Society of Mary in 1816.

1944 Nazi soldiers invaded the home of Dutch Christian Corrie ten Boom, and arrested the family for the charge of harboring Jews. The Jews she had in her home at the time escaped unharmed. Corrie's father and sister died soon after in Nazi prison camps.

1947 U.S. Senate Chaplain Peter Marshall prayed: "Let not the past ever be so dear to us as to set a limit to the future. Give us the courage to change our minds when that is needed."

1949 The Christian Missionary Fellowship was incorporated in Topeka, Kansas, by founder James C. Smith. Headquartered since 1980 in Indianapolis, Indiana, this interdenominational mission agency is engaged in evangelism, church planting and medical and missionary support. Its major centers are located in Kenya, Brazil, Mexico and Indonesia.

February 29

468 Death of Pope St. Hilary (a.k.a. Hilarus, Hilarius), 46th Bishop of Rome according to Roman Catholic tradition. Hilary's pontificate began seven years earlier, on Nov. 19, 461. During his reign he reaffirmed the earlier church councils of Nicea (325), Ephesus (431), and Chalcedon (451), from which the definitive creeds of the early church were established.

1528 Death of Patrick Hamilton (b.ca.1504), Scottish reformer and martyr. Charged with promoting heresy the year before, he fled to Germany where he spent time with Martin Luther and William Tyndale. Returning to Scotland, he vigorously promoted the doctrines of the Reformation and was arrested. Condemned as a heretic, he was burned at the stake for his faith—one of the first martyrs of the Scottish Reformation.

1604 Death of John Whitgift (b.ca.1530), the Anglican archbishop who attended Queen Elizabeth I on her deathbed and crowned James I king of England. Whitgift was also present at the Hampton Court Conference of 1603, where the motion was passed to issue a version of the Bible in English, authorized for use in the churches. The resulting work was the King James (or authorized) Version of 1611.

1692 The Salem Witch Trials in colonial Massachusetts began when Tituba, the female Indian servant of the Rev. Samuel Parris family, and Sarah Good were both accused of witchcraft.

1736 Birth of Ann Lee, religious mystic, in Manchester, England. In 1758 she joined a splinter group of the Friends called the "Shaking Quakers." By 1770 she was one of the leading spokespersons for the movement. Known soon after as "Mother Ann," she, her family, and her followers emigrated to the American colonies in 1774, where she founded the religious sect which called themselves "The United Society of Believers in Christ's Second Appearing." To the rest of the world, the group came to be called the Shakers.

1948 Birth of Karen Lafferty, contemporary Christian composer and musical artist. She wrote the popular Christian songs "Seek Ye First" and "Father of Lights."

1948 American missionary and Auca Indian martyr Jim Elliot emphasized in his journal: "Redemption marks the new beginning of life. Men do not live at all until they have life eternal."

1960   Death of Thomas O. Chisholm (b.1866), American Methodist hymnwriter. After his conversion at age 27, Chisholm wrote more than 1,200 poems, many of which were used as hymn texts. Two of these hymns that still remain popular are "Great Is Thy Faithfulness" and "Living for Jesus."

March

March 1

1562 French Protestants (Huguenots) were slaughtered at the Massacre of Vassy, thus touching off the first of eight religious wars between the Huguenots and the Roman Catholics in France. These wars ended 36 years later, in 1598, when Henry IV of Bourbon issued the Edict of Nantes, which granted political toleration of the Huguenots.

1633 Death of George Herbert (b.1593), Anglican poet and clergyman. He taught at the University of Cambridge between 1615–27, and for a time was courtier to King James I, until he was ordained in 1630. He was fond of music, and wrote hymns for lute and viola. One hymn of his endures: "The God of Love My Shepherd Is."

1767 The Jesuits were expelled from Spain by Emperor Charles III. Originally approved by Pope Paul III in 1540, the Society of Jesus thereafter increased rapidly in size and influence. In the second half of the 18th century, ministers of the Bourbon courts opposed the religious order and succeeded in having the Jesuits expelled from Portugal, France and Spain. Finally, a brief extorted from Pope Clement XIV in 1773 suppressed the order throughout the world. Later, in 1814, Pope Pius VII reestablished the Society of Jesus, and the order has continued to the present time.

1815 Georgetown College in Washington, D.C., was established, under Roman Catholic auspices.

1861 Birth of Carrie E. Rounsefell, New England song evangelist who wrote the hymn tune MANCHESTER ("I'll Go Where You Want Me to Go"), in Merrimack, New Hampshire. Though married to a bookkeeper for a paint and wallpaper firm, she traveled throughout New England, accompanying herself on the autoharp. A member of the Church of God in her later years, she composed several hymn tunes.

1889 Death of William H. Monk (b.1823), Anglican Church organist. After working in London as an organist and choir director for 11 years, he was appointed organist at St. Matthias Church, at Stoke Newington, in 1852, and held the post for the remainder of his life. Monk composed two enduring hymn tunes: EVENTIDE ("Abide with Me") and VICTORY ("The Strife Is O'er, the Battle Done").

1958 Pope Pius XII appointed Samuel Cardinal Stritch (Archbishop of Chicago) to head the Vatican office of the Sacred Congregation for the Propagation of the Faith. Cardinal Stritch thus became the first American to be appointed to the Papal Curia. On May 26, less than two months later, Cardinal Stritch died in Rome at the age of 70.

1966 Swiss Reformed theologian Karl Barth explained in a letter: "In the Bible the world is all humanity. If Jesus is and does what we read in 1 John 2:2, then He prays for all men: for those who already pray and for those who do not yet pray."

March 2

1791 Death of John Wesley (b.1703), English-born founder of Methodism. Ordained an Anglican priest in 1728, he and his brother Charles soon developed methodical procedures for worship, Bible study and prayer. Dubbed "Methodies" by early critics, John Wesley's theological method was later influenced by both the Moravians and English revivalist George Whitefield. The official separation between Methodism and the Anglican/Episcopal Church took place in the American colonies in 1784, with the formal organization of the Methodist Episcopal Church. In England, Methodism became an officially recognized denomination, separate from Anglicanism, after 1795.

1810 Birth of Gioacchino Pecci, Roman Catholic cardinal, near Anagni, Italy. He was ordained a priest in 1813, made a nuncio to Brussels in 1843, and on Feb. 20, 1878, was elected Pope Leo XIII, the 255th pontiff of the Roman Catholic Church. He served as pope for the next 25 years, until his death on July 20, 1903.

1811 Birth of John S.B. Monsell, Anglican clergyman, in Londonderry, Ireland. He published 11 volumes of poetry and nearly 300 hymns during his life, including the two hymns "Fight the Good Fight with All Thy Might" and "Light of the World, We Hail Thee."

1832 Birth of William H. Doane, in Boston. He penned the hymn "Ancient of Days, Who Sittest Throned in Glory," in 1886 for the bicentennial celebration of the city of Albany, New York.

1867 The Freedmen's Bureau in Washington, D.C., chartered Howard Normal and Theological Institute for the Education of Teachers and Preachers. Named for the Director of the Freedmen's Bureau, Oliver Otis Howard, Howard University has become the most prestigious institution of higher learning with a predominantly black student body.

1876 Birth of Eugenio Pacelli, Roman Catholic cardinal, in Rome. Pacelli was ordained in 1899, worked as a nuncio in Berlin 1919–29, was made a cardinal in 1929, and on March 2, 1939, was elected Pope Pius XII, the 259th pontiff of the Roman Catholic Church. He remained in office for 19 years, until his death on Oct. 9, 1958.

1909 Death of Daniel March (b.1816), American Congregational clergyman. March traveled widely in support of missionary endeavors around the world. For many years, in fact, his son F.W. March was a missionary to Syria. The elder March published several written works, but is remembered for writing one hymn (the only hymn he was ever known to have written): "Hark, the Voice of Jesus Calling."

1934 Birth of Dottie Rambo, popular contemporary Gospel singer and songwriter; author of country Gospel hymns as "In the Valley He Restoreth My

Soul," "Build My Mansion Next Door to Jesus" and "I Just Came to Talk with You, Lord."

1948 U.S. Senate Chaplain Peter Marshall prayed: "O God, forgive the poverty and the pettiness of our prayers. Listen not to our words but to the yearnings of our hearts. Hear beneath our petitions the crying of our need."

1959 American Presbyterian apologist for the Christian faith, Francis A. Schaeffer, claimed in a letter: "Christianity is the greatest intellectual system the mind of man has ever touched."

1969 The United Missionary Fellowship moved into its new headquarters in Sacramento, California. Founded in 1948 under the name Pioneer Bible Mission, the U.M.F. is a fundamentalist interdenominational missionary agency engaged in evangelism, church planting, and theological education. Its primary bases are in Lebanon, Cyprus, Mexico, Honduras and New Zealand.

March 3

1547 The Seventh Session of the Council of Trent decreed: "If anyone says that one baptized cannot, even if he wishes, lose grace, however much he may sin, unless he is unwilling to believe, let him be anathema."

1744 Colonial missionary to the New England Indians David Brainerd recorded in his journal: "In the morning, spent an hour in prayer. Prayer was so sweet an exercise to me that I knew not how to cease, lest I lose the spirit of prayer."

1787 English founder of Methodism, John Wesley, assured in a letter: "If God sends you, he will make a way for you. The hearts of all men are in His hands."

1870 Birth of Lettie B. (Mrs. Charles E.) Cowman, American missionary and author, in Iowa. In 1901 she and her husband went to Japan as missionaries, where they founded the Oriental Missionary Society. After her husband's death (1924), Lettie became president of the society in 1928 and led the work until her retirement in 1949. Her devotional guide *Streams in the Desert*, first published in 1925, has been translated into 15 foreign languages.

1877 Birth of Rev. William M. Strong, founder of the Gospel Mission of South America (1923). Located originally in Chile, the G.M.S.A. headquarters moved to the U.S. in the early 1930s, and has been located in Ft. Lauderdale, Florida, since 1975. G.M.S.A. is an evangelical, interdenominational mission organization of Baptist tradition. Engaged primarily in Bible translation and educational ministries, her missionaries work in 18 countries worldwide.

1887 A congressional act was passed giving the U.S. government power to seize and administer the property of the Mormon church. The seized property was not returned until 1896 when the church renounced the practice of polygamy.

1931 American pioneer language educator Frank C. Laubach, while serving as a Congregational missionary to the Philippines, concluded in a letter: "Oh, if we only let God have His full chance He will break our hearts with the glory of His revelation. That is the privilege which the preacher can have above others. It is his business to look into the very face of God until he aches with bliss."

1943 The Navigators were incorporated in San Pedro, California, by founder Dawson E. Trotman. The Navigators is an evangelical, interdenominational organization engaged primarily in personal evangelism, training and discipleship, and Bible memorization. Headquartered since 1954 in Colorado Springs, Colorado, they support over 1,500 workers in the U.S. and in 30 other countries.

1948 American missionary to Ecuador and Auca Indian martyr Jim Elliot lamented in his journal: "Lord, I have an Israelite's unbelief, wondering at times if it were not better to have a grave in Egypt than struggle in this wilderness. But You have promised. I believe."

1950 Modern-born Trappist monk Thomas Merton commented in *Sign of Jonas*: "The Christian life. . . is a continual discovery of Christ in new and unexpected places. And these discoveries are sometimes most profitable when you find Him in something you had tended to overlook or even despise."

March 4

1681 England's King Charles II granted Quaker William Penn a patent for territory in North America, much of which eventually became the state of Pennsylvania.

1738 Moravian missionary Peter Bohler said to John Wesley (founder of Methodism): "Preach faith until you have it; and then, because you have it, you will preach faith."

1845 Birth of William H. Parker, English Baptist hymnwriter, in New Basford, Nottingham. A construction worker in New Basford, Parker was also an active member of the Chelsea Street Baptist Church in Nottingham. He wrote many hymns for the Sunday school; one still popular is "Tell Me the Stories of Jesus."

1866 Death of Alexander Campbell (b.1788), Scottish clergyman. In 1809 Alexander and his father Thomas Campbell emigrated to America. The younger Campbell was ordained to the Baptist ministry in 1812, but became increasingly concerned that the church no longer followed many practices once instituted in the early church. By 1827 the two Campbells had developed a "Restoration Movement" among the Baptists that became known as the Disciples of Christ. Campbell gave the New Testament higher inspirational value than the Old Testament. Of his many writings, perhaps the most important was his book *The Christian System* (1835).

1870 Death of John McClintock (b.1814), American Methodist scholar and clergyman. He was first president of the newly organized Drew Theological Seminary in Madison, New Jersey. His most important work was the 12-volume *Cyclopaedia of Biblical, Theological, and Ecclesiastical Literature*, which he co-edited with James Strong. Only 3 volumes of the work were published before McClintock's death.

1875 Death of John E. Gould (b.1822), sacred music composer and publisher. Born in New England, Gould owned and operated several music stores in the

New York and Philadelphia areas. He composed many tunes, including PILOT, to which we sing "Jesus, Savior, Pilot Me."

1890 Death of Franz Delitzsch (b.1813), German Lutheran Old Testament scholar. Born of Hebrew ancestry, Delitzsch taught at the universities of Rostock, Erlangen and Leipzig from 1846 until his death 44 years later. His greatest contribution to biblical scholarship was the Old Testament commentary he published in collaboration with J.F.K. Keil (1861).

1901 Death of Daniel W. Whittle (b.1840), American evangelist. Formerly a Union major in the American Civil War, Whittle resigned his commission in 1873, under D.L. Moody's influence, to become an evangelist. He was assisted by three outstanding song evangelists of that day: P.P. Bliss, James McGranahan and George C. Stebbins. Whittle authored several hymns that still remain popular, including "There Shall Be Showers of Blessing," "Have You Any Room for Jesus?" (arr.), "I Know Whom I Have Believed" and "Moment by Moment."

1942 Birth of Gloria Gaither, wife of contemporary sacred songwriter Bill Gaither and female vocalist of the Bill Gaither Trio. Gloria coauthored the lyrics to such popular Christian songs as "Because He Lives," "Something Beautiful" and "The King Is Coming."

1944 Birth of Edwin Dale Drake, author of the hymn "Others."

1956 The religious TV program *American Religious Town Hall* aired for the first time over ABC television. Seen on Sunday afternoons and moderated by Episcopal Bishop James A. Pike, the program consisted of a panel debating religious and moral topics of the day. It ran through June 9, 1957.

1968 American Presbyterian apologist for the Christian faith, Francis A. Schaeffer, acknowledged in a letter: "My joy is in seeing many who have such little hope come to the place not only of being saved for eternity, but of being more human in the present life."

March 5

1555 French-born Swiss reformer John Calvin admonished in a letter to Philip Melanchthon: "It behooves us to accomplish what God requires of us, even when we are in the greatest despair respecting the results."

1743 Editor Thomas Prince published the first issue of the weekly *The Christian History*, the first religious journal published in America, in Boston.

1778 Death of Thomas A. Arne (b.1710), English sacred composer. His compositions include 2 oratorios, 13 operas and several hymn tunes. Considered the outstanding English composer of the 18th century, Arne's hymn tune ARLINGTON is sung with two popular hymns: "Am I a Soldier of the Cross?" and "O for a Faith That Will Not Shrink."

1850 Birth of Daniel B. Towner, American music evangelist, in Rome, Pennsylvania. In 1885 he worked with D.L. Moody and was made head of the Music Department at Moody Bible Institute in 1893. He composed over 2,000 hymn tunes, including AT CALVARY ("Years I Spent in Vanity and Pride"), MOODY

("Marvelous Grace of Our Loving Lord"), and TRUST AND OBEY ("When We Walk with the Lord").

1907 Death of Friedrich W. Blass (b.1843), German philologist and grammarian. He taught at the universities of Kiel and Halle, and wrote extensively in the areas of Classical and New Testament Greek. His 1896 *Grammatik des Neutestamentlichen Griechisch* is the basis of the popular *Grammar of the Greek New Testament* (1961) by Blass, Debrunner and Funk.

1919 This day became March 18 in Rumania when that nation adopted the Gregorian calendar (created by Pope Gregory XIII in 1582) to replace the older, inaccurate Julian calendar (created by Julius Caesar in 46 B.C.).

1920 Greek Orthodox Rumania and eastern Russia adopted the Gregorian calendar on this date, jumping the calendar ahead to March 18.

1951 The religious program *Circuit Rider* debuted on ABC television. Broadcast on Monday nights between 11:00–11:30, the program featured guests, biographies of evangelists and musical selections. Produced by Franklin W. Dyson, *The Circuit Rider* ran only two months, through May 7, before being cancelled.

1984 The U.S. Supreme Court ruled that a city may utilize a manger scene as part of an official Christmas display without violating the separation of government and organized religion, as set down in the Constitution.

March 6

1475 Birth of Michelangelo Buonarroti, Italian Renaissance artist, in Caprese, Italy. His monumental style made him the giant of the High Renaissance era in art. His greatest works include the sculptures *Pieta* (1498), *David* (1504), *Moses* (1508), his frescos on the ceiling of the Sistine Chapel (1508–12), and his painting *The Last Judgment* (1534–41).

1735 English revivalist George Whitefield wrote in a letter: "The renewal of our natures is a work of great importance. It is not to be done in a day. We have not only a new house to build up, but an old one to pull down."

1919 Death of Julia H. Johnston (b.1849), American Presbyterian Sunday school leader. Born in Ohio, she lived most of her life in Peoria, Illinois, where she served as Superintendent of the Children's Department of the First Presbyterian Church for 41 years. She wrote about 500 hymns during her lifetime, including "Grace Greater Than Our Sin" (a.k.a. "Marvelous Grace of Our Loving Lord").

1933 Death of Amos R. Wells (b.1862), American Christian educator. From 1891–1933 he was the editorial secretary for the newly organized United Society of Christian Endeavor (forerunner of the modern church Youth Fellowship organizations). Additionally, from 1901 until his death, he was also editor of *Peloubet's Notes for the International Sunday School Lessons*.

1984 Death of Martin Niemoller (b.1892), German theologian. In 1931 Niemoller joined with Dietrich Bonhoeffer and others to oppose Nazi control of the German Evangelical Church. Because of his outspoken opposition to Hitler, he was arrested and imprisoned at the Sachsenhausen and, later, Dachau concentration camps (1937–45).

March 7

1274 Death of St. Thomas Aquinas (b.ca.1224), greatest philosopher and theologian of the Medieval Church. Born in Italy, he became a Dominican in 1244, thereafter spending the greater part of the rest of his life as a teacher in Paris. During his lifetime, Thomas generated an enormous literary output. No doubt the greatest of his writings was the *Summa Theologica* (1265–73), which was an attempt to exhaustively systematize the data of Christian revelation according to the Aristotelian categories of thought popular in that day.

1638 Colonial churchwoman Anne Hutchinson and 19 other exiles from Massachusetts Bay Colony settled on Rhode Island, at the site of modern Portsmouth.

1782 Ohio Territory militiamen began a two-day massacre of the Moravian-founded Indian settlement of Gnadenhutten (modern New Philadelphia, Ohio). They slaughtered 96 Christian Indians of the Delaware (Leni-Lenape) tribe in retaliation for Indian raids elsewhere in the Ohio territory.

1825 Birth of Alfred Edersheim, English biblical scholar, in Vienna, Austria. Born a Jew, Edersheim converted to Christianity before the age of 20 and was ordained a Presbyterian clergyman in 1846. Thirty years later, in 1875, he transferred his ordination to the Church of England. Of his many writings, the most widely read is undoubtedly his *Life and Times of Jesus the Messiah* (1883–90), still in print.

1867 Birth of Peter Cameron Scott, American pioneer missionary and founder of the African Inland Mission. Scott led the little band of missionaries (5 men and 3 women, including Peter's sister Margaret) that first reached Mombasa, Kenya, on Oct. 17, 1895. A month later, the group had traveled 250 miles inland to Nzawi, where they set up their first base. Peter's father and mother also joined the mission. But Peter came down with blackwater fever the following year and on Dec. 4, 1896, died at the age of 29. He was buried at Nzawi. Over 700 missionaries currently follow in Scott's footsteps. As members of Africa Inland Mission, they serve the Gospel of Christ in 11 African countries.

1915 Birth of Geoffrey Bromily, one of the major translators of Swiss Reformed theologian Karl Barth's works into English in Lancaster, England.

1966 Swiss Reformed theologian Karl Barth assured in a letter: "We all can and should be glad to have a God who, without any merit on our part, says 'Yes' to each of us in His own way."

March 8

1522 German reformer Martin Luther explained in a letter: "Human authority is not always to be obeyed, namely, when it undertakes something against the commandments of God; yet it should never be despised but always honored. Christ did not justify Pilate's verdict; but He did not depose him or the emperor, nor did He show any contempt for him."

1607   Birth of Johann Rist, German Lutheran scholar and clergyman, at Ottensen, near Hamburg. Dedicated at his birth to the ministry, Rist entered the pastorate in 1635. During his lifetime he wrote nearly 700 hymns, and his "Break Forth, O Beauteous Heavenly Light" is still sung today.

1698   The first meeting of the British group which formed the Society for Promoting Christian Knowledge (S.P.C.K.) convened.

1887   Death of Henry Ward Beecher (b.1813), American Congregational clergyman, and son of Lyman Beecher and brother of Harriet Beecher Stowe. Though he became world-famous for his wit and drama in the pulpit, Henry Ward Beecher was an unabashed advocate of abolition as well as women's rights. He pastored the Plymouth Church (Brooklyn, New York) for 40 years, from 1847 until his death.

1898   The British organization, S.P.C.K. (Society for Promoting Christian Knowledge), established 1698, celebrated its 200th anniversary.

1948   Religious education within the public schools was declared a violation of the First Amendment by the U.S. Supreme Court. In particular, the court ruled that the practice of "release time"—a scheduling arrangement whereby public school children could, with parental consent, receive religious instruction during school hours, and in school buildings—was a violation of the separation of church and state.

1968   Pope Paul VI appointed Bishop Terence J. Cooke Archbishop of New York, succeeding the late Francis Cardinal Spellman. Archbishop Cooke was formally installed on April 4 at St. Patrick's Cathedral.

March 9

1839   Birth of Phoebe Palmer Knapp, American Methodist hymnwriter, in New York City. The daughter of Walter C. Palmer, a well-known Methodist evangelist of that day, Phoebe, at 16, married Joseph F. Knapp, founder of the Metropolitan Life Insurance Company. Both were members of John Street Methodist Church of New York City, whose membership also included blind hymnwriter Fanny Crosby. Phoebe Palmer Knapp published more than 500 hymn tunes during her lifetime, but her most famous work is the tune for Fanny Crosby's "Blessed Assurance."

1843   Church of Scotland minister Robert Murray McCheyne reminded a friend in a letter: "You will never find Jesus so precious as when the world is one vast howling wilderness. Then He is like a rose blooming in the midst of the desolation, a rock rising above the storm."

1875   Birth of Martin Fallas Shaw, English church organist, in Kennington. He was the Director of Music for the Anglican diocese of Chelmsford 1935–45. Among other publications, he was editor of *The Oxford Book of Carols* (1928). He composed the hymn tune GENTLE JESUS, to which we sing Charles Wesley's hymn "Gentle Jesus, Meek and Mild."

1922   Death of Williston Walker (b.1860), American church historian. He spent the last 22 years of his life as professor of ecclesiastical history at Yale (1901–

22), the successor of George Park Fisher. Of his many writings, *History of the Christian Church*, first published in 1918, is now in its fourth edition (1985).

1930 Pioneer language teacher Frank C. Laubach, while serving as a Congregational missionary in the Philippines, commented in a letter: "It seems to me now that the very Bible cannot be read as a substitute for meeting God soul to soul and face to face."

1931 The World Radio Missionary Fellowship was incorporated in Lima, Ohio, by co-founders Clarence W. Jones and Reuben Larson. Today, this interdenominational mission organization is headquartered in Opa Locka, Florida, and broadcasts the Gospel in 15 languages to South America and throughout Europe.

1948 Death of Civilla D. Martin (b.1866), American hymnwriter. As the wife of Walter S. Martin, a busy evangelist, Civilla frequently aided her husband as a teacher, evangelist, and as a pastor's wife. She also collaborated with him in authoring many Gospel songs. Of these, she is best remembered as the author of "God Will Take Care of You."

March 10

1528 Martyrdom of Balthaser Hubmaier (b.1480), German religious leader and chief writer for the Anabaptist movement. Originally a supporter of the Swiss Reformation, Hubmaier came to disagree with Zwingli on the subject of infant baptism, and wholeheartedly joined the Anabaptist movement in 1523. Because he was closely associated with Thomas Munzer (who touched off the Peasants' War), after the bloody defeat of the peasants, Hubmaier fled to Moravia in 1525. When the Catholics came into power there, Hubmaier was thrown into prison, then condemned at Vienna and burned at the stake.

1681 English Quaker William Penn received a charter from Charles II, which made him the sole proprietor of the colonial American territory known today as the state of Pennsylvania.

1823 Birth of John B. Dykes, Anglican clergyman and writer of nearly 300 hymns, in Hull, England. Many of his hymns first appeared in *Hymns Ancient and Modern*. He is one of the best-remembered Victorian composers. We still sing his tunes DOMINUS REGIT ME ("The King of Love My Shepherd Is"), LUX BENIGNA ("Lead, Kindly Light"), MELITA ("Eternal Father, Strong to Save") and NICAEA ("Holy, Holy, Holy, Lord God Almighty").

1880 The first English Salvation Army mission to the U.S. landed at New York City.

1898 Death of George F. Mueller (b.1805), English philanthropist and evangelist. Himself a converted profligate, Mueller carried on mission work among the Jews, but is better remembered for the work he did among the poor children of England. During his 93 years, he is said to have cared for more than 10,000 orphans.

1905 Death of James R. Murray (b.1841), American music editor and hymnwriter. Trained in music early in life, Murray spent most of his last 40 years as a music teacher and as editor of 2 popular music periodicals: *The Song*

Messenger (1865–71) and *The Musical Visitor* (1881–1905). During his lifetime, Murray composed a great number of Sunday school songs, Gospel songs and religious anthems. One of his tunes that remains as popular today as when he wrote it in 1887 is MUELLER ("Away in a Manger").

1917 Death of Folliott S. Pierpoint (b.1835), English classics instructor and hymnwriter. During his lifetime he wrote a number of hymns, including "For the Beauty of the Earth," and published several volumes of verse.

1937 English historian Arnold J. Toynbee commented: "In this really very brief period of less then 2,000 years Christianity has in fact produced greater spiritual effects in the world than have been produced in a comparable space of time by any other spiritual movement that we know of in history."

March 11

1314 Jacques de Molay, the last Grand Master (leader) of the Knights Templar (the first Roman Catholic military religious order, founded in 1118 during the Crusades), was burned at the stake in Paris. Because of their great wealth, the Knights Templar had attracted the attention of Philip the Fair of France who slyly persuaded Pope Clement V to suppress the order. Philip then condemned the leaders of the order and seized most of their former wealth.

1738 English revivalist George Whitefield pointed out in his journal: "Suffering times are a Christian's best improving times; for they break the will, wean us from the creature, prove the heart."

1845 Wittenberg College was chartered in Springfield, Ohio, under Lutheran auspices.

1847 Death of Jonathan ("Johnny Appleseed") Chapman (b.1774), American "patron saint of orchards and conservation." He planted many apple nurseries from the Alleghenies to central Ohio and beyond from 1800 on. He preached a Gospel incorporating teachings from Swedenborgianism: the then-popular belief that the human spirit could be reconciled with the natural world.

1860 Birth of H. Frances Davidson, pioneer American missionary. As the first woman in the Brethren in Christ Church to have earned an M.A. degree (1892), she began a teaching career at McPherson College in Kansas. In 1897 she became one of her denomination's first missionaries to the African continent, helping to found the Matopo Mission in modern Zimbabwe. Remaining in Africa until 1923, she returned to the U.S. and taught at Messiah College in Grantham, Pennsylvania, until 1932. She died in 1935.

1897 Death of Henry Drummond (b.1851), Scottish biologist and religious writer. Persuaded by D.L. Moody to suspend his teaching long enough to help him with his first evangelistic campaigns in England, Drummond returned to the classroom to influence hundreds of students for the Gospel. Though he published several definitive works in biology, Drummond is best remembered for his classic meditation on 1 Corinthians 13 entitled *The Greatest Thing in All the World*.

1923 Death of Mary Ann Thomson (b.1834), English-born American hymnwriter. Raised during her early years in England, she later came to America to settle in Philadelphia with her husband, John Thomson (who served as the first librarian of the Free Library in Philadelphia). During her life, Mrs. Thomson published many original poems and hymns in periodicals such as *The Churchman* (New York) and *The Living Church* (Chicago). Her most enduring poem is one she wrote in 1868 at the age of 34: "O Zion, Haste, Thy Mission High Fulfilling."

March 12

604 Death of Pope St. Gregory I ("the Great") (b.ca.540), 64th pontiff in the history of the Roman Catholic papacy. Gregory was instrumental in the conversion of the Anglo-Saxons (through the missionary St. Augustine of Canterbury). According to tradition, the Gregorian Chant is named after him. He is ranked by Roman Catholic theologians as fourth among the great teachers of the early Western church, taking his place after Augustine, Jerome and Ambrose.

1607 Birth of Paul Gerhardt, German Lutheran clergyman and hymnwriter, near Wittenberg, Saxony. He suffered much political and domestic misfortune during his life, including dismissal from the Lutheran pastorate for refusing to consider union with the Reformed Church. Four of his five children died in childhood, and his wife died in 1668. During his life, Gerhardt wrote over 130 hymns. His music marks the transition in Lutheran hymnody from confessional and high-church hymns to personal hymns of devotional piety. His most popular hymn today is "O Sacred Head, Now Wounded."

1622 Pope Gregory XV (233rd pope of the Roman Catholic Church) canonized Ignatius Loyola (founder of the Jesuits), Philip Neri (Italian co-founder of a medical religious order), Teresa of Avila (a Spanish Carmelite nun), and Francis Xavier (the apostle of eastern Asia).

1710 Birth of Thomas A. Arne, noted English composer, in London. Though his music compositions were worthy of his times, he lived in a day when the popularity of Handel's music in England overshadowed all native English compositions. Nevertheless, Arne was considered the outstanding English composer of the 18th century. He is remembered for his hymn tune ARLINGTON, to which we sing the hymn "Am I a Soldier of the Cross?"

1826 Birth of Robert Lowry, American Baptist clergyman and hymnwriter, in Philadelphia. He pastored churches in Pennsylvania, New York, and New Jersey between 1854 and his death 45 years later (1899). During the 1860s he became interested in writing sacred music and he later collaborated with William H. Doane in the publication of nearly two dozen hymnals. Lowry is chiefly remembered as the author and composer of "Christ Arose" and "Nothing but the Blood of Jesus." He also composed the hymn melodies for "We're Marching to Zion," "All the Way My Savior Leads Me" and "I Need Thee Every Hour."

1872 Death of Konrad Kocher (b.1786), German chorister and hymnwriter who wrote the melody DIX, to which we sing "For the Beauty of the Earth." During his life he did much to popularize four-part singing in the churches, and helped bring about much-needed reforms in German church music. His influence remains through the hymn tune DIX, which he composed in 1838, at the age of 52.

March 13

1804 Birth of James Waddell Alexander, American Presbyterian clergyman, English teacher and hymnwriter. Though he pastored from 1829 until his death in 1859, he also taught rhetoric and church history and had a great interest in hymnology. His translations of several Latin and German hymns were published posthumously in 1861. It was Alexander who gave us the English text of Paul Gerhardt's immortal hymn "O Sacred Head, Now Wounded."

1868 Birth of Charles E. Cowman, missionary pioneer, in Toulon, Illinois. In 1901 he sailed with his wife (Lettie B. Cowman, who authored *Streams in the Desert*) to Japan, where they incorporated the Oriental Missionary Society and Bible Training Institute in 1910. Cowman continued in the work he started in Japan until 1917. He died in 1924.

1925 The governor of Tennessee signed into law an act making it "unlawful for any teacher (in the state educational system) to teach any theory that denied the story of the divine creation of man as taught in the Bible."

March 14

1559 French-born Swiss reformer John Calvin asked in a letter to a pastor whom he was inviting to accept a pastorate in Geneva: "If your labors, where you now are, are sterile, and if here an abundant harvest awaits them, which is the most forcible tie? the one by which God draws you hither, or the one that detains you there?"

1826 Birth of William F. Sherwin, American music scholar and chorister, in Buckland, Massachusetts. A Baptist layman, he taught in Boston at the New England Conservatory of Music, as well as organized and directed many amateur choruses. During his life he composed several hymn tunes, including BREAD OF LIFE ("Break Thou the Bread of Life") and CHAUTAUQUA ("Day Is Dying in the West").

1835 Birth of William F. Moulton, biblical scholar, at Leek, in Staffordshire, England. Coming from a strong Methodist family, Moulton excelled in biblical languages and grammar. In 1870 he translated Winer's definitive German *Grammar of New Testament Greek* into English. In 1870 he was appointed the youngest member of the committee working on the English Revised Version of the Bible (1881,1885). In 1897 he and A.S. Geden published *A Concordance of the Greek Testament*.

1835 Birth of Henry Barclay Swete, Anglican Bible scholar, in Bristol. In addition to pastoring several parishes, he also taught at King's College, London, and at Cambridge, remaining there 25 years. His best writing was in the field of biblical language. In 1887–91 he published perhaps his greatest treatise: *The Old Testament in Greek*.

1897 The Polish National Catholic Church of America was formally organized at Scranton, Pennsylvania. A strictly American church, the denomination was begun by Polish Roman Catholic immigrants to America who complained there were no bishops and few priests who were Polish, and that under an 1884 Catholic ruling, they were not permitted to establish parishes of their own. With a beginning membership of 20,000, this was the only break of considerable size from the Roman Catholic Church in the U.S. Today, the denomination numbers a little over 32,000 members.

1902 The Nathaniel W. Taylor Lectureship was established at the Yale University Divinity School, in memory of the Rev. Nathaniel W. Taylor (B.A. 1807), who was professor of systematic theology and chairman of the faculty, 1822–58. The lectures were to be on some topic in the field of theology. Some of the better-known guest lecturers have included Walter Rauschenbusch (1917), John Baillie (1936), and H. Richard Niebuhr (1940).

1912 Death of Albert L. Peace (b.1844), English church organist. He was one of the noted Scottish organists of his day, enjoying great popularity as a recitalist. He composed cantatas, service music, organ pieces and hymn tunes. His most enduring hymn tune has been ST. MARGARET, to which we sing George Matheson's "O Love That Will Not Let Me Go."

1937 English Bible expositor A.W. Pink admonished in a letter: "Neither the nearness nor the remoteness of Christ's return is a rule to regulate us in the ordering of our temporal affairs. Spiritual preparedness is the great matter!"

1949 Dr. Robert P. Evans chartered the European Bible Institute, in Chicago, Illinois. In 1952 its name was changed to Greater Europe Mission; its headquarters were relocated to Wheaton, Illinois, in 1979. Today, this interdenominational, evangelical organization is engaged primarily in evangelism, theological education and literature distribution, and has helped establish new churches in a dozen nations throughout Europe.

1961 The New English Bible New Testament was published simultaneously by Oxford and Cambridge University Presses. (The Old Testament was completed nine years later, in 1970.)

1979 Death of A.W. Ruscoe (b.1897), founder of the North American Worldwide Evangelization Crusade. Originally established in 1913 when C.T. Studd sailed from England to the African Congo, this evangelical and interdenominational mission organization was incorporated in the U.S. in 1939. Its name changed to Worldwide Evangelization for Christ International in 1984. The organization engages primarily in evangelism, church planting and theological education. Its major mission bases are located in 21 different countries.

March 15

1729 The Ceremony of Profession was held for Sister St. Stanislaus Hachard at the Ursuline Convent in New Orleans. She was the first Roman Catholic to become a nun in America.

1839 Scottish clergyman Robert Murray McCheyne maintained in a letter: "All my ideas of peace and joy are linked in with my Bible; and I would not give the hours of secret converse with it for all the other hours I spend in this world."

1856 Haverford College was chartered in Haverford, Pennsylvania—the first college in the U.S. to be established under Quaker auspices.

1875 Archbishop John McCloskey became the first American to be named a cardinal by the Roman Catholic Church at St. Patrick's Cathedral in New York City.

1934 English Bible expositor A.W. Pink commented in a letter: "It is the tendency of youth to be speculative, and to accept what others say without much examination. But as one grows older, one becomes more cautious, and slower to accept man's interpretations. We all need to give more heed to 1 Thess. 5:21 ('Prove all things; hold fast that which is good')."

1950 American missionary to Peru and Auca Indian martyr Jim Elliot concluded in his journal: "The believer is a displaced person. He loses the controlling features of both environment and heredity."

1962 Swiss Reformed theologian Karl Barth reminded a friend in a letter: "The time must come when we—our generation—will have had our time and opportunity and made it more or less fruitful."

March 16

1517 Pope Leo X closed the Fifth Lateran Council. Leo had decreed a crusade against the Turks as well as a three-year tax on benefices to finance it. But he never enforced the Council's legislation on these and other reforms.

1621 Birth of George Neumark, German educator and hymnwriter, at Langensalza. Twice in life he lost everything he owned: once by robbers, another time by fire. He wrote both music and poetry and is best remembered as the author and composer of the hymn "If Thou but Suffer God to Guide Thee."

1641 A General Court convened (lasting until March 19), which declared the state of Rhode Island to be a democracy, adopting a new constitution granting religious freedom to all its citizens.

1823 Birth of William H. Monk, English church organist and sacred music composer, in London. In 1852 Monk became organist at St. Matthias Church, in Stoke Newington, a position he held until his death in 1889. Monk's fame rests on the editorial work he did on the best-known hymnal in England: *Hymns Ancient and Modern*. He composed fifty tunes for the 1861, 1875 and 1889 editions of the hymnal. His most enduring tune has been EVENTIDE ("Abide with Me").

1827 Birth of John Baptiste Calkin, English church organist, in London. At age 56, he was appointed to the faculty of the Guildhall School of Music. He is remembered chiefly as the composer of the hymn tune WALTHAM, which we use for the Christmas carol "I Heard the Bells on Christmas Day."

1889 Death of Alfred Edersheim (b.1825), European biblical scholar. Born to Jewish parents in Vienna, he emigrated to Scotland, where he converted to Christianity, and in 1846 entered the Presbyterian ministry. In 1875 he joined the Church of England. Of his many writings, the one most popular today is *The Life and Times of Jesus the Messiah* (1883–90).

1895 Death of John Albert Broadus (b.1827), American Baptist preacher and scholar. He was president of Southern Baptist Theological Seminary in Louisville, Kentucky, from 1889–95, and was a member of the International Lesson Committee from 1878 until his death. His *Commentary on the Gospel of Matthew* is one of his better-known writings.

1909 Death of Marianne Hearn, English Baptist religious teacher and editor who wrote the hymn "Just As I Am, Thine Own to Be." She was a prolific writer and poet during her lifetime; her collected literary works comprising 20 volumes when published.

1915 Birth of Dr. Robert H. Bowman, missionary pioneer. In 1945 he, with John Broger and William J. Roberts, co-founded the Far East Broadcasting Company. With its headquarters in La Mirada, California, since 1979, F.E.B.C. currently engages in Christian radio broadcasting and Bible correspondence courses, reaching thousands of Pacific island-clusters with the Gospel.

1952 The first religious program on TV, *This Week in Religion*, debuted on Dumont television, airing Sunday nights from 6 to 7 p.m. It was the only ecumenical program of the early religious television offerings, and ran for two and a half years, until Oct. 18, 1954.

1960 The Bethel Baptist Assembly was incorporated in Indiana. Founded in 1934 as the Evangelistic Ministerial Alliance at Evansville, the denomination presently consists of approximately 4,000 members and 25 churches.

1966 Swiss Reformed theologian Karl Barth confessed in a letter: "It is not just today but in every age that such poor witness has been given in the Christian Church. The Gospel has always proved to be stronger; if only there were still people who would believe its truth simply but firmly and cheerfully and who would try to live according to its direction."

1970 The complete translation of the entire New English Bible was first published, simultaneously by the Oxford and Cambridge Presses. The translation was the work of British scholars from all the major Protestant denominations. (The N.E.B. New Testament was first published nine years earlier, on March 14, 1961.)

March 17

1734 Forty-two families (78 persons)—Protestant refugees from Salzburg, Germany—arrived in the American colonies, landing in Georgia. Sponsored by the S.P.C.K. (Society for the Promotion of Christian Knowledge), a British missionary organization, the refugees soon established the town of Ebenezer, thirty miles from Savannah, Georgia.

1737 The Charitable Irish Society of Boston hosted the first municipal celebration of St. Patrick's Day in America. Prior to this time, St. Patrick's Day had been celebrated only in a religious context. (Municipal celebrations of this holiday were later initiated in Philadelphia in 1780 and in New York in 1784.)

1789 Birth of Charlotte Elliott, English devotional writer, in Clapham, England. A serious illness at the age of 33 left Miss Elliott an invalid the rest of her 50 years, during which she devoted herself to religious and humanitarian writings. She wrote 150 hymns, including her most popular "Just As I Am," written in 1834 while she was living in Brighton, England.

1841   Birth of James R. Murray, American sacred music editor, in Andover, Massachusetts. A veteran of the Union Army during the Civil War, Murray afterward edited the *The Song Messenger*, and later *The Musical Visitor*. He is best-remembered for his hymn tune MUELLER ("Away in a Manger").

1890   Birth of Julius R. Mantey, coauthor (with H.E. Dana) of a popular intermediate New Testament Greek grammar in 1927. The work is still popular.

1897   Emilie Grace Briggs became the first woman graduate from an American Presbyterian theological seminary when she received her Bachelor of Divinity degree from Union Theological Seminary in New York City.

1902   Death of George W. Warren (b.1828), an outstanding American organist who served at several large Episcopal churches in Albany, Brooklyn, and New York City, New York, between 1846–90. In addition to composing anthems and service music, he also wrote hymn tunes, one of which endures today: NATIONAL HYMN ("God of Our Fathers, Whose Almighty Hand").

1911   Death of Joseph Y. Peek (b.1843), American sacred music instrumentalist. In his early years he worked as a carpenter, farmer, druggist's clerk and florist. In 1904 (at the age of 61) he became a Methodist lay preacher, and was fully ordained on Jan. 22, 1911—the realization of his dream—only 60 days before his death. He is remembered chiefly for composing the hymn tune PEEK, to which we sing "I Would Be True."

March 18

1123   The First Lateran Council opened in Rome. Known also as the Ninth Ecumenical (or General) Council, the First Lateran Council was the first of the Ecumenical Councils to be held in the West. The council settled the right of investiture (i.e., the right to choose replacement clergy) by a treaty between Pope Calixtus II and Holy Roman Emperor Henry V. Basically, the convocation did little more than sanction the decrees made a year earlier in 1522 at the Concordat of Worms, in which Henry V renounced the right to elect bishops.

1314   Thirty-nine French Knights Templars (a medieval Roman Catholic military religious order) were ordered burned at the stake by Philip the Fair. Most experts in church history believe these and other hostilities shown against the organization during the first half of the 14th century were caused by the greed and cunning of Philip the Fair, who conspired to gain the massive wealth this religious order had amassed in the centuries following the Crusades.

1612   Death of Bartholomew Legate (b.ca.1575), English merchant. His theology was questioned in several key Protestant religious circles: Mennonite, Quietist and Anglican. Arrested the year before for heresy, Legate was condemned and publicly executed for his unorthodox theology. Legate has the dubious distinction of being the last man in England to be burned at the stake for his religious beliefs.

1673   Lord Berkeley of England sold his half of the American colony of New Jersey to the Quakers.

1767 Anglican clergyman and hymnwriter John Newton assured in a letter: "The more you know Him, the better you will trust Him; the more you trust Him, the better you will love Him; the more you love Him, the better you will serve Him. . . Remember: the growth of a believer is not like a mushroom, but like an oak, which increases slowly indeed, but surely."

1861 The Metropolitan Tabernacle was opened in London. This was the sanctuary of the famous English Baptist preacher, Charles H. Spurgeon. During his son Thomas's pastorate at the same church 38 years later, on the night of April 20, 1899, the Metropolitan Tabernacle burned to the ground.

1985 Death of Merrill C. Tenney (b.1904), American evangelical Bible scholar and educator. He served as Dean of the Wheaton College (Illinois) Graduate School 1947–71. His most popular publication, no doubt, is his *The New Testament: A Survey* (1953), which has been translated into Spanish, Portuguese, German, Chinese and Bengali. He also served on the New Testament committee of the New International Version of the Bible (N.T.: 1973, O.T.: 1978).

March 19

1641 The General Court (which had convened three days earlier) that declared Rhode Island to be a democracy ended. It adopted a new constitution granting religious freedom to all Rhode Island's citizens.

1684 Birth of Jean Astruc, French physician and the founder of modern Pentateuchal criticism, at Sauve, Languedoc, France. His father was a Huguenot pastor who turned Roman Catholic when the Edict of Nantes (1598) was revoked in 1685. Having studied at Montpellier, Astruc taught medicine there, as well as at Toulouse and Paris. In 1753 he published an anonymous theological treatise which sought to demonstrate that Moses made use of earlier documents in writing the Pentateuch—the two primary sources used "Yahweh" and "Elohim," respectively, as divine names. Though his hypothesis was initially met with ridicule, it was later expanded on by J.G. Eichhorn.

1711 Death of Thomas Ken (b.1637), Anglican clergyman and poet who wrote "Praise God from Whom All Blessings Flow." His frankness in preaching the Gospel led to his dismissal from a royal chaplaincy, and later to imprisonment in the Tower of London. His entire collection of poetry was published in four volumes.

1813 Birth of David Livingstone, Scottish missionary and explorer, in Blantyre, near Glasgow. He was converted at 17 and soon after dedicated his life to Christian missions. In 1840 he was sent to Robert Moffat's mission station in South Africa by the London Missionary Society. In 1845 he married Moffat's daughter Mary and soon after became as much an explorer as a missionary. He discovered Victoria Falls in 1855. He returned to Africa for the last time in 1865 and spent his last eight years of life there. It was during this exploration, in 1871, that Henry M. Stanley of the *New York Herald* found him at Ujiji (addressing him with his famous words, "Dr. Livingstone, I presume."), when he was believed lost to the world. Livingstone traveled over 30,000 miles in Africa.

1825 Death of John J. Husband (b.1760), English-born American music teacher and sacred music chorister. His methods of teaching were said to help simplify the process of learning vocal music. He also composed a number of anthems and hymn tunes, including REVIVE US AGAIN, to which we sing the hymn by the same name.

1928 Birth of Hans Kung, German Roman Catholic theologian, in Switzerland. He has taught at the University of Tubingen since 1960, and was appointed by Pope John XXIII as the official theologian of the Vatican II Ecumenical Council (1962–65). Kung has become a leading Roman Catholic spokesman for the reunification of Christianity.

1930 Death of Arthur James Balfour (b.1848), British statesman and philosopher. He was Britain's Prime Minister from 1902–05. In 1917 he became the first British subject ever to address an American Congress. In 1917 he also produced the *Balfour Declaration*, which committed Great Britain to securing "a national home for the Jewish people" in Palestine.

1937 Pope Pius XI issued the encyclical *Divini Redemptoris*, which condemned Russian Bolshevik Communism for its materialism, its conceptions of man and society, its atheism and terrorism. It declared: "There would be neither Socialism nor Communism today if the rulers of the nations had not scorned the teachings and material warnings of the Church."

1944 German Lutheran theologian and Nazi martyr Dietrich Bonhoeffer declared in a letter from prison: "We can have abundant life, even though many wishes remain unfulfilled."

March 20

1739 English founder of Methodism, John Wesley, wrote in a letter: "I look upon all the world as my parish."

1747 David Brainerd, colonial American missionary, ended his labors among the Indians of New Jersey because of his deteriorating health. He had started two and a half years earlier, in 1744, but was continually plagued with illness. (Brainerd died of tuberculosis seven months later.)

1810 Birth of John McCloskey, American Roman Catholic archbishop, in Brooklyn, New York. Ordained to the priesthood in 1834, he became the first bishop of the newly created diocese of Albany in 1847. In 1864, he succeeded Archbishop Hughes in the archdiocese of New York (including New York, New Jersey and New England). McCloskey attended the 1870 Vatican I Ecumenical Council. In 1875 he was made a cardinal, the first American-born cardinal.

1840 Scottish clergyman Robert Murray McCheyne explained in a letter: "The more God opens your eyes, the more you will feel that you are lost in yourself."

1852 At the age of 41, American abolitionist and author Harriet Beecher Stowe published her classic antislavery novel *Uncle Tom's Cabin*. The controversy sparked by the book eventually contributed heavily to the start of the American Civil War.

1885 Death of Christopher Wordsworth (b.1807), Anglican clergyman and nephew of English poet William Wordsworth. Recognized as one of the outstanding Greek scholars of his day, he published several works, including a commentary on the entire Bible. Interested also in hymnology, he wrote over 115 hymns, including "O Day of Rest and Gladness."

1889 Death of Albrecht Ritschl (b.1822), the leading German Protestant theologian of the latter half of the 19th century. His thought was characterized (in addition to other influences) by caution about Christian doctrines that went beyond verifiable history. For Ritschl, religion was ultimately social, the individual benefiting from his faith only in community with Christ's people, the church.

1897 Birth of Frank Sheed, Roman Catholic lay theologian and founder of Sheed and Ward, publishers of books in the areas of biography, history, philosophy, theology and literature.

1928 Birth of Fred M. Rogers, American Presbyterian clergyman and host of public television's longest-running children's program: *Mr. Rogers' Neighborhood*, in Latrobe, Pennsylvania. His show premiered in 1965. Through this half-hour series, Rogers and his guests gently teach young viewers to handle personal problems such as anger and impatience, as well as minor crises such as the death of a pet.

March 21

1098 The monastery in Citeaux, France, was founded by St. Robert, abbot of Molesme and a Benedictine monk. This was the origin of the Roman Catholic religious order known as the Cistercians.

1146 Bernard of Clairvaux had been preaching for a second crusade, and King Louis VII of France took up the cause and led the ill-fated mission.

1556 Death of Thomas Cranmer (b.1489), Anglican Archbishop of Canterbury from 1533. He was burned at the stake during the reign of Queen Mary while she attempted to restore England to Roman Catholicism.

1656 Death of Archbishop James Ussher (b.1581), Irish priest and scholar. His 1650–54 *Annales Veteris et Novi Testamenti* first demonstrated his interpretation of biblical chronology. His dates have since been included in many editions of the Bible.

1747 Twenty-two-year-old sea captain John Newton, on a slave ship bound for England, was dramatically converted to saving Christian faith during a violent storm at sea. This was more than "foxhole religion," for he eventually gave up slave-trading and the sea (1755). From 1764 until his death 43 years later, he devoted his life to the work of the clergy in the Anglican Church.

March 22

According to the decision of the Council of Nicea in A.D. 325, Easter (the day which celebrates the resurrection of Jesus Christ from the dead) is observed on the first Sunday following the first full moon after the spring equinox (March 21). This reckoning places Easter between March 22 and April 25 on any given year. Easter should fall on any one of these dates from three to six times per century, a minimum of 60 times during the past 2,000 years. However, a March 21 full moon is rare. Thus, between the years 33 and 2000, there have been only 15 occurrences of Easter on March 22: 72, 319, 414, 509, 604, 851, 946, 1041, 1136, 1383, 1478, 1573, 1598, 1761, and 1818. Easter will not be celebrated a single time on March 22 during the 20th century.

1312 Pope Clement V (1305–14), at the Council at Vienne, dissolved the military Order of Knights Templars by an administrative ordinance (*Vox Clamantis*). As the papacy at this time was located in Avignon, France (1305–77), the pope was under tremendous pressure from French monarch Philip IV (1285–1314), who coveted the wealth of the Templars to the point of discrediting their motives and morals in the eyes of the papacy. Clement assigned the wealth and property of the Templars to another military religious order, the Hospitallers (Knights of St. John of Jerusalem). In practice, however, Philip kept their wealth until his death two years later.

1621 In colonial Massachusetts, the Plymouth Colony made a treaty with the neighboring Indians that both sides kept for fifty years.

1758 Death of Jonathan Edwards (b.1703), called by Perry Miller "the greatest philosopher-theologian yet to grace the American scene." Under Edward's powerful preaching (as demonstrated in his sermon *Sinners in the Hands of an Angry God*), colonial America continued to experience the Great Awakening (1734–35). Edwards had been president of Princeton only one month when he died from the effects of a smallpox vaccination.

1819 Birth of Joseph Philbrick Webster, American music teacher and sacred music composer, in Manchester, New York. In addition to being a talented musician who could play the flute, violin and piano, Webster also composed over 1,000 pieces of music, including SWEET BY AND BY ("There's a Land That Is Fairer Than Day").

1836 Birth of Edgar Page Stites, American Methodist frontier preacher and missionary, in Cape May, New Jersey. For more than 60 years Stites was a member of the First Methodist Episcopal Church of Cape May. He is remembered as author of the hymns "Beulah Land" and "Trusting Jesus."

1920 Death of George S. Fisher (b.1855), founder of the Gospel Missionary Union in Topeka, Kansas, in 1892. Headquartered since 1978 in Kansas City, Missouri, this interdenominational mission organization of Baptist tradition currently works in 18 countries worldwide, engaging in evangelism, Bible translation, church planting, educational ministries, and leadership training.

March 23

During the last three centuries, Easter Sunday has fallen on March 23 in only five years: 1704, 1788, 1845, 1856, and 1913. Easter will not occur on March 23 again until the 21st century—in the year 2008.

1540 Waltham Abbey in Essex, England became the last monastery in that country to surrender its allegiance to the Roman Catholic Church and support King Henry VIII and the emerging Church of England.

1836 Birth of Crawford Howell Toy, American Hebrew scholar, at Norfolk, Virginia. Raised in a Southern Baptist family, Toy taught at Richmond College in Virginia, Furman University at Greenville, South Carolina, Southern Baptist Theological Seminary, and Harvard University. His most important literary accomplishments include *The Jewish Encyclopedia*, which he edited and the *International Critical Commentary* volume on Proverbs, which he wrote.

1867   Birth of Samuel M. Zwemer, American Dutch Reformed missionary, in Vriesland, Michigan. Influenced during his youth by the Student Volunteer Movement, in 1888–89 Zwemer and others formed the Arabian Mission in 1888–89 for the evangelization of the Muslims. Zwemer became a missionary to Arabia under the mission in 1890. With his headquarters eventually established at Cairo, he traveled across most of the Islamic world, arousing both American and European interest in bringing Muslims to Christ. Before his death in 1952, Zwemer authored more than 50 volumes in English, and several others in Arabic.

1892   Birth of George Arthur Buttrick, Presbyterian pastor and educator, at Seaham Harbor, Northumberland, England. Ordained in the U.S. in 1915 he served four pastorates, the last being at the Madison Avenue Presbyterian Church in New York City (1927–54). He also taught at both Union Theological Seminary and Harvard University. He was the chief editor of *The Interpreter's Bible* (1952–57).

1966   The Archbishop of Canterbury visited Rome and met with Pope Paul VI—the first such meeting between the heads of these two churches since Henry VIII first broke from Rome to form the Church of England over 400 years before.

March 24

During the last three centuries, Easter Sunday has fallen on March 24 only twice: 1799, and 1940. Easter will not occur on March 24 again until the year 2091.

1267   King Louis IX of France (1214–70) called his knights to Paris, in preparation for the Eighth Crusade (his second), directed against Tunis in North Africa. Canonized in 1297 for his deep spiritual devotion and selfless rule, "St. Louis" had earlier launched the Seventh Crusade against Damietta in Egypt in 1264. Louis had been captured, but was later freed for ransom. He died of fever while on this Eighth Crusade.

1603   Accession of King James VI of Scotland to the English throne, known thereafter as James I of England. His descent from Henry VIII (through his great-grandmother Mary Tudor and his mother Mary Queen of Scots) made him the nearest heir to the English throne when England's Queen Elizabeth I died earlier that year. (The two kingdoms of England and Scotland were not united until 1707.) It was James I who, at the 1604 Hampton Court Conference, authorized the translation project that became the 1611 King James (authorized) Version of the Bible.

1661   William Leddra became the last Quaker to be executed in Boston. His crime: returning from banishment. The Massachusetts Bay Colony Puritans had greeted the first Quakers to arrive in America (July 1656) with beatings, imprisonment and banishment. They were despised for their lack of patriotism. Two years before Leddra's hanging, two other Quakers, William Robinson and Marmaduke Stevenson, were hanged.

1774 Anglican clergyman and hymnwriter John Newton concluded in a letter: "What a mercy it is to be separated in spirit, conversation, and interest from the world that knows not God."

1812 Death of Johann Jacob Griesbach (b.1745), German New Testament scholar. He was one of the pioneers of textual (or lower) criticism. His two-volume critical edition of the Greek New Testament (1775–77) laid the foundation for all scholarly work that has since been done on the Greek text.

1816 Pioneer American Methodist Bishop Francis Asbury delivered the last sermon of his long life. Speaking at the Old Methodist Church in Richmond, Virginia, Asbury preached from Rom. 9:28: "For he will finish the work, and cut it short in righteousness: because a short work will the Lord make upon the earth." The sermon lasted an hour, even though Asbury preached while lying on a table because of his weakened condition. A week later, on March 31, 1816, Asbury died at the age of 71 at Spottsylvania, Virginia.

1818 Influential early American politician and statesman Henry Clay wrote: "All religions united with government are more or less inimical to liberty. All separated from government are compatible with liberty."

1820 Birth of Fanny J. Crosby, popular American hymnwriter, in Putnam County, New York. Blind from the age of six weeks, she spent most of her life in New York City, belonging to the John Street Methodist Episcopal Church. She did not begin writing sacred verse until she was in her 40s, yet before she died at 95, she had produced over 2,000 hymns. Over fifty of these are still popular, including "To God Be the Glory," "Blessed Assurance," "Rescue the Perishing," "Draw Me Nearer," "He Hideth My Soul," "Pass Me Not, O Gentle Savior," "Thou, My Everlasting Portion" and "Praise Him! Praise Him! Jesus Our Blessed Redeemer."

1880 The American branch of the Salvation Army was founded when George Railton and seven women established a command post in Philadelphia. (The organization was first established in London 15 years earlier, in 1865, under the name The Christian Mission.)

1882 Death of Henry Wadsworth Longfellow (b.1807), American poet. Although more popularly celebrated for his secular writings—"The Village Blacksmith" (1842), *The Song of Hiawatha* (1855), *The Courtship of Miles Standish* (1858), "Paul Revere's Ride" (1860)—he also undertook a major Christian literary project after 1861. His wife Fanny had perished in a tragic fire and, as a source of solace, Longfellow began an English translation of Dante's *Divine Comedy*.

1890 Birth of Harold Henry Rowley, English Old Testament scholar, at Leicester. After pastoring for five years, he taught at Christian University in Shantung, China (1924–49), at the University of Cardiff (1930–34), the University of Bangor, in Wales (1935–45), and at Manchester University (1945–59). He authored and edited many valuable contributions to biblical linguistics. Among his most highly acclaimed writings are the *The Aramaic of the Old Testament* (1929) and *The Growth of the Old Testament* (1950).

1921   Death of James Cardinal Gibbons (b.1834), Archbishop of Baltimore and first chancellor of the Catholic University in Washington, D.C.

1940   Dr. Samuel McCrea Cavert, of the Federal Council of the Churches of Christ in America, officiated at a Protestant Easter service in New York City. This was the first religious program broadcast on television. It was televised over NBC affiliate station W2XBS in New York City.

March 25

During the last three centuries, Easter Sunday has fallen on March 25 in only five years: 1731, 1742, 1883, 1894, and 1951. Easter will not occur on March 25 again until the year 2035.

1409   The First Council of Pisa was assembled, for the primary purpose of deposing two rival popes, Benedict XIII (antipope 1394–1417) and Gregory XII (1406–1415). The return of the papacy to Rome from Avignon, France (1309–77), created the Great Schism (1378–1417), which saw as many as three rival popes, each claiming legitimate papal powers. The Council of Pisa elected antipope, Alexander V, on June 26.

1533   German reformer Martin Luther, during one of his "Table Talks," was heard to say: "That the Creator himself comes to us and becomes our ransom—this is the reason for our rejoicing."

1625   Death of King James I (b.1566), Scottish-born English monarch. At the death of England's Elizabeth I, James VI of Scotland assumed the throne of England as James I. He authorized a translation of the Scriptures in 1604, which became the 1611 King James (authorized) Version of the Bible.

1740   Construction began on the Bethesda Orphanage in Savannah, Georgia— the oldest existing orphanage in America. It was built and paid for from contributions raised by English revivalist George Whitefield through his public preaching both in England and America.

1822   Birth of Albrecht Ritschl, a leading German Protestant theologian of the last half of the 19th century, in Berlin. He taught at Bonn (1852–64) and Gottingen (1864–89). His early career was heavily influenced by Hegel and F.C. Baur; his later career by Kant and Schleiermacher. Many scholars were in turn influenced by Ritschl, including Adolf Harnack and Nathan Soderblom.

1823   Birth of Godfrey Thring, Anglican clergyman, in Alford, Somerset, England. Ordained in 1846, he served at different times as curate, rector and prebendary (a cathedral staff member) until his retirement in 1893. During his life he also wrote several hymns, including the still-popular "Crown Him with Many Crowns."

1837   Birth of John R. Sweney, American Methodist pastor and sacred music chorister, in Lime Hill, Pennsylvania. During his lifetime, he composed over 1,000 Gospel songs. A half dozen of his hymn tunes are still used: I SHALL KNOW HIM ("When My Life-Work is ended, and I Cross the Swelling Tide"), STARS IN MY CROWN ("I Am Thinking Today of That Beautiful Land"), STORY OF JESUS ("Tell Me the Story of Jesus"), SUNSHINE ("There is Sunshine in My Soul Today"), SWENEY ("More About Jesus Would I Know"), and "A Child of the King."

1843 Death of Robert Murray McCheyne (b.1813), Church of Scotland minister. Ordained in 1835, McCheyne was appointed the following year as pastor of St. Peter's Church, Dundee. He served there until his premature death from poor health at age 29. Among his popular writings is the hymn "When This Passing World Is Done."

1876 The Home Mission Board of the Northern Presbyterian Church sent its first missionaries to the American Indians.

1877 Death of John H. Stockton (b.1813), American Methodist pastor and hymnwriter. His pastorates were in the New Jersey Conference, and though he was often feeble, he devoted much energy to writing and composing hymns, including ONLY TRUST HIM ("Come, Every Soul by Sin Oppressed"), GLORY TO HIS NAME ("Down at the Cross Where My Savior Died") and GREAT PHYSICIAN ("The Great Physician Now Is Near").

1890 William Ashley ("Billy") Sunday, famed left fielder for the Chicago White Sox, gave up his successful career in baseball following his conversion to Christ. He soon became one of the most popular evangelists of his day. It is estimated that over 300,000 souls were converted through his evangelistic ministry before his death in 1935.

1906 Birth of Dawson E. Trotman, founder of the Navigators, in Bisbee, Arizona. In 1933 he opened his home to disciple converted Navy men, calling his group the Navigators the following year. In 1943 he incorporated the work in California. (Since 1954 the Navigators has been headquartered in Colorado Springs, Colorado. Its work has since become established worldwide.) Trotman died in 1956 while saving a drowning girl.

1951 American missionary to Ecuador and Auca Indian martyr Jim Elliot advised in his journal: "When it comes time to die, make sure that all you have to do is die."

March 26

During the last three centuries, Easter Sunday has fallen (or will fall) on March 26 nine times: 1758, 1769, 1780, 1815, 1826, 1837, 1967, 1978, and 1989.

1827 Death of Ludwig van Beethoven (b.1770), Austrian composer. He performed in public at the age of eight and composed music by the age of ten, later coming under the influence of Bach, Mozart and Haydn. While Beethoven wrote no hymn tunes, many of his music pieces have been adapted to hymns. The most widely used is HYMN TO JOY, to which we sing "Joyful, Joyful, We Adore Thee."

1840 Birth of George Smith, English Assyriologist, in London. In early life he was a banknote engraver, but gained an increasing interest in Oriental languages and explorations. He made several expeditions to the site of ancient Nineveh. During the first two (1873, 1874), he unearthed over 3,000 cuneiform tablets, including portions of the ancient Deluge (Noah's Flood) story. His skill at deciphering the writing led to his coauthoring Sir Henry Rawlinson's third volume of *Cuneiform Inscriptions* (1875).

1862 Hymnwriter Joseph H. Gilmore penned the words to "He Leadeth Me, O Blessed Thought."

1886 Birth of John Baillie, Scottish theologian. He held several theological teaching positions in the U.S. and Canada from 1919–34, before becoming professor of divinity at the University of Edinburgh from 1934–56. His published works are few, but his classic (and most reprinted) volume was undoubtedly his 1948 treatise *God Was in Christ*.

1957 Dr. Basil W. Miller founded the Basil Miller Foundation in Altadena, California. In 1959 the name was changed to World-Wide Missions; and its headquarters was moved to Pasadena, California, in late 1963. Today, this interdenominational, evangelical organization supports national Christian workers and churches in over 30 countries worldwide, with medical relief.

March 27

During the last three centuries, Easter Sunday has fallen on March 27 ten times: 1701, 1712, 1785, 1796, 1842, 1853, 1864, 1910, 1921, and 1932. Easter will not occur on March 27 again until the 21st century—in the year 2005.

1536 Swiss Protestants in Strasbourg and Constance signed the First Helvetic Confession. It became the first of two documents that set forth the common faith of the Swiss Protestant churches. In time, this first confession proved both too short and too Lutheran in tone to be very definitive or popular. In 1562–64 a similar document was written by Heinrich Bullinger for his own use. It was soon adopted throughout Switzerland, Poland, France, Hungary and Scotland, becoming one of the most widely recognized confessions of the Reformed Church.

1625 Death of King James I (b.1566), the English monarch who authorized the 1611 translation of the King James Version of the English Bible.

1667 English poet and theologian John Milton published his great work *Paradise Lost*. A product of both the Protestant Reformation and the Renaissance, Milton's theology stressed the freedom of the human will, which flew in the face of the Calvinist doctrine of predestination.

1816 Birth of George J. Elvey, English organist and chorister, in Canterbury. At 19, he became the organist and master of the boys at St. George's Chapel in Windsor, the home church of the royal family, devoting the next 47 years of his life to that one work. He composed two enduring hymn tunes: DIADEMATA ("Crown Him with Many Crowns" and "Soldiers of Christ, Arise"), and ST. GEORGE'S WINDSOR ("Come, Ye Thankful People, Come").

1840 Scottish clergyman Robert Murray McCheyne challenged in a letter: "No person can be a child of God without living in secret prayer; and no community of Christians can be in a lively condition without unity in prayer."

1842 Birth of George Matheson, Scottish clergyman and devotional writer, in Glasgow. Impaired vision left him nearly blind by age 18, yet he pastored from 1866–99, wrote many books on theology and a volume of verse. Respected as one of the outstanding Presbyterian ministers of his day, he is best remembered as author of "O Love That Wilt Not Let Me Go" and "Make Me a Captive, Lord."

1858 Birth of Peter C. Lutkin, American organist, choral conductor and lecturer on sacred music, in Thompsonville, Wisconsin. He became a church organist at the age of 14 and was awarded the D.Mus. degree by Syracuse University in 1900. He served as an assistant editor of both the *Methodist Hymnal* (1905) and of the *Episcopal Hymnal* (1918). His greatest legacy in the church today, however, is no doubt the hymn tune LANIER, which Lutkin composed for the *Methodist Hymnal*, and to which we sing Sidney Lanier's hymn "Into the Woods My Master Went."

1920 Death of Francis Nathan Peloubet (peh-LOO-bet) (b.1831), American Congregational clergyman and Sunday school lesson writer. Ordained in 1857, he pastored four different churches in Massachusetts before dedicating the rest of his life to preparing and publishing materials for use in the Sunday school. Before his death, he authored 46 annual volumes of *Select Notes on the International Sunday School Lessons* (1875–1920).

1934 Death of Carrie E. Breck (b.1855), author of "Face to Face with Christ My Savior." A devoted housewife and mother of five, she was a member of the Presbyterian church and frequently translated her Christian devotion into poetry.

March 28

During the last three centuries, Easter Sunday has fallen on March 28 eight times: 1717, 1723, 1728, 1869, 1875, 1880, 1937, and 1948. Easter will not occur on March 28 again until the year 2027.

1747 Colonial American missionary to the New England Indians David Brainerd affirmed in his journal: "Oh, how happy it is, to be drawn by desires of a state of perfect holiness!"

1886 Death of Richard Chenevix Trench (b.1807), Church of Ireland Archbishop of Dublin. He served as curate or rector in several different churches (1830–45), as chaplain at Oxford (1845), as professor of divinity at King's College (1846–58) and dean of Westminster (1856–63). He was Archbishop of Dublin from 1864–84. Noted as a theologian, a religious poet, and a philologist his most reprinted work is *New Testament Synonyms* (1854).

1895 Birth of Donald Grey Barnhouse, American Presbyterian clergyman and pioneer radio preacher, in Watsonville, California. In 1927 he began a 33-year pastorate at Tenth Presbyterian Church in Philadelphia. During this time, he became a noted radio preacher and authored some 30 books. He was also the founding editor of *Eternity* magazine (1950–1960).

1915 Birth of Kurt Aland, German Lutheran New Testament textual scholar. He co-edited the two most definitive critical editions of the Greek New Testament: *The Greek New Testament* and Eberhard Nestle's *Novum Testamentum Graece*.

1929 Death of Katherine L. Bates (b.1859), American English teacher. The daughter and granddaughter of Congregational ministers, she authored more than 20 learned works. She is primarily remembered today, however, as author of the patriotic hymn "America the Beautiful."

1929 Death of F.B. (Frederick Brotherton) Meyer (b.1847), English Baptist clergyman and devotional writer. A close friend of Dwight L. Moody after 1872, Meyer engaged primarily in social and temperance work. In later years, Meyer became a popular speaker at Northfield and Keswick. His devotional writings, still in print, are widely read to this day.

1936 Birth of Bill Gaither, contemporary Gospel songwriter and music artist. Together with his wife Gloria, he has written some of the most popular Christian music of the past two decades, including "Because He Lives," "The King Is Coming," "I Am Loved," "The Longer I Serve Him" and "Something Beautiful."

1945 Death of Harry Strachan (b.1872), missions pioneer. In 1921 he founded the Latin America Evangelization Campaign, in Stony Brook, New York. Known today as the Latin America Mission, this interdenominational, evangelical mission is headquartered in Coral Gables, Florida. Working in eight Central and South American countries, L.A.M. is engaged primarily in evangelism and literature production. It also assists other mission agencies.

1954 The weekly religious program *The Fourth R* was first aired on NBC television. A Sunday morning series produced by several cooperating religious organizations, the fourth "*R*" stood for "religion." The program aired for over three years, and was broadcast for the last time on May 26, 1957.

1961 English Christian apologist C.S. Lewis explained in *Letters to an American Lady*: "Surely the main purpose of our life is to reach the point at which 'one's own life as a person' is at an end. One must in this sense 'die,' relinquish one's freedom and independence. 'Not I, but Christ that dwelleth in me'—'He must grow greater and I must grow less'—'He that loses his life shall find it.' "

1981 American-born Christian "apostle to the intellectual," Francis Schaeffer, acknowledged in a letter: "Unhappily it must be said that often churches do not have a combination of a clear doctrinal teaching and yet, at the same time, a practicing community. Certainly such churches do exist, but it also is true that often they are not easy to find."

1987 Death of Maria von Trapp (b.1905), matriarch of the Von Trapp Family Singers. Born in Vienna, Austria, Maria aspired early in life to become a nun, but later abandoned the convent to become an Austrian baroness. In 1938 she and her family fled Nazi-occupied Austria. Until 1956, she and the Von Trapp Family Singers toured the world with their music. Maria's early life was immortalized by Julie Andrews in the 1965 film version of the Rodgers and Hammerstein musical *The Sound of Music*.

March 29

During the last three centuries, Easter Sunday has fallen on March 29 eight times: 1739, 1750, 1807, 1812, 1891, 1959, 1964, and 1970. Easter will again fall on March 29 in the year 2043.

1523 German reformer Martin Luther commented in a letter: "I realize that there has never been a great revelation of God's Word unless God has first prepared the way by the rise and the flourishing of languages and learning, as though these were forerunners, a sort of John the Baptist."

1788 Death of Charles Wesley (b.1707), brother of the English founder of Methodism John Wesley, and himself known as "the sweet singer of Methodism." During his lifetime he wrote over 7,200 hymns, giving full expression to an evangelical, biblical faith. Among the dozens of his hymns that remain classics in Protestant hymnody are: "A Charge to Keep I Have," "Hail, Thou Long-Expected Jesus," "Jesus, Lover of My Soul," "O for a Thousand Tongues to Sing," "Soldiers of Christ, Arise" and "Christ the Lord Is Risen Today."

1847 Birth of Winfield Scott Weeden, American sacred music chorister and hymnwriter, in Middleport, Ohio. During his life he taught singing schools, undertook evangelistic work and led music for the Y.M.C.A., Christian Endeavor and Epworth League conventions. He composed several Gospel songs, but is primarily remembered for "I Surrender All."

1866 Death of John Keble (b.1792), English poet and leader of the Oxford Movement. Ordained an Anglican priest in 1816, Keble's famed 1833 sermon, *National Apostasy*, set in motion the Anglo Catholic Party (a.k.a. the Oxford Movement). Comprised chiefly of Keble, R.H. Froude, J.H. Newman and E.B. Pusey, the movement published 90 *Tracts for the Times*. Though some of these Tractarians eventually joined the Roman Catholic Church, Keble remained an Anglican. His most lasting contribution to the church is the hymn "Sun of My Soul, Thou Savior Dear," written by Keble at age 28.

1882 The Roman Catholic lay fraternal society, the Knights of Columbus, was chartered in New Haven, Connecticut. It was founded to encourage patriotism, religious and racial tolerance and benevolence, as well as to promote the interests of the Roman Catholic Church.

March 30

During the last three centuries, Easter Sunday has fallen (or will fall) on March 30 nine times: 1755, 1766, 1777, 1823, 1834, 1902, 1975, 1986, and 1997.

1135 Birth of Moses Maimonides, medieval Jewish scholar, in Cordova, Spain. Considered the foremost Jewish Talmudist of the Middle Ages, Maimonides' most important writing was probably his *Guide to the Perplexed* (1190) in which he attempted to harmonize rabbinic Judaism with the increasingly popular Aristotelian philosophy of his day. Curiously, he attempted to make Aristotle as unsystematic and contradictory as possible, thus demonstrating the limitations of philosophy in knowing God. Maimonides taught that God could not be fully known, but could be appreciated and loved through His creation. "Revelation" by his definition consisted in teaching the believer how to know God through the natural order, not in imparting distinctive truths.

1771 English founder of Methodism John Wesley admonished in a letter: "Suffer all, and conquer all."

1799 Birth of Friedrich A.G. Tholuck, German Lutheran theologian, at Breslau. In 1826 he became professor of dogmatics and exegesis at the University of Halle, where he taught until his death 51 years later. A steadfast opponent of rationalism in biblical and theological studies, he published commentaries on John, Romans, Hebrews and the Psalms, and wrote several other volumes, including *The Old Testament in the New*. Tholuck, through his connection with the revival movement of that time, did much to further the cause of conservative biblical scholarship in his day.

1820 A group of Protestant missionaries from New England first arrived on the Sandwich Islands, now known as the Hawaiian Islands. They were welcomed by King Kamehameha II.

1894 Birth of Roland Bainton, American church historian, at Ilkeston, Derbyshire, England. Emigrating to America with his family in 1902, Bainton taught ecclesiastical history at Yale University from 1920 until his retirement in 1962. Of his many publications, Reformation scholarship was his strongest subject, the most popular of his writings being *Here I Stand: A Life of Martin Luther* (1950).

March 31

During the last three centuries, Easter Sunday has fallen (or will fall) on March 31 thirteen times: 1709, 1720, 1771, 1782, 1793, 1839, 1850, 1861, 1872, 1907, 1918, 1929, and 1991.

1146 French monastic reformer and theologian Bernard of Clairvaux preached for the Second Crusade at Vezelay, France. Eventually, Emperor Conrad III and King Louis VII of France led the crusade (1147–1149). On the whole, the Second Crusade was a failure.

1492 By royal edict of Ferdinand II, all Jews were expelled from Spain. Spain's conquest of Granada earlier in the year marked the end of Muslim influence in the country and was followed by a rising mood for additional religious conquest or "purification." The royal edict came out of this fervor.

1567 Death of Philip of Hesse (b.1504), the most eminent of the Protestant German princes during the Reformation. In 1525 Philip adopted the reformed faith, and thereafter sought to bring together the followers of Luther and Zwingli.

1631 Death of John Donne (b.1572), English divine and metaphysical poet. His writings, neglected by most today, influenced W.B. Yeats, T.S. Eliot, and W.H. Auden. A convert to Anglicanism, Donne became an eloquent and influential preacher, and was dean of St. Paul's Cathedral from 1621–31. No doubt his best remembered line of poetry begins "No man is an island..." (from *Devotions Upon Emergent Occasions*, 1624).

1732 Birth of Franz Joseph Haydn, music composer, in Rohrau, Austria. He was the mentor of both Beethoven and Mozart. He himself composed operas, chamber music, symphonies, keyboard music and masses. Perhaps his greatest music contribution to the church was his 1798 oratorio *The Creation*.

1770 Birth of John Wyeth, American printer and publisher, in Cambridge, Massachusetts. During the earlier years of independence in the U.S., Wyeth was the editor of a federalist newspaper, and was appointed postmaster of Harrisburg, Pennsylvania, under President George Washington. In 1813 Wyeth composed and published the hymn tune NETTLETON, to which we sing Robert Robinson's hymn of invocation "Come, Thou Fount of Every Blessing."

1787 English founder of Methodism, John Wesley, emphasized in a letter: "When the witness and the fruit of the Spirit meet together, there can be no stronger proof that we are of God. . . . Were you to substitute the deductions of reason for the witness of the Spirit, you never would be established."

1816 Death of Francis Asbury (b.1745), pioneer American Methodist bishop. Sent to America by John Wesley in 1771, his work did much to assure the existence of the Methodism in the new world. Membership in the new denomination grew from less than 500 to over 200,000 by the time of his death.

1856 In Mexico, the property of the clergy was seized by the government. A new program of political and religious reform had begun the year before which included legislation designed to strip the churches of their accumulated wealth.

1860 Birth of Rodney ("Gipsy") Smith, popular 19th-century American evangelist. Smith was once quoted as saying: "Anyone can preach to a crowd, but it takes the grace of God to preach to one man."

1950 American missionary to Ecuador and Auca Indian martyr Jim Elliot declared in his journal: "How the Savior suffered in the sinner's place! What tormented Him in time menaces the sinner for eternity."

1958 English Christian apologist C.S. Lewis confessed in *Letters to an American Lady*: "What most often interrupts my own prayers is not great distractions but tiny ones—things one will have to do or avoid in the course of the next hour."

1975 The Evangelical Union of South America merged with the Gospel Missionary Union. Today, the G.M.U. is an interdenominational mission organization of Baptist tradition whose chief activities include evangelism, church planting, Bible translation, literature distribution and radio broadcasting. Its foreign personnel are located in 19 countries.

1976 American Presbyterian apologist for the Christian faith, Francis A. Schaeffer, warned in a letter: "You must not lose confidence in God because you lost confidence in your pastor. If our confidence in God had to depend upon our confidence in any human person, we would be on shifting sand."

April

April 1

During the last three centuries, Easter Sunday has fallen on April 1 eleven times: 1714, 1725, 1736, 1804, 1866, 1877, 1888, 1923, 1934, 1945, and 1956. Easter will not occur on April 1 again until the year 2018.

1548 The British Parliament ordered the first printing of the English *Book of Common Prayer*.

1745 Colonial American missionary David Brainerd began his four-year work among the New England Indians at Kaunaumeek (between Stockbridge and Albany, Massachusetts). The number of Indians converted during Brainerd's endeavors probably never exceeded 200, and growing illness forced him to retire from the work (he died six months later), but his *Journal* has become a devotional classic, influencing hundreds to become missionaries.

1834 English Anglo-Catholic Tractarian John Keble asked in a letter to John H. Newman: "When shall we give up expecting one another to be consistent?"

1834 Birth of Arthur H. Messiter, Anglo-American church organist and sacred music chorister. Hired in 1866 as organist of the prestigious Trinity Church in New York City, Messiter devoted 31 years to the position. He maintained the highest standards of English cathedral music, and his men's and boys' choirs became models for many other Episcopal churches in this country. Perhaps Messiter's most abiding legacy is his hymn tune MARION, to which we sing "Rejoice, Ye Pure in Heart."

1854 Birth of Augustine Tolton, first American black to be ordained a Roman Catholic priest (1886), in Ralls County, Missouri. Before the Civil War, most black Catholics were in the larger eastern cities. By the end of the 19th century, there were nearly 100,000 throughout the U.S., and 2 newspapers (*St. Joseph's Advocate* of Baltimore and the *American Catholic Tribune* of Cincinnati) devoted themselves to the interests of black Catholics.

1925 British statesman Lord (Arthur James) Balfour inaugurated Hebrew University at Jerusalem.

1927 The Eastern European Mission was founded in Chicago. This interdenominational and evangelical mission agency is presently headquartered in Pasadena, California, and specializes in support of national churches through radio, literature and relief work. The organization changed its name to Eurovision in 1985, and works primarily in ten European countries.

1932 Gerhard Kittel published the first fascicle (partial volume) of the *Theologisches Worterbuch zum Neuen Testament*. The English translation is known as TDNT (*Theological Dictionary of the New Testament*). This major publishing project (comprising ten large volumes) began in 1931. Because of World War II and Kittel's death in 1948, the work was not completed until the late 1960s.

1949 American missionary and Auca Indian martyr Jim Elliot commented in his journal: " 'The law of Jehovah is perfect, restoring the soul' (Ps. 19:7). Most laws condemn the soul and pronounce sentence. The result of the law of my God is perfect. It condemns but forgives. It restores—more than abundantly—what it takes away."

1956 Death of William R. Newell (b.1868), American Congregational pastor and Bible teacher. As one-time assistant superintendent of Moody Bible Institute, he conducted interdenominational Bible classes in several major American cities. He is better remembered today as the author of the hymn "At Calvary" (a.k.a. "Years I Spent in Vanity and Pride").

1973 Death of Gordon Lindsay (b.1906), who founded Christ for the Nations, Inc., in 1948. This evangelical and interdenominational mission agency is headquartered in Dallas, and specializes in raising funds for the production of literature and the construction of local churches.

April 2

During the last three centuries, Easter Sunday has fallen on April 2 ten times: 1705, 1741, 1747, 1752, 1809, 1820, 1893, 1899, 1961, and 1972. Easter will not occur on April 2 again until the year 2045.

1524 At the age of 40, Swiss reformer Ulrich Zwingli publically married the widow Anna Reinhard. Their marriage lasted until his death in the Battle of Kappel in 1531.

1860 Birth of George Milligan, Scottish biblical scholar in Fife, Scotland. He taught at Glasgow University 1910–32. In 1926, he was elected the first chairman of the Scottish Sunday School Union. Most of his published writings were on New Testament language. His *opus magnum* was *The Vocabulary of the Greek Testament* (1914–30), coedited by James Hope Moulton.

1877 Birth of Mordecai Ham, American evangelist of the early 20th century. He would stay in one location many months, thus increasing his credibility and impact of the Gospel. His life's motto was "Love all men, fear no man." It was under his preaching in the late 1930s that Billy Graham was led to Christ.

1888 Birth of Paul Althaus, Lutheran biblical scholar, at Obershagen, Germany. He taught at Gottingen (1914–), Rostock (1920–) and Erlangen (1925–). His expositions of Paul's epistles and study of the synoptic problem are his most noteworthy works in biblical studies. In the area of theology, he specialized in justification by faith, the relationship between law and Gospel, church-state relations and eschatology.

1894 Death of William D. Longstaff (b.1822), English philanthropist. A close friend of Moody and Sankey, Longstaff became active in their work in England. The full extent of his original writings is not known, but he is remembered primarily for the hymn "Take Time to Be Holy."

1911 English-born Congregational clergyman John Henry Jowett began his first and only American pastorate at the Fifth Avenue Presbyterian Church in New York City. He returned to England seven years later.

1914 The Assemblies of God was organized at an 11-day constitutional convention that began on this date in Hot Springs, Arkansas.

1955 English Christian apologist C.S. Lewis responded in *Letters to an American Lady*: "Fear is horrid, but there's no reason to be ashamed of it. Our Lord was afraid (dreadfully so) in Gethsemane. I always cling to that as a very comforting fact."

1971 The European Evangelistic Crusade, Inc. (founded by Rev. James Stewart in 1943), changed its name to Global Outreach Mission. Headquartered today in Buffalo, New York, this interdenominational and evangelical mission supports national churches in over a dozen European and African countries.

April 3

Between 1700 and the year 2000, Easter Sunday will have occurred on April 3 ten times: 1763, 1768, 1774, 1825, 1831, 1836, 1904, 1983, 1988, and 1994.

1593 Birth of George Herbert, English clergyman and poet, in Montgomery, Wales. For a time he served at the court of King James I. Very fond of music, he was known as the "poet of Anglican theology," writing many hymns for lute and viol accompaniment, including the still-popular "The King of Love My Shepherd Is."

1759 Anglican clergyman and hymnwriter John Newton commented in a letter: "I believe that love to God, and to man for God's sake, is the essence of religion and the fulfilling of the law."

1769 Death of Gerhard Tersteegen (b.1697), German Protestant poet and mystic. Denied a seminary education by the death of his father when he was six, he went to work as an apprentice at a young age. Tersteegen went through seasons of deep spiritual despondency, but in 1724 he experienced a solemn spiritual change and devoted the rest of his life to ministering to others in the name of his faith. He lived the rest of his life away from the Reformed tradition of his childhood, yet he never made an effort to start a new denomination. Rather, he lived the quiet life of a celibate and ascetic. Tersteegen's most enduring gift to later generations has been the hymn he wrote at age 38, "God Calling Yet! Shall I Not Hear."

1826 Death of Reginald Heber (b.1783), English clergyman. In 1823 he was consecrated the Anglican bishop of Calcutta. The diocese comprised all of India, Ceylon, Mauritius and Australasia. He wrote about 60 hymns, 3 of which have endured: "Holy, Holy, Holy," "From Greenland's Icy Mountains" and "The Son of God Goes Forth to War."

1897 Death of Johannes Brahms (b.1833), celebrated German composer. He wrote in almost every musical genre except opera. Though essentially not a church musician, Brahms was grounded in historic Lutheran church music, and he did compose a few sacred motets. His choral compositions are usually given the highest praise by critics. Undoubtedly, his greatest choral masterpiece is *A German Requiem*, first performed in 1868. Its lyrics come entirely from the German Bible, and it is regarded by some as the greatest major sacred choral work of the 19th century.

1950 Death of Ira B. Wilson (b.1880), American sacred choral composer. In 1905 he began working for the Lorenz Publishing Co. of Dayton, Ohio, both as an editor and composer of choral music. The professional tradition begun by Wilson was carried on by his son Roger C. Wilson, also a member of the Lorenz editorial staff. Ira Wilson's most enduring sacred composition has been the hymn "Out of the Highways and Byways of Life" (a.k.a. "Make Me a Blessing").

April 4

Between 1700 and the year 2000, Easter Sunday will have fallen on April 4 nine times: 1706, 1779, 1790, 1847, 1858, 1915, 1920, 1926, and 1999.

397 Death of Ambrose (b. ca. 339), Bishop of Milan, Italy. He began his bishopric in 374, laboring indefatigably during his remaining 23 years. Ambrose was influential in encouraging monasticism in Italy, in introducing congregational singing, and showing deference to the bishop of Rome, which helped develop the polity of the Catholic church. Perhaps Ambrose's greatest influence was his witness to Augustine of Hippo, whose eventual fame as a theologian eclipsed even his own.

1507 Martin Luther was ordained a priest in Erfurt, Germany, a year after he had been consecrated a monk within the Augustinian Order. In 1517, ten years later, Luther nailed his *95 Theses* to the door of the Wittenberg Castle church, the symbolic beginning of the Protestant Reformation in Germany.

1541 Ignatius of Loyola (1491–1556) was elected the first General of the Society of Jesus (the Jesuits), the Roman Catholic order that he had founded. Loyola had become a Dominican at age 30. But like Luther, he found that mortifying the flesh could not appease his troubled soul. He finally found peace by yielding himself wholly to the church, its traditions and to the authority of the pope. In 1534 Loyola and six companions formed the Society of Jesus. The order was approved by Pope Paul III in 1540, and Loyola was canonized by the church in 1622, by Pope Gregory XV.

1748 Birth of William White, American patriarch of the Protestant Episcopal Church, in Philadelphia. Ordained an Anglican priest in England in 1772, he soon sided with the Colonies during the American Revolution, even serving as chaplain of the Continental Congresses. White first coined the name "Protestant Episcopal." In 1786 he was chosen the first bishop of the American denomination, and he exercised his episcopal office for the next fifty years, until his death in 1836.

1862 Birth of Ernest W. Shurtleff, American Congregational pastor, missionary and student chaplain, in Boston. After holding several American pastorates from 1898–1905, he organized the American Church at Frankfurt, Germany, in 1905. The following year he began working with American students in Paris. During his life, he published several books of poetry, and authored the hymn "Lead on, O King Eternal."

1889   Death of Asa Mahan (b.1800), American Congregational clergyman and philosopher. He was president of Oberlin College in Ohio from 1835–50 and sought to make the institution interracial. He was also the first president to give degrees to women under the same conditions as men. In 1871 he retired to England to write, but continued to preach to large congregations. Several of his more important publications include *Scripture Doctrine of Christian Perfection*, *Science of Natural Theology*, and *Critical History of Philosophy and Theology*.

1944   Jewish Holocaust victim and Dutch diarist Anne Frank affirmed: "I want to go on living even after my death! And therefore I am grateful to God for giving me this gift. . . of expressing all that is in me."

1965   German theologian Jurgen Moltmann admitted in a letter to Karl Barth: "Polemics always makes one a little one-sided."

April 5

During the last three centuries, Easter Sunday has fallen on April 5 thirteen times: 1711, 1722, 1733, 1744, 1795, 1801, 1863, 1874, 1885, 1896, 1931, 1942, and 1953. Easter will not occur on April 5 again until the 21st century—the year 2015.

1784   Birth of Louis (Ludwig) Spohr, German violin virtuoso and composer, in Brunswick, Germany. As a composer, he wrote violin concertos, chamber music, operas and oratorios that were highly acclaimed in Germany. Today he is known for the hymn tunes GERALD ("I Want a Principle Within") and SPOHR ("All Things Bright and Beautiful").

1802   Pioneer American Methodist bishop Francis Asbury commented in his journal: "I am often drawn out in thankfulness to God, who hath saved a mother of mine, and, I trust, a father also, who are already in glory, where I hope to meet them both, after time, and cares, and sorrows shall have ceased with me."

1811   Death of Robert Raikes (b.1735), English philanthropist and founder of the modern Sunday school movement. Raikes set up an experimental "Sabbath school" in 1780 for the neglected children of his native Gloucester, England. The idea caught fire, and other schools were soon opened on both sides of the Atlantic. The first Sunday-school teachers were paid, but volunteers were used as the movement grew. The movement's success led to the establishment of the first Sunday School union in 1803.

1969   Pope Paul VI abolished the use of the red hat (*galero*) and red shoes and buckles by Roman Catholic cardinals.

April 6

During the last three centuries, Easter Sunday has fallen on April 6 eleven times: 1738, 1749, 1760, 1806, 1817, 1828, 1890, 1947, 1958, 1969, and 1980. Easter will not occur on April 6 again until the 21st century—in the year 2042.

1123   The First Lateran Council closed, under Pope Callixtus II (1119–24). Just before the council, the right of investiture (establishing a person in high office by either the state or church) was settled by treaty between the Pope and Emperor Henry V of the Holy Roman Empire. (There were a total of five ecumenical councils held at the Lateran Palace in Rome. The palace was named for the Laterani family, who occupied the site in ancient times.)

1528 Death of Albrecht Durer (b.1471), European artist of the Reformation era. Durer is best known for pioneering advanced woodcut engraving. Theologically, he consciously sided with Lutheranism, yet his art has deeper affinity with the Christian piety and humanism of Erasmus. Durer's most popular work is *Praying Hands*.

1801 The General Conference of the Methodist Episcopal Church recognized the new African Methodist Episcopal Church. The denomination was formed by blacks who had been denied membership and/or recognition within the white Methodist churches, particularly in Philadelphia and New York. The A.M.E. church became the prototype for the American Methodist Episcopal Zion Church, established in 1820.

1810 Birth of Edmund H. Sears, American Unitarian clergyman, in Sandisfield, Massachusetts. Though educated a non-Trinitarian, Sears once wrote: ". . . I believe and preach the divinity of Christ." He authored a number of deeply spiritual books, but he is immortalized for having authored the Christmas hymn "It Came upon the Midnight Clear" in 1849.

1830 The Church of Jesus Christ of Latter-day Saints (Mormons) was founded by Joseph Smith in Manchester, New York. The Mormons are not considered an orthodox denomination of Protestantism, but their history has intimate connections with the history of Christendom in America.

1851 Anglican churchman and Archbishop of Westminster Henry E. Manning converted to Roman Catholicism. His conversion stemmed from an increasing commitment to the principles of the Oxford Movement (ca. 1833–45), then influencing the English national church. In 1860 Manning became the chief English defender of the pope's temporal power. He was made Archbishop of Westminster in 1865, and in 1875 he became a cardinal in the Roman Catholic Church.

1877 Death of Alexander R. Reinagle (b.1799), a distinguished English church organist in Oxford, 1822–53. His most enduring sacred composition is the hymn tune ST. PETER ("In Christ There Is No East or West.")

1889 Death of Benjamin H. Kennedy (b.1804), English educator who published the English translation of the lyrics to the hymn "Ask Ye What Great Thing I Know" in 1863.

1893 The Mormons dedicated their Salt Lake City Temple in Utah after 40 years of construction.

1952 American missionary to Ecuador and Auca Indian martyr Jim Elliot maintained in his journal: "Faith makes life so even, gives one such confidence, that the words of men are as wind."

1966 Death of Swiss theologian Emil Brunner (b.1889). He was one of the most influential theologians between the two world wars. He pastored from 1916–24, after which he taught theology at Zurich from 1924–53. A contem-

porary of Karl Barth, Brunner's theology was deeply influenced by Kierkegaard's dialectic and Martin Buber's *I-Thou* concept.

April 7

During the last three centuries, Easter Sunday has fallen on April 7 eight
times: 1765, 1776, 1822, 1833, 1844, 1901, 1912, 1985, and will fall on April 7
again in 1996.

1199 Death of King Richard I (b.1157), ruler of England from 1189. Known as
"Richard the Lionhearted," he was one of the three principal leaders of the
Third Crusade (1189–92).

1541 Spanish Roman Catholic missionary and founder of the Jesuits, Francis
Xavier and three companions departed Lisbon, Portugal, for Goa (India), the
first of a long line of Roman Catholic missionaries to travel to India and the
East Indies.

1872 Birth of Kirsopp Lake, British biblical scholar. Most of his writings cover
Greek textual criticism. His greatest work is no doubt the co-edited *The Beginning of Christianity. Part I: The Acts of the Apostles* by Lake and F.J. Foakes
Jackson (1920–33). The book is still a standard reference tool for students of
the New Testament.

1884 Birth of C.H. Dodd, English Congregational clergyman and New Testament scholar. Having taught at Mansfield College and Cambridge, Dodd became the most influential British New Testament scholar of the mid-20th century. In his popular *The Parables of the Kingdom* (1934), Dodd emphasized
"realized eschatology" in the teaching of Jesus. After his retirement from
teaching in 1940, Dodd wrote more than a dozen additional books and he
served as general director for the New English Translation of the Bible.

1917 Death of James Hope Moulton (b.1863), English Methodist clergyman
and biblical Greek scholar. Though he pastored for 16 years before teaching,
his fame rests on his work in New Testament Greek. He published the first of
four volumes, the Prolegomena, of the *Grammar of New Testament Greek*
(1906). Together with G. Milligan, he wrote the first two fascicles (part-vol-
umes) of the definitive *Vocabulary of the Greek New Testament: Illustrated
from the Papyri and other Non-Literary Sources* (1914–30) before he was killed
by enemy fire in World War I.

1928 Birth of James C. Smith, who was General Director of Christian Missionary Fellowship for over 19 years. C.M.F. is an evangelical mission agency
founded in 1949, and headquartered in Indianapolis, Indiana. Its missionaries
work primarily in Brazil, Kenya, Indonesia, and Mexico.

1953 Swedish diplomat and Christian statesman Dag Hammarskjold was
elected Secretary General of the United Nations. Hammarskjold endeared himself to Christian readers through the posthumous publication of his life-journal
Markings (1964).

1968 In a letter penned during his 83rd and final year of life, Karl Barth wrote:
"How one learns to be thankful for each day on which one can still do
something."

April 8

During the last three centuries, Easter Sunday has fallen on April 8 ten times: 1703, 1708, 1787, 1792, 1798, 1849, 1855, 1860, 1917, and 1928. Easter will not occur on April 8 again until the 21st century—in the year 2007.

1546 At its Fourth Session, the Council of Trent adopted Jerome's Latin *Vulgate* as the official biblical text of the Roman Catholic Church. By its decision, the church also accepted the 15 apocryphal books in the *Vulgate* as part of the Old Testament canon of Scripture. (These writings were rejected as authoritative by Martin Luther and most Protestant groups because, among other reasons, their oldest manuscripts were written in Greek rather than in the Hebrew/Aramaic of the other 39 Old Testament writings.)

1730 The first Jewish congregation in America, Shearith Israel, consecrated its synagogue in New York City. The congregation traces its roots back to 1654, when Sephardic Jews, refugees from Portugal, emigrated to America and settled in the colony which at that time was called New Amsterdam.

1743 Colonial American missionary to the New England Indians, David Brainerd, admitted in his journal: "Of late I have thought much of having the kingdom of Christ advanced in the world; but now I saw I had enough to do within myself."

1847 Birth of Frederick Brotherton Meyer, English Baptist clergyman and devotional writer, in London. In 1881 Meyer opened Melbourne Hall in Leicester, a center for social and evangelistic activity that afterwards became the source of Meyer's most popular achievements. He became a popular convention speaker at Northfield and Keswick and penned a number of devotional studies, many of which are still reprinted.

1868 Blind Scottish hymnwriter George Matheson was ordained pastor of the Clydeside parish of Innellan, in Argyllshire, Scotland. He remained at this post for 18 years. Matheson eventually became one of the outstanding Scottish Presbyterian ministers of his day. It was he who wrote the haunting hymn "O Love That Will Not Let Me Go."

1886 Birth of Charles H. Marsh, American church musician and educator, in Magnolia, Iowa. He belonged to the American Guild of Organists and was known equally well for his poetry and painting as well as his music. We remember him as the composer of the hymn tune CHAPMAN, to which we sing "One Day When Heaven Was Filled with His Praises."

1912 The American Theological Society was organized at Union Theological Seminary in New York City. Its membership included theologians and philosophers, meeting annually for the discussion of theological problems. Among the 15 charter members were A.M. Dulles, R.C. Knox, D.C. Mackintosh, and E.W. Lyman.

1935 Death of Otto Rahlfs (b.1865), German Lutheran Septuagint (Greek Old Testament) scholar. Rahlfs devoted the greater part of his professional life to the preparation of a critical edition of the Greek Old Testament—*Septuaginta*—which was not published until the year of his death.

1945 Dietrich Bonhoeffer, before he was hanged the following morning in Flossenburg, Germany, by the Nazis, said: "This is the end—for me the beginning of life."—his last recorded words.

1957 American Roman Catholic Bishop Fulton J. Sheen's religious TV program *Life Is Worth Living* was broadcast for the last time. The series had begun five years earlier, on Feb. 12, 1952.

1966 Child Evangelism Fellowship, Inc., was incorporated, in Chicago, Illinois. The history of this interdenominational mission, however, goes back to 1916, when founder Jesse I. Overholtzer had his first child convert. Later, in 1937, Overholtzer established a forerunner ministry in California, called the Christian Training Association, in which he trained adults to reach children for Christ. Today, this evangelical sending agency works in over 60 foreign countries.

April 9

During the last three centuries, Easter Sunday has fallen on April 9 seven times: 1719, 1730, 1871, 1882, 1939, 1944, and 1950. Easter will not occur on April 9 again until the 21st century—in the year 2023.

1598 Birth of Johann Cruger, German Lutheran church chorister, in Gross-Briesen, Prussia. He was appointed cantor of the Lutheran Cathedral of St. Nicholas, Berlin, in 1622, and remained there until his death 40 years later. He composed a great number of significant sacred choral melodies during his lifetime; the most enduring being NUN DANKET, to which we sing "Now Thank We All Our God."

1761 Death of William Law (b.1686), English devotional writer. An independent, controversial churchman all his life, Law wrote several powerful books. His most influential work is no doubt his *Serious Call to a Devout and Holy Life* (1728), which influenced the lives of many early evangelicals, including George Whitefield, Henry Martyn, and John and Charles Wesley.

1813 Birth of Jane Borthwick, translator of the hymns "My Jesus, As Thou Wilt" and "Be Still, My Soul", in Edinburgh, Scotland. Together with her sister Sarah, Jane made many English translations of German hymns.

1816 The African Methodist Episcopal (A.M.E.) Church was founded in Philadelphia. The original members of the denomination had withdrawn from St. George's Methodist Episcopal Church in Philadelphia in 1787, in protest of what they considered racial discrimination. Soon after officially organizing, the church consecrated Richard Allen the first bishop of this all-black Christian denomination.

1945 Martyrdom of Dietrich Bonhoeffer (b.1906), German Lutheran clergyman and theologian. During World War II, his opposition to Hitler led him to involvement in the resistance movement, and later to his arrest by the Gestapo in April of 1943. He was executed by the Nazis two years later on the charge of treason.

April 10

During the last three centuries, Easter Sunday has fallen on April 10 ten times: 1735, 1746, 1757, 1803, 1814, 1887, 1898, 1955, 1966, and 1977. It will fall on April 10 again in the year 2039.

1583 Birth of Hugo Grotius, Dutch lawyer, statesman and theologian, at Delft, Holland. Though trained and working in the political world, Grotius chose to involve himself in the theological conflict between Calvinism and Arminianism that was agitating Holland at that time. His sympathy for Arminian views caused him to be sentenced for life, although he escaped two years later and fled to Paris. He spent the last ten years of his life in the service of the Swedish government.

1802 Birth of Johann Peter Lange, German Reformed New Testament exegete, in Elberfeld, Prussia. He pastored from 1825–41, after which he taught at the University of Zurich, then in Bonn. His monumental *Theologische-homiletisches Bibelwerk* was later edited into 25 English volumes by Philip Schaff as *A Commentary on the Holy Scriptures, Critical, Doctrinal, and Homiletic*.

1816 Richard Allen became the first elected bishop of the new African Methodist Episcopal (A.M.E.) Church. The all-black denomination traced its beginnings to the 1790s, when blacks organized a movement in reaction to segregation attempts by some whites of St. George's Methodist Church in Philadelphia.

1829 Birth of William Booth, founder and first General of the Salvation Army, in Nottingham, England. Working first as a Methodist minister and evangelist, Booth and his able wife Catherine began tackling social evils at the same time as engaging in direct evangelism. In 1865 Booth began a Christian mission in east London. By 1878 the mission and its work had evolved into the full-grown organization of the Salvation Army. By the time he died in Aug. 1912, he had traveled 5 million miles, preached 60,000 sermons and drawn some 16,000 enlisted soldiers into his Army.

1838 Birth of Edward Kremser, German chorister, in Vienna, Austria. He composed numerous vocal and instrumental works during his lifetime, including the hymn tune KREMSER, to which we sing "We Gather Together."

1899 Death of John R. Sweney (b.1837), American chorister. He composed over 1,000 Gospel songs during his lifetime, including the hymn tunes I SHALL KNOW HIM ("When My Life-Work Is Ended"), STARS IN MY CROWN ("Will There Be Any Stars?"), STORY OF JESUS ("Tell Me the Story of Jesus"), SUNSHINE ("There Is Sunshine in My Soul Today"), and SWENEY ("More About Jesus").

1905 Birth of Joseph Fletcher, American Episcopalian, in Newark, New Jersey. He taught ethics and pastoral theology at Episcopal Theological School, in Cambridge, Massachusetts, beginning in 1944. He is known for his controversial book *Situation Ethics* (1966).

1933 Death of Henry Van Dyke (b.1852), American Presbyterian clergyman. He is remembered for two writings: *The Story of the Other Wise Man* (1896) and the hymn lyrics for "Joyful, Joyful, We Adore Thee." (1908), set to fit the last movement of Beethoven's *Ninth Symphony*.

1945 U.S. armed forces liberated the Nazi concentration camp at Buchenwald, Germany.

1955 Death of Pierre Teilhard de Chardin (b.1881), French Jesuit priest and paleontologist. He combined his field work and Roman Catholic theology to formulate an evolutionary hypothesis, which taught that the world developed according to a law of increasing complexity and consciousness. His *The Phenomenon of Man* (1959) was originally prohibited because of its unusual evolutionary views. His ideas, which only today are beginning to be fully understood, bear a resemblance to process theology.

April 11

According to Christian tradition, Jesus Christ was crucified, and raised again from the dead in A.D. 33—the first Easter! During the last three centuries, Easter Sunday has fallen (or will fall) on April 11 thirteen times: 1700, 1751, 1762, 1773, 1784, 1819, 1830, 1841, 1852, 1909, 1971, 1982, and 1993.

146 Birth of Septimus Severus, Emperor of Rome from A.D. 193–211. He persecuted the Christian Church, although he had once been friendly to the Christian cause.

1506 The foundation stone of the new St. Peter's Basilica was laid under the patronage of Pope Julius II. The church was not completed until 1626. The cost of the building was to be paid by the sale of indulgences—which was bitterly criticized by the Protestant reformers, most memorably Martin Luther.

1598 King Henry IV of France issued the Edict of Nantes, which recognized non-Catholic religions in France, granted freedom of conscience to Protestants and ended the persecution of the Huguenots (French Protestants). The Edict remained in effect until Louis XIV revoked it in 1685.

1816 The first Negro bishop in America, Rev. Richard Allen, was ordained in Philadelphia by Francis Asbury to head the new African Methodist Episcopal Church.

1834 Birth of Marcus Dods, Scottish clergyman and biblical scholar, in Northumberland, England. Ordained in 1864, he pastored until called to teach New Testament at New College, Edinburgh, in 1889. He published several important works in New Testament studies which helped popularize modern biblical scholarship.

1836 English philanthropist George Mueller opened his famous orphanage on Wilson Street, Bristol, in two rented houses. Each building housed 30 children. By 1875 Mueller's orphanage at Ashley Down was providing care and a happy home for over 2,000 children.

1844 Birth of James Orr, Scottish theologian, in Glasgow. He pastored for 17 years before beginning a teaching career that lasted from 1891 until his death in 1913. His best known written work is *The Virgin Birth of Christ* (1907).

1941 French-born American trappist monk Thomas Merton affirmed in his *Secular Journal*: "If we are willing to accept humiliation, tribulation can become, by God's grace, the mild yoke of Christ, His light burden."

1952 Birth of Nancy (Hennenbaum) Honeytree, popular contemporary Christian vocalist and songwriter. One of her popular pieces has been *Diamond in the Rough*.

1967 The Full Gospel Fellowship of Churches and Ministers International, formed five years earlier in Dallas, changed its name to Christ for the Nations, Inc. This interdenominational, charismatic mission agency specializes in raising funds to support church construction and literature distribution both in America and overseas.

April 12

During the last three centuries, Easter has fallen (or will fall) on April 12 ten times: 1716, 1789, 1846, 1857, 1868, 1903, 1914, 1925, 1936, and 1998.

1204 The treacherous Genoese forces of the Fourth Crusade captured the allied city of Constantinople and ravaged it for three days. They took a booty of over $7.5 million and insured the eventual collapse of the Byzantine Empire.

1572 French-born Swiss reformer Theodore Beza, John Calvin's successor, commented in a letter to Scottish reformer John Knox: "They whose citizenship is in heaven ought to have their whole dependence on heaven."

1716 Birth of Felice de Giardini, Italian chorister who wrote the hymn tune for "Come, Thou Almighty King" (ITALIAN HYMN TRINITY), at Turin, Italy. Throughout his life he worked as a violinist, music instructor, conductor and opera singer. Among the music scores he composed are four hymn tunes, including ITALIAN HYMN TRINITY.

1850 Death of Adoniram Judson (b.1788), American Baptist missionary and Bible translator. In 1812 Judson left America to go to India and later to Burma as a missionary. In 1834 he completed the first translation of the Scriptures into the difficult Burmese language. Judson returned to America only once (1845–47) before his death while at sea in 1850.

1867 Birth of Samuel M. Zwemer, American Dutch Reformed missionary, at Vriesland, Michigan. Under the influence of Robert Wilder, he became one of the first members of the Student Volunteer Movement, and later one of its leaders. In 1888–89 Zwemer helped found The Arabian Mission, which he worked with thereafter around the Arabian Gulf. He authored about fifty writings in English and a number in Arabic.

1901 Death of Louis A. Sabatier (b.1839), French Protestant theologian. Expelled as a professor from Strassburg University in 1873, Sabatier joined the Protestant theological faculty at the Sorbonne in Paris. His writings, though not well received in Germany, helped pave the way in France for the acceptance of modern scholarship.

1902 Death of T. DeWitt Talmage (b.1832), American Presbyterian clergyman. Ordained in 1856, he pastored churches in New Jersey, New York, Pennsylvania, and Washington, D.C., until his retirement in 1899. His later sermons were simultaneously published in over 3,500 papers in the U.S. and abroad.

1912 Death of Clara Barton (b.1821), founder of the American Red Cross. Her heroic service to American Civil War wounded led to a nervous collapse in 1869, followed by a trip to Europe to recuperate. While there, she worked with the International Red Cross movement. Returning to America, she organized the American chapter of the Red Cross in 1881, serving as its first president from 1881–1904. She was also an advocate of temperance, women's suffrage and better social conditions for women.

1914 An 11-day constitutional convention, which saw the founding of the Assemblies of God, ended at Hot Springs, Arkansas.

1956 Death of Charles H. Marsh (b.1886), American Congregational pastor and composer of the hymn tune CHAPMAN, to which we sing "One Day When Heaven Was Filled with His Praises."

1968 American Presbyterian apologist Francis A. Schaeffer explained in a letter: "The Bible says that God is not caught in the machine aspect of the universe which He has made, and that man is not caught in the machine either. Man is able by choice to interrupt the machine portion of the universe. Thus, from the biblical viewpoint, when I pray, God does hear and He can act into the cause and effect universe in answer to my prayer."

April 13

According to Christian tradition, Jesus Christ was crucified and raised again from the dead in A.D. 33. During the last three centuries, Easter has fallen on April 13 nine times: 1721, 1727, 1732, 1800, 1873, 1879, 1884, 1941, and 1952. Easter will not occur on April 13 again until the year 2025.

1059 At a Lateran synod, Pope Nicholas II issued the momentous decree establishing the election of the Pope by cardinal bishops only.

1742 George F. Handel's immortal oratorio *Messiah* premiered, in Dublin, Ireland.

1776 Anglican clergyman and hymnwriter John Newton revealed in a letter: "When everything we receive from Him is received and prized as fruit and pledge of His covenant love, then His bounties, instead of being set up as rivals and idols to draw our heart from Him, awaken us to fresh exercises of gratitude and furnish us with fresh motives of cheerful obedience every hour."

1828 Birth of J.B. (Joseph Barber) Lightfoot, English churchman and textual critic. He was ordained in 1858 and consecrated Bishop of Durham in 1879, filling that office until his death in 1889. Quiet and shy by nature, Lightfoot nevertheless wrote enduring critical works on the New Testament and early church fathers. His commentaries on Galatians, Philippians, Colossians with Philemon (1865–75), as well as his editions of the *Apostolic Fathers* (1869,1885) are still in print.

1836 Birth of A.J. (Adoniram Judson) Gordon, American Baptist clergyman, educator and writer, in New Hampton, New Hampshire. Ordained to the pastorate in 1863, Gordon was called to the Clarendon Street Baptist Church in Boston in 1869, and remained there until his death in 1895. He raised great sums of money for foreign missions and engaged in home missions in Boston for Jews, blacks, Chinese, fallen women and dock workers. His memory is preserved in his hymn tune GORDON, to which we sing "My Jesus, I Love Thee."

1853 Loyola College in Baltimore was chartered under Roman Catholic support.

1908 The New England Conference of the Methodist Episcopal Church voted to remove its ban on dancing, card-playing, and theater-going.

1928 Death of Ernest A. Kilbourne (b.1865), American missionary to the Orient. In 1902 he went to Japan with Charles and Lettie Cowman, where they organized the Oriental Missionary Society in 1907. Known today as O.M.S. International, this interdenominational and evangelical organization (head-quartered since 1966 in Greenwood, Indiana) presently works in church planting and development in over a dozen nations on three continents.

April 14

Easter has fallen on April 14 ten times during the last three centuries: 1743, 1748, 1754, 1805, 1811, 1816, 1895, 1963, 1968, and 1974. Easter will fall on April 14 again in 2047.

73 According to the Jewish historian Josephus, 967 Jewish zealots under the leadership of Eleazar ben Jair committed mass suicide within the fortress of Masada the night before it was successfully besieged by the attacking Roman Tenth Legion. Two women and five children survived by hiding in a cistern, and were later released unharmed by the Romans.

1582 The University of Edinburgh, in Scotland, was chartered.

1759 Death of George Frederick Handel (b.1685), German composer of oratorios, chamber music and concertos. Handel is remembered for the most performed major choral work of the modern Christian era: *Messiah* (1741).

1771 English founder of Methodism, John Wesley, commented in a letter: "No part of Christian history is so profitable, as that which relates to great changes wrought in our souls: these therefore should be carefully noticed, and treasured up for the encouragement of our brethren."

1796 Death of Joseph Swain (b.1761), author of "O Thou in Whose Presence My Soul Takes Delight."

1875 Birth of William Charles Poole, American Methodist clergyman and hymnwriter, in Easton, Maryland. He was converted at age 11, ordained to the Methodist ministry at 25, and served various pastorates in the Wilmington Conference for 35 years. Inspired by Charles H. Gabriel, Poole began writing Gospel song texts. One which remains popular is "Just When I Need Him, Jesus Is Near."

1888 Death of William F. Sherwin (b.1826), American sacred chorister. A Baptist layman, Sherwin's extraordinary music directing ability once made him the choice for musical director at the Chautauqua Assembly in New York. His most enduring hymn tunes are BREAD OF LIFE ("Break Thou the Bread of Life") and CHAUTAUQUA ("Day Is Dying in the West").

1940 English Bible expositor A.W. Pink concluded in a letter: "Nothing is too great and nothing is too small to commit into the hands of the Lord."

April 15

Within the last three centuries, Easter has fallen (or will fall) on April 15 nine times: 1759, 1770, 1781, 1827, 1838, 1900, 1906, 1979, and 1990.

1452 Birth of Leonardo da Vinci, Italian Renaissance artist. A profound thinker and scholar, da Vinci was one of the greatest minds of his day, being classed with Dante, Beethoven and Shakespeare as one of the four greatest intellects in the world of art and literature. The church remembers him as the artist who painted *The Last Supper*, on which he labored three years (1494–97).

1610 Death of Robert Parsons (b.1546), leader of the English Jesuits. He left Oxford during his 20s to become a Roman Catholic, and in 1575 joined the Jesuits. In 1580 he and St. Edmund Campion led a mission to his native England, but he was forced to flee the following year. Thereafter a trusted counselor of popes, Parsons' most famous writing is perhaps his spiritual treatise *The Christian Directory* (1582).

1729 German composer Johann S. Bach conducted the first and only performance of his monumental *Passion of Our Lord Jesus Christ According to Saint Matthew* (a.k.a. *St. Matthew Passion*) during his lifetime. Some consider this musical work to be Western civilization's supreme musical achievement. Bach's single performance occurred during Good Friday Vespers at the St. Thomas Lutheran Church in Leipzig, Germany.

1746 Colonial American missionary to the New England Indians David Brainerd cried out in his journal: "My soul longed for more spirituality; and it was my burden that I could do no more for God. Oh, my barrenness in my daily affliction and heavy load! Oh, how precious is time, and how it pains me to see it slide away, while I do so little to any good purpose. Oh, that God would make me more fruitful and spiritual."

1862 Birth of Lelia Naylor Morris, American Methodist minister's wife and hymnwriter, in Pennsville, Ohio. She began writing words and music for religious songs in her 30s. She was totally blind during the last 15 years of her life, but has left a legacy of several Christian hymns which remain popular. She wrote the words and music to "What If It Were Today?," "Let Jesus Come into Your Heart," "Sweeter As the Years Go By," and "Nearer, Still Nearer."

1882 Death of Bruno Bauer (b.1809), German radical scholar. He was one of the most negative New Testament and theological critics of his day. His license to teach had been revoked in 1842, so he spent the last 40 years of his life denying that there ever was an historical Jesus. He also taught that Christianity stood in the way of fulfilled and liberated humanity. Neglected by theologians of his own day, his writings have received more attention recently.

1888 Death of Matthew Arnold, English poet. Known most popularly for his poetry during his lifetime, Arnold also attacked many religious attitudes of his time, including the posture of relying on unprovable assumptions to the neglect of reason. He also stressed the personal and moral sides of Christian faith.

1889 Death of Father Joseph Damien (b.1840), Belgian Roman Catholic priest. Ordained in 1864, Fr. Damien volunteered nine years later to serve as a missionary to the lepers on Molokai Island, Hawaii. He remained at his post for 16 years, until he himself died a victim of the disease.

1892 Birth of Corrie ten Boom, Dutch Christian devotional author and speaker. During World War II, her family was arrested in Holland by the Gestapo for having hidden Jewish refugees in their home.

1905 Death of John B. Calkin (b.1827), English church organist and music educator. In 1872 he composed the hymn tune WALTHAM, which was originally written for different words, but today is commonly sung to the words of H.W. Longfellow's poem, "I Heard the Bells on Christmas Day."

1958 English Christian apologist C.S. Lewis confessed in *Letters to an American Lady*: "I had been a Christian for many years before I really believed in the forgiveness of sins, or more strictly, before my theoretical belief became a reality to me."

1983 Death of Corrie ten Boom (b.1892), Dutch devotional writer and Christian survivor of the Nazi persecutions in her native country. Corrie died on her 91st birthday.

April 16

According to Christian tradition, Jesus Christ was crucified, and raised again from the dead in A.D. 33. During the last three centuries, Easter has fallen (or will fall) on April 16 fourteen times: 1702, 1713, 1724, 1775, 1786, 1797, 1843, 1854, 1865, 1876, 1911, 1922, 1933, and 1995.

1521 German reformer Martin Luther arrived at the Diet of Worms where he defended his *Ninety-Five Theses* (first advanced in 1517). Standing before the emperor and the estates of the empire, Luther refused to recant his ideas "unless overcome by Scripture."

1772 Anglican clergyman and hymnwriter John Newton commented in a letter: "Though I rest and live upon the truths of the Gospel, they seldom impress me with a warm and lively joy. . . . However, I think there is a scriptural distinction between faith and feeling, grace and comfort. . . . The degree of the one is not often the just measure of the other."

1829 Death of Carl G. Glaser (b.1784), German choral master and author of the hymn tune AZMON, to which we sing "O for a Thousand Tongues to Sing."

1879 Death of St. Bernadette Soubirous (b.1844), the French Roman Catholic peasant girl of Lourdes who in 1858 had a series of visions in a grotto (river cave) by the River Gave. She believed that during some of her 18 visions, the Virgin Mary appeared and spoke to her. She was initially mistrusted by Catholic authorities, but Bernadette's visions were later affirmed and she herself was beatified in 1925 by Pius XI, and canonized (made a saint) in 1933. Lourdes itself has since become one of the great Roman Catholic centers of pilgrimage in Europe.

1904 Birth of Merrill C. Tenney, American Baptist New Testament scholar. In addition to his several famous scholarly writings, Tenney was dean of the Wheaton College Graduate School in Illinois from 1947–71.

1958 Christians in Action, Inc., was incorporated in Compton, California. Founded by Rev. Lee Shelley in 1957 in Huntington Park, California, this interdenominational and evangelical mission agency, headquartered today in Woodlake, California, is presently working to establish national churches in 16 foreign countries.

April 17

During the last three centuries, Easter has fallen on April 17 eleven times: 1718, 1729, 1740, 1808, 1870, 1881, 1892, 1927, 1938, 1949, and 1960. It will not occur on April 17 again until the year 2022.

1521 At the Diet of Worms, German reformer Martin Luther was cross-examined about his writings by Papal Nuncio Aleander. Ultimately refusing to retract any of his teachings, Luther was to be officially pronounced a heretic the following month (May 25, 1521).

1640 Reorus Torkillus, from Sweden, became the first Lutheran pastor to arrive in North America, landing at Fort Christie, in Delaware.

1776 English founder of Methodism John Wesley assured in a letter: "You have now such faith as is necessary for your living unto God. As yet you are not called to die. When you are, you shall have faith for this also. Today improve the faith you have, and trust God with tomorrow."

1833 English historian and statesman Thomas B. Macaulay declared: "The whole history of Christianity proves that she has little indeed to fear from persecution as a foe, but much to fear from persecution as an ally."

1920 Birth of Robert G. Bratcher, principal translator of the American Bible Society's *Today's English Version*, also known as the *Good News Bible*.

1941 The *Zamzam*, a freighter flying the Egyptian flag, was shelled and sunk by the German raider *Tamesis* (*Atlantis*). Though the *Zamzam* carried 201 passengers, including 144 missionaries and their families bound for Africa, there were no casualties. The survivors were picked up by the raider and transferred to the *Dresden*, which landed them at St. Jean de Luz in German-occupied France on May 20.

1960 Death of Mrs. (Charles) Lettie B. Cowman (b.1870), pioneer missionary to Japan. In 1902 she and her husband traveled to Tokyo to help establish a Bible training institute. This effort led to the founding of the Oriental Missionary Society in 1907. Known today as O.M.S. International (and headquartered since 1966 in Greenwood, Indiana), this interdenominational evangelical organization presently works in church planting and nurturing in over a dozen nations on three continents.

1960 Swedish Christian and Secretary General of the United Nations Dag Hammarskjold remarked in his *Markings*: "Forgiveness breaks the chain of causality because he who 'forgives' you—out of love—takes upon himself the consequences of what you have done. Forgiveness, therefore, always entails a sacrifice."

1987 Cornelius Van Til, reformed apologist, died at age 91. He had taught more than 40 years at Westminster Theological Seminary in Philedelphia and was a leading defender of the reformed faith.

April 18

Easter has fallen on April 18 nine times during the last three centuries: 1745, 1756, 1802, 1813, 1824, 1897, 1954, 1965, and 1976 but will not fall on April 18 again until the year 2049.

1506 Commissioned by Pope Julius II, the foundation stone was laid for the new St. Peter's Basilica in Rome. (*Basilica* is the Latin word for *church*. A basilica-shaped church generally consists of a long hallway with the nave and aisles separated by column-supported arches.) Julius's plan to pay for construction costs by the sale of indulgences prompted Martin Luther to raise bitter criticism of indulgences in his *Ninety-Five Theses* in 1517.

1521 German reformer Martin Luther declared the biblical foundation of his theological position when he declared, at the Diet of Worms: "Hier stehe ich; ich kann nicht anders. Gott mir helfen. Amen." ("Here I stand! I can do nothing else! God help me! Amen.")

1587 Death of John Foxe (b.1516), English Protestant historian and martyrologist. Early in his life, Foxe abandoned Catholicism for the principles of the Reformation. In 1563 Foxe published the first edition of his *Acts and Monuments of the Church*—published today under the more popular title *Foxe's Book of Martyrs*.

1874 The remains of Scottish missionary David Livingstone, who died the year before in Africa (May 1, 1873), were interred in Westminster Abbey in England.

1882 Birth of George S. Schuler, American evangelical music educator and composer of the music for the hymn "Make Me a Blessing," in New York City. For 40 years he served as a faculty member at Moody Bible Institute in Chicago. He composed a number of Gospel songs during his lifetime, but is remembered particularly for the hymn tune SCHULER ("Make Me a Blessing").

1906 New York Episcopal clergyman, Algernon S. Crapsey, went on trial for heresy in Batavia, charged with having preached against the divinity of Christ. On Dec. 5, he was found guilty, and defrocked.

1914 Birth of Freda Schimpf, co-founder of Christ for the Nations, Inc. Converted to Christ at age 18, she married Gordon Lindsay in 1937. Together they founded Christ for the Nations, Inc., in Shreveport, Louisiana, in April 1948. This evangelical, interdenominational mission agency is headquartered today in Dallas, Texas.

1930 American linguistic pioneer Frank C. Laubach, while serving as a Congregational missionary in the Philippines, declared in a letter: "When I have tasted a thrill in fellowship with God, the thrill of filth repels me, for I know its power to drag me from God. And after an hour of close friendship with God, my soul feels clean as new fallen snow."

April 19

During the last three centuries, Easter has fallen (or will fall) on April 19 ten times: 1767, 1772, 1778, 1829, 1835, 1840, 1908, 1981, 1987, and 1992.

1054 Death of Pope Leo IX (b.1002, pope 1049–1054). He was the first pope in medieval times to actively seek an end to the marriage of priests. Leo is credited with causing the final break between the Eastern and Western (Byzantine and Roman) church, even though the conventional date for the event is set at July 16, 1054, three months after Leo's death. One of the most famous pilgrims to Rome during Leo's pontificate was King Macbeth of Scotland.

1529 At the second (of four) Diet of Spires, the assembled Lutherans set down these words in protest of Charles V's attempt to crush Lutheranism in Germany: "In matters concerning God's honor and the salvation of souls, each one must for himself stand before God and give account." It was from this written protest that Lutherans in Europe took the name "Protestants."

1560 Death of Philip Melanchthon (b.1497), German reformer and humanist. Early in his teaching career, Melanchthon became Martin Luther's fellow worker; and he eventually became known as the formulating genius of the Reformation. He personally composed the Augsburg Confession of 1530 and became the recognized leader of the German Reformation after Luther's death in 1546. As a reformer, Melanchthon was known for his moderation, caution and love of peace.

1813 Birth of John H. Stockton, American Methodist pastor and sacred composer, in New Hope, Pennsylvania. Converted at 19, Stockton was ordained into the New Jersey Conference of the Methodist Church, where during his several pastorates (and while often in feeble health) he wrote a number of hymn tunes. Three endure today: STOCKTON ("Come Every Soul by Sin Oppressed"), GLORY TO HIS NAME ("Down at the Cross Where My Savior Died") and GREAT PHYSICIAN ("The Great Physician Now Is Near").

1823 Birth of Anna L. Waring, Welsh Anglican hymnwriter, in Glamorganshire, South Wales. In addition to her special ministry to prisoners in the jails, she wrote nearly 40 hymns during her lifetime. One we still sing is "In Heavenly Love Abiding."

1836 Birth of A.J. Gordon, American Baptist clergyman, in New Hampton, New Hampshire. Ordained a Baptist pastor in 1863, he pastored Clarendon Street Baptist Church in Boston from 1869 until his death in 1895. His congregation raised many funds for home and foreign missions. His fame rests in his hymn tune GORDON ("My Jesus, I Love Thee, I Know Thou Art Mine.") Gordon was a close friend of D.L. Moody and assisted him during Moody's evangelistic efforts in Boston.

1854 Nineteen-year-old English Baptist preacher, Charles Haddon Spurgeon, was called to pastor the New Park Chapel in London. It was one of the three largest of the 113 Baptist churches in London at that time.

1876 Death of Samuel S. Wesley (b.1810), grandson of Charles Wesley and composer of the hymn tune AURELIA ("The Church's One Foundation").

1887 The Catholic University of America was chartered, in Washington, D.C.

1908 The Roman Catholic decree *Ne Temere*, officially went into effect. Issued in Aug. 1907 by the Vatican's Sacred Congregation of the Council, its publication was intended to clarify the church's laws on marriages. Its chief article decreed that marriages between Catholics were thereafter null unless celebrated before a qualified priest and at least two witnesses. The same law applied when only one party was a Catholic, yet it did not bind those who were not and had not been Catholic.

1930 American linguistic pioneer Frank C. Laubach, while serving as a Congregational missionary to the Philippines, explained in a letter: "Fellowship with God is like a delicate little plant, for a long nurturing is the price of having it, while it vanishes in a second of time, as soon as we try to seat some other unworthy affection beside Him."

April 20

Easter has fallen on April 20 eight times since 1700: 1710, 1783, 1794, 1851, 1862, 1919, 1924, and 1930. The year 2003 will bring us the next April 20th Easter.

1494 Birth of Johann Agricola, Saxon theologian and reformer, one-time close friend and ardent associate of Martin Luther from 1519 on. Around 1539, he began espousing what Luther termed as "antinomianism," that the moral law had no place in Christian experience. After 1540, he severed his closest ties with Lutheranism. Agricola died in 1566.

1718 Birth of David Brainerd, colonial American missionary to the New England Indians, in Haddam, Connecticut. In 1744 the Scottish Society for the Propagation of Christian Knowledge appointed Brainerd a missionary to the Algonquin Indians in eastern Pennsylvania, Maryland and New Jersey. He endured hardship for three years. Brainerd retired from the work in 1647 but died soon after of tuberculosis. During his life and work among the Indians, Brainerd kept a detailed diary of his spiritual and missionary endeavors. The publication of *Brainerd's Journal* after his death by Jonathan Edwards has influenced hundreds to become missionaries.

1767 English founder of Methodism, John Wesley, challenged in a letter: "Certainly the point we should always have in view is, what is best for eternity?"

1826 Birth of Erastus Johnson, American hymnwriter, in Lincoln, Maine. Poor health and eyesight interrupted early seminary studies, and he spent much of his life farming and ranching in the West. A student of the Bible all his life, Johnson penned the hymn "O Sometimes the Shadows Are Deep" (a.k.a. "The Rock That Is Higher Than I").

1855 Rev. Henry Lipowsky, a former lieutenant in the Austrian Army, opened the first Bohemian-American church in the U.S.: St. John Nepomuk Church of St. Louis, Missouri.

1899 The great Metropolitan Tabernacle in London, where Thomas Spurgeon (son of the great Charles Haddon Spurgeon) pastored from 1894–1908, burned to the ground. The cause was an overheated flue in the Pastors' College building next door. Construction on a new building began immediately, and on Sept. 19, 1900, the new tabernacle was opened.

1963 Death of Mrs. Agnes Paynter (b.1863), seven months before her 100th birthday. At the age of 34, Agnes and her husband Rev. Arthur S. Paynter (1862–1933) founded the India Christian Mission, Inc., in the Kumoan District of North India. Today, the I.C.M. organization is headquartered in Nuwara Eliya, in Ceylon.

April 21

During the last three centuries, Easter has fallen on April 21 nine times: 1715, 1726, 1737, 1867, 1878, 1889, 1935, 1946, and 1957. Easter will not occur on April 21 again until the 21st century—in the year 2019.

1512 The Second Council of Pisa suspended Julius II as Pope. To counter the political consequences of this action, Julius convened the Fifth Lateran Council in Rome less than a month later, on May 3.

1649 The Toleration Act was passed by the Maryland Assembly, after strong support by Lord Baltimore, the Roman Catholic proprietor of Maryland. The act protected Roman Catholics within the colony against Protestant harassment, which was rising due to Cromwell's rise to power in England in 1642.

1783 Birth of English churchman and hymnwriter Reginald Heber, in Cheshire, England. While serving as a parish priest in Shropshire, Heber nurtured an increasing desire to write hymns, publishing his first in 1811. But he was unable to secure approval of his writings by the ecclesiastical heads of his day. They waited until 1827, the year after his untimely death as Bishop of Calcutta, India, to approve them. Some of Heber's popular hymns include "From Greenland's Icy Mountains," "Holy, Holy, Holy, Lord God Almighty" and "The Son of God Goes Forth to War."

1828 English churchman John Henry Newman, reflecting on the death of his sister Mary, wrote in a letter to another sister, Harriett: "May I be patient! It is so difficult to realize what one believes, and to make these trials, as they are intended, real blessings."

1855 Boston Sunday-school teacher Edward Kimball led 18-year-old shoe clerk, Dwight L. Moody, to a saving faith in Jesus Christ, at the Holton Shoe Store in Boston. A year and a half later, Moody moved to Chicago where he embarked on a preaching career, eventually becoming the most successful Gospel evangelist in his day.

1856 Birth of Johnson Oatman, Jr., American Methodist hymnwriter who wrote "Count Your Blessings," near Medford, New Jersey. At about the age of 36, he began writing religious poetry which soon came into great demand by such well-known sacred music composers of his day as William J. Kirkpatrick, Charles H. Gabriel and E.O. Excell. One hymn of his that still endures is "Higher Ground" ("I'm Pressing on the Upward Way").

1862 Birth of Anna Belle Russell, active American Methodist laywoman, in Pine Valley, New York. She spent most of her life in the First Methodist Church of Corning, New York, where she made her home with her sister. Together, they wrote a number of hymns. One which is still sung begins "There Is Never a Day So Dreary."

1891 Birth of Georgia E. Harkness, American theological instructor, in Harkness, New York. She was ordained into the Methodist ministry in 1926, afterwards going on to become a recognized scholar in the field of theology. She is better remembered as the author of "Hope of the World, Thou Christ of Great Compassion."

1897 Birth of A.W. Tozer, influential pastor and devotional writer of the Christian and Missionary Alliance Church.

1898 Birth of Norman H. Snaith, Methodist Old Testament scholar, in Oxfordshire, England. His greatest contribution to biblical studies were the texts he produced on the Psalms (1934, 1938, 1945, 1951).

1930 Death of Robert S. Bridges (b.1844), the hymnwriter who rendered the English translation of the text to the popular hymn "When Morning Gilds the Skies."

April 22

During the last three centuries, Easter has fallen on April 22 eight times: 1753, 1764, 1810, 1821, 1832, 1962, 1973, and 1984. Easter will fall on April 22 again in the year 2057.

1418 The Council of Constance was concluded, having first convened Nov. 5, 1414. Known as the "high water mark of the Conciliar Era," this conclave ended the Great Schism within the Roman Catholic Church by deposing three rival popes (John XXIII elected at the Council of Pisa, Gregory XII elected in Rome and Benedict XIII elected in Avignon, France). On a darker side, the council also condemned and executed the two Bohemian reformers, John Huss in 1415 and his close friend and disciple, Jerome of Prague, in 1417.

1541 St. Ignatius of Loyola (1491–1556), the Spanish church reformer who founded the Roman Catholic religious order the Society of Jesus (the Jesuits) in 1534, was elected its first general by the members of the order.

1724 Birth of Immanuel Kant, German philosopher, in Konigsberg, Prussia, where he remained all his life. Born into a Pietist family, he taught logic and metaphysics at the university there beginning in 1770. Kant believed that metaphysical knowledge (including knowledge of God) is impossible. Moreover, neither reason nor sense-experience can provide knowledge by themselves. To Kant, this denial of the possibility of knowledge is what makes room for faith. God himself, though unknowable, becomes a reasonable hypothesis. Thus "rational faith" is merely seeing our duties as divine commands. Kant's ideas strongly influenced such later philosophers and theologians as F.D.E. Schleiermacher, Albrecht Ritschl and Karl Barth.

1776 Pioneer American Methodist Bishop Francis Asbury declared in his journal: "I found Christ in me the hope of glory; but felt a pleasing, painful sensation of spiritual hunger and thirst for more of God."

1864 The motto "In God We Trust" first appeared on U.S. coinage, being struck on a bronze two-cent piece. The motto was conceived during the American Civil War, both as a way of confessing that the resolution of the conflict lay in the hands of God and as a means of bolstering northern economic morale.

1879 The world's largest Jewish daily newspaper, *The Forward*, was first published.

1913 Birth of Jack Wyrtzen, popular contemporary Christian songwriter and music evangelist.

1960 A constitutional convention opened in Minneapolis, Minnesota, during which three major Lutheran bodies in the U.S. formally merged to form the American Lutheran Church, with a resulting total membership of about two million. The three denominations merging included the original American

Lutheran Church, the Evangelical Lutheran Church and the United Evangelical Lutheran Church.

1979 The Far East Broadcasting Co., Inc., founded in 1945, moved to its present headquarters in La Mirada, California. Serving as an interdenominational radio-broadcasting agency, F.E.B.C. presently works in nearly a dozen countries.

1987 Death of Dr. J. Edwin Orr, revival historian. Orr had been a professor at Fuller School of Missions. His work in history showed him that all revivals had sprung from prayer meetings, and he shared this vision wherever he went.

April 23

Christian tradition says that Jesus Christ was crucified and raised again from the dead in A.D. 33—the first Easter. During the last three centuries, Easter has fallen (or will fall) on April 23 only four times: 1848, 1905, 1916, and 2000.

1586 Birth of Martin Rinkart, German clergyman, Latin scholar and chorister who wrote the hymn "Now Thank We All Our God," in Eilenburg, Saxony. Acquainted with the sufferings of the Reformation during much of his life, Rinkart was a prolific writer of prose and verse. His most enduring piece is the brief verse now translated into English, which begins "Nun danket alle Gott. . ." ("Now thank we all our God").

1779 Anglican clergyman and hymnwriter John Newton affirmed in a letter: " 'What Thou wilt, when Thou wilt, how Thou wilt.' I had rather speak these three sentences from my heart in my mother tongue than be master of all the languages in Europe."

1789 What is believed to have been the first Roman Catholic newspaper in America, the *Courrier de Boston*, published its first issue. The periodical lasted only until Oct. 15 of the same year.

1828 Birth of F.J.A. Hort, English New Testament textual critic and biblical scholar. He and B.F. Westcott edited the famous 1881 critical edition of the Greek New Testament, which has become the textual foundation for nearly all modern translations of the Bible.

1843 Followers of the farmer-prophet William Miller, forerunner of the Seventh-Day Adventists, gathered throughout the U.S. to await the return of Christ and the end of the world, just as Miller had predicted. After much anticipation, nothing happened.

1888 Death of Edward Hopper (b.1816), American Presbyterian clergyman and author of the hymn "Jesus, Savior, Pilot Me." With the exception of 11 years, he spent his entire ministry in his home town of New York City, pastoring at the Church of the Sea and Land.

1942 Anglican high-church clergyman William Temple was appointed Archbishop of Canterbury at age 61. Ordained in 1908, Temple's leadership within the English National Church combined philosophical skill with theological acuteness and social awareness. He was a pioneer in ecumenical affairs, presiding at the meeting which inaugurated the British Council of Churches.

1960 A three-day constitutional convention ended in Minneapolis. Three major American Lutheran denominations were merged to form the American Lutheran Church.

1968 The 10.3 million-member Methodist Church and the 750,000-member Evangelical United Brethren Church declared a "declaration of union" during a 14-day conference in Dallas, Texas. The plan for the merger had been adopted by the two churches on Nov. 11, 1966. Each denomination was also the product of earlier reunification movements. This merger made the new United Methodist Church the second largest Protestant denomination (the largest being the Southern Baptist Convention, with 13 million members).

April 24

During the last three centuries, Easter has fallen on April 24 only three times: 1707, 1791, and 1859 (not once during the 20th century) and will not occur on April 24 again until the year 2011.

387 St. Augustine was baptized on the eve of Easter. He told the story of his conversion from a profligate life in his autobiography *Confessions*. He went on to become bishop of Hippo, in North Africa, and one of the theological leaders of the early church.

1547 The forces of Holy Roman Emperor Charles V defeated the army of the Schmalkaldic League, the forces of an alliance of German Lutheran princes, at the Battle of Muhlberg.

1575 Birth of Jacob Boehme, German Lutheran pietist and mystic, near Goerlitz, Germany. Though he spent nearly his entire life as an uneducated shoemaker, Boehme experienced many mystical visions beginning in 1600. He published two writings on these experiences during his lifetime: *The Beginning of Dawn* (1612) and *The Way to Christ* (1623). His theology shifted much in his writings, and no single theory fits all his work. Nevertheless, his life and writings greatly influenced both German pietism and English theologians such as William Law.

1576 Birth of St. Vincent de Paul, French Catholic priest, in Landes, France. Having served royalty during his earlier years, he decided by 1617 to seek God rather than pastoral comforts. He founded several religious organizations during the remainder of his life, the most famous being the Lazarists. Vincent de Paul was canonized in 1737 by Pope Clement XII.

1649 The Toleration Act was passed in Maryland, under the administration of Protestant deputy governor William Stone, which provided for religious freedom for all Christians, including Roman Catholics.

1870 At the Vatican I Ecumenical Council, the dogmatic constitution *Dei filius* was passed, stating the church's official position on creation, revelation, faith, and the relationship between faith and reason. The decree declared, in effect, that God could be known by reason.

1875 Death of Samuel P. Tragelles (b.1813), English New Testament textual critic. His greatest literary efforts included his work on G.V. Wigram's famous *Englishman's Greek and Hebrew Concordances*, and the translation of Gesenius's *Hebrew Lexicon* into English (1847). Tregelles went from his early Quaker heritage to join the Plymouth Brethren. Later, he worshiped with the Presbyterians, and finally with the Church of England.

1920   Death of Eliza E. Hewitt (b.1851), American Presbyterian Sunday school leader and hymnwriter. Hymns she wrote that are still sung today include "I Am Thinking Today of That Beautiful Land," "More About Jesus," Sing the Wondrous Love of Jesus," and "Sunshine in My Soul."

1982   Death of William Cameron ("Uncle Cam") Townsend, founder of one of the world's largest privately funded mission agencies: the 4,500-member Wycliffe Bible Translators. Born in 1896, Townsend was a missionary linguist for 65 years, beginning in 1917 when he started as a 21-year-old Bible salesman. Wycliffe Bible Translators works among nearly 750 minority language groups.

April 25

According to Christian tradition, Jesus Christ was crucified and raised again from the dead in A.D. 33—the first Easter! Today is also the very latest day on which Easter can occur. During the last three centuries, Easter has fallen on April 25 only three times: 1734, 1886, and 1943. Easter will not be celebrated on April 25 again until the year 2038.

1530   The Augsburg Confession was read publicly in German at the Diet of Augsburg, convened by Charles V. Written principally by Philip Melanchthon, the confession comprised a summary of the Lutheran faith, one which hoped to bring about reconciliation between Catholics and Protestants. This first public reading of the confession took two hours.

1599   Birth of Oliver Cromwell, English Lord Protector, in Huntingdon, England. He early became a zealous advocate of tolerance and freedom in religious matters. From 1640, he began verbal attacks against abuses by the church and state under King Charles I. When Parliament executed Charles in 1649, England established a Commonwealth (1649–60) and Cromwell was made Lord Protector of the government.

1792   Birth of John Keble, English clergyman and poet who wrote "Sun of My Soul, Thou Savior Dear," in Gloucestershire, England. Ordained into the Church of England in 1816, Keble is credited with having founded the Oxford Movement in 1833. (In its beginning, the Oxford Movement sought to restore the historic significance of the church as well as to revive several of its liturgies and ceremonies. It ended soon after 1845, when several of its founders converted to Roman Catholicism.) Keble was also known for his poetry.

1800   Death of William Cowper (b.1731), English hymnwriter. Though related to and associated with several great people in English history, Cowper was himself a victim of frequent mental illness and deep depression. For 19 years he was a close associate of John Newton's, with whom in 1779 he co-published *Olney Hymns*, one of the most significant collections in English hymnody. Recognized at one time as the greatest poet of his day, Cowper's literary legacy includes at least three hymns we sing today: "God Moves in a Mysterious Way," "Oh, for a Closer Walk with God" and "There Is a Fountain Filled with Blood."

1839 Birth of Samuel J. Stone, Anglican clergyman and author of the hymn "The Church's One Foundation Is Jesus Christ Her Lord," in Staffordshire, England. He was ordained in 1862 and served until his death in 1900. During his lifetime he published six collections of hymns.

1879 Renowned English New Testament textual scholar J.B. Lightfoot was consecrated Bishop of Durham, having left Cambridge and a life of scholarship to devote the remaining ten years of his life to church administration.

1887 Birth of Charles E. Fuller, American Baptist radio evangelist, in Los Angeles. Ordained in 1925, Fuller began his radio ministry in 1937. His *Old Fashioned Revival Hour* was eventually heard over 625 stations. In 1947 he helped found Fuller Theological Seminary, in Pasadena, California.

1929 The Romanian Orthodox Episcopate of America was organized at a church congress that convened in Detroit. Previously, the parishes in the U.S. were under the jurisdiction of the Patriarchate in Bucharest. But the insurgence of Communism in Eastern Europe forced the new church's separation from its parent body. Today, the group is under the Orthodox Church in America.

April 26

1518 German reformer Martin Luther stated in his disputation at Heidelberg: "Grace is given to heal the spiritually sick, not to decorate spiritual heroes."

1745 Colonial American missionary to the New England Indians, David Brainerd lamented in his journal: "There are many with whom I can talk about religion; but alas! I find few with whom I can talk religion itself."

1834 Birth of Horatio R. Palmer, American Congregational clergyman, in Little Compton, Rhode Island. He was the author of 15 hymns and several volumes of religious verse and devotional essays. Three of his hymns still in use are "Yield Not to Temptation," "Jesus, Thou Joy of Loving Hearts" (translated from the Latin hymn by Bernard of Clairvaux) and "My Faith Looks Up to Thee."

1877 Residents of Minnesota observed this date as a statewide day of prayer, asking for deliverance from a plague of grasshoppers that had been ravishing thousands of acres of farm crops that year. The plague ended during that summer.

1955 The Roman Catholic television program *Life Is Worth Living* was broadcast for the last time on Dumont television. Premiering Feb. 12, 1952, it was one of the most successful religious programs ever to air over television. It won its host, Bishop Fulton J. Sheen, an Emmy Award in 1952 for "the most outstanding personality" on television.

1956 English Christian apologist C.S. Lewis declared, in *Letters to an American Lady*: "One of the many reasons for wishing to be a better Christian is that, if one were, one's prayers for others might be more effectual."

1984 Phase III of the Far East Broadcasting Company's "Open Door to China" project was realized when radio station KFBS, Saipan, went on the air. F.E.B.C. was founded 1945 in California by Robert Bowman, John Broger and William Roberts. This interdenominational mission is engaged primarily in radio broadcasting and Bible correspondence courses. Its major bases of operation lie among ten "island-chain" nations of South East Asia and the Pacific.

April 27

1541 The 26-day-long Ratisbon Conference opened at modern Regensburg, Germany. Convened by Charles V, it was a meeting of three Catholic and three Protestant theologians seeking reunion between rival political parties. The unsuccessful conference closed on May 22, making the Protestant movement a permanent force in 16th century Europe.

1667 English poet John Milton sold the copyright to his epic *Paradise Lost* for ten English pounds (less than $30).

1775 Death of Peter Bohler (b.1712), Moravian minister and missionary. Set apart by Zinzendorf in 1737, Bohler was sent by way of London to the American colonies to work among the blacks in Georgia. While in London, he met John Wesley, to whom Bohler conveyed a complete self-surrendering faith, instantaneous conversion and a joy in believing. Bohler's positive, assuring faith became the permanent mark upon Wesley's life and has characterized historic Methodism ever since.

1859 Death of George W. Doane (b.1799), American Episcopal clergyman and author of the hymns "Fling Out the Banner! Let It Float" and "Softly Now the Light of Day."

1950 The modern state of Israel was recognized by the British government.

April 28

1521 German reformer Martin Luther remarked in a letter: "The authority of Scripture is greater than the comprehension of the whole of man's reason."

1832 At the end of a two-day conference in New York, the American Baptist Home Missionary Society was organized.

1839 Birth of Vernon J. Charlesworth, English clergyman and headmaster of Charles Spurgeon's Stockwell Orphanage. He is remembered as author of the hymn "A Shelter in the Time of Storm."

1872 English devotional writer Frances Ridley Havergal penned the words to her still-popular hymn "Lord, Speak to Me That I May Speak."

1874 Birth of Susan Strachan, missions pioneer. Working together with her husband, Harry Strachan, she founded the Latin America Mission, Inc., in 1921 at Stony Brook, New York. Headquartered today in Coral Gables, Florida, the Latin America Mission specializes in evangelism, church planting and literature production in eight different Central and South American countries.

April 29

1607 The first Anglican (Episcopal) church in the American colonies was established, at Cape Henry, Virginia.

1751 Birth of John Rippon, English Baptist clergyman. He served as pastor at the Carter Lane Baptist Church in London for 63 years. He also published several volumes of Bible expositions and sermons, and it was Rippon who gave us the modern revision of the lyrics to Edward Perronet's "All Hail the Power of Jesus' Name." He also wrote "How Firm a Foundation."

1834 Birth of Joseph H. Gilmore, American Baptist clergyman and Hebrew instructor, in Boston, Massachusetts. Ordained in 1862, he pastored several churches during the next five years. In 1868 he began teaching at the University of Rochester, New York, where he remained until his retirement in 1911. He is remembered as the author of the hymn "He Leadeth Me, O Blessed Thought."

1933 The Navigators trace their origin to this date when Dawson Trotman began work with the first Navy man, Lester Spencer, in San Pedro, California. This interdenominational organization was formally incorporated in 1943, and is headquartered in Colorado Springs, Colorado. It works primarily in discipleship, Bible literacy and memorization in over 30 countries.

1945 U.S. troops liberated the Nazi concentration camp at Dachau, Germany.

1952 Death of Samuel M. Zwemer (b.1867), American Dutch Reformed missionary to the Muslims. In 1888 Zwemer and others helped found The Arabian Mission. He himself served as a missionary to Egypt between 1890–1905. He later visited India and China. During his lifetime, he authored over 50 volumes in English, and a number in Arabic.

April 30

1562 Two ships carrying 150 settlers from France arrived off the coast of northeast Florida. Jean Ribault, with the approval of Charles IX of France, led these Huguenot (French Protestant) emigrants to America to found a colony. The group eventually established a settlement at Parris Island, South Carolina, named Port Royal, but abandoned it two years later (1564) when essential supplies failed to arrive.

1841 Birth of Orville J. Nave, the U.S. Armed Services chaplain who authored *Nave's Topical Bible*, which is still in print.

1854 Death of James Montgomery, British clergyman and poet, in Ayrshire, Scotland. For many years he served as the only Moravian minister in Scotland. Later, as a newspaper editor, he became an advocate of humanitarian causes, including abolition of slavery and support of foreign missions. During his lifetime, he penned over 350 hymns, including the Christmas carol "Angels from the Realms of Glory."

1867 Death of Ithamar Conkey (b.1815), popular English bass vocalist. He also composed the still-popular hymn tune, RATHBUN, to which we commonly sing the hymn "In the Cross of Christ I Glory."

1904 Birth of John T. Benson, Jr., religious composer and president of Heartwarming Music Co. His best-known compositions include the music for the hymn "Love Lifted Me."

1944 English literature scholar J.R.R. Tolkien wrote in a letter to his son Christopher, a British soldier during World War II: "Evil labors with vast power and perpetual success—in vain: preparing always only the soil for unexpected good to sprout in. So it is in general, and so it is in our own lives."

May

May 1

1501 Pope Alexander VI, in the encyclical "Ad ea quae circa decorem," sanctioned the Roman Catholic religious order of Minims, founded by Francis of Paula in 1435.

1740 English revivalist George Whitefield recorded this prayer in his journal: "Lord, show that Thou dost love me, by humbling and keeping me humble as long as I live. The means I leave to Thee."

1782 Birth of Charles Meineke, church organist and composer of the music to which we sing the doxology "Glory Be to the Father. . . ," the GLORIA PATRI (second tune), in Germany. He emigrated to America in 1810 and became the organist for St. Paul's Episcopal Church in Baltimore, Maryland, in 1836. He published several volumes of hymn tunes during his life.

1845 The Methodist Episcopal Church, South was organized as a distinct Methodist denomination by a convention at Louisville, Kentucky.

1858 Birth of A.J. Showalter, American music teacher, in Chattanooga, Tennessee. He began teaching and publishing music from the age of 22, eventually opening his own music publishing company. He also conducted singing schools in over a dozen southern states. Though he composed many songs, he is perhaps best remembered for the hymn tune SHOWALTER, to which we sing the hymn "Leaning on the Everlasting Arms."

1873 Death of David Livingstone (b.1813), Scottish missionary and explorer. He began to study medicine and theology at age 17, and arrived as a missionary in South Africa ten years later. In 1857 he resigned from his sponsoring agency, the London Missionary Society, but returned to Africa under the British government to search for the source of the Nile and to eradicate the slave traffic. When he died, the natives found him on his knees. His body was returned to England, but his heart was buried in Africa.

1881 Birth of Pierre Teilhard de Chardin, French Jesuit philosopher and paleontologist, in Sarcenat, France. As a paleontologist, he assisted in the discovery of the Peking man during his explorations in China (1923–45). Theologically, he attempted to wed evolutionary science with traditional Christian beliefs, arriving at a theology resembling process philosophy. Having linked Christ to the evolutionary process, Teilhard was forbidden by his superiors in the Catholic church from publishing his theological writings during his lifetime. His best-known (posthumous) publications have been *The Phenomenon of Man* (1959) and *The Divine Milieu* (1960).

1933 The first issue of *The Catholic Worker*, a monthly newspaper, was published. Founded by Dorothy Day and Peter Maurin, the periodical promoted social reconstruction through shared farming, and housing for the urban poor. Within three years, the paper's circulation grew to 150,000, while the cost of each issue stayed at a penny.

1939 The *Back to the Bible Broadcast* was launched by founder, Theodore Epp, in Lincoln, Nebraska. Nearly 600 radio stations nationwide carry the program. The Back to the Bible Mission Agency, a subsidiary organization, works in missionary radio broadcasts and literature distribution from offices in eight countries.

1965 Swiss Reformed theologian Karl Barth noted in a letter: "It is puzzling that in the Gospels there is hardly a passage where one can think of Jesus as having laughed. There must be a reason for this but off-hand I could not name it."

May 2

1507 German reformer Martin Luther, two years after entering the Augustinian monastery at Erfurt, was consecrated a priest. Luther remained in the order until 1521, when he was excommunicated from the Roman Catholic Church.

1519 Death of Leonardo da Vinci (b.1452), Italian artist and inventor. Although skilled in many of the arts, Leonardo preferred painting as the best medium for representing nature to the human senses. Today, he is known for such works as the *Mona Lisa* and *The Last Supper*.

1872 A lectureship was established at Yale University Divinity School in memory of Lyman Beecher who graduated from Yale with a B.A. in 1797. The lectures were to cover topics on preaching and the work of the Christian ministry. Some of the better-known lecturers have included Henry Ward Beecher (1872,73,74), Phillips Brooks (1877), A.M. Fairbairn (1892), and Harry E. Fosdick (1924).

1922 Birth of Bob Finley, who chartered the Christian Aid Mission in 1953, in Washington, D.C. This evangelical organization is headquartered today in Charlottesville, Virginia. It works in nearly 40 countries, and supports national Christian workers, indigenous mission boards, and other Christian organizations.

1949 American missionary and Auca Indian martyr Jim Elliot recorded in his journal: "The man who will not act until he knows all will never act at all."

May 3

1512 The Fifth Lateran Council (1517) opened under Pope Julius II (1503–13). He convened the council to reestablish peace among the various European Catholic princes, to promote holy war against the Turks and to reform the Catholic church "in its head and members."

1515 The papal encyclical *Inter Sollicitudines* was published by Pope Leo X. It stated that all writings were to be examined by the Catholic church prior to their printing.

1675 A Massachusetts law was enacted requiring that church doors be locked during the worship service—too many people were leaving before the long sermon was completed.

1738 British revivalist George Whitefield first arrived in America. He stayed until Aug. 28, in all paying seven visits to America.

1814 Death of Thomas Coke (b.1747), first English bishop of the Methodist Church. Raised and ordained a deacon in the Church of England, Coke joined the Methodist movement in 1777. He was so irrepressible as an itinerant minister, John Wesley set him apart in 1784 as superintendent for the American branch of the Methodist movement. Arriving in America that same year, Coke ordained Francis Asbury as co-bishop. Coke crossed the Atlantic eighteen times before leaving the American mission completely in the hands of Asbury in 1803.

1850 Sixteen-year-old Charles H. Spurgeon made his public profession of faith in Jesus Christ, in the Artillery Street Primitive Methodist Chapel, in Colchester, England. The following year, he began a preaching career that did not end until his death in 1892.

1878 Death of William Whiting (b.1825), English poet and music instructor. He was master of Winchester College Choristers' School for more than 20 years. He also published a book of poetry in 1851. He is known to have written only one hymn during his lifetime, but its popularity has endured to modern times: "Eternal Father, Strong to Save."

1895 Birth of Cornelius Van Til, Christian Reformed theological educator, in the Netherlands. He came to America in 1905 and taught theology at both Princeton and Westminster Theological seminaries beginning in 1928. A categorical supporter of classic Calvinism, Van Til vigorously opposed neoorthodoxy throughout his teaching career.

1900 Birth of Johannes Quasten, early church historian, at Homberg, Germany. In 1938 he began teaching ancient church history in America, at the Catholic University of America in Washington, D.C. He authored the definitive series on the theology and spokesmen of the early church: *Patrology* (1950–1983).

1928 Birth of Donald Bloesch, American evangelical author and theological scholar.

1983 In the U.S., the National Conference of Catholic Bishops voted 238 to 9 to approve a pastoral letter entitled *The Challenge of Peace: God's Promise and Our Response*. The letter condemned the international nuclear arms race.

May 4

1256 Pope Alexander IV (1254–61) founded the Roman Catholic religious order of the Augustine Hermits.

1608 The Protestant Union was formed at Aushausen, Germany under the leadership of Frederick IV of the Palatinate.

1773 Anglican clergyman and hymnwriter John Newton observed in a letter: "Unless the Lord shines, I cannot retain today the light I had yesterday; and though His presence makes a delightful difference, I have no more to boast of in myself at one time than another."

1784 Birth of Carl Gotthilf Glaser, German music teacher, in Weissenfels, Germany. He moved to Barmen after completing his education and became a teacher of piano, violin and voice. He composed many choral pieces during his career, but is remembered primarily for his hymn tune, AZMON, to which we sing the hymn "Oh, for a Thousand Tongues to Sing."

1889 Birth of Francis J. Spellman, American Roman Catholic cardinal, in Whitman, Maryland. Ordained into the priesthood in 1916, he was made a cardinal in 1946 under the pontificate of Pius XII.

1962 English novelist and Christian apologist C.S. Lewis observed in *Letters to an American Lady*: "It is sometimes hard to obey St. Paul's 'Rejoice.' We must try to take life moment by moment. The actual present is usually pretty tolerable, if only we refrain from adding to its burden that of the past and the future."

May 5

1525 Death of Frederick III (b.1463), Elector of Saxony. His reputation for justice won him the name "Frederick the Wise." His court at Wittenberg, Germany, patronized the artistic talents of men like Albrecht Durer and Lucas Cranach, but perhaps his greatest role was in serving as the protector of German reformer Martin Luther during his controversy with the Roman church, beginning in 1518.

1766 Death of Jean Astruc (b.1684), French physician and pioneer in modern Pentateuchal criticism. His father was a Huguenot (French Protestant) pastor who converted to Roman Catholicism when the Edict of Nantes was revoked in 1685. While doing research on medical laws in the Bible, Astruc discovered the different contexts that surrounded *Elohim* and *Yahweh*, two of the names for God in the Pentateuch. His 1753 treatise, *Conjectures on the Original Memoirs of Moses*, laid the groundwork for the documentary theory of the Pentateuch's origins, which was developed further by J.G. Eichhorn 130 years later.

1813 Birth of Soren Kierkegaard, Danish philosopher, in Copenhagen. His writings attacked formal, state Christianity as being indifferent to the real issues of the Gospel. He believed New Testament Christian faith made personal, life-changing demands on every one of its followers. To Kierkegaard, personal spiritual commitment was described as "existence," which he contrasted with mere everyday life, or "essence." Essence is attained by thought and logic, but existence can be reached only by moral and religious decision. Kierkegaard's writings strongly influenced the later movements of existential philosophy and neoorthodox theology.

1815 Birth of Ithamar Conkey, New England music artist and composer of RATHBURN, the tune to which we sing "In the Cross of Christ I Glory," in Shutesbury, Maryland. His life career took him from church organist to vocal (bass) soloist and finally to church choir conductor.

1846 Birth of Henryk Sienkiewicz, Polish novelist, in Wola Orkrzejska, Poland. He wrote several colorful historical novels and is remembered most for his 1895 masterpiece, *Quo Vadis?*

1888 Death of Johann K.F. Keil (b.1807), German Lutheran Old Testament scholar. He taught biblical exegesis at the University of Dorpat from 1833 until his retirement in 1858. His chief contribution to the church is his Old Testament commentary, which he began in 1861 in collaboration with Franz Delitzsch. Theologically, Keil ignored modern literary biblical criticism, maintaining that the Old and New Testaments were divinely revealed.

1899 The Religious Tract Society (founded in 1799) celebrated its 100th anniversary in Exeter Hall, London. The Society had published literature in 271 languages and dialects in its first hundred years.

1925 Tennessee biology teacher John T. Scopes was arrested for teaching the theory of evolution in his Dayton, Tennessee, classroom.

1933 The Unevangelized Fields Mission was founded, in Philadelphia, Pennsylvania, by the Rev. and Mrs. E.J. Pudney. The name for this interdenominational, mission organization was changed to U.F.M. International in 1980, and its headquarters moved to Bala Cynwyd, Pennsylvania. U.F.M. International works in over a dozen countries and is engaged in evangelism, church planting, Bible translation and theological education.

1950 American missionary and martyr to the Auca Indians Jim Elliot stated in his journal: "The conflict of science and religion is fought between the errors of both camps."

May 6

1527 Forty thousand soldiers hired by Cardinal Pompeo Colonna, mainly German Lutherans and a Spanish contingent, sacked the city of Rome, butchering clergy and laity alike, and forcing Pope Clement VII to flee to Orvieto disguised as a gardener.

1638 Death of Cornelius Jansen (b.1585), Dutch Roman Catholic theologian. Based on an intense study of Augustine, Jansen sought to reform the church. His ideas resembled the Puritan movement within the Church of England and he opposed both Jesuit semi-Pelagianism and the philosophy of Thomas Aquinas, urging in their place an Augustinian doctrine of irresistible grace. Although Jansen repeatedly affirmed he was not a Protestant, his writings and teachings were condemned as heretical by Pope Innocent X in 1653.

1746 Death of William Tennent (b.1673), Irish-born colonial American clergyman. In 1735 he began training other young men for the ministry in the "Log College" built on his property. Tennent's influence contributed much to both American Presbyterian history and the Great Awakening in the American colonies between 1725–60.

1800, 1804, 1808 The Third, Fourth, and Fifth General Conferences of the Methodist Episcopal Church all began on this date in Baltimore, Maryland.

1818 Birth of Karl Marx, father of Marxism. He was born a Jew, although his father converted to Lutheranism in 1924. Marx studied law at Bonn and Berlin, but studied philosophy for a Ph.D. at Jena (1841). He went to Paris, where he met Friedrich Engels and became a socialist. Marx expressed his dialectical materialism, the theory that the inevitable evolution of culture would bring the triumph of the working class, in his 1848 *Communist Manifesto*. His views took him to exile in London, where he lived in poverty and illness. He died in 1883.

1835 Birth of John T. Grape, American Methodist layman and composer of the tune for the hymn "Jesus Paid It All" (ALL TO CHRIST), in Baltimore, Maryland. Grape was a successful coal merchant in Baltimore, as well as choir director at two different Methodist churches. He wrote a number of hymn tunes during his life.

1840 Death of Father Demetrius A. Gallitzin (b.1770), "Apostle of the Alleghenies." The son of a Russian scientist, he emigrated to America in 1792. After attending Baltimore Seminary and being ordained a priest in the Roman Catholic Church, Gallitzin devoted the remainder of his life to establishing churches in the Allegheny Mountain region.

1867 Birth of George Washington Truett, American Southern Baptist preacher, in Clay County, North Carolina. He began a pastorate at the First Baptist Church in Dallas in 1897 and remained there until his death 47 years later, leaving a church membership of 7,800. Truett was one of the best known and most capable preachers and evangelists of his era.

1986 The Rev. Donald E. Pelotte, age 41, was ordained in Gallup, New Mexico. He is the first American Indian Roman Catholic bishop.

May 7

1530 Birth of Louis de Bourbon, Prince of Conde, the first great leader of the Huguenots (French Protestants).

1833 Birth of Johannes Brahms, celebrated German composer, in Hamburg. Though not a church musician, he composed several beautiful sacred motets. The words to his great choral masterpiece, *A German Requiem*, are taken entirely from the German Bible. The piece is regarded by many as the greatest major sacred choral work of the 19th century.

1839 Birth of Elisha A. Hoffman, American clergyman in the Evangelical Church, in Orwigsburg, Pennsylvania. In addition to pastoring Evangelical and Presbyterian churches for a number of years in both Ohio and Michigan, Hoffman was a prolific writer of Gospel songs. He wrote the words and music to "What a Wonderful Savior," "I Must Tell Jesus" and "Are You Washed in the Blood?" He also authored the texts of "Glory to His Name" and "Leaning on the Everlasting Arms."

1840 Birth of Peter I. Tchaikovsky, Russian composer, in Votkinsk, Russia. Though better known for his classical ballet scores such as *Swan Lake* (1877), *Sleeping Beauty* (1890), and *The Nutcracker* (1892), he also composed sacred music, including "O Praise Ye the Name of the Lord."

1851 Birth of Adolf von Harnack, German Lutheran Church historian, in Dorpat, Livonia (modern Estonia). In 1890 he joined the faculty of the University of Berlin, remaining there for the next 38 years. Though a voluminous writer in many areas, Harnack's main expertise was early church thought. He published a monumental seven-volume *History of Dogma* (1894–99). He also became one of the spokesmen for critical theology, and in 1900–01 published a short writing that quickly became a controversial bestseller: *What Is Christianity?*

1900 Death of Richard S. Willis (b.1819), American music scholar. His studies took him to Boston Latin School and Yale, as well as to Germany for six years and Nice, Italy for four. He published several volumes of music compositions during his lifetime, but is famous for two hymn tunes: CAROL ("It Came upon the Midnight Clear") and his arrangement of CRUSADERS' HYMN ("Fairest Lord Jesus").

1951 *The Circuit Rider*, a religious television program sponsored by America for Christ, Inc., was broadcast for the last time. Produced by Franklin W. Dyson, the program featured sacred music, biographies of great evangelists and special guests. Premiering on March 5, 1951, the series lasted only two months before it was cancelled.

1964 Swiss Reformed theologian Karl Barth observed in a letter: "Human history takes a terribly long breath to achieve but one of those seemingly simple and necessary steps. God knows better what is really happening. But there may be moments and opportunities for human knowledge and action, which should not be missed."

1978 Death of Basil W. Miller (b.1897), mission pioneer. In 1957 Miller incorporated the Basil Miller Foundation in Altadena, California. The name of the organization was changed to World-Wide Missions in 1959, and its headquarters was moved to Pasadena, California, in 1963. W.W.M. International is engaged in supporting national Christian workers and churches as well as supplying relief and medical aid to mission fields in 30 countries worldwide.

May 8

1816 The American Bible Society was organized in the Dutch Reformed Church on Garden Street in New York City. It was a product, in part, of the late 18th-century movement in world missions. The nonprofit society was instituted to promote wider circulation of the Scriptures by publishing Bibles without notes or comments.

1824 German composer Ludwig van Beethoven's choral work *Missa Solemnis*, a mass in D (opus 123), was first performed in Vienna.

1828 Birth of Henri Dunant, Swiss philanthropist, in Geneva. In addition to founding the Red Cross (1864), Dunant also founded the Young Men's Christian Association (Y.M.C.A.), took part in the first Geneva Convention (1864), and won the first Nobel Peace Prize (1901).

1895 Birth of Archbishop Fulton J. Sheen, American Roman Catholic priest, in El Paso, Illinois. Ordained in 1919, Sheen taught philosophy at Catholic

University from 1926–50. His radio broadcasts of *The Catholic Hour* (1930–52) were heard around the world. But he attained his highest popularity during his weekly television broadcast of *Life Is Worth Living* between 1951–57.

1902 Birth of Ethelbert Stauffer, German Lutheran New Testament scholar, in Friedelsheim, Germany. He taught at Halle, Bonn and Erlangen. His most popular publication was perhaps his *Theologie des Neuen Testaments* (*Theology of the New Testament*, 1941).

1917 Birth of Kenneth Taylor, editor and publisher of *The Living Bible*. In 1968 Taylor founded Living Bibles International, an interdenominational agency engaged in translation, production and distribution of the Living Bible. By 1987, 50 foreign-language versions of the Living New Testament had been published.

1920 Death of Handley C.G. Moule (b.1841), British New Testament scholar. Moule believed in the authority of the Scriptures, and in later years associated himself with the Keswick Movement. Firmly evangelical, Moule nevertheless earned the respect of Bible scholars from every perspective; and though a profound scholar, he could write for the layman. During his lifetime, he prepared expositions and commentaries on nearly every New Testament epistle.

1948 American missionary and Auca Indian martyr Jim Elliot recorded this prayer in his journal: "Either take me to be with Thee, Savior, or put out the life of this old man as I draw near Thee in the flesh. Consume me, Fiery Lover, as Thou dost choose."

May 9

1619 The Synod of Dort closed, in the Dutch community of Dordrecht. Convened as a general conclave of the Calvinist churches on Nov. 13, 1618, the council voted unanimously to condemn the Articles of the Remonstrance, a document defending Arminianism that had been signed by 45 Calvinist ministers, and to banish the ministers who had signed the document.

1760 Death of Count Nikolaus Ludwig von Zinzendorf (b.1700), founder of the Moravian Brethren. Born in Dresden, Germany, of an Austrian nobleman, Zinzendorf was raised by his pietist maternal grandmother. In 1722 he began welcoming Bohemian, Hussite refugees to his private estate, where he formed the Christian community called "Herrnhut." He spent the rest of his life traveling throughout Europe and America attempting to unify diverging groups of German Lutherans and Moravians. Although his organizational efforts were not very successful, he had a strong influence on Moravian missions.

1828 Birth of Andrew Murray, South African Dutch Reformed clergyman, at Graaff-Reinet, South Africa. Murray was a conservative theologian with mystical inclinations and profound devotional life. Although a great traveling spokesman for the church in his own day, Murray is better remembered for his more than 250 devotional works. His most famous book is *Abide in Christ* (1860–64).

1852 The first plenary council of all Roman Catholic bishops and archbishops in the U.S. and territories was held at the Cathedral of Baltimore in Maryland.

1900 Birth of V. Raymond Edman, Wheaton College president, in Chicago Heights, Illinois. Graduating from Boston University in 1923, he served as a missionary in Ecuador until 1928 when illness forced him to return home. Earning his Ph.D. from Clark University in 1935, he taught political science at Wheaton College in Illinois from 1936–40. Beginning in 1940, Edman served as president of Wheaton College until he was appointed its first chancellor in 1965. Edman traveled widely and wrote over 20 devotional books before his death in 1967.

1905 Birth of Merrill Dunlop, American sacred music chorister, in Chicago, Illinois. Dunlop was music director at the Chicago Gospel Tabernacle for many years. He was also one of the best-known hymnwriters of his generation. One of his most memorable works is the hymn "My Sins Are Blotted Out, I Know."

1911 Death of Katherine Hankey (b.1834), English social reformer and hymn-writer. Influenced by the spirit of William Wilberforce, "Kate" organized a Bible class at age 18 for London shop girls. In later years she gave much of her literary income for foreign missions. She was also active in hospital vis-itation in London. Her fame endures as the author of two popular hymns: "Tell Me the Old, Old Story" and "I Love to Tell the Story."

1914 President Woodrow Wilson officially proclaimed the second Sunday in May to be Mothers' Day.

1918 Death of John B. Sumner (b.1838), American Methodist clergyman. For a number of years, before entering the Methodist ministry in 1869, he taught singing schools. His rich tenor voice was often heard at Methodist confer-ences. He composed eleven hymn tunes, including BINGHAMTON ("My Father Is Rich in Houses and Lands," a.k.a. "I'm a Child of the King").

1960 Death of Charles R. Erdman (b.1866), American Presbyterian homiletics and pastoral theology professor. Ordained in 1891, Erdman pastored in Penn-sylvania until 1905. From 1906–36, he was the professor of practical theology at Princeton Seminary. He also served as president of the Presbyterian Board of Foreign Missions from 1928–40. Many of his expository commentaries on books of the Bible are still popular.

May 10

1812 Birth of Frances Elizabeth Cox, translator of the English version of the hymn, "Sing Praise to God Who Reigns Above."

1818 Birth of Arthur Cleveland Coxe, American Episcopal clergyman and au-thor of the hymn "O Where Are Kings and Empires Now?", in Mendham, New Jersey. The son of a well-known Brooklyn Presbyterian minister, Coxe was ordained in the Episcopal Church in 1842. He served three churches: in Hart-ford, Connecticut; Baltimore, Maryland; and in New York City. During his youth, Coxe wrote some poetry and several of those verses were set to hymn tunes later in his life.

1828 Roman Catholic Cardinal John Henry Newman grasped for a definition of his feelings in a letter: "I wish it were possible for words to put down those indefinite, vague, and withal subtle feelings which quite pierce the soul and make it sick. What a veil and curtain this world of sense is. Beautiful, but still a veil."

1859 Birth of William Wrede, German Lutheran New Testament scholar, at Buecken, Germany. After studying at Leipzig and Gottingen (1877–81), he taught at both Gottingen and Breslau (1891–1906). He believed in applying strict historical criticism to the study of the New Testament, contending that the Gospels represented the theology of the primitive church rather than the true history of Jesus; and that the Apostle Paul was the real founder and formulator of 1st-century Christianity. Therefore, Wrede's name appeared on the 1906 critical theological classic written by Albert Schweitzer, *The Quest of the Historical Jesus: From Reimarus to Wrede.*

1886 Birth of Karl Barth, Swiss Reformed theologian, in Basel. Educated in Germany, Barth served as a liberal pastor of two different Swiss churches (1909–21). World War I, however, shook his liberal tendencies and the publication of his commentary on Romans (*Romerbrief*) in 1919 catapulted him to world prominence as a theologian. He taught at several German universities beginning in 1921 until he was ejected by the Nazi regime. He taught at Basel from 1935–62. Barth authored over 500 books, articles and papers during his lifetime. *Romerbrief* is his most famous shorter work, but his unfinished 14–volume *Church Dogmatics* is his "opus magnum."

1910 Death of Anna L. Waring (b.1823), English Quaker-turned-Anglican social reformer and hymnwriter. During her later years, she was active in prison visitation; but the legacy she left for the larger church community is her hymn "In Heavenly Love Abiding."

1917 Death of Henry Barclay Swete (b.1835), Anglican Bible and early church scholar. He was regius professor of divinity at Cambridge University from 1890–1915, during which time he published many scholarly biblical works. In 1899 he helped found the *Journal of Theological Studies.* Perhaps his most scholarly writing is *The Old Testament in Greek According to the Septuagint.*

1939 The Declaration of Union reunited the Methodist Church in the U.S. after 109 years of division. The Methodist Protestant Church separated from the Methodist Episcopal Church in 1830, and in 1844 the Methodist Episcopal Church, South separated. The Declaration of Union brought these three major divisions back together.

1952 The offices of Eurovision moved to their present headquarters in Pasadena, California. Incorporated in 1927 in Chicago, Illinois, under the name Eastern European Mission by Paul B. Peterson, Eurovision adopted its present name in 1985. The interdenominational, evangelical mission is engaged in shortwave radio broadcasting, literature production and distribution and relief support, with foreign offices located in ten European and Asian countries.

May 11

1610 Death of Matteo Ricci (b.1552), Italian Jesuit missionary to China. Ordained in 1571, Ricci first arrived at Macao in south China about 1583. In his zeal to evangelize, he adopted Chinese dress and customs. His expertise in science and mathematics won his confidence with government officials in

Peking, who thereafter permitted him to preach the Gospel freely throughout the province.

1682 The General Court of Massachusetts repealed two laws passed in May 1680: one forbade the keeping of Christmas; the other required capital punishment for Quakers who returned after being banished.

1824 St. Regis Seminary was opened in Florissant, Missouri, under the direction of Father Van Quickenborne. It was the first Roman Catholic school established in America for the higher education of American Indians. Located in three buildings that cost about $2,000, the school enrolled 40–60 students.

1825 The American Tract Society was organized in New York City, the first national tract society in America. It was formed by the merger of 50 smaller societies.

1949 The country of Israel joined the United Nations.

May 12

1310 Fifty-four Knights Templars were burned at the stake as heretics in France. This military order was originally founded in Jerusalem in 1119 to protect pilgrims traveling to the Holy Land. After the era of the Crusades (1096–c.1300), the order drew increasing antagonism from Rome until Pope Clement V officially dissolved it in 1312 at the Council of Vienna. The Knights Templars took its name from the claim that its headquarters was located on the site of Solomon's Temple in Jerusalem.

1671 Birth of Erdmann Neumeister, Lutheran pastor, at Uchteritz, Germany. He spent his creative energies opposing the "subjective novelties" and influences of the Pietists and Moravians upon the Lutherans of his day. On the positive side, Neumeister developed the church cantata in about 1700. He also authored the hymn "Christ Receiveth Sinful Men."

1861 "The Battle Hymn of the Republic," written by Julia Ward Howe, was first performed at a flag-raising ceremony for northern recruits at Fort Warren, near Boston, during the U.S. Civil War.

1891 The Presbytery of New York voted to put Rev. Dr. Charles A. Briggs, the new professor of biblical theology at Union Theological Seminary, on trial for heresy.

1907 Birth of Sidney N. Correll, founder and first General Director (1946–71) of United World Mission, Inc. Headquartered in St. Petersburg, Florida, since 1960, U.W.M. is an interdenominational organization involved in a dozen countries worldwide. Its primary areas of work are in evangelism, church planting and Christian education, as well as medical assistance and support of national churches.

1919 Death of Crawford H. Toy (b.1836), American Hebrew scholar. After teaching for 15 years at 4 different southern U.S. schools, Toy joined the faculty of Harvard in 1880 as professor of Hebrew and other Oriental languages, remaining there until his retirement in 1909. Two of his more enduring literary productions include the *Jewish Encyclopedia* (which he edited) and the *International Critical Commentary* volume on Proverbs (1899).

1945 Death of H. Wheeler Robinson (b.1872), English Baptist scholar. After serving six years as a Baptist pastor (1900–06), Robinson became professor of the philosophy of religion at Rawdon Baptist College in Leeds (1906–20), then principal of Regent's Park College (1920–42). He published several important works during his academic career.

1946 On his 39th birthday, Dr. Sidney N. Correll founded the United World Mission in Dayton, Ohio. (See 1907)

1952 Death of George (Gregory) Dix (b.1901), Anglican scholar. After teaching at Oxford for three years (1923–26), Dix began a monastic life among the Anglican Benedictines at Nashdom Abbey. His most important contribution to scholarship is his exhaustive study of Christian worship, *The Shape of the Liturgy* (1945).

1985 Amy Eilberg, age 30, became the first woman Conservative rabbi when she was ordained during graduation ceremonies at Jewish Theological Seminary in New York City.

May 13

1836 The Baptists withdrew from the American Bible Society to form a denominational Bible society of their own.

1839 Birth of William P. Mackay, Scottish physician and pastor, in Montrose, Scotland. Educated at the University of Edinburgh, Mackay practiced medicine for a number of years before becoming a Presbyterian pastor. He wrote several hymns during his life, including "Revive Us Again."

1842 Birth of Arthur S. Sullivan, English music composer, at Bolwell Terrace, Lambeth, England. Though he wrote a great deal of church music, it was his association with Sir W.S. Gilbert (of Gilbert and Sullivan) and the Savoy Operas that gained him international fame. Nevertheless, two of his hymn tunes still enjoy popularity: ST. GERTRUDE ("Onward, Christian Soldiers") and ST. KEVIN ("Come, Ye Faithful, Raise the Strain").

1917 Three shepherd children near Fatima, Portugal, reported that the Virgin Mary had appeared to them. Since October of 1930, this appearance has come to be known as Our Lady of Fatima.

1925 The Florida House of Representatives passed a bill requiring daily Bible reading in all public schools.

1963 Death of A.W. Tozer (b.1897), American devotional writer affiliated with the Christian and Missionary Alliance Church.

1981 Ali Agca (AH-jah), 23-year-old Turkish gunman, shot and nearly killed Pope John Paul II in St. Peter's Square, Rome.

May 14

1491 The modern observance of the Jewish Passover began.

1752 Birth of Timothy Dwight, American Congregational clergyman, in Northampton, Maryland. A grandson of Jonathan Edwards, Dwight became an educator and served as the eighth president of Yale College from 1795 until his death in 1817.

1854 Death of Thomas Kelly (b.1769), Irish clergyman and author of the hymn "Look, Ye Saints. The Sight Is Glorious." Trained in law, Kelly was converted and ordained into the Irish Episcopal Church in 1792. However, his ardent evangelical zeal alienated the Archbishop of Dublin, and Kelly left the Irish church to establish his own religious movement. Kelly was a great preacher, a social reformer, a master of both Scripture and classical languages and a hymnwriter as well. Over 750 of his hymns were published during his lifetime.

1932 Death of John Hughes (b.1873), Welsh railway official and church worker. Hughes was a lifelong member of Salem Baptist Church in Llantwit Fardre, Wales, and a deacon, like his father before him. He composed a number of Sunday school marches, anthems and hymn tunes. His CWM RHONDDA, to which we sing "Guide Me, O Thou Great Jehovah," is still popular.

1950 American missionary and Auca Indian martyr Jim Elliot acknowledged in his journal: "To believe is to act as though a thing were so. Merely saying a thing is so is no proof of my believing it."

May 15

1265 Birth of Alighieri Dante, Italian poet, in Florence. He became a soldier in 1290. About 1302, Dante lost his property and was forced into exile by political changes. He never saw his wife or home in Florence again. Acclaimed worldwide for his literary achievements, Dante is best remembered as the author of *The Divine Comedy*, a poetic view of the moral universe describing the three conditions of man: sin, repentance and salvation. The writing is considered history's first great Christian poem.

1525 A violent faction of Anabaptists led by Thomas Munzer was defeated at the Battle of Frankenhausen.

1553 French reformer John Calvin revealed in a letter: "The time draws nigh when the earth shall disclose the blood which has been hid, and we, after having been disencumbered of these fading bodies, shall be completely restored."

1686 Rev. Robert Ratcliffe arrived in Boston with orders from England's King Charles II to found the Anglican Church in Massachusetts.

1816 Birth of Sylvanus Dryden Phelps, New England Baptist clergyman, in Suffield, Connecticut. Phelps pastored churches in Connecticut and Rhode Island between 1846–76 before retiring to write poetry and prose. Among his several publications was the famous hymn "Savior, Thy Dying Love."

1820 Birth of Florence Nightingale, English nurse, in Florence, Italy. Known as "the lady with the lamp" because she believed that a nursing care was a day and night job, she founded trained nursing, as well as pioneering improved forms of military nursing and hospital care.

1872 Death of Thomas Hastings (b.1784), religious music writer and editor. He spent his life developing church music in America, writing more than 600 hymns, 1,000 hymn tunes, and publishing more than 50 collections of religious music. Two of his hymn tunes which are still popular are TOPLADY ("Rock of Ages, Cleft for Me") and ZION ("Guide Me, O Thou Great Jehovah").

1879 Birth of Gustaf Aulen, Swedish theologian, at Ljungby, Sweden. He taught 20 years at the University of Lund (1913–33), then served as Church of Sweden's Bishop of Strangnas until his retirement in 1952. In his classic publication, *Christus Victor* (published from lectures delivered in 1930), Aulen interpreted Christ's death with a modern version of the medieval "ransom to Satan" theory of atonement.

1886 Death of Emily Dickinson (b.1830), reclusive American poet. The daughter of a prominent Amherst, Maryland, attorney, Ms. Dickinson retired almost completely from society by age 30. When she died 25 years later, a hoard of 1,800 poems and countless letters were found among her belongings. Virtually none of these writings (many of them treating religious themes) were published until after her death.

1889 A two-day Methodist youth conference in Cleveland, Ohio, ended. The conference organized the Epworth League of the Methodist Episcopal Church, the foundation of current Methodist youth programs movements. The conference brought representatives from various young people's societies together.

1943 German Lutheran theologian Dietrich Bonhoeffer declared in a letter from prison: "I read the Psalms every day, as I have done for years; I know them and love them more than any other book."

1948 Death of Father Edward Flanagan (b.1886), founder of Boys Town in Omaha, Nebraska. An Irish Roman Catholic immigrant who came to the U.S. in 1904, Flanagan was ordained a priest in 1912. In 1922 he organized his Home for Homeless Boys, which was later called Boys Town. He was elevated to Monsignor in 1937, and helped found institutions like Boys Town in both Europe and Japan. Flanagan believed there is "no such thing as a bad boy."

1984 Death of Francis A. Schaeffer (b.1912), American Presbyterian missionary and evangelical Christian apologist. An intellectual defender of the Christian faith from his earliest adult years, Schaeffer and his wife Edith relocated in Switzerland in the late 1940s and began a ministry to neighbors, travelers and students. He distilled his ideas in several books and two documentary film series: *How Should We Then Live?* (1977) and *Whatever Happened to the Human Race?* (1979).

May 16

1540 German Reformer Martin Luther remarked: "In the worst temptations nothing can help us but faith that God's Son has put on flesh, is bone, sits at the right hand of the Father, and prays for us. There is no mightier comfort."

1850 Birth of Arthur H. Mann, English church organist, at Norwich, England. He served a record 53 years as organist at King's College Chapel, Cambridge, where he became a skillful director of boys' choirs and an authority on Handel.

He wrote much sacred music, including the hymn tune ANGEL'S STORY, to which we sing "O Jesus, I Have Promised."

1866 Founder of the Missouri Synod Lutheran Church, C.F.W. Walther, observed in a letter: "God carries on His work through men with whom it sometimes seems as if one would go to the right and the other to the left and the third one would hold back, and yet the work progresses."

1869 Death of Karl H. Graf (b.1815), German Protestant Old Testament scholar. Though he was more influential through his teaching than his writings, he further developed the theory that the final form of the Pentateuch was post-exilic (published after 587 B.C.) rather than Mosaic (written in its entirety by Moses, ca. 1250 B.C.). This "documentary hypothesis" was ably explained in writing by one of Graf's students, Julius Wellhausen (1844–1918), near the end of the 19th century. The theory is sometimes referred to as the "Graf-Wellhausen Hypothesis."

1905 Birth of Werner Georg Kummel, German United Evangelical New Testament scholar, at Heidelberg. He taught at the universities of Marburg (1930–32), Zurich (1932–51) and Mainz (1951). His most famous work, *Introduction to the New Testament* (19th ed., 1978), is the most popular N.T. introduction available in English.

1906 Death of Edward H. Bickersteth (b.1825), Anglican clergyman. It was on a Sunday afternoon in Aug. 1875 when Bickersteth wrote the lyrics to the hymn "Peace, Perfect Peace."

1931 Death of George Foote Moore (b.1851), American Old Testament scholar. He taught Hebrew and history of religions at Andover Seminary from 1883–1902, then transferred to Harvard University, where he remained until his retirement. His technical writings are still highly respected, including such titles as *Literature of the Old Testament* (1914) and *Judaism in the Christian Era* (1927).

1945 Death of G. Campbell Morgan (b.1863), British Congregational minister. During his career, Morgan pastored several churches, traveled widely and even taught briefly at the college level. Morgan's most enduring gift was his expository writing. His output of Bible notes, sermons and commentaries was immense, with over 60 titles to his credit. Many of these are still in print.

1955 Death of Cyril A. Alington (b.1872), author of the Christmas hymn "Good Christian Men, Rejoice."

May 17

1844 Birth of Julius Wellhausen, German biblical scholar, in Hameln, Westphalia. His investigation into the sources of the Pentateuch created controversy among orthodox Lutherans of his day and led to his resignation from the faculty at Greifswald. He went on to teach at Halle, Marburg and Gottingen. His publications on the Old Testament built upon the work of earlier scholars. In his 1878 *History of Israel*, he presented the Pentateuch as a compilation of four literary sources, which he labelled "J" (Jahwist), "E" (Elohist), "D" (Deuteronomist), and "P" (Priestly Editor). This teaching has become foundational to critical Old Testament studies and has been called the JEDP Hypothesis, the Documentary Hypothesis and the Graf-Wellhausen Hypothesis.

1847 Birth of Charles C. Luther, New England Baptist evangelist and hymn-writer, in Worcester, Maryland. Ordained in 1886, Luther pursued evangelistic activities most of his life, taking two years out (1891–93) to pastor a Baptist church in Bridgeport, Connecticut. He also wrote about 25 hymns, including "Must I Go, and Empty-Handed?"

1881 The English Revised Version (R.V. or E.R.V.) New Testament was first published in England.

1881 Birth of Carl McIntyre, militant American evangelist and political communicator. McIntyre has been called American Protestantism's "self-styled number one anti-Communist," a firebrand radio evangelist who preaches a combination of biblical fundamentalism and hawkish patriotism.

1947 Birth of John W. Fischer, author of "The All Day Song" ("Love Him in the morning. . . .").

1947 The Conservative Baptist Association of America was formally established at Atlantic City, New Jersey. Created by former members of the American Baptist Convention, C.B.A.A. founders opposed what they considered the encroachment of liberal tendencies within the parent organization. There are approximately 300,000 members within 1,100 C.B.A.A. churches today.

1964 The Vatican II Ecumenical Council created the Secretariat for Non-Christian Religions.

May 18

1291 Acre, the last Christian territory in the Holy Land taken by the Crusades, fell to the Sultan of Egypt.

1631 The General Court of Massachusetts Bay Colony, at their second meeting, decreed that "no man shall be admitted to the body politic but such as are members of some of the churches within the limits" of the colony.

1692 Birth of Joseph Butler, English bishop and scholar, at Wantage, Berkshire, England. He was ordained Bishop of Bristol in 1738 and of Durham in 1750. Butler's *Analogy of Religion*, which he had been writing for many years, appeared in 1736 when the deist controversy in England was at its height. Using empirical argument (argument from experience), Butler wrote that the God of nature was also the God of revelation. The order in nature parallels the order in revelation, and the difficulties in Christianity bear close analogy with those we encounter in nature. Butler's *Analogy* did more to discredit Deism than any other writing of that day.

1766 The Church of the United Brethren in Christ was organized in Lancaster, Pennsylvania, under the leadership of Martin Boehm and Philip William Otterbein.

1843 By the secession of nearly half the member churches of the National Church of Scotland, the Free Church of Scotland was founded.

1864 Death of César H.A. Malan (b.1787), Swiss Reformed pastor and evangelist. Ordained in the Reformed Church in 1810, Malan's outspoken criticism of the church's formalism and apathy forced him to resign, whereupon he built a chapel on his own property and preached there for 43 years. Malan also wrote more than 1,000 hymns, including the tune HENDON ("Ask Ye What Great Thing I Know" and "Take My Life, and Let It Be").

1901   Death of Maltbie D. Babcock (b.1858), American Presbyterian clergyman. He pastored three prominent churches in Maryland and New York state. But he is better remembered for authoring the hymn "This Is My Father's World."

1920   Birth of Karol Wojtyla, Roman Catholic bishop, in Wadowice, Poland. On Oct. 16, 1978, at age 58, he was elected the 263rd pontiff of the Roman Catholic Church, taking the name John Paul II.

1926   The controversial kidnapping of female revivalist Aimee Semple Mc-Pherson took place near Los Angeles. By 1922 she had developed the tenets of her "foursquare Gospel": Christ as Savior, Christ as Healer, a Holy Spirit Baptism with tongues and the Second Coming of the Savior. She disappeared for a month in 1926 and claimed to have been kidnapped. A Los Angeles grand jury challenged her story, but finally dismissed the case.

May 19

804   Death of Alcuin (b.ca. 735), medieval Christian scholar. A prolific author, he wrote Bible commentaries, dogmatic treatises and controversial tracts. Laboring to raise the intellectual labor of the monks, he developed the Caroline minuscule style of handwriting, a system utilizing both small and capital letters for easier reading. Alcuin also led a group of scholars who published a critically revised and updated text of the Vulgate (Jerome's Latin Bible), thus halting accidental scribal corruptions.

1662   England's King Charles II approved a bill requiring all ministers to assent publicly to the Anglican *Book of Common Prayer*.

1740   English revivalist George Whitefield noted in a letter: "True faith is not merely in the head, but in the heart."

1775   English founder of Methodism John Wesley asserted in a letter: "In all other judgments of God, the inhabitants of the earth learn righteousness. When a land is visited with famine, or plague, or earthquake, the people commonly see and acknowledge the hand of God. But wherever war breaks out, God is forgotten."

1885   The complete English Revised (E.V. or E.R.V.) Version of the Bible was published in England. This version is little used today because of its Anglicisms. After waiting a promised 20 years, American scholars on the E.R.V. committee published an "Americanized" edition of this translation, known from 1905 on as the American Revised Version or American Standard Version (A.S.V.) of the Bible.

1894   Birth of Esther Kirk Miller, mission pioneer. In 1950 she and her husband Basil William Miller founded World-Wide Missions in Altadena, California. Headquartered in Pasadena, California, W.W.M. supports personnel working in 30 nations and engages primarily in relief aid, medicine and church planting.

1914 Death of Thomas Koschat (b.1845), Austrian music composer. Although most of his compositions are best labelled "classical," his score POLAND is utilized by the church for the hymn "The Lord Is My Shepherd."

1939 Death of Howard B. Grose (b.1851), American Baptist leader and author of the hymn "Give of Your Best to the Master." Ordained in 1883, he pastored local churches until 1890, when he became president of South Dakota State University. He also worked with American Baptist publications and home missions before his retirement in 1933.

1971 *Godspell* first opened at the Cherry Lane Theater in New York City. The musical by Stephen Schwartz is based on the New Testament Gospel of Matthew and is still produced by secular and religious theater groups today.

May 20

325 The Council of Nicea, the first ecumenical church council, convened.

1232 Anthony of Padua (d.1231) was canonized by Pope Gregory IX. Born in 1195 in Lisbon, Portugal, St. Anthony became a member of the newly instituted Franciscans about 1220. A brilliant orator and preacher, Anthony eventually become the most celebrated of the followers of St. Francis of Assisi.

1506 Death of Christopher Columbus, modern discoverer of America. He was born in Genoa, Italy, but sailed from Spain in 1492 on a voyage to find a western route to the spice islands. He discovered, instead, the Americas. His discovery paved the way for colonial expansion and mission activity by the church in the New World.

1530 German reformer Martin Luther affirmed in a letter: "God's friendship is a bigger comfort than that of the whole world."

1690 Death of John Eliot (b.1604), colonial missionary to the American Indians. Born in England, Eliot emigrated to America in 1631 and began working among the Algonquin Indians of Maryland in 1646. By 1663 Eliot had translated the entire Bible into the Algonquin language. The number of Indian converts peaked at about 3,600 in 1674. Due to the hostilities of King Philip's War (1675–76), however, their numbers declined rapidly. Soon after Eliot's death, the evidences of his missionary work completely vanished.

1754 Columbia University was chartered as King's College in New York City under the Episcopal Church. After a division within the school in 1784, the name was changed to Columbia College. In 1896 the name was finally changed to Columbia University.

1878 Death of William R. Featherstone (b.1846), Canadian Wesleyan Methodist who authored the hymn "My Jesus, I Love Thee."

1884 Death of Silas J. Vail (b.1818), New England businessman. Although music was more of a hobby for him, Vail composed a number of hymn tunes, including CLOSE TO THEE ("Thou My Everlasting Portion").

1920 Death of Henry L. Gilmour (b.1836), Irish-born American dentist and U.S. Civil war veteran. A devoted lay member of the Methodist Church in Wenonah, New Jersey, he was known chiefly for his musical gifts. Gilmour wrote and composed many Gospel songs, but perhaps none is better known than "The Haven of Rest."

1937 Jesse I. Overholtzer chartered Child Evangelism Fellowship, Inc., in Chicago, Illinois. This interdenominational mission agency of Baptist tradition is the outgrowth of evangelistic work Overholtzer began with children in California as far back as 1916. Today, C.E.F. headquarters is located in Warrenton, Missouri. The organization works in radio and TV broadcasting, evangelism, literature production and distribution, and Bible correspondence courses in 63 countries around the world.

1950 Death of Grant C. Tullar (b.1869), New England song evangelist. At the age of 24 (1893), he helped found a successful sacred music publishing business: Tullar-Meredith Publishing Co., in New York. He is better remembered as the composer of the hymn tune FACE TO FACE (". . . With Christ, My Savior").

May 21

1471 Birth of Albrecht Durer, German engraver, in Nuremberg. A friend of Philip Melanchthon, Durer consciously sided with Lutheranism, although he never renounced his Catholic faith. His art also displayed close affinity with the Christian humanism of Erasmus. He designed more than 100 woodcuts, many based on religious subjects. Exerting a marked influence on later Flemish painters, Durer's name endures as the greatest German artist of the Renaissance period.

1527 Michael Sattler, a former monk of St. Peter in Freiburg who had become a convert and spokesman for the Anabaptists, was burned at the stake in Rottenburg, Germany.

1536 The General Assembly of Geneva officially embraced Protestantism by accepting the evangelical faith of the Swiss reformers.

1739 Methodist hymnwriter Charles Wesley, on the first anniversary of his religious conversion, wrote "Oh, for a Thousand Tongues to Sing."

1740 English revivalist George Whitefield explained the nature of Jesus' character in a letter: "He was God and man in one person, that God and man might be happy together again."

1813 Birth of Robert Murray McCheyne, Scottish clergyman, at Edinburgh. Licensed to preach in 1835, McCheyne served under Rev. Andrew Bonar for a year before being ordained to the pastorate of St. Peter's Church, Dundee, a post he held until his early death seven years later. McCheyne's many popular writings include the hymn "When This Passing World Is Done."

1832 Birth of J. Hudson Taylor, English pioneer missionary, in Yorkshire. Converted at age 17, Taylor felt a missionary call to China. He arrived in Shanghai in 1854, and soon after made several evangelistic tours through the closed interior of China. In 1865 he founded the interdenominational China Inland Mission; and 30 years later, C.I.M. was supporting over 640 missionaries in China, about half of the Protestant force in that country. Taylor retired from his work in 1901 and died four years later at Changsha, capital of the last province opened by C.I.M. In 1965 his organization was renamed the Overseas Missionary Fellowship.

1841 Birth of Joseph Parry, Welsh religious composer, at Merthyr Tydfile, Wales. He began his musical training at age 13, and eventually taught music at the Welsh University colleges at Aberystwyth, Swansea and at Cardiff. During his lifetime, Parry wrote many pieces of music, including over 400 hymn tunes. One of his pieces which maintains its popularity is ABERYSTWYTH, to which we sing "Jesus, Lover of My Soul."

1881 New England humanitarian Clara Barton, age 60, founded the American Red Cross. The International Red Cross had been founded 17 years earlier (1863–64) in Geneva by Swiss philanthropist Jean Henri Dunant.

1922 Birth of Doris Akers, religious songwriter and author of the chorus "Sweet, Sweet Spirit."

1924 The theory of evolution was ruled untenable by the General Assembly of the Presbyterian Church at San Antonio, Texas.

1944 German Lutheran theologian Dietrich Bonhoeffer assured in a prison letter: "God alone protects; otherwise there is nothing."

1950 The religious TV program *Faith for Today* was first aired over ABC television. One of the longest running of all religious series, the program was produced in cooperation with the Seventh-Day Adventist Church and hosted for many years by Rev. William A. Sagal.

1972 Deranged attacker Laszlo Toth damaged one of the world's most celebrated sculptures, Michelangelo's *Pieta*, in the Vatican at Rome. Wielding a hammer, Toth broke off the left arm, shattered the hand and chipped the nose and left eye of the Madonna.

May 22

337 Death of Constantine I (the Great), the Roman emperor whose conversion to Christianity changed the entire face of the early Church. Born ca. 280, Constantine was converted to the Christian faith in 312 when, battling the troops of Maxentius (who was trying to seize the Roman throne), Constantine claimed to see a cross in the heavens bearing the inscription "In this sign conquer," in Latin.

1944 The Gospel Mission of South America was incorporated by founder William M. Strong in Concepcion, Chile. Its headquarters was moved to Ft. Lauderdale, Florida, in 1975. The G.M.S.A. is an interdenominational mission agency of Baptist tradition engaged in evangelism, church planting, Gospel broadcasting and Bible correspondence courses. It maintains offices in Chile, Argentina and Uruguay.

1541 The Ratisbon Conference met for its last day after a month of sessions. After the failure of this religious conference to reunify the Catholic church, the Protestant movement became permanent.

1690 Death of Johann Jacob Schutz (b.1640), German Lawyer and the hymnwriter who penned "Sing Praise to God Who Reigns Above." Born in Frankfurt-am-Main, he studied law at Tubingen, then returned to Frankfurt, where he distinguished himself as an excellent lawyer.

1740 English revivalist George Whitefield wrote in a letter: "We must all have the spirit of martyrdom, though we may not all die martyrs."

1789 The first American Presbyterian general assembly convened in Philadelphia, Pennsylvania.

1851 Birth of Edwyn Hoskins, Anglican clergyman, at Aston-Tirrold, Berkshire. As Bishop of Southwell, England, from 1905 until his death in 1925, he devoted himself to improving labor conditions for the working class.

1868 Birth of William R. Newell, pastor and devotional writer, in Savannah, Ohio. Beginning in 1895, he worked with Moody Bible Institute in Chicago, and even conducted interdenominational Bible classes in American and Canadian cities. Though he published several expository works on the Bible, we remember him as the author of the hymn "At Calvary" ("Years I spent in vanity and pride. . .").

1967 The General Assembly of the Presbyterian Church in the United States (P.C.U.S.) adopted the Confession of 1967. It was the first major confession adopted by the Presbyterians since the Westminster Confession of 1647.

May 23

1430 Joan of Arc, French national peasant heroine, was captured by the Burgundians at Reims. She was later turned over to the English, who were fighting France. Condemned on false charges of witchcraft and heresy, she was burned at the stake the following year in Rouen at age 19.

1498 Death of Girolamo Savonarola (b.1452), Italian reformer, who was hanged then burned at the stake in Florence. Eight years earlier he had successfully preached repentance to the city's leaders, pleading also the cause of the poor and oppressed. But when he denounced Pope Alexander VI, he was excommunicated from the church and soon lost his following. Savanarola was tried for heresy, found guilty, and executed.

1848 Birth of George C. Hugg, who composed the melody to the hymn "No, Not One."

1862 Birth of Hermann Gunkel, German Protestant Bible scholar, in Springe, Hanover. He taught from 1888–1927 at the German universities of Gottingen, Halle, Berlin and Giessen. He was one of the pioneers in formulating form criticism as applied to the Old Testament. His two classic commentaries on Genesis (1901) and the Psalms (1926–28) demonstrate the emergence of this relatively new concept in biblical analysis.

1889 Birth of Mary Susanne Edgar, national Y.W.C.A. leader, at Sundridge, Ontario. She wrote a number of hymns during her years of Christian camping ministry with girls, including "God, Who Touchest Earth with Beauty."

1903 Death of Henry Blodget (b.1825), Congregational missionary. Under the sponsorship of the American Board of Missions, Blodget served 40 years as a missionary to China (1854–1894) helping to translate the New Testament into the colloquial Mandarin language of Peking.

1926 Birth of Wilbur Nelson, Christian radio host, in Denver, Colorado. For years Nelson has worked with the *The Morning Chapel Hour*, originating in Paramount, California.

1955 The General Assembly of the Presbyterian Church in the United States first announced that it would permit the ordination of women ministers.

1965 Death of Henry Halley in Chicago, Illinois. He was the creator of *Halley's Bible Handbook*, which is still in print in a variety of editions.

May 24

1738 English founder of Methodism, John Wesley, inscribed the classic account of his religious conversion at Aldersgate Chapel, London, in his journal: "I felt my heart strangely warmed. . . ."

1740 English revivalist George Whitefield wrote in a letter: "Those that have been most humbled, I find, always make the most solid, useful Christians."

1747 Colonial American missionary to the New England Indians David Brainerd wrote in his journal: "I have often remarked to others, that much more of true religion consists in deep humility, brokenness of heart, and an abasing sense of barrenness and want of grace and holiness, than most who are called Christians imagine."

1752 Robert Robinson, author of the hymn "Come Thou Fount of Every Blessing," was born again under the preaching of English revivalist George Whitefield.

1768 Death of Joseph Hart (b.1712), English clergyman and hymnwriter. Though raised in a Christian home, he was not converted to believing faith until age 45. He became an ardent Calvinist preacher and wrote the hymn "Come, Ye Sinners, Poor and Needy" (a.k.a. "I Will Arise and Go to Jesus"), first published in 1759.

1844 The world's first long-distance telegraph message was sent, from the U.S. Supreme Court room in Washington, D.C., to Baltimore, Maryland, by Samuel F.B. Morse, inventor of the telegraph. The words of that message were: "What hath God wrought."

1865 Birth of Emily Divine Wilson, American Methodist clergyman's wife, in Philadelphia. Her fame outlives her husband's because of her composition HEAVEN, to which we sing the hymn "Sing the Wondrous Love of Jesus."

1878 Birth of Harry Emerson Fosdick, American Baptist minister, near Buffalo, New York. A popular spokesman of Christian liberalism, the psychology of religion and biblical criticism, Fosdick played a prominent role in the modernist-fundamentalist controversy of 1920–40. He pastored 20 years at the influential Riverside Church in New York City. During this time he published his most famous writings, including the popular hymn "God of Grace and God of Glory."

1891 Birth of William Foxwell Albright, American Near Eastern scholar, of Methodist missionary parents, in Coquimbo, Chile. His career as a distinguished scholar in Semitics and Old Testament archeology spanned 40 years (1920–59). He wrote over 800 articles and books on archeological and biblical subjects. Perhaps his greatest contribution to conservative Christianity was substantiating the historical accuracy of many biblical dates and times discredited earlier by 19th-century Protestant liberalism.

1892 Birth of Earl B. Marlatt, religious educator and hymnologist, in Columbus, Indiana. He taught college from 1925 until his retirement in 1957 at both Boston and Southern Methodist Universities. He authored the hymn " 'Are Ye Able?' Said the Master."

1930 Frank C. Laubach, pioneer developer of E.S.L. (English as a Second Language) instruction methods, while serving as a Congregational missionary in the Philippines, related in a letter: "As one makes new discoveries about his friends by being with them, so one discovers the 'individuality' of God if one entertains him continuously."

May 25

1085 Pope Gregory VII (b.ca.1025), 156th Bishop of Rome, died in exile. Gregory's mortal enemy, German Emperor King Henry IV, had set up antipope Clement III in 1084 and soon after captured Rome. Gregory was forced to move south with the Normans, and died the following year in Salerno, Italy.

1521 Holy Roman Emperor Charles V pronounced Martin Luther an outlaw and heretic for refusing to recant his teachings at the Diet of Worms, held the previous month on April 17.

1793 Fr. Stephen Theodore Badin was ordained in Baltimore, Maryland. He was the first Roman Catholic priest to be ordained in the U.S. Following his ordination, Fr. Badin served in Kentucky, dedicating the first Roman Catholic chapel in Lexington in 1800.

1805 Death of William Paley (b.1743), English theologian. Between 1767–95 he served in various churches as rector, vicar and prebendary. His greatest influence came through his writings, including the very popular *View of the Evidences of Christianity* (1794) and *Natural Theology* (1802). In his writings, Paley sought to prove the existence of God through the biblical evidence: in Christ and in miracles.

1816 Death of Samuel Webbe (b.1740), English Roman Catholic musician and hymnwriter. He was organist at the chapels of the Sardinian and Portuguese embassies in London, two of the few respectable organ positions then open to a Roman Catholic organist in England. He published several collections of hymn tunes in about 1792. One of his hymn tunes that still remains popular is CONSOLATION ("Come, Ye Disconsolate, Where'er Ye Languish").

1824 The American Sunday School Union was established in Philadelphia, Pennsylvania. Its purpose was to promote and coordinate Sunday school activity in America.

1865 Birth of John R. Mott, American Y.M.C.A. leader, in Livingston Manor, New York. A Methodist layman, Mott spent over 40 years serving the Y.M.C.A. in America, both as Student Secretary for the National Committee (1888–1915) then as General Secretary (1915–31). In his day, the Y.M.C.A. was much more evangelistic, and Mott was known as a zealous soul-winner as well as a strong supporter of student Christian missions.

1868 Death of Billy Bray (b.1794), English Methodist evangelist. In his earlier years he was a drinking and smoking miner, a profligate by most Christian standards. Converted at age 29 (1823), he soon joined the fight against the use of alcohol and tobacco. He was a powerful evangelist in the Methodist Bible Christian Church in his native town in Cornwall, England; but his major soul-winning work was done outside the pulpit, among his fellow miners.

1876 The Reformed Presbyterian Church of Scotland united with the Free Church of Scotland to form the new Free Church of Scotland. The Reformed Presbytery had been organized in 1743 and the Free Church, in 1843, by splits from the Church of Scotland. In 1929 the Free Church merged with the Mother Church, retaining the name Church of Scotland.

May 26

1232 Pope Gregory IX sent the first Inquisition team to Aragon in Spain. Gregory had organized the Inquisition and turned it over to the Dominicans the year before.

1647 A Massachusetts law forbidding any Jesuit or Roman Catholic priest from entering territory under Puritan jurisdiction was enacted. First-time offenders would be banished; second-time offenders, executed.

1700 Birth of Nikolaus Ludwig von Zinzendorf, German reformer, in Dresden. The son of a Lutheran high official in Saxony, Zinzendorf spent his life organizing and uniting the Moravian Brethren. In 1721–22 he purchased and converted an estate in Berthelsdorf into a Christian community for Bohemian Protestant refugees, naming it *"Herrnhut"* ("House of the Lord"). Eventually Zinzendorf succeeded in creating a missionary-minded, service-oriented and state-independent Christian denomination united by mutual love and deep expression of religious devotion.

1773 Birth of Hans G. Nageli, Swiss author of the tune DENNIS, to which we sing "Blest Be the Tie That Binds," in Wetzikon (near Zurich). Establishing a music publishing firm at age 19, Nageli went on to become the founder and president of the Swiss Association for the Cultivation of Music.

1808 The Fifth (U.S.) General Conference of the Methodist Episcopal Church closed, in Baltimore, Maryland. The three-week conference had ordained William McKendree the first American bishop of the Methodist Episcopal Church.

1811 Birth of William Hunter, American Methodist clergyman, in County Antrim, Ireland. His family emigrated to America when he was six, settling in Pennsylvania. After his ordination, he served in the Pittsburgh, Virginia and East Ohio Conferences until 1855, when he was appointed professor of Hebrew at Allegheny College, where he remained for 15 years. Hunter wrote and published three collections of hymns during his lifetime, including the hymn "The Great Physician Now Is Near."

1823 Birth of Frank Bottome, author of the hymn "The Comforter Has Come."

1858 The Associate and the Associate Reformed Presbyterian churches merged in Pittsburgh, Pennsylvania, forming the United Presbyterian Church of North America.

1863 Birth of Shailer Mathews, American Baptist educator, in Portland, Maine. He taught at Colby College from 1887–93 and at the University of Chicago from 1894–33. Though the author of about 30 books, his best remembered work is the *Dictionary of Religion and Ethics* (1921), which he compiled with G.B. Smith.

1925 Death of Ernest DeWitt Burton (b.1856), American Baptist educator. He taught New Testament at the University of Chicago from 1892–1923. Burton's most enduring publication is his *Syntax of the Moods and Tenses in the New Testament Greek* (1893).

1957 The religious television program *The Fourth R* aired for the last time over NBC. Produced by several different religious organizations, the short-lived series aired on Sunday mornings after its debut on March 28 of that year.

May 27

735 Death of the Venerable Bede (b.ca.673), English monk, scholar and church historian. He spent his early life in the monastery teaching, preaching and writing. He was well-versed in the Scriptures and the Latin fathers and became a much-loved teacher as well as a prolific writer. He wrote his best-known work, *Ecclesiastical History of the English Nation*, in 731. The history is so valuable that it is still in print today.

1525 Death of Thomas Munzer (b.ca.1490), militant German reformer. As a theology student at Leipzig, he began embracing the doctrines of the Reformation, but carried them to such excess that he was deposed from preaching. In 1522 he joined with Carlstadt in revolutionary turmoil. Soon after, he began leading riotous attacks on monasteries, espousing the ruthless killing of all the "ungodly." Munzer helped inspire the bloody Peasants' War (1524–25), during which he was captured and beheaded.

1564 Death of John Calvin (b.1509), French reformer. Calvin's interest in the Reformation began in 1532. In 1536 he published the first edition of his famous *Christianae Religionis Institutio*. A short summary of the Christian faith by a virtually unknown author, the *Institutes of the Christian Religion* soon became the popular Protestant apology of the Reformation doctrines. Calvin revised the work five times before the definitive edition appeared in 1559. The first edition contained only six chapters; the final edition, 79.

1799 Birth of George Washington Doane, American Episcopal clergyman, in Trenton, New Jersey. He was one of the foremost promoters of the Episcopal missionary movement of his day. He also authored many hymns, including "Fling Out the Banner. Let It Float" and "Softly Now the Light of Day."

1814 Birth of Charles W. Everest, American Episcopal clergyman and author of the hymn "Take Up Thy Cross, The Savior Said," at East Windsor, Connecticut. Ordained in 1842, Everest served as Rector of Hampden, near New Haven, Connecticut, from 1842–73.

1819 Birth of Julia Ward Howe, American writer and social reformer, in New York City. Prior to the U.S. Civil War, she helped edit an antislavery newspaper. But her most famous writing became the theme song of the Union Armies: "Battle Hymn of the Republic."

1902 Birth of Peter Marshall, American Presbyterian U.S. Senate Chaplain, in Coatbridge, Scotland. He emigrated to the U.S. in 1927, was ordained to the Presbyterian ministry in 1931 and held pastorates in Georgia before becoming pastor of Washington, D.C.'s New York Avenue Presbyterian Church in 1937. He was made chaplain of the Senate in 1947, but died less than two years later. His life's story was immortalized in his wife Catherine's 1950 biography *A Man Called Peter.*

1924 The general conference of the Methodist Episcopal Church, meeting at Springfield, Maryland, gave up its ban on dancing and theater attendance.

1927 Birth of Ralph Carmichael, popular contemporary composer of Christian music. Among many popular pieces, Carmichael is the author and composer of "He's Everything to Me" and "The Savior Is Waiting."

1933 Death of Joseph S. Cook (b.1859), Canadian clergyman. Born in England, Cook came to Canada where he entered the Methodist ministry. Later he transferred into the United Church of Canada. He is remembered as the author of the Christmas hymn "Gentle Mary Laid Her Child."

1948 Death of Luther B. Bridgers (b.1884), American Methodist clergyman and author and composer of the hymn "There's Within My Heart a Melody" (SWEE-TEST NAME). He began preaching at the age of 17, and later became a pastor and evangelist of the Methodist Episcopal Church, South, serving churches in Kentucky, Georgia and North Carolina.

1975 The headquarters of the Gospel Mission of South America moved from Paterson, New Jersey, to its present location in Ft. Lauderdale, Florida. Incorporated in the U.S. by founder William M. Strong in 1940, this interdenominational mission organization of Baptist tradition works in the areas of evangelism, Gospel broadcasting and theological education, and has offices in three South American countries: Chile, Argentina and Uruguay.

May 28

1577 The Formula of Concord was issued, the last of the Lutheran confessions which were later incorporated into the *Book of Concord.* The Formula was chiefly the work of Jacob Andrea and Martin Chemnitz. Its 12 articles steered a careful middle course between extremists on both sides, reaffirming the basic teaching of the Augsburg Confession (1530).

1725 English founder of Methodism John Wesley asserted in a letter to his mother: "I can't think that when God sent us into the world He had irreversibly decreed that we should be perpetually miserable in it."

1775 Anglican hymnwriter John Newton in a letter: "If a transient glance exceed all that the world can afford . . . , what must it be to dwell with Him? If a day in His courts be better than a thousand, what will eternity be in His presence?"

1779 Birth of Thomas Moore, Irish Catholic lawyer, in Dublin. His prolific writings endeared him to the literary and social circles of London. He is better remembered for his hymn "Come, Ye Disconsolate, Where'er Ye Languish."

1835 Birth of Annie Sherwood Hawks, American Baptist homemaker and author of "I Need Thee Every Hour," in Hoosick, New York. A resident of Brooklyn for many years, Mrs. Hawks was an active member of Hanson Place Baptist Church. One of her pastors was the well-known sacred music composer Robert Lowry. Through his encouragement, Mrs. Hawks wrote more than 400 hymns during her lifetime.

1841 Edwin Moody, father of Dwight L. Moody, died, leaving his wife Betsy Holton Moody to raise seven boys and two girls alone. Dwight Lyman was only four years old (b.1837) at the time of his father's death, but he grew up to become the most successful American evangelist of his generation.

1869 Death of Ernst W. Hengstenberg (b.1802), German Lutheran scholar. He taught at the University of Berlin beginning in 1824; but after 1840 he became an outspoken proponent of Lutheran orthodoxy. His writings helped balance, if not defeat, the rationalism of his day; his publications included several outstanding Old Testament studies.

1898 The Shroud of Turin was first photographed by Secundo Pia in Turin's cathedral, where the shroud had rested for 320 years.

1958 The Presbyterian Church in the United States merged with the Presbyterian Church of North America, forming the United Presbyterian Church in the United States of America.

May 29

1453 Constantinople, capital city of Eastern Christianity since 324, fell to the Turks, marking the end of the Middle Ages. They named it Istanbul and made it the capital of the Ottoman Empire.

1698 Construction began on Old Swedes (Holy Trinity) Church in Wilmington, Delaware. Built for 800 pounds-sterling, the church has been used continuously as a place of worship since it was built.

1774 Early American Methodist Bishop Francis Asbury recorded this prayer in his journal: "Lord, keep me from all the superfluity of dress, and from preaching empty stuff to please the ear, instead of changing the heart."

1788 In Philadelphia, the Westminster Larger and Shorter Catechisms were approved as part of the constitution of the Presbyterian Church.

1837 Birth of Charles William Fry, English musician, in Salisbury. Fry was a successful building contractor when the Salvation Army began its work in Salisbury in 1878. Fry and his three sons soon offered their instrumental musical talents and played for the outdoor meetings. This was the first Salvation Army brass band. Fry is also remembered as the author of the hymn "Lily of the Valley" (a.k.a. "I Have Found a Friend in Jesus").

1865 Birth of Otto G.A. Rahlfs, Lutheran Old Testament scholar, near Hanover, Germany. He taught at the University of Gottingen between 1891–1935. Rahlfs

devoted his entire academic life to the preparation of a critical edition of the
Septuagint (the Greek translation of the Hebrew Old Testament). The first
completed edition was published in 1935, the year of Rahlfs' death.

1874 Birth of G.K. (Gilbert Keith) Chesterton, English scholar and novelist, in
London. A convert from Anglicanism to Roman Catholicism, even his lighter
writings were heavily influenced by religious themes. His theological writings,
such as *Heretics* (1905) and *Orthodoxy* (1908), interpreted the Christian faith
from a mystical Catholic viewpoint, setting it apart from, yet intimately relating
it to, contemporary thought.

1944 Lutheran theologian and Nazi martyr Dietrich Bonhoeffer declared in a
letter from prison: "How wrong it is to use God as a stop-gap for the incom-
pleteness of our knowledge. If in fact the frontiers of our knowledge are being
pushed further and further back, then God is being pushed back with them,
and is therefore continually in retreat. We are to find God in what we know,
not in what we don't know; God wants us to realize His presence, not in
unsolved problems, but in those that are solved."

May 30

339 Death of Eusebius (b.ca.265), the father of early church history. Born in
Palestine, he went to Egypt, then to Asia, where he was elected Bishop of
Caesarea about 314. Attending the Council of Nicea in 325, it was Eusebius
who proposed that the baptismal creed of Caesarea be accepted as the
church's creedal statement; it was rejected in favor of what became the Nicene
Creed. He sided with Athanasius, who stood for the deity of Christ, in his
opposition to Arius, but for the most part held a moderate position in the
controversy. Eusebius became the voice of the era of Constantine I through
his several histories. The most famous and best known of all his works was
his *Historia Ecclesiastica* (325), which contains much information on the first
three centuries of the early church found nowhere else in ancient literature.

1135 The Council of Pisa opened. St. Bernard of Clairvaux successfully
pleaded the cause of Pope Innocent II, winning support for him rather than
antipope Anacletus II from the cardinals.

1431 Death of Joan of Arc (b.1412), French saint and heroine. An illiterate
though devout peasant girl, at age 13 she began hearing inward voices prompt-
ing her to deliver France from its English aggressors. For two years (1428–30)
she fought with the French army before being taken prisoner by the English
at Compiegne. The following year she was condemned for witchcraft and
heresy and burned at the stake in the marketplace at Rouen.

1518 German reformer Martin Luther declared in a letter: "Without Christ's
command not even a pope can speak, nor is the heart of a king in his own
hand."

1640 Death of Peter Paul Rubens (b.1577), Flemish painter. Born in Westphalia, Germany, Rubens studied painting in Italy under such masters as Titian
and Michelangelo before returning to his home country and settling in Antwerp. He became the most sought-after painter in Europe, producing more

than 1,200 paintings during his lifetime. His most famous is *The Descent from the Cross*, which hangs today in the Antwerp Cathedral.

1819 Anglican Bishop Reginald Heber penned the lines to the famous missionary hymn "From Greenland's Icy Mountains."

1934 The two-day Barmen Synod ended in Germany. The synod signed the Barmen Declaration, which declared the German Confessing Church's opposition to the Nazis' German Christian Church. Written largely by reformed theologian Karl Barth, the declaration's theme was that Jesus Christ is the true Word of God, and the church is not to recognize other powers as representing divine revelation.

1968 Death of Martin Noth (b.1902), German Lutheran Old Testament scholar. Noth's contributions to Old Testament scholarship include his theory that before Israel had a king, it was a tribal federation with its worship focused on a central sanctuary, rather than on several shrines. Noth was also the first scholar to note that First and Second Samuel and First and Second Kings contain virtually no mention of the classic prophets (Isaiah, Jeremiah, Amos, Hosea, etc.).

May 31

1680 Death of Joachim Neander (b.1650), German hymnwriter. Born in Bremen, he spent most of his life balanced between rebellion against society and teaching in society's schools. He once spent several months living in a cave. While in his 20s, he came under the influence of the Pietists and became a close friend of Jacob Spener. Though he only lived to the age of 30, he wrote and composed about 60 hymns. After his death, he became known as "the Paul Gerhardt of the Calvinists," and is still regarded as the outstanding hymnwriter of the German Reformed Church.

1701 Birth of Alexander Cruden, Scottish author and editor of *Cruden's Concordance*, in Aberdeen. Cruden originally prepared to study for the ministry, but suffered several mental breakdowns that led to his confinement in an asylum in 1720, 1738 and 1753. Between hospitalizations, Cruden worked as a tutor, a bookseller and a proofreader. The first edition of his most famous concordance bore the title *A Complete Concordance to the Holy Scriptures of the Old and New Testament* and was published in 1737.

1769 Anglican hymnwriter John Newton declared in a letter: "He fulfills His promise in making our strength equal to our day; and every new trial gives us a new proof how happy it is to be enabled to put our trust in Him."

1809 Death of Joseph Haydn (b.1732), Austrian composer. Though he spent his greatest energies in writing for the symphony and for string quartets, Haydn composed at least a dozen masses as well, including six which were written after his last symphony and are considered by some critics to be Haydn's greatest musical achievements. His great oratorio *The Creation* (1789) was inspired by Handel's influence on Haydn.

1821 The Cathedral of the Assumption of the Blessed Virgin Mary in Baltimore, Maryland, was dedicated by John Carroll. This was the first Roman Catholic cathedral built in the U.S. The cornerstone had been laid in 1806.

1857 Birth of Achille Ratti, Roman Catholic bishop, near Monza, Italy. On Feb. 6, 1922, he was elected pontiff, and served the Roman Catholic Church as Pope Pius XI for the next 17 years, until his death on Feb. 10, 1939.

1898 Birth of Norman Vincent Peale, American clergyman, in Bowersville, Ohio. A prominent religious author, Peale is best known for the theological emphases embodied in his most popular writing, *The Power of Positive Thinking* (1952).

June

June 1

1657 Five Quakers from England arrived on Manhattan Island and were immediately imprisoned by the local government. Eight days later they were released on condition that they leave the area and go to Rhode Island.

1689 Spanish missionaries formally established the mission of San Francisco de los Tejos in Texas.

1741 The methods used for revivals during the Great Awakening brought a schism in the Presbyterian church, dividing the denomination into the "Old School" and the "New School." Seventeen years later, in 1758, the two factions reunited.

1793 Birth of Henry Francis Lyte, Scottish clergyman who wrote the hymns "Abide with Me" and "Jesus, I My Cross Have Taken." Ordained in 1815, he served several churches, even though he was often in poor health.

1794 Birth of William (Billy) Bray, English Methodist evangelist, in Cornwall, England. During his early years as a coal miner, Bray was a heavy smoker, a drunkard and a profligate, until converted at age 29 under the influence of John Bunyan's *Visions of Heaven and Hell*. Bray was enrolled as a local Methodist preacher the following year, although he did most of his soul-winning outside the pulpit.

1798 Birth of Simeon B. Marsh, American chorister and newspaper editor, in Sherburne, New York. As a devoted Presbyterian layman, he taught singing schools in the churches of the Albany Presbytery for thirty years. He wrote several hymn tunes during his life, including MARTYN, to which we sing "Jesus, Lover of My Soul."

1849 Birth of James H. Fillmore, American music publisher, in Cincinnati, Ohio. He founded the Fillmore Brothers Music House in Cincinnati, which later became widely known throughout the Midwest. Fillmore is remembered through two hymn tunes he composed: HANNAH ("I Know That My Redeemer Liveth") and RESOLUTION ("I am Resolved No Longer to Linger").

1893 The General Assembly of the Presbyterian Church defrocked the Rev. Dr. Charles Augustus Briggs (professor of biblical theology at Union Theological Seminary, in New York City) on conviction of teaching heresy.

1910 Birth of Kenneth Strachan, son of Harry and Susan Strachan, who founded the Latin America Mission in 1921. Kenneth was general director of this evangelical, interdenominational mission organization for 15 years, 1950–65. L.A.M., presently headquartered in Coral Gables, Florida, is involved in eight Latin American countries planting churches, providing literature and education and supporting other related agencies.

1922 Birth of Ray Knighton, who founded the Medical Assistance Programs in Chicago in 1954 and served as its president until 1980. Today, this interdenominational mission agency is headquartered in Brunswick, Georgia, under the name M.A.P. International. It provides medical supplies, health training, emergency aid and related resources in cooperation with other agencies to 82 countries.

1923 Bible Literature International was incorporated, in Columbus, Ohio. Founded by Don R. Falkenberg, this interdenominational mission agency engages in supplying Christian evangelistic, discipleship and church growth literature to many countries overseas.

1930 Pioneer linguistic educator Frank C. Laubach, while serving as a Congregational missionary to the Philippines, insisted in a letter: "I must talk about God, or I cannot keep Him in my mind. I must give Him away in order to have Him. That is the law of the spirit world. What one gives one has, what one keeps to oneself one loses."

1934 Birth of Pat Boone, contemporary Christian entertainer who rose to fame during the 1960s.

1953 The Christian Aid Mission was chartered, in Washington, D.C., by founder Bob Finley. With its present headquarters in Charlottesville, Virginia, this evangelical mission agency works in 40 foreign countries, engaging primarily in transmitting funds to support national workers and indigenous mission boards.

1972 Death of Watchman Nee (b.1903), Chinese devotional writer. Born Ni Shu-Tsu, he adopted the Plymouth Brethren teachings on the victorious Christian life, and began street preaching in 1924. His testimony and writings ran counter to his country's Communist ideology, and he spent the last 20 years of his life in prison.

1977 The Rev. Beverly Messenger-Harris, one of the first women to be ordained to the priesthood in the Episcopal Church in the U.S.A., became that denomination's first female rector at age 28, when she took up her duties at Gethsemane Episcopal Church in Oneida, New York.

1978 The Evangelical Free Baptist Church was incorporated by the state of Illinois, in Du Page County. The denomination withdrew from the Southern Baptist Convention, following a doctrinal dispute, and presently has 22 churches and about 2,600 members.

June 2

597 St. Augustine, missionary to England (not to be confused with the theologian St. Augustine, Bishop of Hippo), baptized Ethelbert, the Saxon king of Kent. Ethelbert had been converted through the influence of his Christian wife Bertha. Thereafter, the Christian faith spread rapidly among the Angles and the Saxons. Augustine became the first Archbishop of Canterbury.

1738 English revivalist George Whitefield asserted in his journal: "The good Mr. John Wesley has done in America, under God, is inexpressible. His name is very precious among the people; and he has laid such a foundation that I hope neither men nor devils will ever be able to shake."

1826 Death of Jean Frederic Oberlin (b.1740), German Lutheran philanthropist. At age 27, he began a ministry among the poverty-stricken in a desolate area between Alsace and Lorraine, a work he would continue for the next 60 years. His name is preserved in America through the Ohio town and college which bear his name.

June 3

1098 The armies of the First Crusade (1095–1204) captured the city of Antioch (in modern Syria). The original purpose of this crusade, proclaimed by Pope Urban II, was to relieve pressure by the Seljuk Turks on the Eastern Roman Empire and to secure safe access for pilgrims to Jerusalem.

1726 Birth of Philip William Otterbein in Dillenburg, Germany. After serving as a German Reformed pastor in his own country for a time, he traveled to America in 1752. After many years of itinerant preaching and church building, Otterbein co-founded, along with Mennonite preacher Martin Boehm, the Church of the United Brethren in Christ, in 1800. In 1946 the denomination merged with the Evangelical Church to form the Evangelical United Brethren, which merged with the Methodist Church in 1968 to form the United Methodist Church.

1851 Birth of Theodore Baker, German-born musicologist and biographical scholar. In 1900 he published *Baker's Biographical Dictionary*. In the realm of sacred music, he is remembered as the translator of the English version of "We Gather Together to Ask the Lord's Blessing."

1853 Birth of W.M. Flinders Petrie, English Egyptologist, in Kent, England. His principal archeological work was between 1880–1924 and 1927–38. The author of nearly 75 volumes, he was regarded by his generation as the greatest archeological genius of modern times.

1853 Central College was chartered in Pella, Iowa, under Baptist auspices. It awarded its first degrees in 1861. In 1916, the university passed from Baptist to Dutch Reformed control.

1879 Death of Frances Ridley Havergal (b.1836), English devotional writer. In frail health all her life, she nevertheless wrote some of the most beautiful hymns in the English language: "I Gave My Life for Thee," "Like a River Glorious," "Lord, Speak to Me That I May Speak," "Take My Life, and Let It Be" and "Who Is On the Lord's Side?"

1905 Death of J. Hudson Taylor (b.1832), English missionary to China. In 1865 he founded the China Inland Mission. At his death, he left over 200 mission stations, 850 missionaries and over 125,000 Chinese Christians in the organization. In 1965 this evangelical mission agency changed its name to Overseas Missionary Fellowship (O.M.F.) and is presently headquartered in Robesonia, Pennsylvania.

1930 Linguistic education pioneer Frank C. Laubach, while serving as a Congregational missionary to the Philippines, concluded in a letter: "As we grow older all our paths diverge, and in all the world I suppose I could find nobody who could wholly understand me excepting God."

1934 English Bible expositor A.W. Pink asserted in a letter: "The Word is an intensely practical Book. It is the chart by which we are to steer through the dangerous sea of life."

1936 Death of H.R. Mackintosh (b.1870), Church of Scotland theologian. Ordained in 1896, Mackintosh was professor of systematic theology at New College, Edinburgh, from 1904 to 1935. The theological emphasis of his writings was that forgiveness of sins is the center of the Gospel. His best-known work was *The Doctrine of the Person of Jesus Christ* (1912).

1963 Death of Pope John XXIII, 260th pontiff of the Roman Catholic Church. Born Angelo Giuseppe Roncalli on Nov. 25, 1881, he was elected to the papacy on Oct. 28, 1958. His most notable achievement was the calling of the Vatican II Ecumenical Council (1962–65), which was completed by his successor, Pope Paul VI.

1972 Sally J. Priesand, age 25, became the first woman rabbi in the U.S. when she was ordained in Cincinnati, Ohio.

June 4

1820 Birth of Elvina M. Hall, American Methodist hymnwriter, in Alexandria, Virginia. A member of the Monument Street Methodist Church in Baltimore, Maryland, for more than 40 years, she penned a verse in 1865 that was later set to music: "Jesus Paid It All" (a.k.a. "I Hear the Savior Say").

1826 Death of Carl Maria von Weber (b.1786), famed German operatic composer. He composed the hymn tune JEWETT, to which we sing the hymn "My Jesus, As Thou Wilt."

1878 Birth of Frank N. Buchman, American social theologian, in Pennsburg, Pennsylvania. Originally ordained a Lutheran minister, his lack of success in evangelism turned him to world travel. In 1908 he experienced a religious conversion in Keswick, England. He soon began developing new methods of evangelism as a means of effecting world change. He founded the First Century Christian Movement (1921), the Oxford Group (1929) and the Moral Re-Armament Movement (1938). He upheld the four absolutes of love, purity, honesty and unselfishness in his teaching.

1900 Birth of Nelson Glueck, American Jewish archeologist, in Cincinnati, Ohio. He was director of the American School of Oriental Research in Jerusalem 1932–33, 1936–40 and 1942–47. During this time, he explored and dated more than one thousand ancient sites in Palestine and the Near East.

1948 The first radio station built by the Far East Broadcasting Company went on the air for the first time, in Manila, Philippines. Founded in 1945 by Dr. Robert H. Bowman and Dr. John Broger, F.E.B.C. is an evangelical, interdenominational mission agency engaged in overseas Christian radio broadcasting and correspondence courses. Its headquarters has been in La Mirada, California, since 1979.

June 5

1940 Death of Alfred F. Loisy (b.1857), the French founder of modernism in the Roman Catholic Church. Throughout his life, the lack of intellectual honesty within Roman Catholicism disturbed him profoundly. A lifelong student of biblical criticism, Loisy revealed some extraordinary insights, yet he shifted too frequently in his views to arrive at any permanent theological conclusions. Shaken in his faith from 1886, he was excommunicated in 1908. He went on to teach the history of religions in the College de France (1909–30) and died without being reconciled to his church.

1944 German Lutheran theologian and martyr, Dietrich Bonhoeffer, commented in a letter from prison: "Certainly one must try everything, but only to become more certain what God's way is."

1960 Pope John XXIII, having earlier announced an ecumenical council (1959, 1960), established through his motu proprio, *Superno Dei Nutu*, the preparatory commissions and secretariats for the Vatican II Council (1962–1965).

1967 Beginning of the Arab-Israeli Six-Day War, during which Israel occupied the Sinai Desert, Jerusalem, and the west bank of the Jordan River. A ceasefire arranged by the United Nations ended the conflict on June 10.

June 6

1799 Birth of Alexis F. Lwoff (also spelled Lvov), Russian soldier and church musician, in Reval, Estonia. While serving at the Imperial Chapel (1837–67), he edited a well-received collection of church music based on the Greek Orthodox Church's ecclesiastical seasons of the year. One hymn tune is still in use in the West: RUSSIAN HYMN, to which is sung "God the Almighty One! Wisely Ordaining."

1844 The Young Men's Christian Association (Y.M.C.A.) was founded in London, England, by George Williams. (The first American branch was founded seven years later, 1851, in Boston.) Originally, the Y.M.C.A. was a lay, interdenominational Protestant organization that sought to win young men to Christ while developing their powers of body, mind and spirit.

1871 Death of Henry J. Buckoll (b.1803), the translator of the English version of the hymn "Come, My Soul, Thou Must Be Waking."

1882 Blind Scottish clergyman George Matheson penned the words to the haunting hymn "O Love That Wilt Not Let Me Go."

1907 Dropsie College for Hebrew and Cognate Learning, a graduate college for biblical and rabbinical studies, was chartered in Philadelphia, Pennsylvania.

1915 Death of William H. Cummings (b.1831), famed English musicologist and composer. He composed the hymn tune MENDELSSOHN, to which we sing the Christmas carol "Hark! the Herald Angels Sing."

June 7

1099 The armies of the First Crusade reached the walls of Jerusalem.

1863   Death of Franz Gruber (b.1787), Austrian church organist, and composer of the hymn tune STILLE NACHT ("Silent Night, Holy Night"). Gruber wrote more than 90 music compositions during his lifetime, yet it was this one melody he put to Joseph Mohr's words, on Christmas Eve, 1818, in the little chapel at Oberndorf, Germany, that secured his place among the ranks of the world's most beloved hymnwriters.

1891   English Baptist preacher Charles H. Spurgeon preached his last sermon at the London Metropolitan Tabernacle. He died the following January. During his 38-year ministry at the Tabernacle, he added over 14,000 new members to the original congregation of 6,000.

1913   Ohio-born Methodist evangelist George Bennard introduced his famous hymn, "The Old Rugged Cross," for the first time at one of his special evangelistic meetings in Pokagon, Michigan.

1934   Wycliffe Bible Translators held its first linguistic training course, at Camp Wycliffe in Sulphur Springs, Arkansas. The study lasted three months, extending to Sept. 7 of that year.

1959   English literary scholar and Christian apologist C.S. Lewis explained in *Letters to an American Lady*: "If we really think that home is elsewhere and that this life is a 'wandering to find home,' why should we not look forward to the arrival?"

June 8

632   The prophet Mohammed is believed by Muslims to have ascended into heaven from a rock in Jerusalem where the ancient Temple of Solomon once stood. The Muslim shrine later constructed on the site is known as the Dome of the Rock.

1191   King Richard I ("the Lionhearted") of England arrived at the beseiged Palestinian port city of Acre (Acco) during the Third Crusade (1189–1192).

1612   Death of Hans Leo Hassler (b.1564), musician and hymnwriter who wrote the Lenten hymn tune PASSION CHORALE for "O Sacred Head, Now Wounded." One of the eminent organists of his day, Hassler was the first notable German musician to be educated in Italy.

1810   Birth of Robert A. Schumann, German composer, at Zwickau, Saxony. During his prodigious music career, he wrote symphonies and chamber music and was an early leader in the Romantic school of 19th-century music. One hymn tune of his which still endures is CANONBURY, to which we sing the hymn "Lord, Speak to Me That I May Speak."

1913   Death of Charles A. Briggs (b.1841), American clergyman and biblical scholar. For over 30 years he taught at Union Theological Seminary in New York City. Ordained a Presbyterian pastor in 1870, he was defrocked in 1892 by that denomination on the dubious charge of heresy. In 1900 Briggs was ordained in the Episcopal Church. Among the many scholarly works he published, one of the best known was *A Critical and Exegetical Commentary on the Book of Psalms* (1906–07).

1942 U.F.M. International was first incorporated in the U.S., in Philadelphia, Pennsylvania. Formerly called The Unevangelized Fields Mission, this evangelical, interdenominational mission agency is primarily engaged in evangelism, church planting, theological education, Bible translation and medical assistance. Headquartered in Bala Cynwyd, Pennsylvania, U.F.M. International (the new name it adopted in 1980) works in a dozen countries in Latin America, Europe and Africa.

1978 After nearly 150 years of religious discrimination against Blacks, president of the Mormon church, Spencer W. Kimball, sent a copy of the new policies to all general and local priesthood officers of the Church of Jesus Christ of Latter-Day Saints throughout the world. The letter stated, ". . . all worthy male members of the Church may be ordained to the priesthood without regard for race or color." Two days later, Joseph Freeman, 26, a Salt Lake City telephone repairman and father of three, became the first black man ordained into the priesthood in the Mormon church.

June 9

68 Death of Nero Claudius Caesar (b.37), the Caesar to whom the Apostle Paul appealed for justice in Acts 25:10. Nero was the first Roman emperor to persecute the Christians, and is traditionally linked to the martyrdom of both Peter and Paul. Nero later alienated the entire nation of Rome, and died by his own hand rather than be captured and executed by his enemies.

597 Death of St. Columba (b.521), pioneer missionary to Scotland. Born of a noble Irish family, he founded several churches and monasteries in his own country before departing in 563 for the Scottish Isle of Iona. From this base, Columba evangelized the mainland of Scotland and Northumbria.

1549 In the recently established Church of England, the first Act of Uniformity was enacted. It imposed exclusive use of the Book of Common Prayer in all public religious services, laying down penalties for those clerics who failed to comply.

1732 James Edward Oglethorpe received a royal charter for the formation of the American colony of Georgia. The colony was to be a place of refuge for persecuted Protestant sects in England as well as for the law-abiding poor.

1784 Father John Carroll was appointed superior of the American missions by Pius VI. This was the first step toward the organization of the Roman Catholic Church in the U.S. There were approximately 25,000 Catholics living in America, among a general population of 4 million. Five years later, in 1789, Fr. Carroll was placed in charge of the Diocese of Baltimore, becoming the first bishop ordained in the U.S.

1790 Death of Robert Robinson (b.1735), English Calvinist clergyman. Robinson was converted to the Christian faith in 1755, following three years of turmoil after hearing George Whitefield preach. He wrote many theological works during his life, but is remembered principally as the author of a single hymn: "Come, Thou Fount of Every Blessing."

1834 Death of William Carey (b.1761), English Baptist missionary. The Baptist Missionary Society was founded in 1792 largely through his influence. In 1793 he sailed for India; and completed a translation of the entire Bible into Bengali by 1809. Before his death, he had published complete Bibles and portions into 24 other languages and dialects, rendering the Scriptures accessible to more than 300 million people. Carey is referred to as "the father of modern missions."

1855 Birth of Gustaf H. Dalman, German Bible scholar. Moravian in background, he held teaching posts in both Germany and Palestine. His extensive research into the language and customs of 1st-century Judaism established that Jesus' ordinary language was Aramaic, not Greek. One of Dalman's famous works is the book *The Words of Jesus* (1898).

1911 Death of Carry Nation (b.1846), American temperance leader. After an unhappy marriage to a drunkard, she joined the prohibitionists. In 1899 she began her notorious career by wrecking all the saloons in Medicine Lodge, Kansas. She used an ax in her 1901 crusades against the saloons in Wichita and Topeka. She did much to help the prohibition movement in the U.S.

1957 The religious TV program *American Religious Town Hall* aired for the last time over ABC television. A panel show debating religious and moral topics, it was moderated by James A. Pike, and seen Sunday afternoons. The program was canceled after 15 months on the air.

1970 Death of Mrs. (William) Esther K. Miller (b.1894), who with her husband co-founded the Basil Miller Foundation, in Altadena, California, in 1957. In 1959 its name was changed to World-Wide Missions. This evangelical, interdenominational missionary organization, headquartered today in Pasadena, California, engages in relief, medical and other aid for national churches in over 30 countries.

June 10

1692 Bridget Bishop became the first person hanged for witchcraft during the 20-month ordeal known today as the "Salem Witch Trials." Nineteen people were hanged and one was pressed to death in the isolated Puritan community of Salem, Massachusetts.

1850 The American Bible Union was founded, organized by Baptists who had seceded from the American and Foreign Bible Society.

1877 Death of Friedrich A.G. Tholuck (b.1799), German Lutheran Bible scholar. His influence did much to check the domination of rationalistic scholarship in Germany.

1921 Death of Edwin O. Excell (b.1851), American hymnwriter. Converted at a Methodist revival, Excell turned his energies toward sacred music. For the rest of his life he was active in the publication of Gospel songbooks and leading music at Sunday School conventions. He wrote both words and music to more than 2,000 Gospel songs, three of which still remain popular: "Since I Have Been Redeemed" (a.k.a. "I Have a Song I Love to Sing"), "I'll Be a Sunbeam" and "Count Your Blessings" (a.k.a. "When Upon Life's Billows You Are Tempest-Tossed").

1925 The United Church of Canada was formed, uniting both the Methodist and the Presbyterian Churches of Canada. Merger talks began in 1902, and the formal union took in about 3,000 Congregational churches in Canada as well as other union churches in the western part of the country.

1967 The Six-Day Arab-Israeli War (begun June 5) ended when Israel successfully captured Jordanian territory on the west bank of the Jordan River, the Arab quarter of Jerusalem, the Gaza strip on the west coast of Palestine and the Egyptian Sinai Peninsula.

1983 The Presbyterian Church (U.S.A.) (with three million members) was formed in Atlanta, Georgia, through the re-unification of the United Presbyterian Church in the U.S.A. (U.P.C.U.S.A.) and the Presbyterian Church in the U.S. (P.C.U.S.). The two groups had separated 122 years before because of the American Civil War.

June 11

1739 English founder of Methodism John Wesley stated in his journal: "I look upon all the world as my parish."

1799 Richard Allen (1760–1831), the first black bishop in the U.S., was ordained a deacon in the Methodist Episcopal Church.

1860 Birth of Charles Hurlburt, who served as general director of the Africa Inland Mission, Inc., for 28 years (1897–1925). It was Hurlburt who pioneered the work of A.I.M. in East Africa and the Congo (modern Zaire). A.I.M. was founded in 1895 in Philadelphia, Pennsylvania, by missionary Peter Cameron Scott.

1912 Birth of David C. Cook, American evangelical publisher, in Elgin, Illinois. Cook was founder and first president of the David C. Cook Publishing Company, a Sunday School materials publisher headquartered in Elgin.

1936 Led by Dr. J. Gresham Machen, the Presbyterian Church of America was organized in Philadelphia, Pennsylvania. The denomination was formed by local congregations within the United Presbyterian Church (U.S.A.), who felt there were too many liberal tendencies in the larger body. A lawsuit by the parent body forced the group to change its name to the Orthodox Presbyterian Church in 1938.

1978 Joseph Freeman of Salt Lake City, Utah, a 26-year-old telephone repairman and father of three, became the first black ordained to the priesthood in the nearly 150-year history of the Mormon church.

June 12

1458 The College of St. Mary Magdalen was founded at Oxford University in England.

1720 Birth of Isaac Pinto, translator of the first Jewish prayerbook published in America.

1744 David Brainerd was ordained a missionary at Newark, New Jersey, by American representatives of the Society of Scotland for Propagating Christian Knowledge. Brainerd later became a missionary to the Indians of colonial New England (1744–47).

1819 Birth of Charles Kingsley, Anglican clergyman and novelist, in Devon-shire, England. His disparaging remarks to Anglican-turned-Catholic John Henry Newman in 1863 (he said that Newman had little respect for truth) motivated Newman to write his famous *Apologia Pro Vita Sua*. Kingsley's novels were generally formulated around social issues. Several are still read today, including *Westward Ho* and *The Water Babies*.

1890 At the opening of the annual session of the Norwegian Lutheran Church of America, three synods of the church united to form the United Norwegian Lutheran Free Church of America.

1898 Death of Sanford F. Bennett (b.1836), American hymnwriter and author of the hymn "Sweet By and By" (a.k.a. "There's a Land That Is Fairer Than Day").

1909 Birth of Charles Feinberg, fundamentalist American theologian. He taught at Dallas Theological Seminary, The Bible Institute of Los Angeles (B.I.O.L.A.), and at Talbot Theological Seminary.

1914 The first edition of A.T. Robertson's monumental *A Grammar of the Greek New Testament in the Light of Historical Research* was published by Hodder & Stoughton. Five editions have followed the original.

1919 Death of John H. Sammis (b.1846), American Presbyterian clergyman and author of the hymn "Trust and Obey" (a.k.a. "When We Walk with the Lord").

1929 Birth of Anne Frank, a Jewish teenager famous for her diary, in Frankfort-am-Main, Germany. At the age of four, she and her family left Germany for Amsterdam, Netherlands, to escape Nazi persecution. In July 1942 her family and four others were forced into hiding, and managed to evade detection until Aug. 1944. Taken into custody by German occupation forces, Anne died in March 1945 at the Bergen-Belson German concentration camp. Anne's diary was later discovered in the family's hiding place, and first published in 1947.

1950 American missionary and Auca Indian martyr Jim Elliot warned in his journal: "Earthly blessing is no sign of heavenly favor. Behold how many wicked prosper."

June 13

1231 Death of St. Anthony of Padua (b.1195), a celebrated scholarly friar. A member of the Augustinian Canons earlier in his life, Anthony later joined the Franciscans and was appointed by St. Francis of Assisi to be the first teacher of the new order. A year after his death at 36, Anthony was canonized by Pope Gregory IX.

1525 German reformer Martin Luther (1483–1546) married Katherine von Bora (1499–1552), a former nun. She was 26, he was 42. Their 21-year marriage was a happy one, which saw the birth of six children. Kate outlived her husband by six years.

1742 English founder of Methodism John Wesley cautioned in his journal: "Oh, let none think his labor of love is lost because the fruit does not im-mediately appear!"

1816   Birth of Edward F. Rimbault, English church organist and music scholar, in London. He composed the hymn tune HAPPY DAY, to which we sing the hymn "O Happy Day, That Fixed My Choice."

1840   Birth of John Stainer, church organist and choral master, in London, England. During his lifetime, he wrote over 150 hymn tunes. Two are still in use today as the tunes for the "Four-fold Amen" and the "Seven-fold Amen."

1861   Birth of Karl P. Harrington, American classics scholar, in Somersworth, New Hampshire. Recognized also as an accomplished musician, Harrington also served in various Methodist churches as organist and choir director. He contributed twelve hymn tunes to the 1905 edition of the Methodist hymnal. One of these, CHRISTMAS SONG ("There's a Song in the Air"), is still popular.

1876   The Presbyterian Church of England merged with the United Presbyterian Church of Scotland.

1897   Birth of Reuben Larson, missions pioneer. In 1931 Larson co-founded the World Radio Missionary Fellowship in Lima, Ohio, with Clarence W. Jones. In 1969 the W.R.M.F. headquarters was moved to Opa Locka, Florida.

1909   Birth of Cyril C. Richardson, English church historian, in London, England. Raised an Episcopalian, Richardson is best known for his definitive compilations of early Christian writings. One work is still in print: *The Early Christian Fathers* (1953).

1965   Death of Martin Buber (b.1878), Jewish religious philosopher. Influenced by Kierkegaard's Christian existentialism, Buber developed the description of the "I-Thou" relationship, for which he saw Judaism as uniquely suited. The value of this concept for the Christian faith is that personalized religious truth is dynamic, not doctrinal. One believes in God by holding fast to God, by experiencing God, not by knowing propositional truth about God. To Buber, God was the "Eternal Thou."

1972   American Presbyterian apologist Francis Schaeffer declared in a letter: "As Christians we are called upon to exhibit the character of God, and this means the simultaneous exhibition of His holiness and His love."

June 14

1744   Colonial American missionary to the New England Indians David Brainerd in his journal: "God is very gracious to me, both in health and sickness, and intermingles much mercy with all my afflictions and toils."

1811   Birth of Harriet Beecher Stowe, American novelist, in Litchfield, Connecticut. The daughter of Lyman Beecher and the sister of Henry Ward Beecher, she was converted to Christ at age 13. In 1852 she published her best-known novel, *Uncle Tom's Cabin*. The work solidified antislavery sentiment and helped to precipitate the American Civil War.

1827   Death of Johann G. Eichhorn (b.1752), German Old Testament scholar. Eichhorn was among the early source critics attributing the Book of Genesis to the conflation of two previous sources: the "Yahwist" (J source) and the "Elohist" (E source). He also held that the three New Testament Synoptic

Gospels were all based on a single, lost Aramaic Gospel. Eichhorn's most important writing was his three-volume *Introduction to the Old Testament* (1780–83). The accuracy of some of his work has been questioned by modern scholars.

1837   Birth of William C. Dix, English insurance agent who authored "As with Gladness Men of Old," in Bristol.

1901   Death of Ralph E. Hudson (b.1843), American Methodist clergyman and music publisher. Devoting much of his time to evangelistic work, Hudson published several volumes of original Gospel songs. Three of his hymns that we still sing are "At the Cross" (a.k.a. "Alas, and Did My Savior Bleed"), "Blessed Be the Name" and "I'll Live for Him."

1936   Death of G.K. (Gilbert Keith) Chesterton (b.1874), English journalist and author. Converted from Anglicanism to the Roman Catholic faith in 1922, his writings interpreted the Christian faith from a mystical Catholic viewpoint. It was his belief that the church was the only institution in which a true humanism could develop.

1966   The Vatican announced that its "Index of Prohibited Books" had been abolished. The Index, originally created by Pope Paul IV in 1557, listed books which Catholics were forbidden to read, possess or sell under penalty of excommunication. After 1966 the Index no longer had the force of law within the Catholic church.

1984   The Southern Baptist Convention passed a resolution opposing the ordination of women for ministry in the Baptist church. The resolution was made nonbinding for local congregations, and did not apply to women who had already been ordained for ministry.

June 15

1215   King John of England set his seal to preliminary demands of the barons at Runnymede. The resulting document, called the *Magna Carta*, established some basic rights for the people of England. One clause insured: "No free man shall be taken or imprisoned or dispossessed, or outlawed, or banished, or in any way destroyed . . . except by the legal judgment of his peers or by the law of the land."

1520   Pope Leo X issued the papal encyclical *Exsurge Domine*, which condemned Martin Luther as a heretic on 41 counts and branded him an enemy of the Roman Catholic Church.

1649   Margaret Jones of Charlestown, Massachusetts, became the first person tried and executed for witchcraft in Massachusetts.

1803   Catholics in Massachusetts were finally granted religious freedom by the state constitution of June 15, 1780.

1807   Birth of William Nast, founder of German Methodism, at Stuttgart, Wurttemberg, Germany. Nast came to America in 1828 and was ordained in 1835 to the Ohio Annual Conference of the Methodist Episcopal Church. He worked to organize German settlers in America into churches. He founded a successful Methodist mission in Germany and also helped found Wallace College in Berea, Ohio (which later merged to become Baldwin-Wallace University).

1834 English cardinal John Henry Newman observed in a letter: "Would we could so command our minds as to make them feel as they ought! But it is their very disease. . . that they are excited by objects of this world, not by the realities of death and judgment, and the mercies of the Gospel."

1893 Death of John Ellerton (b.1826), Anglican clergyman and hymnwriter. His hymns and interest in hymnology earned him great respect among his peers, and his counsel was sought by compilers of every major hymnal published in the last half of the 19th century. One hymn of his which is still sung is "Savior, Again to Thy Dear Name We Raise."

1950 American missionary and Auca Indian martyr Jim Elliot asserted in his journal: "A man without Christ has his roots only in his own times, and his fruits as well."

1979 The Greater Europe Mission moved its headquarters from Chicago to Wheaton, Illinois. Founded by Robert P. Evans in 1949 (as the European Bible Institute), G.E.M. is today an interdenominational, evangelical mission organization supporting missionaries in over a dozen European countries, and is engaged chiefly in evangelism, church planting, literature distribution and theological education.

June 16

1539 German reformer Martin Luther declared: "Faith justifies not as a work, or as a quality, or as knowledge, but as assent of the will and firm confidence in the mercy of God."

1752 Death of Joseph Butler (b.1692), Anglican clergyman and theologian. Ordained in 1718, he held various pastorates until 1750, when he was made Bishop of Durham, the wealthiest diocese in England. Butler lived during the "golden age of deism," and sought to combat his generation's contempt for revealed religion. To this end he penned his famous *The Analogy of Religion, Natural and Revealed, to the Constitution and Course of Nature* (1736). Butler's *Analogy* demonstrated the strong probabilities of the existence of a theistic, caring God over that of a deistic, disinterested Creator God. Butler's text was long used as required reading in Christian apologetics in universities both in England and America.

1804 Anglican missionary to Persia Henry Martyn confessed in his journal: "My soul, alas, needs these uneasinesses in outward things, to be driven to take refuge in God."

1833 Anglican-turned-Catholic Cardinal John Henry Newman, while on a ship traveling from Italy to France, penned the words to the hymn of trust "Lead Kindly Light, Amid th' Encircling Gloom."

1909 Death of Erastus Johnson (b.1826), American rancher and farmer who wrote the hymn "The Rock That is Higher Than I" (a.k.a. "O Sometimes the Shadows Are Deep") in 1873. Throughout his active life he remained a devoted Christian and student of the Bible.

1948 Death of Rufus M. Jones (b.1863), American Quaker theologian. He did much to advance the cause and organization of Quakerism in America, his influence reaching far beyond just his denomination. He wrote 56 books and hundreds of articles on the general theme of translating mystical experience into redemptive social action. Jones helped found the American Friends Service Committee in 1917 and served as its chairman for over 20 years.

June 17

1700 A Massachusetts law was passed which allowed three months for any Roman Catholic priest to leave the colony. If he remained, he would be arrested as "an enemy to the true Christian religion." If found guilty, he could be imprisoned for life or executed.

1703 Birth of John Wesley, founder of Methodism, in Epworth, England. Ordained in the Anglican Church in 1728, he joined his brother Charles the following year in their "Holy Club," which developed methodical procedures in meeting, study, prayer and weekly communion. He did not claim an experiential faith until 1738, after which he embarked on a career in evangelism and church planting. Eventually forced out of Anglican pulpits, Wesley officially chartered the Methodist Episcopal denomination in 1784. From small beginnings in 1760, the Methodist movement eventually spread widely in America. Eighteenth-century England was no doubt spared divine judgment by the revival generated by the Wesley brothers.

1812 Pioneer American Baptist missionary Adoniram Judson and his wife, Ann Hasseltine Judson, first arrived in Calcutta, India. The following year, they went to Rangoon, Burma, where Judson served during the remaining 37 years of his life.

1822 The first elders were elected in what later became the African Methodist Episcopal (A.M.E.) Zion Church, in New York City. Abraham Thompson, James Varick and Leven Smith were ordained by three elders of the Methodist Episcopal Church.

1846 Iowa College was chartered in Davenport, Iowa, under the joint sponsorship of the Congregational and Presbyterian churches. In 1859 the school moved to Grinnell, Iowa, and was renamed Grinnell College in 1909.

1852 Birth of Fredrik Franson, who founded The Evangelical Alliance Mission (T.E.A.M.) in Chicago, Illinois, in 1890. T.E.A.M. is an interdenominational mission agency working in 25 countries, and committed primarily to evangelism, church planting and development. The organization is also involved in providing Christian education, literature, linguistic training, radio and medical assistance.

1859 Birth of J. Wilbur Chapman, U.S. Presbyterian pastor and evangelist, in Richmond, Indiana. In addition to his active ministry, Chapman was also the first director of the Winona Lake Bible Conference, in Indiana, and was later instrumental in founding similar conferences at Montreat, North Carolina, and Stony Brook, New York. He authored a number of hymns, including "Jesus! What a Friend of Sinners!" (a.k.a. "Our Great Savior") and "One Day When Heaven Was Filled with His Praises."

1963 English literary scholar and Christian apologist C.S. Lewis asked in *Letters to an American Lady*: "Can you not see death as the friend and deliverer? . . .Has this world been so kind to you that you should leave it with regret? There are better things ahead than any we leave behind."

1963 The U.S. Supreme Court ruled that classroom prayer and Bible reading in public schools was unconstitutional.

June 18

1429 Joan of Arc, "the Maid of Orleans," led the French army to victory over the English at Patay.

1464 Pope Pius II took up the cross to begin a crusade against the Turks. Making his way to the rendezvous city of Ancona, Italy, he became ill and died before the rest of his allies arrived. Although the last of the seven major crusades ended in 1274, the idea persisted for another two centuries. With Pius's death, the crusades mentality came to an end.

1819 Birth of Samuel Longfellow, American clergyman and hymnwriter, in Portland, Maine. The brother of poet and author Henry Wadsworth Longfellow, Samuel also wrote and published verses. Several have since become the texts of popular hymns, including "Father, Give Thy Benediction."

1830 Birth of Elizabeth C. Clephane, Scottish poetess, in Edinburgh, Scotland. Orphaned at an early age and in poor health throughout her short life (she died in 1869), she was nevertheless known for her humanitarian relief of the poor and sick in her community. One of the few female poets from Scotland, she left a rare legacy to Christian hymnody. Two of her haunting poems have been set to music and are sung in the church today: "Beneath the Cross of Jesus" and "The Ninety and Nine."

1849 Death of William B. Tappan (b.1794), American Sunday school promoter. Orphaned at twelve, Tappan learned clockmaking and followed it until 1822, when a growing interest in the Sunday school movement led to his employment with the American Sunday School Union—an association he maintained until his death. A prolific poet, he published ten volumes of verse. One became a hymn that is still popular: "'Tis Midnight, And on Olive's Brow."

1906 Birth of Gordon Lindsay, who with his wife, Freda, founded Christ for the Nations, Inc.; in Shreveport, Louisiana, in 1948. Christ for the Nations, Inc., is a charismatic, interdenominational mission agency headquartered in Dallas, Texas. It assists missions by raising funds for church construction and literature production.

1956 Death of Dawson E. Trotman (b.1906), founder and first president of the Navigators. This interdenominational organization, headquartered since 1954 in Colorado Springs, Colorado, is engaged in ministry to servicemen here and overseas, and works in 30 countries in individual training in personal evangelism, discipleship, and Bible memorization.

June 19

325 The First Council of Nicea opened, the first ecumenical council in the history of the church. The council formulated the Nicene Creed, established the method for calculating Easter, and condemned the heretical views of Arianism.

1566 Birth of King James I of England (James VI of Scotland). He ascended the Scottish throne in 1657 on the abdication of his mother, Mary Queen of Scots. He received the English throne in 1603 at the death of Elizabeth I. At the 1604 Hampton Court Conference, he authorized a translation of the Bible into English, which was published in 1611 and has become known as the King James Version.

1623 Birth of Blaise Pascal, mathematician, scientist and religious thinker, in Clermont, France. By age 20, he had invented a calculating machine, a machine which eventually led to development of the electronic computer. He discovered Pascal's Law, the principle behind all modern hydraulic operations. Theologically, he defended the Jansenists, conservative reformers within the French Roman Catholic Church who opposed the liberalism of the Jesuits. Pascal died at 39, before publishing a systematic collection of his theological reflections and insights. These remarkable, scattered notes were collected under one cover by others and published under the title *Pensees* (*Thoughts*) as early as 1670, eight years after his death.

1834 Birth of Charles Haddon Spurgeon, English Baptist preacher, in Essex, England. Converted at age 16 (1850), the following year he embarked on his illustrious career as a pastor. Crowds overflowed his churches so he built the London Metropolitan Tabernacle in 1859. Spurgeon remained in London the rest of his life, adding over 14,000 new members to the Metropolitan Tabernacle before an early death at age 58 took him in 1892.

1848 Birth of Henry Adeney Redpath, English Old Testament scholar. His greatest work, co-edited by Edwin Hatch, was an exhaustive list of all the words used in the ancient Greek translation of the Old Testament, the *Septuagint*. Published in three volumes from 1892–1906, this monumental work bore the full title *A Concordance to the Septuagint and the other Greek Versions of the Old Testament (Including the Apocryphal Books)*. It is still in print and continues to stand as a classic in textual scholarship, unequaled by any project similarly produced by computer.

1954 Death of William P. Merrill (b.1867), American Presbyterian clergyman who wrote the hymn "Rise Up, O Men of God." Widely known from his pastorate at the Brick Presbyterian Church in New York City (1911–38), Merrill authored a number of books, as well as several other hymns.

1977 Pope Paul VI canonized 19th-century Redemptorist John Nepomucene Neumann, fourth Bishop of the Philadelphia diocese, who was known for his development of the parochial school. Neumann became the first American-born male to achieve sainthood in the Catholic church.

June 20

1336 In an effort to correct abuses which had crept into the Catholic church, Pope Benedict XII issued the encyclical *Summi Magistri*, which reconstituted the ancient religious order of the Benedictines. This constitution remained in effect until the Council of Trent (1545–63).

1529 Pope Clement VII and Holy Roman Emperor Charles V signed the Peace of Barcelona, which ended attacks on Rome by the Lutheran armies.

1599 The Synod of Diamper, held on the coast of southwest India, reunited the Indian church with Rome. Discovered by the Portuguese in 1498, this pocket of Christians supposedly dated back to the missionary efforts of the Apostle Thomas. The Diamper Synod was convened to root out the Nestorian heresy perpetuated in the Indian church while in isolation and bring it into greater theological conformity with the western (Roman) church.

1772 English founder of Methodism John Wesley warned in a letter: "Of all gossiping, religious gossiping is the worst: It adds hypocrisy to uncharitableness, and effectually does the work of the devil in the name of the Lord."

1776 Anglican clergyman and hymnwriter John Newton explained in a letter: "A Christian is not of hasty growth, like a mushroom, but rather like the oak, the progress of which is hardly perceptible, but in time becomes a great deep-rooted tree."

1779 Birth of Dorothy Ann Thrupp, English hymnwriter, in London. She wrote several hymns, but left some of them unsigned. One that is known to be hers is the hymn "Savior, Like a Shepherd Lead Us."

1809 Birth of Isaac August Dorner, Lutheran theologian, in Wurttemberg, Germany. His multi-volume work *History of the Development of the Doctrines of the Person of Christ* was first translated into English in 1861, and made him the distinguished German Christological scholar of his generation. His work is still considered important today.

1885 A band of Moravian missionaries landed on the shores of Alaska and founded the Bethel Mission.

June 21

1639 Birth of Increase Mather, colonial American minister, in Dorchester, Massachusetts. Ordained in 1657, he became pastor of North Church in Boston in 1664, and remained there until his death nearly 60 years later, in 1723. Also president of Harvard College 1684–1701, Mather published nearly 100 books. He is credited with helping end executions for witchcraft in colonial America.

1745 David Brainerd, colonial American missionary to the New England Indians, declared in his journal: "O blessed be God, who lays me under a happy, a blessed necessity of living upon himself!"

1821 Birth of Henry W. Baker, Anglican hymn compiler, in London, England. He was the originator (and editorial chairman for 20 years) of *Hymns Ancient and Modern*—the unofficial Anglican church hymnal. Among his many editorial contributions to hymnody, Baker authored the enduring hymn based on Psalm 23: "The King of Love My Shepherd Is."

1821 The newly formed African Methodist Episcopal Zion Church held its first Conference in Zion Church in New York City. At the conference, a limited episcopacy was established, and James Varick was elected the first bishop (thereafter called "superintendent").

1836 Birth of Sanford Fillmore Bennett, American newspaper editor and pharmacist, in Eden, New York. The author of many poems, Bennett penned the words to the hymn "Sweet By and By" (a.k.a. "There's a Land That Is Fairer Than Day").

1892 Birth of Reinhold Niebuhr, American theologian, in Wright City, Missouri. From 1928–60 he was professor of applied Christianity at Union Theological Seminary in New York City. Though influenced by Karl Barth's rejection of liberalism, Niebuhr rejected Barth's nonparticipation in society and sought to make biblical faith real in the secular world. Niebuhr's most enduring writing was *The Nature and Destiny of Man* (1941,1943).

1897 Death of Clara H. Scott (b.1841), American music educator. A creative teacher and hymnwriter, she published *The Royal Anthem Book* in 1882, the first collection of anthems published by a woman. She also penned the words and music to the hymn "Open My Eyes, That I May See."

1963 Italian Cardinal Giovanni Battista Montini was elected Pope Paul VI, in Rome—the 261st pontiff of the Roman Catholic Church.

1968 Swiss Reformed theologian Karl Barth declared in a letter: "Faith in God's revelation has nothing to do with an ideology which glorifies the status quo."

1975 The six-part miniseries *Moses the Lawgiver* premiered on CBS television. This Italian-English production featured Burt Lancaster as Moses, Anthony Quayle as Aaron, Irene Papas as Zipporah, and Laurent Terzieff as Pharaoh. Filmed in Israel, this series on the life of Moses ran weekly through Aug. 2.

June 22

1559 Queen Elizabeth's Prayer Book was issued, a revision of the Second Prayer Book of Edward VI. Elizabeth I, daughter of Henry VIII and Anne Boleyn, was the third and last of Henry's children to occupy the throne. During her 45-year reign (1558–1603), she adopted the 39 Articles of the Anglican Church, presided over the defeat of the Spanish Armada, and restored popular confidence in the monarchy.

1714 Death of Matthew Henry (b.1662), English Presbyterian Bible commentator. Ordained in 1687, he pastored for the next 25 years at Chester, in Cheshire County, England. He wrote the Bible commentary *Exposition of the Old and New Testaments*—first begun in 1704 and completed by others soon after his death. This monumental work is still published as *Matthew Henry's Commentary*. The value of his commentary lies more in its devotional and practical emphasis than for its critical textual insights.

1745 Colonial American missionary to the New England Indians David Brainerd recorded in his journal: "I am often weary of this world, and want to leave it on that account; but it is more desirable to be drawn, rather than driven out of it."

1750 New England colonial preacher Jonathan Edwards was dismissed from his pulpit at the Congregational Church in Northampton, Massachusetts, after serving there 23 years. A controversy had erupted over the requirements for admission to full membership in the church. Edwards took the more restrictive view, in scrupulous alignment with his theology. For his unyielding stand, he was released from the pastorate.

1850 Death of William Walford (b.1772), English Congregational clergyman and religious writer. He published several works, including a translation of the Psalms. In the late 1830s he penned the lines to "Sweet Hour of Prayer."

1870 The committee of New Testament scholars appointed to work on the Revised Version of the Bible began its work. The complete New Testament of the R.V. (more commonly termed the English Version or English Revised Version) was published in 1881, and the Old Testament was completed in 1885. The American Standard Version of 1901 built on the R.V.

1874 Death of Lydia Baxter (b.1809), American Baptist lay worker and hymnwriter. Though an invalid most of her life, her home became a gathering place for preachers, evangelists, and Christian workers. She wrote and published religious verse and popular Gospel hymns, including the hymn "Take the Name of Jesus with You."

1930 Pioneer linguistic educator Frank C. Laubach, while a missionary to the Philippines, commented in a letter: "People ought to take a walk every evening all alone where they can talk aloud without being heard by anyone, and during this entire walk they ought to talk with God, allowing Him to use their tongues to talk back—and letting God do most of the talking."

1963 Reformed Swiss theologian Karl Barth commented in a letter: "Perhaps in heaven what is now hidden from me will be disclosed, but it is a pity it doesn't happen how."

June 23

1415 Bohemian reformer and martyr John Huss remarked in a letter: "Surely it is difficult to rejoice without perturbation, and to esteem it all joy in various temptations. It is easy to talk about it and to expound it, but difficult to fulfill it."

1516 German reformer Martin Luther stated in a letter: "It is not the man whom nobody bothers who has peace. That kind of peace is the peace of the world. It is that man whom everybody disturbs and everything harasses and yet who joyfully and quietly endures them all."

1683 English Quaker William Penn signed his famous treaty with the Indians of Pennsylvania. Voltaire said the agreement was the only treaty never sworn to and never broken.

1738 Birth of Samuel Medley, Baptist clergyman, in Hertfordshire, England. He wrote many hymns during his lifetime, including "O Could I Speak the Matchless Worth."

1775 Anglican hymnwriter John Newton explained in a letter: "The truths of Scripture are not like mathematical theorems which present exactly the same ideas to every person who understands the terms. . . . True religion is not a science of the head so much as an inward and heartfelt perception. . . . Here the learned have no real advantage above the ignorant; both see when the eyes of the understanding are enlightened; till then, both are equally blind."

1942 Death of Emily D. Wilson (b.1865), American Methodist pastor's wife and talented songwriter. She wrote the hymn tune HEAVEN, to which we sing "When We All Get to Heaven" (a.k.a. "Sing the Wondrous Love of Jesus").

June 24

1415 Imprisoned Bohemian reformer John Huss, shortly before his death at the stake, mentioned in a letter: "I take it for certain that God has given you as angels to me, comforting me, weak and wretched, in greatest trials."

1519 Birth of Theodore Beza, French-born Swiss reformer, at Vezelay in Burgundy. In 1548 at age 29, Beza renounced Catholicism for Calvinism. At Calvin's invitation, he became professor of Greek at Lausanne, serving from 1549–58. Upon Calvin's death in 1564, Beza became the acknowledged leader of the Swiss Calvinists. In 1565 he brought out his first critical edition of the Greek New Testament.

1803 Birth of George J. Webb, American sacred music organist, near Salisbury, England. Moving to the U.S. in 1830, he was church organist at Old South Church in Boston for 40 years (1830–70). He helped compose, compile and edit several music collections during his lifetime. One of his popular hymn tunes is WEBB ("Stand Up, Stand Up for Jesus").

1813 Birth of Henry Ward Beecher, American Congregational clergyman, in Litchfield, Connecticut. He was the son of Lyman Beecher and brother of Harriet Beecher Stowe. Henry was ordained in 1837 and held only three pastorates during his 50-year ministry. He was an active abolitionist, but condemned violent methods of winning freedom for the slaves.

1917 Death of Orville J. Nave, U.S. Armed Services chaplain and editor of *Nave's Topical Bible*.

June 25

1115 St. Bernard (1090–1153) founded the fourth house of the Cistercians in Clairvaux, France, and was also made the first abbot. The monastery at Clairvaux became one of the main centers of the Cistercian religious order. The order flourished until the 15th century, when the Reformation and European civil wars contributed to its decline.

1580 The German *Book of Concord* was published containing all the official confessions of the Lutheran Church: the three ecumenical creeds (Apostles', Nicene and Athanasian), Martin Luther's Small and Large Catechisms (1529), the Augsburg Confession of 1530, the Augsburg Apology of 1531, the Smalcald Articles and the *Tract Concerning the Power and Primacy of the Pope* (1537), and the *Epitome and Thorough Declaration of the Formula of Concord* (1577). No English translation of the entire work appeared before 1851.

1744 The first Methodist conference in history convened, in London. It set the standards for doctrine, liturgy and discipline. The need for the conference was John Wesley's successful efforts to organize converts of his and George Whitefield's "Evangelical Revival" (starting in 1739) into regularly meeting groups which would sustain the new converts and the revival. England's 18th-century revival continued for the next 50 years, principally under Wesley's leadership.

1845 The Lutheran Synod of Buffalo was organized. Eighty-five years later, on Aug. 11, 1930, its group merged with two other synods to form the American Lutheran Church.

1865 Pioneer missionary J. Hudson Taylor founded the China Inland Mission in Great Britain. The headquarters moved to the U.S. in 1901. In 1965 the organization changed its name to Overseas Missionary Fellowship. O.M.F. supports over 150 missionaries in 9 Southeast Asian and Pacific countries.

1957 The United Church of Christ was established by a general synod uniting the Congregational Christian churches and the Evangelical and Reformed Church. The merger became official in July 1961, with the adoption of a constitution at Philadelphia, Pennsylvania.

1962 The U.S. Supreme Court ruled six to one that reciting a 22-word prayer in the New York State public schools violated the First Amendment of the U.S. Constitution.

1981 American Presbyterian apologist Francis Schaeffer wrote in a letter: "The Lord made everything, and Christ died to redeem everything. And though full restoration will not come until Christ returns, it is our calling, looking to Christ for help, to try to bring substantial restoration in every area of life."

June 26

1097 The armies of the First Crusade occupied the ancient Byzantine city of Nicaea (the modern village of Iznik, in northwest Turkey). Before the crusade ended, the armies went on to capture Antioch (1098) and Jerusalem (1099), where they set up the Latin Kingdom (1099–1143).

1702 Birth of Philip Doddridge, English Nonconformist clergyman, in London. The youngest of 20 children (18 of whom died in infancy), Doddridge was orphaned at the age of 13. He went on to become a man of great learning, and authored 370 hymns, most of which were published posthumously. One of his most popular hymns today is "O Happy Day That Fixed My Choice."

1839 Scottish clergyman and missionary Robert Murray McCheyne declared in a letter: "Joy is increased by spreading it to others. Thus Christ's joy and glory are increased by making us partakers of it."

1892 Birth of Pearl S. Buck, American Presbyterian missionary to China and author of the best-seller *The Good Earth* (1931).

1901 Birth of Heinrich Bornkamm, Lutheran historical scholar, in Saxony, Germany. His teaching career began in 1927, with his longest appointment at the University of Heidelberg (1948–). His publications cover Luther, the Reformation, mysticism, 18th-century church history, and modern Catholicism.

1934 Two religious bodies with Swiss and German roots—the Evangelical Synod of North America and the Reformed Church in the U.S.—merged in

Cleveland, Ohio, to form the Evangelical and Reformed Church. The Reformed Church in the U.S. was originally organized in 1725 by John Philip Boehm in Montgomery County, Pennsylvania. The Evangelical Synod of North America had been organized in 1840 in St. Louis County (Mehlville), Missouri.

June 27

444 Death of Cyril (b.376), Alexandrian patriarch and theologian. He was a member of the synod which condemned John Chrysostom for opposing Nestorius and his teachings and for vigorously defending both the Trinity and Mary as *theotokos* (mother, or bearer, of God).

1299 Pope Boniface VIII, in his encyclical *Scimus, fili,* claimed Scotland owed allegiance to the Catholic church.

1519 The Disputation of Leipzig opened (lasting through July 16). It was a debate arranged by John Eck (Martin Luther's friend-turned-adversary) in an attempt to discredit Luther's theology by tricking the reformer into espousing heresy. Luther first affirmed that church councils may not only err, but have in fact erred; and that the "power of the keys" had been given to the faithful members of the church rather than to the Pope. The disputation prepared the way for Luther's condemnation by the Diet of Worms the following year.

1739 English revivalist George Whitefield declared in a letter: "Christ's servants have always been the world's fools."

1760 English founder of Methodism John Wesley assured in a letter: "Every one, though born of God in an instant, yet undoubtedly grows by slow degrees. . . . God can do His work by pleasure, as well as by pain."

1844 Joseph Smith (founder of the Mormon church in 1830) and his brother Hyrum were killed by an armed mob in Carthage, Illinois, while the Smiths sat in jail on charges of immorality. Smith had authorized the practice of polygamous marriage for the Mormon community the year before by authority of a divine revelation.

1933 Death of James Mountain (b.1844), English revivalist. A pastor to royalty during his early years, in 1897 he became a Baptist. He was well known for his religious writings, which included a number of hymn tunes. Three are still in use: TRANQUILLITY ("Jesus, I am Resting, Resting"), WYE VALLEY ("Like a River Glorious") and the melody to "I Am His, and He Is Mine."

1944 German Lutheran theologian and Nazi martyr Dietrich Bonhoeffer affirmed in a letter from prison: "This world must not be prematurely written off; in this the Old and New Testaments are one."

1944 Death of James Moffatt (b.1870), Scottish New Testament scholar. He lived in the U.S. from 1927–39 as professor of church history at Union Theological Seminary in New York City. A writer in many fields, he is best remembered for his translation of the Bible into modern English. Moffatt's New Testament was published in 1913, the Old Testament in 1924, and the complete work was revised in 1935.

June 28

1577 Birth of Peter Paul Rubens, Flemish painter, in Westphalia, Germany. He moved to Antwerp, Belgium, where he began his artistic training at age ten. He became one of the most popular painters in Europe but lived an unusually successful and happy life, with no hint of deterioration in either artistic powers or mental clarity. However, he was ill much of the time in his later years. His most famous canvases include *Descent from the Cross* and *Erection of the Cross*.

1814 Birth of Frederick W. Faber, English theologian, hymnist and member of the Oxford movement, in Yorkshire, England. In 1845 he converted from the Anglican to the Roman Catholic Church. An author of some 150 hymns, Faber sought to produce religious music which appealed to Roman Catholics with the same popularity as that which appealed to Protestants. Three of his hymns which succeeded are "Faith of Our Fathers," "There's a Wideness in God's Mercy" and "My God, How Wonderful Thou Art."

1851 Birth of Eliza E. Hewitt, American hymnwriter, in Philadelphia, Pennsylvania. For many years she was Sunday school superintendent of the Northern Home for Friendless Children and an active member of Olivet Presbyterian Church, both in Philadelphia. Many of her hymns were set to music by some of the best-known composers of her time. Four of her hymns, which still endure, are "Will There Be Any Stars?" (a.k.a. "I am Thinking Today of That Beautiful Land"), "More About Jesus Would I Know," "When We All Get to Heaven" (a.k.a. "Sing the Wondrous Love of Jesus") and "Sunshine in the Soul."

1910 Westminster Cathedral was consecrated in London.

1914 Birth of Lester Roloff, U.S. evangelist. For years he served as a radio evangelist, but in later life he founded the "City of Refuge," a work specializing in reforming children who come from broken homes.

1962 The Lutheran Church in America was formed with the merger of four Lutheran synods: the United Lutheran Church in America, the Augustana Evangelical Lutheran Church, the American Evangelical Lutheran Church and the Finnish Evangelical Lutheran Church. The consolidated denomination comprised a religious body of two million members.

June 29

1757 Anglican clergyman and hymnwriter John Newton stated in a letter: "Whatever we may undertake with a sincere desire to promote His glory, we may comfortably pursue: nothing is trivial that is done for Him."

1810 The first American foreign missionary society, the American Board of Commissioners for Foreign Missions, was organized, in Massachusetts. The organizational plan was devised by Dr. Samuel Spring and the Reverend Samuel Worcester, and afterward adopted by the General Association of Massachusetts Proper, a body of conservative Congregational ministers, at Bradford, Massachusetts. (The A.B.C.F.M. became part of the United Church Board for World Ministries in 1961, after the merger of the Congregational Christian churches with the Evangelical and Reformed Church.)

1894 Death of Frank Bottome (b.1823), author of the hymn "The Comforter Has Come."

1908 Birth of Cyrus H. Gordon, American Jewish archeological scholar, in Philadelphia. He was professor of Assyriology and Egyptology at Dropsie College in Philadelphia starting in 1946. His scholarly and technical writings include the *Ugaritic Handbook* (1947).

1931 U.F.M. International was first founded, in England. Originally called the Unevangelized Fields Mission, this interdenominational mission agency is engaged in evangelism, church planting, theological education, Bible translation and medical assistance. It operates in a dozen countries in Latin America, Europe and Africa as well as in Haiti and Indonesia. Headquartered in Bala Cynwyd, Pennsylvania, since May 1954, U.F.M. International adopted its present name in 1980.

1961 World Missionary Press, Inc., was incorporated in Winona Lake, Indiana, by the Rev. & Mrs. G. Watson Goodman. Headquartered in New Paris, Indiana, since 1970, this interdenominational missionary agency is primarily involved in Bible distribution and memorization programs. W.M.P. presently produces portions of the Scriptures in 214 different languages, distributing them in nearly 180 countries.

1968 Pope Paul VI issued the *Creed of the People of God*, an authoritative modern Catholic statement of faith.

June 30

1764 English founder of Methodism, John Wesley, clarified the basis of salvation in a letter: "It is certainly right. . . to abstain from all outward occasions of evil. But this profits only a little: the inward change is the one needful for you. You must be born again, or you will never gain a uniform and lasting liberty."

1872 Birth of Harry Strachan, founder of the Latin America Mission. Strachan and his wife Susan first named their mission The Latin America Evangelization Campaign when they founded it in 1921 in Stony Brook, New York. Today, this interdenominational mission agency (headquartered in Coral Gables, Florida) engages in evangelism, church planting and literature production in eight Latin American nations.

1949 American missionary and Auca Indian martyr Jim Elliot commented in his journal: " 'Grace *and* truth came by Jesus Christ.' Only truth, the law, came by Moses."

1963 Italian Cardinal Giovanni Battista Montini was crowned Pope Paul VI at Vatican City. Born in 1897, Montini was ordained in 1920 and made a cardinal by John XXIII in 1958. At the conclave of June 1963, attended by 80 cardinals, Montini was elected John's successor on the 5th ballot, becoming the 261st pope.

1973 The Far East Broadcasting Company began broadcasting from HLAZ, its first radio station, in Korea. F.E.B.C., founded in 1945, is an evangelical, interdenominational mission agency specializing in radio broadcasting and Bible correspondence courses. It is active in nearly a dozen countries and islands in eastern Asia and the Pacific.

July

July 1

1097 The Islamic Seljuk Turks were defeated by the armies of the First Crusade at Dorylaeum (the site of an ancient Phrygian city southwest of Constantinople in Asia Minor). The next city attacked by the Crusaders was Antioch.

1643 The Westminster Assembly first convened, in Westminster Abbey. This designated advisory body to the "Long Parliament" was comprised of 121 English and Welsh clergymen, intent on reforming the Church of England. The most important documents to emerge from this short-lived synod were the Westminster longer and shorter catechisms, in 1648. Soon abandoned by the Anglican Church, these two catechisms were nevertheless adopted by the General Assembly of the Church of Scotland, and have since been regarded as the highest doctrinal formulation of the Presbyterian churches.

1654 Jacob Barsimon first arrived on Manhatten Island, the first Jew to settle in America, and the first of 23 Jewish immigrants to come to Manhatten that year.

1800 The earliest recorded Methodist camp meeting in America was held in Logan County, Kentucky, near the Gaspar River Church.

1813 Birth of Samuel Wolcott, American Congregational missionary and clergyman. He was a missionary in Syria from 1840–42 and later pastored churches in Rhode Island, Illinois, and Ohio. He wrote his first hymn at age 56. By the time of his death 17 years later, he had written more than 200 hymns, including "Christ for the World! We Sing."

1824 American Congregational revivalist Charles G. Finney was ordained at age 32. After pastoring and holding revival campaigns for several years, he went to Oberlin College in Ohio as professor of theology in 1835. He taught there until his death in 1875.

1825 Birth of William H. Walter, composer of "Rise Up, O Men of God!"

1878 Death of Catherine Winkworth (b.1827), English educator. She actively promoted educational and social issues and pioneered in higher education for women. She was also regarded as one of the best translators of German in her time, translating the English versions of at least three German hymns which remain popular: "Lift Up Your Heads, Ye Mighty Gates," "Now Thank We All Our God" and "Praise to the Lord, the Almighty."

1881 The American Red Cross was incorporated, and founder Clara Barton was elected its first president (1881–1904).

1892 Death of Charles Haddon Spurgeon (b.1834), famed English Baptist preacher. By age 22, he was the most popular preacher of his day. In 1861 he built the Metropolitan Tabernacle in London, which seated 6,000 people. From this pulpit, Spurgeon ministered for his remaining 30 years.

1896 Death of Harriet Beecher Stowe (b.1811), American abolitionist and author. Daughter of Presbyterian clergyman Lyman Beecher, Harriet married Rev. C.E. Stowe, professor of Hebrew at Lane University in Ohio, in 1836. She published her most famous novel *Uncle Tom's Cabin* (or *Life Among the Lowly*) in 1852. The book helped crystalize antislavery sentiment, which eventually led to the American Civil War.

1899 The Gideons International (a Bible-distributing organization) was established by three commercial business travelers—John H. Nicholson, Samuel E. Hill, and William J. Knights—at the Janesville, Wisconsin, Y.M.C.A. Organized under the original title "Christian Commercial Men's Association of America," the Gideons placed their first Bibles in the Superior Hotel of Iron Mountain, Montana, in Nov. 1908. This interdenominational laymen's association is presently headquartered in Nashville, Tennessee, and is active in both personal evangelism and Bible distribution in 133 countries throughout the world.

1909 Birth of Hugh T. Kerr, Jr., American Presbyterian theologian, in Chicago, Illinois. He taught systematic theology at Princeton Theological Seminary starting in 1940 and authored several popular theology books, including *Compendium of Calvin's Institutes* (1939) and *Compendium of Luther's Theology* (1943). He was once editor of the religious quarterly *Theology Today*.

1925 Firebrand American fundamentalist evangelist Lester Roloff was converted to faith in Jesus Christ. It is said that Roloff's favorite Scripture was Heb. 10:38: "Now the just shall live by faith: but if any man draw back, my soul shall have no pleasure in him."

1942 Birth of Andrae Crouch, Black American sacred music artist. His most popular Christian songs include "My Tribute" ("To God Be the Glory") and "Soon and Very Soon."

1970 The Christian Aid Mission was incorporated in Washington, D.C. Established in 1953 by founder Bob Finley, the organization was originally a division of International Students, Inc. (I.S.I.), known as A.I.D. (Assisting Indigenous Developments). Headquartered since 1976 in Charlottesville, Virginia, Christian Aid Mission supports Christian organizations and Christian national workers in 40 countries throughout the world.

1974 The headquarters of Overseas Missionary Fellowship (O.M.F.) moved to its present location in Robesonia, Pennsylvania. Founded in 1865 in Great Britain by J. Hudson Taylor, this evangelical, interdenominational missions agency engages in evangelism, church planting, theological education and literature distribution in nine Far Eastern countries.

July 2

1489 Birth of Thomas Cranmer, first Protestant Archbishop of Canterbury, in Nottinghamshire, England. Cranmer's 1529 suggestion that the question of Henry VIII's divorce from Catherine be handled by theologians rather than the Catholic church led to his rapid political and ecclesiastical advancement, and he was appointed archbishop in 1533. Cranmer's most positive endeavor was to promote the circulation of the Scriptures in vernacular English. He was also the main author of the *Book of Common Prayer* and what became "the Thirty-Nine Articles," the doctrinal statement of the Anglican Church.

1778 Death of Jean-Jacques Rousseau (b.1712), French philosopher. His religious writings stressed the idea that primitive man was free and happy, unencumbered with the idea of human inequalities. Rousseau was a deist who advocated a utopian program of education, far from the corrupting influences of society. After his death, his writings became one of the most powerful influences on philosophy and religion in all Europe.

1916 Death of Arthur H. Messiter (b.1834), American sacred music organist. For 31 years he served as organist for Trinity Episcopal Church of New York City. During this time he composed a number of anthems, including the hymn tune MARION, to which we sing "Rejoice, Ye Pure in Heart."

1918 Death of Washington Gladden (b.1836), American Congregational clergyman and author of the hymn "O Master, Let Me Walk with Thee." Gladden was an advocate of the positive social impact of the Gospel. He authored "O Master, Let Me Walk with Thee," in 1879 for the magazine *Sunday Afternoon*.

1930 Pioneer linguistic educator Frank C. Laubach, while a Congregational missionary to the Philippines, disclosed in a letter: "[God said to me,] 'If I do not speak to you in words at times, it is because the reality all about you is greater than the imperfect symbols of things which you have in words.' "

July 3

529 The Synod of Orange convened in Arausio, in southern France. Caesarius of Arles presided over the council of 13 bishops. Caesarius successfully submitted a declaration on grace and free will outlining and upholding St. Augustine's doctrines on the nature of grace. The synod ended the struggle against semi-Pelagianism (as advocated by Faustus of Riez and John Cassian) in Southern Gaul. The signed documents from this council were formally approved in 531 by Pope Boniface II.

1756 English founder of Methodism, John Wesley, declared in a letter: "One who lives and dies in error, or in dissent from our Church, may yet be saved; but one who lives and dies in sin, must perish."

1894 Birth of Don R. Falkenberg, founder and first president of Bible Literature International. Falkenberg incorporated this specialized service ministry in 1923 in Columbus, Ohio, under the name Mid-West Businessmen's Council of the Pocket Testament League. In 1941 the name was changed to Bible Meditation League, and in 1967, to Bible Literature International. This interdenominational organization provides Christian evangelistic, discipleship and church-growth literature to mission agencies in over 200 countries.

1904 Death of Theodor Herzl (b.1860), Hungarian-born journalist and founder of political Zionism. In 1897 he founded the Congress of the Zionist Organizations. He also established the Zionist newspaper *Die Welt*, and negotiated with both Turkey and Britain for a mass Jewish settlement in Palestine. His most important treatise was no doubt *Der Judenstaat* (*The Jewish State*), published in 1896. It laid the philosophical foundations for a modern Jewish nation, foundations that led to the establishment of modern Israel in May 1948.

1907 Pope St. Pius X, in the encyclical *Lamentabili*, formally condemned the modernist intellectual movement within the Roman Catholic Church.

1960 Death of Alfred H. Ackley (b.1887), American Presbyterian clergyman and hymnwriter. Ordained to the ministry in 1914, Ackley served churches in Pennsylvania and California, all the while becoming increasingly involved in the field of sacred music. He wrote about 1,500 songs during his lifetime. His tune HE LIVES, to which we sing "I Serve a Risen Savior," remains popular.

1981 Death of William Chapman, mission pioneer. In 1938 he founded the World Home Bible League in Chicago, Illinois. With its headquarters in South Holland, Michigan, since 1969, this interdenominational service organization aims at placing Bibles in ever home in over 70 countries throughout the world.

July 4

1187 Saladin, leader of the united Muslim forces, defeated the armies of the Third Crusade at Tiberius, in Syria.

1552 French reformer John Calvin cautioned England's King Edward VI in a letter: "How much danger kings and princes are in, lest the height to which they are raised should dazzle their eyes, and amuse them here below, while making them forgetful of the heavenly kingdom."

1755 Death of John Cennick (b.1718), English clergyman. Cennick's life reads like the diary of an ecumenical pilgrim. He was born of Quaker parents, raised in the Anglican Church, worked within the Methodist movement under John Wesley, left Wesley to work with George Whitefield, and finally, in 1745, joined the Moravian Brethren, being ordained by them in 1749. Cennick published several collections of hymns during his lifetime. One hymn from those collections is the popular table grace "Be Present at Our Table, Lord."

1765 English poet and hymnwriter William Cowper observed in a letter: "How naturally does affliction make us Christians!"

1831 The American patriotic hymn "America," written by Baptist clergyman Samuel Francis Smith, was first sung at worship services, at Park Street Church in Boston, Massachusetts. Smith had taken the tune from a German songbook and was unaware that it was also the tune of the British national anthem "God Save the King (Queen)."

1840 Birth of James McGranahan, American sacred music songwriter and music pioneer, in Adamsville, Pennsylvania. He served as song leader for popular 19th-century evangelist Major D.W. Whittle. He also wrote, edited and compiled many songs during his long ministry (1862–87). Several of his most famous hymn tunes include: CHRIST RETURNETH ("It May Be at Morn") EL NATHAN ("I Know Not Why God's Wondrous Grace"), MY REDEEMER ("I Will Sing of My Redeemer"), NEUMEISTER ("Christ Receiveth Sinful Men"), and SHOWERS OF BLESSING.

1870 Birth of James Moffatt, New Testament scholar, in Glasgow, Scotland. After pastoring for Scotland's Free Church from 1894–1907, he taught at Mansfield College in Oxford (1911–15), at Glasgow (1915–27), and finally at Union Seminary in New York City (1927–39). Moffatt translated both the Old and New Testaments into modern colloquial English (N.T.: 1913, O.T.: 1924, revision of the whole: 1935).

1918 Birthday of the Friedman twins, Esther Pauline and Pauline Esther, in Sioux City, Iowa. When they were in their late 30s, the two each became competing advice columnists. Esther Pauline wrote under the pen name "Ann Landers," beginning in 1955, while her twin sister, Pauline Esther, became "Dear Abby" (Abigail Van Buren) in 1956.

1970 American Presbyterian apologist Francis Schaeffer observed in a letter: "If standards are raised which are not really scriptural, and especially if these are put forth as the spiritual standard for which we should strive, it can only lead to sorrow. If we try to have a spirituality higher than the Bible sets forth, it will always turn out to be lower."

1975 The Slavic Gospel Association moved its headquarters from Chicago to nearby Wheaton, Illinois. Founded in 1934 by Rev. Peter Deyneka, Sr., S.G.A. is an interdenominational mission agency whose ministry is focused on Slavic peoples. The organization is engaged primarily in radio broadcasting, evangelism, literature production and Bible distribution in eight countries in Europe and South America.

July 5

1768 English founder of Methodism John Wesley affirmed in a letter: "We are reasonable creatures, and undoubtedly reason is the candle of the Lord. By enlightening our reason to see the meaning of the Scriptures, the Holy Spirit makes our way plain before us."

1835 Irish Anglican clergyman Richard C. Trench (1807–1886) was ordained into the Anglican priesthood. He had been ordained a deacon in 1832. Trench added teaching responsibilities to his pastoral career in 1845. Archbishop of Dublin from 1864–84, Trench was a noted theologian, a religious poet and a philologist. His *New Testament Synonyms* (1854) is still in print.

1865 English Methodist clergyman William Booth began his labors among the unchurched and poverty-stricken masses in London's East End under the name The Christian Mission. In 1878 he changed the name of his growing ministry to The Salvation Army.

1903 Death of William Burt Pope, English Methodist theologian. Ordained in 1842, he became a successful linguist and translator of German anti-rationalist critics. He taught at Didsbury Wesleyan College in Manchester, England, from 1867–86. His greatest work, the three-volume *Compendium of Christian Theology* (1875–76), set forth the most powerful arguments for the holiness doctrine of all Methodist systematic theologies of that day, and fully answered many destructive criticisms of Methodist doctrine.

1962 Death of Helmut Richard Niebuhr (b. 1894), American neoorthodox theologian. He was professor of Christian ethics at Yale University from 1931–62.

More scholarly than his elder brother Reinhold, Niebuhr sought to grapple with the nature of religious experience, and to determine the relationships between Christian faith and one's attitude toward civilization. A prolific writer, Niebuhr's most popular work is *Christ and Culture* (1951), a theological classic that explores the available options of Christian association with the world.

July 6

1415 Death of John Huss (b.1373), Bohemian (Czech) reformer. Ordained to the priesthood in 1402, he was later made rector of the University of Prague. Huss antagonized both secular and religious authorities alike when he began preaching radical sermons condemning the morals of the Roman Catholic clergy. He was excommunicated by· antipope John XXIII in 1412. The king soon removed him from the university. Promised safe conduct to the Council of Constance in 1414, Huss was instead taken captive, thrown into prison, and condemned for heresy and burned at the stake the following year.

1439 The Council of Basel (Florence), while meeting in Florence, Italy, issued the decree *Laetentur Coeli*. This *Decree of Union* united (at least in theory) the Latin and the Greek Catholic churches. Greek Orthodoxy was severed permanently from Roman Catholicism only 14 years later, at the fall of Byzantium on May 29, 1453, to the Turks.

1535 Death of Sir Thomas More (b.1478), English Roman Catholic statesman. More was elevated to Lord Chancellor of England by Henry VIII in 1529. His fortune turned when he opposed Henry's divorce. Resigning the Chancellorship in 1532, More was imprisoned two years later when he refused to take the oath on the Act of Succession. Fifteen months later, he was accused of treason and beheaded for opposing the Act of Supremacy, which required the acknowledgment of Henry VIII as head of the English church.

1757 Birth of William McKendree, colonial American Methodist bishop, in King William County, Virginia. Converted when nearly 30, McKendree was ordained an elder by Francis Asbury in 1791. In 1808 he was ordained the first American-born bishop of the Methodist Episcopal Church. McKendree College in Lebanon, Illinois, was named in his honor.

1770 English founder of Methodism, John Wesley, assured in a letter: "What can hurt those that trust in Him?"

1813 Death of Granville Sharp (b.1735), English abolitionist. It was Sharp who argued the James Somersett case in 1772, resulting in the landmark decision that "any slave stepping on the soil of England was free." Sharp was also a biblical Greek scholar. He formulated an important grammatical rule called the Granville Sharp Rule.

1846 Birth of John H. Sammis, American Presbyterian clergyman, in Brooklyn, New York. Ordained in 1880, Sammis held pastorates in Iowa, Indiana, Michigan, and Minnesota. Later in life, he joined the faculty of the Los Angeles Bible Institute, where he taught until his death in 1919. Sammis is remembered as author of the hymn "Trust and Obey" (a.k.a. "When We Walk with the Lord").

1879 Death of Henry T. Smart (b.1813), English church organist. Largely self-taught, Smart served as the organist in four prominent London churches, starting in 1831. He also wrote a large number of sacred compositions, both instrumental and choral, including the hymn tunes LANCASHIRE ("Lead On, O King Eternal") and REGENT SQUARE ("Angels from the Realms of Glory").

1888 Death of George Duffield (b.1818), American Presbyterian pastor. Ordained in 1840, he served churches in New York, New Jersey, Pennsylvania, Illinois and Michigan. He was the author of *English Hymns, Their Authors and History* (1886). He also authored the hymn "Stand Up, Stand Up for Jesus."

1905 Birth of Harold J. Ockenga, American evangelical leader. Ockenga is credited with having helped shape the intellectual credibility of modern evangelicalism in America. In addition to having pastored at Boston's Park Street Church for 33 years (1936–69), Ockenga was the first president of the National Association of Evangelicals (N.A.E.) and co-founder and first president of Fuller Theological Seminary in Pasadena, California.

1935 American Presbyterian apologist Francis A. (August) Schaeffer, age 23, married Edith Rachel Seville, age 20. They had met three years earlier, on June 26, 1932, at the First Presbyterian Church of Germantown, Pennsylvania. Their marriage yielded four children: Priscilla (6/18/37), Susan (5/28/41), Deborah (5/3/45) and Franky (Francis August IV, 8/3/52). Francis and Edith were married for 49 years, until his death from cancer in May 1984.

1941 English Bible expositor Arthur W. Pink observed in a letter: "It is those who walk the closest with God who are most conscious of their sins."

1961 Swiss Reformed theologian Karl Barth explained in a letter: "Eternal life is not another and second life, beyond the present one. It is this life . . . in relation to what God has done for the whole world, and therefore for us too, in Jesus Christ."

1970 American Presbyterian apologist Francis Schaeffer noted in a letter: "There are indeed many reasons why we should go on living, and the largest one is that God really is there. He really does exist, and He made us for himself. . . To know that we can speak and that there is Someone who will answer fills the vacuum of life that would otherwise be present."

July 7

1538 German reformer Martin Luther remarked: "I have learned this art: When I have nothing more to say, I stop talking."

1586 Birth of Thomas Hooker, colonial American pastor. He fled his native England in 1630 to escape persecution for his Puritan faith. In 1633 he arrived in New England, and in 1636 he and several members of his church founded the colony of Hartford, Connecticut. In 1639 Hooker proposed the idea of a federal government to Governor Winthrop, which led to the organization of The United Colonies of New England in 1643—the earliest system of federal government in America. Hooker died four years later.

1647 Death of Thomas Hooker, whose concept of a federal government resulted in the first such system of rule in America.

1787 Birth of H.A. Cesar Malan, distinguished French sacred music composer, in Geneva, Switzerland. Ordained to the Reformed Church ministry in 1810, his outspoken preaching against spiritual apathy and empty formalism forced him out of the Reformed Church. He therefore built a chapel on his own property and preached there for 43 years. Malan became famous as a preacher, touring evangelist, artist, printer, poet and musician. He wrote over 1,000 hymn tunes and has been compared with Isaac Watts for providing the first impulse toward the general recognition of hymns in French public worship, and with Charles Wesley for providing the devotional expression for the great religious movement which affected his own generation. Malan is remembered for composing the tune HENDON, in 1823, which we sing with "Ask Ye What Great Thing I Know" (words written in 1741) and "Take My Life, and Let It Be" (written 1874).

1851 Birth of Charles A. Tindley, Black American Methodist preacher, in Berlin, Maryland. Tindley was orphaned by age 5, but still learned to read and write by age 17. He was ordained into the Methodist ministry in 1885, and served churches in Delaware, New Jersey and Maryland. In 1902 he was called to pastor Philadelphia's Calvary Methodist Episcopal Church, where he preached for 30 years. Tindley also wrote the words and music to many popular Gospel songs, including "Nothing Between," "By and By," "Leave It There," and "Stand by Me." His "I'll Overcome Some Day" inspired the civil rights song "We Shall Overcome."

1870 The Vatican I Council held its last general meeting. This 20th Ecumenical council first opened Dec. 1869, and held four public sessions and 89 general meetings. Opened under Pope Pius IX, Vatican I was attended by about 800 bishops and other prelates of Roman Catholicism. During its sessions, it defined papal primacy and infallibility in a dogmatic constitution. The council suspended sessions in Sept. 1 of the same year and was adjourned Oct. 20.

1907 Death of James McGranahan (b.1840), American sacred music artist. He served as song leader for popular 19th-century evangelist Major D.W. Whittle. McGranahan also wrote, edited and compiled many songs during his long ministry in music (1862–87). Several of his more famous hymn tunes include: CHRIST RETURNETH ("It May Be at Morn"), EL NATHAN ("I Know Not Why God's Wondrous Grace"), MY REDEEMER ("I Will Sing of My Redeemer"), NEUMEISTER ("Christ Receiveth Sinful Men"), and SHOWERS OF BLESSING.

1935 English Bible expositor Arthur W. Pink replied in a letter: "It is not how much of the Scriptures we know with our heads, but how much of them is written on our hearts and is regulating and transforming our lives."

1944 Death of George Washington Truett (b.1867), American Southern Baptist preacher. Ordained in 1890, Truett was called to the First Baptist Church of Dallas in 1897. He continued there until his death 47 years later. During his long pastorate, the membership grew from 700 to 7,800.

1946 In ceremonies presided over by Pope Pius XII, Mother Frances Xavier Cabrini was canonized—the first American citizen to be elevated to sainthood in the Roman Catholic Church. Born 1850 in Lombardy, Italy, Cabrini founded the Missionary Sisters of the Sacred Heart in 1880 and was sent by Leo XIII to the U.S. in 1889 to do charity work among Italian immigrants. She became an

American citizen in 1909. Before her death in Chicago in 1917, she established hospitals, schools, orphanages and convents in several major American cities.

1948   American missionary and Auca Indian martyr Jim Elliot recorded this meditation in his journal: "Psalms 104:4: 'Who maketh. . . his ministers a flaming fire.' Am I ignitible? God deliver me from the dread asbestos of 'other things.' Saturate me with the oil of the Spirit that I may be a flame."

1959   English Christian apologist C.S. Lewis remarked in *Letters to an American Lady*: "I 'believed' theoretically in the divine forgiveness for years before it really came home to me. It is a wonderful moment when it does."

July 8

1115   Death of Peter the Hermit (b.ca.1050), spiritual propagandist of the First Crusade (1096–99). Returning from a pilgrimage to Jerusalem in 1093, he reported to Pope Urban II the atrocities the Seljuk Turks were inflicting on Christian pilgrims to the Holy Land. Urban's fiery pronouncement at the Council of Clermont in 1095, and Peter's subsequent stirring messages to the European people led to the organized Christian military forces which routed the Muslims of Nicaea, Antioch and Jerusalem in 1097–99. Peter entered Jerusalem with the Crusaders in 1099 but returned to Europe and become prior of an Augustinian monastery he helped to found.

1663   Following the restoration of the monarchy in England, the New England colony of Rhode Island was issued a new charter guaranteeing religious freedom regardless of "differences in opinion in matters of religion."

1741   Colonial American theologian Jonathan Edwards preached his classic sermon *Sinners in the Hands of an Angry God*, at Enfield, Connecticut. Under the influence of Edwards' preaching—primarily at the Congregational Church of Northampton, Massachusetts—a "Great Awakening" was taking place throughout New England, having begun in 1734–35. After 1740 the revival spread throughout the Colonies.

1835   The American Liberty Bell first cracked while tolling the death of Chief Justice John Marshall. The bell was first cast in England in 1752. Earlier that year, the Pennsylvania Provincial Assembly voted that its inscription read: "Proclaim liberty throughout all the land unto all the inhabitants thereof"— the text taken from Leviticus 25:10.

1862   Birth of Rev. Arthur Stephen Paynter, mission pioneer. In 1897 he founded the India Christian Mission in the Kumoan District of North India. In 1904 the I.C.M. headquarters moved to Nuwara Eliya, Sri Lanka (Ceylon). This evangelical, interdenominational agency supports agriculture, education and orphanage work in both India and Sri Lanka by transmitting funds.

1884   Death of Isaac A. Dorner (b.1809), German Lutheran theologian. He taught at several German universities for the last fifty years of his life. Deeply influenced by Schleiermacher, Hegel and Kant, Dorner brought their philosophic insights into the study of theology, which he interpreted in a traditional, evangelical sense. His theological emphasis was Christological, and his greatest writing was *History of the Development of the Doctrines of the Person of Christ* (1861–65).

1884 Death of Johann Peter Lange (b.1802), German Reformed theologian and exegete. After pastoring from 1825–41, he taught in the universities of Zurich and Bonn. A prolific writer, Lange's *Theologische-homiletisches Bibelwerk* was later edited and translated by Philip Schaff into 25 English volumes under the title *A Commentary on the Holy Scriptures*. It is this publication that has made Lange's name familiar to students of the Scriptures in the English-speaking world.

1959 Representatives of the Congregational Christian Churches and the Evangelical and Reformed Church adopted a united statement of faith in Oberlin, Ohio. The two groups merged and formed the United Church of Christ in 1961.

1969 A plan calling for the merger of the Methodist and Anglican churches in England was defeated by the Anglican convocations. The concept of church leadership as an office (the Methodist view) and not as an order (the Anglican view) proved unacceptable to the Anglicans.

July 9

1228 Death of Stephen Langton (b.ca.1155), Archbishop of Canterbury. Langton was one of the chief instructors (magisters) and theologians at the University of Paris prior to his ecclesiastical promotion to archbishop in 1206. By the end of his 20-year career of teaching scriptural studies (ca. 1185–1205), Langton had developed the modern biblical chapter divisions.

1441 Death of Jan Van Eyck (b.ca. 1390), Flemish painter. Van Eyck's great emphasis on detail, it is said, "has the effect of spiritualizing the subject so that the division between secular and religious art is virtually done away with." Van Eyck's best-remembered religious painting is the Ghent altarpiece (1432), which dramatizes the redemption of man in 20 panels. The work is both realistic and symbolic.

1530 German reformer Martin Luther remarked in a letter: "This is a definite sign that we are God's children, because we are men of peace."

1838 Death of Robert Grant, Indian-born English lawyer. In 1818 he entered Parliament, and in 1834 he became Governor of Bombay, India. He wrote 12 hymns during his lifetime, all published posthumously. One which we still sing today is "O Worship the King, All Glorious Above."

1838 Birth of Philip P. Bliss, American Gospel singer and hymnwriter, in Clearfield, Pennsylvania. In 1860 he began teaching music professionally. He began work in the music publishing business five years later. Both he and his wife died in a tragic train accident in 1876. Musicologist John Julian states that Bliss stands next to Fanny Crosby for the brilliance of his Gospel hymns. Among the many popular hymn tunes (and their texts), Bliss penned over a hundred years ago, several are used even today: "Wonderful Words of Life," "Almost Persuaded," "Whosoever Will," "I Will Sing of My Redeemer," "Let the Lower Lights Be Burning," KENOSIS ("I Gave My Life for Thee") and VILLE DU HAVRE ("It Is Well with My Soul").

1843 Birth of Ralph E. Hudson, sacred music writer and publisher, in Napoleon, Ohio. A veteran of the American Civil War, Hudson later set up a music publishing business in Alliance, Ohio. He was also a licensed preacher in the

Methodist Episcopal Church and spent much time in evangelistic work. Of his original hymns, he is best remembered for the words to "I'll Live for Him" (a.k.a. "My Life, My Love I Give to Thee") and for the words and music to "At the Cross" and "Blessed Be the Name."

1896   Birth of William Cameron Townsend, American missionary-linguist. He began his career in 1917 as a 21-year-old Bible salesman in Guatemala. Later he also worked in Mexico and Peru. In 1942 Townsend incorporated the Wycliffe Bible Translators in Glendale, California. The organization has since grown to over 4,500 members. W.B.T. is an interdenominational mission agency involved primarily in Bible translation, linguistics and literacy. Headquartered since 1974 in Huntington Beach, California, W.B.T. works in nearly 750 minority languages in over 40 countries throughout the world.

July 10

1509   Birth of John Calvin, French Protestant reformer, in Noyon, France. In 1536 he published the first edition of his classic *Christianae Religionis Institutio*. Originally a brief summary of the Christian faith by an unknown author, the *Institutes of the Christian Religion* eventually became the most popular Protestant doctrinal statement of the Reformation. Calvin revised the *Institutes* five times before the definitive edition appeared in 1559. The first edition contained only 6 chapters; the final edition, 79.

1518   German reformer Martin Luther explained in a letter: "The word of Christ has been of such a kind that whoever wants to carry it into the world must necessarily, like the Apostles, renounce everything and expect death at any and every hour. If it were not so, it would not be the word of Christ."

1629   The first non-Separatist Congregational Church in America was established, in Salem, Massachusetts. It was founded by Francis Higginson and Samuel Skelton, two newly arrived ministers from England.

1851   The California Wesleyan College was chartered in Santa Clara, California, under Methodist auspices. It was renamed University of the Pacific in 1852, transferred to San Jose, California, in 1871, merged with Napa College of Napa, California, in 1896, and renamed the College of the Pacific in 1911. The main campus moved to Stockton, California, in 1924 and the college readopted the name University of the Pacific in 1961.

1863   Death of Clement C. Moore (b.1779), American writer and educator. With part of a family inheritance, Moore established General Theological (Episcopal) Seminary in 1819, where he taught Greek and Hebrew Literature for 28 years (1823–50). Ironically, Moore's name endures not as a great theologian, but as the author of the completely mythical Christmas story which begins: "'Twas the night before Christmas..." (*A Visit from St. Nicholas*, 1823).

1888   Birth of Eduard Thurneysen, Swiss Protestant theologian, at Wallenstaat, Switzerland. Beginning in 1913, Thurneysen maintained correspondence with fellow pastor Karl Barth. Their written communications helped both develop and elaborate on the dynamics of dialectical theology. While Barth eventually went on to explore the academic avenues of this new discipline, Thurneysen remained in the local church, interpreting dialectical theology at its pastoral and social levels.

1908 Death of Phoebe Palmer Knapp (b.1839), active American lay Methodist. The daughter of the respected Methodist evangelist Walter C. Palmer, Phoebe married J.F. Knapp, founder of the Metropolitan Life Insurance Co. She published more than 500 Gospel songs, including the hymn tune ASSURANCE, to which we sing "Blessed Assurance, Jesus Is Mine."

1925 The famous Scopes "Monkey Trial" began in Dayton, Tennessee. High school biology teacher, John T. Scopes was arrested on May 5 for teaching Darwin's theory of evolution to his students. His trial defense was conducted by Clarence Darrow, with fundamentalist orator William Jennings Bryan acting as prosecuting attorney. Scopes was found guilty, but was fined only $100. Two years later, the Tennessee Supreme Court reversed the trial decision on a legal technicality, and in 1967, the statute broken by Scopes was repealed.

1950 Jim Elliot, American missionary and Auca Indian martyr, stated a goal in his journal: "I am just trying to deliver familiar truth from the oblivion of general acceptance."

July 11

1319 Death of Jean de Joinville (b.ca.1225), French historian. Joinville accompanied French King Louis IX (St. Louis) to Egypt and Palestine on the Sixth Crusade (1248–54). In 1250 Joinville and Louis were taken prisoner at Damietta by the Turan Shah. After 1254, when Louis was ransomed and returned to France, Joinville wrote a famous biography of the king.

1533 Pope Clement VII excommunicated King Henry VIII of England from the Roman Catholic Church for remarrying after his divorce. Clement also annulled Henry's divorce and remarriage.

1656 Having sailed from the Barbados, Ann Austin and Mary Fisher landed in Boston—the first Quakers to arrive in America. The two women were immediately imprisoned for their Quaker beliefs by Massachusetts authorities; five weeks later, they were deported to England.

1895 Death of Alexander Ewing (b.1830), Scottish soldier. He spent 12 years in the foreign service, enlisting in 1855 at the outbreak of the Crimean War. Before this time, Ewing had studied law and music. The only music he is known to have composed is the hymn tune EWING ("Jerusalem, the Golden").

1952 American missionary and Auca Indian martyr Jim Elliot recorded this prayer in his journal: "Teach me, Lord Jesus, to live simply and love purely, like a child, and to know that You are unchanged in your attitudes and actions toward me. Give me not to be hungering for the 'strange, rare, and peculiar' when the common, ordinary, and regular, rightly taken, will suffice to feed and satisfy the soul."

1955 American Presbyterian apologist Francis A. Schaeffer concluded in a letter: "No price is too high to pay to have a free conscience before God."

July 12

526 Felix IV was elected pope of the Roman Catholic Church. He served slightly more than four years before his death in 530. St. Benedict of Nursia established the Benedictine Order in 528 with the foundation of Monte Cassino during Felix's rule. St. Benedict's rule became the pattern for all subsequent religious orders within the Roman Catholic Church. At least 24 popes have been members of the Benedictine order.

1191 The armies of the Third Crusade (1189–92), led by England's King Richard I ("The Lionhearted"), captured the Syrian seaport of Acre.

1536 Death of Desiderius Erasmus (b.ca.1466), Dutch humanist and Greek scholar. He was the leading humanist of the Protestant Reformation, and sought to reform the church through scholarship and Christian instruction. He lived in Basel, Switzerland, for part of his professional life (1521–29). Erasmus was the first popular author after the advent of printing. His critical satire *In Praise of Folly* (1509) demonstrated the need for reform in the church. His *Greek New Testament* (1516) demonstrated that the church could go beyond her Latin (Vulgate) roots. Because Erasmus laid foundations for reform but had neither the call nor radical courage to build on them, it is said that Erasmus laid the egg that Martin Luther hatched.

1840 Famed English preacher Frederick W. Robertson (1816–53) was ordained into the Anglican Church by the Bishop of Winchester. During his remaining 13 years, he brought evangelical passion to his pulpit. He was known for his psychological approach to biblical characters, in which he sought to understand their motivations and to relate these to the motivations of his hearers.

1843 Joseph Smith, founder of the Mormon church, announced that a divine revelation had been given him sanctioning polygamy. This announcement stirred up bitterness within both the Mormon community and among non-Mormons around Nauvoo, Illinois, where Smith's followers were settled. Less than 12 months later (June 27, 1844), Smith and his brother Hiram were murdered by a mob in Carthage, Illinois—principally for practicing and teaching the doctrine of polygamy.

1871 A riot between Irish Catholics and Irish Protestants in New York City left 52 dead and many wounded.

1898 Birth of Rev. Peter Deyneka, Sr., founder of The Slavic Gospel Association. The S.G.A., founded in 1934, is an evangelical, interdenominational mission agency whose ministry is focused on Slavic peoples. The organization is engaged primarily in radio broadcasting, evangelism, literature production and Bible distribution in eight countries in Europe and South America.

1963 Swiss Reformed theologian Karl Barth admonished in a letter: "Do not stop testing and correcting your insights by holy scripture. Then, being sound in what really counts, you can live and represent a comforted life."

July 13

1105 Death of Rashi (b.1040), medieval Jewish Bible scholar. His name is an abbreviation, a Hebrew acrostic for Rabbi Sholomon ben Isaac. He was the leading rabbinic commentator on the Old Testament in his day. In contrast to contemporary methods of exegesis, it was Rashi's aim to interpret the Old Testament according to its literal sense. His commentaries have been influential among Jewish and Christian exegetes since his time.

1769 Birth of Thomas Kelly, Irish Episcopal clergyman who wrote the hymn "Praise the Savior, Ye Who Know Him!", in County Queens, Ireland. Ordained in 1792, his fervent evangelicalism quickly brought him into disfavor with the Archbishop of Dublin, and Kelly soon left the church. He devoted the rest of his life to working with the poor and establishing an independent church. He wrote 765 hymns during his lifetime.

1778 Anglican hymnwriter and former slave-trader John Newton noted in a letter: "It is perhaps the highest triumph we can obtain over bigotry when we are able to bear with bigots themselves."

1854 Birth of Edmund S. Lorenz, American sacred composer who wrote the hymns "Tell It to Jesus" and "The Name of Jesus."

1886 Birth of Father Edward Flanagan, Roman Catholic parish priest, in Roscommon, Ireland. He came to the U.S. in 1904 to receive his education, and was ordained 1912. Flanagan served churches in Nebraska from 1912–16. Feeling an increasing need to help boys before they became hardened in crime and believing there was "no such thing as a bad boy," Flanagan organized his Home for Homeless Boys outside Omaha, Nebraska, renaming it Boys Town in 1922. It was his aim to develop character in the boys by supplementing vocational training with social and religious education. Flanagan later helped found similar institutions in both Europe and Japan.

July 14

1274 Death of St. Bonaventura (b.ca.1217), Italian Roman Catholic theologian and mystic. Joining the Franciscans in his 30s, Bonaventura became close friends with Thomas Aquinas. Becoming general of the religious order in 1257, Bonaventura helped settle many of its internal problems. As a theologian, he taught that Christian illumination (special revelation) was superior to human reason (general revelation). Canonized by Pope Sixtus IV in 1482, Bonaventura had a lasting influence on the Roman Catholic Church as a spiritual writer.

1773 The first American Annual Conference of the Methodist Church convened at St. George's Church in Philadelphia, Pennsylvania.

1775 Anglican hymnwriter John Newton remarked in a letter: "The knowledge of God cannot be attained by studious discussion on our parts; it must be by revelation on His part—a revelation, not objectively of new truth, but subjectively of new light in us."

1800 Birth of Matthew Bridges, English clergyman, in Essex, England. Raised in the Anglican Church, Bridges came under the influence of the Oxford Movement. In 1848 he followed John Henry Newman and others in joining the Roman Catholic Church, and spent the latter part of his life in Quebec, Canada. Bridges wrote several hymns during his lifetime, including "Crown Him with Many Crowns."

1833 Anglican clergyman John Keble preached his famous sermon on the subject of national apostasy, marking the beginning of the Oxford Movement in England. Keble was joined by John Henry Newman and E.B. Pusey, who led this effort to purify and revitalize the Anglican Church of their day. These men aroused great interest through their *Tracts for the Times* series (1833–41), reviving the ideals and practices of the pre-Reformation English (Catholic) church.

1875 Death of Simeon B. Marsh (b.1798), American Presbyterian chorister who wrote the hymn tune MARTYN ("Jesus, Lover of My Soul") at age 36. Gifted in music, Marsh taught in his first school of singing at the age of 19, and continued to teach in many churches of the Albany, New York, Presbytery for over 30 years.

1892 The Baptist Young People's Union held its first annual national convention in Detroit, Michigan. Organized the previous year, this new denominational organization for young people was inspired by the founding of the first official organization for church youth, called the Christian Endeavor Society, in 1881. It was established by Dr. Francis E. Clark, pastor of the Congregational Church of Portland, Maine.

July 15

1099 The Muslim citizens of Jerusalem surrendered their city to the armies of the First Crusade. In response, thousands of unarmed men, women and children were massacred by the zealous though misguided Christian soldiers.

1606 Birth of (Harmenszoon van Rijn) Rembrandt, Dutch painter, in Leiden, Holland. Famous as a portrait artist by age 25, he moved to Amsterdam where his wife died in 1642. Subsequent financial difficulties led to bankruptcy, which appeared to deepen the spiritual dimensions of his art. Rembrandt's greater understanding of the passion of Christ led him to make it the theme of nearly 90 paintings and etchings.

1779 Birth of Clement C. Moore, theological educator and writer, in New York City. With his family inheritance, Moore established the Episcopal General Theological Seminary in 1819, where he taught Greek and Hebrew literature for 28 years (1823–50). Ironically, Moore's fame is not as a great theologian, but as the author of the completely mythical Christmas story that begins: "'Twas the night before Christmas. . . ." He published it in 1823, at age 44, under the title *A Visit from St. Nicholas*.

1814 Birth of Edward Caswall, English clergyman, in Hampshire, England. In 1848 Caswall left the Anglican Church to become a Roman Catholic, and was ordained a priest in 1850. He published *Lyra Catholica* about this time, a collection of 197 English translations of Latin hymns. Because of doctrinal differences, few of Caswall's hymns have been used outside the Roman Catholic Church. Two hymns, however, have become popular in both Catholic and Protestant traditions: "Jesus, the Very Thought of Thee" and "When Morning Gilds the Skies."

1828 Birth of Josiah K. Allwood, American clergyman and author of the hymn "O They Tell Me of a Home Far Beyond the Skies," in Harrison County, Ohio.

He spent many years as a circuit rider for the United Brethren in Christ, and later as a presiding elder. About 1890 Allwood was returning home on a clear moonlit night when he wrote the words and composed the melody to the song "O They Tell Me of a Home Far Beyond the Skies" (THE UNCLOUDED DAY).

July 16

1054 The Roman and Greek Catholic churches excommunicated each other when Michael Cerularius, Patriarch of Constantinople, repudiated the claims of Pope Leo IX as universal head of Christendom. This "Great Schism" between the Western and Eastern churches persisted for 911 years. On Dec. 7, 1965, Pope Paul VI and Eastern Orthodox Patriarch Athenagoras I met to declare an end to the schism and to express the mutual hope for eventual reunification.

1228 Pope Gregory IX, who greatly favored the new mendicant religious orders—the Franciscans and the Dominicans—canonized St. Francis of Assisi.

1519 The Disputation of Leipzig ended after three weeks. It had been arranged by John Eck in an attempt to discredit Martin Luther's theology and force Luther into dangerous anti-papal statements. During the second of three separate debates, Luther made the controversial affirmation that church councils may not only err, but in fact had done so; that the "power of the keys" (cf. Matt. 16:19) was given to the church (i.e., the community of the faithful) rather than to the pope; and that belief in the preeminence of the Roman Catholic Church was not necessary to salvation.

1769 Spanish Franciscan friar Father Junipero Serra founded the San Diego de Alcala mission in California. San Diego was the first permanent Spanish settlement on the west coast of America. During the next 15 years, Father Serra founded 8 more missions, extending as far north as San Francisco Bay.

1863 Birth of Howard E. Smith, American church organist and author of the hymn tune for "Love Lifted Me." Little is known of Smith's life. Before his death in Norwalk, Connecticut, on Aug. 13, 1918, he was for many years a church organist in Connecticut. He composed a number of hymn tunes during his 55 years, including SAFETY ("Love Lifted Me").

1931 Death of C.T. (Charles Thomas) Studd (b.1862), English pioneer missionary. Converted under the ministry of D.L. Moody at age 21, while a student at Cambridge, Studd dedicated his inherited wealth and his life to Christ. He became one of the group of young men known as the "Cambridge Seven" who offered themselves to missionary service. He worked in China, India and central Africa. In 1913 he founded the Worldwide Evangelization Crusade, known today as Worldwide Evangelization for Christ, International.

1944 German Lutheran theologian and martyr of the Nazi persecution Dietrich Bonhoeffer observed in a letter from prison: "One has to live for some time in a community to understand how Christ is 'formed' in it (Gal. 4:19)."

1962 Swiss Reformed theologian Karl Barth pointed out in a letter: "In no case is God a 'what' that one may peep at close up or at a distance and value or disparage as one pleases. God is a 'Who.' "

1986 Death of Joe Bayly (b.1920), Christian writer and lecturer. Besides authoring nearly a dozen books, Bayly wrote a column for *Eternity* magazine for 25 years, edited *His* magazine from 1952–60 and served as president of the David C. Cook Publishing Co., near Chicago, Illinois. One of his most popular books, first published in 1960, was *The Gospel Blimp*, a humorous satire on how not to engage in Christian evangelism.

July 17

431 The Council of Ephesus adjourned. The third of the 21 ecumenical councils of the church, the council condemned Nestorianism (which denied the real unity of the divine and human natures in the Person of Christ), defined Mary's title as *"Theotokos"* (*"Bearer of God"*), and condemned Pelagianism (the belief that human nature could take the initial steps toward salvation by self-effort, unaided by divine grace).

1245 The First Council of Lyons adjourned, having held three sessions after convening on June 28. The 13th of the church's 21 historic ecumenical councils, Lyons I was opened by Pope Innocent IV, and attended by approximately 150 bishops. The council confirmed the deposition of Emperor Frederick II.

1274 The Second Council of Lyons adjourned, having held six sessions after convening on May 7. Convened by Pope Gregory X and attended by approximately 500 bishops, Lyons II achieved a temporary reunification of Rome and the separated eastern churches as well as issuing regulations for papal elections. Lyons II was the 14th Ecumenical Council.

1505 Twenty-one-year-old Martin Luther entered the Augustinian monastic order at Erfurt, Germany.

1674 Birth of Isaac Watts, pioneer in modern English hymnody, at Southampton, England. He became assistant pastor at a dissenting church in Mark Lane, London, in 1698, took over the pastorate three years later and remained at the same church the rest of his life. Publishing his first hymn book in 1707, Watts not only redefined the subject matter of adult hymns, but he also published the first hymnal for children in 1720. He wrote about 600 hymns, many among the finest in the English language. Some of his most popular include: "At the Cross," "Am I a Soldier of the Cross?" "Come, We That Love the Lord," "Jesus Shall Reign Where'er the Sun," "Joy to the World!," "O God, Our Help in Ages Past," "When I Survey the Wondrous Cross" and "We're Marching to Zion."

1836 Death of William White (b.1748), American patriarch of the Protestant Episcopal Church. Ordained in England in 1772 for the Anglican priesthood, White sided with the American colonies during the Revolutionary War. It was White who first coined the name "Protestant Episcopal." In 1786 he was chosen first bishop of the new American denomination—remaining in office for the next 50 years.

1856 A disastrous railroad accident near Philadelphia, Pennsylvania, took the lives of 66 children during a Sunday-school outing.

1917 American Baptist radio evangelist Charles E. Fuller was converted to a saving faith in Jesus Christ. Fuller was ordained in 1925, and in 1937 began a pioneer radio program called *The Old Fashioned Revival Hour*. In 1947 Fuller helped to found Fuller Theological Seminary in California.

1939   Death of Judson W. Van DeVenter (b.1855), American Methodist evangelist and author of the hymn "All to Jesus I Surrender" (1896). Having served as an active music layman in the Methodist Church for many years, Van DeVenter felt a call to the ministry. Licensed to preach, he began active evangelistic work, preaching throughout the U.S., England, and Scotland.

1942   The New Tribes Mission was organized, in both Los Angeles and Chicago, by Paul W. Fleming. Headquartered since 1978 in Sanford, Florida, N.T.M. is an interdenominational, fundamentalist mission agency engaged in establishing churches, training missionaries, and working in Bible translation and distribution. N.T.M. has over 1,000 staff members in 18 countries around the world.

1949   American missionary and Auca Indian martyr Jim Elliot recorded in his journal: "It is dangerous to get the cart before the horse, but essential in God's program to get the heart before the course."

1950   Death of Evangeline Cory Booth (b.1865), Salvation Army General. The daughter of founder William Booth, Evangeline supervised the field operations of the Army in Great Britain, Canada, and Alaska. In 1904 she was promoted to head the American branch of the denomination. She was elected General of the World Wide Salvation Army in 1934 and kept her position until retirement in 1939. She authored many popular Salvation Army hymns.

July 18

1100   Death of Godfrey of Bouillon (b.ca.1060), French Crusader. He led a German army during the First Crusade (1096–99). Three years later, he helped besiege and capture Jerusalem. He was elected Jerusalem's first Christian king, but died later that same year. In legend, Godfrey is depicted as the personification of the ideal Christian knight.

1323   Pope John XXII canonized Italian philosopher and Dominican theologian Thomas Aquinas (c.1225–74).

1504   Birth of Henry Bullinger, Swiss reformer, in the Swiss canton of Argau. In 1523 he joined the forces supporting Ulrich Zwingli's reformation of Zurich. After Zwingli's death in the fateful Battle of Kappel (1531), Bullinger succeeded him as chief pastor of Zurich, remaining at that post for the next 40 years. Bullinger enjoyed great prestige in England; he was a close associate of Cranmer, Melanchthon, Calvin and Beza. In 1566 he wrote the Second Helvetic Confession. He died at Zurich on Sept. 17, 1575.

1681   Death of George Neumark (b.1621), German educator and hymnwriter. Twice during his life he lost everything he owned—once to robbers and again to fire. These losses contributed much to the depth of his religious verse. We remember Neumark as the author and composer of the hymn "If Thou but Suffer God to Guide Thee."

1697   Death of Antonio Vieira (b.1608), Portuguese Jesuit missionary. Raised in Brazil, he returned to Lisbon in 1641. Eleven years later, he was sent back to Brazil as a missionary. He was responsible for the conversion of the Nheengai'bas Indians on the Island of Marajo.

1838 Death of Christmas Evans (b.1766), Welsh Baptist preacher. Born on Christmas Day to a cobbler, Evans grew up with little formal education. Ordained in 1789, he pastored in Anglesea between 1791–1826. By tradition, he is revered as one of the three greatest Welsh preachers—along with John Elias and William Williams. Though somewhat erratic in his theological opinions, Evans' gift for preaching derived from his skill in oratory as well as his great imagination.

1870 The Vatican I Council issued the proclamation *Pastor Aeternus*, which declared the pope's primacy and infallibility in deciding faith and morals. Vatican I was the 20th ecumenical council in the history of the Roman Catholic Church. Pope Pius IX presided and 800 bishops from around the world attended.

1876 American philosopher and essayist Ralph Waldo Emerson noted: "Great men are they who see that spiritual is stronger than material, that thoughts rule the world."

1889 Death of Elvina M. Hall (b.1820), American Methodist hymnwriter. She was a member of the Monument Street Methodist Church in Baltimore, Maryland, for more than 40 years. In 1865 at age 45, she penned the words to the hymn "Jesus Paid It All" (a.k.a. "I Heard the Savior Say").

1944 German Lutheran theologian and martyr Dietrich Bonhoeffer explained in a letter from prison: "It is not the religious act that makes the Christian . . . The religious act is always something partial; 'faith' is something whole, involving the whole of one's life. Jesus calls men not to new religion but to life."

July 19

1649 Edward Winslow, governor of the Plymouth Colony, helped organize the Society for Propagating the Gospel in New England, in London. The purpose of the society was to promote and support the conversion of the New England Indians to Christianity. The society was formed as a result of the interest created by the published story of John Eliot (1604–90), "Apostle to the American Indians."

1692 In the Massachusetts colony of Salem, five women were convicted and hanged for witchcraft: Sarah Good, Sarah Wildes, Elizabeth Howe, Rebecca Nourse, and Susannah Martin. (In the preceding month, Bridget Bishop became the first Salem resident executed for witchcraft.) Twenty persons died that year—the last on Sept. 22. All were convicted on charges brought against them by 15 young girls in the Salem community who claimed to have been bewitched by them and by as many as 140 other citizens in the area.

1799 Death of Samuel Medley (b.1738), English Baptist preacher. Converted after reading a sermon by Isaac Watts, Medley pastored in two different Baptist churches in Liverpool between 1767–99. An accomplished hymnwriter, one of Medley's hymns endures to this day: "O Could I Speak the Matchless Worth."

1825 The American Unitarian Association was founded by members of the liberal wing of the Congregational churches in New England. The movement was inspired by a sermon preached in 1819 by William Ellery Channing in Boston. In 1961 the organization changed its name to the Unitarian Universalist Association after merging with the Universalists.

1835 Birth of Jesse Engle, pioneer missionary. In 1898 he led the first party of five missionaries to Africa under the sponsorship of the Brethren in Christ Missions (headquartered today in Mount Joy, Pennsylvania).

1848 More than 300 men and women assembled in the Wesleyan Chapel at Seneca Falls, New York, for the first formal convention to discuss "the social, civil and religious condition and the rights of women." The event has been called the birthplace of the women's rights movement.

1904 Construction began on the Liverpool Cathedral in England. The work was completed and the cathedral consecrated 20 years later, on this same date in 1924.

1938 Death of Paul Rader (b.1879), American evangelist. He was pastor of the Moody Memorial Church in Chicago, Illinois (1914–21), pastor of the Chicago Gospel Tabernacle (1922–29), and president of the Christian and Missionary Alliance (1921–33). Rader was also a pioneer in radio evangelism.

1943 The city of Rome was bombed by nearly 500 Allied planes. During World War II, the city's networks of railroads and freight yards had made it a highly strategic location. Rome had previously been spared from attack by the Allies because of the city's immense cultural and religious significance.

1961 Swedish statesman and U.N. Secretary-General Dag Hammarskjold recorded a prayer in *Markings*: "Give us a pure heart, That we may see Thee, A humble heart, That we may hear Thee, A heart of Love, That we may serve Thee, A heart of faith, That we may live Thee, Thou, Whom I do not know, but Whose I am."

1970 The religious program *Frontiers of Faith* aired for the last time over NBC television. First broadcast in Oct. 1951, this long-running religious series was sponsored by the National Council of Churches. For several years, it shared its time slot with two other religious programs: *The Catholic Hour* and *The Eternal Light*.

July 20

1559 Scottish reformer John Knox asserted in a letter to Queen Elizabeth I: "Neither the consent of people, process of time, nor multitude of men, can establish a law which God shall approve. But whatsoever He approveth (by His eternal Word) that shall be approved, and whatsoever He dampeneth shall be condemned, though all men on earth would hazard the justification of the same."

1877 Birth of Jesse Irvin Overholtzer, mission pioneer. In 1937 Overholtzer incorporated Child Evangelism Fellowship in Chicago, Illinois. This evangelical mission agency works in over 60 countries throughout the world, and is engaged primarily in radio and TV broadcasting, evangelism, literature production and Bible correspondence courses.

1886 Birth of Paul Tillich, German Lutheran theologian, in Starzeddel, Prussia. Ordained to the Lutheran ministry in 1912, he served as a chaplain in the German forces during World War I. In 1933 his opposition to Hitler forced him to leave Germany and he settled in the U.S. He taught at Union Seminary and Columbia University in New York (1933–55), at Harvard (1955–62), and at the University of Chicago (1962–65). A prolific writer, Tillich's best-known work is his *Systematic Theology* (1951–63). Tillich's theology has been criticized because of its idealism, which hints of a pantheistic and impersonal God. Tillich seemed unable to grasp or faithfully represent, the "sola scriptura" principle of Protestant tradition.

1910 The Christian Endeavor Society of Missouri began a campaign to ban all motion pictures that depicted kissing between nonrelatives.

1962 Pope John XXIII sent invitations to all "separated Christian Churches and Communities" (all non-Catholic Christian denominations), asking each to send delegate-observers to the upcoming Vatican II Ecumenical Council in Rome.

July 21

1542 Pope Paul III issued the encyclical *Licet ab Initio*, which instituted the Congregation of the Roman Inquisition or the Holy Office. It was given the punitive powers of censorship as the central authority for combating heresy. (This is not to be confused with the Spanish Inquisition—urged by King Ferdinand and approved by Pope Sixtus IV in 1478—which sought to "convince" Spanish Jews of their heresy. Its unusual cruelties and political overtones lingered into the early 19th century.)

1816 Birth of Daniel March, American Congregational clergyman, in Millbury, Massachusetts. Ordained in 1845, he served churches in Connecticut, New York, Pennsylvania and Massachusetts. He also traveled and spoke widely in support of foreign missions. March is known to have written only one hymn: "Hark, the Voice of Jesus Calling."

1829 Birth of Priscilla Jane Owens, American public-schoolteacher, in Baltimore, Maryland. She spent her entire life in Baltimore where she taught public school for 49 years. A member of the Union Square Methodist Episcopal Church, she had particular interest in the work of the Sunday school. She published several articles and poems during her lifetime, including the hymn texts "We Have an Anchor" and "Jesus Saves" (a.k.a. "We Have Heard the Joyful Sound").

1925 Biology teacher John T. Scopes was convicted of teaching evolution in his Dayton, Tennessee, classroom. He was fined $100.

1936 Birth of Bill McChesney, American missionary to Africa. While serving in the Belgian Congo (modern Zaire) under the Worldwide Evangelization Crusade, he was martyred by rebels on Nov. 25, 1964, at the age of 28.

1958 English Christian apologist C.S. Lewis asserted in *Letters to an American Lady*: "What the devil loves is that vague cloud of unspecified guilt or unspecified virtue by which he lures us into despair or presumption."

July 22

1620 A small congregation of English Separatists who had previously taken refuge in the Netherlands with their minister John Robinson, left Leiden, Holland, bound for England. From there they emigrated to the New World. We refer to these persecuted religious emigrants as "the Pilgrims."

1680 French mystic Madame (Jeanne Marie Bouvier de la Motte) Guyon (1648–1717) achieved a "unitive state with the divine." She was a close friend of Archbishop Francois Fenelon (1651–1715). Her life and writings were marked by a fervent devotion to Jesus. The publication of her mystical visions, revelations and spiritual experiences ultimately led to her arrest and imprisonment by the Roman Catholic Church.

1822 Birth of Gregor Mendel, Austrian monk and botanist, in Heinzendorf, Austria (modern Czeckoslovakia). During the early 1860s, he discovered the basic laws of biological inheritance. His work explained the principles of natural selection but was ignored and almost forgotten before it was rediscovered by Dutch botanist Hugo M. DeVries in 1900.

1836 Birth of Emily E.S. Elliott, Anglican missions supporter, in Brighton, England. Daughter of the brother of Charlotte Elliott (author of the hymn "Just As I Am"), Emily was active in mission work. The hymns she wrote were first used in the church where her father was rector. One which we still sing today is the hymn "Thou Didst Leave Thy Throne."

1865 Birth of Peter P. Bilhorn, music composer and evangelist, in Mendota, Illinois. His father died in the American Civil War three months before Peter's birth. Peter was converted to saving faith at age 18 and began combining his love for music with evangelism. He composed many Gospel songs during his lifetime, and eventually became a well-known publisher of sacred music. He produced more than 1,400 Gospel songs and is remembered as composer of "I Will Sing the Wondrous Story" and as author and composer of the hymn "Sweet Peace, the Gift of God's Love."

1893 Birth of T.W. (Thomas Walter) Manson, British Presbyterian New Testament scholar, at Tynemouth, Northumberland. He taught New Testament at Mansfield College at Oxford (1932–36) and at Manchester University (1936–58). Manson's most important writings cover Jesus and the Gospels. His greatest contributions to New Testament scholarship were *The Teaching of Jesus* (1931) and *The Sayings of Jesus* (1949).

July 23

1742 Death of Susannah (nee Annesley) Wesley (b.1669), mother of John and Charles Wesley. Born the 25th child in a clergyman's family, Susannah is one of the most notable mothers in Christendom. It is difficult to imagine how different the lives of John and Charles Wesley might have been lived without her disciplined upbringing. Susannah Wesley was a devoted pastor's daughter, pastor's wife and pastors' mother.

1764 Death of Gilbert Tennent (b.1703), Irish Presbyterian preacher. He emigrated with his father, William Tennent, to America in about 1717. Ordained in 1726, Tennent supported the work of English revivalist George Whitefield in 1740 when he came to America to preach revival. Criticized by Presbyterian colleagues for his fiery zeal, Tennent preached his famous "Nottingham Sermon," which led to a division within the Presbyterian church—the "Old School" (conservatives) vs. the "New School" (those favoring innovations). Tennent helped reconcile the two sides in 1758. He served as pastor of the newly organized Second Presbyterian Church of Philadelphia, composed largely of converts and followers of George Whitefield, during his last 19 years (1743–64).

1779   Pioneer American Methodist Bishop Francis Asbury recorded in his journal: "Arose, as I commonly do, before five o'clock in the morning, to study the Bible. I find none like it; and find it of more consequence to a preacher to know his Bible well, than all the languages or books in the world—for he is not to preach these, but the Word of God."

1808   Death of Francois H. Barthelemon, French violinist and composer. A member of the Swedenborgian church, he toured Germany, Italy and France with his music. Barthelemon wrote five operas, one oratorio and six symphonies, as well as concertos and violin sonatas. Ill health plagued him during his last years and he died a brokenhearted paralytic. Two of his compositions have become hymn tunes: AUTUMN ("Hail, Thou Once Despised Jesus") and BALERMA ("Oh, for a Closer Walk with God").

1846   Birth of William R. Featherstone, Canadian Methodist, in Montreal, Quebec. Little is known of his life, except that he was a member of the St. James United Church in Montreal and that he wrote the hymn "My Jesus, I Love Thee, I Know Thou Art Mine" sometime before he reached the age of sixteen.

1860   Birth of William Washington McConnell, pioneer American missionary. He was the first missionary to be sent out by the Central American Mission after its founding in 1890. McConnell arrived in Costa Rica in Feb. 1891.

1918   Death of Joseph H. Gilmore (b.1834), American Baptist clergyman. Ordained in 1862, he pastored several churches until 1868 when he was invited to teach at the University of Rochester in New York. He remained there until he retired in 1911. Respected and loved in both religious and educational circles, he is also remembered for authoring the hymn "He Leadeth Me!" which he wrote when he was 28.

July 24

1550   French-born Swiss reformer John Calvin advised in a letter: "If you make a constant study of the word of the Lord, you will be quite able to guide your life to the highest excellence."

1725   Birth of John Newton, Anglican clergyman and hymnwriter, in London, England. For ten years of his early life, he was a slave shipmaster. Converted about 1747, he began to study for Anglican ordination. He was appointed curate at Olney in 1764, where he became an intimate friend of poet William Cowper. Together they published *Olney Hymns* (1779), to which Newton contributed 280 hymn texts. Among Newton's best-loved hymns are: "Amazing Grace," "Glorious Things of Thee are spoken" and "How Sweet the Name of Jesus Sounds."

1819 Birth of Josiah G. Holland, American writer and author of the Christmas hymn "There's a Song in the Air," in Belchertown, Massachusetts. After a brief career in medicine, Holland established a weekly newspaper, but later joined the editorial staff of the Springfield, Massachusetts *Republican*. Holland eventually helped establish *Scribner's Magazine* and served as its editor until his death.

1874 Birth of Oswald Chambers, evangelical Bible teacher, in Aberdeen, Scotland. The son of a Baptist pastor, Chambers was converted under the ministry of C.H. Spurgeon. In 1906–07, he toured the world, preaching among Methodist and Pentecostal Holiness groups, and worked with the Pentecostal League of Prayer from 1907–10. The last ministry of his brief 42 years was as chaplain to the British troops stationed in Egypt. Chambers has been called an "evangelical mystic" by some; and nowhere does this dimension of his faith come out more prominently than in his devotional classic *My Utmost for His Highest*.

1921 The Latin America Evangelization Campaign was founded at Stony Brook in New York City, by Harry Strachan. Headquartered originally in Philadelphia, this evangelical, interdenominational mission agency is now known as the Latin American Mission, Inc., with its headquarters in Coral Gables, Florida. L.A.M. works in eight Central and South American countries and is engaged primarily in evangelism and literature production. It also offers additional support for other missionary agencies.

1921 Death of C.I. (Cyrus Ingersoll) Scofield (b.1843), editor of the *Scofield Reference Bible*. Converted at age 36, Scofield was ordained into the Congregational ministry in 1882. He served at the First Church of Dallas, Texas (1882–95; 1902–07), and at the Moody Church in Northfield, Massachusetts (1895–1902). He also founded the Central American Mission in 1890.

July 25

1741 English revivalist George Whitefield asserted in a letter: "Your extremity shall be God's opportunity."

1825 Birth of Henry Blodget, American Congregational missionary. Under the sponsorship of the American Board of Commissioners for Foreign Missions, Blodget became a missionary to China from 1854–94. During his 40 years in the field, he helped translate the New Testament into the colloquial Mandarin of Peking.

1848 Birth of A.J. (Arthur James) Balfour, British statesman and philosopher, near Edinburgh, Scotland. Britain's Prime Minister from 1902–05, he later served as foreign secretary and issued the *Balfour Declaration* (1917), which favored the creation of "a national home for the Jewish people" in Palestine. Balfour died in 1930, 18 years before the modern state of Israel became a reality (1948).

1854 Birth of Francis H. Rowley, American Baptist clergyman and humanitarian, in Hilton, New York. Ordained in 1878, Rowley served Baptist churches in Pennsylvania, Massachusetts, and Illinois. In addition, he was president of the Massachusetts Society for the Prevention of Cruelty to Animals for over 35 years. The Rowley School of Humanities at Oglethorpe University in Atlanta, Georgia was named in his honor. Rowley is more widely known for authoring the hymn "I Will Sing the Wondrous Story."

1899 Birth of Stuart W.K. Hine, English missionary. In 1923, while he and his wife were ministering to the people of the Ukraine, they were introduced to a Russian version of the Swedish hymn "O Store Gud." They sang it as a duet and it had a telling effect on the unsaved everywhere they went. Later, while crossing the Carpathian Mountains into southern Russia, the beauty of the surrounding mountains inspired them to write original English lyrics to the song. They entitled it "How Great Thou Art." In 1974 a *Christian Herald* magazine poll named "How Great Thou Art" the most popular hymn in America.

1918 Death of Walter Rauschenbusch (b.1861), American Baptist clergyman. Born in Rochester, New York, of German immigrant parents, he pastored the Second German Baptist Church in New York City from 1886–97, where he both saw and entered into the plight of immigrants and others who were socially and economically disadvantaged. After 1897 he taught at Rochester Theological Seminary, first New Testament (1897–1902), then church history (1902–1918). With a lifelong interest in the social implications of the Gospel, Rauschenbusch emphasized economic and political programs as methods of realizing the Kingdom of God on earth.

1968 Pope Paul VI published the encyclical *Humanae Vitae*, which condemned artificial methods of birth control. The document disappointed many in the church because the majority of those on the Pontifical Commission, appointed in 1963 to study the subject, had reported in favor of contraception under certain circumstances.

July 26

1603 James I was crowned King of England. He had already been Scotland's King James VI since 1567. When Elizabeth I of England died, his descent from Henry VII made him the nearest heir to the English throne. It was James I who sponsored the English Bible translation that was published in 1611 and came to be called the King James Version.

1741 English revivalist George Whitefield encouraged in a letter: "Venture daily upon Christ, go out in His strength, and He will enable you to do wonders."

1802 Birth of Gottfried Thomasius, German Lutheran theologian. He taught at the University of Erlangen, where he developed a Christology around the *"kenosis"* ("emptying") of Christ at His incarnation (based on the Greek verb in Phil. 2:7). Thomasius' most important published work is his *Christi Person und Werk* (1852–61).

1817 Death of John Fawcett (b.1740), English Baptist clergyman and educator. Ordained in 1763, he later founded the Northern Education Society, now known as Rawdon College. He penned over 150 hymns, most of them intended to be sung at the conclusion of the worship service. Two of these hymns that we still use in this manner are "Blest Be the Tie That Binds" and "Lord, Dismiss Us with Thy Blessing."

1926 The Sanctuary of Our Lady of Victory, in Lackawanna, New York, became the first Roman Catholic Church in the U.S. to be consecrated as a basilica.

1933 Death of Charles A. Tindley (b.1851), Black American Methodist preacher. Born of slave parents and orphaned by age 5, Tindley taught himself to read and write by age 17. He studied theology and in 1885 was ordained to the Methodist ministry. After serving a number of smaller country churches throughout the New England area, he was called to Philadelphia's Calvary Methodist Episcopal Church in 1902. Under his leadership, the membership grew to 12,500. Tindley, known as "the distinguished Negro Methodist pastor from Philadelphia," was also a talented writer of Gospel songs. Four of his most moving hymns include "By and By," "Leave It There," "Nothing Between" and "Stand by Me."

1935 The Open Bible Standard Churches, Inc., was formed by the merger of two separate revival movements: Bible Standard, Inc. (founded in Eugene, Oregon in 1919), and Open Bible Evangelistic Association (founded in Des Moines, Iowa, in 1932). Today, the organization is headquartered in Des Moines, Iowa, and is comprised of 275 churches with approximately 35,000 members. The church is "fundamental in doctrine, evangelical in spirit, missionary in vision and pentecostal in testimony."

July 27

1741 Birth of Francois H. Barthelemon, French violinist and composer, in Bordeaux, France. A member of the Swedenborgian church, he toured Germany, Italy and France with his music. Barthelemon wrote five operas, one oratorio and six symphonies, as well as concertos and violin sonatas. Ill health plagued him during his last years and he died a brokenhearted paralytic. Two of his compositions have since become hymn tunes: AUTUMN ("Hail, Thou Once Despised Jesus") and BALERMA ("Oh, for a Closer Walk with God").

1861 Birth of Cyrus S. Nusbaum, American Methodist clergyman, in Middlebury, Indiana. Ordained in 1886, Nusbaum served six different pastorates in Kansas, was appointed by President Woodrow Wilson to inspect the American Red Cross in France during World War I, and traveled through the Midwest as a conference evangelist for a while. He wrote and composed several hymns during his lifetime, including "Would You Live for Jesus, and Be Always Pure and Good?"(a.k.a. "His Way with Thee").

1901 Death of B.F. (Brooke Foss) Westcott (b.1825), English New Testament textual scholar. Ordained in the Church of England in 1851, Westcott was appointed Regius Professor of Divinity at Cambridge in 1870. He lectured the first three years on early church history and for the next five years on church doctrine. After that, he taught on specific books or passages in the New Testament. He was appointed Bishop of Durham in 1890, to succeed J.B. Lightfoot, and remained at this post until his death eleven years later. In 1881 Westcott published his most memorable work. Having made a scientific evaluation of the many ancient biblical manuscripts that had been discovered, Westcott and his colleague F.J.A. Hort edited the most precise critical text of the Greek New Testament compiled to that date. This work has since become the foundation stone of almost all subsequent editions of the New Testament.

1903 Death of Caroline ("Lina") V. Sandell Berg (b.1832), Swedish hymnwriter. She lost her father at sea when she was 26, and afterward wrote some of the most beautiful hymns that ever flowed from her pen. She has been called the "Fanny Crosby of Sweden." Two of her best-loved hymns in English translation are "Children of the Heavenly Father" and "Day by Day."

1933 Death of Rev. Arthur Stephen Paynter (b.1862), missions pioneer. In 1897 he and his wife Agnes founded the India Christian Mission in the Kumoan District of north India. In 1904 the I.C.M. headquarters moved to Nuwara Eliya, Ceylon (modern Sri Lanka). Today, this evangelical, interdenominational fund-transmitting agency supports agriculture, education and orphanage work in both India and Sri Lanka.

July 28

1750 Death of Johann Sebastian Bach (b.1685), German composer. A devout Lutheran, Bach was unquestionably the greatest organ composer of all time. His toccatas, preludes and fugues, and over 100 pieces based on Lutheran chorales, were written for various functions in the church liturgy. (Unfortunately, the performance of these compositions is largely confined to the concert hall.) Bach's two great monumental works are his *Mass in B Minor* (1724–46) and the *St. Matthew Passion* (1729), the latter considered by some to be "Western civilization's supreme musical achievement." Of his other choral works *The Magnificat* and *The Christmas Oratorio* are the most celebrated.

1847 The Mormon community that followed Brigham Young across the plains chose the site for their future temple (and present-day headquarters) on the Great Salt Lake in Utah. The huge Mormon Tabernacle was constructed from 1853–93.

1881 Birth of J. (John) Gresham Machen, American Presbyterian theologian, in Baltimore, Maryland. Having taught at Princeton Seminary from 1906–29, Machen and other fundamentalists founded Westminster Seminary, where Machen served as president and professor of New Testament from 1929–37. In 1936 Machen and sixteen others established the Orthodox Presbyterian Church. Machen was an active scholar and writer who never married. Two of his many books, both still in print, are *New Testament Greek for Beginners* (1923) and *The Virgin Birth of Christ* (1930–32).

1942 Death of W.M. (William Matthew) Flinders Petrie (b.1853), English archeologist. He was regarded by W.F. Albright as "the greatest genius among biblical archeologists." Petrie headed the British School of Archaeology in Egypt, and directed its excavations in Egypt and Palestine between 1880–1937. He published over 100 books, most of them excavation reports.

1960 American Trappist monk Thomas Merton wrote in a letter: "I can depend less and less on my own power and sense of direction—as if I ever had any. But the Lord supports and guides me without my knowing how, more and more apart from my own action and even in contradiction to it. It is so strange to advance backwards and get to where you are going in a totally unexpected way."

July 29

1776 Pioneer American Methodist Bishop Francis Asbury remarked in his journal: "My present mode of conduct is as follows—to read about a hundred
pages a day; usually to pray in public five times a day; to preach in the open
air every other day; and to lecture in prayer-meeting every evening. And if it
were in my power, I would do a thousand times as much for such a gracious
and blessed Master."

1833 Death of William Wilberforce (b.1759), English philanthropist and abolitionist. Converted to an evangelical faith at a young age, Wilberforce was
encouraged to serve Christ through politics, which he entered in 1790. He
became interested in various social reforms, but his main concern was the
abolition of slavery. In 1807 he succeeded in having a law passed abolishing
slave trade. A bill abolishing slavery itself passed in 1833. Wilberforce was
also instrumental in founding the Church Missionary Society in 1799 and the
British and Foreign Bible Society in 1804.

1856 Death of Robert A. Schumann (b.1810), German composer. Schumann
enjoyed a prodigious musical career, during which he wrote symphonies and
chamber music, being an early leader in the Romantic school of 19th-century
music. One of his compositions, CANONBURY, has endured today as a hymn
tune. To it is sung the popular hymn of preparation "Lord, Speak to Me That
I May Speak."

1866 Birth of T.O. (Thomas Obediah) Chisholm, American Methodist, in Simpson County, Kentucky. He had several different careers; he taught grade
school, was editor of his hometown newspaper, served briefly as a Methodist
pastor and did some farming. From 1909–53, he was a life insurance salesman. Chisholm wrote more than 1,200 religious poems during his lifetime,
and published more than 800. Several later became hymn texts, including
"Great Is Thy Faithfulness" and "Living for Jesus a Life That Is True."

1905 Birth of Dag Hammarskjold, Swedish diplomat, in Jonkoping, Sweden.
Hammarskjold gained international prominence during his eight years as Secretary-General of the United Nations. But he endeared himself to Christians
everywhere when his personal journal was published in 1964, three years after
his untimely death in a plane crash. The journal is a spiritual diary, and was
published under the title *Markings*.

1957 Death of William M. Runyan (b.1870), American Methodist clergyman
and sacred music editor who composed the hymn tune for "Great Is Thy
Faithfulness" (FAITHFULNESS). Ordained at age 21, he served in Kansas pastorates for 12 years before increasing deafness forced him to resign from the
ministry. From 1925 until his retirement in 1948, Runyan was closely associated with Moody Bible Institute and Hope Publishing Company, both in
Chicago. When he was 53 and still living in Kansas, Runyan composed the
hymn tune FAITHFULNESS.

1974 The first eleven women priests in the Episcopal Church were ordained,
in Philadelphia's Church of the Advocate. This ordination was ruled invalid
by the House of Bishops on Aug. 15; but on Oct. 17, the same body approved
the ordination of women as priests in principle.

July 30

1715 Death of Nahum Tate (b.1652), English poet, playwright and author of "While Shepherds Watched their Flocks by Night." Born in Dublin, he emigrated to England to seek literary fame. He wrote many plays, achieving fame through his adaptation of others' works rather than by creating his own. Appointed Poet Laureate of England in 1692, Tate's chief claim to fame was his 1696 metrical version of the Psalms, which he coauthored with Nicholas Brady.

1718 Death of William Penn (b.1644), founder of Pennsylvania. Raised an Anglican, Penn became a Quaker in 1667, and sought to found a colony in America for Quakers and others suffering religious oppression. In 1682 he obtained a grant of land for the area constituting modern Pennsylvania and Delaware. The constitution he drew up for the new colony permitted all forms of public worship compatible with monotheism and religious liberty. Penn was governor of Pennsylvania from 1682–1718, with the exception of 1683.

1726 Birth of William Jones of Nayland (b.1726), Anglican divine. Ordained in 1649, Jones held several pastorates before being appointed as perpetual curate of Nayland in 1777, in Suffolk, England. During his ministry, Jones sought to keep alive the high church traditions among Anglicans who otherwise rejected the Oxford Movement. Jones was skilled at articulating complex theological ideas, and in 1756 published *The Catholic Doctrine of the Trinity*, in which he sought to prove from Scripture that the church's belief in the Trinity is not mere tradition.

1784 Death of Denis Diderot (b.1713), key French promoter of the Enlightenment. Educated by the Jesuits, Diderot went on to study literature, languages and science in Paris. The request from a bookseller for a French translation of a popular encyclopedia suggested the need of a new French encyclopedia to Diderot. The work occupied most of the rest of his life; the first volume appeared in 1751 and the last in 1772. The *Encyclopedie, ou Dictionnarei Raisonne des Sciences, des Arts, et des Metiers* was 28 volumes long, with eight more added later. Diderot's encyclopedia offended the church of his day because it advocated religious toleration and democracy.

1860 Death of August F.C. Vilmar (b.1800), German Lutheran theologian. He began his teaching career in 1823 as a rationalist and liberal. His studies in the church fathers and Lutheran confessions led him to break with these movements and to become leader of the theological conservatives in Hesse. His theology was best represented in his 1856 *Die Theologie der Tatsachen wider die Theologie der Rhetorik*. Vilmar stressed the objective facts of salvation and their effect in human experience. He decried theology which was mere talk, or "intellectual knowledge." Vilmar also stressed the mediation of salvation through the ministerial office over the priesthood of all believers. He regarded the institutional church as the last wall of defense against the disruptive political and theological forces at work in the Europe of his day.

1871 Death of Henry Longueville Mansel (b.1820), Anglican clergyman and dean of St. Paul's from 1868. Ordained in 1844, Mansel taught at Oxford from 1859. He achieved fame as a teacher of logic, although his real interest lay in the field of metaphysics and psychology. In his Bampton Lectures of 1858,

Mansel argued that the human intellect acquired knowledge of the nature of God from special revelation alone. This thesis brought Mansel into a protracted conflict with F.D. Maurice and John Stuart Mill.

1956 "In God We Trust" became the official motto of the U.S., by an act of Congress signed by President Dwight D. Eisenhower.

1976 Death of Rudolf Bultmann (b.1884), German Lutheran New Testament scholar. As professor at Marburg (1921–51), his 1921 publication *History of the Synoptic Tradition* made him one of the three major pioneers in modern form criticism of the Gospels. (The other two were M. Dibelius and K.L. Schmidt.) Form criticism argues that the Gospels contain smaller textual units which had developed independently during the early years of oral preaching in the church. During his later years, Bultmann published *Kerygma and Myth* (1941), which advocated the need to "demythologize," to remove and/or rework, obsolete metaphors in the Gospels (such as the conception of the physical universe, the values of a monarchy, militaristic symbols, the virgin birth of Christ, etc.) so that the central message of the Gospel (the *kerygma*) might be made meaningful to modern humanity. Modern evangelicals reject much of Bultmann's work because he accepted few of Christ's words or acts as reality.

July 31

1367 Death of Giovanni Colombini (b.ca.1300), Roman Catholic religious leader. He devoted himself to serving the poor and sick. About 1360 he founded the religious order "Clerici Apostolici S. Hieronymi," more commonly known as the Gesuati. Approved by Pope Urban V in 1367, the year Colombini died, the congregation lasted a little more than 300 years before it was dissolved by Pope Clement IX in 1668.

1556 Death of Ignatius Loyola (b.1491), Spanish Roman Catholic reformer and founder of the Jesuits. In 1534 he and six companions made a vow of poverty and chastity, devoting their lives to apostolic labors. Six years later, in 1540, the Society of Jesus was officially sanctioned by Pope Paul III in the bull *Regimini Militantis Ecclesiae*. Ignatius was unanimously chosen the first general of the order and drew up the Constitutions of the Society (1547–50). He was canonized in 1622 by Pope Gregory XV. Today, with their emphasis on education and ecclesiastical preparation, the Jesuits comprise some of the most learned members of the Roman Catholic Church.

1773 Anglican hymnwriter John Newton declared in a letter: "Duty is our part; the care is His."

1776 Francis Salvador, a plantation owner from South Carolina, became the first Jew to die for American independence when he was killed in a skirmish with the British.

1828 English Catholic John Henry Newman asserted in a letter: "Most pious men who have gone out, have hardly had that flexibility and elasticity of religious principle which can accommodate itself to the world, and have worked stiffly."

1859 Death of James Waddell Alexander (b.1804), American Presbyterian cler-gyman, teacher and hymnwriter. After his ordination, Alexander pastored sev-eral large Presbyterian churches in New Jersey and New York between 1829 and his death. Maintaining a lifelong interest in hymnology, he especially enjoyed translating Latin and German hymn texts. His most famous hymn is "O Sacred Head, Now Wounded," translated from a Latin hymn originally attributed to Bernard of Clairvaux (1091–1153).

1886 Death of Franz Liszt (b.1811), Hungarian composer and piano virtuoso. In his youth he studied under Beethoven; he later formed close friendships with H. Berlioz, F. Chopin, N. Paganini and R. Wagner. The combination of his sensitive spirit, his mother's early religious training and broken romance drove Liszt to radical ascetic practices which almost cost him his life. In 1865 he joined the Franciscans. Regarded by some as "perhaps the greatest pianist of all time," he advanced the playing technique and methods of composition for the piano in his more than 1,200 works. His interest in religious music is not often noted, but Liszt composed three large-scale settings of the Mass, two oratorios and a variety of other sacred works.

1889 Death of Horatius Bonar (b.1808), the Scottish preacher-poet who wrote the hymn "I Heard the Voice of Jesus Say." Ordained in the Church of Scotland in 1837, he joined the new Free Church in 1843. In 1866 he began pastoring the Chalmers Memorial Free Church in Edinburgh. In theology, Bonar was conservative and premillenarian. He authored many books, but is today re-membered chiefly as a hymnwriter. Of the more than 600 hymns he penned, 100 are still in use.

1908 Death of Winfield S. Weeden (b.1847), American sacred chorister. Wee-den taught singing schools, did evangelism, worked for the Y.M.C.A., spoke at Christian Endeavor and Epworth conventions and all the while composed numerous Gospel songs. He is remembered primarily for one hymn tune: SURRENDER ("I Surrender All").

1968 The National Council of Catholic Bishops issued a statement on birth control in support of Pope Paul VI's encyclical of the previous week. The statement reiterated the Pope's condemnation of artificial methods of birth control—in spite of the sentiment of several priests and laymen who publicly disagreed with the Pope's position.

1970 The complete New American Standard Version of the Bible (N.A.S.B.) was first published. (The New Testament had been published in 1963.)

August

August 1

1521 German reformer Martin Luther stated in a letter: "Be a sinner and sin boldly, but believe and rejoice in Christ even more boldly, for He is victorious over sin, death, and the world. . . . No sin will separate us from the Lamb. . . . Do you think the purchase price that was paid for the redemption of our sins by so great a Lamb is too small?"

1558 French-born Swiss reformer John Calvin declared in a letter: "The most noble and the most excellent have to glory in their littleness in order to be classed among the subjects of Jesus Christ who are rejected and despised."

1779 Birth of Francis Scott Key, American patriot. Key is most popularly known as the author of "The Star Spangled Banner," which he wrote on Sept. 14, 1814, during the War of 1812, and which became the official U.S. national anthem in 1931. But Key was also a devout Christian, a member of the Protestant Episcopal Church. From 1814–26, he was a delegate to the general conventions of his denomination. He was also one of the first to help in the American Sunday School Union.

1834 Death of Robert Morrison (b.1782), first Protestant missionary to China. Having studied the Chinese language in England, the London Missionary Society ordained him in 1807 and sent him to Canton, where he became a translator for the British East India Company, a position he held for the next 25 years. His missionary labors were largely literary. He translated the New Testament into Chinese (1814), constructed a Chinese grammar (1815), founded an Anglo-Chinese college (1820), edited a six-volume Chinese dictionary (1821), and in 1823 completed a translation of the entire Bible into Chinese.

1843 Birth of William Sanday, English New Testament scholar. Ordained in 1869, he spent much of his life teaching at the universities of Durham and Oxford. Theologically, Sanday was a moderate conservative who brought European continental biblical criticism into English scholarship. Of his many scholarly writings, Sanday is best remembered for the definitive commentary on Romans (1895) for the *International Critical Commentary* series that he coauthored with A.C. Headlam. He also published many works on Christology, including his 1911 *Oxford Studies in the Synoptic Problem*.

1890 Birth of Walther Eichrodt, Reformed Old Testament scholar, in Baden, Germany. He taught at the universities of Erlangen and Basel, starting in 1918. Eichrodt is highly regarded by Christian evangelicals for his three-volume *Theology of the Old Testament* (1933–39).

1953 English scholar and Christian apologist C.S. Lewis defended holy living in *Letters to an American Lady*: "How little people know who think that holiness is dull. When one meets the real thing, it is irresistible."

August 2

1776 English founder of Methodism, John Wesley, admonished in a letter to his sister: "Use all the ability which God giveth, and He will give you more."

1908 Death of Fredrik Franson (b.1852), missions pioneer. In 1890 Franson founded The Evangelical Alliance Mission in Chicago. T.E.A.M. is an evangelical, interdenominational mission agency, headquartered in Wheaton, Illinois. Working with 929 staff in 26 overseas countries, T.E.A.M. is committed to evangelism, church planting and development. The staff members are also involved in education, linguistics, medicine, radio, and other special services.

1930 Death of Jesse L. Hurlbut (b.1843), U.S. Methodist clergyman and author of *Hurlbut's Story of the Bible*. After holding several pastorates between 1865–79, Hurlbut worked closely with the American Sunday School Union for twenty years. He was also one of the founders of the Methodist Epworth League in 1889 (forerunner of the modern U.M.Y.F., or youth fellowship).

1948 Jim Elliot, American missionary and Auca Indian martyr, recorded this petition in his journal: "Father, teach me the speed of eternity. Synchronize my movements with the speed of Thine Own heart—then, hasting or halting, I shall be in good time."

1975 The last segment of *Moses, the Lawgiver* aired over CBS television. The six-part miniseries on the life of Moses was an Italian-English production filmed in Israel. The first segment aired in June, and featured Burt Lancaster as Moses, Irene Papas as Zipporah, and Anthony Quayle as Aaron.

1982 American Presbyterian apologist Francis Schaeffer, two years before his death from cancer, explained in a letter: "I do believe that at times the Lord gives direct healing. But there is the constant, pernicious danger of this slipping into the idea that if a person is a true believer and has sufficient faith, he will always be healed. This is clearly not what the Bible teaches."

August 3

1739 English revivalist George Whitefield clarified his theology in a letter: "I am no friend to sinless perfection. I believe the being (though not the dominion) of sin remains in the hearts of the greatest believers."

1836 Birth of Augustus H. Strong, U.S. Baptist theologian, in Rochester, New York. Ordained in 1861, Strong pastored for 11 years. From 1872–1912, he was president of Rochester Theological Seminary. Highly regarded by his generation as a teacher and leader, Strong was also president of the American Baptist Missionary Union (1892–95) and first president of the Northern Baptist Convention (1905–10). He published his three-volume *Systematic Theology*, which is still in print, in 1886.

1858 Birth of Maltbie D. Babcock, U.S. Presbyterian clergyman, in Syracuse, New York. He pastored three prominent churches in Maryland and New York

City. Remembered today as a hymnwriter, Babcock wrote a 16-verse poem that was published posthumously in 1901. Later reduced to four verses and set to music, Babcock's poem became the hymn "This Is My Father's World."

1897 Death of Emily E.S. Elliott (b.1836), Anglican missions supporter and hymnwriter. She was the daughter of Edward B. Elliott, rector of St. Mark's Anglican Church in Brighton, England. Gifted in music, most of her hymns were first used in her father's church. One, which was based on Luke 2:7, was written to teach children the meaning of the Advent and Christmas seasons: "Thou Didst Leave Thy Throne."

1902 Birth of Martin Noth, Lutheran Old Testament scholar, in Dresden, Germany. His research concentrated on the "history-of-traditions" approach to understanding the documents of the Old Testament.

1933 Death of Adam Geibel (b.1885), sacred music editor. An improperly treated eye infection left him blind from age eight. But because of his deep love of music, Geibel studied in Philadelphia and became a skilled organist, conductor and composer. He wrote both sacred and secular music and founded the Adam Geibel Music Company, which later merged to become the Rodeheaver Company. His many hymn tunes include GEIBEL, to which we sing the hymn "Stand Up, Stand Up for Jesus."

1944 German Lutheran theologian and Nazi martyr Dietrich Bonhoeffer commented in a letter from prison: "The Church must not underestimate the importance of human example (which has its origin in the humanity of Jesus and is so important in Paul's teaching); it is not abstract argument, but example, that gives its word emphasis and power."

1959 English scholar and Christian apologist C.S. Lewis remarked in *Letters to an American Lady*: "When we lose one blessing, another is often most unexpectedly given in its place."

August 4

1874 Methodist minister John H. Vincent and manufacturer Lewis Miller established the Chautauqua Assembly: a two-week summer retreat combining summer recreation with the training of Sunday-school teachers and church workers. This first assembly ran through Aug. 18 and was held on the shore of Lake Chautauqua in northwest New York state.

1884 Birth of Sigmund O.P. Mowinckel, Bible scholar, at Kjerringoy, Norway. He taught Old Testament theology at Oslo University from 1917–54. Of his many contributions to Old Testament studies, Mowinckel's most important publications include *The Royal Psalms in the Bible* (1916), *Psalmenstudien* (1921–24), and *The Psalms in Israel's Worship* (1951; English translation 1963).

1892 English medical missionary Sir Wilfred T. Grenfell (1866–1940) first arrived in Labrador, Newfoundland. For 42 years he labored as a physician and missionary among the fisherfolk, and was instrumental in building orphanages, hospitals, cooperative stores and other community organizations. In 1927 King George V of England knighted him for his work.

1959 Swedish Christian statesman Dag Hammarskjold observed in *Markings*: "We encounter a world where each man is a cosmos, of whose riches we can only catch glimpses."

August 5

1540 Birth of Joseph Justus Scaliger, French history scholar, in Agen, France. He was raised a Roman Catholic by his Italian parents, but became a Huguenot (French Protestant) in 1562. For 30 years he pursued private research under the patronage of nobleman Louis Chasteigner. Scaliger escaped the St. Bartholomew's Day Massacre of 1572 by retreating to Geneva, Switzerland, to teach. His editions of Latin authors helped develop the ground rules for the science of textual criticism. His 1583 *On the Correction of Chronology* also helped place historical chronology on scientific ground. Scaliger's most famous disciples include Daniel Heinsius (1480–1655) and Hugo Grotius (1583–1645).

1570 A group of Spanish Jesuit missionaries, led by Fray Batista Segura, arrived in the Chesapeake Bay area of America for the purpose of converting the Indians to Christianity. (Unfortunately, six months later, in Feb. 1571, everyone in the Segura group was murdered by the Indians, leading to the withdrawal of other Jesuit missionaries from the Virginia area.)

1579 Death of Stanislaus Hosius (b.1504), Polish cardinal and Counter-Reformation leader. Ordained to the priesthood in 1843, Hosius was made Bishop of Ermland in 1551, where one of his main tasks was to combat Protestantism. He exercised his polemic skill against Protestant reformers such as Johann Brenz and Jan a Lasco, making him one of the greatest of the Polish counter-reformers. Hosius's 1553 theological classic *Confessio Catholicae Fidei Christiana* sought to prove that Catholicism and Christianity were identical. In 1561 Pope Pius IV made him a cardinal and appointed him papal legate at Trent, where Hosius became a leading voice in the doctrinal discussions of the final sessions of the Council of Trent.

1604 Baptism of John Eliot, American apostle to the American Indians. Born in Hertfordshire, England, Eliot graduated from Cambridge in 1622, after distinguishing himself in language skill. His increasingly nonconformist views led him to America in 1631. He began teaching in the church at Roxbury, Massachusetts, in 1632, and kept the position during his remaining 58 years. He began his work among the American Indians in 1646. By 1674 he had organized his "praying Indians" into 14 self-governing communities. (The work at Natick, Massachusetts, where the first Indian church was founded, continued until the death of its last native pastor in 1716.) Eliot also helped prepare and publish the Bay Psalm Book (1640), the first American metrical version of the Psalms, and the first book printed in America. Eliot translated the Bible into the Algonquin language in 1661–63. Renowned for his learning, piety, evangelistic zeal and practical wisdom, Eliot's missionary zeal led to the formation of the Society for the Propagation of the Gospel in New England in 1649.

1656 Eight Quakers from England arrived in Boston. They were immediately imprisoned without trial by the Puritans of the Massachusetts Bay Colony, and kept until the vessels that brought them were readied to return to England. (Similar incidents occurred in 1657 and 1659.)

1835 Death of Thomas McCrie (b.1772), Scottish divine and church historian. In 1796 he was ordained minister of the Second Associate Church at Edinburgh. In 1806 McCrie and three other ministers left the General Association Synod and formed the Constitutional Association Presbytery. Deposed by his church in 1809, McCrie's congregation withdrew and built the West Richmond Street Church for him, where he pastored until his death in 1835. His greatest literary achievement was a two-volume biography, *The Life of John Knox.*

1869 Birth of Grant Colfax Tullar, U.S. Methodist music evangelist, in Bolton, Connecticut. Named after President Grant and Vice-President Schuyler Colfax, Tullar was converted at a Methodist camp meeting at age 19. For ten years, he was the song leader for evangelist Major George A. Hilton, but in 1893 he helped found the Tullar-Meredith Publishing Co. in New York, which produced church and Sunday-school music. Tullar composed the popular hymn "Face to Face with Christ, My Savior."

August 6

1651 Birth of Francois Fenelon, Roman Catholic priest, in Perigord, France. His life and writings are tied to several theological currents then prominent in France. Educated by the Jesuits, he spent three years seeking to convert the Huguenots (1686–88). In 1689 he was appointed tutor to Louis XIV's grandson, the young Duke of Burgundy. In 1695 he was consecrated the Archbishop of Cambrai, France. In 1697 he published his famous *Explication des Maximes des Saints* (still in print under the title *Christian Perfection*), which provided a reasoned defense of mystical spirituality. But this association with the Quietist followers of Madame Guyon soon brought Fenelon into disfavor with the Pope. His resulting recantation of Quietism was not necessarily sincere. In the Jansenist-Jesuit controversy, Fenelon defended the infallibility of the church. Throughout his professional life, Fenelon displayed a marvelous mixture of both ecclesiastical authoritarianism as a priest and a broad humanitarianism as a man.

1774 Religious leader Ann Lee and her small band of followers first arrived at New York City, from Liverpool, England. The sect called itself the United Society of Believers in Christ's Second Coming; but its followers were more popularly known as the "Shaking Quakers" or "Shakers." They established their headquarters at New Lebanon, New York.

1801 The Great Religious Revival of the West began at a Presbyterian camp meeting in Cane Ridge, Kentucky.

1809 Birth of Alfred Lord Tennyson, Victorian poet, in Lincolnshire, England. The fourth son of an Anglican rector, his spiritual development found its fullest expression in a poem dedicated to the memory of his best friend, Arthur Henry Hallam, who had just passed away. Tennyson's poetry is permeated by a religious spirit. He authored the hymn "Ring Out the Old, Ring in the New."

1821 Birth of Edward H. Plumptre, Anglican theologian and author of the hymn "Rejoice, Ye Pure in Heart," in London, England. Ordained in 1846, he soon after became popular both as a preacher and a scholar. He taught at King's College between 1847 and 1881. Plumptre published many works on theology, biblical criticism and biography. He was also a member of the Old Testament committee for the 1881 English Revised Version of the Bible.

1866 Death of John Mason Neale (b.1818), Anglican clergyman. Through the influence of the Oxford Movement, he became a high churchman and his suspicious superiors appointed him warden of a home for indigent old men from 1846–63. Nevertheless, his love for ancient liturgies and early church practices occupied his mind and he became one of the first to translate medieval Latin and Greek hymns into English, including "The Day of Resurrection," "Good Christian Men, Rejoice," "Jerusalem, the Golden," "O Come, O Come, Emmanuel" and "All Glory, Laud, and Honor."

1895 Death of George F. Root (b.1820), American sacred chorister and composer. He began his music career at 19, when he alternately played the organ, taught singing, studied music and worked as an editor for sacred publishing companies. At one time, Gospel song writer Fanny Crosby was his student. He composed several hundred songs and helped publish 75 music collections. Today, he is remembered primarily for the composition JEWELS ("When He Cometh").

1955 Death of Jesse Irvin Overholtzer (b.1877), founder and first director of Child Evangelism Fellowship. Overholtzer founded C.E.F. in 1937 in Chicago, although his work in youth evangelism went back as far as 1916. C.E.F., Inc., is an interdenominational mission agency of Baptist tradition, and is engaged primarily in radio and TV broadcasting, evangelism, literature production and Bible correspondence courses. The organization works with over 100 overseas staff in 62 countries around the world.

1966 Swiss Reformed theologian Karl Barth affirmed in a letter: "Since God does in fact address man in His Word, He obviously regards him as addressable in spite of the fact that man as a sinner closes his ears and heart to Him. . . . But He is greater than our heart, making the deaf to hear and the blind to see."

August 7

117 Death of Marcus Ulpius Trajan (b.52), Roman emperor (98–117). In A.D. 97, Emperor Nerva adopted Trajan as a son. After Nerva's death the following year, the Senate chose Trajan as his successor. His attitude toward the church was relative toleration; however, when Christians refused to obey state laws of worship, he legalized their punishment. Letters to him from Pliny the Younger (ca.112), governor of Pontus and Bithynia in Asia Minor, offer rare insight into imperial policies toward the church in the early second century. During Trajan's rule Ignatius of Antioch was martyred.

1409 The Council of Pisa was dissolved. Convened in March of this year, the council had been convened to end the Great Schism (1378–1417) caused by the election of two rival popes, one in Avignon, France, the other in Rome. The council's solution was to elect a third pope, Alexander V, on June 26. Alexander, whose reign lasted only until May 1410, has generally been regarded as one of the antipopes.

1831 Birth of F.W. (Frederic William) Farrar, Dean of Canterbury, in Bombay, India. Ordained in the Anglican Church in 1857, he preached at Charles Darwin's funeral in 1882. In 1885, he visited the U.S., where he became a close friend of Phillips Brooks. Farrar published many books, including individual volumes for several Bible commentary series: *The Expositor's Bible*, *Ellicott's Commentary* and *The Cambridge Bible*. He introduced philological (word origins) research into modern biblical studies.

1852 Birth of Franklin L. Sheppard, U.S. Presbyterian organist and denominational leader, in Philadelphia, Pennsylvania. He maintained a lifelong interest in music, and in 1915 edited a Presbyterian Sunday-school songbook entitled *Alleluia*. He also served on the editorial committee for the 1911 edition of the Presbyterian *Hymnal*. Sheppard's popularity endures as the composer of TERRA PATRIS, to which we sing the hymn "This Is My Father's World."

1878 Founder of the Lutheran Church Missouri Synod, C.F.W. Walther, admonished in a letter: "Do not deny the Word of God when it speaks to you."

1899 Death of A.B. (Alexander Balmain) Bruce, Scottish Free Church theologian. After the death of Patrick Fairbairn in 1875, Bruce taught apologetics and New Testament at the University of Glasgow. During this time, he produced his major scholarly writings, including *St. Paul's Conception of Christianity* (1894) and the volumes on the Synoptic Gospels (1897) and Hebrews (1899) for the *Expositor's Greek Testament*.

1902 The Education Act was passed in British Parliament, requiring that all religious training in the secular schools be done according to the parents' faith.

1922 Death of William H. Jude (b.1851), English sacred organist. He began his career in Liverpool. In 1889 he became organist at Stretford Town Hall, near Manchester. A popular recitalist, he toured both England and Australia, and was editor of several sacred periodicals and hymn collections. Jude composed the hymn tune GALILEE, to which "Jesus Calls Us o'er the Tumult" is sung.

1961 Death of Frank N. Buchman (b.1878), American theologian. Ordained a Lutheran minister, he soon resigned from the pastorate in disillusionment. While on a visit to England, he underwent a personal conversion and embarked on a lifelong endeavor to "change lives and enlist life-changers" through personal evangelism. He established the beginnings of the Moral Re-Armament movement as early as 1921, though the organization was not called by that name until 1938. Buchman's theology stressed home gatherings, private confession and strong mysticism (spiritual guidance).

August 8

1471 Death of Thomas a Kempis (b.ca.1380), Dutch mystic and devotional writer. Born near Cologne, Germany, into a Catholic family, Thomas was nevertheless educated by the Brethren of the Common Life, who influenced him toward a life of contemplation. About 1400, he entered the Augustinian convent of Mount St. Agnes, near Zwolle, Holland. The rest of his 90 years were outwardly uneventful. He practiced piety, taught novices, read, preached, and copied the entire Bible no less than four times. His inner life was one of simple, mystical devotion, evidenced by his book *The Imitation of Christ*. This classic in Christian literature is still in print, a guide to promoting inner spiritual sensitivity.

1518 German Reformer Martin Luther advised in a letter: "The Lord will provide with the trial a way out."

1845 Birth of Thomas Koschat, Austrian composer of sacred music, near Klagenfurt, Austria. Though many of his works are better labeled "classical," one of Koschat's scores has been arranged as the hymn tune POLAND, to which we sing "The King of Love My Shepherd Is."

1852 The roots of the Baptist General Conference were established when Swedish-born immigrant minister Gustaf Palmquist baptized his first three converts in the Mississippi River, at Rock Island, Illinois. The B.G.C. claims 138,000 members and over 800 churches in 16 different states.

1877 Birth of Walter Bauer, Lutheran theologian and lexicographer, in Koenigsberg, Germany. He taught New Testament at Marburg (1903–13), Breslau (1913–16) and Gottingen (1916–45). Although Bauer's work in theology bore some fruit, his literary monument is *A Greek-English Lexicon of the New Testament and other Christian Literature* (*Griechischdeutsches Worterbuch...*), which is the standard biblical Greek lexicon on library shelves today. The fourth edition (1952) was translated into English by W.F. Arndt and F.W. Gingrich (1957, rev. 1979).

August 9

1765 English founder of Methodism, John Wesley, preached with his pen in a letter: "You have but one Pattern; follow Him inwardly and outwardly. If other believers will go step for step with you, well; but if not, follow Him!"

1788 Birth of Adoniram Judson, American Baptist missionary, in Malden, Massachusetts. In 1812 Judson was appointed a missionary by the American Board of Commissioners for Foreign Missions. He and five fellow Congregational seminary students and their wives soon set sail for India and Burma. En route, Judson's theological views changed, and he joined the Baptists. After three years in Burma, Judson completed a grammar of the Burmese language. By 1834 he had completed a translation of the entire Bible into Burmese. He took his first and only furlough from the mission field in 1845–47, after over 30 years in service. Judson died in 1850 while aboard a ship, trying to recoup his failing health, and was buried at sea.

1883 Death of Robert Moffat (b.1795), Scottish missionary. In 1817 he first arrived in Cape Town, South Africa, under the London Missionary Society. He worked among various tribes, not returning to England again until 1839–43. While on furlough, Moffat inspired David Livingstone to go to Africa. After arriving on the field, Livingstone married Moffat's daughter. Returning to Africa himself, Moffat completed a translation of the Bible into the Sechvana language in 1859.

1884 Birth of Kenneth Scott Latourette, U.S. Baptist and church historian, in Oregon. Educated at Yale University, he taught in China until ill health forced him home in 1912. He was a professor at Yale from 1921–53. The author of many writings on Christian missions and church history, Latourette's greatest literary achievements are his seven-volume *History of the Expansion of Christianity* (1937–45) and five-volume *Christianity in a Revolutionary Age* (1958–62). He died a bachelor in 1968.

1933 Death of William H. Draper (b.1855), Anglican clergyman and translator of the English text for the hymn "All Creatures of Our God and King." Ordained in 1880, he served as curate of St. Mary's in Shrewsbury, vicar of Alfreton, vicar of the Abbey Church in Shrewsbury, rector of Adel in Leeds, Master of the Temple in London and vicar of Axbridge in Somerset. He wrote more than 60 hymns during his lifetime, including some of the finest English translations from the ancient Greek and Latin.

1942 English Bible expositor Arthur W. Pink explained in a letter: "Waiting on (upon) the Lord (Isa. 40:31, etc.) describes an attitude of soul when we are engaged in true prayer, but waiting for the Lord is the exercise of patience while His answer tarries."

August 10

1742 English revivalist George Whitefield observed in a letter: "It is a very uncommon thing to be rooted and grounded in the love of Jesus. I find persons may have the idea, but are far from having the real substance."

1760 Philip Embury first arrived in New York from England—the first Methodist clergyman to come to America. A carpenter by trade, he erected the first building of the present-day John Street United Methodist Church in 1766–68—one of the oldest Methodist churches in the New World. After other Methodist missionaries from England immigrated, Embury moved to Camden, New York, where he formed a congregation that grew into the influential Troy Conference.

1806 Death of Johann Michael Haydn (b.1737), Austrian chorister. The younger brother of Franz Joseph Haydn, Johann became music director for Archbishop Sigismund of Salzburg, Austria, in 1762, where he remained until his death. He was a devout Christian, composing over 500 sacred music works, including the hymn tune LYONS ("O Worship the King, All Glorious Above").

1841 Birth of Mary A. Lathbury, American Methodist leader who wrote the hymns "Break Thou the Bread of Life" and "Day Is Dying in the West," in Manchester, New York. The daughter of a Methodist preacher, she became an artist and published many original poems in several Methodist publications. She served as secretary for the Methodist Sunday School Union and was active in the summer Chautauqua assemblies in New York.

1855 Birth of F.J. (Frederick John) Foakes-Jackson, Anglican theologian, in Ipswich, England. Ordained in 1880, he became a divinity lecturer in 1882 and a fellow in 1886. He was dean of Jesus College, Cambridge, from 1895–1916; and later, professor of Christian institutions at Union Seminary in New York (1916–34). His numerous publications were primarily in the area of church history. His best remembered work was done in collaboration with

Kirsopp Lake: *The Beginnings of Christianity, Part I: The Acts of the Apostles* (five volumes, 1919–33).

1886 Death of Joseph M. Scriven (b.1819), Irish Plymouth Brethren hymnwriter. He spent his life performing menial work for the underprivileged and destitute. A man of frequent misfortune, his plans for marriage were cut short twice by tragedy. In Ireland, his bride-to-be drowned the evening before their wedding. In Canada, another fiancee died suddenly, shortly before their wedding, after a brief illness. Scriven was plagued by failing health, a meager income and prolonged fits of depression in later life. It was never ascertained whether his death by drowning was an accident or suicide. In spite of Scriven's lifelong hardships, he left the world the beautiful hymn "What a Friend We Have in Jesus."

1897 Death of William Walsham How (b.1823), Anglican clergyman who wrote the hymns "We Give Thee but Thine Own" and "For All the Saints." Ordained in 1845, he served several churches before becoming chaplain of the English church at Rome (1865). In 1888 he became the first bishop at Wakefield. An unassuming man, How was best known for his work among the poor in East London, where he was known as the "poor man's bishop." During his lifetime, he wrote more than 50 hymns.

1933 The mission organization Wycliffe Bible Translators was first set in motion at the Day of Prayer for the tribes of Latin America, in Keswick, New Jersey. Incorporated in 1942 by founders W. Cameron Townsend and L.L. Legters, W.B.T. is one of the largest interdenominational mission agencies in America. It claims a home staff of 1,000 and an overseas staff of over 3,000, many of whom work on translation projects in over 40 nations throughout the world.

August 11

1519 Death of Johann Tetzel (b.ca.1465), Roman Catholic commissioner of indulgences. He entered the Dominican Order about 1490. He was famous for his preaching before he began promoting indulgences in 1501, a task he continued for the rest of his life. In 1516 Pope Leo X made him commissioner of indulgences for all Germany. In 1517 Archbishop Albert of Brandenburg commissioned Tetzel to sell indulgences in order to raise money for both local expenses and for the building of St. Peter's Church in Rome. Tetzel's shameful manner of selling pardon for sin compelled German Augustinian monk Martin Luther to post his *95 Theses* in Wittenberg on Oct. 31, 1517, touching off the Protestant Reformation.

1699 Death of German nobleman Friedrich R.L. Canitz (b.1654), author of the hymn "Come, My Soul, Thou Must Be Waking."

1775 Anglican hymnwriter John Newton explained in a letter: "Scriptural faith is a very different thing from a rational assent to the Gospel. . . . Christ is not only the object, but the Author and Finisher of faith."

1778 Death of Augustus M. Toplady (b.1740), Anglican clergyman. Converted under the Methodists, he nevertheless was ordained in the Church of England in 1762, becoming an ardent Calvinist and an outspoken critic of Wesleyan theology. Today, his name endures as author of the popular hymn: "Rock of Ages, Cleft for Me."

1872 Death of Lowell Mason (b.1792), American composer of sacred music. By the time he was 16, Mason was leading village choirs and teaching singing schools. He studied music in Savannah, Georgia (1812–27), then returned to Boston to direct the choir of Bowdoin Street Church for fourteen years. In 1832 he established the Boston Academy of Music. His publication of church music was prolific, with over 1,500 sacred compositions to his credit. A majority of his original hymn tunes took their titles from the Old Testament—35 from Joshua 15 alone. A brief survey of his most popular tunes includes BETHANY ("Nearer, My God, to Thee"), HAMBURG ("When I Survey the Wondrous Cross"), OLIVET ("My Faith Looks Up to Thee"), DENNIS ("Blest Be the Tie That Binds"), UXBRIDGE ("Be Present at Our Table, Lord") and "Work, for the Night Is Coming."

1890 Death of Cardinal John Henry Newman (b.1801), author of the hymn "Lead, Kindly Light." Ordained an Anglican in 1824, he later became a zealous leader of the Oxford Movement, which sought to restore high church principles to the Church of England. In 1843 he severed connections with the Anglicans and became a Roman Catholic. He was made a cardinal in 1879.

1914 Birth of Rev. Lee Shelley, missions pioneer. In 1957 he founded Christians in Action Missions International in Huntington Park, California. Headquartered today in Woodlake, California, Christians in Action International is an interdenominational, evangelical mission agency working in seventeen foreign countries, and engaged primarily in evangelism, church establishing and missionary orientation.

1930 In Toledo, Ohio, the Evangelical Lutheran Synods of Iowa, Buffalo and Ohio merged to form the American Lutheran Church. In 1960 the A.L.C. merged with the Evangelical Lutheran Church and the United Evangelical Lutheran Church, retaining its name. Before its 1988 merger with the Lutheran Church in America to form the Evangelical Lutheran Church in America, U.S. membership in the denomination stands at about 2.5 million.

1933 Birth of Jerry Falwell, U.S. Baptist clergyman. He is pastor of the Thomas Road Baptist Church in Lynchburg, Virginia. An active political lobbyist, Falwell was until recently head of the Liberty Federation, which was formerly called the Moral Majority.

1968 American Presbyterian apologist Francis Schaeffer noted in a letter: "We live in an abnormal world and all kinds of things do exist, but this does not make them right."

August 12

1715 Death of Nahum Tate (b.1652), Irish-born English writer. Graduating from Trinity College in Dublin in 1668, he moved to London to seek literary fame. Writing mostly for the stage, he was better skilled at adapting the works of others than in creating his own plays. Failing to achieve financial success, Tate died in a debtors' refuge. One of his brief verses survives today as the Christmas carol "While Shepherds Watched Their Flocks by Night." This metrical version of Luke 2:8–14 was first published in 1700.

1827 Death of William Blake (b.1757), English poet and artist. His major literary works include "Songs of Innocence" (1789) and "Songs of Experience" (1794). He engraved and illustrated most of his books by hand. Blake's artistry shows us his very private system of belief. His art spurned both nature and reason by exalting human imagination; his religion opposed the doctrines and asceticism of much of the religion he saw. Blake's theology professed a sympathy with all living things, which he believed was identified with the forgiveness of sins proclaimed by the Gospel.

1838 Birth of Joseph Barnby, English sacred chorister, in York, England. An organist by age 12 and a choirmaster by 14, Barnby's two most important appointments were as organist and choirmaster at St. Andrew's, Wells Street, London (1863–71), and at St. Ann's Soho (1871–76). He later worked at Eton College and Guildhall School of Music. He edited five hymnbooks and wrote 246 hymn tunes during his lifetime. His sacred melodies, which are still popular, include LAUDES DOMINI ("When Morning Gilds the Skies"), LONGWOOD ("Spirit of God, Descend Upon My Heart"), MERRIAL ("Now the Day Is Over") and ST. ANDREW ("We Give Thee but Thine Own").

1859 Birth of Katherine Lee Bates, U.S. English teacher, in Falmouth, Massachusetts. The daughter and granddaughter of Congregational ministers, she taught high school for six years (1880–86), then taught at Wellesley College, where she later was made head of the English Department. She authored more than 20 books, but is remembered for authoring the hymn of patriotism: "O Beautiful for Spacious Skies."

1891 Death of James Russell Lowell (b.1819), American poet and statesman. A Harvard graduate in law, Lowell's interests turned to literature, and he taught modern languages for a short while at Harvard. He later became editor of the *Atlantic Monthly* (1857–62), editor of the *North American Review* (1863–72), U.S. minister to Spain (1877–80) and ambassador to England (1880–85). Though his reputation as an essayist, poet and critic is dominant, he left the church with a verse we sing as the hymn "Once to Every Man and Nation."

1912 Death of William G. Fischer (b.1835), New England bookbinder and sacred chorister. While learning the bookbinding trade at J.B. Lippincott's in Philadelphia, he studied music at night. He became professor of music at Girard College (1858–68). Fischer wrote a number of Gospel songs, though none were ever published during his lifetime. Three of his hymn tunes remain popular: FISCHER ("Whiter Than Snow"), HANKEY ("I Love to Tell the Story") and ROCK OF REFUGE ("O Sometimes the Shadows Are Deep" a.k.a. "The Rock That Is Higher Than I").

1942 William Cameron Townsend and Rev. L.L. Legters incorporated the Wycliffe Bible Translators in Glendale, California. This evangelical, interdenominational mission agency is headquartered today in Huntington Beach, California, and is the parent organization for 21 national mission agencies involved in Bible translation, linguistics, literacy and missionary orientation/training. W.B.T.'s affiliates include the Summer Institute of Linguistics (S.I.L.), Jungle Aviation and Radio Service (J.A.A.R.S.) and Wycliffe Associates (the fund-raising arm of W.B.T.).

1943 German Lutheran theologian and Nazi martyr Dietrich Bonhoeffer observed in *Letters from Prison*: "I fear that Christians who stand with only one leg upon earth also stand with only one leg in heaven."

1952 American missionary and Auca Indian martyr Jim Elliot recorded this prayer in his journal: "I must come to be aware of Satan. He may never get me into hell, but he may cause God shame in defeating me. Preserve me from the lion, Lord. Let him not swallow me up."

August 13

1587 The first American Indian converted to Protestantism was baptized. Manteo was baptized into the Church of England by members of Sir Walter Raleigh's expedition to Roanoke, Virginia. Raleigh later named him Lord of Roanoke.

1667 Death of Jeremy Taylor (b.1613), Anglican clergyman and writer. In 1638 he was appointed by Archbishop of Canterbury William Laud to the rectory at Uppingham, but Taylor lost his position four years later when the British Commonwealth replaced the monarchy. He was taken prisoner in 1644, during the English Civil War. Released a year later, Taylor spent the following ten years in retirement in Wales, teaching and writing. During this decade, he produced his famous *The Rule and Exercise of Holy Living* (1650) and *The Rule and Exercise of Holy Dying* (1651). These classic expressions of Anglican spirituality insist on a well-ordered piety with a stress on temperance and moderation.

1682 The first Welsh immigrants to the America colonies arrived in Pennsylvania. They were Quakers, and later settled just north of modern Philadelphia.

1878 Death of Elizabeth P. Prentiss (b.1818), U.S. schoolteacher and poet. Raised in Portland, Maine, she taught in the local public schools for a number of years. In 1845 she married a Congregational minister who later taught homiletics at Union Seminary, New York City. She contributed the first of many articles to the *Youth's Companion* periodical at age 16, but she is better remembered for writing the hymn "More Love to Thee, O Christ."

1908 Death of Ira D. Sankey (b.1840), U.S. song evangelist. He spent his early years working with his father, who was a tax collector. In 1870 he met Dwight L. Moody at a Y.M.C.A. convention in Indianapolis, and six months later joined his evangelistic team. He was Moody's song evangelist during revival crusades for the next quarter century. Throughout his career, Sankey wrote music for many verses as new situations were encountered. Many of his hymn tunes are still used today, including HIDING IN THEE ("O Safe to the Rock That Is Higher Than I"), SANKEY ("Faith Is the Victory") and TRUSTING JESUS ("Simply Trusting Every Day").

1910 Death of Florence Nightingale (b.1820), English nurse. Known as the "Lady with the Lamp," she was a pioneer in the development and improvement of civil and military nursing and hospital care (1856–60). Her example led to the use of trained nursing care.

1918 Death of Howard E. Smith (b.1863), American sacred music organist who composed the hymn tune SAFETY ("Love Lifted Me"). Little is known of his life except that for many years he was a church organist in Connecticut. During his 55 years, he composed a number of hymn tunes.

1919   Birth of Rex Humbard, Ohio-based radio and television evangelist.

August 14

1727   Death of William Croft (b.1678), English choirmaster and organist. During his earlier life, he composed music for the secular theater. Later, however, he devoted himself completely to sacred music. Croft is one of the great names in the sacred music history of England. He pioneered the writing of the English psalm tune, including ST. ANNE, to which we sing "O God, Our Help in Ages Past."

1739   English revivalist George Whitefield pointed out in a letter: "Our extremity is God's opportunity."

1810   Birth of Samuel Sebastian Wesley, grandson of Charles Wesley, in London, England. During his lifetime, he served as organist at five parish churches and four cathedrals (Hereford, Exeter, Winchester and Gloucester). An avid fisherman, he reportedly chose positions according to the quality of the fishing in the area. He composed a large amount of service music, publishing over 130 original hymn tunes. His best-remembered tune is AURELIA, to which "The Church's One Foundation" is sung.

1824   Death of Hugh Wilson (b.1766), Scottish tradesman. He learned shoemaking from his father. In his spare time, he studied mathematics and music. Later, he worked as a draftsman. Throughout his life he was active in the various churches he attended, and founded the first Sunday school in Duntocher, Scotland. He composed and arranged many psalm tunes, including AVON ("Alas, and Did My Savior Bleed," a.k.a. "At the Cross").

1848   Death of Sarah F. Adams (b.1805), English devotional writer. Her health kept her from seeking a career in theater. Rather, she published verse and prose in *The Repository*, a periodical edited by her minister. In 1845 she published *The Flock at the Fountain*, a catechism with hymns for children. One of those hymns has remained popular even to this day: "Nearer, My God, to Thee."

1944   German Lutheran theologian and martyr Dietrich Bonhoeffer declared in a letter from prison: "God does not give us everything we want, but He does fulfill all His promises . . . leading us along the best and straightest paths to Himself."

August 15

1096   The armies of the First Crusade set out from Europe to deliver Jerusalem from the occupying forces of Islamic Turks. The Crusaders were under the leadership of Godfrey of Bouillon, Baldwin of Flanders, Raymond of Toulouse and Bohemund of Tarentum. The crusade had been promoted by Peter the Hermit three years earlier, and this date of departure had been set in 1095 by Pope Urban II at the Council of Clermont.

1534 The Roman Catholic Society of Jesus (the Jesuits) was founded by St. Ignatius of Loyola. The order's twin purposes were to foster reform within the church and to undertake mission work among the heathen. The society was formally approved in 1540 by Pope Paul III.

1549 The first Christian missionaries to reach Japan landed at Kagoshima. They were Spanish Jesuits led by Francis Xavier.

1613 Birth of Jeremy Taylor, Anglican clergyman and writer, in Cambridge, England. Two of Taylor's devotional writings are classic expressions of Anglican spirituality: *The Rule and Exercise of Holy Living* (1650) and *The Rule and Exercise of Holy Dying* (1651). They insist on piety, temperance and moderation.

1790 Father John Carroll was consecrated at Lulworth Castle in England as the first Roman Catholic bishop in the U.S. Chosen by Pope Pius VI, Carroll had founded Georgetown University the previous year. Pius chose Baltimore as the first diocese in America, with its boundaries co-extensive with those of the U.S. In 1811 Carroll was made the first archbishop in the U.S. His efforts at achieving greater autonomy for the Roman Catholic Church in America made him the most important leader in early U.S. Catholic history.

1853 Death of Frederick W. Robertson (b.1816), Anglican clergyman. Ordained bishop at Winchester in 1840, Robertson's ministry was mainly among the working classes. His lasting popularity derived from a sincere, spiritual insight and a capacity for analyzing and understanding human motives and character.

1954 The second assembly of the World Council of Churches convened at Evanston, Illinois.

August 16

1661 Death of Thomas Fuller (b.1608), Anglican historian. As a preacher, he was very popular in the 1630s and 1640s. During the English Civil War, he escaped persecution from Oliver Cromwell. His fame rests chiefly on his books *A Church History of Britain* (1650) and *Worthies of England*, published the year after his death. Fuller is reputed to have been one of the first Englishmen to make writing a source of income.

1773 Pope Clement XIV published the brief *Dominus ac Redemptor Noster* in which he decreed the complete dissolution of the Jesuit Order. The Jesuits had earlier been expelled from Portugal (1759), France (1764) and the Spanish Empire (1769) because of increasing fear over their growing power. But while officially suppressed, the order continued its work under state protection in Austria, Prussia, Western Russia, and England. In 1814 the society was formally restored by Pope Pius VII through the encyclical *Sollicitudo Omnium Ecclesiarum*.

1815 Birth of St. John Bosco, Roman Catholic educator, in Becchi, Italy. Ordained in 1841, he worked in Turin, Italy, where the plight of poor boys in the city led him to pledge his life to their betterment. In 1859 he founded the Society of St. Francis of Sales, known today as the Salesians. His educational philosophy supported a minimum of restraint. Known as the "preventive system," it taught "as far as possible, avoid punishing. . . . Try to gain love before inspiring fear." Bosco died in 1888 and was canonized in 1934 by Pope Pius XI.

1852 Birth of Adolf von Schlatter, Swiss Protestant New Testament scholar, in St. Gall, Switzerland. After pastoring briefly, he taught at Bern (1880–88), Griefswald (1888–93), Berlin (1893–98) and Tubingen (1898–1922). His book *The History of Christ* (1921) defended the view that the only solid foundation for systematic theology lay in biblical exegesis. Von Schlatter opposed all speculative and idealistic interpretations of the Christian faith, and stressed that neither theology nor history must forget God. He died in 1938.

1875 Death of Charles G. Finney (b.1792), American revivalist. Originally trained in law, Finney was converted to faith at age 29 (1821) and was ordained by the Presbyterians in 1824. He conducted revivals the next eight years, then in 1832 served briefly as pastor of the Second Presbyterian Church in New York City. In 1835 he began teaching theology at Oberlin College in Ohio, and spent the rest of his life in close affiliation with the school, serving as its president from 1851–66. Theologically, Finney fit no single pattern. Calling himself a "New School Calvinist," he laid heavy stress on man's ability to repent and to attain sanctification in this life.

1942 Birth of Don Wyrtzen, popular contemporary Christian songwriter. His most popular songs have included "Yesterday, Today, and Tomorrow" and "Worthy Is the Lamb."

August 17

1635 Richard Mather first arrived in Boston. He became the founder of the "Mather Dynasty," three generations of New England ministers who dominated the religious policies of the Puritan communities of their day.

1761 Birth of William Carey, English missionary to India. While still a teenager, he already could read the Bible in six languages. He joined the Baptist church in 1783, and soon began advocating the cause of missions. In 1792 he preached the memorable sermon: *Expect Great Things from God; Attempt Great Things for God.* The following year, he went to India as one of the first missionaries under the English Baptist Missionary Society. He became professor of Oriental languages at the newly founded Fort William College of Calcutta in 1801 and held the position the rest of his life. The Serampore Press that Carey helped found made the Bible accessible to more than 300,000,000 people.

1775 Anglican hymnwriter John Newton observed in a letter: "It is no great matter where we are, provided we see that the Lord has placed us there, and that He is with us."

1780 Birth of George Croly, Irish churchman, in Dublin, Ireland. Ordained in 1804, Croly went to London six years later to devote himself to literary endeavors. He published numerous writings: biographical, historical and religious in nature. His theology was strongly conservative. In 1835 he was appointed to St. Stephen's Church in London's poorer section, where no services had been conducted for years. The boldness of Croly's preaching greatly increased the attendance. Croly also wrote the hymn "Spirit of God, Descend upon My Heart."

1806 Birth of Peter Richard Kenrick, Archbishop of St. Louis from 1847–96. Kenrick helped preserve the separation of church and state in America by appealing the case of one of his priests who had been imprisoned for violating a Missouri law that required any clergyman officiating at weddings or preaching to swear loyalty to the state. The U.S. Supreme Court ruled the law unconstitutional.

1809 Thomas Campbell and a group of followers formed the Christian Association of Washington, in Pennsylvania. Campbell, a dissident Presbyterian from Scotland, was joined by his son Alexander the following month. Soon after, the Campbellite Movement began to spread. In 1832 it united with other similar groups and they chose to be called the Christian Churches. Today, the denomination is called the Disciples of Christ.

1828 Birth of George W. Warren, American organist of sacred music who composed the tune for "God of Our Fathers," in Albany, New York. Largely self-taught, Warren became one of the outstanding American organists of his day. He served 44 years as organist in the Episcopal churches of St. Peter's in Albany (1846–58), St. Paul's in Albany (1858–60), Holy Trinity in Brooklyn (1860–70) and St. Thomas's in New York City (1870–90). He composed the tune NATIONAL HYMN in 1887 in honor of the centennial of the American Constitution, but the melody is used today as the hymn tune to which we sing "God of Our Fathers."

1839 Birth of Hubert P. Main, American sacred music editor, in Ridgefield, Connecticut. His entire professional life was spent in the sacred music publishing business. In 1867 he joined the William B. Bradbury Co., which became the firm of Biglow and Main after Bradbury's death the following year. Biglow and Main was purchased by the Hope Publishing Co. of Chicago in 1920. H.P. Main is credited with having written more than 1,000 hymn compositions, including ELLESDIE, to which we sing the hymn "Jesus, I My Cross Have Taken."

1851 Birth of Henry Drummond, Scottish biologist and religious writer, at Stirling, Scotland. In 1884 he was ordained into the Free Church of Scotland and made a full professor at the Free Church College in Glasgow. He made three visits to the U.S. in the interest of student missions. Of Drummond's several writings, none has been more popular than *The Greatest Thing in the World*, his meditation on 1 Corinthians 13.

August 18

1688 English Christian author John Bunyan preached his last sermon in London. Bunyan (b.1628) authored *Pilgrim's Progress* (1678), a Christian allegory that describes the journey of the man Christian from the City of Destruction to the Celestial City. Bunyan was imprisoned twelve years for unlicensed preaching. Bunyan died on Aug. 31, three months before his 70th birthday and thirteen days after preaching his last sermon.

1756 Death of Erdmann Neumeister (b.1671), German Lutheran clergyman. In 1715 he became pastor of St. James's Church in Hamburg, where he remained

41 years, until his death. He was outspoken in the pulpit against the Pietists and Moravians. He penned nearly 650 hymns, including "Sinners Jesus Will Receive" (a.k.a. "Christ Receiveth Sinful Men"), and is recognized as the first to use the church cantata (ca.1700).

1856 Birth of Charles H. Gabriel, American sacred music artist, in Wilton, Iowa. He spent his first 17 years on the farm. After moving to California for two years, he settled in Chicago, Illinois, in 1892. He edited an extraordinary number of music collections, including 35 Gospel songbooks, 8 Sunday school songbooks, 7 books for men's chorus, 6 books for ladies' voices, 10 children's songbooks, 19 collections of anthems and 23 cantatas! Gabriel left a great legacy to modern hymnody. Just a few of his many popular hymns— to which he wrote both words and music—include: "Oh, It Is Wonderful!," "He Lifted Me," "I Stand Amazed in the Presence," "More Like the Master," "Send the Light" and "O That Will Be Glory."

1922 Death of Marvin R. Vincent (b.1834), American Presbyterian Bible scholar. He entered the Methodist ministry in 1860 but joined the Presbyterians in 1863. He pastored two churches in New York state: Troy (10 years) and New York City's Church of the Covenant (14 years). In 1887 he was made professor of New Testament exegesis and criticism at Union Theological Seminary in New York. His most popular work is the four-volume *Word Studies in the New Testament* (1887–1900).

1927 Christian radio pioneer Theodore Epp (1907–85) repented and accepted Jesus as his Savior. Epp later became a pastor and evangelist. He also authored many Christian books, booklets and magazine articles. In 1939 Epp founded *Back to the Bible Broadcast* in an effort to reach the people of Nebraska with the Gospel. Today the radio program is heard on nearly 600 radio stations around the world.

1963 Swiss Reformed theologian Karl Barth declared in a letter: "Even if there is cause for great dissatisfaction with one's church, one should stay in it in the hope that new movements will come, and resolve to do one's best in relation to these. Only in this way could I myself have been, and continue to be, a member of the Evangelical Reformed Church."

August 19

1099 The armies of the First Crusade (1096–99) defeated the Saracens at the Battle of Ascalon (an historic Palestinian city on the Mediterranean), one month after they had recaptured Jerusalem. Muslim resistance to Christian occupation of the Holy Land afterward came to an end until the period of the Second Crusade (1147–49).

1662 Death of Blaise Pascal (b.1623), French scientist and religious thinker. Already successful as an inventor of a primitive mechanical "computer," Pascal also took part in the religious ferment of his day, defending the Jansenists against the power of the Jesuits. He intended to write a complete work on apologetics, but rapidly failing health made it impossible for him to do more than write scattered, nonconnected thoughts. These were collected and published posthumously under the title *Pensees* (*Thoughts*). Pascal spent his last months as an ascetic and mystic. He died at the age of 39.

1692 Five citizens of Salem, Massachusetts, were hanged for witchcraft: George Burroughs (a graduate of Harvard College), John Proctor (former minister of Salem), John Willard, George Jacobs and Martha Carrier. This unparalleled witch hunt began on Feb. 29 of the same year and lasted until Sept. 22, when the last of the 20 convicted victims was hanged.

1775 Anglican hymnwriter John Newton asserted in a letter: "We are never more safe, never have more reason to expect the Lord's help, than when we are most sensible that we can do nothing without Him."

1835 William Nast (b.1807–1899), founder of German Methodism, was appointed a missionary to Germans in Ohio. Born in Stuttgart, Germany, Nast came to America in 1828. Nast organized hundreds of German converts into Methodist churches. He later helped found Wallace College (now known as Baldwin-Wallace) in Berea, Ohio.

1843 Birth of C.I. (Cyrus Ingersoll) Scofield, American Bible teacher, in Lenawee County, Michigan. He worked as a lawyer in Kansas and Missouri from 1869–82. Converted to Christ at 36, Scofield was ordained to the Congregational ministry in 1882. He served several pastorates between 1882–1902, and founded the Central American Mission in 1890. His great legacy to students of the Scriptures was his dispensational and premillennial *Scofield Reference Bible*, first published in 1909.

1856 Birth of James M. Black, chorister of sacred music who wrote the hymn "When the Roll Is Called Up Yonder," in South Hill, New York. Following an early education in music, Black made his living teaching singing schools. He was editor of more than a dozen hymnals published by the Methodist Book Concern and other sacred music publishers. He was a member of the Pine Street Methodist Church in Williamsport, Pennsylvania, from 1904 until his death in 1938.

1883 Birth of Howard A. Walter, Congregational missionary and pastor, in New Britain, Connecticut. He taught English in Japan for a short time. Returning to the U.S., he pastored a Congregational church in Hartford, Connecticut, from 1910–13. Later in life, he joined the executive staff of the Y.M.C.A. and worked with Islamic students in India and Ceylon. He expressed his commitment to Jesus in his hymn "I Would Be True."

1886 The Christian Union was founded by Richard G. Spurling, a Baptist minister, in Monroe County, Tennessee. Numbering only eight members when it was founded, after 1923 the organization became known as the Church of God, Cleveland, Tennessee. Membership in this Pentecostal denomination is currently over 450,000.

1929 Death of A.S. (Arthur Samuel) Peake (b.1865), English Bible scholar. He began his teaching career in 1889, and in 1904 was made the first Rylands professor of biblical exegesis at Manchester University and the first dean of its theological faculty. His many books, though scholarly, were directed to the popular rather than the technical reader. Best known of his writings was the one-volume *Commentary on the Bible* (1919), which introduced many students and laymen to the benefits of biblical criticism. (This work should not be confused with a completely different work edited by M. Black and H.H. Rowley, entitled *Peake's Commentary*, 1962.)

1934 English Bible expositor Arthur W. Pink remarked in a letter: "It is not words which God pays attention to, but heart-groans and tears!"

August 20

1153 Death of Bernard of Clairvaux (b.1090), French theologian and monastic reformer. He joined the Cistercians in 1113 and within three years had established his own monastic community, from which he attacked the disciplinary decadence of the religious orders of his day. It was Bernard's personality, rather than his intellect, which made him the dominant figure in 12th-century Latin Christendom. He wrote several popular hymns, including "Jesus, the Very Thought of Thee," "O Sacred Head Now Wounded" and "Jesus, Thou Joy of Loving Hearts."

1384 Death of Gerard (Geert) Groote (b.1340), Dutch founder of the Brethren of the Common Life. At the age of 34, after a serious illness, Groote joined the monastic Carthusians near Arnhem, but became dissatisfied with their forms of piety. In 1380 he formed his own group for the cultivation of spiritual living in Deventer. His most famous pupil from this "school of faith" was Thomas a Kempis (c.1380–1471).

1553 French-born Swiss Reformer John Calvin assured in a letter: "Seeing that a Pilot steers the ship in which we sail, who will never allow us to perish even in the midst of shipwrecks, there is no reason why our minds should be overwhelmed with fear and overcome with weariness."

1636 Scottish pastor and theologian Samuel Rutherford began his two-year exile in Aberdeen, Scotland, forbidden by the Scottish crown to preach. Born around 1600, it was Rutherford who is credited with having written the Westminster Shorter Catechism of 1643. Three of his other famous works are *An Apology for Divine Grace* (1636), *Lex Rex* (*The Law and the Prince*), and his famous exile *Letters*, published after his death in 1661.

1745 Birth of Francis Asbury, pioneer American Methodist bishop, near Birmingham, England. Converted at age 13, he joined the Methodist movement in England and in 1771 was appointed by John Wesley to be a missionary to America. In 1784 the American church became a separate organization and Asbury and Thomas Coke were ordained the first two bishops of American Methodism. Asbury's remaining 42 years were devoted to superintending the Methodist churches in his charge. As administrator of 224 annual conferences, Asbury traveled nearly 300,000 miles by horseback, right up to the day of his death in 1816. As with many early Methodist clergymen, Asbury never married. He received an annual salary of $64.

1884 Birth of Rudolf Bultmann, German Lutheran New Testament scholar. Professor at Marburg 1921–51, Bultmann pioneered New Testament form criticism with his book *History of the Synoptic Tradition* (1921). (Form criticism argues that smaller units of independent oral tradition once circulated independently. In time they were gathered into the larger written compilations we now call "Gospels.") In later years, Bultmann advocated the need to strip away obsolete metaphors (such as ancient conceptions of the universe) and/ or reword them in modern images so that the central message of the Gospel (the *kerygma*) might be made meaningful to modern generations. His 1941 publication *Kerygma and Myth* best summarized these later views.

1886 Birth of Paul Tillich, Lutheran philosophical theologian, in Starzeddel, Germany. Between World War I and 1933 he taught at the German universities of Berlin, Marburg, Dresden, Leipzig and Frankfurt. During Hitler's rise to power, he emigrated to America, where he taught at Union Seminary in New York, Harvard and the University of Chicago until his death in 1965. His *Systematic Theology* (1951–63) depicted God as a "Ground of Being," to whom man relates existentially by affirming oneself in the face of nonbeing. In the area of epistemology (theories of how we know what is true), Tillich was a leading advocate of *myth* as a signpost, participating in the reality to which it points. Evangelicals have leveled criticism against Tillich for his pantheistic views of God and his failure to grasp the "sola Scriptura" principle of the Lutheran tradition in which he stood.

1888 Famed English expository preacher G. Campbell Morgan, at the age of 25, married his wife Nancy (nee Annie Morgan). It is said that Morgan hesitated to propose because all he could offer a wife was the life of an itinerant evangelist. But her response was "If I cannot start with you at the bottom of the ladder, I should be ashamed to meet you at the top."

1908 Birth of Gerhard Friedrich, German Lutheran New Testament scholar, at Jodszen, East Prussia. He taught at the universities of Tubingen, Bloestau and Bethel Bielefeld. After the death of Gerhard Kittel (1888–1948), Friedrich became the editor of the famed *Theologisches Worterbuch zum Neuen Testament* (*TWNT*), first published in 1933. The English edition of this work is better known as the *Theological Dictionary of the New Testament* (ten volumes, 1964–76), affectionately called *TDNT* among those who use it.

1912 Death of General William Booth (b.1829), English founder of the Salvation Army. Converted under the Methodists, Booth was ordained in 1858 but left Methodism soon after because of infighting within the denomination. In 1865 he began mission work among the poor of East London. By 1878 the work had grown into a military-like spiritual organization, and Booth named it The Salvation Army. Before his death, Booth saw the new denomination spread to 55 countries around the world. He himself traveled some five million miles for the work and preached nearly 60,000 sermons.

August 21

1245 Death of Alexander of Hales (b.ca.1170), English scholastic theologian. In 1220 he earned his doctorate and became a teacher in Paris; then in 1236 he joined the Franciscans. He began a famous school in Paris that attempted to understand the rediscovered writings of Aristotle, his philosophy and its implications in theology. Alexander is regarded as the founder of the Franciscan school of theology even though the *Summa Theologica* that is attributed to him is only partly his.

1799 Birth of Alexander R. Reinagle, British church organist, in Brighton, England. Descended from a distinguished line of musicians, Reinagle served as organist of St. Peter's-in-the-East in Oxford from 1822–53. During his extended tenure, he composed many works of sacred music, including ST. PETER ("In

Christ There Is No East or West"). He also published *Psalm Tunes for the Voice and the Pianoforte* (1830).

1866 Birth of Civilla D. Martin, teacher and songwriter, in Jordan, Nova Scotia. After teaching village schools for several years, she married evangelist Walter S. Martin. She assisted her husband in his work as a pastor, teacher and evangelist. She also collaborated with him in writing several Gospel songs. She authored the hymn "God Will Take Care of You" (a.k.a. "Be Not Dismayed Whate'er Betide").

1874 Famous 19th-century preacher Henry Ward Beecher (father of Harriet Beecher Stowe, author of *Uncle Tom's Cabin*) was sued for $100,000 by Theodore Tilton, who accused Beecher of committing adultery with his wife. A pretrial investigation by members of Beecher's Boston congregation exonerated him of the charge. The trial itself ended with a nine-to-three jury decision in favor of the defendant.

1890 Death of Frederick H. Hedge (b.1805), the New England clergyman who translated Luther's "A Mighty Fortress Is Our God." Ordained a Unitarian minister in 1829, Hedge served several New England churches while teaching at Harvard in the areas of ecclesiastical history (1857–76) and German (1872–81). He made a significant contribution to hymnody with his 1853 publication *Hymns for the Church of Christ*.

1930 American linguistic pioneer Frank C. Laubach, while a Congregational missionary in the Philippines, concluded in a letter: "If this entire universe has a desperate need of love to incarnate itself, then 'important duties' which keep us from helping little people are not duties but sins."

1980 American Presbyterian apologist Francis A. Schaeffer remarked in a letter: "What a delicate balance it is not to see death as less than a present enemy, and yet not to be overcome by the sorrows of death when it comes to a very dear loved one. The balance is not easy, but is the only balance that makes sense in the midst of the world, broken and sorrowing as it is."

August 22

1752 Death of William Whiston (b.1667), English theologian, historian and translator. In 1703 he succeeded Isaac Newton as professor of mathematics, but his theology was questionable, so after seven years he was expelled from Cambridge on the charge of Arianism. Impoverished because Anglicans shunned him, Whiston joined the Baptists in 1747. He is best known as the English translator of the works of Josephus, which are still in print. Whiston completed the mammoth project in 1737 at the age of 70.

1800 Birth of Edward B. Pusey, Tractarian leader, in Pusey, England. Ordained in the Anglican Church in 1829, Pusey became a noted scholar in Hebrew and biblical studies. In 1833 he formally marked his identification with the Oxford Movement by writing *Tracts for the Times*. When J.H. Newman converted to Roman Catholicism in 1845, leadership of the Oxford Movement fell to Pusey. Starting in 1839, he worked for the establishment of religious orders in Anglicanism. In 1845 he helped found the first Anglican sisterhood. He wrote several works promoting union between the Anglican and Roman Catholic churches; but his hopes were lost when the Vatican I Ecumenical Council established the doctrine of papal infallibility (1869–70).

1831 Birth of William H. Cummings, English musicologist, in Devonshire, England. Having once sung under composer Felix Mendelssohn, he later succeeded Joseph Barnby as principal of the Guildhall School of Music. An accomplished vocalist, he toured the British Isles and was especially skilled at singing Bach's passion music. He was professor of singing at the Royal Academy of Music from 1879–96. In 1855 he adapted a theme from the second movement of Mendelssohn's *Festgesang* (1840), which we sing today with "Hark, the Herald Angels Sing."

1885 Death of William P. Mackay (b.1839), Scottish Presbyterian clergyman and author of the hymn "We Praise Thee, O God, for the Son of Thy Love" (a.k.a. "Revive Us Again"). After practicing medicine for a number of years, Mackay abandoned his career and was ordained a pastor of the Prospect Street Presbyterian Church in Hull in 1868. He published 17 hymns in W. Reid's *Praise Book* (1872), including "We Praise Thee, O God, for the Son of Thy Love."

1948 The Constitution of the World Council of Churches was ratified in Amsterdam, Holland.

1952 Death of Lewis Sperry Chafer (b.1871), American Presbyterian theologian and educator. Ordained in 1900, he was a traveling evangelist from 1900–14, a Bible lecturer from 1914–24 and in 1924 he founded the Evangelical Theological College in Dallas, Texas. Today the institution is known as Dallas Theological Seminary. From 1924 until his death, Chafer was president and professor of systematic theology. His greatest literary legacy is his eight-volume *Systematic Theology* (1947), one of the most detailed discussions of dispensational, pre-millennial theology ever written.

August 23

1723 Death of Increase Mather (b.1639), American colonial clergyman. Ordained in 1657, he pastored the North Church of Boston from 1664 until his death 59 years later. He was also president of Harvard College from 1684–1701. He received the first diploma in America granting the Doctor of Divinity degree. Mather published nearly 100 books, the most significant being one that brought an end to executions for witchcraft in New England: *Cases of Conscience Concerning Witchcraft* (1693). He was the father of Cotton Mather.

1882 Death of Charles W. Fry (b.1837), English Salvation Army worker. Converted to Christ at 17, Fry followed his father's profession and became a builder, in Salisbury. His three sons also participated in the business with him. When The Salvation Army began its work in the community, Fry and his sons volunteered their talents as brass players for the outdoor meetings—the beginning of the Salvation Army brass band. Fry eventually closed his business and he and his family devoted themselves to full-time service to the church. It was Fry who penned the words to the hymn "I Have Found a Friend in Jesus" (a.k.a. "Lily of the Valley").

1926 Death of Russell K. Carter (b.1849), the American Methodist clergyman who authored the hymn "Standing on the Promises." He graduated from the

Pennsylvania Military Academy in 1867 and returned two years later to teach. In 1887 he resigned his teaching position to become ordained into the Methodist ministry. Identifying himself with the Holiness movement, Carter became active in camp meeting activities. He was also a prolific writer in the areas of math, science and religion. In 1891 he co-edited, with A.B. Simpson, *Hymns of the Christian Life.*

1952 Death of Sir Frederick George Kenyon (b.1863), British archeologist and philologist. With close ties to the British Museum throughout his professional life, Kenyon devoted himself to discovering biblical parallels in ancient Greek papyri. He was skilled at making his discoveries intelligible to laymen and in convincing readers that science does not disprove the Bible. One of Kenyon's most reprinted works is *Our Bible and the Ancient Manuscripts* (1895, rev. 1939).

August 24

79 The Roman city of Herculaneum was completely buried in volcanic ash by the volcanic eruption of Mt. Vesuvius.

410 Visigoth King Alaric and his armies ransacked the city of Rome in retaliation for Rome's refusal to grant the Goths the land on which they wanted to settle in modern Hungary. The event disillusioned both the Christians and pagans who believed Rome's piety bestowed on her a divine favor protecting her from political and social upheaval. St. Augustine tackled the dilemma in his *City of God* (ca.413–27). Alaric himself died in southern Italy one month after his attack.

1456 The printing of the famed Gutenberg Bible was completed. Published in Mainz, Germany, by printer and inventor Johannes Gutenberg (ca.1398–1468), it was the first complete book to be printed using movable type.

1572 St. Bartholomew's Day Massacre. During the night in Paris and throughout France, over 10,000 Huguenots (French Protestants) were murdered by the troops of Catherine de Medici, the Queen mother, and for 30 years the real ruler of France. The St. Bartholomew's Day Massacre precipitated the Fourth Huguenot War and quickened the spirit of French Protestant religious emigration soon after.

1683 Death of John Owen (b.1616), English Puritan clergyman. Owen was a Reformed theologian who favored the Congregational form of church government. During the English Civil War, he favored Parliament and served as Cromwell's chaplain 1649–51. In 1651 Parliament appointed him dean of Christ Church in Oxford. For 23 years, after the restoration of the British monarchy, Owen was the acknowledged leader of Protestant Nonconformity. His writings were treasured by many Christians of his day, and have been constantly reprinted since.

1759 Birth of William Wilberforce, English philanthropist, in Yorkshire, England. He became a Christian in early life and entered politics in 1790. Wilberforce, John Newton and Thomas Clarkson brilliantly undermined the arguments for slavery. Complete abolition of slavery came just before his death in 1833. He was also instrumental in the founding of the Church Missionary

Society in 1799 as well as the British and Foreign Bible Society in 1804. Wilberforce College in Ohio (founded in 1856), the second oldest institution for black higher education in the U.S., was named after him.

1795 Death of Samuel Stennett (b.1727), English dissenting (non-Anglican) clergyman. Raised in the Gospel by his pastor father, Stennett himself preached for 20 years (1736–56) at the Sabbatarian ("Saturday-worshiping") Baptist Church in London. One of the outstanding dissenting preachers of his day, Stennett was a personal friend of England's King George III (of American Revolutionary War notoriety). Stennett contributed 39 hymns to John Ripon's famous 1787 *Selection of Hymns*, including "Majestic Sweetness Sits Enthroned" and "On Jordan's Stormy Banks I Stand."

1854 The Evangelical Lutheran Synod of Iowa was organized by German Lutherans. In 1930 this synod merged with the synods of Ohio and Buffalo, to form the American Lutheran Church.

1895 Birth of Richard J. Cardinal Cushing, American Roman Catholic leader, in Boston, Massachusetts. As Archbishop of Boston from 1944 until his death in 1970, Cushing was also the highly successful director of the Boston office of the Society for the Propagation of the Faith (the Jesuits). He has been called "the most persuasive social force" in Boston during the late 1940s and early 1950s.

1939 The Worldwide Evangelization Crusade International (U.S.A.) was incorporated in Seattle, Washington, by North American founder A.W. Roscoe (1897–1979). W.E.C. International was originally founded in 1913 when missionary C.T. Studd sailed from England to the Congo. W.E.C. American headquarters have moved to Washington, Pennsylvania. This evangelical, interdenominational missions agency is engaged primarily in evangelism, church planting, theological education, Bible translation, and medicine, and works with staff located in 26 countries around the world.

1952 Robin Elizabeth Rogers, the child of Roy and Dale Evans Rogers, about whom Dale wrote the book *Angel Unaware*, died.

1964 The first Roman Catholic mass conducted completely in English was celebrated in St. Louis, Missouri, in Kiel Auditorium. The service was conducted by the Rev. Frederick Richard McManus of the Catholic University of America.

August 25

325 The General Council of Nicea ended. The first of 20 ecumenical councils in the history of the church, the Nicene Council was attended by 300 bishops. During its three months of meeting, the council condemned Arianism (the heresy denying the deity of Christ), established the formula for choosing Easter Sunday and formulated the Nicene Creed.

1560 Protestantism was formally adopted at the first General Assembly of the Church of Scotland. During the month of August, the Scottish parliament accepted a Calvinistic confession of faith drafted by John Knox, declared the Pope had no jurisdiction in Scotland and forbade the mass. Knox also drew up plans for a presbyterian (rule by elders) system of church government.

1817 German clergyman Joseph Mohr, author of "Silent Night," began his assistant pastorate at St. Nicholas Church in Oberndorf, Austria. Ordained to the Roman Catholic priesthood in 1815, Mohr's association with the St. Nicholas Church lasted only until October, 1819. However, during his time at St. Nicholas, on Christmas Eve 1818, Mohr prepared the text of a Christmas poem for which his organist, Franz Gruber, composed a fitting melody. This song, "Silent Night," written for two voices and a guitar (because the organ was broken), was sung at that evening's service for the first time.

1935 English Bible expositor Arthur W. Pink observed in a letter: "None but the Lord himself can afford us any help from the awful workings of unbelief, doubtings, carnal fears, murmurings. Thank God one day we will be done for ever with 'unbelief.' "

August 26

1498 In Rome, Italian artist Michelangelo was commissioned by Pope Alexander VI to carve the *Pieta* (the marble sculpture of Mary lamenting over the dead body of Jesus which she holds across her lap). The sculpture was completed in 1501 and gracefully harmonizes classic beauty and Christian austerity. Michelangelo has been classed with Dante, Shakespeare and Beethoven as one of the four greatest intellects in the world of art and literature.

1832 Death of Adam Clarke (b.1762), English Methodist clergyman. Appointed a circuit preacher in 1782, Clarke gained fame as a traveling evangelist, after which he served as president of the British Methodist Conference three different times. Clarke's eight-volume commentary on the Bible (1810–26 and still in print) is very popular.

1901 The American Standard Version (A.S.V.) of the New Testament was first published, by Thomas Nelson and Sons. This literal Bible translation was the American spin-off of the 1881 English Revised Version (R.V. or E.R.V.) New Testament, on which several American scholars worked. (An updated version of the A.S.V., the "New American Standard" N.A.S. Bible, was completed in 1971.) The overly precise literalism of the R.V. and A.S.V. made these versions ironically unsuitable for devotional or liturgical use, and thereby kept them from gaining wide acceptance, even though they were the first nondenominational revisions of the English Bible since the publication of the King James Version in 1611.

1948 Death of Maud Ballington Booth (b.1865), English-born American religious and welfare leader. In 1882 she joined the Salvation Army and married the founder's son, Ballington Booth, in 1886. The following year they were given command of the Salvation Army's American branch. A period of growing tension ensued in which the couple disagreed with the British authoritarian structure of the Army. In 1896 Maud and Ballington resigned their S.A. membership and founded the Volunteers of America. Ballington Booth was repeatedly elected General of the new organization until his death in 1940. Maud Booth, a lifelong worker among the poor, devoted her remaining years to one of the branches of the new parent organization: the Volunteer Prison League. She was also a founder of the Parent-Teacher Association, which she served as honorary vice-president starting in 1943.

1956 Swedish Christian statesman Dag Hammarskjold recorded in his journal: "Bless your uneasiness as a sign that there is still life in you."

1958 Death of Ralph Vaughan Williams (b.1872), English composer. He composed nine symphonies, several major works for chorus and orchestra, ballet, opera, chamber music and film music and three organ preludes based on Welsh hymn tunes. Some say only two composers in music history concerned themselves expressly with composing hymn tunes specifically for religious texts: J.S. Bach and Ralph Vaughan Williams. Called by some "one of the most significant English composers of the 20th century," Williams wrote the hymn tune SINE NOMINE (1906) for William W. How's sacred text "For All the Saints."

August 27

1556 Charles V (1500–58), emperor of the Holy Roman Empire (1519–55), stepped down from his throne. Tired and discouraged, he divided his empire between his son Philip (Spain, the Netherlands, Sicily) and Ferdinand (the Hapsburg hereditary lands), while he himself retired to the San Yuste monastery in Estremadura, Spain, to live out his remaining two years.

1660 Books by John Milton (1608–74) were ordered burned in London because of his attacks on the English monarchy. His indictment revolved around his theology, his advocating presbyterian (elder ruled) rather than episcopal (bishop ruled) church government. With the restoration of the monarchy to England in 1660, Milton was punished with a fine and a short term in prison for supporting the Parliament. Afterward, he lived in retirement and wrote his greatest work, *Paradise Lost* (1667).

1770 Birth of Georg W.F. Hegel, German philosopher. Having taught earlier at Bern and Frankfurt (1793–1901), Jena (1801–07), and Nurnberg (1808–16), he moved to the University of Berlin in 1818, where he rapidly gained the reputation as the foremost German philosopher of his day. Hegel believed God seeks to manifest himself in history through the process of reconciling contradictions. Hegel's three-part process started with a thesis and antithesis, resolved by a synthesis of the two. Religion, he said, is an imaginative presentation of philosophical truth, but the lowest form of truth accessible to humans. Christianity, he believed, is the highest form of religious truth. Hegel was basically pantheistic and he is noteworthy for his great influence on Karl Marx's social theories.

1830 English Cardinal John Henry Newman declared in a letter to his mother: "It is our great relief that God is not extreme to mark what is done amiss, that He looks at the motives, and accepts and blesses in spite of incidental errors. What, indeed, else would become of any of us?"

1876 Famed English clergyman G. Campbell Morgan, at age 13, preached his first sermon in the Monmouth Methodist Chapel in Tetbury, England. The theme of his sermon was "Salvation." He grew to become one of the most famous expository preachers of late 19th-century England and America.

1877 Birth of Lloyd C. Douglas, American Lutheran minister and religious novelist, in Columbia City, Indiana. Ordained to the pastorate in 1903, Douglas pastored until 1933 in Indiana, Ohio, Washington D.C., Michigan, California and Montreal, Quebec. He published his first religious novel in 1929: *Magnificent Obsession*. Later bestsellers included *The Robe* (1942) and *The Big Fisherman* (1948).

1910   Birth of Mother Teresa (nee Agnes Bojoxhiu), missionary nun, of Albanian parents in Yugoslavia. In 1928 she entered the convent at Loreto Abbey, in Rathfarnham, Ireland. Sent to India to begin her novitiate, she soon after became deeply involved in working among the poor in Calcutta's slums. She formed a religious order, the Missionary Sisters of Charity (M.C.) in 1948, which received pontifical recognition in 1965. In 1971 she received the Pope John XXIII Peace Prize for her work in Calcutta, where she and other sisters tend the sick and destitute, work among lepers and give shelter to those incurables whom no one else will help.

August 28

430   Death of St. Augustine of Hippo (b.354), early church theologian. Born of a pagan father and Christian mother in north Africa, he lived a philosophically diversified and morally profligate younger life, before seriously turning to Christianity in 387 (at age 33). In 395 he was consecrated Bishop of Hippo. During his remaining years, Augustine wrote many deep works which are still in print. As a churchman, he dealt with three major heresies: Manicheeism, Donatism, and Pelagianism. His two most celebrated writings are *Confessions* (ca.397–401), the story of his conversion to the Christian faith, and *City of God* (ca.413–27), written after the destruction of the "holy places" in Rome during Alaric's sack of the city in 410.

1645   Death of Hugo Grotius (b.1583), Dutch statesman and theologian. Professionally established in the political world, Grotius chose to join the theological conflict between Calvinism and Arminianism that was dividing his native Holland. His sympathy for Arminian views led to Grotius' life imprisonment. He escaped to Paris two years later and spent the last ten years of his life serving the Swedish government.

1774   Birth of Elizabeth Ann (nee Bayley) Seton, American Roman Catholic leader. Born in New York City of non-Catholic parents, Seton joined the Catholic church in 1805. In 1809 she founded the Sisters of Charity, a women's religious order. About this same time, Seton is credited with laying the foundation for the first Catholic parochial school system in the U.S. Mother Elizabeth Bayley Seton was canonized by Pope Paul VI in 1975, making her the first American-born Roman Catholic saint.

1796   Birth of William H. Bathurst, Anglican clergyman. He entered the ministry in 1818, and was rector of Barwick-in-Elmet, near Leeds, England, from 1820–52. In 1852 he resigned his religious credentials over personal conflict with the doctrines of the Anglican Book of Common Prayer, particularly regarding baptismal and burial services. Retiring to his family estate in 1863, Bathurst died in 1877. Among several important religious verses he wrote, we sing "O For a Faith That Will Not Shrink."

1828   Birth of Leo Tolstoy, Russian novelist and social reformer, in south-central Russia (Yasnaya Polyana). After the publication of his famous novels

War and Peace (1869) and *Anna Karenina* (1877), Tolstoy renounced secular literary ambition. Rejecting the deity of Christ and the New Testament way of salvation, he became a critic of the formalism of the Russian Orthodox Church, and was excommunicated in 1901. He sought to live his remaining years (he died 1910) in austere simplicity, renouncing even his property and family life. The key to Tolstoy's later theology was taken from the Sermon on the Mount; he believed man's greatest religious good was to love one another.

1840   Birth of Ira D. Sankey, American music evangelist, in Lawrence County, Pennsylvania. Beginning in 1870, he was closely associated with the great revival campaigns of D.L. Moody for a quarter century. It was Sankey who composed the tunes to such perennial Gospel favorites as "The Ninety and Nine," "When the Mists Have Rolled Away" and "Faith Is the Victory."

1906   Death of George Matheson (b.1842), Scottish clergyman and devotional writer. Impaired vision left him nearly blind from age 18, yet he actively pastored churches between 1866–99 and published several theological works. Regarded as one of the outstanding Presbyterian preachers of his day, Matheson is remembered for writing the hymns "O Love That Wilt Not Let Me Go" and "Make Me a Captive, Lord."

1928   Dr. W.A. Criswell, popular American southern pastor, was ordained into the Baptist church. He presently pastors the First Baptist Church of Dallas, Texas.

1953   Campus Crusade for Christ was incorporated in Los Angeles, California, by founders Bill and Vonette Bright. C.C.C. is an interdenominational, evangelical missions agency headquartered today in Arrowhead Springs, California, and works in over 90 countries around the world. The organization engages primarily in evangelism, Christian education, small group discipleship and the training of nationals for Christian leadership.

1977   *Marshall Efron's Illustrated, Simplified and Painless Sunday School* last aired over CBS television. Efron, a former regular on PBS, hosted this multi-part religious series for young children on Saturday mornings on an irregular basis between 1973–77.

August 29

1632   Birth of John Locke, English philosopher, in Somersetshire, England. He spent the first 34 years of his life in relative obscurity as a medical student. He then lectured at Oxford in philosophy from 1660–66, followed by service to Lord Ashley, first earl of Shaftsbury, from 1666–83. His first major writing was *An Essay Concerning Human Understanding* (1690), which brought him great recognition. His 1695 *The Reasonableness of Christianity* was generally in line with Christian orthodoxy, insofar as it taught that the only secure basis of Christianity is its reasonableness. Yet Locke's theology spawned four later major philosophies: empiricism, English sensationalism, English deism and English moralism. Locke became the foremost advocate of free inquiry and religious toleration in late 17th-century England (though his toleration did not extend to atheists or Catholics).

1792   Birth of Charles G. Finney, American revivalist and educator, in Warren, Connecticut. Originally trained in law, he was converted to Christianity in 1821 after studying the Bible for himself. He soon turned from the legal profession and received Presbyterian ordination in 1824. For eight years he conducted successful revival campaigns in the eastern U.S. In 1835 he became professor of theology at Oberlin College in Ohio and continued a close affiliation with the school until his death in 1875. He was president of Oberlin from 1851–66. Finney's theology was a mixture. He labeled himself a Calvinist (Presbyterian/Congregational), yet he also emphasized man's ability to repent, and went so far as to make attainable sanctification a trademark of Oberlin's teaching.

1877 Death of Brigham Young (b.1801), American Mormon leader. Born in Vermont, he left the Methodist Episcopal Church in 1832 to join the newly organized Mormon church. After the death of Mormon founder Joseph Smith in 1844, Young led most of Smith's followers to Utah, where they reconstituted themselves as the Church of Jesus Christ of Latter-day Saints. In 1850 Young became the first territorial governor of Utah. He reaffirmed the Mormon doctrine of celestial marriage and polygamy on his 51st birthday (Aug 29, 1852), and began construction on the great Mormon Tabernacle in 1853. By the time of his death, Young had over 20 wives, and had fathered 51 children.

1908 Death of Lewis H. Redner (b.1830), American Episcopal organist and active Sunday-school leader. Redner became a wealthy real estate broker early in life in his hometown of Philadelphia. A devoted churchman, he served as organist at Holy Trinity Episcopal Church, was Sunday-school superintendent for 19 years, and maintained a keen interest in music all his life. Redner gave us the hymn tune ST. LOUIS, to which we sing "O Little Town of Bethlehem."

1917 Death of Ernest W. Shurtleff (b.1862), American Congregational clergyman and author of the hymn "Lead On, O King Eternal." He pastored churches in California, Massachusetts and Minnesota from 1898–1905. Later he organized the American Church at Frankfurt, Germany. The following year, he began conducting evangelistic work among American students in Paris. Shurtleff died during World War I while doing relief work with his wife.

August 30

1637 American colonial religious leader Anne Hutchinson was banished from the Massachusetts Bay Colony, having been charged with "traducing the ministers and the ministry." Having immigrated from England three years earlier (1634), Hutchinson's theological teachings soon brought her into conflict with the local civic/religious leaders. She was banished because of her supposedly "antinomian" view that God's "covenant of grace" superseded His "covenant of works." Anne and her family moved to Rhode Island in 1638. In 1642 her husband died and she moved her family to New York. The next year, Indians killed Anne and her family, leaving only one daughter alive.

1770 Anglican hymnwriter John Newton wrote in a letter: "The exercised and experienced Christian, by the knowledge he has gained of his own heart and the many difficulties he has had to struggle with, acquires a skill and compassion in dealing with others; and without such exercise, all our study, diligence, and gifts in other ways would leave us much at a loss in some of the most important parts of our calling."

1820 Birth of George F. Root, American chorister and composer of sacred music, in Sheffield, Massachusetts. He began a diversified music career at age 19. He alternately served as an organist, taught singing, studied music theory and worked as an editor for sacred music publishing companies. He composed several hundred songs and helped in the publication of 75 music collections. He composed the hymn tune JEWELS, to which we sing "When He Cometh."

1854 Birth of Edmond L. Budry, author of the hymn "Thine Be the Glory."

1856 Wilberforce College was founded in western Ohio by the Methodist Episcopal Church. It was the second institution of higher learning in the U.S. to be established for Negroes. (Ashmun Institute in Pennsylvania, founded two years earlier, was the first.)

1874 Birth of I. Allen Sankey, son of D.L. Moody's famous song evangelist Ira D. Sankey. He composed the hymn "Never Give Up."

1894 American evangelist and educator Bob Jones, Sr. was converted to a saving Christian faith. Born in 1883 in Alabama, Jones was licensed to preach by the Methodists at age 15. Starting in 1920, he was an ardent evangelist. In 1926 he founded Bob Jones University (located in Greenville, South Carolina), which reflects the spirit of his lifelong militantly fundamentalist understanding of the Christian faith. Before his death in 1968, he had preached over 12,000 sermons in all 50 states and in 30 foreign countries.

August 31

1667 Death of Johann Rist (b.1607), German Lutheran clergyman and hymnwriter. Dedicated to the ministry at birth by his parents, Rist entered the pastorate in 1635 at age 28. During his lifetime he wrote nearly 700 hymns. One which remains popular is "O Living Bread from Heaven."

1688 Death of John Bunyan (b.1628), English Puritan writer and preacher. Imprisoned several times between 1660–72, his relative isolation enabled him to pen his literary masterpieces *Grace Abounding to the Chief of Sinners* (1666) and *Pilgrim's Progress* (1678). Theologically, Bunyan held a Calvinist view of grace, but was a Separatist in his views of baptism and the church.

1740 Birth of Jean Frederic Oberlin, German Lutheran minister and philanthropist, in Alsace. He commanded the respect of the various French regimes and powers (his lifetime spanned the French Revolution) for his educational work with small children and for his philanthropic work. While he is little known or remembered in America, his name is preserved by the town and college he helped endow, in Oberlin, Ohio.

1757 Anglican clergyman and hymnwriter John Newton declared in a letter: "I am persuaded that love and humility are the highest attainments in the school of Christ and the brightest evidences that He is indeed our Master."

1820 Birth of Anna B. (Bartlett) Warner, New England hymnwriter, on Long Island, New York. Daughter of a prominent New York lawyer, she never married, but made her home with her older sister Susan and their father near the U.S. Military Academy at West Point. During her lifetime (she died at the age of 95) she published two collections of verse. She wrote a verse in 1860 within the pages of a novel she coauthored with her sister: *Say and Seal*, which has long since gone out of print. But her poem has become one of the most beloved of all children's hymns in the church: "Jesus Loves Me, This I Know."

1828 Birth of Lewis Hartsough, New England Methodist clergyman, in Ithaca, New York. Ordained at the age of 25, Hartsough pastored within the New York Oneida Conference for years. For health reasons, he moved to western U.S. Methodist conferences: Utah, Wyoming, Iowa and the Dakotas. He wrote a number of hymns during his life, including "I Am Coming, Lord."

1861 Birth of Jesse B. (Brown) Pounds, American hymnwriter, in Hiram, Ohio. From the age of 15, she wrote regularly for religious periodicals. At the age of 36 (1897) she married the Rev. John E. Pounds, pastor of the Indianapolis Central Christian Church. During her lifetime she published 9 books, 50 cantatas and more than 400 religious song texts. Three of her hymns, which still remain popular, are "Anywhere with Jesus," "I Know That My Redeemer Liveth" and "The Way of the Cross Leads Home."

1870 Birth of Maria Montessori, Italian educator, in Chiaravalle, Italy. She developed the theory of education that stresses the nurture and reinforcement of initiative, training of the muscles and the senses and stressing the freedom of the child. She opened her first school in Rome in 1907. Her approach to elementary education has since been named the *Montessori Method*.

1970 The religious program *Catholic Hour (Guideline)*, last aired over NBC television. Having debuted 17 years earlier (Jan. 1953), this long-running religious series shared its time slot with 2 other programs of similar nature *Frontiers of Faith* and *The Eternal Light*. It was produced by NBC in cooperation with the National Council of Catholic Men.

September

September 1

1558 Dutch reformer Menno Simons admitted in a letter: "There is nothing upon earth which my heart loves more than it does the church."

1159 Death of Adrian IV (b.ca.1100), the 168th pope of the Roman Catholic Church. Born in England as Nicholas Breakspear, he traveled to France as a poverty-stricken priest, where he became abbot of a monastery near Avignon in 1137. He was later brought to Rome, where he was made a cardinal by Pope Eugenius III. When Eugenius died in 1153, Anastasius IV reigned briefly (1153–54); but after his death, Adrian was elected pope. Adrian IV is the only English pope in Roman Catholic history.

1646 The Cambridge Synod of Congregational Churches was convened by the General Court of Massachusetts. The synod led to the adoption of the *Cambridge Platform*, a document setting down the religious government of the Congregational churches in Massachusetts, Plymouth, New Haven, and Connecticut. The synod voted to adopt a congregational form of church government (leadership by local, independent congregational officers) and endorsed the doctrines of the Westminster Confession.

1728 Birth of Philip Embury, English Methodist, in Ballingrane, Ireland. He was converted to Methodism in 1752 and emigrated to America in 1760—the first Methodist clergyman in America. In 1766 he began preaching in his own house while he was constructing a chapel on the site of the present John Street Church in New York City. The chapel was completed in 1768, and Embury moved to Camden, New York, the following year. The congregation he formed there grew into the influential Troy Conference. Embury died in 1773.

1785 Birth of Peter Cartwright, American pioneer Methodist circuit rider, in Virginia. Raised in Kentucky, he was converted in an 1801 camp meeting. He was ordained an elder by Bishop McKendree of the Methodist Church in 1808, and served several circuits in Kentucky and surrounding states. In 1824 he transferred to Illinois, where he served as presiding elder for 45 years. Cartwright was characterized as rough, uneducated, and eccentric; but he possessed unusual stamina, a quick wit, and a clear perception of human nature. He also demonstrated profound devotion to the work of God.

1803 In Boston, the Massachusetts Society for Promoting Christian Knowledge was instituted. It was the first tract society to be formed in North America.

1836 A wagon train of Presbyterian missionaries reached the site of modern Walla Walla, Washington, at the Columbia and Snake rivers. The group was led by Dr. Marcus Whitman. His wife was the first white woman to cross the North American Continent.

1880 The Northfield Christian Workers' Conference, more commonly known as the Northfield Bible Conference, was instituted by American evangelist Dwight L. Moody (1837–99) at Northfield, Massachusetts. The conference was held to encourage and edify Christian clergy and laity in the work of the Gospel. Over 300 attended the first conference; and its popularity and influence grew throughout Moody's lifetime.

1904 American fundamentalist preacher John R. Rice (1895–1980) was converted. At the time of his death, Rice was a radio pastor whose program aired over 60 stations. He started editing the Christian newspaper *The Sword of the Lord* in 1934.

1925 Birth of John M. Moore, English Baptist clergyman, in Dunbartonshire, Scotland. Converted to Christ at age 16, he soon entered the evangelistic ministry of the Scottish Baptist Church. He also served pastorates in Glasgow and Inverness. His later years of ministry were spent in Willowdale, Ontario. A prolific writer of Gospel music, Moore penned "Burdens Are Lifted at Calvary" at the age of 27.

1936 Death of Lewis E. Jones (b.1865), American Y.M.C.A. leader. He graduated from Moody Bible Institute in the same class as Billy Sunday and became active in the Y.M.C.A. Hymnwriting was his hobby, and he produced many songs that were published, including POWER IN THE BLOOD ("Would You Be Free from Your Burden of Sin?").

1985 The headquarters of the Friends of Israel Gospel Ministry moved to its present location in Bellmawr, New Jersey. This interdenominational, fundamentalist mission organization was founded in 1938 by Victor Buksbazen, who also served as its first director (1938–73). Originally headquartered in Philadelphia, Pennsylvania, the organization was first named Friends of Israel Missionary and Relief Society. F.I.G.M. is engaged primarily in evangelism and literature distribution.

September 2

1784 English clergyman Thomas Coke (1747–1814) was consecrated the first "bishop" of the Methodist Episcopal Church, by founder John Wesley. An indefatigable itinerant minister who joined the denomination in 1777, Coke afterward journeyed to America where he ordained Francis Asbury as his co-superintendent (the title "bishop" was never formally approved by Wesley). In executing his responsibilities, Coke crossed the Atlantic 18 times (the last in 1803), all at his own expense.

1884 Birth of Frank C. Laubach, American Congregational missionary and linguistic pioneer, in Benton, Pennsylvania. Ordained in 1914, he was dean of Union Seminary, in Manila, from 1922–26. In 1929 he began developing methods of teaching reading by phonetic symbols, which eventually led to the publication of literacy primers in over 300 languages. The Laubach slogan of literacy education, now world famous, is "Each one teach one."

1930 American linguistic pioneer, Frank C. Laubach, while a Congregational missionary in the Philippines, noted in a letter: "God is always awaiting the chance to give us high days. We so seldom are in deep earnest about giving Him His chance."

1973 Death of J.R.R. (John Ronald Reuel) Tolkien (b.1892), English philological scholar and novelist. After World War I, he taught Anglo-Saxon and English literature at Oxford. His two most popular writings are *The Hobbit* (1937) and the trilogy *Lord of the Rings* (1954–55). The trilogy describes a war between good and evil in which evil is routed through courage and sacrifice.

September 3

590 St. Gregory I ("the Great") was consecrated the 64th pope of the Roman Catholic Church, governing 14 years. A member of the Benedictines, Gregory's administration was responsible for the conversion of the Anglo-Saxon tribes of England, chiefly under missionary St. Augustine of Canterbury. Gregory is considered one of the four great moral theologians of the Roman Catholic Church, taking his place after Ambrose, Augustine and Jerome. His *Book of Morals*, a commentary on Job, was Gregory's longest work, and was highly valued in the study of ethics during the Middle Ages.

1658 Death of Oliver Cromwell (b.1599), English statesman. Elected to Parliament in 1640, he built up a well-trained army which defeated the royal forces when the English Civil War broke out in 1642. Afterward, he was among the signers of the death warrant for King Charles I (1649). England was reconstituted as a commonwealth (1649–60), and Cromwell was elected Lord Protector (1653). A zealous advocate of religious freedom, it was Cromwell's dream that England be ruled by Parliament and not by absolutist kings.

1752 In Great Britain (England, Scotland, Ireland, Wales and the English colonies in America), this date became Sept. 14 when the British government officially adopted the Gregorian Calendar (developed by Pope Gregory XIII in 1582) to replace the older, inaccurate Julian Calendar (devised by Julius Caesar in 46 B.C.).

1776 Anglican hymnwriter John Newton asserted in a letter: "The love I bear Christ is but a faint and feeble spark, but it is an emanation from himself: He kindled it and He keeps it alive; and because it is His work, I trust many waters shall not quench it."

1894 Birth of H. Richard Niebuhr, American neoorthodox theologian, in Wright City, Missouri. He was professor of Christian ethics at Yale University from 1931–62. More scholarly than his elder brother Reinhold, he sought to determine the relationships between faith and civilization. Though much published, his most enduring writing is undoubtedly *Christ and Culture* (1951), which explores the ways a Christian can associate with the world.

1934 Evangeline Cory Booth, daughter of founder General Booth (1865–1950), became the fourth elected commander and the first woman general in the Salvation Army, in London, England.

1939 Death of American Presbyterian evangelist W.E. Biederwolf (b.1867). Converted to saving faith at age 20, he was ordained into the Presbyterian ministry in 1897. After pastoring in Indiana for 3 years, then serving 1 year as a chaplain during the Spanish-American War, Biederwolf took up the work of an evangelist in 1900 and continued for the next 39 years. He also served as president of Winona College (1917–19), director of the Winona Lake Bible School of Theology (1923–33) and founder and general director of the Family Altar League (1909–39). During his last ten years, he was pastor of the Royal Poinciana Chapel at Palm Beach, Florida.

1946 Founder Dr. Sidney N. Correll incorporated the United World Mission in Dayton, Ohio. Headquartered since 1960 in St. Petersburg, Florida, the U.W.M. is an interdenominational, evangelical mission organization which specializes in evangelism, church planting and Christian education. With over 60 staff members working in 13 foreign countries, U.W.M. also supplies medical assistance and provides support for national churches.

1958 Death of B.D. Ackley (b.1872), American sacred music composer. After serving as a church organist during his 20s and 30s, Ackley joined the Billy Sunday evangelistic team in 1907, traveling as its pianist and secretary for a number of years. He later worked as a composer and editor for the Rodeheaver Publishing Co. In 1930 he met famous Canadian pastor Oswald J. Smith. Together they collaborated on more than 100 Gospel songs. Ackley composed more than 3,000 hymn tunes in all, including the music for Oswald J. Smith's hymn "God Understands Your Sorrow."

September 4

1645 The first Lutheran church building in America was dedicated, near Essington, Pennsylvania.

1735 Birth of Robert Raikes, English newspaper editor, philanthropist and founder of the modern Sunday school. As owner of the *Gloucester Journal*, Raikes was moved by the neglected condition of the local children, especially by their behavior on Sundays. He began a "Sabbath school" experiment in his local parish for the purpose of teaching the children religion, reading and other elementary subjects. Word of positive effects on the children and their families traveled throughout England. Raike's experiment quickly became the model for a far-reaching movement, one which spread rapidly within and without the institutional churches. By the time Raikes retired from the work, 30 years later, many Sunday schools had been established throughout both England and America.

1802 Birth of Marcus Whitman, American pioneer medical missionary, in Rushville, New York. He grew up in the Congregational church but later became a Presbyterian elder. Having completed his studies in medicine, he was sent to explore regions west of the Mississippi River in 1835, with a view toward opening a mission to the Indians. Whitman, his wife Narcissa and a small band of others became the first white Americans to reach the Pacific coast by wagon train. They set up a mission in the Walla Walla River Valley of the Oregon Territory, which included modern Washington, Oregon, Idaho and parts of Montana and Wyoming. The Cayuse Indian tribe initially responded to the teaching of the missionaries. But in 1847 an epidemic of measles broke out among the Indians; and in superstitious retaliation, a band of the Cayuse attacked and murdered Whitman, his wife and 12 others.

1804 Anglican missionary to Persia, Henry Martyn, asserted in his journal: "With all my worthlessness, and deadness, and stupidity, I would not wish to exist unless I hoped to live entirely for God."

1813 *The Religious Remembrancer*, later called *The Christian Observer*, was first published, in Philadelphia, Pennsylvania. It was the first weekly religious newspaper in the U.S. and in the world. It is still being published.

1824 Birth of Phoebe Cary, American writer and devotional poet, in Cincinnati, Ohio. In 1852 she and her sister Alice moved to New York City, where they lived the rest of their lives. Phoebe's most famous poem is her "Nearer Home," which begins "One sweetly solemn thought . . ."

1835 Birth of Edwin Hatch, Anglican clergyman and biblical scholar. He began a teaching career in 1859, and in 1884 began teaching ecclesiastical history at Oxford. Of his several scholarly publications, his most famous is the *Concordance to the Septuagint* (1897), which he edited with H.A. Redpath. Published eight years after Hatch's death, this work of two (originally three) large volumes lists every occurrence of every word in the Greek Old Testament, and remains the definitive writing in its field.

1844 Death of Oliver Holden (b.1765), American Puritan clergyman. In 1786 he moved from his native Boston to Charlestown, Massachusetts, where he became a carpenter. After acquiring some property, he began dealing in real estate. He built a Puritan church and became its pastor. He was also a state representative for eight terms (1818–33). His love for music led to the publication of several hymn books. In 1792, at age 27, he wrote CORONATION, the tune to which we still sing the hymn "All Hail the Power of Jesus' Name."

1847 Anglican clergyman Henry Francis Lyte first revealed his words to his hymn "Abide with Me." He had served 24 years as curate of a church in Devonshire, England. Lyte preached his final sermon to the congregation and later in the evening shared the verses of this text with a close relative. The hymn was later published in 1850 in a volume of Lyte's *Remains*.

1965 Death of Albert Schweitzer (b.1875), French theologian, musician and medical missionary. Following publication of his theological classic *The Quest of the Historical Jesus* (1906, English translation 1910), Schweitzer began the study of medicine. In 1913 he founded a native hospital at Lambarene, in French Equatorial Africa (modern Gabon). Here, except for the years 1917–24, he devoted the rest of his life as a medical missionary.

September 5

1529 Death of George Blaurock (b.ca.1492), early Swiss Anabaptist evangelist. He responded to Zwingli's preaching in 1523, after having been a priest for some time. He embraced Anabaptist views, and initiated the practice of believer's baptism in Zurich, founding the first Anabaptist congregation in 1525. In 1527 he was exiled from Zurich and became a successful itinerant evangelist, planting the Anabaptist faith throughout central Europe. He was eventually arrested by church officials in Hapsburg, Germany, and burned at the stake for heresy.

1692 Colonial clergyman Increase Mather received the first Doctor of Sacred Theology degree (S.T.D.) awarded in America, at Harvard College in Cambridge, Massachusetts.

1802 Birth of Frederick Oakeley, English clergyman, in Shrewsbury, England. Oakeley was one of the Tractarian authors during the Oxford Movement (which advocated that certain Roman Catholic practices be restored in the Church of England). His involvement with the movement created great controversy, leading to his resignation from the Church of England in 1845. He later joined the Roman Catholic Church. Oakeley translated the popular 18th-century Latin carol "Adeste Fidelis" into English, entitling it "O Come, All Ye Faithful."

1807 Birth of Richard Chenevix Trench, Irish clergyman and scholar, in Dublin, Ireland. Ordained a priest in the Church of Ireland in 1835, Trench added teaching responsibilities to his pastoral career in 1845. He was appointed Dean of Westminster Cathedral in 1858 and Archbishop of Dublin in 1864. Trench's best-known writings include *Notes on the Parables of our Lord* (1841) and *Notes on the Miracles of our Lord* (1846).

1810 The American Board of Commissioners for Foreign Missions was formally organized by the Congregational Churches of New England, at Farmington, Connecticut.

1851 Birth of Howard B. Grose, American Baptist leader, in Millerton, New York. Ordained in 1883, he pastored several churches before working with higher education. He also worked with his denomination's publishing house and was editorial secretary of the American Baptist Home Mission Society (1904–10). His interests have left the church with the hymn "Give of Your Best to the Master," for which he wrote the words.

1870 Three American Roman Catholic universities were founded on this same date: St. John's in New York City, Loyola in Chicago and Canisius in Buffalo, New York.

1888 At age 26, American baseball player-turned-evangelist Billy Sunday (1862–1935) married his wife, later known affectionately as "Ma Sunday."

1900 Death of John Henry Yates (b.1837), American clergyman. He began his professional career as a shoe salesman, later becoming a hardware store manager. From 1886–96 he edited a local newspaper in his hometown of Batavia, New York. He was licensed to preach by the Methodists in 1858, but was later ordained into the Baptist ministry. His poetic ability attracted the attention of Moody's song evangelist Ira D. Sankey, and under his encouragement, Yates wrote the text of the still-popular hymn "Faith is the Victory."

1909 Birth of G. (George) Ernest Wright, American Presbyterian archeologist, in Zanesville, Ohio. He received his Ph.D. from Johns Hopkins in 1937. He taught at McCormick Theological Seminary beginning in 1939, then at Harvard. He founded the periodical *The Biblical Archaeologist*, and served as its editor for 29 years. Wright directed archeological digs at Shechem (1956–68) and Gezer (1964–74).

1950 Baptist Bible College was founded in Springfield, Missouri, under the auspices of the Baptist Bible Fellowship. The school is one of the largest Bible colleges in America, with an enrollment of over 2,000.

September 6

1711 Birth of Henry Melchior Muhlenberg, Father of American Lutheranism, in Hanover, Prussia. He received his theological training at Gottingen and Halle. In 1742 he was sent to America to organize struggling Lutheran congregations in Pennsylvania. Muhlenberg was a man of immense physical strength and organizational ability. He was also an expert linguist and a tireless traveler. Filled with evangelistic zeal, he ministered in the Philadelphia area from 1742–79, organizing the Evangelical Lutheran Ministerium of Pennsylvania and Adjacent States in 1748. Muhlenberg spent the Revolutionary War years in semiretirement and died in 1787.

1839 Birth of Samuel H. Kellogg, American Presbyterian missionary and scholar, at Quogue, New York. Ordained in 1864, he sailed to India the following year as a Presbyterian missionary. While there, Kellogg studied Hindi dialects and taught at his church's Theological School of the India Synod. He published *A Grammar of the Hindi Language and Dialects*. Following his wife's death in 1875, Kellogg returned to the U.S. where he pastored from 1885–92. He returned to India in 1892 to help revise the Hindi translation of the Old Testament. He lived until 1899.

1850 Birth of F. Buhl, the Danish Semitics scholar who helped edit the 13th-14th editions of Gesenius' Hebrew lexicon. The first English edition of this classic appeared in 1907 under the supervision F. Brown, S.R. Driver and C.A. Briggs. *A Hebrew and English Lexicon of the Old Testament* is frequently referred to as *Brown-Driver-Briggs*.

1869 Birth of Henry W. Davies, composer of the hymn "God Be in My Head."

1934 Students completed the first linguistic training course for Wycliffe Bible Translators at Happy Valley Farm in Sulphur Springs, Arkansas. W.B.T. was founded the year before by W. Cameron Townsend and Rev. L.L. Legters in Glendale, California. Wycliffe has grown to become the parent organization for 21 national mission agencies involved in Bible translation, linguistics, literacy and missionary orientation.

1938 The Academy Award-winning movie *Boys Town* was first released by Metro-Goldwyn-Mayer film studios. Starring Spencer Tracy, the film depicted the 1922 founding of the famous character-building Boys Town vocational institution in Nebraska by Roman Catholic parish priest Father Edward J. Flanagan.

1950 American missionary and Auca Indian martyr Jim Elliot recorded in his journal: "Principles of guidance: (1) Never allow plans to be so 'scheduled' that you find it difficult to respond to the Spirit's working. Let your walk be flexible. (2) Work where God is working. Don't hammer at unprepared soil when there is ready ground nearby."

1974 American Presbyterian apologist Francis A. Schaeffer acknowledged in a letter: "I have learned something in life, including married life, that it is only the one who has been hurt that can bring healing. The other person cannot. It is the one who has been hurt who has to be willing to be hurt again to show love, if there is to be hope that healing will come."

September 7

1640 Birth of Johann Schutz, German lawyer. A resident of Frankfurt, Schutz was an authority on civil and canon law. He was closely allied with the Pietist movement, being acquainted with Pietist founder Philip Jacob Spener. Schutz wrote a number of religious publications during his time, and also five hymns, including "Sing Praise to God Who Reigns Above."

1724 The first American congregation of German Baptists, or Dunkards, met in Philadelphia, Pennsylvania.

1812 Birth of George N. Allen, music scholar and educator, in Mansfield, Massachusetts. After graduating from Oberlin College in Ohio in 1838, Allen taught music there until his retirement in 1864. His teaching laid the foundations for the Oberlin Conservatory of Music, which was established in 1865. Allen composed several hymn tunes during his career, including MAITLAND, to which we sing the hymn "Must Jesus Bear the Cross Alone?"

1833 Death of Hannah More (b.1745), English philanthropist and devotional writer. She began writing verse at an early age, engaged in dramatic writing between 1762–79, then turned her attention to writing religious literature. During the height of the French revolution, she penned a series of essays known as the *Cheap Repository Tracts*, through which she sought to counteract the disintegrating influences of the revolution on English religion and morals. Nearly two million of her tracts were distributed, laying the foundation for England's Religious Tract Society.

1845 St. Louis, Missouri, became the site of the first Hebrew synagogue to be built in the Mississippi Valley.

1881 Death of Sidney Lanier (b.1842), American poet of the Confederacy and author of the hymn "Into the Woods My Master Went." A Georgian by birth, he fought for the South during the American Civil War. Lanier's poor health from imprisonments during the war led to his death at age 39. Yet Lanier published 24 volumes of writings, including 10 volumes of poetry.

1892 Death of John Greenleaf Whittier (b.1807), American Quaker poet, abolitionist and newspaper editor. Although he never imagined any of his religious verse could be set to music, we sing his words in the hymn "Dear Lord and Father of Mankind," which is based on his poem "The Brewing of Soma."

1897 Death of Jane Borthwick (b.1813), British hymnwriter, in Edinburgh, Scotland. She was a member of the Church of Scotland and a great supporter of home and foreign missions. Jane and her sister Sarah devoted themselves to making English translations of favorite German hymns. Jane's translations are ranked by some as second in quality only to Catherine Winkworth. Two of Jane's English texts that remain popular are: "Be Still, My Soul," and "My Jesus, As Thou Wilt."

September 8

70 After a six-month siege, the city of Jerusalem surrendered to the Roman armies of Titus. His forces numbered 60,000 soldiers. Jewish historian Josephus says that as many as 1,100,000 Jewish citizens perished in the siege. After capturing the city, the Romans sold 97,000 Jews into slavery.

1500 Birth of Pietro Vermigli (Peter Martyr), Italian reformer, in Florence, Italy. He joined the Augustinians at age 16 and headed the order by age 41. His later acquaintance with Valdes, Zwingli and Bucer brought him accusations of heresy. Vermigli fled to Switzerland in 1542. He went to England in 1547 at Archbishop Cranmer's invitation. While there, he became professor of divinity at Oxford and took part in the preparation of the *Book of Common Prayer*. After Mary's accession to the throne in 1553, persecution forced Vermigli to flee to Strassburg, Germany. In 1556 he became professor of Hebrew at Zurich, a position he held until his death in 1562.

1565 The parish of St. Augustine, Florida, was founded by Father Don Martin Francisco Lopez de Mendozo Grajales, who was chaplain of the conquering Spanish forces. It was the first Roman Catholic parish established in America.

1636 Harvard College was established—the first institution of higher education in America.

1784 Death of Ann Lee, English-born American religious mystic. In 1758 she joined a splinter group of English Friends known as the "Shaking Quakers." The acknowledged leader of the group by 1770, "Mother Ann," her family and followers emigrated to America in 1774. Here she founded "The United Society of True Believers in Christ's Second Appearing." The movement came to be called the "Shakers." Because the group demands celibacy, even of new converts who had been married, fewer than a half-dozen members belong to the organization today.

1809 Birth of Lydia Baxter, American Baptist hymnwriter. After her conversion, she and her sister established a Baptist church in their hometown of Petersburg, New York. Later in life, she became an invalid and opened her home as a gathering place for preachers, evangelists and other Christian workers. She published much religious poetry and many immediately popular Gospel songs, including "Take the Name of Jesus with You," which she wrote four years before her death in 1874.

1845 English clergyman and Oxford Movement Tractarian, John Henry Newman (1801–90), was received into the Roman Catholic Church. Ordained an Anglican priest in 1824, Newman resigned from the Church of England, convinced that it had severed itself from its ancient episcopal moorings and true apostolic succession. In 1879 Newman was elevated to the Roman Catholic office of cardinal.

1907 Pope Pius X issued the encyclical *Pascendi*, which refuted the errors of the modernists, the inductive theological critics among the biblical scholars within the Roman Catholic Church.

September 9

1561 The Religious Colloquy of Poissy convened near Paris. Comprised of an assembly of French Roman Catholic prelates and reformed Protestant theologians and clergy led by Theodore Beza, the council prepared the way for a 1562 edict that gave official royal acceptance and a measure of freedom to the French Protestants.

1598 A celebration was held for the newly completed church at San Juan de los Caballeros—the first church in New Mexico. The town was a former Indian pueblo in the Chama River Valley.

1747 Birth of Thomas Coke, the first English Methodist bishop, in Brecon, Wales. Ordained into the Anglican Church in 1770, he joined the emerging Methodist movement seven years later. In 1784 he was consecrated by founder John Wesley as superintendent for America. (His title was later changed to "bishop," although this term was never strictly approved by Wesley.) Coke crossed the Atlantic 18 times, each time at his own expense, while carrying out his administrative duties (1784–1803). He died in 1814 while on a missionary voyage to India, and was buried at sea.

1803 Birth of Henry J. Buckoll, the translator of the English text of the hymn "Come, My Soul, Thou Must Be Waking."

1863 Song evangelist for D.L. Moody, Ira D. Sankey (1840–1908), married Fanny V. Edwards, daughter of the Honorable John Edwards, a member of the Pennsylvania State Senate. Married for 45 years, they had two sons, one of whom became a songwriter like his father: Ira H. Sankey.

1898 Death of William C. Dix (b.1837), English insurance agent and author of the Christmas hymn "As with Gladness Men of Old." Educated at Bristol Grammar School for a mercantile career, Dix became the manager of a marine insurance company in Glasgow, Scotland. He wrote a large number of hymns during his lifetime, most of which were published before his death.

1952 The religious drama series *This Is the Life*, premiered on Dumont (later ABC) television. This long-running program aired on Friday nights from 8:00–8:30 p.m., and was produced under the auspices of the Missouri Synod Lutheran Church, and in cooperation with the National Council of Churches.

September 10

1224 The Franciscans first arrived in England. They were called "Grey Friars" because of their grey habits. The Franciscan habit is brown today. (The order was founded by St. Francis of Assisi in 1209 and was officially approved by Pope Honorius III in 1223.)

1734 English revivalist George Whitefield concluded in a letter: "Pain, if patiently endured, and sanctified to us, is a great purifier of our corrupted nature."

1777 Anglican clergyman and hymnwriter John Newton admitted in a letter: "Perhaps it is better to feed our people like chickens, a little and often, than to cram them like turkeys till they cannot hold one gobbet more. Besides, overlong sermons break in upon family concerns and often call off the thoughts from the sermon to the pudding at home, which is in danger of being overboiled."

1794   Blount College was established in Knoxville, Tennessee, by the Presbyterians. In 1806 the school became a state school and in 1807 it was renamed
East Tennessee College. Its present name is the University of Tennessee.

1819   Birth of Canadian hymnwriter Joseph Scriven, in Seapatrick, County
Down, Ireland. He was schooled in Dublin but moved to Canada in 1844. He
was engaged in Ireland when his bride-to-be drowned the night before their
wedding. In Canada, a second fiancee died after a brief illness shortly before
she was to have married him. The depression of later years may have led to
his own accidental drowning in 1886. He is remembered for authoring the
hymn "What a Friend We Have in Jesus."

1937   Death of B.H. Streeter (b.1874), Anglican New Testament textual scholar.
Involved in several related causes during his lifetime, Streeter's greatest con-
tribution was in the field of New Testament studies. His 1924 publication *The
Four Gospels: A Study of Origins* is still widely used today in biblical research.

1965   Death of Father Divine (b.ca.1882), American black religious cult leader.
He is thought to have been George Baker, born near Savannah, Georgia. To
members of his Peace Mission (Kingdom of Peace), he was God in the flesh.
His popularity flourished during the 1930s and 1940s. His followers stressed
communal living, peace, asceticism and celibacy.

September 11

506   The Council of Agde was held in southern France under the leadership
of Caesarius of Arles. Attended by 35 bishops, the council published 71 canons. The canons dealt with clerical celibacy, the age of ordination, relationships between bishops and their diocesan synods, intoxication of clergyman
and religious obligations of the faithful.

1834   Birth of Marvin R. Vincent, American Presbyterian Bible scholar, in
Poughkeepsie, New York. He entered the Methodist ministry in 1860, but three
years later was ordained into the Presbyterian church, pastoring at Troy, New
York (1863–73), and Church of the Covenant in New York City (1873–87). In
1887 he began teaching New Testament at Union Theological Seminary in
New York City. Vincent is remembered for his four-volume set of Greek *Word
Studies in the New Testament* (1887–1900). He also wrote the *International
Critical Commentary* on Philippians and Philemon.

1857   Mormon fanatic John D. Lee was angered over President James Buchanan's order to remove Brigham Young from the governorship of the Territory
of Utah. In retaliation, Lee incited a band of Mormons and Indians to massacre
120 California-bound emigrants in Mountain Meadows, Utah.

1952   The European Bible Institute changed its name to Greater Europe Mission. Founded in 1949 in Chicago by Robert P. Evans, G.E.M. is headquartered
today in Wheaton, Illinois. The mission is interdenominational and evangelical, supporting over 250 overseas personnel in nearly a dozen European
countries. G.E.M. is engaged in evangelism, church planting, literature distribution and theological education.

1962   American Trappist monk Thomas Merton observed in a letter: "We have
not known and tasted the things that have been given to us in Christ. Instead

we have built around ourselves walls and offices and cells and chambers of all sorts, and filled them full of bureaucratic litter, and buried ourselves in dust and documents, and now we wonder why we cannot see God, or leap to do His will."

September 12

1729 Birth of John W. Fletcher, early English Methodist theologian, at Nyon, Switzerland. He moved to England while in his teens, and became an English tutor. Converted under the Methodists, he was nevertheless ordained an Anglican priest in 1757. During the Calvinism-Arminianism controversy stirring England about this time, Fletcher became the chief defender of evangelical Arminianism, writing his famous *Checks to Antinomianism* (1771–75). A lifelong model of Christian reconciliation, Fletcher's character exemplified the holiness he preached. His greatest compliment was that Wesley wanted him for his successor; but Fletcher died in 1785, and Wesley in 1791.

1771 Pioneer Methodist Bishop Francis Asbury, while on his maiden voyage to the American colonies, wrote these words of resolve in his journal: "Whither am I going? To the New World. What to do? To gain honor? No, if I know my own heart. To get money? No, I am going to live to God, and to bring others so to do."

1788 Birth of Alexander Campbell, Scottish-born American clergyman. He and his father Thomas Campbell emigrated to America in 1809. Originally associated with the Baptists, Alexander grew increasingly concerned over the loss of many practices instituted in the early church. By 1827, the two Campbells had developed a restoration movement which came to be known as the Disciples of Christ. The group merged with the 10,000 members of Barton Stone's Christian Church in 1832. In 1840 Alexander Campbell founded Bethany College, serving as its president until his death 26 years later. The Disciples of Christ give the New Testament higher inspirational value and authority than the Old Testament.

1805 Birth of Johann Jakob Herzog, German reformed theologian. He taught between 1835–77 at the universities of Lausanne, Halle and Erlangen. His monumental work was the publication of a 22-volume religious encyclopedia (1853–68), to which he himself contributed 529 articles. This encyclopedia was revised, condensed and translated by Philip Schaff (1882–84), and published under the English title *The Schaff-Herzog Encyclopedia of Religious Knowledge*.

1818 Birth of George Duffield, American Presbyterian clergyman, in Carlisle, Pennsylvania. Ordained in 1840, he spent 44 years in the pastorate, serving churches in New York, New Jersey, Pennsylvania, Illinois and Michigan. He authored the hymn "Stand Up, Stand Up for Jesus," which he published in 1858.

1851 Birth of Francis E. Clark, American Congregational clergyman, in Aylmer, Quebec. At age 29, Dr. Clark founded the first Young People's Society of Christian Endeavor. It was organized at the Williston Congregational Church of Portland, Maine on Feb. 2, 1881. The new concept of a "church youth fellowship" led to the organization of similar groups in the Methodist (1889),

Baptist (1891) and Lutheran (1895) churches. Clark devoted 44 years of his life to the new movement, traveling around the world five times in the interests of his work. He died in 1927.

1922 The House of Bishops of the U.S. Protestant Episcopal Church voted 36–27 to delete the word *"obey"* from the denomination's official marriage service.

1928 Pocket Testament League International was incorporated in Birmingham, England. The U.S. branch of this interdenominational Christian outreach is located in Lincoln Park, New Jersey. The Pocket Testament League has a staff of 17 working in 16 countries and specializing in Scripture distribution, evangelism and Christian discipleship.

September 13

1635 The Massachusetts General Court ordered Separatist preacher Roger Williams into exile. He was banished for his criticism of the Massachusetts Bay Company charter and for repeatedly advocating the separation of church and state.

1748 English statesman Lord Chesterfield observed in a letter: "We read every day, with astonishment, things which we see every day without surprise."

1771 English founder of Methodism, John Wesley, advised in a letter: "It is right to pour out our whole soul before Him that careth for us. But it is good, likewise, to unbosom ourselves to a friend, in whom we can confide. This also, is an appointed means which it generally pleases God to bless."

1827 Birth of Catherine Winkworth, English educator, in London, England. An activist in the social and educational issues of her day, Winkworth was a pioneer in the higher education of women. She was also regarded as one of the best translators of German verse. She rendered at least three popular German hymns into English: "Lift Up Your Heads, Ye Mighty Gates," "Now Thank We All Our God" and "Praise Ye the Lord, the Almighty."

1845 William W. Walford's hymn "Sweet Hour of Prayer," first appeared in print, in the *New York Observer*. Walford, a blind lay preacher, had written the poem three years earlier in the village of Coleshill, England.

1865 Birth of Maud Ballington Booth, American religious and welfare leader, in Surrey, England. Joining The Salvation Army in 1882, she married the founder's son Ballington Booth four years later. The following year, in 1887, they were given command of the American branch of the denomination. A period of tension ensued in which the younger Booths disagreed with the British authoritarian cast of the Army being used in America. In 1896 the couple resigned from the parent denomination and formed the Volunteers of America, over which Ballington Booth was repeatedly elected general until his death in 1940. Maud was a lifelong worker among the poor and devoted her own remaining years to one of the branches of the new denomination: the Volunteer Prison League. She was also a founder of the Parent-Teachers Association, serving as an honorary vice-president of the P.T.A. from 1943 until her death in 1948.

1903 Death of Godfrey Thring (b.1823), Anglican clergyman and author of the hymn "Crown Him with Many Crowns." Ordained in 1846, he served several churches before succeeding his father in 1858 as rector of Alford. In 1876 he became prebendary of East Harptree in Wells Cathedral, where he remained for 17 years, until his retirement in 1893. He published several books of hymns during his lifetime.

1904 Death of Frederick Whitfield (b.1829), Anglican clergyman. He published nearly 30 volumes of prose and verse, including the hymn "Oh, How I Love Jesus" (a.k.a. "There Is a Name I Love to Hear").

1962 Swiss Reformed theologian Karl Barth commented in a letter: "God, according to 2 Cor. 5:19, reconciled the world to himself, not himself to the world."

September 14

407 Death of John Chrysostom (b.ca.347), early church theologian. He was born and educated in Antioch, Syria, and wrote most of his greatest works in that city. For 12 years (386–98) he delivered an outstanding collection of sermons on various books of the Bible (which earned him his 6th-century Greek name *"Chrysos-stomos"* or "golden-mouthed"). In 398 he was unwillingly appointed patriarch of Constantinople. His frankness from the pulpit incurred the wrath of the empress, who banished him. He was later recalled, then exiled to Pontus, where he died. No doubt due to his intimate association with the theologians of Antioch, Chrysostom opposed allegorical interpretations (a method of explaining the Bible especially popular in Alexandria) and insisted that Scripture must be interpreted literally. Chrysostom enjoyed wider popularity among the Protestant reformers than any other ancient church father except Augustine.

1321 Death of Dante Alighieri (b.1265), Italian poet. Born in Florence, he began writing poetry as well as involving himself in political life at an early age. After a fall from favor with a political faction in the church, Dante was banished from Florence in 1302. He never saw his wife or the city again. Dante's greatest literary achievement was his *Divine Comedy*. Composed of 100 cantos, this poetic view of the moral universe is divided into "The Inferno," "The Purgatory," and "The Paradise," each representing the three conditions of humankind: sin, repentance and salvation. *The Divine Comedy* is generally regarded as the first great Christian poem in literary history.

1737 Birth of Johann Michael Haydn, German sacred music chorister, in Rohrau, Austria. Younger brother of Franz Joseph Haydn, Johann became music director for the Archbishop of Salzburg in 1762, and remained there until his death 44 years later (1806). He composed the hymn tune LYONS, to which we sing "O Worship the King."

1741 German composer George Frederic Handel (1685–1759), age 56, finished his oratorio *Messiah*. He completed the score only 24 days after starting work on it.

1765 Anglican hymnwriter John Newton remarked in a letter: "How unspeakable are our obligations to the grace of God."

1814 American patriot Francis Scott Key, while a British prisoner during the bombarding of Ft. McHenry during the War of 1812, penned the words to "The

Star-Spangled Banner." The song became the official U.S. national anthem in 1931.

1883 Birth of Martin Dibelius, German Lutheran New Testament scholar, in Dresden. Educated at the universities of Leipzig, Tubingen and Berlin, he taught at the universities of Berlin (1910–15) and Heidelberg (1915–47). Dibelius laid great emphasis on preaching as the original means of spreading the Gospel, saying that our written Gospels contain "kernels" of these public messages. Along with K.L. Schmidt, H. Gunkel and R. Bultmann, Dibelius's 1919 publication *From Tradition to Gospel* (English translation 1934), helped to lay foundations for New Testament form criticism. But Dibelius viewed the New Testament evangelists as compilers of traditional material rather than as independent authors, tending to be more conservative in his judgments than many others in the early form criticism school.

1918 The Evangelical Lutheran Joint Synod of Wisconsin, Ohio and other states was founded when several midwestern U.S. German Lutheran synods merged. This new denomination later merged with two other synods in 1930 to form the American Lutheran Church.

1927 Bob Jones University opened in Greenville, South Carolina. Eighty-eight students registered for the first year.

1964 Pope Paul VI opened the third session of the Second Vatican Council in Rome. This session lasted through Nov. 21. Vatican II, the 21st ecumenical council, met between Oct. 1962 and Dec. 1965 in four sessions.

1965 Pope Paul VI opened the fourth and last session of the Second Vatican Council in Rome. This session lasted through Dec. 8, when the council was formally adjourned. Sixteen major documents were prepared and published by the 2,860 priests who participated in the various council proceedings. The overall spirit of Vatican II reflected an attitude of renewal and reform within the Roman Catholic Church.

1975 Mother Elizabeth Ann Bayley Seton (1774–1821) was canonized by Pope Paul VI, making her the first U.S. citizen to be made a saint in the Roman Catholic Church.

September 15

1770 English founder of Methodism, John Wesley, noted in a letter: "To use the grace given is the certain way to obtain more grace. To use all the faith you have will bring an increase of faith."

1853 Antoinette L. Brown was ordained a pastor in the Congregational church in South Butler, New York, making her the first ordained woman pastor in the U.S. Miss Brown was an 1847 graduate of Oberlin College before she went on to become its first female theology student.

1885 Birth of Adam Geibel, American sacred music publisher, in Baden, Germany. An improperly treated eye infection left him nearly blind from age eight. However, he studied music and became a church organist, conductor and prolific composer. He formed the Adam Geibel Music Company, which later grew into the Rodeheaver Hall-Mack Company. Of his many original hymn tunes, one of the most popular is GEIBEL ("Stand Up, Stand Up for Jesus").

1905   Death of Samuel G. Green (b.1822), English Baptist preacher. He began pastoring in 1844, but switched to teaching in 1851. He later worked with both the London Religious Tract Society and the John Rylands Library. His most important book is the *Handbook to the Grammar of the Greek Testament*, written for beginning Greek students.

1920   Pope Benedict XV published the encyclical *Spiritus Paraclitus*, which restated the Roman Catholic position on the inspiration of Scripture: " . . . the Bible, composed by men inspired of the Holy Ghost, has God himself as its principal author, the individual authors constituted as His live instruments. Their activity, however, ought not be described as automatic writing."

1932   Death of Charles H. Gabriel (b.1856), American sacred music composer. He spent his first 17 years on a farm in Iowa. He moved to California in 1890, but settled in Chicago two years later. Between 1895–1912, Gabriel published an extraordinary number of music collections, including 35 Gospel song-books, 8 Sunday school songbooks, 7 books for men's voices, 6 books for women's voices, 19 collections of anthems and 23 cantatas. Gabriel joined Rodeheaver Publishing Co. in 1912, remaining with the firm until his death. He left a tremendous legacy to modern hymnody. A partial list of only his most popular hymns includes "More Like the Master," "Send the Light," "O That Will Be Glory," "He Lifted Me," "Oh, It Is Wonderful" and "I Stand Amazed in the Presence."

1935   Birth of Jay Kesler, American youth leader, in Barnes, Wisconsin. He has worked with the Youth for Christ International since 1955. He has written several popular books for teens, including *I Never Promised You a Disneyland* (1975). He was also a member of the editorial review committee for the New King James Version of the Bible (1979, 1982).

1935   In Germany, the Nuremberg Laws were enacted by the Nazi Party. These regulations deprived Jews of German citizenship and prohibited intermarriage with Jews.

1952   The European Bible Institute, founded in 1949 by Robert P. Evans, adopted the new name Greater Europe Mission. This evangelical, interdenom-inational mission organization operates with a staff of over 250 in 12 countries around the world. It specializes in evangelism, church planting, literature distribution and theological education. Since 1979 its headquarters has been located in Wheaton, Illinois.

1961   The Baptist World Mission was founded in Chicago, Illinois. Today, B.W.M. is headquartered in Decatur, Georgia, with a staff of 95 personnel working in 17 countries. This independent mission agency of fundamentalist Baptist tradition specializes in evangelism and church planting.

1966   The American Bible Society published its first edition of *Good News for Modern Man*, the New Testament of Today's English Version of the Bible. It marked the end of a two-and-a-half year translation effort led by Robert G. Bratcher. The complete Good News Bible was published in 1976.

September 16

681 The Constantinople (III) Council adjourned under the leadership of Pope St. Leo II. The sixth ecumenical council, it was attended by approximately 170 bishops who met in 16 sessions starting in Nov. 680. The council condemned Monothelitism, a heresy that taught that Christ's will was only divine, not human. Constantinople III is also called the Trullan Council, because its sessions were held in the domed hall (Latin *"trullus"*) of the imperial palace of that city.

1224 St. Francis of Assisi (ca.1181–1226) received the stigmata, the crucifixion scars of Christ, on the Mount Alvernia, Italy, during an extended period of prayer and fasting.

1498 Death of Tomas de Torquemada (b.1420), Spanish Grand Inquisitor. Having joined the Dominican order at an early age, he became confessor (personal pastor) to the Spanish King Ferdinand and Queen Isabella in 1474. In 1478 Pope Sixtus IV permitted the Spanish monarchy to establish an inquisition, and Torquemada was given full power to organize the tribunals. His organization was so effective that it lasted three centuries, and was not abolished until 1820. Some historians write that under Torquemada's command, over 2,000 executions occurred, as he sought to impose his own austere religious character on those of other beliefs. The victims of this persecution included Moors (Spanish Muslims), Jews, Marranos (Jewish converts), Moriscos (Islamic converts), and other religious adherents whose beliefs or practices deviated from strict Roman Catholic norms.

1620 The English ship *Mayflower*, a former whaling vessel, set sail from Plymouth, England, bound for the New World. On board were 48 crew members and 101 colonists, including 35 who were Separatists from Leiden, Holland, known as the Pilgrims. Also included on the ship's roster were 14 indentured servants, several hired craftsmen, Separatist leaders William Brewster and William Bradford, and Miles Standish, who was appointed to organize defenses of the new American colony. During the three-month voyage, two of the passengers died and two babies were born.

1692 Death of 80-year old Giles Corey, in Salem, Massachusetts. Accused of witchcraft, he refused to plead guilty, and he was accidentally pressed to death while authorities interrogated him. Corey and 19 other victims were executed between June 10 and Sept. 22, 1692 during the civil chaos that surrounded the infamous Salem Witch Trials.

1840 Famous Scottish pastor Robert Murray McCheyne affirmed in a letter: "Grace fills us with very different feelings from the possession of anything else. A man who has much money is not very anxious that all the world should be rich; one who has much learning does not long that all the world were learned; but if you have tasted the grace of the Gospel, the irresistible longing of your hearts will be, 'Oh, that all the world might taste its regenerating waters.' "

1882 Death of Edward B. Pusey (b.1800), English Tractarian. Ordained into the Anglican Church in 1829, Pusey became a noted biblical scholar. In 1833 he formally attached himself to the Oxford Movement, an effort to bring doctrines and practices of the early Catholic church back into the Anglican liturgy.

When John H. Newman converted from Anglicanism to Catholicism in 1845, leadership of the movement fell to Pusey. He sought to achieve closer union between the two religious traditions, but his hopes were dashed when the Vatican I Council (1869–70) declared the doctrine of papal infallibility.

1906   Birth of J.B. (John Bertram) Phillips, Anglican clergyman. Ordained in 1930, he wrote *Your God Is Too Small* (1951). He also translated the *New Testament in Modern English*, first published in 1967.

1920   Death of William Sanday (b.1843), English Bible scholar. He pastored from 1869–76 before teaching at Durham (1876–82) and later at Oxford (1882–1919). Most of his writings were studies of the four Gospels and Christology. His most detailed work was the *International Critical Commentary* volume on Romans (1895), coauthored by A.C. Headlam. Sanday also contributed to the *Oxford Studies in the Synoptic Problem* (1911), which is still in print.

1926   Birth of Robert H. Schuller, American Reformed clergyman, in Alton, Iowa. In 1955 he became founder of the *Hour of Power* television ministry, headquartered in Garden Grove, California. Known as the "theologian of self-esteem," Schuller's teachings promote "possibility thinking." Included among his many writings are: *You Can Become the Person You Want to Be* (1973), *Self-Esteem: The New Reformation* (1982), and *Tough-Minded Faith for Tenderhearted People* (1984). His theology has drawn criticism for its lack of emphasis on repentance.

1942   Birth of Stormie Omartian, contemporary Christian music artist. She has written over 400 Christian songs, including "Praise the Lord, He Never Changes." Stormie has been in active Christian leadership for 15 years and is involved in both prison and child abuse ministries.

1976   In Minneapolis, Minnesota, the 65th triennial General Convention of the Episcopal Church officially approved the ordination of women. This allowed the official recognition of the 15 women previously ordained in Philadelphia and Washington. Three and a half months later, Mrs. Jacqueline Means of Indianapolis, Indiana, became the first woman ordained into the Episcopal Church in the U.S.A. after its official sanction.

September 17

1575   Death of Henry Bullinger (b.1504), Swiss reformer. In 1523 he joined the forces supporting Zwingli's reformation of Zurich. After Zwingli's fateful death at the Battle of Kappel (1531), Bullinger succeeded him as chief pastor of Zurich and remained in this position for the next 40 years. Bullinger enjoyed great popularity in England and was a close acquaintance of Thomas Cranmer, as well as with Melanchthon, Calvin and Beza on the Continent. In 1566 Bullinger played a key role in writing the Second Helvetic Confession.

1656   The colonial federal commissioners recommended severe laws against Quakers, which were then enacted by Massachusetts. Quakers arriving in America were to be committed to a house of correction and kept at hard labor until placed on a ship and transported back to England. At that time, government and religion were intensely interwoven, the line between blasphemy and treason being almost nonexistent. Thus the Quakers were despised because their dislike for religious pageantry and sacraments gave the impression that they also hated the government.

1717 The first Presbyterian synod in America met in Philadelphia.

1787 The U.S. Constitution was ratified on this date by a convention of the states. The document insures freedom of religion, and states in Article 6, Section 3: "No religious tests shall ever be required as a qualification to any office or public trust under the United States."

1868 Birth of Walter Gowans, mission pioneer, in Canada. In 1893 he and two others (Rowland Bingham and Thomas Kent), sharing a burden for the unsaved in the African Sudan, founded the Sudan Interior Mission in Toronto, Canada. In 1982 the organization merged with the Andes Evangelical Mission and changed its name to S.I.M. International. This interdenominational, evangelical organization is headquartered in Charlotte, North Carolina. It manages a staff of over 650 in 15 countries who work primarily with African nationals. S.I.M. International specializes in church planting, theological education, medicine and broadcasting. It also supports the establishment of independent indigenous churches and community development.

September 18

52 Birth of Marcus Ulpius Trajan, Emperor of Rome from 98–117. He was the third Roman emperor, after Nero (ruled 54–68) and Domitian (ruled 81–96), to persecute the early Christian Church. During his reign, the apostolic father Ignatius of Antioch was martyred (117).

1643 Birth of Gilbert Burnet, British prelate, in Edinburgh, Scotland. He pastored in Scotland from 1661, taught at Glasgow University from 1669–74, then moved to England. In 1688 he became chaplain to the English rulers William and Mary, and was made Bishop of Salisbury the following year. In office, he was a model of zeal and activity. He was liberal in his toleration of religious beliefs but an outspoken anti-Roman Catholic. Burnet helped inaugurate the ecclesiastical provision known as Queen Anne's Bounty, which helped augment the income of the poorer Anglican clergy.

1765 Birth of Oliver Holden, early American Puritan, near Boston, Massachusetts. In 1786 he moved to Charlestown, Massachusetts, where he became a successful carpenter. Later, he began dealing in real estate, built a Puritan church and became its pastor. He was also a state representative for eight terms (1818–33). His love for music led to the publication of several hymnbooks, which included the hymn tune CORONATION ("All Hail the Power of Jesus' Name"), which he wrote in 1792 at age 27.

1905 Death of George MacDonald (b.1824), Scottish novelist and poet. He pastored a Congregational church in 1850, but resigned three years later to avoid a split in the church over his doctrine of eternal punishment. (MacDonald taught that sinners cast into hell will still have the chance to choose to love God, and will all eventually come to the decision to follow Jesus.) He spent the rest of his life supporting his family through lecturing, teaching, writing and occasional preaching. While he stood against the popular Calvinism of his day, MacDonald never became a violent radical nor a theological liberal. He was at his best as a storyteller, and the cheerful goodness of MacDonald's writings later captured C.S. Lewis's imagination, convincing him that true Christian righteousness is not dull.

1930 Death of Carrie E. Rounsefell (b.1861), music evangelist from New England. The wife of a bookkeeper for a wallpaper firm in Manchester, New Hampshire, she traveled throughout New England, accompanying herself on the autoharp and singing the Gospel. She composed the hymn tune MANCHESTER, to which we sing "I'll Go Where You Want Me to Go."

1961 Death of Dag Hammarskjold (b.1905), Swedish statesman. Hammarskjold gained international prominence during the eight years he served as Secretary-General of the United Nations, but he was killed in a plane crash in Africa. Three years after his death, his personal journal *Markings* (1964) was published, revealing him to be an individual of intense, inner Christian faith. The spiritual jottings in this private diary have endeared Hammarskjold to Christians everywhere.

1962 The Full Gospel Fellowship of Churches and Ministers International (F.G.F.C.M.I.) was established in Dallas, Texas, by Gordon and Freda Lindsay. In 1967 its name was changed to Christ for the Nations. This interdenominational, charismatic service agency specializes in supporting foreign missions by raising funds for church construction and literature distribution.

September 19

1787 Pioneer Methodist Bishop Francis Asbury recorded this observation in his journal: "I lamented the gaiety of the children of Methodists; but yet they do not appear to be so full of enmity against God and His people as other children."

1853 Baptist missionary pioneer J. Hudson Taylor set sail from England for China at age 21, sent by the Chinese Evangelization Society. The inefficiency of the mission society caused Taylor to sever connections with them a short while later. In 1865 Taylor founded the interdenominational China Inland Mission, which is today known as the Overseas Missionary Fellowship.

1948 American missionary and Auca Indian martyr Jim Elliot inscribed this prayer in his journal: "Father, make of me a 'crisis man.' Bring those I contact to decision. Let me not be a milepost on a single road. Make of me a fork, so that men must turn one way or another on facing Christ in me."

1967 American Trappist monk Thomas Merton (1915–68) wrote in a letter: "The solitude that has been granted me here is certainly a precious gift and I value it most highly. The long hours of complete silence are the best thing in the world and I appreciate them more than I can say. Pray that I use them well." (Merton entered the Trappist Abbey of Gethsemani in 1941. The Trappist order imposes absolute silence on its monks.)

1971 Death of William F. Albright (b.1891), American Methodist archeologist. For nearly 30 years he was professor of Semitic languages at Johns Hopkins University (1929–58). He was also director of the American School of Oriental Research at Jerusalem (1920–29, 1933–36), and editor of the *Bulletin of the American School of Oriental Research* for 38 years (1931–68). He penned over

1,000 articles and books on archeological subjects and led several Near Eastern expeditions, which excavated at Gibeah, Bethel, Petra and Debir (Tell Beit Mirsim). Often called "the dean of biblical archeologists," Albright's work did much to substantiate the geographical and historical accuracy of the Bible.

September 20

1883 Birth of Albrecht Alt, German Lutheran Old Testament scholar, in Stuebach, Bavaria. He taught at the Universities of Greifswald, Basel, Halle and Leipzig. His most important literary contribution is *Biblia Hebraica*, which he edited with R. Kittel. It has been the standard critical text of the Hebrew Old Testament among students of the Bible for many years (13th ed., 1962).

1900 Birth of Joachim Jeremias, Lutheran New Testament scholar, in Dresden, Germany. He taught at the universities of Berlin, Greifswald and Gottingen. One of Jeremias' most popular contributions to New Testament scholarship has been his *New Testament Theology* (1971).

1908 Death of Walter C. Smith (b.1824), Scottish clergyman. Ordained into the Free Church of Scotland, he pastored in London (1850–57), in Edinburgh at the Roxburgh Free High Church (1857–76), and the First Free High Church (1876–94). The hymns he wrote were first published in *Hymns of Christ and the Christian Life* (1876), including the classic "Immortal, Invisible, God Only Wise."

1909 Death of Will L. Thompson (b.1847), American sacred music writer. His early music education included studies at Mt. Union College in Ohio, at the Boston Conservatory of Music and special studies in Leipzig, Germany. He established the Will L. Thompson & Co. music publishing firm in his native East Liverpool, Ohio and in Chicago. His musical genius was expressed in at least two hymns which are still popular. He wrote both words and music to "Jesus Is All the World to Me" (ELIZABETH) and "Softly and Tenderly Jesus Is Calling" (THOMPSON).

1921 Death of William J. Kirkpatrick (b.1838), American Methodist sacred music composer. Trained in music by his father, he published his first hymn collection at age 21. A Union veteran of the American Civil War, he went into the furniture business in 1862, but left it after his wife's death in 1878 to devote himself full time to music. He served as music director at Grace Methodist Episcopal Church in Philadelphia from 1886–97, remaining an active member until his death. Several of Kirkpatrick's hymn tunes remain popular to this day: JESUS SAVES ("We Have Heard the Joyful Sound"), KIRKPATRICK ("He Hideth My Soul"), REDEEMED ("Redeemed, How I Love to Proclaim It") TRUST IN JESUS ("'Tis So Sweet to Trust in Jesus") and both the words and music to "Lord, I'm Coming Home."

1932 In England, several branches of Methodism united to form the Methodist Church of Great Britain and Ireland. The merging bodies included the United Methodists (1907), the United Methodist Free Churches (1857), the Wesleyan Methodists (1784) and the Primitive Methodists (1811).

1948 American missionary and Auca Indian martyr Jim Elliot recorded this personal challenge in his journal: "I am Thine at terrible cost to Thyself. Now

Thou must become mine—as Thou didst not attend to the price, neither would I."

1957 Death of Jean Sibelius (b.1865), Finland's best-known composer. His music is characterized by a fervent nationalism. One movement of his 1899 tone poem "Finlandia" has become the music for Katharine von Schlegel's hymn "Be Still, My Soul." (Jane L. Borthwick gave us the English translation.)

September 21

1452 Birth of Girolamo Savonarola, Italian reformer, in Ferrara, Italy. In 1474 he joined the Dominicans and became famous for his religious zeal and extraordinary piety. In 1481 he began preaching in Florence, Italy; and for 14 years, he boldly attacked the evils in that city. Savonarola was elevated to city manager in 1494, which marked a degree of reformation in the city. But he also attacked the evils of Pope Alexander VI and his court, for which he was excommunicated. Savanarola's followers soon turned against him, and in 1498, he was convicted of heresy, hanged and his body burned.

1522 Martin Luther's German translation of the New Testament was first published.

1558 Death of Charles V (b.1500), Holy Roman emperor. At his election in 1519, his empire consisted of Spain and the Spanish Empire, Naples, the Netherlands and Burgundy. It was Charles who called the Diet of Worms in 1521 to discuss the teachings of German reformer Martin Luther. The council banned Luther's teachings, but other difficulties prevented Charles from following up with consistent action. In 1555, at the Diet of Augsburg, the Protestant princes forced him to accept the principle of "cuius regio, eius religio" ("in a prince's country, the prince's religion"). Charles abdicated the throne in 1556, two years before his death.

1935 Death of James M. Gray (b.1851), American Bible teacher and author. Ordained in the Episcopal Church, he pastored 14 years in Boston before resigning to become a Bible teacher. In 1904 Gray became dean of Moody Bible Institute; and in 1925 he became president. He served as one of the original editors of the Scofield reference Bible. He also wrote several popular hymns, including "Nor Silver Nor Gold" and "Only a Sinner."

September 22

1566 Death of Johann Agricola (b.1494), German theologian and reformer. In 1519 he became a good friend of Martin Luther, but the relationship soured after 1540 over the authority of the Mosaic Law in the lives of the believer and the nonbeliever. Agricola fled to Berlin and the elector Joachim II of Brandenburg took him into his favor, appointing him court preacher and general superintendent, offices which he held until his death. Agricola's career in Brandenburg became one of great activity and influence.

1601 The first priests, Sebastian Chimura and Aloysius Niabara, of the newly established Christian Church (Roman Catholic) in Japan were ordained in their hometown of Nagasaki.

1692 The last 8 of 20 condemned "witches" were hanged in Salem, Massachusetts, during the famous witch trials of 1692. The last eight victims of these infamous trials were: Martha Cory, Mary Esty, Alice Parker, Mary Parker, Ann Pudeator, Wilmot Reed, Margaret Scott and Samuel Wardwell. Thirteen women and seven men were executed.

1827 According to the narrative of Mormon founder Joseph Smith, the angel Moroni revealed the golden tablets containing the text of the *Book of Mormon* to him. They were hidden on Cumorah Hill near the Smith family farm, near Palmyra, New York. Joseph's English translation of the strange hieroglyphics on these plates became the foundation for his new religion.

1865 Birth of Ambrose J. Tomlinson, American church leader, in Westfield, Indiana. Converted at age 27 in a Quaker meetinghouse, Tomlinson became a bookseller for the American Bible Society. Coming under the influence of Richard G. Spurling, he joined the Pentecostal Church of God in 1896. He rose to leadership within the group from 1903–23 and was general overseer of the Church of God (Cleveland, Tennessee) from 1923 until his death in 1943. Afterward, the denomination split over the choice of his successor. Some say as many as 40 new denominations were generated before the controversy finally settled.

1871 Death of Charlotte Elliott (b.1789), English devotional writer and author of the classic hymn "Just As I Am." A serious illness at age 33 left her an invalid her remaining 50 years. She devoted her time to religious and humanitarian concerns; and, through pain and suffering, pursued an active literary career, writing over 150 hymns.

1950 Founders Basil W. and Esther K. Miller incorporated the Basil W. Miller Foundation in Altadena, California. In 1959 the name was amended to World-Wide Missions, and in 1963 its headquarters was moved to Pasadena, California. This interdenominational, evangelical mission organization specializes in relief aid and medicine, as well as general support for national workers and churches. Its overseas staff of 15 supervises the group's work in 31 countries.

1978 Death of Gaines S. Dobbins (b.1886), American Baptist Church scholar and writer. After a brief pastorate in Mississippi, Dobbins worked within the educational and administrative structures of the Southern Baptist Church. For 46 years he taught at Southern Baptist Theological Seminary in Louisville, Kentucky (1920–56, professor emeritus 1968–78). He authored many books on developing the local church, including *Building Better Churches* (1947), *A Church at Worship* (1962) and *Learning to Lead* (1968).

September 23

1595 The Spanish crown launched an intensive missionary campaign in the American southeast, led by Fray Juan de Silva. The area was divided into mission provinces comprising Florida, Georgia and South Carolina. During the next two years, about 1,500 Indians were converted to the Catholic faith. Missionary efforts such as this reflected the Spanish—and general European—belief that conversion to Christianity was a more effective method of pacifying the Indians than the use of arms.

1888 Birth of Gerhard Kittel, Lutheran Bible scholar, in Breslau, Germany. He taught at the universities of Kiel, Leipzig, Greifswald and Tubingen. He devoted himself to studying the Jewish background of the New Testament. He believed that the Hebrew element prevailed over the Hellenistic (Greek) element in the making of the New Testament books. Kittel's greatest literary contribution was his work as first editor of the ten-volume *Theologisches Worterbuch zum Neuen Testament* (1933–76). Kittel died in 1948 before the work could be completed, and G. Friedrich followed him as editor. The English translation of Kittel's monumental work was edited by G.W. Bromily and is entitled *Theological Dictionary of the New Testament* (1964–76), or *T.D.N.T.* for short.

1897 Death of Frances E. Cox (b.1812), the hymnwriter who translated into English the German text of the hymn "Sing Praise to God Who Reigns Above."

1907 Death of John S. Norris (b.1844), English-born American clergyman and composer of the hymn tune NORRIS ("I Can Hear My Savior Calling"). In 1868 he was ordained into the Methodist ministry in Canada. After serving ten years in churches in Canada, New York and Wisconsin, he became a Congregational pastor in 1878 and pastored churches in Wisconsin and Iowa (1878–1901). In 1901 he moved to Chicago, where he remained until his death. Norris wrote over 100 hymns in all.

September 24

787 The Nicaea II general council began under the support of Pope Hadrian I. The 7th of the church's 21 ecumenical councils, the 8 sessions of Nicaea II were attended by 300 bishops. The council condemned iconoclasm (the belief that the veneration of Christian images and relics was idolatry). Nicaea II is regarded by the Eastern Orthodox churches as the last of the ecumenical councils.

1868 Death of Henry H. Milman (b.1791), Anglican clergyman and scholar. Ordained in 1817, he was also a poet and historian. He wrote 13 hymns, which he first published in hymnals in 1827 and 1837. Milman wrote the Palm Sunday hymn "Ride On! Ride On in Majesty!"

1904 Death of William True Sleeper (b.1819), American Congregational clergyman. After ordination, he engaged in home mission work in Massachusetts and then in Maine, where he established three new churches. In 1876 he returned to pastor the Massachusetts church he founded, remaining there 30 years. He published a book of verse in 1883, including two poems which became hymns: "Ye Must Be Born Again" (a.k.a. "A Ruler Once Came to Jesus by Night") and "Jesus, I Come" (a.k.a. "Out of My Bondage, Sorrow and Night").

1924 Death of Charles Cowman (b.1867), founder of the Oriental Missionary Society. (See 1939 entry.)

1934 Death of A.T. (Archibald Thomas) Robertson (b.1863), American Baptist New Testament scholar. Converted at age 13 he was ordained into the Baptist ministry in 1888. In 1895 he was appointed to teach at Southern Baptist Theological Seminary in Louisville, Kentucky. He remained at the school for 39 years. He published 45 books, but in 1914 Robertson published his most famous work, the 1,454-page *Grammar of the Greek New Testament*, for years the most complete New Testament Greek grammar available. Robertson spent 26 years writing it.

1939 Death of Juji Nakada (b.1870), Japanese evangelist. In 1901 he invited Charles and Lettie Cowman of the U.S. to help establish a Bible institute in Japan. As a result of Nakada's vision, the Oriental Missionary Society (today known as O.M.S. International) was founded in Tokyo, Japan, that same year. This interdenominational mission organization of Wesleyan tradition specializes in evangelism, church planting, radio/TV broadcasting, and theological education. Headquartered in Greenwood, Indiana, O.M.S. operates in over a dozen countries, with a total overseas staff of more than 250 personnel.

September 25

1493 Twelve Spanish missionaries set sail for the New World to formally introduce Christianity to America.

1555 The Peace of Augsburg was signed following the defeat of Emperor Charles V's forces by Protestant princes in Germany (1552). The agreement officially recognized the Lutheran church in Germany; but its wider significance meant that both the political unity of Germany and the medieval unity of Christendom were permanently dissolved.

1643 In London, the Westminster Assembly signed the Solemn League and Covenant. It was intended to preserve the Reformed faith of the Church of Scotland, to bring the churches of England and Ireland to Reformed theology and to abolish church government by bishops. In 1646 the British Parliament ordered the establishment of this Presbyterian form of church government, but the act was never carried out.

1789 The U.S. Constitution was amended by Congress to prohibit any establishment of a state religion or interference with freedom in the exercise of religion.

1827 Birth of Emma F. Bevan, English writer and translator of the German hymn "Christ Receiveth Sinful Men" (a.k.a. "Sinners Jesus Will Receive"), in Oxford, England. In 1856 she married a London banker. Her greatest contributions to English hymnody were her translations of German verse.

1866 Birth of Cleland Boyd McAfee, American Presbyterian clergyman and scholar. He served as pastor of College Church in Parkville, Missouri, for 20 years (1881–1901). He also served as professor of systematic theology for 18 years in Chicago (1912–30). He wrote the words and music to the hymn "Near to the Heart of God" ("There Is a Place of Quiet Rest").

1869 Birth of Rudolf Otto, German Lutheran theologian, in Hanover, Germany. Educated at Erlangen and Gottingen, he taught theology at Gottingen (1907–14), Breslau (1914–17) and Marburg (1917–37). Otto's most important work was *Das Heilige* (1917; English translation *The Idea of the Holy*, 1923), which he wrote in an effort to deepen public worship in Lutheranism by stressing the surpassing holiness of God. God's holiness was largely neglected by liberal Protestantism but it greatly influenced the theology of Otto's generation.

1872 Death of Peter Cartwright (b.1785), early American Methodist circuit rider. He was raised in Kentucky, where he was converted at an 1801 camp meeting. Ordained an elder by Methodist Bishop McKendree in 1808, Cartwright served several circuits in Kentucky and surrounding states. In 1824 he transferred to Illinois, where he served as presiding elder for 45 years. Cartwright was characterized as rough, uneducated, and eccentric; but he possessed great physical stamina, a quick wit and a clear perception of human nature. He also demonstrated profound devotion to the work of God, in that he spent over 70 of his 97 years spreading the Gospel through the frontiers in the Midwest.

1890 Polygamy was officially banned by the Mormon church. The federal government had mounted increasing campaigns against Mormon polygamy following the Civil War; and in 1887 the church was disincorporated and its properties confiscated. An 1890 Supreme Court ruling which denied all privileges of citizenship to members of the Mormon church undoubtedly led to this official pronouncement.

1908 Death of Henry A. Redpath (b.1848), English Old Testament textual scholar. He was co-editor of the monumental three-volume concordance of the Greek Old Testament, the Septuagint. He and Edwin Hatch worked on *A Concordance to the Septuagint and the Other Greek Versions of the Old Testament* from 1892–1906.

1926 Birth of Jack Hyles, American Baptist clergyman, in Italy, Texas. For years he has pastored First Baptist Church in Gary, Indiana.

September 26

1626 Death of Lancelot Andrewes (b.1555), Anglican church leader. Ordained to the priesthood in 1580, Andrewes was thoroughly devoted to episcopacy (oversight of churches by a bishop, as opposed to supervision by an assembly) and to the monarchy. He took a leading part in the Hampton Court Conference of 1604, and was one of the first scholars appointed by King James I to work on the Bible translation committee for what has become known as the King James Version. Andrewes was one of the most learned men of his time, as well as a man of austere piety, rigorous in private devotion and liberal in his giving. He was a major influence in the development of Anglican theology.

1774 Birth of Jonathan Chapman ("Johnny Appleseed"), pioneer American environmentalist, in Leominster, Massachusetts. He chose the life of an itinerant, and wandered throughout pioneer settlements from the Alleghenies to the central Ohio Valley, distributing religious tracts and scattering apple seeds wherever he went. Chapman's theology is believed to have been patterned after the teachings of Emmanuel Swedenborg (1688–1772), which spoke of an empathy with the natural world. Chapman also introduced and encouraged people to raise medicinal herbs.

1863 Death of Frederick W. Faber (b.1814), English clergyman. Ordained in 1842, he soon came under the influence of the Oxford Movement, and in 1846 resigned from the Church of England to enter the Roman Catholic Church. He founded a religious community in Birmingham and served as its leader during his last years. Greatly influenced by the hymns of John Henry Newman and William Cowper, Faber himself penned 150 hymns, including "Faith of Our Fathers" and "There's a Wideness in God's Mercy."

1876 Death of Edward F. Rimbault (b.1816), English organist and scholar. In his early years he served as organist in four different churches around London. He became a respected music scholar and was awarded honorary doctorates from the Universities of Stockholm, Harvard and Gottingen. He wrote the hymn tune HAPPY DAY, to which we sing "O Happy Day That Fixed My Choice."

1896 Death of William G. Tomer (b.1833), American Methodist hymnwriter. A Union veteran of the U.S. Civil War, Tomer worked as a government employee in Washington, D.C. for 20 years. He also served as Music Director of the Grace Methodist Episcopal Church in Washington, D.C. He spent the last years of his life as a schoolteacher in New Jersey. Tomer is remembered as composer of the hymn tune FAREWELL ("God Be with You Till We Meet Again").

1897 Birth of Giovanni Battista Montini, Italian cardinal, near Brescia, Italy. Ordained in 1920, he was named a cardinal by Pope John XXIII in 1958. When John XXIII died in 1963, the conclave elected Montini his successor on June 21. He chose a name suggesting Christian outreach: Pope Paul VI. His 15 years as pontiff, until his death in 1978, were instrumental in bringing the Vatican II Council to a confident conclusion in 1965.

September 27

1540 Through the encyclical *Regimini Militantis Ecclesiae*, Pope Paul III officially approved the Society of Jesus (the Jesuits), founded six years earlier by Ignatius of Loyola.

1660 Death of St. Vincent de Paul (b.1581), Roman Catholic religious. After pastoring for several years, Vincent abandoned his search for power and position, and embarked on a life of serving the poor. In 1617 he founded the first Confraternity of Charity. In 1525 he founded the Congregation of the Mission (Vincentians or Lazarists), and in 1533 he established the Daughters of Charity, the first nonmonastic women's order given completely to care of the sick and poor. He was canonized in 1737 by Clement XII, and in 1885 was named patron saint of all works of charity.

1735 Birth of Robert Robinson, English clergyman and author of the hymn "Come, Thou Fount of Every Blessing," in Norfolk, England. At age 20 he was converted under the preaching of George Whitefield. Robinson began preaching; initially at a Calvinistic Methodist chapel in Suffolk, then in an independent church in Norwich, and finally at the Stone Yard Baptist Church in Cambridge, remaining there from 1761–90. Though lacking formal education, Robinson became a popular preacher and theologian.

1805 Birth of George Mueller, English philanthropist, near Magdeburg, Germany. In 1825 he was converted from the life of a prodigal to Christian faith under the Moravians. He began to preach and did evangelistic work among the Jews and children. He moved to Bristol in 1832 and made it his permanent home. His next 66 years were devoted to the care of orphan children, relying entirely on private prayer and voluntary offerings to support the work. By 1875 over 2,000 children were being housed, fed and instructed in the Christian life. When Mueller died at 93, his worldly possessions were valued at less than $1,000. Nevertheless, during his lifetime, he had dispersed over $8 million in donated funds, and over 10,000 orphans had been welcomed into his homes.

1829 Mt. Ararat, the mountain in Turkey that is believed to hold the remains of Noah's Ark, was first climbed in modern times by Dr. J.J. Parrot.

1867 Birth of W.E. Biederwolf, American Presbyterian evangelist, in Monticello, Indiana. Converted to saving faith at age 20, he was ordained in 1897 to the Presbyterian ministry. He pastored in Indiana for three years, then served one year as a chaplain during the Spanish-American War. In 1900 Biederwolf took up evangelistic work, continuing for the next 39 years. He also served as president of Winona College (1917–19), director of the Winona Lake Bible School of Theology (1923–33) and founder and general director of the Family Altar League beginning in 1909. During his last ten years, he was pastor of the Royal Poinciana Chapel at Palm Beach, Florida.

1872 Birth of B.D. Ackley, American sacred composer, in Spring Hill, Pennsylvania. During his early career, he served as an organist in several churches. In 1907 Ackley joined the Billy Sunday evangelistic team and traveled with them as pianist and secretary for a number of years. He later worked as a composer and editor for the Rodeheaver Publishing Co. In 1930 he met famous Canadian pastor Oswald J. Smith and they collaborated on more than 100 Gospel songs. Ackley composed more than 3,000 hymn tunes, including the melody he wrote for Smith's hymn "God Understands Your Sorrow."

1899 Death of James Ellor (b.1819), English-born American hatmaker who wrote the hymn tune DIADEM ("All Hail the Power of Jesus' Name.") He came to the U.S. at age 24 to continue the hatmaking trade he learned early in life. He possessed a natural musical talent, and by the time he was 18, he was leading local church choirs.

1901 Birth of F. Wilbur Gingrich, American Evangelical United Brethren (United Methodist) New Testament scholar, in Annville, Pennsylvania. He taught at Albright College in Pennsylvania from 1923. In 1957 he and W.F. Arndt edited *A Greek-English Lexicon of the New Testament*. The most useful language tool Gingrich himself left for New Testament Greek students was his *Shorter Lexicon of the Greek New Testament* (1965), which is based on the larger 1957 work, but also contains Bible references and listings of irregular Greek verb forms.

1914 Birth of Catherine (nee Wood) Marshall LeSourd, American Christian writer, in Johnson City, Tennessee. She became a bestselling author with the publication of *A Man Called Peter*, a biography of her first husband, Peter Marshall, Chaplain of the U.S. Senate. She became a regular contributor to *Guideposts* magazine. She and her second husband, Leonard LeSourd, were owners of Chosen Books Publishing Co. She was almost finished with her novel *Christy* when she died in 1983 at age 69.

1921 At age 26, American fundamentalist evangelist John R. Rice (1895–1980) married Lloys McClure Cook.

1944 Death of Aimee Semple McPherson (b.1890), founder of the Church of the Foursquare Gospel. An itinerant revivalist from 1916–23, she was the best-known woman evangelist of her day. In 1923 she founded the Church of the

Foursquare Gospel, and built the Angelus Temple in Los Angeles, serving as minister there from 1923 until her death. She was a spell-binding faith healer, whose followers remained faithful through her several marriages and divorces and a sensational (though dubious) kidnapping in 1926.

1947 The Church of South India was officially formed by the merger of three denominations: the Anglican Church (dioceses of Madras, Tinnevelly, Travancore and Cochin, and Dornakal plus dioceses of the Church of India, Burma and Ceylon); the South India province of the Methodist Church; and the South India United Church (formed originally by a 1908 union of Presbyterian and Congregational churches). The merger was an historic event: the first union ever between episcopal (bishop-led) and non-episcopal (congregation-led) bodies.

1957 The half-hour dramatic anthology series *Crossroads* aired for the last time over ABC television. Depicting the work of clergymen, the series had premiered two years earlier in Oct. 1955.

September 28

1740 English revivalist George Whitefield noted in a letter: "Exercise the talents you have, and that is the way to get more. Thus has God dealt with me for these eleven years. 'To him that hath, shall be given.' "

1774 Anglican hymnwriter John Newton mentioned in a letter: "We are always equally in danger in ourselves and always equally safe under the shadow of His wings."

1808 Andover Theological Seminary was opened in Massachusetts under Congregational auspices.

1839 Birth of Frances E. Willard, American educator and temperance leader, in Churchville, New York. She graduated from Northwestern Female College in Evanston, Illinois, in 1859, and returned to teach from 1869–74. She became interested in temperance and women's suffrage, and in 1879 she was elected president of the National Women's Christian Temperance Union, holding the office until her death in 1898. In 1883 she founded the World W.C.T.U., serving as its president from 1891–98. The passage of both the 18th and 19th Amendments to the U.S. Constitution (Prohibition and Women's Suffrage) was partially a result of her efforts.

1903 Death of Samuel A. Ward (b.1847), American music publisher. He received training in music early in life in New York City. He later settled in Newark, New Jersey, where he established a successful retail music store and became active in the music life of the city. In 1880 he became organist at the Grace Episcopal Church of Newark, and held the position for several years. From his pen came the hymn tune MATERNA, to which we sing "America the Beautiful" ("O Beautiful for Spacious Skies").

1934 The first issue of the fundamentalist Christian newspaper *The Sword of the Lord* was published. Founded by American evangelist John R. Rice, it was the largest independent Christian weekly for many years, and was recognized by liberals as the voice of fundamentalism. Five thousand copies were printed for the first edition.

1978 Death of Pope John Paul I (b.1912), 262nd pontiff of the Roman Catholic Church. Born Albino Luciani, he was ordained a priest in 1935. Named patriarch of Venice in 1969, he hosted five ecumenical conferences during his nine-year tenure, including an important doctrinal meeting between the Roman and Anglican churches. Following Paul VI's death on Aug. 6, 1978, Luciani was elected to succeed him on the third ballot on the first day of the papal conclave. His choice of the name "John Paul" was said to express his desire to combine John XXIII's progressiveness, and Paul VI's traditionalism. He was invested Sept. 3 in St. Peter's Square, but died only three weeks later, of a heart attack, while reading a devotional in bed.

September 29

1770 The day before he died, English revivalist George Whitefield prayed: "Lord Jesus, I am weary in Thy work, but not of it."

1773 English founder of Methodism, John Wesley, acknowledged in a letter: "Grace in one sense will make all things new. And I have sometimes known this done to such a degree that there has been no trace of the natural temper remaining. But generally the innocent natural temper does remain: only refined, softened, and cast into the mould of love."

1803 The first Roman Catholic Church in Boston was formally dedicated. Catholics had been granted religious freedom by the Massachusetts Constitution of June 15, 1780.

1838 The Missionary Board of the Reformed (German) Church in the United States was organized. The board supported missionaries sent by other agencies until 1865, when it began sending its own missionaries to the Winnebago Indians in Wisconsin and to Japan.

1890 The Chicago Presbytery petitioned the Chicago Board of Education to have the Bible read in the public schools.

1903 Birth of Texan Red Harper, self-taught composer and singer. He wrote the Gospel songs "Each Step of the Way" and "Lord, Keep Your Hand on Me." He appeared in several early films produced by the Billy Graham Evangelistic Association.

1963 Pope Paul VI opened the second session of the Vatican II Council in Rome. This session lasted through Dec. 4. Vatican II was the 21st of the church's ecumenical councils. The council met in four sessions between Oct. 1962 and Dec. 1965. The general attitude of the council revealed a desire for reformation within the Roman Catholic Church.

1967 Swiss Reformed theologian Karl Barth commented in a letter: "God has very different people who like one another to different degrees."

September 30

420 Death of St. Jerome (b.ca.345), early Bible translator. At age 12 he went to Rome to learn Latin and Greek. At 19 he became a Christian and spent the next several years in semi-asceticism, learning Hebrew while living five years as a hermit in the Syrian desert. In 382 Pope Damasus urged him to begin a translation of the Scriptures into the common (vulgar) Latin tongue. Jerome completed a translation of the entire Bible, later known as the Latin *Vulgate*, into contemporary Latin. The Roman Catholic Church recognized the *Vulgate* as its authorized version of the Bible in the 8th century. Jerome also wrote commentaries on virtually every book of the Bible.

1770   English revivalist George Whitefield (b.1714) died in Newburyport, Massachusetts. His last words were "I had rather wear out, than rust out." While at Oxford, he had come under the influence of the Wesley brothers and followed them to Georgia, where he established an orphanage in Savannah. Returning to England, he found Anglican Church doors closed to his preaching, so he began preaching as an itinerant evangelist. He broke ties with the Wesleys after 1743 to form the Calvinist Methodist Society. During his lifetime, he traveled throughout the British Isles and paid seven visits to America. He is regarded as the most striking orator to have come out of 18th century English revivalism.

1882   Death of Johann Jakob Herzog (b.1805), German Reformed theologian. He taught between 1835–77 at the Universities of Lausanne, Halle and Erlangen. His greatest work was the 22-volume religious encyclopedia *Realencyklopadie fur Protestantische Theologie und Kirche* (1853–68), to which he contributed 529 articles. This standard reference work was later revised and translated by Philip Schaff, and published under the English title *The Schaff-Herzog Encyclopedia of Religious Knowledge* (1882–84).

1943   Pope Pius XII issued the encyclical *Divino Afflante Spiritu*, which emphasized, among other things, the great importance of textual criticism in biblical studies. It permitted Catholic scholars to devote more attention in their teaching, exegesis and writing to the historical background of the original texts of Scripture. One of the results of the encyclical was the preparation of the New American Bible translation.

1946   The International Military War Tribunal at Nuremberg, Germany, having convened in Nov. 1945, ended its investigations with the conviction of 22 Nazi leaders for war crimes committed against the Jewish people. Eleven were sentenced to death by hanging. One of those convicted, Hermann W. Goering, committed suicide in his prison cell two hours before his scheduled execution.

1951   Billy Graham's television program *Hour of Decision* first aired over ABC. It was broadcast on Sunday nights from 10:00–10:30 p.m. EDT. The program ran through Feb. 1954, but was syndicated for broadcast afterward.

1952   The complete Revised Standard Version of the Bible was first published, by Thomas Nelson and Sons.

1963   The U.S. Congress declared this date Annual Bible Translation Day.

1970   The complete New American Bible was published in Patterson, New Jersey. It was the first Catholic-sponsored English translation of the Scriptures taken directly from the original Greek and Hebrew and was intended to replace the 1610 Douay version of the Bible.

October

October 1

1529 The Marburg Colloquy convened in the Marburg Castle of Philip of Hesse. During its four days of meetings, Protestant theologians Martin Luther, Philip Melanchthon, Ulrich Zwingli and Oecolampadius debated various theological issues separating them in order to form a united front against the Roman Catholic threat. The efforts at harmony were consistently frustrated by disagreements over how Christ is present at the Lord's Supper. At the end of the colloquy, 15 articles were issued expressing the doctrines on which general agreement was held. Despite the common ground, the colloquy served to divide the Protestant movement rather than unite it, setting a pattern for denominational division that has persisted into the 20th century.

1878 The Regions Beyond Missionary Union (founded 1873) opened Harley College in Bow, Ireland. By 1915 over 1,500 missionaries had been trained and sent out. Originally called the Livingstone Inland Mission, this evangelical Baptist mission organization first established itself in the U.S. in 1948. Its present name, R.B.M.U. International, was adopted in 1981. Headquartered today in Philadelphia, Pennsylvania, the agency works with over 100 overseas personnel in 5 foreign countries: Peru, Chile, the Philipines, Indonesia and Zaire. R.B.M.U. is engaged primarily in Bible translation, evangelism, church planting and support of national churches.

1883 American religious leader A.B. Simpson founded the first Bible school in America to train missionaries, in New York City. Its name became the Missionary Training Institute in April 1894. The school changed its name to Nyack College in 1972.

1889 Birth of Ralph W. Sockman, American Christian writer, in Mount Vernon, Ohio. He was an associate professor at Union Theological Seminary starting in 1950. He authored many devotional writings, but perhaps is best remembered today for the poem which begins "I met God in the morning, when my day was at its best. . . ."

1921 The Latin America Mission was incorporated in Philadelphia by founders Harry and Susan Strachan. Originally called the Latin America Evangelization Campaign, the organization moved to its present headquarters in Coral Gables, Florida, in April 1977. Today, this interdenominational, evangelical mission organization specializes in evangelism, church planting, literature production and the support of other mission agencies. Over 125 foreign staff work with L.A.M. in 8 Central and South American countries.

1946 World Literature Crusade was founded in Prince Albert, Saskatchewan, by Rev. Jack McAlister (president from 1946–79). Headquartered since 1975 in Chatsworth, California, this evangelical, interdenominational missions organization works in 43 foreign countries and is engaged primarily in Bible and literature distribution, church planting and Bible correspondence courses.

1963 World-Wide Missions moved its headquarters to Pasadena, California. Founded in 1950 by Basil W. & Esther K. Miller, this evangelical, interdenominational missionary organization operates in nearly 30 countries, and is engaged primarily in providing medicine, relief aid and financial support of national workers and churches.

October 2

1792 The Baptist Missionary Society was founded in London, England. It was started principally by William Carey and was the first modern mission society.

1808 Birth of Allen W. Chatfield, Anglican clergyman, in Cambridgeshire, England. Ordained in 1832, he served as vicar at Stotfold (1833–47) and as vicar at Much-Marcle in Herefordshire from 1847 until his death 49 years later (1896). His best-remembered writings include the English translation of the hymn "Lord Jesus, Think on Me."

1918 Birth of Don Hustad, organist for the Billy Graham Evangelistic Association. He accompanied Graham as organist for his worldwide crusades during 1961–67.

1921 Birth of Robert Runcie, Anglican clergyman. In Jan. 1980 he replaced F. Donald Coggan as the Archbishop of Canterbury, Primate of the Anglican Church in England.

1984 Grace Ministries International was incorporated in Grand Rapids, Michigan. Originating in 1951, G.M.I. began as Bethesda Mission, a sending extension of the Bethesda Church of Minneapolis. In 1964 Bethesda Mission merged with the Worldwide Grace Testimony Mission (founded in 1939), and was renamed Grace Mission. G.M.I. is an interdenominational, evangelical mission agency engaged primarily in church planting, theological education, literature production and provision of medical supplies. G.M.I. supports 55 overseas staff working in Zaire, Africa and 9 other nations.

October 3

1226 Death of St. Francis of Assisi (b.ca.1182), Italian religious leader. In 1208 Francis set out on a life of evangelistic preaching and mendicant living. He and a band of his followers drew together a religious rule based on sayings from the Gospels and formed the beginnings of the Franciscan Religious Order. The Franciscans were officially approved by Pope Innocent III in 1223.

1690 Death of Robert Barclay (b.1648), Scottish Quaker theologian. In 1667 he followed his father in leaving the Church of Scotland to join the Society of Friends. He then traveled as an evangelist throughout Great Britain, Holland and Germany. In 1673 he penned *A Catechism* and *Confession of Faith*, the nearest document to a confession of faith ever produced by the Quakers. But Barclay's fame rests on his 1676 writing *An Apology for the True Christian Divinity*. This systematic presentation of the mystical piety on which Quakerism is based defends the doctrine of the "Inner Light" against the supremacy of external authorities. The writing became the classic exposition of Quaker principles, and made Barclay the most prominent theologian of the early Quaker faith.

1778 Anglican hymnwriter John Newton affirmed in a letter: "A real conviction of our weakness we cannot learn merely from books or preachers. The providence of God concurs with His Holy Spirit in His merciful design of making us acquainted with ourselves."

1832 Birth of Carolina ("Lina") Sandell Berg, Swedish Lutheran hymnwriter, in Froderyd, Smaland, Sweden. At the age of 12, she was miraculously healed of a childhood paralysis. From the experience, she began writing verses expressing her love and gratitude to God. She wrote about 650 hymns before her death at 71 (1903) and she has come to be known as "the Fanny Crosby of Sweden." Two of her songs that continue in popularity are "Day by Day, and with Each Passing Moment" and "Children of the Heavenly Father."

1875 Hebrew Union College was founded in Cincinnati, Ohio under Jewish auspices. It was the first Jewish college in the U.S. established to train men for the rabbinate.

1892 Death of Samuel Longfellow (b.1819), American clergyman and brother of Henry Wadsworth Longfellow. Like his brother, Samuel also wrote and published collections of verse. One of his poems has endured as the text of the hymn "Father, Give Thy Benediction."

1919 Death of Daniel B. Towner (b.1850), American music evangelist. He worked with the evangelistic team of D.L. Moody in 1885, and in 1893 was made head of the Music Department at Moody Bible Institute in Chicago, Illinois. Towner composed more than 2,000 songs during his lifetime, including MOODY ("Marvelous Grace of Our Loving Lord"), CALVARY ("Years I Spent in Vanity and Pride"), and TRUST AND OBEY ("When We Walk with the Lord").

1929 The Church of Scotland merged with the United Free Church of Scotland, retaining the name Church of Scotland. Though it maintains an official state connection, its government is presbyterian in nature.

1958 American Presbyterian apologist Francis Schaeffer observed in a letter: "It seems to me that we do tend to have two creeds—the one which we believe in our intellectual assent, and then the one which we believe to the extent of acting upon it in faith. More and more it seems to me that the true level of our orthodoxy is measured by this latter standard rather than the former."

October 4

1529 The Marburg Colloquy closed. Disagreement over what actually takes place at the Eucharist (The Lord's Supper) prevented union among Martin Luther, Philip Melanchthon, Ulrich Zwingli and Oecolampadius, the Protestant reformers. Switzerland remained Reformed, Germany remained Lutheran and no united European front against Roman Catholic domination was ever consolidated.

1535 The printing of Miles Coverdale's (1488–1568) English version of the Bible was completed in London. Coverdale later supervised the printing of the Anglican Church's *Great Bible* (1538–39) and helped edit *Cranmer's Bible* (1540). Coverdale published little original material during his lifetime, but was a good translator. He also gained popularity as a Lutheran preacher.

1582 Death of St. Teresa of Avila (b.1515), Spanish Carmelite nun. She first entered the convent at age 20 (1535). Beginning in 1555 she began experiencing ecstatic visions and receiving prophecies. She tried to combine her mystical experience with a practical explanation of what occurred. She was the first writer to differentiate between states of prayer: simple meditation and deep ecstasy (which she termed "mystical marriage").

1858 Birth of Dorothy Frances (Blomfield) Gurney, English devotional writer, in London, England. The daughter of an Anglican rector, Miss Blomfield married an Anglican clergyman, Gerald Gurney. In 1919 they both left the Church of England to join the Roman Catholic Church. Mrs. Gurney published two volumes of verse and also a devotional work: *A Little Book of Quiet*. In 1883, while preparing for her sister's wedding, Dorothy penned the text to the only hymn she ever wrote: "O Perfect Love, All Human Thought Transcending." It was included in the Anglican hymnal six years later.

1880 Birth of Homer A. Rodeheaver, American song evangelist and publisher, in Union Furnace, Ohio. From 1909–31 he was a music evangelist and choir director for Billy Sunday's evangelistic campaigns. In 1942 he became music director at Bob Jones College, then in Tennessee (now Bob Jones University in Greenville, South Carolina). He later became a music editor at the Rodeheaver Hall-Mack Company, publishers of Gospel music, in Winona Lake, Indiana. Rodeheaver published several collections of Gospel music in addition to writing some hymns. He spent his final years, before his death in 1955, directing a Florida ranch for underprivileged boys.

1901 Birth of Gregory Dix, Anglican Benedictine scholar. Born George Eglinton Alston, he taught at Oxford from 1923–26, then entered the monastic life. Although he is known widely for his radio broadcasts, his most important contribution lies in his comprehensive study of Christian worship, *The Shape of the Liturgy* (1945). Two convictions pervaded his theological thinking: "Religions pray," and "History happens through men and women, not through abstractions."

1965 Pope Paul VI arrived at New York City, the first pope in history to visit the Americas. On this first day of his visit, the pope celebrated a mass in Yankee Stadium and addressed the United Nations on the need for peace in the world. While speaking at the U.N., Paul published a document exonerating the Jews of all blame in the death of Christ.

October 5

1582 In Italy, Spain, Portugal and (Austrian and German) Poland, this date became Oct. 15, as these Roman Catholic nations officially instituted the Gregorian calendar. The Gregorian system of marking time had been formulated earlier in the year by Pope Gregory XIII. His new calendar marked a revision of the former, inaccurate Julian calendar, first implemented by Julius

Caesar in 46 B.C., and officially adopted by the Christian world at the Council of Nicea in 325. In order to maintain accuracy, the Gregorian calendar decreed that no year ending in "00" should be a leap year unless divisible by 400. Thus, 1700, 1800 and 1900 were not leap years, but the year 2000 will be. Without this adjustment, the Julian calendar had lost ten days against the solar year.

1703   Birth of Jonathan Edwards, colonial American theologian, in East Windsor, Connecticut. By age 13 he knew Latin, Greek, and Hebrew well enough to enter Yale College. He graduated in 1720 with highest honors. In 1724 he began a 26-year pastorate at the Northampton Congregational Church in Massachusetts. While he was in Northampton, the Great Awakening of 1734–44 broke out. Edwards' sermons, such as *Sinners in the Hands of an Angry God* (July 8, 1741), had a powerful influence on his audiences. In 1751 Edwards became pastor of the Congregational Church in Stockbridge, Massachusetts. Six years later, he was elected president of Princeton College in New Jersey, but died of smallpox five weeks after his inauguration in 1758.

1744   Colonial American missionary David Brainerd, following his ordination, began three years of missionary labors among the Indians on the Susquehannah River at Opeholhaupung, New Jersey.

1833   Birth of William G. Tomer, American Methodist hymnwriter. A veteran of the U.S. Civil War Union Army, Tomer worked for 20 years as a U.S. government employee in Washington, D.C. He also served as musical director at Grace Methodist Episcopal Church in Washington. Tomer composed several hymn tunes during his work at the Grace Church, including FAREWELL, to which we sing the hymn "God Be with You Till We Meet Again."

1969   Death of Harry Emerson Fosdick (b.1878), American Baptist clergyman. Ordained in 1903, Fosdick pastored in New Jersey from 1903–15. He also taught at Union Theological Seminary in New York from 1908–46 and pastored Riverside Church in New York City from 1926–46. His preaching focused on the clash between fundamentalists and liberals ("modernists"), taking his stand between the two extremes. Fosdick authored the hymn "God of Grace and God of Glory."

October 6

1536   Martyrdom of William Tyndale (b.ca.1494), English reformer and translator of the English Bible. Ordained about 1521, he came under the influence of Erasmus's Greek New Testament and Luther's writings. Desiring to give the English people the Bible in their own language, Tyndale went to Hamburg to learn Hebrew. His English New Testament was printed from 1525–26 in Worms, Germany, then smuggled back into England by English merchants. In 1534 he moved to Antwerp, Belgium, but was soon after arrested, tried for heresy and convicted. Tyndale was strangled to death, then burned in the prison yard. His last words were "Lord, open the eyes of the King of England."

1552   Birth of Matteo Ricci, Italian Jesuit missionary, in Macerata, Italy. He joined the Jesuit order in 1571, was sent as a missionary to India in 1578, and about five years later went to Macao in South China. In order to be "all things to all men," Ricci adopted Chinese dress and customs, and won many converts by introducing Christianity through Chinese concepts. After Ricci's death in 1610, his evangelistic methods were the subject of heated controversy in the Roman Catholic Church on the legitimacy and limits of "accommodation" in the preaching of the Gospel. Ricci's excessive accommodations were condemned by his church in 1704 and 1715.

1583   In Tyrol (Austria) and Bavaria, this date became October 16 when these governments officially adopted the Gregorian Calendar.

1683   A group of German settlers in America arrived at Philadelphia. These 13 linen weavers and their families were Mennonite refugees from Krefield, Germany. They founded Germantown, the first German settlement in America, near Philadelphia. Their pastor, Francis Daniel Pastorius, was considered by many the most learned man in America at the time.

1816   Birth of William B. Bradbury, American Baptist sacred music composer, in York, Maine. A graduate of the Boston Academy of Music, Bradbury published 59 collections of sacred and secular music during his lifetime. His most enduring hymn tunes include BRADBURY ("Savior, Like a Shepherd Lead Us"), CHINA ("Jesus Loves Me, This I Know"), WOODWORTH ("Just As I Am"), YARBROUGH ("Take My Life and Let It Be") and the melodies to the hymns "He Leadeth Me," "The Solid Rock" and "Sweet Hour of Prayer."

1818   Birth of Silas J. Vail, New England businessman and composer of CLOSE TO THEE ("Thou My Everlasting Portion"), in Brooklyn, New York. Music was a hobby for Vail, yet he composed a number of hymn tunes during his lifetime.

1874   Death of John E. Bode (b.1816), Anglican clergyman. He pastored at Christ Church in Oxford, at Westwell, in Oxfordshire, and at Castle Camps in Cambridgeshire, starting in 1860. His major writings were collections of ballads and poems, including the verse "O Jesus, I Have Promised."

1892   Death of Alfred Lord Tennyson (b.1809), English Victorian poet. The fourth son of an Anglican clergyman, Tennyson's poetry is permeated with a religious spirit, which finds its deepest expression in the poem *In Memoriam*, dedicated to the memory of a dear friend who had recently died: Arthur Henry Hallam. Tennyson also authored the hymn "Ring Out the Old, Ring in the New."

1894   Death of Matthew Bridges (b.1800), English clergyman. Raised in the Anglican Church, Bridges later came under the influence of the Oxford Movement. In 1848 he followed John Henry Newman and others in joining the Roman Catholic Church. He spent the later years of his life in Quebec, Canada. Bridges was the author of several hymns, including "Crown Him with Many Crowns."

1938   Birth of Dannie Bell Hall, contemporary religious artist. Dannie Bell toured with Billy Graham and Andrae Crouch during several of their evangelistic crusades. She is famous for her song "Ordinary People."

1945   Death of George C. Stebbins (b.1846), American Baptist music evangelist. For 25 years he was associated with the work of Dwight L. Moody. Later, he assisted Ira Sankey in compiling several volumes of the *Gospel Hymns* series. Stebbins himself composed hundreds of Gospel songs, many of which we still use as hymn tunes: CALLING TODAY ("Jesus Is Tenderly Calling Thee

Home"), FRIEND ("I've Found a Friend, Oh, Such a Friend"), HOLINESS ("Take Time to Be Holy") and POLLARD ("Have Thine Own Way, Lord").

1979 In Washington, D.C., at the White House, Pope John Paul II met with Jimmy Carter. This was the first meeting in history between a pope and a U.S. president. John Paul II had arrived on Oct. 1 for a six-day visit to the U.S. His major stops included Boston, New York City, Philadelphia, Des Moines, Chicago and Washington, D.C.

1982 American Bible expositor Derek Prince assured in a radio broadcast: "God accepts responsibility for the maintenance of His appointed temple— our body."

October 7

1772 Death of John Woolman (b.1720), American Quaker preacher. Beginning in 1743, he traveled throughout the 13 Colonies preaching against the draft, against taxes for military equipment, against ill treatment of the Indians and in support of Negro rights. His protests bore fruit in 1776 when the representatives at the annual meeting of Friends in Philadelphia voted to end their practice of owning slaves. Woolman's *Journal* (written from 1756 until his death) greatly influenced 19th-century abolitionists. ·

1787 Death of Henry M. Muhlenberg (b.1711), Father of American Lutheranism. Raised in Prussia, he was sent to America in 1742 to organize the struggling Lutheran congregations in Pennsylvania. A man of immense physical strength and organizational ability, Muhlenberg ministered in the Philadelphia area for 37 years (1742–79). In 1748 he organized the Evangelical Lutheran Ministerium of Pennsylvania and Adjacent States. Muhlenberg spent his last years, during the American Revolutionary War, in semiretirement.

1810 Birth of Henry Alford, Anglican Bible scholar, in London, England. Ordained in 1834, Alford pastored during his remaining 37 years. He was an original member of the 1881 English Revised Version New Testament Committee. His greatest publication is the four-volume *Expositor's Greek Testament* (1849–61, and still in print), which he edited. Alford also wrote the hymns "Ten Thousand Times Ten Thousand" and "Come, Ye Thankful People, Come."

1832 Birth of Charles C. Converse, American lawyer and sacred music composer, in Warren, Massachusetts. In 1855 he traveled to Germany where he studied music under such great composers as Plaidy, Richter, Hauptmann, and Franz Liszt. Returning to America in 1859, he completed a degree in law from Albany University (1861). He later worked with William B. Bradbury editing and publishing collections of hymnbooks and Sunday school songbooks. Converse composed the hymn tune CONVERSE ("What a Friend We Have in Jesus").

1835 Birth of Folliott Sanford Pierpoint, classics instructor and author of the hymn "For the Beauty of the Earth," in Bath, England. He published several volumes of verse and penned a number of other hymns.

1887 Death of George J. Webb (b.1803), American organist of sacred music. Coming to the U.S. from England in 1830, he soon after became church organist at Old South Church in Boston—a position he held for 40 years. During this time, Webb wrote and published several music collections. Today, he is remembered primarily for his hymn tune WEBB, to which we sing the hymn "Stand Up, Stand Up for Jesus."

1925 Death of Hubert P. Main (b.1839), American sacred music editor. He spent his entire professional life in the sacred music publishing business. He joined the William B. Bradbury Co. in 1867 (which was eventually bought out by Hope Publishing in 1920). Main is credited with having created more than 1,000 hymn compositions during his lifetime, including ELLESDIE ("Jesus, I My Cross Have Taken").

1930 American Congregational linguist and missionary Frank C. Laubach conceded in a letter: "Beside Jesus, the whole lot of us are so contemptible. I do not see how God stomachs us at all. But God is like Jesus, and like Jesus, He will not give up until we, too, are like Jesus."

1955 The religious drama *Crossroads* first aired over ABC television. This anthology broadcast dramatizations of true experiences of clergymen of all denominations. The series ran for two years, airing its last show in Sept. 1957.

1982 American radio pastor Chuck Smith admitted: "Oh, how horrible our sins look when they are committed by someone else."

October 8

451 The Council of Chalcedon opened near Istanbul. The 4th ecumenical council of the ancient church, it was attended by 450 bishops. Seventeen sessions were held before Nov. 1. The council condemned monophysitism or Eutychianism, the ancient Christological heresy denying the full humanity of Christ by teaching that the incarnate Son of God possessed only one ("*mono*") nature ("*physis*"): the divine. The council also condemned the monophysite Robber Synod of Ephesus (449).

1882 Birth of Walter Russell Bowie, American Episcopalian theologian, in Richmond, Virginia. After completing studies at Harvard Seminary, Bowie pastored from 1908–39. Beginning in 1939, he taught at Union Theological Seminary in New York City and Virginia Theological Seminary. He authored over two dozen books and served on the Revised Standard Version (R.S.V.) translation committee. Bowie also authored the hymn "Lord Christ, When You First Came to Earth."

1901 The American branch of Overseas Missionary Fellowship was chartered. Founded in 1865 in Great Britain by missionary pioneer J. Hudson Taylor, O.M.F. was originally the China Inland Mission. At its centennial celebration in 1965, the organization adopted its present name. This interdenominational, evangelical mission organization operates in nine Far Eastern nations, engaging primarily in evangelism, church planting, theological education and literature distribution.

1914 Birth of Robert W. ("Bob") Pierce, American evangelist and founder of World Vision, in Fort Dodge, Iowa. Ordained in 1940, Pierce was an evangelist beginning in 1937. This took him to Japan, Korea and the Philippines. His compassion for the suffering he saw while in Asia led him to found World

Vision International, a worldwide relief organization, in 1950. In 1967 he resigned as president of W.V.I. and founded Samaritan's Purse, a fund-raising agency supporting relief in Asia. Pierce died of leukemia in 1978.

October 9

1561 The Colloquy of Poissy ended. Held near Paris, this conference between the French Roman Catholic bishops and the Protestant ministers (led by Theodore Beza) paved the way for an edict in 1562 that officially recognized and gave limited freedoms to French Protestantism.

1635 Colonial American Separatist Roger Williams was banished from Massachusetts for preaching that civil government had no right to interfere in religious or ecclesiastical affairs. Williams purchased land from the Indians on the shores of Narragansett Bay the following year and founded Providence. Williams' life-work was to establish freedom of worship through the separation of church and state.

1747 Death of David Brainerd (b.1718), Colonial American missionary to the New England Indians. In 1744 Brainerd was appointed by the Scottish Society for the Propagation of Christian Knowledge (S.P.C.K.) to do evangelistic work among the Indians of Eastern Pennsylvania, Massachusetts, and New Jersey. For three years he endured great physical deprivation and hardship. In 1747 he retired from his missionary work because of tuberculosis, which killed him three months later. Brainerd kept a minutely detailed diary of both his spiritual and missionary endeavors. Following his death, the publication of *Brainerd's Journal* by Jonathan Edwards influenced hundreds to become missionaries after him.

1747 Birth of Thomas Coke, pioneer English Methodist bishop, in Brecon, Wales. Ordained an Anglican in 1770, Coke joined the Methodist movement in 1777, and in 1784 was made superintendent (later called "bishop") of America by John Wesley. That same year Coke arranged the Conference of Baltimore, where he ordained Francis Asbury as co-superintendent of the American Methodist Church. Coke crossed the Atlantic 18 times for his job. In 1814 he gave the funds to establish a Methodist mission in India, and even sailed with a band of missionaries going there. He died on the voyage and was buried at sea. Coke was an opponent of slavery and had always wished to heal the breach between Methodism and its Anglican parent church.

1776 Spanish missionaries dedicated the first mission chapel on the northern California coast at Yerba Buena. In 1847 the name of the city that grew up around the mission was changed to San Francisco.

1845 English churchman John Henry Newman, co-founder of the Oxford Movement, made his celebrated conversion from Anglicanism to the Roman Catholic Church. Between 1845–62, nearly 250 clergy from the Church of England followed Newman into Catholicism. In 1879 Pope Leo XIII made Newman a cardinal.

1890 Birth of Aimee Semple McPherson, American religious leader, in Ingersoll, Ontario, Canada. An itinerant revivalist from 1916–23, she became the best-known female evangelist of her time. In 1923 she founded the Church of the Foursquare Gospel. She built the Angelus Temple in Los Angeles, serving as its minister from 1923 until her death in 1944. She was a spellbinding faith healer whose followers remained faithful through her several marriages and divorces, as well as her sensational (and somewhat scandalous) "kidnapping" in 1926.

October 10

1560 Birth of Jacob Arminius, Dutch theologian, at Oudewater, Holland. Ordained in 1588, he pastored in Amsterdam until 1603. While studying for a defense of Calvinism, he became convinced that he was defending an illogical position. When the Dutch Republic became an independent state in 1609, Calvinism was declared the official·state religion. Arminius, in opposition, sought to modify Calvinism so that God might not be viewed the author of sin, nor man an automaton in the hands of God. Arminius died in 1609, in the early stages of this theological controversy, before a national synod could be convened in which his views could be clearly stated. Arminian Protestantism takes its name from this Dutch theologian of the early 17th century.

1821 Charles G. Finney (1792–1875) was saved. At age 29, Finney was already a successful lawyer, but he began attending church and reading the Bible. His spiritual conversion was remarkably sudden and thorough. He gave up his law practice and began a 50-year career in the ministry.

1838 Birth of Theodor Zahn, German Lutheran Bible and patristics (study of the early church fathers) scholar, in Mors, Rhenish Prussia. He taught at the universities of Gottingen (1865–77), Kiel (1877–78), Erlangen (1878–88 and 1892–1909) and Leipzig (1888–92). He was the author of many important monographs and commentaries. Nevertheless, his influence was underrated because he defended the conservatives in New Testament studies, opposing the radical critics of the Bible. Among his leading works was his three-volume *Introduction to the New Testament* (1897–99; English Translation 1909).

1841 Birth of William A. Ogden, American sacred music writer, in Franklin County, Ohio. His early studies in music were interrupted by four years of service to the Union Army during the American Civil War. Afterward, he resumed his education, studying under Lowell Mason, Thomas Hastings, E.E. Bailey and B.F. Baker. Ogden became well known as a music teacher and a conductor of music conventions. During his lifetime, he published several collections of Sunday school songs. His progressive music is preserved in the music of the hymn "Bring Them In" and in both his words and music to the hymn "He Is Able to Deliver Thee."

1851 Birth of W. Robertson Nicoll, Scottish theologian and editor, in Aberdeenshire, Scotland. Ordained in 1874, he pastored at two churches before 1885 when ill health forced his resignation. Moving to London, he eventually served as editor of at least five periodicals. He became the library advisor to the publishing house of Hodder and Stoughton. His most enduring literary achievement is *The Expositor's Greek Testament*, a series of 50 volumes that he edited and released between 1888–1905. Nicoll's personal library contained almost 25,000 volumes, including 5,000 biographies.

1903 Emma Moody died. Born Emma Charlotte Revell in 1842, she married American evangelist Dwight L. Moody in 1862. Emma was 19; Moody was 25. Their marriage lasted 37 years, until D.L.'s death in 1899. Emma outlived her husband by only 4 years, living until age 61.

1940 Death of Wilfred T. Grenfell (b.1866), English medical missionary to Labrador. He was converted to Christ at a D.L. Moody crusade in 1885. Seven years later, Grenfell began his famous 42-year medical mission work among the fisherfolk of Labrador and Newfoundland. He retired from the work in 1935 and wrote several books about his missionary experiences.

1958 Death of George Bennard (b.1873), American Methodist evangelist. The son of an Ohio coal miner, Bennard's father's early death forced him to abandon plans for higher education. He later moved his family to Illinois, where he married. After several years of work in the Salvation Army, Bennard joined the Methodist Episcopal Church and spent many years as an evangelist in the U.S. and Canada. Though he wrote over 300 Gospel songs, he is remembered for only one. In 1913, in the midst of evangelistic services in Michigan, Bennard penned the words and music to "The Old Rugged Cross."

October 11

1521 Pope Leo X conferred the title of Fidei Defensor ("Defender of the Faith") upon Henry VIII of England as a reward for Henry's *Defense of the Seven Sacraments*, published in answer to Luther's *Babylonian Captivity*. Three popes and almost exactly 13 years later, Henry established a national Catholic church, the Church of England, itself severing all ties with Rome.

1531 Death of Ulrich Zwingli (b.1484), Swiss reformer. While serving as a parish priest in Zurich, Zwingli secretly married in 1522. He broke with the Roman Catholic Church in 1525, adopting reformed theology in its place. He was soon after engaged in controversy over doctrinal matters with both Anabaptists and Lutherans. Zwingli's final years were marked with increasing political and military involvement. A temporary peace was reached in 1529 between the Reformed and the Catholic canons of Switzerland; but in 1531, the Catholics rebelled, and Zwingli was killed in the Battle of Kappel.

1863 Birth of James Hope Moulton, English Methodist theologian, in Richmond, Surrey. The son of W.F. Moulton, he entered the ministry in 1886, and also began teaching in the college classroom. He taught Classical Greek and Indo-European philology at the University of Manchester from 1908–17. He died in 1917 while returning from a missionary tour to India. His ship was torpedoed and sunk and he died of exposure. Of his many scholarly works, his two greatest publications were undoubtedly the first volume (Prolegomena) of the *Grammar of New Testament Greek* (1906) and his *Vocabulary of the Greek Testament*, which he co-edited with G. Milligan (1914–15, 1930).

1895 Birth of Avis B. Christiansen, sacred music writer, in Chicago, Illinois. Converted to Christ early in life, she married a member of the staff at Moody Bible Institute in Chicago. One of the most prolific hymnwriters of the 20th century, Mrs. Christiansen wrote hundreds of Gospel hymn texts, as well as several volumes of verse. She collaborated with such well-known Gospel composers as Harry Dixon Loes, Wendell Loveless and Haldor Lillenas. Two of her hymns are "Up Calvary's Mountain" and "Precious Hiding Place."

1914 Birth of Kenneth R. Adams, missionary publishing pioneer. In 1941 Adams founded the Christian Literature Crusade, in Colchester, England. C.L.C. is an evangelical, interdenominational service agency which publishes and distributes Bibles and Christian literature in 45 countries.

1954 American Presbyterian apologist Francis Schaeffer wrote in a letter: "Doctrinal rightness and rightness of ecclesiastical position are important, but only as a starting point to go on into a living relationship—and not as ends in themselves."

1962 In St. Peter's Basilica, Pope John XXIII opened the first session of the Vatican II Ecumenical Council. This session lasted until Dec. 8. Three more sessions followed during the next three years. A total of 2,860 priests participated in the council, with an average attendance of 2000–2500 at any one meeting.

October 12

1518 Summoned before Cardinal Thomas de Vio Cajetan (1469–1534), German reformer Martin Luther (1483–1546) refused to recant the 95 theses he had posted the previous Oct. 31 on the chapel door at the Wittenberg castle.

1872 Birth of Ralph Vaughan Williams, one of the most significant English composers of the 20th century. In addition to composing nine symphonies and several other major works for chorus and orchestra, Williams became a pioneer in collecting and publishing English folk music, which greatly influenced many of his own music compositions. Williams composed the music for W.W. How's hymn "For All the Saints."

1881 Death of Josiah G. Holland (b.1819), American news editor and author of the Christmas hymn "There's a Song in the Air." After a brief career in medicine, Holland established a weekly newspaper. Later, he joined the staff of the *Springfield Republican*, in Massachusetts. Holland helped found *Scribner's Magazine*, serving as its editor the rest of his life.

1883 Birth of C. Harold Lowden, American evangelical and reformed sacred music composer. He spent over 60 years in various branches of the sacred music field. He was music editor for the Reformed Church Board. He taught music at the Bible Institute of Pennsylvania. He served 28 years as minister of music at the Linden Baptist Church of Camden, New Jersey. His most popular compositions are GENEVA ("God Who Touchest Earth with Beauty") and LIVING ("Living for Jesus a Life That Is True").

1895 Death of Mrs. Cecil Frances Alexander (b.1823), Irish poet and hymnwriter. In 1850 she married William Alexander, an Irish clergyman who became Primate of Ireland in 1893. During the 1840s and 1850s, Mrs. Alexander published several volumes of poetic verse. Three of her poems are popular hymns: "All Things Bright and Beautiful," "Jesus Calls Us" and "There Is a Green Hill Far Away."

1910 Birth of F.F. (Frederick Fyvie) Bruce, English New Testament scholar, in Elgin, Scotland. He taught at the Universities of Edinburgh (1935–38), Leeds

(1938–47), Sheffield (1947–59) and Manchester (1959–78). He has authored many evangelical commentaries on various books of the Bible and published many articles in theological journals. Some of his better-known books include *The Books and the Parchments* (1950), *The English Bible* (1961), *Paul: Apostle of the Heart Set Free* (1978), and *The New Testament Documents: Are They Reliable*. He was editor of the *Evangelical Quarterly* from 1949–80.

1949 American missionary and Auca Indian martyr Jim Elliot noted in his journal: "For my generation I must have the oracles of God in fresh terms."

1971 *Jesus Christ Superstar* debuted on Broadway. The rock opera by Andrew Lloyd Webber and Timothy Rice opened at the Mark Hellinger Theater in New York City starring Jeff Fenholt, Ben Vereen and Yvonne Elliman. Previously, the opera had been performed across America by two touring companies; and the album recording of the musical had already sold 2.5 million copies.

October 13

1605 Death of Theodore Beza (b.1519), French-born Swiss Reformer. Beza renounced Catholicism for Calvinism at the age of 29 in 1548. The following year, at Calvin's invitation, Beza became professor of Greek at Lausanne, serving until 1558. When Calvin died in 1564, Beza became the acknowledged leader of the Swiss Reformation. In 1565 he published the first edition of his Greek New Testament.

1742 English revivalist George Whitefield related in a letter: "My strength is daily renewed. Still I desire to cry, Grace! Grace!"

1824 Birth of Henry Stephen Cutler, American sacred music chorister, in Boston, Massachusetts. In 1846 he became organist at Grace Episcopal Church in Boston, later moving to the Church of the Advent. During his second appointment, he assembled the first choir with robes in the U.S. In 1858 he became organist at Trinity Church in New York City. He later held positions in Brooklyn, New York; Providence, Rhode Island; and Philadelphia and Troy, Pennsylvania. Cutler composed the hymn tune ALL SAINTS, NEW, to which we sing the hymn "The Son of God Goes Forth to War."

1843 The Jewish fraternal society B'nai B'rith ("Sons of the Covenant") was founded in New York City by a group of German Jews. It is both the oldest and the largest of the Jewish fraternal organizations.

1873 Birth of Louis Berkhof, Dutch Reformed theologian, in Holland. He attended Calvin Seminary in Grand Rapids, Michigan. After other post-graduate work and serving as a pastor, Berkhof was called back to Calvin to teach in 1906. He spent the next three decades teaching systematic theology to almost every Christian Reformed preacher of his day. Berkhof was an extensive writer. Some of his more famous works include *Reformed Dogmatics* (three vols., 1932) and *The History of Christian Doctrine* (1937).

1877 English devotional writer Frances Ridley Havergal (1838–1879) penned the words to the hymn "Who Is on the Lord's Side?" She based her text on 1 Chronicles 12:1–8. The poem was first published in Havergal's *Loyal Responses* (1878).

1934 Death of Theodore Baker (b.1851), German-born American musicologist and biographical scholar. He served as literary editor for G. Shirmer, Inc., from 1892–1926. In 1900 he published his classic *Baker's Biographical Dictionary*. He also gave us the English translation of the German hymn "We Gather Together to Ask the Lord's Blessing."

October 14

1644 Birth of William Penn, American Quaker statesman, in London, England. Penn was raised in the Anglican Church, but became a Quaker in 1655. For years, Penn nourished the hope of establishing a home in America for Quakers and others suffering religious oppression. Starting in 1677, he helped send more than 800 Quakers to New Jersey. In 1682 he obtained a grant of land in the American colonies comprising modern Pennsylvania and Delaware from King Charles II. The constitution Penn drew up for this new colony permitted all forms of public worship which were compatible with monotheism and religious liberty. With the exception of one year, Penn served as governor of Pennsylvania from 1682 to his death in 1718.

1656 The first punitive legislation in Massachusetts against Quakers was enacted. The new laws decreed that a 40-shilling fine be imposed against anyone illegally harboring Quakers. Other regulations prescribed assorted mutilations for those Quakers returning to the colony after they had been banished.

1708 The General Court of Connecticut enacted the Saybrook Platform, later adopted by the colony's Congregational churches. The legislation instituted a form of church government more presbyterian than congregational in nature.

1735 John and Charles Wesley first set sail to America—John, to become a missionary to the Indians, and later to the colonists, of Georgia; Charles, to become secretary to Gov. Oglethorpe of Georgia. It was on this same day that John Wesley began keeping his famous journal. He maintained the journal for over 55 years, its last entry dating Oct. 24, 1790.

1835 Birth of William G. Fischer, American sacred music chorister, in Baltimore, Maryland. He first learned to read music in a church singing class and later studied music at night while learning bookbinding at J.B. Lippincott's in Philadelphia. He taught music at Girard College for ten years (1858–68), and afterward went into the piano business. Fischer wrote a number of Gospel songs, though none were published during his lifetime. Nevertheless, his tunes FISCHER ("Whiter Than Snow"), HANKEY ("I Love to Tell the Story") and ROCK OF REFUGE ("The Rock That Is Higher Than I") endure in modern hymnody.

1876 Birth of Harry A. Ironside, American clergyman, in Toronto, Canada. He was converted at age 14, and although never ordained, immediately began to preach. A Salvation Army officer for a time, he later joined the Plymouth Brethren. From 1930–48, he pastored at the Moody Memorial Church in Chicago—his only pastorate. For over 50 years Ironside traveled widely as an evangelist and Bible teacher. He authored over 60 books, mostly popular Bible commentaries. He died in 1951 at age 75 while on a preaching tour in New Zealand.

1890 The Evangelical Alliance Mission was founded in Chicago, Illinois, by Fredrik Franson. Headquartered today in nearby Wheaton, Illinois, T.E.A.M. is an interdenominational mission agency engaged in evangelism, missionary recruiting, training and orientation and mission-related research.

1891 Protestant Episcopal clergyman Phillips Brooks (1835–93) was consecrated Bishop of the Diocese of Massachusetts in Boston's Trinity Church. His fame rests both in the sermons he published and in his Christmas hymn "O Little Town of Bethlehem."

1897 Death of William A. Ogden (b.1841), American sacred music writer who wrote the music for the hymn "Bring Them In." His early studies in music were interrupted by his service to the Union during the U.S. Civil War. He afterward resumed his music education, studying under Lowell Mason, Thomas Hastings, E.E. Bailey and B.F. Baker. Ogden gained a reputation as a music teacher and a conductor of music conventions. He published several collections of Sunday school songs. His upbeat music is preserved in the music to the hymn "Bring Them In" and in both his words and music to the hymn "He Is Able to Deliver Thee."

1922 In Detroit, Michigan, the Evangelical Association and the United Evangelical Church merged, forming the Evangelical Church. The combined membership at the time of the merger was 260,000.

October 15

1784 Birth of Thomas Hastings, sacred music composer, in Washington, Connecticut. An albino and afflicted with extreme nearsightedness, Hastings taught himself the fundamentals of music. By age 18 he was leading the choir in his local church. Hastings penned more than 600 hymns, composed 1,000 hymn tunes and published more than 50 collections of sacred music. He and Lowell Mason did much to shape church music in 19th-century America. His most popular hymn tunes include ORTONVILLE ("Majestic Sweetness Sits Enthroned"), TOPLADY ("Rock of Ages") and RETREAT ("From Every Stormy Wind That Blows").

1840 In Mehlville, Missouri, the Evangelical Synod of North America was founded. The denomination later merged with the Reformed Church in June 1943 at Cleveland, Ohio, to form the Evangelical and Reformed Church. This group, in turn, merged with the Congregational Christian Church in 1957 to form the United Church of Christ denomination.

1851 Birth of George Foote Moore, American Old Testament scholar, in West Chester, Pennsylvania. He taught at Andover Seminary (1883–1902) and at Harvard (1902–21). Among his several technical writings, two stand out: *History of Religions* (1914, 1919) and *Judaism* (two vols., 1927).

1881 Birth of William Temple, Anglican clergyman, in Exeter, England. Ordained in 1908, he became Bishop of Manchester in 1921, Archbishop of York in 1929 and Archbishop of Canterbury in 1942. He died two years later. Temple combined a keen philosophical mind with deep social concern. He was prominent in England because of his concern with economic and international problems. He was also in the forefront of ecumenical affairs. Temple is sometimes said to have been too much of a philosopher for the theologians and too much of a theologian for the philosophers. Among other works, he wrote *The Faith and Modern Thought* (1915) and *Nature, Man and God* (1934).

1906 Death of Samuel Porter ("Sam") Jones (b.1847), American evangelist. Born in Alabama, Jones was admitted to the Georgia bar in 1869. Though a successful lawyer, his personal life was in shambles from drink. Fulfilling a promise to his dying father, Jones became a Christian and quit his drinking. Soon after, he was licensed to preach in the Methodist Church, and held pastorates from 1872–80. In 1892 he began evangelistic preaching and was soon welcomed in important cities around the country. His crude wit, coarse stories and rural-life parodies captured listeners everywhere.

1946 At Nuremberg, Germany, ten Nazi war criminals were hanged.

1948 American missionary and Auca Indian martyr Jim Elliot commented in his journal: " 'They shall mount up with wings as eagles' (Isa. 40:31). These wings are not so typical of purity as they are of power—strength to live above snares and everything else. Grace to be alone as the eagle. Thanks for wings, Lord."

October 16

1555 English reformers Hugh Latimer (b.1485) and Nicholas Ridley (b.ca. 1500) were burned at the stake for their Protestant beliefs. When Mary Tudor (daughter of Henry VIII) took the English throne in 1553, she sought to restore Roman Catholicism to England. In 1555 Reginald Pole reconciled England to the papacy, and soon afterward the trials for the Protestant heresy began. Latimer was Anglican Bishop of Worcester, and Ridley was Bishop of London. Their deaths placed them among the most celebrated martyrs of Mary's reign. Mary's Spanish marriage, her intolerance of Protestantism and her inability to have children ultimately lost her the affection of the English people. Her rule ended with her death three years later (1558).

1649 The independent government of the colony of Maine passed legislation granting religious freedom to all its citizens, provided that those of contrary religious persuasions behaved acceptably. This tolerance lasted only three years, until Maine was annexed by Massachusetts

1701 The Collegiate School was founded at Saybrook, Connecticut, by Congregational clergy dissatisfied with growing liberalism at Harvard College. The school was named after Elihu Yale, son of one of the founders of New Haven, Connecticut. In 1716 the school moved to New Haven, Connecticut, where it became Yale College. In 1887 the name was changed to Yale University.

1752 Birth of Johann G. Eichhorn, German Lutheran Old Testament scholar, in Dorrenzimmern, Germany. He was a pioneer in "higher criticism," which sought to establish the truth of biblical teachings through literary analysis and historical evidence rather than by unquestioned acceptance of religious tradition. Eichhorn believed at least two independent literary traditions lay behind the written form of the Pentateuch. He was also an early advocate of the "primitive Gospel hypothesis," which holds that Matthew, Mark and Luke are based on a single, lost Gospel written in Aramaic. The accuracy of his work has been questioned by later scholars.

1812 Death of Henry Martyn (b.1781), Anglican missionary to Persia. Martyn first sailed to India in 1805 as a chaplain for the East India Company. His outstanding linguistic gifts led him into his great life's work: the translation of the New Testament into Hindustani. He later translated the New Testament into both Arabic and Persian. He died at age 31 while on a ship returning to England.

1847 Birth of Samuel Porter ("Sam") Jones, American evangelist, in Chambers County, Alabama. Porter was admitted to the Georgia bar in 1869. Although a successful lawyer, his personal life was in shambles from heavy drinking. Fulfilling a promise to his dying father, Jones quit his drinking and became a Christian. Soon after, he was licensed to preach in the Methodist Church and held pastorates from 1872–80. In 1892 he began evangelistic preaching and was soon welcomed in important cities around the country. His crude wit, coarse stories and rural-life parodies captured listeners everywhere. He died in 1906 while in the midst of an evangelistic campaign.

1888 Death of Horatio Gates Spafford (b.1828), American medical lawyer and hymnwriter. A successful Chicago lawyer, he enjoyed close friendships with Moody, Sankey, Pentecost, Bliss and numerous other evangelists of his day. Spafford planned a European vacation for his family in 1873, but unexpected business developments forced him to send his family ahead. While his family was sailing on the S.S. *Ville du Havre*, the ship was struck by another ship and sank immediately. Spafford's wife survived, but his four daughters drowned. Spafford left by ship to meet his wife. While on the ocean, near the scene of the recent tragedy, Spafford penned the lines to the well-loved hymn of consolation "It Is Well with My Soul."

October 17

1651 French scientist Blaise Pascal asserted in a letter: "Jesus Christ suffered and died to sanctify death and suffering; he has been all that was great, and all that was abject, in order to sanctify in himself all things except sin, and to be the model of every condition."

1792 Birth of John Bowring, English statesman and author of the hymn "In the Cross of Christ I Glory," in Exeter, England. He began as an assistant to his father, a woolen goods manufacturer. His involvement in international trade polished his gift for languages. He was an outstanding linguist, claiming to understand 200 languages and able to speak 100 of them. He was actively involved in Parliament beginning in 1835. Although a Unitarian, Bowring was described as being "nearer orthodoxy than the radical wing of his own denomination." A prolific author, Bowring's writings were published in 36 volumes after his death in 1872.

1910 Death of Julia Ward Howe (b.1819), American writer and social reformer. Prior to the War Between the States, she helped edit an abolitionist newspaper. During the U.S. Civil War, she wrote the hymn that became the theme song of the Union armies: "The Battle Hymn of the Republic."

1912 Birth of Albino Luciani, Pope John Paul I, near Belluno, Italy. Ordained to the priesthood in 1935, Luciani was named Patriarch of Venice in 1969.

During his nine years as patriarch, he hosted five ecumenical conferences, including an important doctrinal meeting between Anglican and Roman church officials. Following Pope Paul VI's death on Aug. 6, 1978, Luciani was elected pope on the third ballot on the first day of the conclave, Aug. 26. He chose the name "John Paul" to symbolize his desire to combine John XXIII's progressive qualities and Paul VI's traditional emphases. Luciani was invested Sept. 3, but died of a heart attack only three weeks later.

October 18

1662 Birth of Matthew Henry, English Presbyterian Bible commentator, in Flintshire, Wales. Ordained in 1687, he pastored 25 years in Cheshire County, England. In 1712 he began a pastorate in Hackney, near London, but died only two years later. Twice-married and the father of nine daughters and one son, Henry was a beloved pastor and spiritual father. He is remembered for his *Exposition of the Old and New Testaments* (1708–10), now commonly published in six volumes as *Matthew Henry's Commentary*. The value of Henry's work lies not so much in its critical exegesis as in its devotional and practical emphasis.

1685 The Edict of Nantes was revoked by French King Louis XIV. First signed 87 years earlier (1598) by Henry IV, the edict outlined limited religious tolerance for French Huguenots (Protestants). Louis's revocation of the edict led to a mass exodus of hundreds of thousands of Huguenots from France. Many immigrated to Holland, England, English North America and South Africa. The exodus was a blow to France's industrial economy, possibly hastening the French Revolution.

1877 Death of William Hunter (b.1811), American Methodist clergyman and author of the hymn "The Great Physician Now Is Near." After his ordination, he pastored in the Pittsburgh, Virginia and Eastern Ohio conferences until 1855. From 1855–70 he taught Hebrew at Allegheny College. Hunter published three collections of hymns during his lifetime.

1918 Death of Charles C. Converse (b.1832), American lawyer and sacred music composer. In 1855 Converse went to Germany to study music under such greats as Louis Spohr and Franz Liszt. He returned to America and completed a degree in law at Albany University. He later worked with William B. Bradbury, with whom he edited and published several collections of hymnbooks and Sunday school songbooks. Today, Converse is remembered as composer of the hymn tune CONVERSE, to which we sing "What a Friend We Have in Jesus."

1949 American country songwriter Stuart Hamblen (b. 1908) was converted to Christ. Hamblen gained national attention when his fast-paced song "This Old House," recorded by Rosemary Clooney, topped the music charts in 1954. Some of his better-known Christian songs include: "It Is No Secret What God Can Do," "Open Up Your Heart and Let the Sun(Son) Shine In," "Known Only to Him," "You Must Be Born Again," "How Big Is God?" "They That Wait upon the Lord" and the favorite of many "Beyond the Sunset."

1954 *The Week in Religion*, a Sunday evening religious panel show, aired for the last time over Dumont television. First broadcast in March 1952, this ecumenical religious broadcast ran from 6:00–7:00 p.m. and was divided into 20-minute segments for Protestant, Catholic and Jewish news. The original hosts were Rabbi William S. Rosenbloom, Rev. Robbins Wolcott Barstow, and Rev. Joseph N. Moody.

October 19

1562 Birth of George Abbot, Archbishop of Canterbury, in Guildford, England. His rise to leadership of the Anglican Church (1611) followed his defense of the hereditary monarchy (1606) and his efforts to combine the English and Scottish churches (1608). For years he was the recognized leader of the English Calvinists and demonstrated deep Puritan sympathies. He also took a leading part in the translation of the King James Version of the Bible.

1609 Death of Jacob Arminius (b.1560), Dutch theologian. Ordained in 1588, he pastored in Amsterdam until 1603. In studying to prove Calvinism, he decided that Calvinism was illogical. When the Dutch Republic became an independent state in 1609, Calvinism was declared the official state religion. Arminius, in opposition, sought to modify Calvinism's view of God as the author of sin, and its view of man as a robot without a will in the hands of God. Arminius died in 1609, in the early stages of this theological controversy, before a national synod could be convened in which his views could be clearly stated. Arminian Protestantism takes its name from this Dutch theologian of the early 17th century.

1720 Birth of John Woolman, American Quaker preacher, in Rancocas, New Jersey. Beginning in 1743 he traveled extensively throughout the American colonies preaching in support of Negro rights. His activism bore fruit in 1776 when the members of the annual meeting of Friends in Philadelphia voted to end their practice of owning slaves. Woolman's *Journal*, written from 1756 until his death in 1772, greatly influenced 19th-century abolitionists.

1744 English revivalist George Whitefield arrived at York, Maine, at the start of his second visit from England to America.

1902 Death of William O. Cushing (b.1823), American Christian clergyman and hymnwriter. Over a period of more than 20 years, he pastored 5 churches in the New York area. Following the death of his wife in 1870, ill health forced his retirement from active ministry. During this time, however, he became greatly interested in hymnwriting, authoring more than 300 hymns. Among Cushing's most popular texts are the hymns "Under His Wings," "When He Cometh," "Ring the Bells of Heaven" and "Hiding in Thee."

1921 Birth of Bill Bright, founder and president of Campus Crusade for Christ. Bill and his wife Vonette founded C.C.C. in Feb. 1951 and incorporated the student organization in Aug. 1953 in Los Angeles, California.

1952 Death of E.O. Sellers (b.1869), American Baptist music evangelist and educator. Converted at a Y.M.C.A. meeting, Sellers later enrolled in Moody Bible Institute, Chicago. After serving several Y.M.C.A. and church positions, he returned to Moody to teach music and Christian education (1908–19). At this time, he was also active as a song evangelist for revivalists such as R.A. Torrey, Gipsy Smith, A.C. Dixon and J. Wilbur Chapman. He also published many articles and poems, as well as composing a number of hymn tunes. He authored and composed the hymn "Thy Word Is a Lamp to My Feet" and composed the music for "There Is Never a Day So Dreary" (a.k.a. "Wonderful, Wonderful Jesus").

October 20

1802 Birth of Ernst W. Hengstenberg, German Lutheran Old Testament scholar, in Westphalia, Germany. He was an outspoken defender of evangelical Christianity against the rationalism of his day. He authored several important works in the field of Old Testament studies, the most significant being his four-volume *Christology of the Old Testament* (1829–35), still in print.

1828 Birth of Horatio Gates Spafford, American lawyer and hymnwriter, in North Troy, New York. A successful Chicago lawyer, he enjoyed close friendships with Moody, Sankey, Pentecost, Bliss and numerous other evangelists of his day. Spafford planned a European vacation for his family in 1873 but unexpected business developments forced him to send his family ahead without him. While his family was sailing on the S.S. *Ville du Havre*, the ship was struck by another ship and sank immediately. Spafford's wife survived, but his four daughters drowned. Spafford left by ship to meet his wife. While on the ocean, near the scene of the recent tragedy, Spafford penned the lines to the hymn "It Is Well with My Soul."

1853 Birth of Rudolph Kittel, Old Testament scholar, in Wurttemberg, Germany. He taught at the Universities of Breslau (1888–97) and Leipzig (1898–1924). He was the author or editor of many outstanding works in the field of Old Testament studies. His best-known work is the critical text of the Hebrew Old Testament *Biblia Hebraica* (13th ed., 1962).

1892 Birth of Harry Dixon Loes, American sacred music educator, in Kalamazoo, Michigan. A student at Moody Bible Institute, Loes studied under Daniel Brink Towner. He began composing Gospel songs and later attended the American Conservatory of Music, the Metropolitan School of Music and the Chicago Musical College. He traveled widely throughout the U.S. and Canada as an evangelist for 12 years. From 1927–39, he served as music and educational director at the First Baptist Church of Okmulgee, Oklahoma; then at First Baptist Church in Muskogee, Oklahoma. In 1939 Loes joined the faculty at Moody Bible Institute, where he taught until his death in 1965. He wrote many Gospel songs and choruses, including REDEEMER ("Up Calvary's Mountain, One Dreadful Morn").

1893 Death of Philip Schaff (b.1819), American church historian. Born in Switzerland, he emigrated to America at age 24 (1843) and became an outstanding leader of the German Reformed Church, helping the group make the transition from German traditions and language to a blended American church using the English language. He taught church history at the German Reformed Seminary of Mercersburg, Pennsylvania (1844–63), and at Union Theological Seminary in New York City (1870–93). His literary output was immense, including an eight-volume *History of the Christian Church* (1858–92) and *The Creeds of Christendom* (three vols., 1877). He also produced the English translations of Lange's Bible commentaries (1864–80) and the Schaff-Herzog *En-*

cyclopedia of Religious Knowledge (1884).

1908 Birth of Stuart Hamblen, American songwriter, in Kellyville, Texas. Converted to Christ in 1949, Hamblen gained national fame when his fast-paced song "This Old House," recorded by Rosemary Clooney, topped the charts in 1954. Some of the better-known Christian songs include: "It Is No Secret What God Can Do," "Open Up Your Heart and Let the Sun(Son) Shine In," "Known Only to Him," "You Must Be Born Again," "How Big Is God?" "They That Wait upon the Lord" and the favorite "Beyond the Sunset."

1913 Death of Mary A. Lathbury (b.1841), American Methodist church leader. In addition to serving with the Methodist Sunday School Union, she also wrote for several Methodist magazines. Her association with John H. Vincent brought her to active leadership in the summer Chautauqua assemblies in New York. She authored the hymns "Break Thou the Bread of Life" and "Day Is Dying in the West."

1957 English scholar and apologist C.S. Lewis confessed in *Letters to an American Lady*: "It'll be nice when we all wake up from this life, which has indeed something like a nightmare about it."

1960 The United World Mission, Inc., moved to its present headquarters in St. Petersburg, Florida. Founded in 1946 in Dayton, Ohio, U.W.M. is an interdenominational, evangelical sending agency engaged primarily in evangelism, Christian education, medicine and support of national churches. The agency has 60 workers in 12 countries outside the U.S.

October 21

1532 German reformer Martin Luther declared: "For some years now I have read through the Bible twice every year. If you picture the Bible to be a mighty tree and every word a little branch, I have shaken every one of these branches because I wanted to know what it was and what it meant."

1692 Quaker statesman William Penn was deposed as Governor of Pennsylvania by the throne of England. His overtures of thanksgiving to James II for permitting religious freedom for dissenters of the Church of England led William and Mary, upon taking the throne, to charge Penn with being a papist. Penn was arrested and imprisoned, but later established his innocence. After gaining favor with the new king and queen, Penn was restored to his governorship in 1694.

1808 Birth of Samuel Francis Smith, American Baptist clergyman. A graduate of Andover Theological Seminary in 1834, he pastored at the Baptist Church in Waterville, Maine, from 1834–42 and the Baptist Church of Newton, Massachusetts from 1842–54. Afterward, he was editorial secretary of the American Baptist Missionary Union. Smith had a lifelong interest in hymnology and is credited with about 100 hymns, including "My Country, 'Tis of Thee" (a.k.a. "America"), written at age 23 while he was still in seminary. In 1843 he helped compile *The Psalmist*, the most widely used Baptist hymnal of its day.

1881 Death of Josiah G. Holland (b.1819), American journalist. After a brief career in medicine, Holland established a weekly newspaper. He later joined the editorial staff of the Springfield, Massachusetts *Republican*, and helped found *Scribners Magazine*, serving as its editor until his death. In 1874, at age 55, Holland penned the words to the popular Christmas hymn "There's a Song in the Air."

1892 Birth of James L. Kelso, American Presbyterian archeologist, in Duluth, Minnesota. He taught Semitics and biblical archeology at Pittsburgh-Xenia Theological Seminary beginning in 1923. He also participated in three archeological digs at Tell Beit Mirsim (ancient Debir) (1926, 28, 30), served as president of the staff of the Bethel excavation (1954, 57, 60), and directed the Herodian Jericho and Nitla excavations (starting in 1950). Kelso authored several important texts in the field of biblical archeology, including *Ceramic Vocabulary of the Old Testament*.

1970 Death of John T. Scopes (b.ca.1900), Tennessee high school biology teacher. In 1925 he went to trial for violating the Butler Act, which prohibited the teaching of evolution in Tennessee schools. William Jennings Bryan was prosecuting attorney and Clarence Darrow defended Scopes. The overblown publicity of the case gave rise to its popular nickname, "The Scopes Monkey Trial." Scopes was found guilty and fined $100, but the decision was later overturned by the Tennessee Supreme Court. (Scopes went on to graduate studies at the University of Chicago and became a geologist.)

October 22

1697 Birth of Katharina Von Schlegel, German Lutheran hymnwriter and author of "Be Still, My Soul." Little is known of her life. She may have been the canoness of an evangelical women's seminary in Germany. She contributed lyrics to a collection of hymns published in 1752. "Be Still, My Soul" was translated into English by Jane L. Borthwick 100 years after it was written.

1746 Princeton College was founded in Elizabethtown, New Jersey, by an evangelical faction of the Presbyterian church. The school became a bastion of conservatism during the denomination's bitter conflicts with liberal theology. Originally named the College of New Jersey, the school moved to Newark in 1747 and to Princeton, New Jersey, in 1752. Its name was changed 140 years later, in 1896, to Princeton University.

1811 Birth of Franz Liszt, Hungarian composer, in Raiding, Hungary. Once a student of Beethoven, Liszt later developed close friendships with Berlioz, Chopin, Paganini and Wagner. A sensitive nature contributed to Liszt's later ascetic practices, including his decision to join the Franciscans in 1865. Regarded by some as possibly "the greatest pianist of all time," Liszt greatly advanced both the playing techniques and the compositional methods for the piano. He penned over 1,200 music works. In the realm of religious music, Liszt composed three large-scale settings of the mass, two oratorios and a variety of other sacred works.

1839 Birth of Louis August Sabatier, French Protestant theologian, in Vallon (Andreche), France. He taught at the University of Strasburg (1867–73) and at the Sorbonne starting in 1877. Sabatier taught that theology is best understood through the psychological meanings of religious phenomena. His later views that biblical concepts were mere symbols undermined the authority of scriptural doctrine. Sabatier's most revealing writings are *Outlines of a Phi-*

losophy of Religion (1897) and *The Religions of Authority and the Religion of the Spirit* (1903).

1844 Followers of American religious leader William Miller (1782–1849) predicted this as the date of Christ's return, or Second Advent. Between 50,000–100,000 people disposed of their possessions and waited prayerfully for the Lord to return. When the day came and went, vast numbers lost all interest in "adventism" and returned to their former churches. Others abandoned the Christian faith altogether.

1859 Death of Louis Spohr (b.1784), German composer. Spohr composed many highly acclaimed operas, oratorios and violin. He also composed the hymn tune SPOHR ("All Things Bright and Beautiful").

1876 Birth of Karl Adam, German Roman Catholic theologian, in Bavaria. Ordained to the priesthood in 1900, Adam taught (1908–49) at the universities of Munich, Strassburg and Tubingen. His theology combined full Catholic orthodoxy with a modern empirical, inductive outlook, thereby exercising a wide influence over the lay public. Adam's best-known writing was his *Das Wesen des Katholizismus* (1924), translated into English as *The Spirit of Catholicism*.

1903 Death of Susannah Spurgeon (b.1832), wife of English Baptist preacher Charles Haddon Spurgeon. Born Susannah Thompson in London, she and her famous husband married in 1856. Susannah was 24; Charles, 22. Their marriage lasted 36 years, until Charles' death in 1892. Susannah outlived her husband by 11 years, though she was an invalid her last 35 years.

1922 Death of Lyman Abbott (b.1835), American Congregational clergyman. After a brief career in law (1853–59), Abbott turned to the ministry and was ordained in 1860. He pastored in Indiana (1860–65) and New York (1865–69), then became associate editor of *Harper's Magazine* in 1869. He served as editor of the American Tract Society's *Illustrated Christian Weekly* from 1871–76 and later joined Henry Ward Beecher as editor of the *Christian Union* (1876). He succeeded Beecher as pastor of Plymouth Church in Brooklyn (1888–89). In his latter years, Abbott became especially interested in social reform. He sought to reconcile Darwinian evolution and German biblical criticism with evangelical theology in his preaching and writing. Some of his most significant writings were *The Theology of an Evolutionist* (1897) and *Reminiscences* (1915).

1966 Swiss Reformed theologian Karl Barth observed in a letter: "God makes no mistakes."

October 23

4004 B.C. According to Archbishop James Ussher's conclusions in his chronology of the world, "the heavens and the earth" were created on this date—at 9:00 a.m. (Greenwich time). Ussher (1581–1656) was made Archbishop of Armagh, the Primate of the Irish Church, in 1625. His famous *Annales Veteris et Novi Testamenti* (*Chronologies of the Old and New Testaments*) was first published in 1650–54. His chronology was based on a literal, closed accounting of the biblical genealogies. Ussher's scheme of dating sacred history is generally discounted today, but it ranks as the first serious attempt to formulate a biblical chronology.

1842 Death of H.F.W. Gesenius (b.1786), famed German Hebrew scholar. Having taught Semitics at the University of Halle from 1811 until his death, Wilhelm Gesenius spent his entire professional life concentrating on the problems of Semitic philology, becoming the outstanding Hebrew scholar of his generation. He first published his *Hebraische Grammatik* in 1813. The work has been revised 25 times by several editors. It goes by the shortened name *Gesenius' Hebrew Grammar.*

1871 Birth of Edgar J. Goodspeed, American Greek scholar and Bible translator, in Quincy, Illinois. He taught at the University of Chicago from 1898–1937. He then lectured on history at the University of California (Los Angeles) from 1938–51. He authored over 60 books and 200 scholarly articles. No doubt his most famous publication is his American English translation of the New Testament (1923). It was republished in 1931 as part of *The Bible, An American Translation*, more familiarly titled *Smith and Goodspeed.* J.M.P. Smith (1866–1932) translated the Old Testament portion of the work.

1941 Death of Shailer Mathews (b.1863), American Baptist educator. He taught at the University of Chicago from 1894–1933. He also directed the religious department of the Chautauqua Institute from 1912–34 and edited *The World Today* from 1903–11 and *The Biblical World* 1913–20. Mathews authored about 30 books, including *Dictionary of Religion and Ethics* (1921), which he and Gerald Birney Smith edited.

October 24

1538 French reformer John Calvin warned in a letter: "Among Christians there ought to be so great a dislike of schism, as that they may always avoid it so far as lies in their power. There ought to prevail among them such a reverence for the ministry of the Word and of the Sacraments that wherever they perceive these things to be, there they may consider the Church to exist."

1790 English founder of Methodism John Wesley (1703–91) made the last entry in his journal. He had preached in the morning on "The Whole Armor of God" (Eph. 6:11), and in the afternoon on "One Thing Is Needful" (Lk. 10:42). The last words in Wesley's journal read: "I hope many even then resolved to choose the better part." Wesley had begun keeping his journal almost exactly 55 years earlier, on Oct. 14, 1735.

1826 Death of Ann Hasseltine Judson (b.1789), wife of American missionary Adoniram Judson. Converted to Christ at age 16, Ann married Adoniram in 1812 (he was 24, she was 23), just 12 days before they set sail to India as missionaries. For 14 years, Ann worked on the mission field alongside Adoniram. During her last months, she carried food to her husband while he was ill after being imprisoned by the Burmese during a war against the British. Soon after Adoniram's release, Ann became sick and died at age 37. Her last words were, "It is the will of God. I am not afraid of death."

1875 Death of J.P. Migne (b.1800), French Roman Catholic publisher. Ordained in 1824, he served as a parish priest near Orleans, France, for about a decade. In 1836 he established his own publishing house, which he called Ateliers Catholique. During his remaining 39 years, he published 221 volumes in his *Patrologia Latina* series and 161 volumes in his *Patrologia Graeca* series. The larger series contained the writings of Latin ecclesiastical writers from the 2nd century to Pope Innocent III (1198–1216). The shorter series comprised the writings of all the Eastern fathers of the church.

1932 Death of Palmer Hartsough (b.1844), American sacred music chorister. From 1867–77, he traveled through Michigan, Illinois, Iowa, Ohio, Kentucky and Tennessee as an itinerant teacher of singing schools. In 1877 he opened a music studio in Rock Island, Illinois, where he taught vocal and instrumental music. In 1893 he began to work with the Fillmore Publishing Co. of Cincinnati, Ohio, providing texts for hymns, Gospel songs, cantatas and Sunday school music, including the hymn "I Am Resolved No Longer to Linger." Hartsough produced over 1,000 texts for publication. He remained unmarried, but was devoted to his two sisters.

1956 In Syracuse, New York, Margaret Ellen Towner became the first woman to be ordained in the Presbyterian church.

1958 Death of Martin F. Shaw (b.1875), English sacred music organist. He was director of music for the Anglican diocese of Chelmsford from 1935–45. Among his several publications, he edited *The Oxford Book of Carols* (1928). Today, he is remembered for his hymn tune GENTLE JESUS, to which we sing Charles Wesley's hymn "Gentle Jesus, Meek and Mild."

1978 Gospel Missionary Union moved into its present headquarters in Kansas City, Missouri. Founded in 1892 in Topeka, Kansas, by George S. Fisher, G.M.U. is an interdenominational missionary sending agency of Baptist tradition. Its overseas staff numbers over 400, and works in nearly 20 countries in evangelism, Bible translation, literature distribution, radio broadcasting, medical and educational ministries.

October 25

1147 The German forces in the armies of the Second Crusade (1147–49) were destroyed by the Saracens at Dorylaeum (modern western Turkey). The Crusaders went on with fruitless campaigns against Damascus.

1564 Birth of Hans Leo Hassler, German musician of sacred music, in Nuremberg, Germany. The outstanding organist of his day, Hassler was the first notable German musician to be educated in Italy. His rich musical legacy includes the tune PASSION CHORALE, to which we sing "O Sacred Head, Now Wounded."

1800 Birth of Jacques Paul Migne, French ecclesiastical publisher, near Orleans, France. Ordained in 1824, he served as a parish priest near Orleans, France, for about a decade. In 1836 he established his own publishing house, which he named Ateliers Catholique. During his remaining 39 years, he published 221 volumes in his *Patrologia Latina* series and 161 volumes in his *Patrologia Graeca* series. The larger series contains the writings of Latin ecclesiastical writers from the 2nd century to Pope Innocent III (1198–1216). The shorter series comprises the writings of all the Eastern church fathers.

1812 Birth of Frederic L. Godet, Swiss Reformed theologian, in Neuchatel, Switzerland. Ordained in 1836, he pastored for 22 years, 15 of them in Neuchatel. He then taught theology at the Swiss Reformed seminary at Neuchatel from 1851–73. A prominent representative of Reformed theology, Godet combined deep Christian piety with positive biblical criticism. His work strongly influenced the orthodox Christian position among the Swiss theologians of his day. He authored several important books on biblical studies, but his most famous work in the English-speaking world is his *Commentary on the Gospel of St. John* (1864–65; English translation 1877).

1921 Founders Lewis and Viola Glenn incorporated Evangelistic Faith Missions in Bedford, Indiana. This interdenominational mission organization of Wesleyan tradition utilizes a staff of 28 in its work among nationals of 9 foreign countries. E.F.M. is engaged primarily in evangelism, church planting, education, Gospel broadcasting and medical support.

1963 At the second session of the Vatican II Ecumenical Council, the principle of an immovable date for Easter was approved.

1970 Pope Paul VI canonized forty English and Welsh Roman Catholic martyrs of the 16th and 17th centuries.

October 26

1751 Death of Philip Doddridge (b.1702), English nonconformist clergyman. Doddridge was orphaned at age 13, the youngest of 20 children, 18 of whom died in infancy. He was plagued with poor health all his life. He was offered a free education at Cambridge if he would become ordained into the Anglican Church upon graduation. However, Doddridge declined, and entered a nonconformist seminary. He eventually become one of the most influential, evangelical church leaders of his generation. Doddridge was a voluminous writer, but is best remembered for the 400 hymns he wrote, including "O Happy Day." None of his hymns were published until after his death.

1779 Anglican hymnwriter John Newton declared in a letter: "The Lord is so rich that He easily can—so good that He certainly will—give His children more than He will ever take away."

1813 Birth of Henry T. Smart, English sacred music organist, in London, England. Though largely self-taught, Smart served as organist in four prominent London churches beginning in 1831. He also published many pieces of sacred music. Two of his hymn tunes which are still in popular use are LANCASHIRE ("Lead On, O King Eternal") and REGENT SQUARE ("Angels from the Realms of Glory").

1818 Birth of Elizabeth P. Prentiss, American schoolteacher and poet, in Portland, Maine. At age 16, she contributed the first of many articles to the *Youth's Companion* magazine. One of her poems has become the hymn "More Love to Thee, O Christ." She taught in her local public schools for a number of years before marrying a Congregational minister in 1845.

1889 Birth of Millar Burrows, American archeologist, in Cincinnati, Ohio. He taught at Tusculum College (1920–23), Brown University (1925–34), and Yale. He was also director of the American School of Oriental Research at Jerusalem

(1931–32, 1947–48). His most popular written work is *What Mean These Stones?* (1941).

1911 Birth of Mahalia Jackson, black American Gospel singer, in New Orleans, Louisiana. Her rich voice helped her break into national prominence in the 1930s as she sang such songs as "He's Got the Whole World in His Hands" in cross-country Gospel tours. Her later records sold millions of copies, earning her recognition among all classes. Jackson's singing style presented a close link between the religious and secular roots of jazz.

1928 Death of Reuben A. Torrey (b.1856), American Congregational evangelist and educator. After pastoring for a few years, Torrey was called to Chicago by D.L. Moody to superintend the new Bible Institute of the Chicago Evangelization Society (now the Moody Bible Institute). He remained in the position until 1908, while also pastoring the Chicago Avenue Church (now the Moody Memorial Church). Torrey wielded tremendous influence in the development of these two institutions. From 1912–24, Torrey was dean of the Bible Institute of Los Angeles (Biola) while serving as pastor of the Church of the Open Door in Los Angeles (1915–24). He published 40 religious books, including *The Fundamental Doctrines of the Christian Faith* (1919).

1944 Death of William Temple (b.1881), Anglican Church leader. Ordained in 1908, he was elevated to Bishop of Manchester in 1921, Archbishop of York in 1929 and Archbishop of Canterbury from 1942. Temple combined a keen philosophical mind with deep social concern. He was prominent in England through his concern with economic and international problems. He was also an ecumenical leader. Temple is sometimes said to have been too much of a philosopher for the theologians, and too much of a theologian for the philosophers. Among his more memorable writings are *The Faith and Modern Thought* and *Nature, Man and God* (1934).

1953 The religious drama *This Is the Life* was last aired over ABC television before going into syndication. This half-hour series, produced by the Lutheran Church-Missouri Synod, depicted one Christian family's attempts to deal with the moral problems of everyday life. The program first aired in Sept. 1952 over Dumont television. After 1953, *This Is the Life* ran in syndication. The program has continued to the present day, making it one of the longest-running series in television history.

October 27

1466 Birth of Desiderius Erasmus, Dutch humanist and Greek scholar, in Rotterdam, Netherlands. The leading humanist of the Protestant Reformation, Erasmus sought to reform the church through scholarship and Christian instruction. He spent most of his professional life in Basel, Switzerland (1514–29), where he became the world's first "bestselling author" following the advent of the moveable-type printing press. He wrote the critical satire *In Praise of Folly* (1509), calling attention to a need for reform within the Roman Catholic Church. His *Greek New Testament* (1516) was a demonstration of his desire to find the roots of the church before it had focused on Latin and Rome as the source of truth. Erasmus' methods of reform were, for the main part, intellectual; but history reveals that his *Greek New Testament* greatly motivated the faith of at least three other, more active, religious reformers of his generation: John Wycliffe in England, Ulrich Zwingli in Switzerland and Martin Luther in Germany. It is sometimes said that Erasmus laid the egg that Luther hatched.

1659 William Robinson and Marmaduke Stevenson became the first Quakers hanged in Massachusetts. They had violated the laws of 1658 which forbade Quakers from returning to Massachusetts once they had been banished.

1682 English Quaker colonist and founder of Pennsylvania, William Penn first arrived in America.

1771 Pioneer Bishops Francis Asbury and Richard Wright first arrived in Philadelphia after having been sent from England by John Wesley to preach Methodism in America.

1814 Birth of John McClintock, American Methodist clergyman and scholar, in Philadelphia. He was first president (1867–70) of the newly established Drew Theological Seminary in Madison, New Jersey. His most important writing was the 12-volume *Cyclopaedia of Biblical, Theological, and Ecclesiastical Literature*, which he co-edited with James Strong. Only 3 volumes were published before McClintock's death in 1870.

1889 The first Lithuanian Church in America was organized in Plymouth, Pennsylvania: St. Casimir's Lithuanian Church. The first pastor was the Rev. Alexander Burba.

1977 American Presbyterian apologist Francis Schaeffer explained in a letter: "The unforgivable sin is not something done once for all and which when done is without remedy. It is the constant, unremitting resistance of the gracious work of the Holy Spirit for salvation."

1978 The complete New International Version of the Bible was first published, by Zondervan Publishers of Grand Rapids, Michigan. The New Testament had appeared in 1973.

October 28

312 The outnumbered forces of Roman emperor Constantine (c.280–337) defeated the army of Maxentius, a contender for the throne, at Milvian Bridge. Constantine had trusted in the sign of the cross, which he had seen in a vision with the inscription *In this sign conquer.* Constantine afterward became the first Roman emperor to embrace the Christian faith.

901 Death of Alfred the Great (b.849), king of the Saxons. In 871 he succeeded to the throne of Wessex on the death of his brother Ethelred. During his 30-year reign, Alfred instituted valuable military reforms, held a deep concern for the administration of justice and sought to codify the laws of England for his subjects. His greatest contributions lay in the area of Christian education. Alfred understood the importance of maintaining intellectual links with wider Christendom, and therefore assembled an international band of scholars to translate into English the fundamental writings of theology, philosophy, history and spiritual devotion.

1585 Birth of Cornelius Jansen, Dutch Roman Catholic theologian, in Utrecht province, Holland. Through an intense study of Augustine, Jansen became increasingly convinced that the Roman Catholic Church had strayed from the doctrine of the early church. Jansen and his reform movement became to the Roman Catholic Church what Puritanism was to the Anglican Church. Jansen especially opposed the salvation-seeking pomp of the Jesuits and the Aristotelian philosophy of Thomas Aquinas. He urged a return to Pauline and Augustinian theology, which viewed salvation through grace. Jansen's greatest sphere of influence was around Paris.

1636 The General Court of the Massachusetts Bay Colony founded Harvard College by passing an act that appropriated 400 English pounds to establish the school. The Rev. Henry Dunster was named the first president of the college.

1646 Colonial missionary John Eliot ("Apostle to the New England Indians") conducted the first Protestant worship service for Indians in North America, at Nonantum, Massachusetts. He also delivered the first sermon preached to Indians in their native tongue.

1704 Death of John Locke (b.1632), English philosopher. In early life he was a student of medicine; later, he lectured at Oxford in philosophy (1660–66). He published his first major writing at age 58 (1690): *An Essay Concerning Human Understanding.* His great recognition began from this date. His 1695 *Reasonableness of Christianity* taught that the only secure basis of Christianity was its intellectual integrity. Yet Locke's "theology" also contained the seeds which later spawned four non-Christian philosophies: empiricism, English sensationalism, English deism and English moralism. Locke became England's foremost advocate of religious toleration in the late 17th century, even though his own toleration did not extend to Catholics or atheists.

1777 Anglican hymnwriter John Newton pointed out in a letter: "The Lord usually reserves dying strength for a dying hour."

1820 Birth of John H. Hopkins, author and composer of the Christmas hymn "We Three Kings of Orient Are."

1948 American missionary and Auca Indian martyr Jim Elliot recorded in his journal: "I covenanted with my Father that He would do either of two things— either glorify himself to the utmost in me, or slay me. By His grace I shall not have His second best." The following year, on this same date, Elliot wrote what might almost seem a postscript to this earlier resolve: "He is no fool who gives what he cannot keep to gain that which he cannot lose."

1960 English Christian apologist C.S. Lewis wrote in *Letters to an American Lady*: "I find FEAR a great help—the fear that my own unforgiveness will exclude me from all the promises. Fear tames wrath."

October 29

1794 Birth of William B. Tappan, American Congregational advocate of the Sunday school, in Beverly, Massachusetts. Originally trained in clockmaking, Tappan's increasing interest in the Sunday school movement led to his employment with the American Sunday School Union in 1822, remaining with the organization until his death in 1849. A prolific poet, Tappan published ten volumes of verse during his lifetime, including the verse we sing as "'Tis Midnight, and on Olive's Brow."

1837 Birth of Abraham Kuyper, Dutch Calvinist theologian and statesman, near Rotterdam, Holland. Ordained in the Reformed Church, Kuyper was "converted" to orthodox Calvinism by the deep piety of his first congregation at Beesd (1863–38). He later pastored at Utrecht (1868–70) and Amsterdam (1870–74). Beginning in 1867, Kuyper moved toward making orthodox Calvinism a political force. He was elected to Parliament 1874 and even became prime minister in 1901–05. As statesman, Kuyper's greatest achievement was to give the "common people," the lower-middle class orthodox Calvinist group, both political voice and suffrage. As a theologian, he revived a systematic Calvinism that emphasized "common grace."

1869 Birth of E.O. Sellers, American Baptist music evangelist and educator, in Hastings, Michigan. Converted at a Y.M.C.A. meeting, Sellers soon enrolled at Moody Bible Institute, Chicago. After serving several Y.M.C.A. and church positions, he returned to Moody to teach music and Christian education (1908–19). He was also active as a song evangelist for such famed revivalists as R.A. Torrey, Gipsy Smith, A.C. Dixon and J. Wilbur Chapman. Sellers also published many articles, poems and hymn tunes. He authored and composed the hymn "Thy Word Is a Lamp to My Feet" (a.k.a. "Thy Word Have I Hid in My Heart") and composed the hymn "There Is Never a Day So Dreary" (a.k.a. "Wonderful, Wonderful Jesus").

1870 Birth of Juji Nakada, Japanese Christian evangelist. In 1901 he invited Charles and Lettie Cowman to come and help establish a Bible training institute in Japan. In 1910 the Cowmans incorporated the Oriental Missions Society in Tokyo. Headquartered today in Greenwood, Indiana, O.M.S. International is an interdenominational mission organization of Wesleyan tradition. Its 251-member overseas staff serves in over a dozen countries, engaged primarily in evangelism, church planting, radio and TV broadcasting and theological education, as well as in helping support the national churches.

1889 New York missions pioneer A.B. (Albert) Simpson (1843–1919) incorporated the International Missionary Alliance in New York City. Two years earlier he had organized the Christian Alliance, a home missions society. In 1897 the two organizations were combined under a new name: the Christian and Missionary Alliance. Simpson was president of the denomination until his death. The C& MA is one of the most aggressive denominations within orthodox Protestantism, fully committed to foreign missions.

1900 Death of Frederic L. Godet (b.1812), Swiss Reformed theologian. Ordained in 1836, he pastored for 22 years, 15 of them in his hometown of Neuchatel, Switzerland. He then taught theology at the denominational seminary at Neuchatel from 1851–73. A prominent representative of reformed theology, Godet combined deep Christian piety with positive biblical criticism. His work strongly influenced the orthodox Christian position among the Swiss theologians of his day. The author of several important books on biblical studies, Godet's best-known work in the English-speaking world is his *Commentary on the Gospel of St. John* (1864–65; English translation 1877).

1919 Death of A.B. (Albert) Simpson (b.1843), founder of the Christian and Missionary Alliance. Originally ordained into the Presbyterian ministry, Simpson resigned from the denomination in 1881 to begin missionary work in New York City. In 1883 he founded Nyack College, in 1887 he organized the Christian Alliance Society and in 1889 he founded the International Missionary Alliance. In 1897 the two societies were combined under the new name Christian and Missionary Alliance, which has become one of the most aggressive and missions-minded denominations in Protestantism.

1954 American missionary and Auca Indian martyr Jim Elliot recounted in his journal: "First time I ever saw an Auca—fifteen hundred feet is a long ways if you're looking out of an airplane." Barely ten weeks later, on Jan. 8, 1956, Jim and four other missionaries (Pete Fleming, Ed McCully, Nate Saint and Roger Youderian) were speared to death by the Auca Indians whom they had come to Ecuador to evangelize. The cause of the Aucas' provocation was never fully determined, but several months after Jim and the others died, the first Auca Indian was led to Christ by Jim Elliot's wife Elisabeth.

1954 Death of Anna Belle Russell (b.1862), active American Methodist layperson and author of the hymn "There Is Never a Day So Dreary" (a.k.a. "Wonderful, Wonderful Jesus"). She spent most of her life as a member of the First Methodist Church of Corning, New York, where she lived with her sister. They both wrote a number of hymns.

October 30

1536 Lutheranism was made the official religion in Denmark. During the period from 1523–36, a group of Lutheran ministers brought spiritual revival, which led to the official state adoption of the Protestant faith.

1738 English founder of Methodism, John Wesley, explained in a letter: "By a 'Christian' I mean one who so believes in Christ as that sin hath no more dominion over him."

1768 The Wesley Chapel on John Street in New York City was formally dedicated. It was the first Methodist Church building in America to be erected. The edifice was later rebuilt in 1817 and again in 1840.

1807 Birth of Christopher Wordsworth, Anglican clergyman and scholar, in Lambeth, England. Ordained in 1833, he was made Bishop of Lincoln in 1869. Nephew of poet William Wordsworth, Christopher was recognized as one of the outstanding Greek scholars of his day. He also published many written works, including a commentary on the Bible and 127 hymns. One of his hymns that remains popular is "O Day of Rest and Gladness."

1820 Birth of John F. Young, American Episcopal clergyman, in Pittston, Maine. He served a number of years as bishop in the state of Florida. Throughout his church ministry, he maintained a deep interest in sacred music. Of the several hymn collections he published, one hymn has become famous: his 1863 English translation of Joseph Mohr's German Christmas hymn "Stille Nacht." In English, the hymn is "Silent Night! Holy Night!"

1883 Birth of Bob Jones, Sr., American fundamentalist Methodist evangelist and educator, in Alabama. In 1926 he started his own college for the purpose of promoting earnest fundamentalism. At the time of his death in 1968, Bob Jones University, located in Greenville, South Carolina, had an enrollment of 4,000. Jones's evangelistic preaching took him to every state in the Union and to 30 other countries. His fundamentalist theology, including segregation of the races, came to be identified with southern conservative politics.

1902 Pope Leo XIII established the Pontifical Biblical Commission with the publication of the Apostolic Letter *Vigilantiae Studiique*. The commission was ordered to safeguard the correct interpretation of Scripture, to state positions that had to be held by Catholics on biblical questions, to set up standards for biblical studies and to grant degrees in sacred Scripture.

October 31

1517 German Augustinian monk Martin Luther nailed his 95 theses to the door of the castle church in Wittenberg and touched off the Protestant Reformation. Nine times in the theses he repeated, *"Docendi sunt Christiani!"* ("Christians must be taught!").

1870 Birth of Hugh Ross Mackintosh, Church of Scotland theologian, at Paisley, Scotland. Ordained in 1896, he served parishes in Tayport and Aberdeen until 1904. He then taught systematic theology at New College, Edinburgh (1904–35). His theology emphasized the forgiveness of sins as the center of the Gospel. He is also known for his "kenotic Christology," which he detailed in *The Doctrine of the Person of Jesus Christ* (1912). Other important writings include *The Christian Experience of Forgiveness* (1927) and *Types of Modern Theology* (1937). Mackintosh had a firm grasp of the German theological writers of his day and sought to make their teachings known in Britain. For this he was unfairly judged a liberal.

1907 Death of Daniel C. Roberts (b.1841), American Episcopal clergyman. Ordained in 1865, he served appointments in Vermont and Massachusetts. He became vicar of St. Paul's Church, in Concord, New Hampshire, in 1877, where he remained for the next 30 years. Roberts penned the words to the hymn "God of Our Fathers, Whose Almighty Hand" in 1876.

1912 Birth of Dale Evans (Mrs. Roy Rogers), American singer, actress and songwriter, in Uvalde, Texas. Most of her best films were made in the 1940s, and most were with Roy Rogers, whom she married in 1947. Evans wrote several songs, and at least two remain popular: "The Bible Tells Me So" and "Happy Birthday, Gentle Savior." She has also written numerous articles for religious publications as well as several Christian books, including *Angel Unaware* and *Spiritual Diary*.

1963 Death of Sam Shoemaker (b.1893), American Episcopal clergyman. Ordained in 1921, he became rector of Calvary Episcopal Church in New York City in 1925. A popular counselor and radio speaker, Shoemaker stressed personal evangelism and everyday practice of the Christian faith. He also assisted Alcoholics Anonymous in formulating its "Twelve Steps." His several popular books include *Religion That Works* (1928) and *Twice Born Ministers* (1929).

November

November 1

451 The Council of Chalcedon (in modern Turkey) adjourned. The council is reckoned by Catholic theologians as the church's fourth ecumenical council (Vatican II, the latest, was the 21st). Pope Leo I convened the first session the previous month. During the 17 sessions, the 600 bishops involved condemned monophysitism as heresy. (Monophysitism is sometimes called Eutychianism. It is an ancient heresy which denied the full humanity of Christ by teaching that the incarnate Son of God possessed only one nature: the divine.)

1512 Italian Renaissance artist Michelangelo (1475–1564) unveiled his 5,808–square-feet masterpiece on the ceiling of the Sistine Chapel in the Vatican. Pope Julius II had originally wanted a fresco of the 12 apostles, but commissioned Michelangelo in 1508 to do a work depicting the whole story of the Bible. The artist was 37 at the time of its completion.

1537 German reformer Martin Luther stated: "There are many fluent preachers who speak at length but say nothing, who have words without substance."

1770 Death of Alexander Cruden (b.1699), Scottish editor and compiler of *Cruden's Concordance*. Cruden originally prepared to study for the ministry; but after suffering several mental breakdowns, he was confined to an asylum for brief stays in 1720, 1738 and 1753. Between these hospitalizations, Cruden worked as a tutor, a bookseller and proofreader. He opened his own bookshop in London in 1732. In 1737 he published the first edition of his classic work *A Complete Concordance of the Holy Scriptures of the Old and New Testaments*. He published three editions of the concordance before his death.

1792 The first General Conference of the Methodist Episcopal Church in America convened in Baltimore, Maryland.

1825 Birth of William Whiting, English school principal, in Kensington, England. Whiting was an Anglican clergyman who served for 20 years as headmaster of the Winchester College Choristers' School in Winchester, England. He published a book of verse, *Rural Thoughts* (1851), and wrote several hymn texts, including "Eternal Father, Strong to Save."

1825 English philanthropist George Mueller (1805–98) attended a Moravian mission and was converted to a living Christian faith. Delivered from a profligate life, Mueller dedicated his remaining years to the cause of improving social conditions around him. His best-known work, an orphanage, began in 1832. By the time of Mueller's death at age 93, over 10,000 had been welcomed into his orphan homes in Bristol.

1897 The India Christian Mission was founded by Rev. and Mrs. Arthur Stephen Paynter in the Kumoan District of North India. Additional branches were established in the Himalayas (1901), Ellore in South India (1903), Ceylon (1904), and modern Sri Lanka (1924). Headquartered today in Nuwara Eliya, Sri Lanka, the India Christian Mission is an interdenominational fund transmitting agency engaged primarily in supporting agriculture, education, literature distribution and orphan work.

1905 The Terry Lectureship was established at Yale University by a gift from Dwight H. Terry, for lectures on religion in light of science and philosophy. Terry lecturers have included Robert A. Millikan (1927), Arthur H. Compton (1932) and John Dewey (1934).

1918 Death of Howard A. Walter (b.1883), American Congregational missionary. After graduation from Princeton in 1905, he taught English in Japan for a year, then returned to the U.S. to attend Hartford Seminary. After ordination, he served as an assistant pastor in Connecticut for three years (1910–13). He then joined the Y.M.C.A. and traveled to Lahore, India, to evangelize and teach Muslim students. He died there at an early age, the victim of a severe flu epidemic. While in his 20s in Japan, Walter wrote several poems which were later set to music by J.Y. Peek, including "I Would Be True."

1921 Birth of John Willard Peterson, contemporary American Christian songwriter, in Lindsborg, Kansas. Following World War II, Peterson received music training at Moody Bible Institute and the American Conservatory of Music. Called by some "the dean of contemporary Gospel songwriters," Peterson has received several honorary doctorates in recognition of his contribution to Gospel music. He has composed over 1,200 gospel songs and more than 30 cantatas and musicals. Among his many popular songs are: "So Send I You," "No One Understands Like Jesus," "Shepherd of Love," "Heaven Came Down," "It Took a Miracle," "Springs of Living Waters" and "Over the Sunset Mountains."

1927 The Eastern European Mission was incorporated in Chicago, Illinois, by founder Paul Bernhard Anderson. Headquartered today in Pasadena, California, this interdenominational, evangelical mission organization shortened its name to Eurovision in 1985. Working in 10 European nations, Eurovision is engaged primarily in shortwave radio broadcasting, literature production and distribution, and relief support.

1942 The Rev. Spence Burton, was enthroned Bishop of the Church of England over the diocese of Nassau, Haiti. He was the first American to be made a bishop in the Church of England.

1950 Pope Pius XII proclaimed the dogma of the Assumption of the Blessed Virgin Mary, *Munificentissimus Deus*. (This doctrine teaches that Jesus' mother at the end of her life on earth was taken—body and soul—into heaven to be united with the risen Christ.)

1961 Death of Mordecai Ham, the evangelist under whose ministry Billy Graham was saved. Ham's ministry spanned 61 years.

1963 Christian English scholar J.R.R. Tolkien wrote in a letter: "In the last resort, faith is an act of will, inspired by love."

1963 The first U.S. Christmas stamp went on sale. The design showed a Christmas tree in front of the White House.

1977 The Children of India Foundation was incorporated in Westerly, Rhode Island. This interdenominational mission organization of fundamentalist and Pentecostal tradition is engaged primarily in relief work and the support of national Christian workers in India.

1986 S.I.M. International moved into its new headquarters in Charlotte, North Carolina. Founded in 1893 as the Sudan Interior Mission, the present name was adopted in 1982 when the organization merged with the Andes Evangelical Mission. S.I.M. is an evangelical, interdenominational mission agency engaged primarily in church planting, theological education and Gospel broadcasting. Its overseas staff of over 650 work in 15 countries around the world.

November 2

1164 Archbishop of Canterbury Thomas a Becket began his six-year exile in France. He had opposed the policies of England's King Henry II. Henry permitted Thomas to return to his office in early Dec. 1170; but after another controversy between king and archbishop, Henry sent four of his knights to Canterbury, where they murdered Thomas in the cathedral.

1610 Death of Richard Bancroft (b.1544), who became Archbishop of Canterbury in 1604. Beginning in 1589, he launched a strong attack against Presbyterians and Puritans by promoting an Anglican-style episcopal (rule by bishops) form of government. Bancroft became Bishop of London in 1597, then succeeded John Whitgift as Anglican primate in 1604. It was Bancroft whom King James I appointed supervisor of the translation project that has come to be called the King James Version of the Bible, first published in 1611.

1752 Death of Johann Albrecht Bengel (b.1687), German Lutheran clergyman and Bible scholar. Trained at Tubingen, he taught at the Lutheran seminary in Denkendorf from 1713–41. His chief publication was a critical edition of the New Testament (1734) that marks the beginning of modern textual or lower criticism. In 1742 Bengel published *Gnomon Novi Testamenti*, a word-by-word explanation of the New Testament Greek text. This work was translated and augmented in John Wesley's *Notes Upon the New Testament* (1755). Bengel's *Gnomon* is still in common use among evangelical scholars.

1789 In the chaos of the French Revolution, the property of the church in France was taken over by the state.

1830 In Baltimore, Maryland, a general convention of anti-Episcopal Methodist reformers met to establish the Methodist Protestant Church.

1834 Birth of Harriett Eugenia Peck Buell, American Methodist writer and author of the hymn "I'm a Child of the King," in Cozenovia, New York. For 50 years she was a regular contributor to the *Northern Christian Advocate*. She lived in Manlius, New York, until 1898 as an active member of the Methodist Church there.

1904 Daughter of General Booth, Miss Evangeline Cory Booth (1865–1950) was appointed commander of the Salvation Army in the U.S. In 1934 Miss Booth became the first woman general (the fourth international commander) of the Salvation Army. She held the position until her retirement in 1939.

1915 Death of John T. Grape (b.1835), American church organist and choir director. Grape, a successful coal merchant, was choir director at two Methodist churches in Baltimore, Maryland. He also composed a number of hymn tunes, including ALL TO CHRIST ("Jesus Paid It All").

1917 British Foreign Secretary Arthur J. Balfour approved *The Balfour Declaration*. The document called for "the establishment in Palestine of a national home for the Jewish people."

1978 Rev. M. William Howard, a black American clergyman, was elected president of the National Council of Churches. He was the youngest person to hold that office.

November 3

753 Death of St. Pirminius, the first abbot of the Benedictine monastery at Reichenau. With the protection of Charles Martel, Pirminius founded Reichenau and other monasteries among the Almanni in Baden and in Alsace. His book *Scarapsus* (or *Dicta Pirminii*) is of special interest in liturgical studies as it is the earliest available document containing the Apostles' Creed in its present form.

1534 The British Parliament passed the *Supremacy Act*, whereby Henry VIII and his successors to the English throne were declared "the only supreme head in earth of the Church of England." The legislation officially made England a Protestant nation.

1631 English clergyman Rev. John Eliot (1604–90) first arrived in America, at Boston. He was the first Protestant minister in America to devote himself to the evangelization of the American Indian.

1643 In Boston, Samuel Gorton and six others who had been extradited from Warwick, Rhode Island, were sentenced by the General Court of Massachusetts to confinement at hard labor for blasphemy.

1649 Death of Giovanni Diodati (b.1576), Italian Calvinist theologian. Born in Geneva, Switzerland, he taught Hebrew and pastored there before succeeding Theodore Beza as professor of theology in 1609, a post which he retained until his death. He was later the Genevese representative at the Synod of Dort (1618–19). Diodati's translated the Bible into Italian and published it in 1607; he published a revised edition with notes in 1641. His translation is still commonly used by Italian Protestants. He also produced a French translation of the Bible in 1644.

1723 Birth of Samuel Davies, American Presbyterian leader, near Summit Ridge, New Jersey. Ordained an evangelist in 1747, he was sent to Hanover County, Virginia, to preach to Presbyterian converts of the Great Awakening. In 1753 he accompanied Gilbert Tennent on a trip to England to raise money for the College of New Jersey (now Princeton University). Davies served as president of the school from 1759 until his death in 1761, and considerably raised its standards. He also led the organization of Virginia's Hanover Presbytery in 1775, the first presbytery in the southern U.S.

1784 Thomas Coke (1747–1814) first arrived in America from England, at New York City. He was the first Methodist bishop to come to the New World.

November 4

1646 The Massachusetts Bay Colony passed a law making it a capital offense to deny that the Bible was the Word of God. Any person convicted of the offense was liable to the death penalty.

1740 Birth of Augustus M. Toplady, Anglican clergyman, in Surrey, England. He was converted under the Methodists, but in 1762 was ordained into the ministry of the Church of England. In later years, Toplady was an ardent Calvinist, an outspoken critic against Arminian and Wesleyan theology. Due to frail health, Toplady died of overwork and tuberculosis at the age of 38 (1778). Highly respected as a spiritual and evangelical leader, Toplady authored the hymn "Rock of Ages, Cleft for Me" two years before his death.

1771 Birth of James Montgomery, English newspaper editor, in Ayrshire, Scotland. Raised by the Moravians in Ireland, Montgomery settled in Sheffield, England, where he began working for the *Sheffield Register*. In 1794 he took over the newspaper, editing it for the next 31 years, and changed its name to the *Sheffield Iris*. A public-spirited writer and champion of humanitarian causes, Montgomery was twice imprisoned for expressing unpopular views on national issues in his paper. He was a strong abolitionist and equally strong in his support of the British Bible Society and foreign missions. Montgomery wrote over 350 hymns, including the popular "Go to Dark Gethsemane," "Prayer Is the Soul's Sincere Desire" and "Angels from the Realms of Glory."

1794 Birth of Billy Bray, Cornish Methodist evangelist, in Twelveheads, England. A coal miner during his early years, Bray was also an inveterate smoker and drinker. In 1823, at age 29, he converted to Christ after reading John Bunyan's *Visions of Heaven and Hell*. He became an active opponent of tobacco and alcohol abuse. He influenced many miners for the Gospel by showing an active concern for their lives.

1826 Birth of Timothy R. Matthews, Anglican hymnwriter who wrote the tune MARGARET ("Thou Didst Leave Thy Throne"), in Colmworth, England. After a brief career in teaching, he was ordained in 1853 and served as curate in Nottingham (1853–39). He was later curate (1859–69) then rector (1869–1907) at the church in North Coates, where he served for 48 years. Matthews composed more than 100 hymn tunes.

1838 Birth of Andrew Martin Fairbairn, British Congregational theologian, in Fife, Scotland. Ordained in 1860, he served churches in Bathgate and Aberdeen through 1877, then as principal of Airedale Theological College in Bradford, Yorkshire (1877–86). In 1886 he became the first principal of Mansfield College at Oxford University, remaining at this post for 23 years (-1909). Much in demand as a preacher and lecturer, Fairbairn paid several visits to the U.S. His more popular writings included *Studies in the Life of Christ* (1880), *Christ in Modern Theology* (1893), and *Philosophy of the Christian Religion* (1902).

1847 Death of Felix Mendelssohn (b.1809), German composer and pianist. His compositions, noted for their gracefulness, are light and easily understood. His works include five symphonies and eight books of *Songs without Words*. Among his better-known religious compositions are *St. Paul* (1835), and *Elijah* (1846), which is considered by many to be one of the greatest oratorios of the 19th century, second only to Handel's *Messiah*.

1866 Birth of J. Lincoln Hall, American sacred music composer, in Philadelphia, Pennsylvania. He received his music training at the University of Pennsylvania and was later awarded an honorary Doctor of Music degree from Harriman University. Hall was a highly respected choral conductor, composer and music publisher. He composed the scores for many cantatas, oratorios and anthems, and wrote hundreds of Gospel songs. For many years he worked with the Hall-Mack Publishing Co. in Philadelphia, which later merged with the Rodeheaver Publishing Co. from Winona Lake, Indiana. One of Hall's most memorable hymn tunes is one he composed for a verse by Frank E. Graeff in 1905: "Does Jesus Care?"

1868 Birth of C.F. (Charles Fox) Burney, Anglican Bible scholar. Ordained in 1893, he spent his entire career (32 years) at Oxford as a lecturer in Hebrew (1893–97), university librarian (1897–1908), and Oriel professor of the interpretation of Holy Scripture (1914–25). He was a noted authority on Semitic languages and one of the most original thinkers among scholars of his generation. Burney stressed the importance of recognizing an Aramaic foundation underlying the language of the New Testament Gospels. His most important publications include *Outlines of Old Testament Theology* (1899) and *The Aramaic Origin of the Fourth Gospel* (1922).

1903 Birth of Watchman (Henry) Nee, Chinese Christian author, in Swatow, China. Educated at Trinity College in Foochow, Nee began preaching in 1924. He adopted the Plymouth Brethren teachings of the victorious life, local assemblies, local unpaid ministers and weekly communion. His church was known as the Little Flock. Nee visited the U.S. and Britain several times. Because he opposed the communist Three-Self religious movement, Nee spent his last 20 years in prison (1952–72). He wrote such Christian classics as *The Spiritual Man* and *Rethinking the Work*.

1924 Death of Charles C. Luther (b.1847), American Baptist evangelist. From 1871–86 he was active as a lay evangelist. Ordained in 1886, he continued his work until accepting the pastorate of the Bridgeport First Baptist Church in Connecticut (1891–93). For a number of years he also worked with the state Baptist Mission Board of New Jersey. Luther authored about 25 hymns, including "Must I Go, and Empty-Handed?"

November 5

1414 The Council of Constance was convened in modern West Germany. Termed the "high water mark of the Conciliar Era," this Roman Catholic conclave, which lasted until April 22, 1418, ended the Great Schism within the church by deposing three rival popes (John XXIII, elected at the Council of Pisa; Gregory XII, elected in Rome; and Benedict XIII, elected in Avignon, France). On a darker note, it was also this council that brought to trial and executed the two Bohemian reformers, John Huss (1415) and his close friend and disciple Jerome of Prague (1416). This council also anathematized the teachings of English reformer John Wycliffe (c.1329–1384).

1439 Duke Amadeus VIII of Savoy, in southeastern France, was elected Pope Felix V by one cardinal and eleven bishops of the Roman Catholic Church. Felix was the last of the church's antipopes (men whose election to the papal

office has been traditionally viewed as irregular by Roman Catholic historians). Felix eventually abdicated his papal office in April 1449 in deference to
Pope Nicholas V, who had been elected to the office two years earlier (March
1447) by an official college of Cardinals. Felix V died in 1451.

1851 Birth of Benjamin B. Warfield, American Presbyterian Bible scholar, in
Lexington, Kentucky. Ordained into the ministry in 1879, he pastored only a
year before securing his first teaching position. From 1887 until his death in
1921, Warfield was professor of theology at Princeton Theological Seminary.
He was an ardent Calvinist and a strict fundamentalist, holding to the plenary
("full" or "whole") inspiration of the Bible. He published several pamphlets
and addresses, and a score of books on theology and the Bible, including *An
Introduction to the Textual Criticism of the New Testament* and *The Divine
Origin of the Bible.*

1887 Birth of Donald M. Baillie, Scottish theologian, at Gairloch, Ross-shire,
Scotland. He pastored several churches in Scotland (1918–34), then taught
systematic theology in the University of St. Andrews his remaining 20 years
(1934–54). His theological position was between the old liberalism and the
neoorthodoxy. Though teaching took precedence over writing for Baillie, his
book *God Was in Christ* (1948) went through many editions and is regarded
by some as the most significant book of its time in the area of Christology.

1907 Death of Daniel C. Roberts (b.1841), American Episcopal clergyman. A
Union veteran of the U.S. Civil War, Roberts was ordained in 1865. After serving
churches in Vermont and Massachusetts, he became vicar of St. Paul's Church
in Concord, New Hampshire, where he served almost 30 years. It was during
Roberts' first pastorate in Brandon, Vermont, that he penned a verse to com-
memorate the 100th anniversary of the signing of the Declaration of Independence. It was sung for the first time at Brandon's Fourth of July celebration.
The hymn went unsung until 1892, when it was included in the new edition
of the Episcopal hymnal with a different tune called NATIONAL HYMN. Roberts' text has since been used exclusively with this tune to the present time,
yielding the hymn as we know it today: "God of Our Fathers."

1912 Birth of Roy Rogers, Christian country and western artist, in Cincinnati,
Ohio. Born Leonard Slye, the "King of the Cowboys" began his career as a
western singer. In 1932 he formed the music group Sons of the Pioneers. From
1935 to the mid-sixties, he starred in over 100 western films. He and his wife,
Dale Evans, co-starred in the TV series *The Roy Rogers Show*, from 1951–57.
Roy and Dale have won special acclaim from Christians for their charitable
work, especially among children. They adopted and raised a large family of
their own, including many children who had been severely handicapped from
birth.

1935 The Cooperative General Association of Free Will Baptists (northern
U.S.) and the General Conference of Free Will Baptists (southern U.S.) merged
in Nashville, Tennessee, to form the National Association of Free Will Baptists.
In contrast to the more traditional Calvinistic beliefs in Baptist theology, Free
Will Baptists hold the doctrine that Christ gave himself a ransom for all, not
just for the elect; God calls all people to repentance and "whosoever will"
may be saved.

1960   Death of Donald Grey Barnhouse (b.1895), American Presbyterian clergyman and pioneer radio preacher. He worked in France as a missionary from 1919–27, then returned to the U.S. In 1927 he began a 33-year pastorate and radio ministry at the Tenth Presbyterian Church in Philadelphia. During his last 10 years, Barnhouse edited *Eternity* magazine, which he had founded. He authored over 30 books on the Scriptures and on the Christian life.

1970   Francis Schaeffer, American Presbyterian apologist for the Christian faith, pointed out in a letter: "The Bible does not minimize sexual sin, but neither does it make it different from any other sin."

November 6

1777   Anglican hymnwriter John Newton explained in a letter: "God often takes a course for accomplishing His purposes directly contrary to what our narrow views would prescribe. He wounds in order to heal, kills that He may make alive, brings a death upon our feelings, wishes and prospects when He is about to give us the desire of our hearts."

1804   Birth of Benjamin H. Kennedy, Anglican educator, in Summer Hill, England. Ordained in 1829, he pastored briefly before devoting himself to educational activities. He taught at St. John's College (1828–36), Shrewsbury School (1836–66), and Cambridge (1867). He also wrote several hundred hymns, as well as translating several from German. His greatest legacy is the English translation of the hymn "Ask Ye What Great Thing I Know."

1850   Death of Charles Meineke (b.1782), German-born American church organist who wrote the tune GLORIA PATRI. He emigrated from Germany to England in 1810, then to America in 1822. For eight years he was organist at St. Paul's Episcopal Church in Baltimore, Maryland. Meineke published several volumes of hymns during his life, including the GLORIA PATRI, to which we sing the doxology, "Glory be to the Father. . ."

1853   The first Chinese Presbyterian Church in the U.S. was organized, in San Francisco, California.

1863   Birth of A.T. (Archibald Thomas) Robertson, American Baptist New Testament scholar, near Chatham, Virginia. Converted at age 13, he was licensed to preach at age 16. In 1895 he was elected to succeed John A. Broadus as professor of New Testament interpretation at Southern Baptist Theological Seminary in Louisville, Kentucky. He held this position until his death in 1934. Robertson's greatest contribution to biblical scholarship was in the field of New Testament Greek. In 1914 he published his monumental 1,454-page *Grammar of the Greek New Testament*, the largest and most comprehensive New Testament grammar ever published. It went into five editions by 1931. Robertson also authored 45 other books.

1876   Death of James Nicholson (b.ca.1828), Irish-born American Methodist layman and author of the hymn "Lord Jesus, I Long to Be Perfectly Whole" (a.k.a. "Whiter Than Snow"). Emigrating to the U.S. in the early 1850s, Nicholson lived in Philadelphia, Pennsylvania, for 20 years, where he was an active member of the Wharton Street Methodist Episcopal Church. He worked with the U.S. Post Office in Washington, D.C. In 1872 Nicholson and William

G. Fischer published a 16-page pamphlet entitled *Joyful Songs No. 4*, which included "Lord Jesus, I Long to Be Perfectly Whole," based on the text of Psalm 51:7.

1893 Death of Peter I. Tchaikovsky (b.1840), Russian composer. He is best known for his classical ballet scores, such as *Swan Lake* (1877), *Sleeping Beauty* (1890), and *The Nutcracker* (1892). However, Tchaikovsky also composed sacred music, including "O Praise Ye the Name of the Lord."

1935 Death of Billy Sunday (b.1862), American Presbyterian revivalist. Orphaned during the Civil War, Sunday spent part of his boyhood in orphanages. From 1883–91 he played major league baseball with Chicago, Pittsburgh and Philadelphia. Converted in 1886 at the Pacific Garden Mission in Chicago, he quit baseball and worked for the Chicago Y.M.C.A. (1891–93). Later, he worked with Presbyterian evangelist J. Wilbur Chapman (1893–95). Ordained to the Presbyterian ministry in 1903, Sunday worked his remaining 42 years (1893–1935) as an evangelist. His fiery, conservative preaching was dramatic and unconventional; yet its unique style attracted huge audiences. Before his death in 1935, Sunday probably held more than 300 evangelistic campaigns, spoke to a total audience of 100 million and led as many as 300,000 souls to Christ.

1950 American missionary and Auca Indian martyr Jim Elliot wisely recorded in his journal: "If only youth knew and age could do, what a wonderful place this would be."

1953 English Christian apologist C.S. Lewis observed in *Letters to an American Lady*: "Our prayers are really His prayers; He speaks to himself through us."

1977 The Barnes Lake Dam burst in Toccoa Falls, Georgia, releasing a flood of water which destroyed the campus of Toccoa Falls Bible Institute. Thirty-eight students and instructors were killed in the tragedy.

November 7

680 The Third Council of Constantinople opened under Pope Leo II. The sixth of the church's 21 ecumenical councils, Constantinople III was attended by 165 bishops. During its 18 sessions (held until Sept. 681), the Council condemned Monethelitism (a heresy which taught that Christ's will was only divine and not human). Constantinople III is sometimes called the Trullian Council because its sessions were held in the domed hall, Trullos, of Constantinople's Imperial Palace.

1637 Colonial American religious leader Anne Hutchinson (1591–1643) was tried and convicted of spreading heresy by the Congregational synod of Newtown, Massachusetts. She taught redemption through faith rather than through works. Banished from the Massachusetts Bay Colony, Mrs. Hutchinson fled to Rhode Island with her family and friends.

1828 Birth of Joseph Henry Thayer, American New Testament lexicographer, in Boston, Massachusetts. After pastoring in the Congregational church for five years (1859–64), Thayer went into teaching, and was affiliated with Harvard his remaining 18 years (1883–1901). Thayer's main interest was New Testament Greek. In 1886 he published his definitive *Greek-English Lexicon of the New Testament*, a work which established Thayer's reputation as a New

Testament scholar. The work was the English standard in New Testament lexicons until 1957, when Bauer's lexicon was translated from German. Thayer served on the revision committees of both the (1881) English Revised Version and the (1901) American Standard Version of the New Testament. He was also responsible, perhaps more than any other individual, for the founding of the American School of Oriental Research in Jerusalem.

1837 Murder of Elijah P. Lovejoy (b.1802), American Presbyterian abolitionist newspaper editor. Converted to Christ at age 30 (1832), Lovejoy was licensed as a Presbyterian preacher in 1833. As editor of the *St. Louis Observer* from 1833–36, he advocated temperance and abolition, turning the Presbyterian weekly periodical into a major abolitionist newspaper with a circulation near 1,700. Anti-abolitionists forced him to move his presses from St. Louis to Alton, Illinois (just across the Mississippi River from St. Louis) in 1836. The following year, the same forces twice destroyed his press, then shot him to death trying to destroy them a third time.

1847 Birth of Will Lamartine Thompson, American songwriter, in East Liverpool, Ohio. His education included studies at Mt. Union College in Ohio, at Boston Conservatory of Music, and special studies in Leipzig, Germany. The author of many secular and patriotic songs, Thompson's major interest was sacred music. He established the Will L. Thompson & Co. music publishing firm. He wrote both words and music to "Jesus Is All the World to Me" (ELIZABETH) and "Softly and Tenderly Jesus Is Calling" (THOMPSON).

1906 Birth of Eugene Carson Blake, American Presbyterian clergyman, in St. Louis, Missouri. Educated at Princeton and Edinburgh, he taught briefly in India, then pastored in the U.S. from 1932–51. Elected president of the National Council of the Churches of Christ in the U.S.A. (1954–57), Blake was elected general secretary of the World Council of Churches in 1966, a position he held until his retirement in 1972.

1918 Birth of William Franklin ("Billy") Graham, American evangelist, in Charlotte, North Carolina. Educated at Bob Jones University, Florida Bible Seminary and Wheaton College, he was ordained into the Baptist ministry in 1940. In 1943 he became the first evangelist of the newly founded Youth for Christ organization. Acquiring national fame in 1948 during his Los Angeles crusade, he founded the Billy Graham Evangelistic Association in 1950 and has since led crusades in nearly every part of the world. Graham has also developed subsidiaries of his ministry. Since 1950, he has led the weekly *Hour of Decision* program on radio and television. He has written several books, including *My Answer* (1960), *World Aflame* (1965) and *Crusade Hymn Stories* (1967). He is also the editor of *Decision* magazine.

November 8

1674 Death of John Milton (b.1608), English poet and theologian. He was an Anglican with moderate Puritan leanings. In later years he turned Presbyterian, but finally turned independent with Arminian inclinations. He went blind about 1652, and wrote with the assistance of a secretary. Milton penned a series of pamphlets on ecclesiastical and social subjects. He defended the Presbyterian system of church government (rule by a group) against the Episcopal (rule by a bishop). From the Restoration (1660) until his death, Milton lived in retirement, writing his greatest work, *Paradise Lost* (1667), followed four years later by *Paradise Regained* and *Samson Agonistes*. Milton was a product of both the Renaissance and the Reformation. His belief in the freedom of the human will lay behind his stand against the Calvinist doctrine of predestination.

1837 Mount Holyoke Seminary first opened in South Hadley, Massachusetts. Founded the previous year by Mary M. Lyon (1797–1849), it was the first college in the U.S. established specifically for the education of women. Mrs. Lyon spent her last 12 years (1737–49) as principal of the new college.

1889 Birth of Oswald J. Smith, Canadian clergyman. For many years he pastored the People's Church of Toronto, Canada, which he had founded. The church has become well known for its great missionary outreach; and Smith's preaching took him to 66 countries. He also authored a number of books and composed more than 1,200 hymns, including "Deeper and Deeper," "Joy in Serving Jesus," "The Song of the Soul Set Free," "Then Jesus Came" and "God Understands."

1904 Emile Combs introduced a bill for the separation of church and state in France. The bill passed in Dec. 1905, thereby ending the Concordat of 1801 and allowing complete liberty of conscience.

1920 Death of Abraham Kuyper (b.1837), Dutch Calvinist theologian and statesman. Ordained in the Reformed Church, Kuyper was converted by the piety of his first congregation at Beesd (1863–68), and thereafter embraced orthodox Calvinism. With an eye toward making his newfound faith into a political force, Kuyper was elected to Parliament in 1874, and even became prime minister (1901–05). Kuyper's theology revived a systematic Calvinism which emphasized "common grace."

1925 Moody Memorial Church in Chicago, Illinois, was dedicated. Its auditorium seats 4,000. It was named after evangelist D.L. Moody (1837–99), who began his evangelistic work in Chicago in 1861.

1951 American Presbyterian apologist for the Christian faith, Francis Schaeffer commented in a letter: "The higher the mountains, the more understandable is the glory of Him who made them and who holds them in His hand."

1970 The new administration building for World Missionary Press, Inc., was dedicated at New Paris, Indiana. Founded by Dr. & Mrs. Watson Goodman in 1961, W.M.P. moved from its original headquarters in Winona Lake, Indiana, earlier in 1970. World Missionary Press is an interdenominational, fundamentalist mission organization engaged primarily in Scripture distribution and memorization. The headquarters produces and distributes Scripture booklets in 214 languages to nearly 180 countries around the world.

1971 The International Board of Jewish Missions moved into its present headquarters in Chattanooga, Tennessee. Founded in 1949 in Atlanta, Georgia, the I.B.J.M. is an interdenominational, fundamentalist mission organization that ministers to Jews in the U.S. and overseas. Its overseas staff of 28 work in 10 countries around the world primarily in church planting, radio broadcasting and literature distribution.

November 9

1538 German reformer Martin Luther declared: "It would be a good thing if young people were wise and old people were strong, but God has arranged things better."

1800 Birth of Asa Mahan, American Congregational clergyman, in Vernon, New York. He pastored in New York and Ohio between 1829 and 1835. From 1835–50 he was president of Oberlin College in Ohio. Mahan was responsible for instituting Oberlin's distinctive policies of encouraging interracial enrollment and granting degrees to women. After several other administrative and pastoral positions, Mahan retired in Essex, England, to write. His greatest contributions to Christian scholarship were in the area of philosophy. His best-known works include *Scripture Doctrine of Christian Perfection*, *Science of Moral Philosophy*, *Critical History of Philosophy*, and his *Autobiography: Intellectual, Moral, and Spiritual*.

1802 Birth of Elijah P. Lovejoy, American Presbyterian newspaper editor, in Albion, Maine. Lovejoy began his career as a schoolteacher in Maine and Missouri. Converted in 1832, he received a license to preach from the Philadelphia Presbytery in 1835. He edited the *St. Louis Observer* from 1833–36, turning the Presbyterian weekly into a major abolitionist newspaper with a circulation of nearly 1,700. In 1836 anti-Abolitionists forced him to move his presses to Alton, Illinois (just across the Mississippi River from St. Louis). The following year, these same forces twice destroyed his presses, then shot him to death trying to destroy them a third time.

1836 Birth of Samuel Hill, Christian businessman and founder of the Gideons. In 1899 Hill and two other businessmen, John Nicholson and W.J. Knights, organized the Gideons. Since its founding, membership has grown to over 30,000 in 133 countries. The goal of the Gideons is to win individuals to faith in Christ, particularly through the distribution of Scripture. Distribution first began in 1908. More than 12 million Bibles and 100 million New Testaments have been distributed.

1837 Moses Montefiore became the first Jew to be knighted in England.

1938 In Nazi Germany, the worst campaign of terror against the Jews by the Third Reich took place. It was organized by the S.S. as a "spontaneous" public demonstration against the assassination of German diplomat Ernst von Rath by Jewish refugee Grynszpan two days earlier. During the night, 267 synagogues were plundered, 7,500 shops were wrecked, 91 Jews were killed and 20,000 others were arrested and sent to concentration camps. The event came to be known as the *Kristallnacht* ("Night of Glass") because of the thousands of windows that were broken by Nazi thugs.

November 10

1483 Birth of Martin Luther, founder of the German Reformation, in Eisleben, Germany. Luther entered the Augustinian order in 1505; three years later, he was sent to teach at the University of Wittenberg. While working out a personal anxiety regarding his own salvation, Luther received a spiritual revelation that God justifies through faith alone, and not works. In 1517 Luther nailed his 95 theses against the practice of indulgences to the castle church doors. The intense reaction of the Roman Catholic authorities led to Luther's excommunication in 1521. Before his death in 1546, Luther translated the Bible into the German language of the common man, a translation that has been the basis for many later German versions. He also penned several hymns, including the immortal "A Mighty Fortress Is Our God."

1735 Birth of Granville Sharp, English lawyer and abolitionist. It was Sharp's legal reasoning that won the famed 1772 James Somersett case, the landmark decision that insured "any slave stepping foot on the soil of England was free." Bible students also know of Sharp's Greek grammatical principle. Granville Sharp's Rule states that when the first element of a series is preceded by *"the"* and connected to the rest of the series by *"and,"* the series is a description of one thing; but when each element in a series is connected by *"and the,"* each element in the series has a separate identity. For example, *"the* tax collectors *and* sinners" is one group of people, but *"the* tax collectors *and the* sinners" are two groups. The rule is important in New Testament translation.

1766 Queen's College was chartered in New Brunswick, New Jersey, under the Dutch Reformed Church. In 1825 the school was renamed Rutgers College. The present name of Rutgers University was adopted in 1924.

1852 Birth of Henry Van Dyke, American Presbyterian clergyman, in Germantown, Pennsylvania. Van Dyke served pastorates in Rhode Island and New York City from 1879–99. He was then appointed professor of English literature at Princeton University, where he remained 23 years. He published a number of books, including *The Story of the Other Wise Man* (1896). Van Dyke also wrote a verse that we sing to the last movement of Beethoven's Ninth Symphony: "Joyful, Joyful, We Adore Thee."

1855 Birth of George S. Fisher, American missions pioneer. In 1890 he founded the Gospel Missionary Union. Headquartered today in Kansas City, Missouri, G.M.U. is an evangelical, interdenominational organization of Baptist tradition. Its overseas staff of nearly 400 works in 20 countries around the world. The Gospel Missionary Union is engaged in evangelism, church planting, leadership training, Bible translation, and special ministries in the areas of literature, radio, medicine and education.

1871 English news correspondent Henry M. Stanley finally discovered Scottish missionary and explorer David Livingstone, who had been missing in Africa for five years. Stanley met him with the question, "Dr. Livingstone, I presume?"

1889 Death of Edwin Hatch (b.1835), Anglican Old Testament scholar. He began his teaching career in 1859 and taught ecclesiastical history at Oxford University from 1884 until his death. He wrote several books, but the most important is his definitive *Concordance to the Septuagint* (1897). Hatch co-edited the project with H.A. Redpath; and the work was published eight years after Hatch's death. Originally published in three large volumes, the concordance lists the occurrence of every word in the Greek Old Testament, and is still in print.

1910 The Gideons placed their first Bible, in the Superior Motel in Iron Mountain, Montana.

1933   Death of James Rowe (b.1865), English-American writer. Emigrating from England in 1890, Rowe worked briefly for the railroad and for the Hudson River Humane Society. He then devoted himself to writing. He wrote song texts and edited music journals, working with Trio Music (Waco, Texas), A.J. Showalter Music (Chattanooga, Tennessee), and James D. Vaughan Music (Lawrenceburg, Tennessee). It is believed he wrote more than 19,000 song texts, including "I Would Be Like Jesus" and "I Was Sinking Deep in Sin" (a.k.a. "Love Lifted Me").

1946   Death of Kirsopp Lake (b.1872), British-American archeologist and bib- lical historian. He served in the Anglican pastorate between 1895–1904, then taught at the Universities of Leiden in Holland (1904–14) and Harvard (1914– 38). He was a member of the archeological expedition that discovered the site of the oldest known Semitic cult on Serabit Plateau in Egypt. For students of the New Testament, he is remembered for *The Beginning of Christianity, Part I: The Acts of the Apostles* (1920–33), which he co-edited with F.J. Foakes-Jackson. Lake also published extensively on the subjects of ancient Greek writing and textual criticism.

1952   English scholar and Christian apologist C.S. Lewis observed in *Letters to an American Lady*: "I believe that, in the present divided state of Christen- dom, those who are at the heart of each division are all closer to one another than those who are at the fringes."

November 11

1215   The Fourth Lateran Council was convened by Pope Innocent III, meeting until Nov. 30. The 12th of the church's 21 ecumenical councils, Lateran IV defined and made official the concept of "transubstantiation," the Roman Catholic belief that the bread and wine of the Eucharist change invisibly into the actual body and blood of Jesus. Lutherans believe in "consubstantiation," wherein the presence of Christ is closely attached to the bread and wine of the Lord's Supper. In contrast to both Catholic and Lutheran theology, many Protestants interpret the Lord's Supper as primarily a memorial, a way of remembering the atoning death of Christ for mankind's sins, a theology de- veloped by the Swiss reformer Ulrich Zwingli.

1760   English founder of Methodism John Wesley wrote about the presence of God in a letter: "You cannot live on what He did yesterday. Therefore He comes today."

1921   Death of P.T. (Peter Taylor) Forsyth (b.1848), English Congregational cler- gyman and theologian. He held five pastorates between 1876–1901. From 1901 until his death, he was principal of Hackney Theological College in Hamstead, London. His teaching brought together the evangelical power of the old school and the intellectual viewpoint of modern liberalism. He stressed the need to utilize the freedoms of theological criticism as a means to understanding evangelical realities. His writings reflected a deep sense of the human need for atonement through the cross, emphasizing the divine initiative of Christ. His greatest book was *The Person and Place of Jesus Christ* (1909).

1947   Death of Martin Dibelius (b.1883), German Lutheran New Testament scholar. Educated at the universities of Leipzig, Tubingen and Berlin, he went on to teach at the Universities of Berlin (1910–15) and Heidelberg (1915–47). Dibelius emphasized preaching as the original means of spreading the Gospel in the early church. He believed that the four written Gospels contain "sermon-kernels" (German "formeln") of the original oral message. Along with K.L. Schmidt, H. Gunkel and R. Bultmann, Dibelius's 1919 publication *From Tradition to Gospel* (English translation 1934) helped establish New Testament form criticism. But while Dibelius viewed the New Testament evangelists as compilers of traditional material rather than as independent authors, he tended to be more restrained on liberal issues than many others in the early school of form criticism.

November 12

1556 Dutch Anabaptist leader Menno Simons explained in a letter: "I can neither teach nor live by the faith of others. I must live by my own faith as the Spirit of the Lord has taught me through His Word."

1615 Birth of Richard Baxter, English Puritan clergyman, at Rowton, England. Sick much of his life, he was self-educated through private study, self-instruction and introspection. Ordained an Anglican in 1638, he began a 20-year pastorate in 1640 near Birmingham. In 1662, passage of the Act of Uniformity forced him out of the Church of England. Baxter continued to preach, but suffered repeated persecution between 1662–87. He was imprisoned briefly in 1685–86. Baxter was known for a lifelong non-partisan stance, which placed him in the unenviable middle ground between the monarchy and the commonwealth, between the Episcopalians and the Presbyterians, between the high church and the independents, and between Calvinism and Arminianism. Baxter left nearly 200 writings when he died in 1691, including his great devotional work *The Saints' Everlasting Rest* (1650).

1701 The Carolina Assembly passed the Vestry Act of 1701, making the Church of England the official religion of the Carolina colony. Active opposition by Quakers and other religious Nonconformists who lived there ultimately convinced the proprietors of the colony to revoke the Vestry Act in 1703.

1808 Birth of Ray Palmer, American Congregational clergyman, in Little Compton, Rhode Island. Ordained in 1835, he served churches in Bath, Maine (1835–50), and Albany, New York (1850–65). From 1855 until his retirement in 1878, he was correspondence secretary for the American Congregational Union, headquartered in New York City. He authored several volumes of religious verse and devotional essays, and penned 15 hymns, including several English translations from Latin texts. Two of Palmer's hymns still used are "My Faith Looks Up to Thee" and the English text to "Jesus, Thou Joy of Loving Hearts."

1818 Birth of Henri Frederick Hemy, English Catholic church organist, at Newcastle-upon-Tyne, England. He was a respected composer and organist at the church at Tynemouth. In 1864 he compiled the popular Catholic hymnal *Crown of Jesus*. He later taught music at St. Cuthbert's College in Durham. Of his several compositions, the best known is the hymn tune ST. CATHERINE (Faith of Our Fathers").

1852 Birth of John Oxenham, English Congregational writer and author of the hymn "In Christ There Is No East or West," in Manchester, England. During his early adult years, he worked as a wholesale merchant; but early literary adventures became so successful that he eventually devoted all his time to writing. He wrote under the pseudonym John Oxenham, even though his real name was William Arthur Dunkerly. He published more than 40 novels and 20 volumes of verse and prose.

1866 Birth of Frederick A. Challinor, English composer, in Longton, Stafford-shire, England. By age 15, Challinor had worked in a brickyard, a coal mine and a china factory. He received his first degree in music in 1897, earning his doctorate in music six years later. An active composer, Challinor published over 1,000 songs. His most enduring piece has been the hymn tune STORIES OF JESUS, to which we sing "Tell Me the Stories of Jesus."

1899 American evangelist Dwight L. Moody (1837–99) began his last evangelistic campaign, in Kansas City, Missouri. He became ill during the last service and was unable to complete his message. He died a few days later.

1932 Death of Edmond L. Budry (b.1854), author of the hymn "Thine Be the Glory."

1954 American Presbyterian apologist for the Christian faith, Francis Schaeffer, warned in a letter: "Loyalty to organizations and movements have always tended over time to take the place of loyalty to the person of Christ."

November 13

354 Birth of St. Augustine, greatest of the early Latin church fathers, at Tagaste in Numidia, North Africa. His father was a pagan and his mother Monica was a praying Christian. Augustine was eventually led to Christ under Ambrose of Milan at age 33. He returned home, giving himself to prayer and study in monasteries at Tagaste and Hippo. In 391 he was chosen priest by the people of Hippo, and in 395 elevated to bishop, an office he held until his death in 430. Augustine became the leading voice of many of the North African synods, including the Synod of Carthage in 397. He exerted a powerful influence as a preacher, bishop, theologian, writer and defender of the faith. He was a Christian for all ages, and still enjoys profound respect from both Catholics and Protestants. Of his many deep writings, two stand out: *Confessions* (ca. 397–401) describes the crises leading to his conversion, and *The City of God* (ca.413–27) was written in response to the sacking of Rome in 410. Augustine died in 430, when Roman Africa fell to the besieging Vandals.

1504 Birth of Philip of Hesse, in Marburg, Germany. He first met Martin Luther in 1521 at Worms, and later began to take an active role in the Reformation. He was one of the founders of the Schmalkald League, and became Elector of Saxony in 1531. His bigamous marriage to Margaret of Saale weakened his position in the Reformation. When the Protestants were defeated in the Schmalkaldic War (1546–47) and the league dissolved, Philip was captured and imprisoned. Released in 1552, he devoted his remaining years to reunifying the Catholics and Protestants in his country.

1564 Pope Pius IV (pope 1559–65) ordered his bishops, superiors and scholars to subscribe to the *Professio Fidei*, the *Profession of the Tridentine Faith* lately fromulated at the Council of Trent (1545–63), as the new and final definition of the Roman Catholic faith.

1618 The Synod of Dort was convened in the Dutch commune of Dordrecht. Ostensibly intended to be a general council of the Calvinist churches, its primary agenda was to pass judgment upon the Arminian controversy. Perhaps it was because the representatives from Holland far outnumbered those from England, the Palatinate, Hesse, Switzerland and Bremen, that the council voted to condemn the five articles of the Remonstrance (a document signed by 45 Calvinist ministers defending Arminianism), and to banish those ministers who had signed it. The synod closed on May 9, 1619.

1804 Anglican missionary to Persia Henry Martyn remarked in his journal: "God and eternal things are my only pleasure."

1874 Death of Edward Mote (b.1797), English cabinetmaker. As a young adult, he settled in Southwark, a suburb of London, where he became a successful cabinetmaker and a devoted pastor. He was a Calvinist, and in 1852 started a 21-year pastorate at the Baptist church at Horsham, Sussex. At the age of 37, Mote penned the lines to the hymn "My Hope Is Built on Nothing Less."

1907 Death of Francis Thompson (b.1859), English poet. Originally educated for the Roman Catholic priesthood, Thompson later began a study of medicine but became a hopeless opium addict who wandered throughout London for three years. Rescued in 1888 by Wilfred Meynell, Thompson published his first volume entitled *Poems* in 1893. In all his writings he forms a unique blend of the wild imagery of the drug addict, the asceticism of the mystic and a sacramental conception of nature. His classic work is "The Hound of Heaven," which portrays God patiently tracking the wayward soul just as a hunting dog tirelessly pursues its prey.

November 14

1558 Dutch Anabaptist patriarch Menno Simons commented in a letter: "We ought not to dread death so. It is but to cease from sin and to enter into a better life."

1739 English revivalist George Whitefield explained in his journal: "We can preach the Gospel of Christ no further than we have experienced the power of it in our own hearts."

1741 English revivalist George Whitefield (1714–70) married the widow Elizabeth Burnell (ca.1705–ca.1768) in Wales. He was 27 and she was about 36.

1831 Death of Georg W.F. Hegel (b.1770), German philosopher. Having taught from 1793–1816 at the universities of Frankfurt, Jena and Nurnberg, Hegel moved to the University of Berlin in 1818. His fame grew rapidly and he became the foremost German philosopher of his day. Hegel believed that God sought to manifest himself in history through the process of reconciling contradictions. Hegel's code words for this process were: "thesis," "antithesis" and "synthesis." Christianity was, to Hegel, the highest synthesis, or solution, of all religious systems. However, he was basically pantheistic.

1890 The Central American Mission was founded by C.I. Scofield in Dallas, Texas. In 1975 it adopted the new name C.A.M. International because of increased geographical expansion. C.A.M. International is an interdenominational, fundamentalist mission engaged in evangelism, church planting, theological education, literature production and Gospel broadcasting. Its overseas staff of over 200 works in seven Central American countries and Spain.

1941 Inter-Varsity Christian Fellowship was incorporated in Chicago, Illinois. Headquartered today in Madison, Wisconsin, I.V.C.F. is an interdenominational, evangelical agency that seeks to establish student fellowship chapters at colleges, universities, schools of nursing and seminaries. From the standpoint of missions, I.V.C.F. is engaged in evangelism, missionary orientation, discipleship and literature distribution. The organization has a combined full- and short-term overseas staff of nearly 400.

1953 Death of Karl P. Harrington (b.1861), American Methodist classics scholar and author of the Christmas hymn "There's a Song in the Air." Well known for his Latin skills, he taught at the universities of North Carolina and Maine, as well as Wesleyan University. He also served in several Methodist churches as organist and choir director, and was one of the music editors for the 1905 edition of the *Methodist Hymnal*.

November 15

1280 Death of Albert Magnus (b.1193), German Dominican theologian. He entered the Dominican order in 1223. His teaching career included lecturing at Dominican schools in Germany (1228–45), teaching at Paris (1245–48), then at Cologne (1248–55). Albert was the first medieval Christian scholar to master the entire body of Aristotle's writings. During his career he wrote 21 massive volumes, mainly commentaries on Aristotle and theological studies based on Aristotelian philosophy. His main interest lay in reconciling philosophy and Christianity. Albert believed that no real truth contradicted Christian revelation; therefore, he invited scholars to use all human knowledge in the investigation of divine mysteries. Albert's theology contributed greatly to the development of Scholasticism. He was St. Thomas Aquinas's teacher.

1731 Birth of William Cowper, English poet, in Hertfordshire, England. Originally trained for the legal profession, Cowper passed the bar in 1754 but never practiced law. Stress led to deep depression, from which Cowper never fully recovered. He made his home with the Rev. Morley Unwin and later with Anglican hymnwriter John Newton in Olney. Cowper and Newton produced *Olney Hymns* (1779), one of the most significant collections of English hymnody. Before his death in 1800, Cowper was recognized as the greatest English poet of his day. Two of his most popular verses are sung as the hymns "Oh, for a Closer Walk with God" and "There Is a Fountain Filled with Blood."

1760 Anglican hymnwriter John Newton remarked in a letter: "Our love to Him is the proof and measure of what we know of His love to us."

1794 Death of John Witherspoon (b.1723), American Presbyterian clergyman. Born and raised in Scotland, Witherspoon was licensed to preach in 1743. In 1768 he accepted the invitation to serve as president of the College of New Jersey (modern Princeton University). During the American Revolution, the college was closed, and Witherspoon was voted to represent New Jersey in the Continental Congress from 1776–82. Witherspoon signed the Declaration of Independence—the only clergyman among the signers. Witherspoon became totally blind in 1790, four years before his death.

1804 Anglican missionary to Persia Henry Martyn commented in his journal: "Corruption always begins the day, but morning prayer never fails to set my mind in a right frame."

1839 Famed Scottish clergyman Robert Murray McCheyne declared in a letter: "I know well that when Christ is nearest, Satan also is busiest."

1890 Birth of Anders Nygren, Swedish Lutheran theologian, in Goteborg, Sweden. Ordained into the Church of Sweden in 1912, he pastored for eight years before turning to teaching. He was active in Lutheran world affairs as well as in the formation of the World Council of Churches. He served as president of the Lutheran World Federation from 1947–52, and was chairman of the W.C.C.'s Faith and Order Commission on Christ and the Church from 1953–63. His best-known books include *Agape and Eros* (1930; English translation 1953), *Christ and His Church* (1955; English translation 1957), and *Meaning and Method* (1972).

1907 Death of Horatio R. Palmer (b.1834), American Congregational clergyman and author of the hymn "Yield Not to Temptation." After being trained in music in New York, Berlin and Florence, Palmer became head of the music department of Rushford Academy in New York in 1857. He also served as organist and choir director in Rushford's Baptist Church. He later edited a music journal, published several writings and conducted music festivals. For 15 years (1877–91) he was dean of the summer school of music at Chautauqua, New York.

1917 Death of Oswald Chambers (b.1874), Scottish Bible teacher and evangelical mystic. The son of a Scottish Baptist pastor, Chambers was converted after hearing C.H. Spurgeon preach. While studying for the Baptist ministry, Chambers met William Quarrier, and from him learned a simplicity of faith and prayer. For three years he worked as a traveling missioner for the Pentecostal League of Prayer (founded by Reader Harris). He then became principal of the League's Bible Training College at Clapham Common in London. Chambers died in 1917 in Egypt, after two years of working as a Y.M.C.A. chaplain among the desert troops. He was a man of mystic faith and intense prayer, who taught that the Christian life was to be a victorious one. His most important book is his classic devotional *My Utmost for His Highest*, still in print and available in several languages.

November 16

1894 Death of James McCosh (b.1811), Free Church of Scotland philosopher and educator. Licensed in the Church of Scotland in 1834, McCosh entered the Free Church of Scotland at the Disruption in 1843. He was professor of logic and metaphysics at Queen's College in Belfast from 1852–68. After an initial visit to America, he was elected president of Princeton College in 1868 and held the position for 20 years. McCosh prepared the way for Princeton College to become a university. He was one of the first orthodox clergymen in America to accept and defend the theory of evolution. A prolific author, one of McCosh's many writings was *The Supernatural in Relation to the Natural*.

1895 Death of Samuel Francis Smith (b.1808), American Baptist clergyman. A graduate of Andover Theological Seminary in 1834, he pastored Baptist churches in Waterville, Maine (1834–42) and in Newton, Massachusetts (1842–54). He later became editorial secretary of the American Baptist Missionary Union. Smith held a lifelong interest in hymnology and is credited with having written about 100 hymns. In 1843 he helped compile *The Psalmist*, the most widely used Baptist hymnal of its day. Today, however, Smith is best remembered as the author of "My Country, 'Tis of Thee" (a.k.a. "America"), written at age 23 while Smith was still in seminary.

1928 The Women's Home Missionary Society of Oak Park, Illinois, canceled a lecture by Miss Maude Royden, an English preacher and Bible teacher, when it learned that Miss Royden smoked cigarettes.

1946 The Evangelical United Brethren Church was organized at Johnstown, Pennsylvania. The new denomination resulted from a merger of the Evangelical Church and the Church of the United Brethren in Christ. The membership of the new denomination was 700,000. (The E.U.B. Church later merged with the Methodists in 1968 to form the United Methodist Church.)

1952 The religious program *Our Goodly Heritage* first aired over CBS television. This Sunday-morning Bible study program was hosted by William Rush Baer of New York University. It was broadcast more than five years, until Jan. 1958.

November 17

3 B.C. According to early Christian theologian Clement of Alexandria (c.155–c.220 A.D.), Jesus Christ was born on this date.

331 Birth of Julian the Apostate, Roman emperor from 361–63. A half brother of Constantine the Great, Julian was raised in a Christian home, but turned to Greek and pagan philosophies by age 25. He was sent to Gaul in 355 by Emperor Constantius II to fight German invaders. While there, he won the Roman troops to his cause, and in 361 marched into Constantinople as the undisputed new emperor. He reigned only 18 months, but set out to reform the government along pagan ideals. By this time, Julian hated Christianity and rejected it as mere superstition. During an expedition against hostile Persians in 363, he was mortally wounded in a battle at Ctesiphon, the Persian capital. Julian was the last emperor to attempt establishing pagan religion in the Roman Empire.

1558 Upon the death of Roman Catholic monarch Mary Tudor, the Church of England was reestablished.

1624 Death of Jacob Boehme (b.1575), German pietist and mystic. Though he spent his life as an uneducated shoemaker, Boehme underwent several mystical visions beginning in 1600. Two of his books, *The Beginning of Dawn* (1612) and *The Way to Christ* 1623), reflect these experiences. His theology shifts much throughout his writings, and no single theory fits all his work.

Nevertheless, his life and writings greatly influenced both German and English Pietism.

1775 Anglican hymnwriter John Newton observed in a letter: "Rational assent may be the act of our natural reason; faith is the effect of immediate almighty power. Faith is always efficacious, whereas assent is often given where it has little or no influence upon the conduct."

1871 A national council of Congregational churches was formed in Oberlin, Ohio.

1874 Birth of B.H. (Burnet Hillman) Streeter, English New Testament scholar, in Croydon, England. He was closely associated with Oxford University from 1899–1933, and was canon of Hereford from 1915–34. Streeter sought to correlate theology with science in his writings. He was an active supporter of the Student Christian Movement, and later Frank Buchman's Oxford Group Movement. While Streeter's main interest was in the philosophy of religion, his most significant book is on New Testament textual studies: *The Four Gospels: A Study of Origins* (1924).

1875 The Theosophical Society of America was founded in New York City by Russian spiritualist Helena Petrovna Blavatsky. Theosophy regards reality as one basic, eternal principle beyond human understanding, yet attainable with help from secret divine wisdom transmitted by "masters" or "mahatmas." Although Theosophy has been influential in popularizing Asian religion in the West, it is regarded by Christian orthodoxy as a heresy, akin to the basic beliefs of the ancient heresy Gnosticism.

1876 English-born Rodney ("Gipsy") Smith (1860–1947) was converted to Christ at age 16. Smith was an English Wesleyan evangelist and singer whose preaching emphasized the love of God.

1981 Death of Reuben Larson (b.1897), missions pioneer. In 1931 Larson and Clarence W. Jones co-founded the World Radio Missionary Fellowship in Lima, Ohio. Headquartered today in Opa Locka, Florida, W.R.M.F. is an interdenominational, evangelical organization that broadcasts the Gospel in 15 languages. Also involved in evangelism, Bible correspondence courses, medicine and literature distribution, World Radio Missionary Fellowship utilizes over 220 overseas staff in eight countries around the world.

November 18

1302 Pope Boniface VIII published the bull *Unam Sanctam* against Philip IV (the Fair) of France, condemning Philip's political interference with the affairs of the Church. The papal decree set in writing for the first time the claim that spiritual power took precedent over temporal power. *Unam Sanctam* was also the first papal document to declare that subjection to the pope is necessary to salvation.

1784 American-born Anglican priest Samuel Seabury (1729–96) was ordained a bishop in Scotland. He returned to the U.S. to help found the American Protestant Episcopal Church (the Episcopalians), a denomination independent from the Church of England. Seabury became the first American-born bishop in the American Episcopal Church.

1804 Anglican missionary to Persia Henry Martyn recorded in his journal: "Had I ten thousand lives, my calm judgment, unruffled by dangers, testifies that they ought all to be spent for Christ. But when the trying hour comes, how shall I feel? Yet I have that promise, 'As thy day, so shall thy strength be.' "

1849 Birth of Russell K. Carter, American Methodist clergyman and author of both words and music to the hymn "Standing on the Promises," in Baltimore, Maryland. Graduating from the Pennsylvania Military Academy in 1867, he returned two years later to begin a 20-year teaching career there. In 1887 he was ordained into the Methodist ministry, and soon after became active in camp meetings with the Wesleyan Holiness movement. A prolific writer, he co-edited *Hymns of the Christian Life* in 1891 with Christian and Missionary Alliance founder, A.B. Simpson.

1866 English hymnwriter Katherine Hankey (1834–1911) penned the verse that we sing as the hymn "I Love to Tell the Story."

1874 Delegates from 17 states met (through Nov. 20) in Cleveland, Ohio, to form the Women's Christian Temperance Union (W.C.T.U.). The organization grew out of an increasing concern by women over liquor traffic in the midwestern states. Mrs. Annie Wittenmyer was elected the first president. Carry Nation (1846–1911) and Frances Willard (1839–98) were later associated with the W.C.T.U.

1893 Pope Leo XIII published the encyclical *Providentissimus Deus*, which strongly encouraged Roman Catholic educators to teach sound courses in biblical introduction and interpretation. The document launched a new era in Roman Catholic biblical studies.

1966 This was the last required meatless Friday for American Roman Catholics. In February of this year, Pope Paul VI made an apostolic decree that prayer or charitable works might be substituted as penance instead of fasting and abstinence, thus authorizing bishops' conferences in each nation to make their own decisions. The U.S. Council of Bishops announced a Dec. 2 end to the ban on this date, but Friday, Nov. 25, followed Thanksgiving Day and was already exempted from the penance by tradition.

1978 In Jonestown, Guyana, 913 members of Jim Jones's People's Temple cult committed suicide by poisoning themselves and their families. Over 200 children were found among the dead. Most of the sect's members were American citizens. The People's Temple had previously been based in San Francisco, California.

November 19

1742 English revivalist George Whitefield advised in a letter: "Plead His promises, be much in secret prayer, and never give God rest, till your soul is filled with all His fulness."

1745 The Earl of Chesterfield encouraged in a letter to his son: "Be wiser than other people if you can, but do not tell them so."

1862 Birth of William Ashley ("Billy") Sunday, American Presbyterian revivalist, in Ames, Iowa. Orphaned during the American Civil War, Sunday spent part of his boyhood in Army orphanages. From 1883–91, he was a professional baseball player with the National League, playing for Chicago, Pittsburgh and Philadelphia. He was converted to Christ in 1886 through the street preaching of Harry Monroe of the Pacific Garden Mission in Chicago. From 1891–93, he worked for the Chicago Y.M.C.A., and from 1893–95, was associated with Presbyterian evangelist J. Wilbur Chapman. In 1903 Sunday was ordained to the Presbyterian ministry. Working as an evangelist from 1893–1935, Sunday's staunch conservative preaching was fiery, dramatic and unconventional. Yet its unique style attracted immense crowds. Before his death in 1935, it is estimated that Sunday held over 300 evangelistic campaigns, spoke to a total audience of 100 million and led as many as 300,000 souls to Christ.

1885 Birth of Haldor Lillenas, American hymnwriter, in Bergen, Norway. Emigrating to the U.S. as a child, Lillenas grew up in the Lutheran church. Converted at age 21, he soon felt called to preach and to write Christian music. He and his wife traveled across the country as evangelists, and later pastored at several Nazarene churches in California, Texas, Indiana and Illinois. In 1924 he founded the Lillenas Music Co. in Indianapolis, Indiana, which merged with the Nazarene Publishing Co. in 1930. Lillenas remained with his company as music editor for 20 years. He wrote approximately 4,000 Gospel texts and hymn tunes, including "Wonderful Grace of Jesus," "It Is Glory Just to Walk with Him," "Jesus Has Lifted Me," "Peace, Peace, Wonderful Peace" and "My Wonderful Lord."

1900 Death of Samuel J. Stone (b.1839), Anglican clergyman. Ordained in 1862, Stone served as curate in two churches (1862–74), then vicar (1874–90) and finally rector of a church in London (1890–1900). During his pastorates, he published five collections of hymns, which included his hymn "The Church's One Foundation."

1929 Death of Arthur H. Mann (b.1850), English organist of sacred music. He served a record 53 years as church organist at King's College Chapel in Cambridge. He also became a skilled director of boys' choirs, and was considered an authority on G.F. Handel. Mann also composed a hymn tune that has remained popular: ANGEL'S STORY ("O Jesus, I Have Promised").

November 20

1572 The first Presbyterian meeting house in England was established at Wandsworth, Surrey.

1786 Birth of Carl Maria von Weber, famed German composer. He founded the German national opera and gained his greatest fame as an opera writer, although he also composed symphonies, masses, cantatas, chamber music and piano compositions. He is best remembered for his hymn tune JEWETT, to which we sing the hymn "My Jesus, As Thou Wilt."

1847 Death of Henry Francis Lyte (b.1793), Scottish clergyman. Ordained in 1815, Lyte was frail his entire life, and in later years had asthma and consumption. During his last 23 years, he pastored a poor parish among the fisherfolk of Lower Brixham, England. There he authored the hymn "Jesus, I My Cross Have Taken." In deteriorating health, Lyte preached his last sermon only six weeks before his death. About this time, he also penned the hymn

"Abide with Me, Fast Falls the Eventide."

1850 Blind American hymnwriter Fanny Crosby (1820–1915) underwent a dramatic conversion experience at a Methodist revival meeting. Though always devout and religious from childhood, Miss Crosby described this special day in her 30th year by saying, "The Lord planted a star in my life and no cloud has ever obscured its light." In 1865 Miss Crosby began writing the first of thousands of hymn texts, many of which remain popular to this day, including "Rescue the Perishing," "Jesus, Keep Me Near the Cross" and "All the Way My Savior Leads Me."

1872 The hymn "I Need Thee Every Hour" by Annie Sherwood Hawks (1836–1918) was first sung at a National Baptist Sunday School Convention in Cincinnati, Ohio.

1945 In Nuremberg, Germany, the trial of 22 German Nazi war leaders began. It was the first such trial under international law. In Sept. 1946 the Nuremberg International Tribunal announced its verdicts. The tribunal acquitted only three of the defendants, convicting the rest of various atrocities against the Jewish people. The sentences ranged from ten years' imprisonment to death.

1961 The Russian Orthodox Church joined the World Council of Churches.

November 21

1620 The first social contract for a New England colony, the Mayflower Compact, was drafted and signed by 41 adult males in Provincetown Harbor, Massachusetts. The Pilgrims did not settle there, but soon went on to Plymouth.

1638 A general assembly at Glasgow (through Dec. 20) abolished the episcopal form of church government, adopted the presbyterian form in its place, settled liturgy and canons, and gave final constitutional form to the Church of Scotland.

1768 Birth of F.D.E. (Friedrich) Schleiermacher, German theologian/philosopher, in Breslau, Germany. Ordained in 1794, he was soon caught up in the romantic movement, the intellectual avant-garde of that day. Schleiermacher rejected the emotion-stripping rationalism of the Enlightenment that swept 18th century Europe. His first major publication was *On Religion: Speeches to Its Cultured Despisers* (1799). Schleiermacher pointed out that the rationalists had reduced religion to mere knowledge and dogma, and morality to mere conscience. He claimed that the true religious element of human experience was located in feeling, which yields an immediate experience of God, not in the cognitive or moral faculties. In *The Christian Faith* (1821), Schleiermacher declared that true religion was "a feeling of absolute dependence" or "God-consciousness." Scripture and theology were merely agents by which to record the religious experiences (feelings) of previous generations. For Schleiermacher, Christ was a sinless man, not God incarnate.

1837 Birth of John Henry Yates, American clergyman, in Batavia, New York. He worked as a shoe salesman and later as a hardware store manager. In 1886 Yates entered the Methodist ministry, then transferred into the Baptist ministry. Under the influence and encouragement of D.L. Moody's song evangelist Ira D. Sankey, Yates wrote several Gospel songs, including "Faith Is the Victory."

1852 Union Institute was chartered by the Methodists in Randolph County, North Carolina, as a normal college. The school was renamed Trinity College in 1859. Its campus moved to Durham, North Carolina, in 1892. Upon receipt of a $40 million endowment from tobacco magnate James B. Duke in 1924, Trinity changed its name to Duke University.

1907 Birth of Jim Bishop, American journalist and author, in Jersey City, New Jersey. Bishop has given new life to great historical moments through his books, including the chronicle *The Day Christ Died* (1957).

1943 German Lutheran theologian Dietrich Bonhoeffer, while imprisoned by the Nazis, observed in a letter: "A prison cell, in which one waits, hopes, does various unessential things, and is completely dependent on the fact that the door of freedom has to be opened from the outside, is not a bad picture of Advent."

1948 The religious program *Lamp unto My Feet* first aired over CBS television. This Sunday morning broadcast featured programs on cultural as well as religious themes. It was produced for CBS News by Pamela Ilott, and became one of TV's longest-running network shows, airing through Jan. 1979.

November 22

1840 Birth of Daniel W. Whittle, American evangelist, in Chicopee Falls, Massachusetts. A Union major in the American Civil War, Whittle became an evangelist in 1873 under D.L. Moody's influence. He was joined in his campaigns by three of the foremost music evangelists of his day: P.P. Bliss, J. McGranahan and G.C. Stebbins. Whittle also wrote a number of hymns during his years of ministry, including "Have You Any Room for Jesus?", "I Know Whom I Have Believed," "Moment by Moment" and "Showers of Blessing."

1849 Austin College was chartered in Huntsville, Texas, by Presbyterians. In 1876 the school campus was moved to Sherman, Texas.

1873 American hymnwriter Horatio G. Spafford's four daughters drowned. The ship on which they were passengers, the S.S. *Ville du Havre*, was struck by the English ship *Lochearn* and sank in less than 12 minutes. Spafford's wife survived the disaster, and wired Spafford of the tragedy. In mid-December Spafford took another ship to meet his wife who had gone to Wales with other survivors. While on the high seas, near the scene of the November tragedy, Spafford penned the words to the hymn "It is Well with My Soul."

1900 Death of Arthur S. Sullivan (b.1842), English composer. He was famous for his work with Sir W.S. Gilbert and the Savoy comic operas. However, Sullivan also composed two hymn tunes which still remain popular: ST. GERTRUDE ("Onward, Christian Soldiers") and ST. KEVIN ("Come, Ye Faithful, Raise the Strain").

1950 Death of Paul William Fleming (b.1910), missions pioneer, in a Wyoming plane crash on his way to South America with a group of missionaries. In

1942 Fleming and Cecil A. Dye co-founded the New Tribes Mission in Los Angeles, California. Headquartered in Sanford, Florida, N.T.M. is an interdenominational, fundamentalist sending agency engaged in missionary training, church planting, literature production and mission aviation. Its overseas staff of nearly 1,500 work in 18 countries around the world. Dye was slain by Indians in 1943.

1963 Death of C.S. Lewis (b.1898), Anglican scholar, novelist and Christian writer. He taught at both Oxford (1924–54) and Cambridge (1954–63) universities. During his early 30s, Lewis was converted from a faith in intellect to Jesus Christ. Of his many books, Lewis is known best for his children's classic *The Chronicles of Narnia* (1950–56), his science fiction novels and Christian apologetical works. Two of his classics include *The Screwtape Letters* (1943) and *The Great Divorce* (1946). Lewis's apologetics, which are largely inductive, appeals greatly to both evangelicals and skeptics. He assumes no dogma except that which has an immediate or ultimate evidence from the natural or conceptual world to support it.

November 23

1742 English revivalist George Whitefield recommended in a letter: "Two things I would earnestly recommend to your constant study: the book of God, and your own heart. These two, well understood, will make you an able minister of the New Testament."

1872 Death of John Bowring (b.1792), English statesman and author of the hymn "In the Cross of Christ I Glory." He began adult life as a woolen goods manufacturer. Increasing involvement in world trade polished his gift for languages. An outstanding linguist of his day, Bowring claimed to understand 200 languages and speak 100. Beginning in 1835, he was actively involved in Parliament. A prolific author, Bowring's writings were published after his death in 36 volumes.

1895 Death of Sylvanus D. Phelps (b.1816), American Baptist clergyman. Ordained in 1846, he pastored churches in Connecticut and Rhode Island for 30 years. In 1876 he became editor of the religious journal *The Christian Secretary*. Phelps published a number of writings during his lifetime, both verse and prose. One of his poems became the text for the hymn "Savior, Thy Dying Love."

1899 Death of Robert Lowry (b.1826), American Baptist clergyman and sacred music composer. He served Baptist pastorates for 45 years (1854–99) in Pennsylvania, New York and New Jersey. Lowry became interested in writing sacred music during the 1860s, and later collaborated with W.H. Doane in publishing nearly two dozen hymnals. Among his many successful compositions are the tunes for the hymns "Marching to Zion," "All the Way My Savior Leads Me," and "I Need Thee Every Hour," as well as the words and music of "Christ Arose," and "Nothing but the Blood of Jesus."

1906 Death of William Wrede (b.1859), German Lutheran New Testament scholar. He taught at the universities of Gottingen and Breslau from 1891–1906. Applying the tenets of strict historical criticism to the New Testament, Wrede contended that the Gospels represented the theology of the primitive church rather than a true biographical history of Jesus; and that the Apostle Paul was the real founder or formulator of 1st century Christianity. Wrede's name appeared in the title of Albert Schweitzer's theological classic: *The Quest of the Historical Jesus: From Reimarus to Wrede* (1906).

1947 E.L. Sukenik of the Hebrew University of Jerusalem received the first information about the discovery of the Dead Sea Scrolls. These documents had been accidentally discovered during the preceding winter (1946–47) by two Bedouin shepherds in the vicinity of Qumran. The scrolls are dated roughly between 200 B.C.—A.D. 70. They are considered by many to be the outstanding archeological find of this century in the field of Old Testament Studies.

November 24

1531 Death of Johannes Oecolampadius (b.1482), German-born Swiss reformer. His early studies took him to Bologna, Heidelberg and Tubingen. In 1515 he was called to Basel, Switzerland, to preach. While there he came under the influence of both Erasmus and Luther. By 1522 he was a strong advocate of the Reformation doctrines. He became pastor at the Church of St. Martin in Basel, where he remained until his death. The following year, he also began teaching Scripture at the university. Oecolampadius promoted Protestantism in his writings throughout Switzerland. His influence, mainly in the area of Zwinglian theology, helped lead to the formation of the Reformed Church.

1572 Death of John Knox (b.ca.1514), Scottish reformer. Ordained to the Roman Catholic priesthood in 1536, he was converted to Protestantism 10 years later under George Wishart. He preached in England until Catholic Queen Mary gained the throne; then he fled to the Continent. In 1553 he met with John Calvin in Geneva, where he thoroughly studied the Presbyterian and Calvinist doctrines. Knox returned to Scotland in 1559 and boldly preached the doctrines of the Reformation. The following year, Protestantism was established as the national religion. Knox's most notable writing is *History of the Reformation of Religion within the Realm of Scotland* (1644).

1703 In Philadelphia, Pennsylvania, the Rev. Justus Falckner became the first Lutheran pastor to be ordained in the U.S.

1713 Birth of Father Junipero Serra, Spanish Franciscan missionary to America, in Majorca, Spain. He first arrived in Mexico in 1749, where he did missionary work for 20 years. He extended his labors to upper California in 1769, and established 9 of the first 21 Franciscan missions founded along the Pacific coast. Serra baptized some 6,000 Indians and became one of the cultural pioneers of California. He died in 1784.

1860 Death of George Croly (b.1780), Irish clergyman and author of the hymn "Spirit of God, Descend upon My Heart." Ordained in 1804, Croly went to London to devote himself to writing. He published several biographies, histories and religious books. He was strongly opposed to liberalism. In 1835 he was appointed to St. Stephen's Church in Walbrook, one of London's poorer sections.

1865 Birth of A.S. (Arthur Samuel) Peake, English Methodist Bible commentator, in Leek, England. He taught at Mansfield College in Oxford from 1889–92. In 1892 he began a lifelong teaching position at Hartley College in Manchester. In 1904 he also became the first Rylands professor of biblical exegesis at Manchester University. Peake's many writings, though scholarly, were directed at the popular reader. His best-known work was the one-volume commentary on the Bible (1919), which he edited. The work was the first to introduce the English layman to the emerging branches of biblical criticism.

1941 American Trappist monk Thomas Merton explained in his *Secular Journal*: "Spiritual dryness is an acute experience of longing—therefore of love."

1964 The U.S. Air Force dropped 600 Belgian paratroopers into Stanleyville, in the Congo, to rescue white hostages held captive by Congolese rebels. Minutes before the paratroopers landed, 29 hostages were executed, including American medical missionary Dr. Paul E. Carlson. Eighty whites were discovered to have been slain by the rebels.

November 25

2348 B.C. According to Archbishop James Ussher's chronology, the Great Deluge, or Noah's Flood, began on this date.

1697 Birth of Gerhard Tersteegen, German hymnwriter, in Prussia. His plans for seminary were thwarted by his father's death, and he became an apprentice to his brother, a shopkeeper. Converted to Christ at age 16, he gave himself to prayer, fasting and almsgiving. For several years he lived alone as a ribbon weaver, suffering bouts of deep spiritual depression. Recovering in 1724, he began doing religious teaching supported by gifts from friends. He lived the remainder of his years as a celibate and ascetic. He wrote the hymn "God Calling Yet. Shall I Not Hear?"

1742 In New York, colonial churchman David Brainerd (1718–47) was examined and approved as a missionary to the New England Indians by representatives of the Scottish Society for the Propagating of Christian Knowledge (S.P.C.K.). Brainerd worked heroically, between April 1743 and Nov. 1746, for the conversion of the Indians of New York and eastern Pennsylvania. He met his greatest success among the Indians of New Jersey. In 1747 he was forced by an advanced case of tuberculosis to relinquish his work. He died in October that same year.

1748 Death of Isaac Watts (b.1674), founder of modern English hymnody. In 1699 he became the assistant, and later the pastor, of a dissenting church in London. Watts published the first of many hymn collections in 1706. His originality redefined English hymnody. He wrote nearly 600 hymns, including "At the Cross," "Come, We That Love the Lord," "Jesus Shall Reign Where'er the Sun," "Am I a Soldier of the Cross?" "When I Survey the Wondrous Cross" and "Joy to the World."

1787 Birth of Franz Gruber, German teacher and church organist, near Hochburg, Austria. From 1807–29, he was a schoolteacher at Arnsdorf. To supplement his income, he served as organist at the St. Nicholas Church in nearby Oberndorf in 1816. Later he became headmaster at Berndorf (1828–32), and from 1833 until his death 30 years later, choirmaster at Hallein, near Salzburg. Gruber penned more than 90 music compositions, but his fame endures for the single tune he wrote in Dec. 1818: STILLE NACHT ("Silent Night, Holy Night").

1807   Anglican missionary to Persia, Henry Martyn, recorded this in his journal: "With thee, O my God, there is no disappointment; I shall never have to regret that I loved thee too well."

1820   English poet and Oxford Movement leader John Keble (1792–1866) penned the words to the hymn "Sun of My Soul."

1846   Birth of Carry A. (Amelia) Nation, American temperance leader, in Garrard County, Kentucky. Following an unhappy marriage to a drunkard, she became a fiery advocate for the cause of temperance. In 1889 the imposing six-foot, 175-pound Nation gained notoriety by wrecking all the saloons in Medicine Lodge, Kansas. In 1901 she added to her reputation by hatcheting saloons in Wichita and Topeka, Kansas. Lecturing widely, she was also an advocate of women's suffrage.

1851   The first Y.M.C.A. was organized in North America, in Boston, Massachusetts. Chapters were soon formed in other American cities. The Y.M.C.A. was originally established in London in 1844 by George Williams and 12 others. The first North American convention of the Y.M.C.A. was held in Buffalo, New York, in 1854.

1854   Death of John Kitto (b.1804), English writer. A fall at age 12 left him permanently deaf. Kitto turned to reading, became a lover of books and began a lifelong writing profession. Between 1824–33, he intermittently served as a missionary. Kitto's most popular publications were written after he returned to England: *Cyclopedia of Biblical Literature* (1843–45) and his eight-volume *Daily Bible Illustrations* (beginning in 1850). His *Cyclopedia* set a new pattern in biblical encyclopedias, combining articles on religion, scholarly biography, rabbinical literature and New Testament archeology in the same work. These elements were soon considered basic ingredients of a good Bible dictionary, and Kitto's work became the conceptual basis for McClintock & Strong's ten-volume *Cyclopaedia of Biblical, Theological, and Ecclesiastical Literature* (1867–81).

1864   British statesman Benjamin Disraeli declared in a speech delivered at Oxford: "Man is a being born to believe, and if no church comes forward with all the title deeds of truth, he will find altars and idols in his own heart and his own imagination."

1877   Death of William H. Bathurst (b.1796), Anglican clergyman and author of the hymn "Oh, for a Faith That Will Not Shrink." Ordained in 1818, he was rector of Barwick-in-Elmet, near Leeds, England, for 32 years (1820–52). He then resigned from the Church of England over conflict with the sacramental doctrines in the *Book of Common Prayer*, particularly regarding the baptismal and burial services. Bathurst retired to his family estate in 1863 and died there 14 years later.

1899   Death of Robert Lowry (b.1826), American Baptist clergyman. Between 1854 and his death, Lowry pastored churches in Pennsylvania, New York and

New Jersey. He began writing sacred music during the 1860s and collaborated with William H. Doane in the publication of nearly two dozen collections of Gospel hymns. Lowry's best-known hymn tunes include: "Marching to Zion," "All the Way My Savior Leads Me," SOMETHING FOR THEE ("Savior, Thy Dying Love") and "I Need Thee Every Hour." Lowry also penned both the words and music to "Christ Arose" and "Nothing but the Blood of Jesus."

1934 Death of George Milligan (b.1860), Scottish Bible scholar. He taught at Glasgow University from 1910–32. In 1926 he was elected the first chairman of the Scottish Sunday School Union. Milligan published many books and articles on biblical languages. His most important contribution to New Testament scholarship is no doubt *The Vocabulary of the Greek Testament* (1914–29), which he co-edited with J.H. Moulton.

1956 Death of Ludwig H. Koehler (b.1880), German reformed Semitics scholar. Ordained into the Swiss Reformed Church in 1904, he began teaching at the University of Zurich in 1908, not retiring until 1947. Of Koehler's many publications, his most important contribution to Old Testament scholarship is his three-volume Old Testament Hebrew lexicon co-edited with W. Baumgartner: *Lexicon in Vetereris Testamenti Libros* (1948–53).

1960 Birth of Amy (Lee) Grant, popular contemporary Christian singer and songwriter. She wrote and recorded such Christian favorites as "Never Give You Up" and "Faith Walking People."

November 26

1900 Death of Willibald Beyschlag (b.1823), German evangelical theologian. A powerful church leader in his day, Beyschlag fought for a broad-minded biblical Christianity. He rejected both Chalcedonian Christology (which stated that Christ was fully God and fully man) and D.F. Strauss's rationalistic *Life of Jesus*. Greatly concerned with national questions as well as with practical piety, Beyschlag asked why the return to traditional confessions had done so little to renew the spiritual life of the church in his day. After 1870, he helped draw up the new constitution of the Prussian Church. He was a strong supporter of the rights of the laity and of the autonomy of the church.

1901 Death of Joseph Henry Thayer (b.1828), American New Testament lexicographer. Ordained into the Congregational ministry in 1859, Thayer pastored, then taught at Harvard for 18 years. His main interest was in the Greek of the New Testament. He translated two famous German grammars by Winer and Buttmann; but the work which established Thayer's reputation as a New Testament scholar is his *Greek-English Lexicon of the New Testament* (1886), which was the standard English, New Testament lexicon for many years.

1909 Birth of Seward Hiltner, a leader in early pastoral psychology, in Tyrone, Pennsylvania. He was ordained into the United Presbyterian Church in 1935, then served three years as executive secretary of the Council for Clinical Training in New York City. He spent 12 years with the Federal Council of Churches' department of pastoral services (1938–50). He taught pastoral psychology at the University of Chicago from 1950–61 and was professor of theology and personality at Princeton Theological Seminary from 1961–80. Hiltner is the author of numerous books, including *Sex and the Christian Life*

(1957), *Preface to Pastoral Theology* (1958) and *Toward a Theology of Aging* (1976).

1914 Death of Edward Kremser (b.1838), German chorister. Kremser was a noted Viennese choir director who composed and published several vocal and instrumental works. In 1877 he adapted a late 16th-century Dutch folk melody to fit Theodore Baker's English translation of a popular religious verse: "We Gather Together to Ask the Lord's Blessing."

1922 Birth of Charles M. (Monroe) Schulz, American cartoonist, in Minneapolis, Minnesota. After serving in World War II, Schulz became a free-lance cartoonist with the *St. Paul Pioneer Press* and the *Saturday Evening Post*. In 1950 he created a strip originally entitled *Li'l Folks*. The strip later was syndicated as *Peanuts*, and has become one of the most successful American comic strips in the mid-20th century. Schulz, a Christian, bases his characters on semiautobiographical experiences. The main character, Charlie Brown, represents a five-year-old version of all of us, a sensitive but otherwise bland and unexceptional child. In recent years, *Peanuts* has been adapted to television, the stage and even two full-length animated films.

November 27

1095 Pope Urban II began promoting the First Crusade at the Council of Clermont. The first armies marched the following year, in 1096. When the crusade ended in 1099, the European soldiers had captured Antioch (1098) and Jerusalem (1099) from the Seljuk Turks, and had set up the Latin Kingdom (1099–1143).

1654 Birth of Friedrich R.L. Canitz, author of the hymn "Come, My Soul, Thou Must Be Waking."

1755 Land for the first Jewish settlement in America was purchased by Joseph Salvador, who bought 100,000 acres near Fort Ninety-Six in southern Carolina.

1787 Birth of Andrew Reed, English Congregational clergyman, in London, England. Ordained in 1811, he served as pastor of the New Road Chapel, St. George's-in-the-East, London, for fifty years (1811–61). Reed was also instrumental in helping to establish the London Orphan Asylum at Clapton, the Reedham Orphanage at Coulsdon, a mental asylum in Earlswood, the Royal Hospital for Incurables in Putney, Surrey, and the Eastern Counties Asylum at Colchester, Essex. Reed also penned several hymns, including "Holy Ghost, with Light Divine."

1862 Birth of Adelaide A. Pollard, the American hymnwriter who wrote "Have Thine Own Way, Lord," in Bloomfield, Iowa. Raised in a Presbyterian home, she taught in several girls' schools in Chicago during the 1880s and later at Nyack Missionary Training School in New York. Although plagued with frail health, Pollard was nevertheless attracted to extreme religious sects and lived the life of a mystic. She wrote a number of hymns during her life.

1874 Birth of Chaim Weizmann, Zionist leader, in Motol, Russia. He participated in the negotiations leading to the Balfour Declaration of 1917. Weizmann served as president of the World Zionist Organization (1920–29, 1935–46). When modern Israel gained its political independence, Weizmann was elected the nation's first president in 1949, serving until his death in 1952.

1950 American missionary and Auca Indian martyr Jim Elliot pointed out in his journal: "What gets me into the Kingdom, from Christ's own statement, is not saying 'Lord, Lord,' but acting 'Lord, Lord.' "

1953 English scholar and Christian apologist C.S. Lewis explained in *Letters to an American Lady*: "Anxiety is not only a pain which we must ask God to assuage but also a weakness we must ask Him to pardon—for He's told us to take no care for the morrow."

November 28

1739 English revivalist George Whitefield wrote in a letter: "Follow after, but do not run before the blessed Spirit; if you do, although you may benefit others, and God may overrule everything for your good, yet you will certainly destroy the peace of your own soul."

1757 Birth of William Blake, English poet and artist, in London, England. A mystic who claimed visions from boyhood on, Blake created his own elaborate system of religious beliefs with his poetry and art. His theology opposed both the doctrines and the asceticism of the religion of his day. His most important works were *Songs of Innocence* (1789), *Songs of Experience* (1794), and *The Marriage of Heaven and Hell* (ca.1790).

1863 Thanksgiving Day was first observed in the U.S. as an official holiday. President Lincoln had proclaimed a month earlier that a national holiday would be observed the last Thursday of November. In 1939 President Franklin Roosevelt moved Thanksgiving back a week, to stimulate Christmas shopping. But in 1941, Congress adopted a joint resolution declaring the fourth Thursday of November to be Thanksgiving Day.

1902 Death of Joseph Parker (b.1830), English Congregational preacher. His formal education all but ceased at age 16. His preaching career began when he was 28. In 1869 he began a ministry at Poultry Chapel, London. The congregation built him the City Temple, which opened in 1874. Parker pastored the church until his death. He was regarded by his generation as one of London's great pulpit masters, ranking alongside Spurgeon and Liddon in popularity. Though living during the period of liberalism in England, Parker remained unbendingly evangelical. During 1883–92, he preached through the Bible. These sermons were published in 25 volumes, under the title, *The Parker's People's Bible* (1885–95).

1904 Death of Jeremiah E. Rankin (b.1828), American Congregational clergyman. Ordained in 1855, he served pastorates in New York, Vermont, Massachusetts, Washington, D.C., and New Jersey. From 1889 until his death, he was president of Howard University. He compiled a number of Gospel songbooks and wrote several hymns, including "Tell It to Jesus" and "God Be with You Till We Meet Again."

November 29

1776 Anglican hymnwriter John Newton encouraged in a letter: "He knows our sorrows, not merely as He knows all things, but as one who has been in our situation, and who, though without sin himself, endured when upon earth inexpressibly more for us than He will ever lay upon us."

1847   Death of Marcus Whitman (b.1802), American pioneer medical missionary. In 1836 he set out with the Presbyterian church to explore and evangelize regions west of the Mississippi River, with a view toward opening a mission to the Indians. Along with his wife Narcissa and a small band of settlers, Whitman's followers were the first Americans to reach the Pacific coast by wagon train. They set up a mission in the Walla Walla River Valley of the Oregon Territory, and initially the Nez Perce, Cayuse, and Flathead Indians responded to their teaching. But when a deadly epidemic of measles broke out among the Indians, a band of superstitious Cayuse retaliated and attacked the settlement, murdering Whitman, his wife and 12 others.

1898   Birth of C.S. Lewis, Anglican scholar and Christian writer, in Belfast, Ireland. Educated at the universities of Malvern and Oxford, Lewis taught at both Oxford (1924–54) and Cambridge (1954–63) universities. Greatly admired by evangelicals for his inductive approach to Christian apologetics, Lewis's best-known writings include *Miracles* (1947), *Mere Christianity* (1952), and his autobiography *Surprised by Joy* (1955). His allegorical *The Chronicles of Narnia* (1950–56) have become classics in children's literature.

1921   Death of Augustus H. Strong (b.1836), American Baptist clergyman and theologian. While a student at Yale, he became a Christian under the preaching of Charles G. Finney. Ordained in 1861, he held pastorates in Haverhill, Massachusetts (1861–66), and in Cleveland, Ohio (1866–72). From 1872–1912, he was president of Rochester Theological Seminary, as well as teaching biblical theology there. He was the first president of the new Northern Baptist Convention (1905–10). Strong's major writings include his 13-volume *Systematic Theology* (1886) and *Philosophy and Religion* (1888).

1950   The National Council of the Churches of Christ (N.C.C.) was formed. The charter roll of 25 Protestant denominations and 5 Eastern Orthodox bodies represented 37 million church members.

1970   In Nagpur, India, a union of six churches merged to form the Church of India. These six denominations included the Anglicans (Church of India, 280,000 members), the United Church of Northern India (230,000), the Baptists (110,000), the Methodists (of the British and Australia conferences, 20,000), the Church of the Brethren (18,000), and the Disciples of Christ (16,000). Efforts toward the union had begun as early as 1929.

November 30

594   Death of St. Gregory of Tours (b.ca.539), French Roman Catholic bishop and historian. Ordained into the priesthood in 569, he governed the diocese of Tours from 573. Gregory's fame is from his *History of the Franks*, a ten-volume work he began writing about 576. It treats history from the Creation through the year 591. The last six volumes deal comprehensively with the history of Gregory's time (ca.575–91). The work comprises the major, if not the only, source of the history of Gaul during the dark and stormy time of the Merovingian kings.

1170 English Archbishop of Canterbury Thomas a Becket returned from a six-year exile in France for his opposition to the policies of Henry II. Four weeks after his return, four of Henry's knights murdered Thomas in the Canterbury cathedral.

1531 German reformer Martin Luther remarked: "Whenever I happen to be prevented by the press of duties from observing my hour of prayer, the entire day is bad for me."

1554 Under the reign of Mary Tudor (daughter of Henry VIII and Catherine of Aragon), England was temporarily reconciled with the Roman Catholic Church. In the process, "Bloody Mary" had Thomas Cranmer, Hugh Latimer, Nicholas Ridley and nearly 300 other Protestant leaders burned at the stake. However, her death in 1558 yielded the English throne to Elizabeth I (daughter of Henry VIII and Anne Boleyn), who again severed ties with Rome and re-established the Church of England.

1628 Birth of John Bunyan, English Puritan preacher and writer, near Bedford, England. In 1649 he married a Christian girl who led him to Christ four years later. Soon after, he began to preach, but at the Restoration was arrested for preaching without a license from the Established Church. Imprisoned intermittently between 1660–72, Bunyan's relative isolation and solitude helped him generate his literary masterpieces: *Grace Abounding to the Chief of Sinners* (1666) and *Pilgrim's Progress* (1678). Bunyan's theology portrayed the world as the scene of spiritual warfare; nothing else matters except the salvation of souls.

1729 Birth of Samuel Seabury, first bishop of the American Protestant Episcopal Church, in Groton, Connecticut. In 1752 Seabury went to England to complete a study of medicine. He was ordained into the Anglican Church there, and returned to America in 1754 a missionary under the Society for the Propagation of the Gospel (S.P.G.). From 1757–75 he was a missionary rector in New York. In 1784 he was consecrated a bishop in Scotland, and returned to the U.S. Following the American Revolution, Seabury helped formulate the documents that constituted the American Protestant Episcopal Church (the Episcopalians) as independent and autonomous from the Church of England.

1892 Death of F.J.A. (Fenton John Anthony) Hort (b.1828), British New Testament textual scholar. Ordained an Anglican priest in 1856, Hort pastored for the next 16 years, then became a full-time instructor at Cambridge. As early as 1853 he began working with B.F. Westcott on a critical edition of the Greek New Testament, which took nearly 30 years to complete (1881). This monumental work makes a scientific evaluation of the tremendous number of ancient New Testament manuscripts, choosing the most probable reading of the original text. Hort and Westcott's Greek New Testament has become the foundation for almost all editions of the New Testament.

1894 In Naperville, Illinois, seven groups (representing 60,000–70,000 members) of the Evangelical Association withdrew from that organization to form the United Evangelical Church. The two denominations reunited in 1922, although a minority from several congregations continued a separate existence under the name United Evangelical Church. This united denomination comprises about 27,000 members in about 160 churches.

1949 United Missionary Fellowship was incorporated in Sacramento, California. This interdenominational, fundamentalist mission organization is engaged in evangelism, church planting, theological education, Bible correspondence courses and special ministries to the deaf and blind. An overseas staff of 17 serves U.M.F. in 5 countries: Lebanon, Cyprus, Mexico, Honduras and New Zealand.

1984 The first volume of the first published Sumerian dictionary was issued by the University of Pennsylvania. Sumerian was the world's first written language. The complete dictionary was projected to run to 17 volumes. Although there are no direct references to Sumer in the Bible, it corresponds to the "land of Shinar" mentioned eight times in the Old Testament. The Sumerian culture appeared about 3,500 B.C. Our knowledge of the Sumerians helps explain some of the social and economic customs in the Old Testament.

December

December 1

1145 Pope Eugene III sent a papal bull to King Louis VII of France (1137–79), proclaiming the Second Crusade. It was written in response to the fall of the crusader outpost Edessa (in modern southeast Turkey) to the Turks the previous year. Three months later, Eugene renewed the bull, commissioning Bernard of Clairvaux to promote the crusade. Ultimately, Emperor Conrad III and Louis VII led the Second Crusade (1147–49). It failed when mistrust between Western and Eastern leaders allowed the Turkish forces to decimate the crusader army in their attempt to retake Damascus.

1635 Death of Melchior Teschner (b.1584), Silesian clergyman. He was appointed cantor of the Lutheran church at Fraustadt in 1609; he also taught in the parish school. In 1614 he became pastor at Oberprietschen; and his son and grandson succeeded him in this appointment. Teschner composed the hymn tune ST. THEODULPH, to which we sing "All Glory, Laud, and Honor."

1764 The French government issued a royal decree abolishing the Jesuit order in that country. The decree came as a result of powerful forces opposing both the Jesuits and Pope Clement XIII. The pope's successor, Clement XIV, formally suppressed the Society of Jesus in 1767; but it was restored again by Pius VII in 1814.

1798 Birth of Albert Barnes, American Presbyterian clergyman and Bible scholar, in Rome, New York. He pastored in Morristown, New Jersey (1825–30), and at the First Presbyterian Church in Philadelphia (1830–67). In 1835 he was examined by the Philadelphia presbytery for espousing an unlimited atonement. Although he was acquitted, his case became a point of discussion within his denomination, and was one of the primary causes for the 1837 split in the Presbyterian Church in the U.S. Barnes was an abolitionist and actively supported the Sunday school movement. He is best-remembered for his 11-volume *Notes on the New Testament* and *Notes on the Old Testament*, both still in print.

1880 Birth of William F. Arndt, American Missouri Lutheran theologian, at Mayville, Wisconsin. Arndt served as professor of New Testament at Concordia Seminary in St. Louis from 1921 until his death in 1957. Among his many writings are *Does the Bible Contradict Itself?* (1926) and *Fundamental Christian Beliefs* (1938). His chief contribution to New Testament scholarship was the English translation of Bauer's Greek-German lexicon, co-edited with F.W. Gingrich and published under the title *Lexicon of the Greek New Testament* (1957, rev. 1979).

1882 Death of Titus Coan (b.1801), American Episcopal missionary to Hawaii. He first reached the islands in 1835 with his wife and six other missionaries.

Coan began preaching on the shores in the native tongue in three months. By 1841 three-quarters of the adult population of Hilo Island had joined the church. Considered one of the greatest missionaries to Hawaii, Coan reported in 1870 that he had baptized and received into the church 11,960 members. He also saw a score of his people go out as foreign missionaries to the dark islands of Micronesia. Coan spent his last years as a pastor of the church at Hilo, and as supervisor of his diocese.

1909   The first Christmas club savings account was opened at a New York City bank.

1917   Nebraska parish priest Father Edward Flanagan founded Boys Town near Omaha. Ordained a Roman Catholic priest in 1912, Father Flanagan (1886–1948) began his life-long work with troubled teens in 1917. He believed there was "no such thing as a bad boy."

1926   Groundbreaking ceremonies were held for Bob Jones College. The Protestant, fundamentalist college was located nine miles from Panama City, Florida. It later relocated in Greenville, South Carolina. Today the school is called Bob Jones University.

1941   Death of Frederick John Foakes-Jackson (b.1855), Anglican biblical scholar. He taught at Cambridge University from 1882–1916, then became a professor at Union Theological Seminary in New York City from 1916–34. The author of numerous books, Jackson wrote primarily in the area of church history. His most enduring publication, which he coauthored with Kirsopp Lake, is *The Beginnings of Christianity, Part I: The Acts of the Apostles* (five vols., 1919–33).

1950   American missionary and Auca Indian martyr Jim Elliot recorded in his journal: "Unwillingness to accept God's 'way of escape' from temptation frightens me—what a rebel yet resides within."

1958   A school fire claimed the lives of 95 children and 3 nuns at the Our Lady of the Angels Parochial School in Chicago, Illinois. It was the third worst school fire in America to that time.

December 2

1381   Death of Jan Van Ruysbroeck (b.1293), Flemish Roman Catholic mystic. Ordained in 1317, he helped establish an Augustinian abbey, where he became prior in 1350. Ruysbroeck's most famous writing is his *The Spiritual Espousals* (1350), a commentary on the biblical sentence, "Behold, the bridegroom cometh" (Matt 25:6). Ruysbroeck's spiritual mysticism deeply influenced later Christian leaders such as John Tauler and Gerard Groote, founder of the Brethren of the Common Life, a mystical group of the 14th—15th centuries. His manner of combining the metaphysical with personal experience earned Ruysbroeck the title, *the Ecstatic Doctor*. He was beatified by Pope Pius X in 1908.

1831   Birth of Francis Nathan Peloubet (puh-LOO-bet), American Congregational clergyman, in New York City. Peloubet was a promoter of the Sunday school, and between 1875 and his death in 1920, he wrote 44 annual volumes of *Select Notes on the International Sunday School Lessons*, known afterward as *Peloubet's Notes*.

1873 The Reformed Episcopal Church was organized in New York City when 8 clergymen and 20 laymen broke from the Protestant Episcopal Church over a debate regarding proper ritual. There are approximately 6,500 members and 64 churches in this denomination today.

1908 The Federal Council of Churches of Christ in America was founded in Philadelphia, Pennsylvania. Thirty Protestant denominations were represented. In Nov. 1950, this ecumenical organization was replaced by the National Council of the Churches of Christ, uniting 29 denominations and 32 million members.

1929 Death of William Henry Parker (b.1845), English Baptist hymnwriter and author of the hymn "Tell Me the Stories of Jesus." Parker constructed machines for a lace company and later headed an insurance company. He was also an active member of the Chelsea Street Baptist Church in Nottingham, England. Parker had a great interest in Sunday school; and he penned several hymns for Sunday school anniversaries.

1946 Rev. E.V. Steele founded the European Christian Orphanage and Mission Society, in Alberta, Canada. In 1953 the name was changed to World Missions Fellowship. Headquartered since 1961 in Grants Pass, Oregon, this evangelical, interdenominational sending agency is engaged in evangelism, orphan care, leadership programs and camping. Its overseas staff of 16 represent W.M.F. in India, Austria, Ireland, Brazil and Japan.

1985 The International Bible Society occupied its new headquarters in Carter House in New York City. Founded in 1809, the I.B.S. is a specialized evangelical agency that translates, publishes and distributes copies of the Scriptures worldwide.

December 3

1841 Birth of Clara H. Scott, American music teacher and composer, in Elk Grove, Illinois. Born Clara Jones, she was married to Henry Clay Scott in 1861. Trained as a teacher of sacred music, she contributed several hymns to the collections published by Horatio R. Palmer. She also authored and composed the hymn "Open My Eyes, That I May See" (SCOTT).

1850 Birth of Frank Mason North, American Methodist clergyman, in New York City. Ordained in 1872, he pastored churches for 20 years in Florida, New York and Connecticut. He was also editor of *The Christian City* from 1892–1912. In 1912 he became corresponding secretary of the Methodist Board of Foreign Missions. North wrote "Where Cross the Crowded Ways of Life" and 11 other hymns, most of them for special occasions.

1902 Birth of Mitsuo Fuchida, Japanese military general, at Kashiwara-Shi, Japan. Fuchida flew the lead plane in the Japanese air attack on Pearl Harbor on Dec. 7, 1941. Through the representatives of the Pocket Testament League, he was converted to Christianity on April 14, 1950, five years after World War II ended.

1908 Birth of C.F.D. (Charles Francis Digby) Moule, Anglican clergyman and New Testament scholar, in Hangchow, China. Ordained in 1933, Moule taught at Cambridge University beginning in 1944. He was canon theologian of the Diocese of Leicester from 1955–76. He has authored numerous books and articles on New Testament studies, including *An Idiom Book of New Testament Greek* (1953), *The Phenomenon of the New Testament* (1967) and *The Origin of Christology* (1977).

1910 Death of Mary Baker Eddy (b.1821), founder of Christian Science. Born Mary Ann Morse Baker, in 1843 she married George W. Glover, who died the following year; Daniel Patterson in 1853, who deserted her; and Asa Gilbert Eddy in 1877, who died five years later. The widow Eddy, age 61, went on to fame and fortune by founding her own church. Its theology is based on "Divine Science," Mrs. Eddy's special doctrine of healing. In 1875 she published her *Science and Health, With a Key to the Scriptures*; and four years later she founded the First Church of Christ, Scientist in Boston, with herself as pastor. Mrs. Eddy's doctrines deny both disease and death as well as the deity of Christ, the Trinity, and Satan.

December 4

1154 Adrian IV (ca.1100–59) was elected the 168th pope of the Roman Catholic Church. Born Nicholas Breakspear near St. Albans, England, he has been the only Englishman to be elevated to the office of pope.

1563 The Roman Catholic Council of Trent, the 19th ecumenical council, was closed. It had been opened 18 years earlier, in 1545, in reaction to the growth of the Protestant movement in Roman Catholic Europe. With intermediate delays, the council consisted of three separate convocations: 1545–47, 1551–52 and 1562–63. At the council's end, the doctrines of the Protestant reformers Luther, Zwingli and Calvin were condemned.

1584 Birth of John Cotton, early Massachusetts Bay pastor, at Derby, England. Ordained an Anglican in 1610, Cotton began altering the liturgy to his Puritan tastes until the resulting controversy forced him to resign from the ministry in 1633. A friend of John Winthrop, Cotton emigrated to Boston that same year and worked in the Boston Puritan Church for the rest of his life (1633–52). Cotton became embroiled in the theological controversies surrounding both Roger Williams (1635) and Anne Hutchinson (1638). Cotton stressed the unconditional nature of election and the inner experience of the Holy Spirit in regeneration.

1642 Death of Armand Jean du Plessis Richelieu (b.1585), French cardinal and politician. Ordained in 1606, he was made a cardinal in 1622 by Pope Gregory XV. Richelieu exemplified the medieval use of power for both ecclesiastical and secular ends. Though a cleric, he strove to secularize politics and to shift the European balance of power from the Hapsburg dynasty to the Bourbons of France. Richelieu persecuted the Huguenots (French Protestants), yet aligned France with the Protestant powers of Germany. In 1629 Richelieu became chief minister, the virtual ruler of France.

1674 French Jesuit missionary Jacques Marquette erected a mission on the shores of Lake Michigan in Illinois. This log cabin became the first building of a settlement that became the city of Chicago, Illinois.

1804 Birth of John Kitto, English writer. A fall at age 12 left him permanently deaf, causing Kitto to turn to reading for self-education. He became a great lover of books and entered a lifelong writing profession. He served intermittently between 1824–33 as a missionary in the East. Kitto's most successful books were penned after his return to England. In 1843–45 he published the *Cyclopedia of Biblical Literature*. The work set a new pattern in for biblical encyclopedias in that it combined articles on religion, scholarly biography, rabbinical literature and archeology in the same work. These elements were later considered standard ingredients of a good Bible dictionary, and Kitto's work became the conceptual basis for McClintock and Strong's ten-volume *Cyclopaedia of Biblical, Theological and Ecclesiastical Literature* (1867–81).

1809 The International Bible Society was founded in New York City as an interdenominational agency for translating, producing and distributing the Scriptures. Since then, I.B.S. has distributed the Word of God to over 150 countries in the world.

1844 Birth of John Samuel Norris, American Methodist clergyman, in West Cowes, Isle of Wight, England. Norris was educated in Canada, where he was also ordained in 1868. He served churches for ten years in Canada, New York and Wisconsin. In 1878 he became a Congregational minister and held pastorates in Wisconsin (1878–82) and Iowa (1882–1901). He wrote more than 100 hymns, including the hymn tune NORRIS ("I Can Hear My Savior Calling"; a.k.a. "Where He Leads Me I Will Follow").

1854 Birth of Mary Reed, American missionary, in Lowell, Ohio. Sponsored by the Women's Missionary Society of the Methodist Episcopal Church, Miss Reed sailed to India in 1885. Her health broke immediately and she went to the Himalyas to recuperate. While there, she visited a leper colony at Chandag, and devoted the rest of her life to working among these people, contracting the disease herself in 1890. Mary Reed died in 1943 after completing 52 years of ministry among the lepers of India.

1859 Birth of Joseph S. Cook, Canadian clergyman and author of the hymn "Gentle Mary Laid Her Child," in Durham, County, England. After emigrating to Canada, Cook entered the Methodist ministry, but later transferred into the United Church of Canada.

1861 At a meeting in Augusta, Georgia, 47 southern presbyteries met to form the Presbyterian Church in the Confederate States of America, separating themselves from the northern Presbyterians. In 1865, following the Civil War, the United Synod Presbyterian Church (formed in 1857) merged with the P.C.C.S.A. to form the Presbyterian Church in the United States (P.C.U.S.). The Kentucky Synod merged with the denomination in 1869 and the Missouri Synod in 1874. The breach between northern and southern Presbyterians was not fully restored until the reunion of 1983.

1893 Rowland Bingham, Walter Gowans and Thomas Kent founded the Sudan Interior Mission in Toronto, Canada. This interdenominational, evangelical mission agency is known today as S.I.M. International. Headquartered in Cedar Grove, New Jersey, the organization is engaged in church planting, theological education, medicine, Gospel broadcasting and support of national churches. Its overseas staff of 650 represents S.I.M. International in over a dozen African nations, including Ethiopia, Kenya, Nigeria and the Sudan.

1896 Death of Peter Cameron Scott (b.1867), American pioneer missionary and founder of the Africa Inland Mission (A.I.M.). Scott led a band of nine missionaries to Mombasa, Kenya in Oct. 1895. The following month, the group set up its first permanent base at Nzawe, 250 miles inland. Peter's father, mother and five others later joined the mission; but before they reached the base, Peter died from blackwater fever at age 29. Over 400 missionaries follow in Scott's footsteps today, helping staff the Africa Inland Mission bases in 11 African nations.

1944 The first missionaries sponsored by Child Evangelism Fellowship, Inc., were sent out from the U.S. to Mexico: Rev. and Mrs. Arthur Phillips of Des Moines, Iowa. C.E.F. was originally organized in 1937 in Chicago by Jesse I. Overholtzer. It is headquartered in Warrenton, Missouri, today.

1963 Officials at the Vatican II Ecumenical Council authorized that the language of the mass and of the sacraments be changed from Latin to the vernacular language—English in the U.S.—demonstrating Rome's desire to make the liturgy a contemporary vehicle of worship.

1966 Swiss reformed theologian Karl Barth reported in a letter: "The good Lord, in spite of reports to the contrary, is not dead."

1976 The Association of Evangelical Lutheran Churches (A.E.L.C.) was formed in Chicago, Illinois. The new denomination of 75,000 members was established by moderates who had broken with the conservative Missouri Synod Lutheran Church over its insistence on a literal interpretation of the Bible.

December 5

1484 Pope Innocent VIII (1484–92) issued his notorious "Witch Bull," *Summis Desiderantes*, ordering the Inquisition in Germany. The decree gave powerful sanction to the bloody persecution of witchcraft by two fanatical Dominican inquisitors. Innocent has the dubious distinction of having first introduced the concept of the "witch hunt."

1791 Death of Wolfgang Amadeus Mozart (b.1756), Austrian musician and composer. His father taught him harpsichord, violin, organ and voice before age six. He was composing music by age five. In 1782 he married Constance Weber, cousin of Carl Maria von Weber, and settled in Vienna. He suffered from poor economic management, ill health, melancholy and depression. Nevertheless, he was a prolific artist, composing over 600 works, many of which were published only after his death. Mozart wrote for the church, the opera and the concert hall. He composed masses, cantatas, operas, symphonies, marches, dances, concertos, quartets, choral and chamber works. Among his chief works were his opera *Don Giovanni* and his unfinished *Requiem*. He also wrote the tune ELLESDIE, the melody to which we sing "Jesus, I My Cross Have Taken."

1824 Birth of Walter C. Smith, Scottish clergyman, in Aberdeen, Scotland. Ordained into the Free Church of Scotland, Smith pastored in London (1850–57), and then at two appointments in Edinburgh (1857–76, 1876–94). He authored several hymns, including "Immortal, Invisible, God Only Wise," which were first published in the 1876 *Hymns of Christ and the Christian Life*.

1834 Birth of Mary Ann Thomson, American hymnwriter and author of the hymn "O Zion, Haste" (1875), in London, England. Having grown up in England, she came to America, where she married John Thomson (first librarian of the Free Library in Philadelphia). For many years she was a member of the Church of the Annunciation in Philadelphia where her husband was also the church treasurer. Mary Thomson published many poems and hymns during her life.

1848 Death of Joseph Mohr (b.1792), Austrian Roman Catholic clergyman. Ordained in 1815, he served as assistant priest at St. Nicholas Church in Oberndorf, Austria, from 1817–19. He later became vicar at Hintersee from 1828–37, then at Wagrein in 1837, where he remained until his death. In the middle of his appointment at Oberndorf, Father Mohr penned the words to a Christmas song that was set to music by the village schoolmaster and church organist, Franz Gruber. The hymn was completed in time for Christmas Eve mass, and on the night of Dec. 24, 1818, "Stille Nacht" ("Silent Night") was sung for the very first time. This Christmas hymn has since been translated into every major language of the world.

1855 Birth of Judson W. Van DeVenter, American Methodist evangelist and author of the hymn "I Surrender All," near Dundee, Michigan. After serving as a Methodist layman for many years, Van DeVenter felt a call to the ministry. Licensed to preach, he began an evangelistic work which took him throughout the U.S., England and Scotland. He first published "I Surrender All" in 1896.

1862 Birth of C.T. Studd, pioneer missionary, in England. Converted at age 21 under the preaching of D.L. Moody, he dedicated his life and inherited wealth to Christ. Giving away about $150,000, he and six others formed the famous "Cambridge Seven," and in 1885 sailed for China for service with the China Inland Mission. Returning to England in 1894 in broken health, Studd returned to missionary labors in India from 1900–06, then in Africa from 1910 until his death in 1931. His influence contributed to the organization of the Worldwide Evangelization Crusade (1919).

1902 Death of Henry Stephen Cutler (b.1824), American Episcopal sacred chorister. About 1850 he became organist and choir director at the Church of the Advent in Boston, where he organized a choir of men and boys after the English tradition, making them the first robed choir in the U.S. Columbia University gave him the Mus.D. degree in 1864. In 1872 Cutler published the hymn tune ALL SAINTS, NEW, to which we sing "The Son of God Goes Forth to War."

1907 Death of Priscilla Jane Owens (b.1829), American Methodist schoolteacher. She spent her entire life in Baltimore, Maryland, where she taught public school for 49 years. A member of the Union Square Methodist Episcopal Church, she was particularly interested in the work of the Sunday school. She published several articles and poems in religious magazines, including two sets of verse which we sing as the hymns "We Have Heard the Joyful Sound" (a.k.a. "Jesus Saves.") and "We Have an Anchor."

1933 The 21st Amendment to the U.S. Constitution repealed the 18th Amendment, legalizing the manufacture and sale of liquor in the U.S once again.

1934 American missionaries John and Betty Stamm were beheaded for their faith, in China. John was born in 1907, Betty in 1906. They met each other while attending Moody Bible Institute. Betty went to China in 1931 and John followed in 1932 under the China Inland Mission. They married in 1933 and were sent to Tsingteh, where they were martyred the following year by the Chinese Communists.

1943 German Lutheran theologian and Nazi martyr Dietrich Bonhoeffer explained in a letter from prison: "It is only when one knows the unutterability of the name of God that one can utter the name of Jesus Christ; it is only when one loves life and the earth so much that without them everything seems to be over that one may believe in the resurrection and a new world."

1951 American missionary and Auca Indian martyr Jim Elliot expressed this concern in his journal: "How sadly and how slowly I am learning that loud preaching and long preaching are not substitutes for inspired preaching."

1983 Death of John A.T. Robinson (b.1919), Anglican clergyman. As Bishop of Woolwich, his *Honest to God* (1963) created so much controversy that many labeled him a heretic, and the Archbishop of Canterbury denounced him. Bishop Robinson taught at Cambridge University and was a visiting professor at Harvard. Other books by Robinson include *The Difference in Being a Christian Today* (1972), *The Human Face of God* (1973), and his autobiography *Roots of a Radical* (1981).

December 6

1538 German reformer Martin Luther was overheard saying: "With all our thoughts we can't get beyond the visible and physical. No man's heart comprehends eternity."

1787 Cokesbury College, the first Methodist college in America, opened in Abingdon, Maryland. The campus consisted of a three-story building 108 feet long and 40 feet wide.

1769 During the illness of his close friend Mrs. Unwin, English poet William Cowper penned the lines to the hymn "Oh, for a Closer Walk with God."

1930 American Congregational missionary and linguistic pioneer Frank C. Laubach noted in a letter: "Sometimes one feels that there is a discord between the cross and beauty. But there really cannot be, for God is found best through these two doorways. . . . A man has not found his highest beauty until his brow is tinged with care for some cause he loves more than himself. The beauty of sacrifice is the final word in beauty."

1950 Death of Susan Strachan (b.1874), who founded the Latin American Evangelization Campaign with her husband Harry in 1921 on Long Island, New York. This interdenominational, evangelical missionary agency is headquartered today in Coral Gables, Florida, under its new name Latin American Mission, Inc.

1955 English Christian apologist C.S. Lewis concluded in *Letters to an American Lady*: "It is a dreadful truth that the state of having to depend solely on God is what we all dread most . . . It is good of Him to force us; but dear me, how hard to feel that it is good at the time."

1964 The Roman Catholic hierarchy in both England and Wales authorized joint prayers with other churches.

1983 In a London auction, a record 7.4 million pounds (14.6 million dollars) was bid for a 12th-century manuscript of the Gospels of Henry the Lion.

December 7

521 Birth of St. Columba, apostle to Scotland. Columba was an Irish-born Celtic missionary who sailed with 12 companions from Ireland to the Scottish island of Iona in 563, where he founded a monastery and evangelistic center. From there, he and his companions evangelized both the Picts and the Scots, founding many churches.

1661 Under pressure from the British Parliament, the Colony of Massachusetts suspended the Corporal Punishment Acts of 1656, which imposed harsh penalties on Quakers and other religious Nonconformists.

1845 Birth of George A. Minor, American Baptist choral leader and author of the hymn tune HARVEST ("Bringing in the Sheaves"), in Richmond, Virginia. A Confederate veteran of the American Civil War, he taught vocal music and led singing schools and music conventions. In 1875 he helped found the Hume-Minor Co. of Richmond and Norfolk, manufacturers of pianos and organs. For many years he was a member of the First Baptist Church of Richmond, where he was also chairman of the music committee.

1874 Death of L.F.K. (Lobegott Friedrich Konstantin) von Tischendorf (b.1815), German biblical and textual scholar. Educated at Leipzig, he came under the influence of J.G.B. Winer, who instilled a combined love for the sacred text with disciplined Greek philology. Tischendorf later taught at Leipzig and traveled throughout Europe, Egypt and Palestine in search of biblical manuscripts. In 1844 in the Monastery of St. Catherine at the foot of Mt. Sinai, he discovered the (4th century) Codex Sinaiticus, the oldest known complete manuscript of the Greek New Testament. During his lifetime, Tischendorf published more critical editions of the Greek New Testament than any other scholar. He also published other important works, including an edition of the Septuagint (Greek Old Testament).

1965 The Roman Catholic and Greek Orthodox churches reconciled themselves, thus ending a mutual excommunication of each other dating back over 900 years, to July 1054.

1973 The Presbyterian Church in America (P.C.A.) established its missionary organization, P.C.A. Mission to the World, in Atlanta, Georgia. This evangelical mission agency was an outgrowth of the new denomination. It is represented by an overseas staff of 263 who work under the P.C.A.M.W. in 35 countries.

December 8

1649 Death of Martin Rinkart (b.1586), German Lutheran clergyman. At age 31 he began a pastorate in his native Eilenburg, Saxony. In the years that followed, the community suffered from the Thirty Years War (1618–48) and the Plague of 1637. Rinkart buried 5,000 victims of the plague, including his wife. In spite of the privations and sufferings of this era, Rinkart penned seven different dramatic productions and wrote 66 hymns. His best-known hymn begins "Nun danket alle Gott . . . ," which we sing in English as "Now Thank We All Our God."

1691 Death of Richard Baxter (b.1615), English Puritan clergyman. In frail health much of his life, Baxter educated himself through private study, self-instruction and introspection. Ordained an Anglican in 1638, he began a 20-year pastorate in 1641 at Kidderminster. The 1662 Act of Uniformity forced him out of the Church of England. Baxter continued to preach, but suffered repeated persecution between 1662–87. He was imprisoned briefly from 1685–86. Baxter was known for his lifelong non-partisan stance, which placed him in the unenviable median between the supporters of the monarchy and the commonwealth, between the Episcopalians and the Presbyterians and between Calvinists and Arminians. Baxter left nearly 200 writings at his death in 1691, including his great devotional work *The Saints' Everlasting Rest* (1650).

1775 Anglican clergyman and hymnwriter John Newton asserted in a letter: "This is faith: a renouncing of everything we are apt to call our own and relying wholly upon the blood, righteousness and intercession of Jesus."

1854 Pope Pius IX affirmed the doctrine of the Immaculate Conception, stating that the Virgin Mary was free from original sin. Pius's announcement stimulated devotion to Mary among Roman Catholics and opened new possibilities for theological development in this direction.

1869 The First Vatican Council opened. Called by Pope Pius IX and attended by approximately 800 bishops and other prelates, a total of 4 public sessions and 89 general meetings were held between this date and July 7, 1870. Vatican I, the 20th ecumenical council of the church, defined papal primacy and infallibility in a dogmatic constitution entitled *Pastor Aeternus*. The document affirmed that the pope possesses infallibility when he speaks *"ex cathedra,"* in his office as pope, when defining doctrine regarding faith and morals.

1903 Death of Henry Clay Trumbull (b.1830), American Congregational Sunday school leader. Ordained in 1862, Trumbull served briefly as a chaplain during the American Civil War. He later worked for the American Sunday School Union (1865–80). In 1872 he called for the national Sunday school convention, which led to the establishment of the International Sunday School Lessons. Trumbull spent his latter years traveling in the Holy Land, writing and lecturing. His 1888 Lyman Beecher Lectures at Yale University were later published under the title, *The Sunday School: Its Origin, Mission, Methods, and Auxiliaries*.

1962 The Rev. John Melville Burgess was consecrated as suffragen Bishop of Massachusetts, the first American Negro bishop of the Protestant Episcopal Church to serve a predominantly white diocese.

1965 The Vatican II Ecumenical Council (begun in 1962) closed. The council had been called by Pope John XXIII, who died in June 1963. Pope Paul VI convened the final 3 of the Council's 4 sessions. The 2,860 priests who participated formulated and published 16 documents: 2 dogmatic constitutions, 2 pastoral constitutions, 9 decrees and 3 declarations, all aimed at renewal and reform in the 20th-century Roman Catholic Church.

1978 Death of Paul Bernhard Peterson (b.1895), American missions pioneer. In 1927 Peterson founded the Eastern European Mission in Chicago, Illinois. He also served as its president for 48 years, from 1930 until his death. This interdenominational, evangelical sending agency has been headquartered in Pasadena, California, since 1985 under the name Eurovision. The organization does shortwave radio broadcasting, literature production and distribution, and relief and support of nationals. Its ·overseas staff works in nine European countries, as well as in the Soviet Union.

1981 The U.S. Supreme Court upheld the constitutionality of student organizations holding religious services at public colleges and universities. This was one of the most significant rulings by the high court on the issue of separation of church and state in several years.

December 9

1608 Birth of John Milton, English poetic theologian, in London. He grew up an Anglican, but later turned Presbyterian and finally Independent. He went blind about 1652, but still wrote—through his secretary—his greatest literary works: *Paradise Lost* (1667), *Paradise Regained* (1671), and *Samson Agonistes* (1671).

1667 Birth of William Whiston, English mathematician and theologian. He entered the Anglican ministry in 1698, but turned to teaching five years later. He succeeded Isaac Newton as professor of mathematics at Cambridge, but his Arian theological views led to his expulsion from the university in 1710. Whiston suffered intensely and lived in considerable poverty. In 1747 he joined the Baptists. Whiston believed the work of the Reformation would remain incomplete until the Ante-Nicene Fathers were translated into English. The way would then be opened for the restoration of primitive Christianity. At age 70 (1737), Whiston completed a translation of the writings of Jewish historian Josephus (A.D. 37–ca.100).

1840 Scottish missionary and explorer David Livingstone set sail on his first journey to Africa. Accepted in 1838 by the London Missionary Society, Livingstone's first goal had been to work in China; but the Opium Wars forced him to change his direction, and he became one of the most famous missionary-explorers ever to work in Africa.

1843 The world's first Christmas card was created, in England.

1863 Birth of G. Campbell Morgan, English Congregational clergyman and Bible expositor, in Gloucestershire, England. Having served several pastorates, Morgan became pastor of the Westminster Congregational Church in London in 1904. It was a dying church that he turned into one of England's most active congregations by the time he left in 1917. Morgan authored more than 60

Bible commentaries and books of sermons, many which are still in print today.

1870 The Society of Biblical Archaeology was founded in London "for the investigation of the archaeology, history, arts, and chronology of ancient and modern Assyria, Palestine, Egypt, Arabia, and other biblical lands; the promotion of the study of the antiquities of these countries; and the record of discoveries hereafter to be made in connection therewith."

1877 Death of George N. Allen (b.1812), American music scholar. After his graduation from Oberlin College in Ohio in 1838, he stayed on to teach music and remained until his retirement in 1864. Allen laid the foundation for the Oberlin Conservatory of Music, which opened in 1865. He also composed several hymn tunes, including MAITLAND ("Must Jesus Bear the Cross Alone?").

1893 Death of George J. Elvey (b.1816), English sacred music chorister and organist. He served at St. George's Chapel in Windsor (home church of the royal family) for 47 years. Elvey composed 2 popular hymn tunes: DIADEMATA ("Crown Him with Many Crowns") and ST. GEORGE'S WINDSOR ("Come, Ye Thankful People, Come").

1905 An Act for the Separation of Church and State became law in France, abrogating the Concordat of 1801 and other related legislation. The new law, first introduced by Emile Combs, guaranteed freedom of conscience, but also severed religious groups from any further economic support by the national government.

1907 Christmas Seals first went on sale, supporting the fight against tuberculosis. Christmas seal income today is used primarily in the fight against birth defects.

1968 Death of Karl Barth (b.1886), Swiss reformed theologian. He was one of the founders of neo-orthodoxy (or dialectical theology). After pastoring two Swiss churches from 1909–21, the horrors of the World War I, the theologies of Calvin and Kierkegaard and personal study of the Bible replaced his liberal optimism with an embryonic crisis theology. Barth's 1919 commentary on Romans (*Romerbrief*) catapulted him into theological prominence. He taught at several German universities until Nazi pressures forced him to flee to Switzerland, where he continued to teach from 1935–62. Barth was a prolific writer. His chief publication is no doubt the unfinished, multi-volumed *Church Dogmatics*, which sets down the philosophical and theological basis for all Barth's beliefs. He had no use for natural revelation in which man is drawn to God through nature or through intellectual stimulation. Barth saw God as totally different from man, as transcendent. The only way man can relate or return to God is through Jesus Christ.

1973 The religious program, *Marshall Efron's Illustrated, Simplified and Painless Sunday School*, first aired over CBS-television. Marshall Efron, who was a regular participant on PBS's *The Great American Dream Machine*, hosted this religious series for young children. Produced by Pamela Ilott and directed by Ted Holmes, the program was broadcast on Sunday mornings until Aug. 1977.

1979 Death of Fulton J. Sheen (b.1895), American Roman Catholic archbishop and broadcaster. Ordained in 1919, he taught philosophy at Catholic University from 1926–50. From 1930–52, his NBC radio broadcasts of the *Catholic Hour* were heard around the world. His program *Life Is Worth Living* was seen by an estimated 30 million viewers each week from 1951–57. He also authored many books on devotional and philosophical topics.

December 10

1520 German reformer Martin Luther publicly burned Pope Leo X's bull *Exsurge Domine.* Leo had issued the bull in June, demanding that Luther recant his "protestant" heresies. Luther had taught earlier that justification was by faith alone, not through purchased indulgences or other papal favors. In response to Luther's burning of the papal encyclical, Leo formally excommunicated him in Jan. 1521 in the bull *Decet.*

1561 Death of Kaspar Schwenkfeld (b.1489), Silesian Anabaptist theologian and writer. Undergoing a spiritual awakening in 1518, Schwenkfeld began introducing his own variety of Lutheran reform into his native Silesia in 1522. Called "Reformation of the Middle Way," Schwenkfeld's theology brought the wrath of both Lutheran and Calvinist authorities, and he was anathematized in 1540 by the Schmalkaldic League. He opposed war and oath-taking, emphasized inward mystical religion, rejected infant baptism and other sacraments and held that spiritual regeneration is effected by grace wrought by the work of the Holy Spirit within the individual. The Schwenkfelder denomination in the U.S. was organized in 1734, and is headquartered today in Philadelphia, Pennsylvania.

1582 This day in France became Dec. 20 (Dec. 10–19 having been skipped) when the new Gregorian calendar was implemented. Earlier in 1582, the committee organized by Pope Gregory XIII had finished a reformation of the old Julian calendar (named for Julius Caesar, who had reformed the old Roman calendar in 46 B.C.), which had lost ten days against the solar year in the 1,628 years since its implementation.

1735 During a visit to England, Georgia governor James Edward Oglethorpe met John and Charles Wesley, students at Oxford University. Impressed by their fervent evangelicalism, Oglethorpe invited them to undertake mission work in the Georgia colony. The Wesleys accepted and arrived in America the following February.

1815 Birth of John Zundel, organist of sacred music, in Hochdorf, Germany. He began his music career as organist at St. Anne's Lutheran Church in St. Petersburg, Russia. Emigrating to America in 1847, he worked in the New York City area for three years. In 1850 he became organist at Henry Ward Beecher's Plymouth Congregational Church in Brooklyn, where he served for the next 30 years. His music became almost as popular as was Beecher's preaching. Zundel published several hymn collections and edited three different musical periodicals. Of the several hymn tunes he composed, one is still popular: LOVE DIVINE ("Love Divine, All Loves Excelling").

1824 Birth of George MacDonald, Scottish novelist and poet, in Aberdeenshire, Scotland. He became a Congregational pastor at Arundel, Sussex, in 1850, but theological controversies with his deacons led to his resignation three years later. He supported himself by lecturing, tutoring, writing and occasional

preaching. Though often in poor health and great poverty, MacDonald's writings show a deep faith in God. C.S. Lewis acknowledged a great debt to
MacDonald's writings, especially his *Phantastes* (1858) and *Lilith* (1895). The
cheerful goodness demonstrated in these works captured Lewis' imagination,
and convinced him that righteousness was not dull.

1862 Birth of Henry Ernest Nichol, the composer of sacred music who wrote
both words and music for the hymn "We've a Story to Tell to the Nations," in
Hull, England. Nichol abandoned study for a career in civil engineering to
study music, and earned his Bachelor of Music degree from Oxford University
in 1888. He authored and composed many sacred songs for special Sunday
school services.

1968 Death of Thomas Merton (b.1915), French-born American Trappist monk.
He died by accidental electrocution while attending a conference of Buddhist
and Catholic monks in Bangkok, Thailand. In 1941, at age 26, Merton abandoned a secular teaching career for monastic living and entered the Trappist
Abbey of Our Lady of Gethsemani in Kentucky. He continued his writing and
publishing, however, and became internationally famous with the publication
of his autobiography, *The Seven Storey Mountain* in 1948. During his 27 years
as a monk, Merton wrote 300 articles and 50 books. He championed nonvi-
olent social justice and international peace.

December 11

1640 The "Root and Branch" petition was introduced by the Puritans in the
Long Parliament in London. It demanded that the English episcopacy, "with
all its dependencies, roots and branches, be abolished."—The imagery came
from Malachi 4:1. Parliament did little with the petition, since moderate Puritans disagreed with radical Presbyterians over its strong demands. But during
the English Civil Wars (1642–52), Anglican bishops, deans and chapters were
abolished, and church lands were confiscated.

1792 Birth of Joseph Mohr, German Roman Catholic clergyman, in Salzburg,
Austria. Mohr was ordained in 1815 and served as assistant priest at St. Nicholas Church in Oberndorf, Austria, from 1817–19. He later became vicar at
Hintersee (1828–37), then vicar at Wagrein (1837–48), where he remained
until his death in 1848. While at Oberndorf, Father Mohr penned the words
to a Christmas song which was set to music by the village schoolmaster and
church organist, Franz Gruber. The hymn was finished in time for Christmas
Eve mass, Dec. 24, 1818, when "Stille Nacht" ("Silent Night") was sung for
the first time.

1895 Birth of American Fundamentalist John R. Rice, in Cook County, Texas.
Raised a Baptist, Rice became a traveling evangelist, holding city-wide campaigns across the U.S. In 1934 he founded the *The Sword of the Lord*, a
monthly fundamentalist newspaper. He edited the paper until his death 46
years later in 1980.

1962 American Presbyterian apologist Francis Schaeffer explained in a letter:
"Our trusting the Lord does not mean that there are not times of tears. I think
it is a mistake as Christians to act as though trusting the Lord and tears are
not compatible."

1975   The Central American Mission changed its name to C.A.M. International after it expanded its missionary efforts into other areas. This interdenominational, evangelical mission organization was founded in Dallas, Texas, in 1890 by Dr. C.I. Scofield (editor of the Scofield Bible). C.A.M. International is engaged in evangelism, church planting, theological education, Gospel broadcasting and literature production. Over 200 overseas personnel represent the mission in 7 Central American countries and in Spain.

December 12

1545   The Council of Trent opened. This 19th of the church's 21 ecumenical councils was held in 25 sessions, between 1545–63, over an 18-year period. The council issued many decrees concerning doctrinal matters opposed by the Protestant reformers. It also mobilized the forces of the Counter-Reformation. The liturgy was reformed and general discipline in the Catholic church was improved. Religious instruction and education of the clergy was promoted through new seminaries. Trent and Vatican II (1962–65) stand as the two greatest ecumenical councils of the Western church.

1562   Death of Pietro Vermigli ("Peter Martyr") (b.1500), Italian reformer. He joined the Augustinian order at age 16 and was leading it by age 41. He became acquainted with Valdes, Zwingli and Bucer, which led to accusations of heresy being leveled against him. Peter fled Italy in 1542. At Archbishop Cranmer's invitation, he went to England in 1547 and became professor of divinity at Oxford. He also took part in the preparation of the *Book of Common Prayer*. After Mary Tudor's accession to the throne in 1553, Peter was again forced to flee the country. In 1556 he became professor of Hebrew at Zurich, Switzerland, where he taught until his death.

1718   Birth of John Cennick, English clergyman and author of the hymn "Be Present at Our Table, Lord," in Reading, England. Born to Quaker parents, Cennick was raised in the Anglican Church. He later came under the influence of John Wesley and became one of the first Methodist lay preachers. He left the Wesleys because of doctrinal differences and joined George Whitefield. In 1745 he joined the Moravian Brethren, and was ordained in 1749. As a Moravian preacher, Cennick spent his later years traveling and preaching in Germany and Ireland.

1767   Anglican hymnwriter John Newton assured in a letter: "Blessed be God, we are in safe hands. The Lord himself is our Keeper. Nothing befalls us but what is adjusted by His wisdom and love. He will, in one way or other, sweeten every bitter cup, and ere long He will wipe away all tears from our eyes."

1805   Birth of Frederick Henry Hedge, New England clergyman, in Cambridge, Massachusetts. Hedge studied music in Germany for four years before graduating from Harvard in 1825. Ordained a Unitarian minister in 1829, he served churches in Massachusetts, Maine and Rhode Island. He also taught ecclesiastical literature and German at Harvard (1857–81). He made a significant contribution to hymnody in 1853 with the publication of his *Hymns for the Church of Christ*. Hedge translated Martin Luther's classic "A Mighty Fortress Is Our God" into English.

1808 The Bible Society of Philadelphia was organized, the first of its kind in America, with the Rev. William White elected its first president. Following an example set in London four years earlier, the new organization purposed to promote and distribute Scriptures.

1842 Death of Robert Haldane (b.1764), Scottish evangelist and philanthropist. He and his brother James were orphaned by age ten. In 1795 both were converted and became interested in lay preaching. Robert resolved to devote his life, talents and fortune to Christ. He built a church in Edinburgh where his brother James, a Congregational preacher, served as pastor for 50 years. Robert wanted to go to India as a missionary at his own expense, but was hindered by the East India Company. He carried on extensive evangelistic work throughout Scotland. From 1816–19 he taught biblical studies in Geneva, Switzerland, and in France. Robert was actively involved with the Bible Society of Edinburgh, and helped form the Society for the Propagation of the Gospel at Home. His book *Exposition of the Epistle to the Romans* (1816–19) has frequently been reprinted.

1888 The American Sabbath Union was organized, "to preserve the Christian Sabbath as a day of rest and worship."

1900 Birth of D. (David) Elton Trueblood, American Quaker theologian, in Pleasantville, Iowa. Having taught at Guilford College in North Carolina and Haverford College in Pennsylvania, Trueblood began his long career at Earlham College, a Quaker school in Richmond, Indiana, in 1946. In 1956 he founded the Earlham School of Religion. He also founded and served as president of the Yokefellow Association. Trueblood has authored dozens of books over the years, each filled with quotations and simple explanations of complex Christian issues.

December 13

1204 Death of Maimonides (Moses ben Maimon) (b.1135), medieval Jewish scholar. The friend and pupil of Spanish-Arabian scholar Averroes, Maimonides moved from Spain to Morocco, Palestine and Egypt. He published a commentary on the *Mishnah* in 1168. His greatest book, however, was *The Guide of the Perplexed* (1190), which attempted to harmonize Aristotelian philosophy with rabbinic Judaism. Maimonides' writings strongly influenced medieval Christian scholasticism. They reintroduced Aristotelian philosophy into Christian theology, especially through Albertus Magnus and his pupil, Thomas Aquinas.

1545 The Council of Trent was opened by Pope Paul III. Between this date and Dec. 1563, 25 sessions were held, debating doctrines opposed by the reformers and mobilized by the Counter-Reformation. Reckoned the 19th Ecumenical Council by church historians, the sessions spanned a total of 18 years, and were convened by 3 popes (Paul III, Julius III, Pius IV). The documents generated covered such topics as faith, justification, grace, original sin, the sacraments, the Mass, the veneration of saints, purgatory, indulgences, and the jurisdiction of the pope within the Catholic Church. The Council of Trent initiated many reforms for renewal and general discipline in the church, including the promotion of religious education among both clergy and laity.

Trent ranks with Vatican II (1962–65) as the greatest ecumenical council held in the West.

1793 Funeral services were held for John Hatton, composer of the hymn tune DUKE STREET ("Jesus Shall Reign Where'er the Sun"), at St. Helens, England. Very little is known about Hatton's life other than that he was born in Warrington, England, lived his life in the English township of Windle and belonged to the local Presbyterian church.

1823 Birth of William Walsham How, Anglican clergyman, in Shrewsbury, England. Ordained in 1845, he served six churches before becoming suffragen Bishop of East London in 1879. In 1888 he became Bishop of Wakefield. Shunning the glory of higher ecclesiastical positions, How was better known for his work among the poor of poverty-stricken East London. He also wrote more than 50 hymns, including "We Give Thee but Thine Own" and "For All the Saints."

1835 Birth of Phillips Brooks, American Episcopal clergyman, in Boston, Massachusetts. In 1859 he was ordained and began his first pastorate in Philadelphia. He transferred to Trinity Episcopal Church in Boston in 1869 and remained there until 1891. Brooks became famous as a preacher of exceptional personality, charm and spiritual force. Liberal in his theology, Brooks' central message was that all men are the children of God. He produced five volumes of sermons; and five more were published after his death in 1893. He also wrote the Christmas carol "O Little Town of Bethlehem" for the children of his Sunday school, after a visit to the Holy Land in 1868.

1851 Birth of E.O. (Edwin Othello) Excell, American sacred music chorister and writer, in Stark County, Ohio. Converted under the Methodists, Excell turned his energies to directing, writing and publishing sacred music. He was also active in the work of the Sunday school, leading the music at Sunday school conventions and helping establish the *International Sunday School Lessons*. He also assisted evangelist Sam P. Jones in his revival meetings for 20 years. Excell published 50 Gospel songbooks and composed over 2,000 Christian songs, including "Since I Have Been Redeemed," "I'll Be a Sunbeam for Jesus" and "Count Your Blessings."

1931 Birth of Flo Price, contemporary American Christian vocalist and songwriter. She has written such Christian music favorites as "Bright New World" and "Gonna Wake Up Singing."

1936 Death of Peter P. Bilhorn (b.1865), American music artist. Converted at 18 under the ministry of evangelist George F. Pentecost and George C. Stebbins, Bilhorn turned his energies toward a music education and studied with F.W. Root and G.C. Stebbins. After touring the American West as a music evangelist, Bilhorn invented a portable organ for use in evangelistic and missionary work. In later life, he was Billy Sunday's song evangelist. He also composed over 2,000 Gospel songs, including the hymn tune WONDROUS STORY ("I Will Sing the Wondrous Story") and "Sweet Peace, the Gift of God's Love."

1950 American missionary and Auca Indian martyr Jim Elliot pondered in his journal: "I think God is to be glorified by asking the impossible of Him."

1974 Death of Don R. Falkenberg (b.1894), American missions pioneer. In 1923 Falkenberg incorporated Mid-West Businessmen's Council of the Pocket Testament League in Columbus, Ohio. In 1967 the name of the organization was changed to Bible Literature International. This interdenominational agency provides Christian literature, with an emphasis on evangelism, discipleship and church growth, for missionary projects in over 200 countries.

December 14

1363 Birth of Jean Charlier de Gerson, French theologian and church leader, near Reims, France. He began studying theology in 1381, securing his doctorate in 1392. In 1395 he succeeded his teacher, Piere d'Ailly, as chancellor of the University of Paris, and was made a canon of Notre Dame. During the great papal schism (1378–1414), Gerson took part in the reform-seeking councils of Pisa (1409) and Constance (1414–18). He believed that a general council was superior to the pope, that a genuine reformation—starting with the papacy—of the church was necessary and that the Bible was the only source and authority of Christian knowledge. Gerson spent his last years in a monastery at Lyons teaching children, composing hymns and writing books on mystical Christian devotion. He died in 1429.

1417 Death of Sir John Oldcastle (b.ca.1378), English leader of the Lollards. He became one of John Wycliffe's Lollard lay preachers in 1410, after holding several government posts. He was a member of Parliament in 1404, and became a baron in 1409. The following year, however, he incurred the wrath of Thomas Arundel, Archbishop of Canterbury, for his Lollard sympathies. The Lollards rejected transubstantiation and confession, denounced the pope as Antichrist and denied the church's right to dictate what a man should believe. In 1413 Oldcastle was accused of heresy, and in 1417 he was taken into custody, hanged and burned.

1586 Birth of George Calixtus, German-Danish Protestant theologian, in Medelby, Schleswig, Germany. He taught theology at the University of Helmstedt from 1614–56. While traveling through Holland, England and France between 1609–13, Calixtus became acquainted with the theologies of the leading Protestant reformers. It became his great aim in life to build a universal theological system. Based on the Scriptures, the Apostles' Creed and the church fathers, Calixtus sought to reconcile the Lutherans, Calvinists and Roman Catholics of his day; making him one of the earliest pioneers of the ecumenical movement. Calixtus suffered the fate of many peacemakers in that he was rejected by the very groups he sought to reconcile. Nevertheless, he persevered in seeking to appreciate unimportant differences in theology, while concentrating on the fundamental articles of the historical, orthodox Christian faith.

1678 Birth of Daniel Neal, English Puritan historian, in London. Ordained in 1706, he pastored the independent congregation on Aldersgate Street in London until his death in 1743. Recognized as one of the best Puritan preachers of his day, Neal also wrote the famous work *History of the Puritans: 1517–1688* (1732–38), an historical compilation with a strong Puritan bias.

1715 Death of Thomas Tenison (b.1636), Archbishop of Canterbury beginning in 1695. Ordained in 1659, Tenison had an outstanding record of ministry within the Anglican Church. Tenison is also remembered for establishing the first public library in London, in 1684. A lifelong supporter of Christian missions, he also played a prominent part in founding the Society for the Propagation of the Gospel.

1773 Birth of Johannes E. Gossner, German clergyman and founder of the Gossner Foreign Missionary Society, in Hausen (near Augsburg), Germany. He was ordained a priest in 1796 and served as a Catholic pastor until 1826. He then left Romanism to join the Lutheran Church. In 1829 he began a pastorate at the Bethlehem Church in Berlin, remaining there for 17 years. In 1842 he established the Gossner Foreign Missionary Society, which sent out over 140 missionaries during his lifetime, principally to the Khols of East India. Retiring from the pastorate in 1846, Gossner devoted his remaining 12 years to a hospital he had founded.

1836 Birth of Frances Ridley Havergal, English devotional writer, in Astley, England. She began writing verse for publication as early as age seven. Her home between 1841–60 was the rectory of St. Nicholas Church in Worcester, where her father was pastor. Throughout her life, Miss Havergal was in frail health. But she was a fruitful writer, and even composed a number of hymn tunes. She wrote the hymns "I Am Trusting Thee, Lord Jesus," "Take My Life, and Let It Be," "Lord, Speak to Me, That I May Speak," "Like a River Glorious," "Who Is on the Lord's Side?", "I Give My Life for Thee" and "True-Hearted, Whole-Hearted."

1847 Death of Dorothy A. Thrupp (b.1779), English hymnwriter. Little is known of her life. She wrote several hymns, including "Savior, Like a Shepherd Lead Us," either anonymously or under the pen name "Iota." She was editor of *Hymns for the Young* (ca.1830), in which all the hymns were published unsigned.

1927 Death of Olivia E.P. Stokes (b.1847), American philanthropist. Olivia and her sister Caroline were born into a prominent New York City banking family that understood its responsibility to be a good steward of wealth. The sisters grew up amid their family's active work for temperance, abolition, Negro education, foreign missions, Bible and tract societies, the Y.M.C.A. and children's hospitals. Neither sister married and Olivia wrote several books, including a biography of her two closest friends: *Letters and Memories of Susan and Anna Bartlett Warner* (1925). (Her friend Anna was the author of the children's hymn "Jesus Loves Me, This I Know.")

December 15

37 Birth of Nero (Claudius Caesar Drusus Germanicus), Roman emperor from 54–68. Nero succeeded Claudius to the throne at the age of 17. Initially a virtuous ruler, he soon fell in with evil opportunists and became a profligate, a spendthrift and a tyrant. When more than a third of Rome was destroyed by fire in 64, Nero blamed the Christians for the action and instituted the first large-scale Roman persecution of the church. According to tradition, both Peter and Paul died in this persecution. But Nero invoked other reigns of terror and caused revolts in Gaul, Spain and Africa by 68. The Roman Senate declared him a public enemy; and at age 31, Nero committed suicide to save himself from capture and execution.

1558 Dutch Anabaptist reformer Menno Simons asserted in a letter: "Wherever there is a pulverized and penitent heart, there grace also is, and wherever there is a voluntary confession not gained by pressure, there love covereth a multitude of sins."

1739 English revivalist George Whitefield admonished in a letter: "My brother, entreat the Lord that I may grow in grace, and pick up the fragments of my time, that not a moment of it may be lost."

1808 Birth of Henry F. Chorley, English music journalist, in Blackley, England. He worked in a merchant's office in Liverpool during his early years. In 1830 he began work with the London *Athenaeum* as its music editor, continuing there for the next 35 years. He was also music critic for *The Times* for many years. Chorley penned the hymn "God the Omnipotent" in 1842.

1830 Birth of Lewis Henry Redner, American Episcopal organist and composer of the hymn tune for "O Little Town of Bethlehem" (ST. LOUIS), in Philadelphia, Pennsylvania. Early in life, Redner became a wealthy real estate broker in his hometown of Philadelphia. A devoted churchman as well, he served as Sunday school Superintendent for 19 years at the Holy Trinity Episcopal Church. He also served as organist for the church.

1837 Birth of Ethelbert William Bullinger, Anglican clergyman, in Canterbury, England. While in college, he studied music under J. Hullah and W.H. Monk. He composed several hymn tunes, including BULLINGER ("I Am Trusting Thee, Lord Jesus").

1843 Birth of A.B. (Albert Benjamin) Simpson, American clergyman, on Prince Edward Island, Canada. Ordained into the Presbyterian ministry, he served pastorates in Canada, Kentucky and New York between 1865–83. He left a prestigious, well-paying ministry to begin a mission church in New York City. Within a decade, Simpson's tabernacle became one of the leading evangelical centers in the city. Simpson founded the Nyack Missionary Training Institute in 1883. He established the Christian Alliance in 1887 and the International Missionary Alliance in 1889. In 1897 these two societies were joined to form the Christian and Missionary Alliance, one of the most mission-minded of today's Protestant denominations.

1900 Birth of Clarence W. Jones, who helped found the World Radio Missionary Fellowship, Inc. with Reuben Larson, in Lima, Ohio, in 1931. In 1969 W.R.M.F.'s headquarters was moved to Opa Locka, Florida. This missionary agency is best known for radio station HCJB, which it has operated in Quito, Ecuador, since Christmas day of 1931.

December 16

1714 Birth of George Whitefield, English revivalist, in Gloucester, England. He met the Wesley brothers at Oxford in 1732, experienced the new birth in 1735 and embarked on his lifelong calling as an evangelist. He usually preached outdoors, to crowds as large as 20,000. He first sailed to America in 1738, where he founded an orphanage near Savannah, Georgia. During the years 1741–43, he broke with the Wesleys over the doctrines of free grace and predestination. Whitefield visited America seven times, and died at Newbury-port, Massachusetts.

1786 Birth of Konrad Kocher, German chorister and composer of the hymn tune for "For the Beauty of the Earth" (DIX), in Dietzingen, Wurttemberg, Germany. He studied music in Russia and Italy. Greatly influenced by the work of Palestrina, Kocher made church choral music the major interest of his career. In 1821 he founded the School of Sacred Song in Stuttgart. He did much to popularize four-part singing in the churches.

1826 Birth of John Ellerton, Anglican clergyman and hymnwriter, in London, England. Ordained in 1850, he wrote his first hymns for the children at his first church, in Brighton. His hymns and his interest in hymnology led the compilers of every significant hymnal published in the last half of the 19th century to consult with him. His own hymns were published in *Hymns, Original and Translated* (1888), which included "Savior, Again to Thy Dear Name We Raise," "God the Omnipotent King, Who Ordainest" and "Welcome, Happy Morning."

1859 Birth of Francis Thompson, English poet, in Lancashire, England. Educated for the Roman Catholic priesthood, Thompson went on to study medicine, but became a hopeless opium addict who wandered London for three years. Rescued in 1888 by Wilfred Meynell, Thompson began writing and published his first volume of *Poems* in 1893. In all his works, Thompson's literary style forms a unique blend of the wild imagery spawned by drug addiction, the asceticism of the mystic and a sacramental conception of nature. His classic "The Hound of Heaven" portrays God pursuing the wayward soul just as a hound tirelessly pursues its prey.

1867 Birth of Amy Wilson Carmichael, Scottish-Irish missionary to India, in Millisle, Ireland. Raised a Presbyterian, she was influenced by the Keswick movement and became a missionary under the Church of England Zenana Missionary Society. She first arrived in India in 1895, and remained there without furlough until her death 56 years later in 1951. She adopted Indian dress, and in 1901 began her work of rescuing girls who had been dedicated without choice to a life of cult prostitution in Hindu temples. In 1918 she also began working with boys. The work led to the establishment of the Dohnavur Fellowship in 1925. In 1931 a fall shattered her leg, leaving her an invalid. She devoted her last 20 years to writing books of devotion and poetry, including *Things As They Are* (1903), *Rose from Brier*, *Though the Mountains Shake* and *Toward Jerusalem*.

1870 The Colored Methodist Episcopal Church of America was established at Jackson, Tennessee. At a general conference four years earlier (1866), a commission from the black membership of the Methodist Episcopal Church South had asked to separate into a church of its own. The request was granted, and the Colored Methodist Episcopal Church was organized. At the general conference of 1954 in Memphis, Tennessee, the name of the denomination was changed to the Christian Methodist Episcopal Church. There are approximately 800,000 members and 3,000 churches belonging to this denomination.

1870 Death of Alexis F. Lwoff (also written Lvov) (b.1798), Russian soldier and sacred music organist. After serving in the Russian army for 19 years

(1818–37), he succeeded his father as director of the Imperial Court Chapel at St. Petersburg, a position which he held for 24 years. An excellent violinist, Lwoff composed several works for the instrument, three operas and many pieces of chamber music. Increasing deafness brought on his retirement in 1867. Lwoff composed the hymn tune RUSSIAN HYMN, to which we sing the hymn "God, the Omnipotent."

1935 Death of Walter Stillman Martin (b.1862), American clergyman, evangelist and composer of the hymn tune for "God Will Take Care of You" (GOD CARES). He was originally ordained into the Baptist ministry, but later joined the Christian Church (Disciples of Christ). In 1916 he began teaching Bible at the Atlantic Christian College in North Carolina. He moved to Atlanta three years later and spent his remaining years conducting Bible conferences and evangelistic meetings across the nation.

December 17

1770 Birth of Ludwig van Beethoven, German composer, in Bonn, Germany. Raised in a Roman Catholic home, he had the best teachers, including Mozart and Hadyn. He composed music for 45 years, beginning at age 11. He began losing his hearing at 30 and was totally deaf by 50. Beethoven suffered much from ill-health, poverty and unhappy family relationships. He never married. Nevertheless, he always believed he had a reason to go on living, saying, "I owe it to . . . the Almighty. I must write music to the glory of God." Beethoven was an innovator, writing many symphonies, sonatas, masses, one oratorio (*Christ on the Mount of Olives*), one opera and many smaller compositions. He once declared, "Music is the only spiritual entrance to a higher world of knowledge."

1796 Death of Felice de Giardini (b.1716), Italian music artist. From 1752–84, he lived in England as an operatic impressario, violinist, music teacher and conductor. He composed ITALIAN HYMN (TRINITY), to which we sing "Come, Thou Almighty King."

1807 Birth of John Greenleaf Whittier, American Quaker poet, abolitionist and hymnwriter. His first book of poems was published in 1831. Two years later he entered politics as an abolitionist and became an important writer in the antislavery movement. Following the American Civil War, poetry became his main interest. Whittier turned to religious verse. The middle verses of one of his longest poems, "The Brewing of Soma," became the hymn "Dear Lord and Father of Mankind."

1834 Birth of Marianne Hearn, English Baptist religious editor and author of the hymn "Just As I Am, Thine Own to Be" in Farningham, England. She was an active member of the College Street Baptist Church in Northampton. She was also editor of *The Sunday School Times*, a weekly publication for Sunday-school teachers in England. A prolific writer and poet, her collected literary works were later published in 20 volumes.

1836 Death of John Rippon (b.1751), English Baptist clergyman. In 1772 he began a pastorate at the Carter Lane Baptist Church in London, remaining there for the next 63 years. One of the most influential ministers of his day, Rippon published many of his sermons and edited several hymnbooks. He revised Edward Perronet's hymn "All Hail the Power of Jesus' Name," and wrote "How Firm a Foundation."

1843 Charles Dickens' *A Christmas Carol* was first published.

1879 American revivalist Gipsy Smith, as an older man, married a very young lady. When someone asked him why, he replied, "I'd rather smell perfume than liniment."

1934 Birth of Kurt (Frederic) Kaiser, American Christian composer and songwriter. His area of special interest has been music for young singers. Kaiser has written the words and music to such contemporary favorites as "Oh, How He Loves You and Me," "Master Designer" and "Pass It On."

1935 Death of Frank Mason North (b.1850), American Methodist clergyman. Ordained in 1872, he served churches for 20 years in Florida, New York and Connecticut. He was also editor of *The Christian City* from 1892–1912. In 1912 he became corresponding secretary of the Methodist Board of Foreign Missions. North wrote 12 hymns during his life, most of them for special occasions. One which we still sing is "Where Cross the Crowded Ways of Life."

1943 German Lutheran theologian and Nazi martyr Dietrich Bonhoeffer confided in a letter from prison: "The consciousness of being borne up by a spiritual tradition that goes back for centuries gives one a feeling of confidence and security in the face of all passing strains and stresses."

December 18

1707 Birth of Charles Wesley, co-founder of Methodism, in Epworth, England. The 18th child of an Anglican pastor, Wesley followed his older brother John to Oxford in 1726. The Wesleys and their friends formed the "Holy Club." The group was derisively dubbed the "Methodists" for their methodical forms of personal piety. Ordained an Anglican priest in 1735, Charles underwent a spiritual conversion three years later (May 20, 1738), three days before John's heart was "strangely warmed" at Aldersgate. Between 1737–42, they published 6 volumes of original hymns. The United Methodist hymnal still contains 73 of the more than 6,500 hymns Charles penned during his lifetime. Among his best-known works are: "Christ the Lord Is Risen Today," "And Can It Be?", "Hark! The Herald Angels Sing," "O for a Thousand Tongues," "Love Divine, All Loves Excelling," "A Charge to Keep I Have" and "Jesus, Lover of My Soul." It was said that one could sing the theology of John in the hymns of Charles.

1789 Death of John Darwall (b.1731), Anglican clergyman and songwriter, in Haughton, England. He spent his last 20 years as vicar of St. Matthew's Parish Church in Walsall, England. His deep interest in music led him to publish two volumes of piano sonatas. He also composed melodies for all 150 Psalms. The tune he penned for Psalm 148 (DARWALL) is still popular. We use it with the hymn "Rejoice, the Lord Is King."

1819 Birth of Isaac Thomas Hecker, American Roman Catholic and founder of the Paulists, in New York City. Baptized a Lutheran as a baby, Hecker associated briefly with the Methodists and later with transcendentalism. In 1844 he was baptized a Roman Catholic, and entered the Redemptorist order the following year. Completing his novitiate in Europe, he returned to the U.S., where he felt the need for an English-speaking order to evangelize American Protestants. In 1858 he formed the Missionary Society of St. Paul the Apostle, known also as the Paulist Fathers or Paulists. Hecker was superior general of the society his remaining 30 years (1858–88). He also founded *The Catholic World* in 1865, the chief Roman Catholic periodical in the U.S. today, editing it until his death.

1834   Emory College was chartered in Oxford, Georgia, under Methodist auspices. In 1915 the name was changed to Emory University, and in 1919 the college was relocated in Atlanta, Georgia.

1835   Birth of Lyman Abbott, American Congregational clergyman, in Massachusetts. After a six-year career in law, Abbott turned to the ministry in 1859 and was ordained the following year. He pastored churches in Indiana (1860–65) and New York (1865–69). From 1871–76, he served as editor of the American Tract Society's *Illustrated Christian Weekly*. In 1888 he succeeded Henry Ward Beecher as pastor of Plymouth Church in Brooklyn, New York. In his latter years, Abbott sought to reconcile evangelical theology with Darwinian evolution and German biblical criticism. His most significant publications are *The Theology of an Evolutionist* (1897) and *What Christianity Means to Me* (1921).

1892   Rabbi H. Rosenberg was expelled from Temple Beth-Jacob in Brooklyn, New York, for eating pork.

1943   German Lutheran pastor and Nazi martyr, Dietrich Bonhoeffer, reminded in a letter from prison: "God will see to it that the man who finds Him in his earthly happiness and thanks Him for it does not lack reminder that earthly things are transient, that it is good for him to attune his heart to what is eternal, and that sooner or later there will be times when he can say in all sincerity, 'I wish I were home.' "

1957   Death of Dorothy Sayers (b.1893), English writer. After graduating from Oxford, she published the first of a long series of detective novels in 1923 that were to make her the most popular mystery writer in England. A close friend of C.S. Lewis, Charles Williams, J.R.R. Tolkien and Owen Barfield, Sayers was a scholar and an expert on the Middle Ages. Her translation of Dante's *Divine Comedy* is unexcelled, especially in its notes revealing the Christian significance of the poem. In 1941 she prepared a series of radio plays on the life of Christ: *The Man Born to Be King*. In her book *The Mind of the Maker*, she excelled as a lay apologist for Christian doctrine, especially the doctrine of the Trinity.

December 19

1808   Birth of Horatius Bonar, Scottish clergyman and poet, in Edinburgh, Scotland. From a long line of Scottish clergy, Bonar was ordained in 1837 in Kelso. He left the State Church in 1843, but remained a minister, serving with the Free Church of Scotland. From 1866 to the end of his life (1889), he was pastor of Chalmers Memorial Church in Edinburgh. Bonar was a prolific writer and poet. He authored several missionary biographies and penned over 600 hymns, including "Here, O My Lord, I See Thee Face to Face" and "I Heard the Voice of Jesus Say."

1855 Birth of William Henry Draper, Anglican clergyman and author of the hymn "All Creatures of Our God and King," in Kenilworth, England. Ordained in 1880, Draper served parishes in Shrewsbury, Leeds, London and Somerset. Before his death in 1933, he published several collections of hymns. He penned over 60 hymns, many of which were translations from Latin and Greek. Draper's most popular translation, "All Creatures of Our God and King," is his English rendition of a Latin text by St. Francis of Assisi.

1860 Birth of Frank E. Graeff, American Methodist clergyman, in Tamaqua, Pennsylvania. Ordained in 1890, he served churches in the Philadelphia Conference. Graeff was always interested in children and became well known for his storytelling ability. He also authored over 200 hymns, including "Does Jesus Care?"

1909 Birth of W.A. (Wallie Amos) Criswell, American Southern Baptist clergyman, in Eldorado, Oklahoma. Ordained in 1928, Criswell pastored Oklahoma churches in Chickasha (1937–41) and Muskogee (1941–44). Since 1944 he has been pastor of First Baptist Church in Dallas, Texas. A former president of the Southern Baptist Convention, Criswell has preached throughout America. He has contributed many articles to religious journals and authored dozens of books on the Bible, including *The Gospel According to Moses* (1950), *Why I Preach the Bible Is Literally True* (1969) and *The Scarlet Thread Through the Bible* (1970). He and his wife, the former Bessie Marie Harris, married on Valentine's Day, 1937.

1944 Birth of Andrew Robert Culverwell, American sacred music songwriter. This contemporary music artist has written such popular Christian songs as "Born Again" and "Come On, Ring Those Bells," both sung by Evie Tournquist Karlsson.

1965 American Presbyterian apologist Francis Schaeffer declared in a letter: "God has given us rules not because He is arbitrary, but because the rules He has given us are fixed in His own character. And He has created man according to His own character . . . Thus, when we sin we break the law of God, but at the same time it is in the direction of destroying what we really are."

December 20

1488 Birth of Thomas Munzer, radical German reformer, in Stolberg, Germany. Munzer studied to be a priest, then briefly allied himself with Martin Luther in 1519. But he felt Luther's political conservatism did little to promote reform and justice for the poor. During a stormy pastorate at Zwickau (1520–23), Munzer instituted radical liturgical changes; but his reliance on direct inspiration from the Holy Spirit brought him into dispute with Luther. Expelled from Zwickau, Munzer began preaching open rebellion, which ultimately led to the Peasants' War (1524–25) against the princes. Munzer led riotous attacks against monasteries and preached the ruthless killing of the ungodly. Philip of Hesse finally defeated Munzer's peasant army in 1525, and Munzer was beheaded.

1552 Death of Katherine von Bora (b.1499), former German nun and wife of German reformer Martin Luther. Her mother died while Katherine was still young. When her father remarried, Katherine was sent to a Cistercian cloister in Nimbschen, Germany, where her aunt was the abbess. Katherine took her vows at age 16. She began hearing of the Augustinian monk, Martin Luther, who lectured on the Bible at Wittenberg. Soon after, monks and nuns began seeking freedom from their monastic living. Katherine and eight others from her convent joined the exodus, and were covertly taken to Wittenberg in a merchant's wagon. All the other woman found husbands; and in 1525, Luther married "Katie." She was 26, he was 42. Biographers agree that their marriage was a happy one. They cared for their six children, as well as Luther's relatives who came to visit and students who attended the university in Wittenberg. Luther died in 1546; Katie, six years later at age 53.

1787 The United Society of Believers in Christ's Second Appearing, the Shaking Quakers or Shakers, began a revival movement in colonial America that ignited religious fervor among other denominations, especially in Kentucky and other frontier regions.

1803 Death of Samuel Hopkins (b.1721), colonial American theologian. Converted under the preaching of George Whitefield and Gilbert Tennant, Hopkins studied theology under Jonathan Edwards. He pastored two Congregational churches during his life: one in Great Barrington, Massachusetts (1743–69), and the other at Newport, Rhode Island (1769–1803). For the last 30 years of his ministry, Hopkins wrote and preached against slavery—the first American Congregational abolitionist. His best-known work was the book *System of Doctrines Contained in Divine Revelation Explained and Defended* (1793).

1822 Birth of Samuel G. Green, English Baptist clergyman, in Falmouth, England. After pastoring from 1844–51, he taught at Rawdon College (1851–63). From 1863–76 he served as president of Rawdon. In 1876 he became the book editor of the Religious Tract Society in London, not retiring from the work until 1899. Green was also a trustee of the John Rylands Library in Manchester, a vice-president of the British and Foreign Bible Society, and president of the Baptist Union of Portsmouth. Green authored many books on the Bible, church history and related subjects. His most important works are *Handbook to the Grammar of the Greek Testament* and *Handbook to the Hebrew of the Old Testament*.

1845 Baldwin Institute was first chartered in Berea, Ohio by Methodists. In 1854 the school changed its name to Baldwin University. In 1914 the college joined with German Wallace College and adopted the new name Baldwin-Wallace University.

1856 Newberry College was chartered in Newberry, South Carolina, under Lutheran auspices. The main campus was transferred to Walhalla, South Carolina, in 1868, but returned to Newberry in 1877.

1863 Birth of C.C. (Charles Cutler) Torrey, American biblical linguist. He taught at Andover Seminary (1892–1900) then at Yale University (1900–32). As first director of the School of Oriental Research in Jerusalem (1900–01), Torrey was a specialist in Aramaic and in apocryphal and pseudepigraphical literatures. His scholarly writings include *The Translations Made from the Original Aramaic Gospels* (1912), *The Composition and Date of Acts* (1916), and *Documents of the Primitive Church* (1946). Torrey believed that Aramaic originals lay behind large portions of the New Testament writings, a theory that has found little favor among modern biblical scholars.

1934 Death of Adelaide A. Pollard (b.1862), American hymnwriter and religious mystic. Raised by Presbyterian parents, Pollard taught in several girls' schools in Chicago during the 1880s, and later at Nyack Missionary Training Institute in New York. Though in constantly poor health, Pollard was attracted to extreme religious sects, living the life of a mystic. She wrote a number of hymns, including "Have Thine Own Way, Lord."

1945 The Far Eastern Broadcasting Company, Inc., was incorporated in California. This international, interdenominational, evangelical radio ministry broadcasts the Gospel primarily to Asia, in over 70 different languages, as well as providing discipleship material and Bible correspondence courses.

1961 Swiss reformed theologian Karl Barth noted in a letter: "What God chooses for us children of men is always the best."

December 21

69 Death of Vitellius, who became Emperor of Rome for a short time in "the year of the Four Emperors." Vitellius ruled only from April to December of this year, and was executed by Vespasian.

1597 Death of Peter Canisius (b.1521), Dutch-born Roman Catholic reformer. He joined the Jesuits in 1543 and founded a Jesuit colony at Cologne. He wrote three Catechisms, which went through 200 editions and were translated into 12 languages. His singular abilities in educational reform, preaching, teaching, apologetics and pastoral work attracted many other talented men to the Jesuit order. More than any other single person, Canisius established the Counter-Reformation in southern Germany and Austria.

1620 The Mayflower anchored off Plymouth, Massachusetts, after a brief exploratory expedition, concluding a 63-day voyage across the Atlantic Ocean. The 102 colonists, including the 35 Pilgrims, began disembarking the day after Christmas. Following the winter at port in Plymouth, the Mayflower set sail for its return trip to England in April 1621.

1672 Birth of Benjamin Schmolck, German Lutheran clergyman, in Brauchitzchdorf, Germany. Ordained in 1701, he was appointed pastor of the Friedenskirche at Schweidnitz in 1702, remaining there until his death in 1737. Because of the Catholic restrictions on the number and locations of Lutheran churches in Silesia, Schmolck's Schweidnitz church had to serve 36 villages. Nevertheless, Schmolck found time to pen over 900 hymns. Schmolck was not a Pietist, yet his hymns reveal the warmth of intimate and practical Christianity. His most popular song is "My Jesus, As Thou Wilt."

1672 Birth of Johann Christoph Schwedler, German clergyman and author of the hymn "Ask Ye What Great Thing I Know," in Krobsdorf, Silesia, Germany. He pastored his last 30 years (1700–30) at Niederweise. His fame as a preacher grew, and great crowds attended his worship services. It is said that he would preach again and again between 5:00 a.m. and 3:00 p.m. without stopping, as worshipers filled the church in succession. Schwedler wrote more than 500 hymns during his life. The major theme of his lyrics was the grace of God available through Christ, and the joy-filled confidence available to every believer.

1776 Anglican clergyman and hymnwriter John Newton explained in a letter: "It is necessary that our sharpest trials should sometimes spring from our dearest comforts, else we should be in danger of forgetting ourselves and setting up our rest here. In such a world . . . we shall often need something to prevent our cleaving to the dust, to quicken us to prayer and to make us feel that our dependence for one hour's peace is upon the Lord alone."

1795 Birth of Robert Moffat, Scottish missionary and translator, in Ormiston, Scotland. His early education was meager; and at 14 he was apprenticed to a gardener. But he was converted and soon became interested in missions. In 1816 he was sent to Cape Town, South Africa, under the London Missionary Society. In 1820 he married Mary Smith, who had come there from London. The couple settled at Kuruman in Bechuanaland in 1825, where they established the headquarters for their next 45 years of mission work. They returned to England from 1839–43, promoting the cause of missions in Africa. Moffat inspired David Livingstone (1813–73) to go. In 1845 Livingstone married Moffat's daughter Mary. Moffat and his wife served as missionaries until failing health forced their retirement in 1870. While on the field, Moffat finished a translation of the Bible into Sechvana in 1859. He also authored a hymn book and published two missionary textbooks on South Africa.

1807 Death of John Newton (b.1725), Anglican clergyman and hymnwriter. Newton began his life as a profligate seaman involved in the slave trade. He was miraculously turned toward God during a storm at sea in March 1748. He abandoned this degrading profession four years later to become a port clerk. Influenced by Charles Wesley and George Whitefield, Newton began studying for the ministry. In 1764, at age 39, Newton was ordained into the Anglican ministry. His first appointment was the parish at Olney, where he remained 16 years (1764–79). English poet William Cowper was a member of Newton's congregation; together they wrote a number of Christian songs, published in 1779 under the title *Olney Hymns*. Newton had written 282 of the 349 selections, including such favorites as "Amazing Grace," "Glorious Things of Thee Are Spoken" and "How Sweet the Name of Jesus Sounds."

1835 Oglethorpe University was chartered in Milledgeville, Georgia, under Presbyterian auspices. In 1913 the campus moved from Milledgeville to Atlanta.

1860 Birth of Henrietta Szold, American Zionist leader, in Baltimore, Maryland. In 1912 Szold founded Hadassah, an American Zionist organization dedicated to health work in Palestine. "*Hadassah*" is the Hebrew name Esther, the name of the Old Testament heroine. Szold served as the first president of Hadassah.

1889 Death of J.B. Lightfoot (b.1828), Anglican clergyman and textual scholar. Following his ordination in 1858, he began teaching at Trinity College, Cambridge. He remained there in various posts until appointed Bishop of Durham in 1879, an office he held for his last ten years. One of the most learned men of his time, Lightfoot was best at assessing facts rather than ideas. His enduring critical works in the areas of biblical studies and patristics won him great fame. He completed three commentaries: *Galatians* (1865), *Philippians*

(1868), and *Colossians / Philemon* (1875). His work on the *Apostolic Fathers* (1869, 1885) set new standards in textual criticism. Although quiet by nature, Lightfoot helped many young graduates in their training for the ministry.

1906 Death of Robert Rainy (b.1826), clergyman and leader in the Free Church of Scotland. Born and educated in Glasgow, Rainy pastored in Aberdeenshire (1851–54) and Edinburgh (1854–62). From 1862–1900, he taught church history at Edinburgh. Reunification of the Scottish Presbyterian churches was a burning issue with Rainy; and he saw the disestablishment of the Church of Scotland as the only means of accomplishing the goal. He found sympathy for his vision with British Prime Minister W.E. Gladstone. In 1900 Rainy led the Scottish Free Church into union with the United Presbyterians.

1918 Birth of Dr. Robert P. Evans, American missions pioneer. In 1949 Evans founded the European Bible Institute. In 1952 its name was changed to Greater Europe Mission. Headquartered since 1979 in Wheaton, Illinois, G.E.M. is an interdenominational, evangelical sending agency engaged in evangelism, church planting, literature distribution and theological education. Its overseas staff of over 250 works in nearly a dozen European countries.

1938 Death of James M. Black (b.1856), American Methodist chorister and composer of the hymn tune for "When the Roll Is Called Up Yonder." Having studied music at an early age, Black made a living by teaching singing schools. He also published more than a dozen Christian songbooks through the Methodist Book Concern. An active Methodist all his life, Black was appointed to the Joint Commission for the *Methodist Hymnal* (1905).

December 22

1216 Pope Honorius III officially approved the *Ordo Praedicatorum* or Order of Preachers (the Dominicans). Known in England as Black Friars, the order was founded earlier in 1216 by St. Dominic. Devoting themselves to study and preaching, the members of the order relinquished ownership of property, gave up manual labor and lived by begging. During the Middle Ages, many leaders of European thought were Dominicans. The papacy also used them for preaching crusades and for staffing the Inquisition. In addition, the Dominicans followed Portuguese and Spanish explorers to the Americas as missionaries.

1552 Death of St. Francis Xavier (b.1506), Spanish Jesuit missionary to the Orient. An aristocrat by birth, he was one of the six young men who joined Ignatius of Loyola in forming the Society of Jesus (the Jesuits) in 1534. Ordained a priest in 1537, Xavier traveled to India as a missionary in 1541. He worked in missions around Goa, but later extended his work into South India and Ceylon. He traveled the Malay Archipelago and sailed for Japan in 1549. He died on the island of Sancian, trying to get into China. Canonized in 1622, he is considered one of the greatest of the Roman Catholic missionaries. The Jesuits credit him with more than 700,000 conversions.

1582 This date became Jan. 1, 1583 in Belgium when that nation officially adopted the new Gregorian calendar. The old Julian Calendar had been designed by Julius Caesar in 46 B.C., and had been the standard calendar of Christian nations from Roman times on. But after 16 centuries, the Julian calendar had lost 10 days against "sun time." The new calendar by Pope

Gregory XIII was designed to keep time with the solar calendar. By 1950, the Gregorian calendar had been adopted worldwide.

1770 Birth of Father Demetrius Augustine Gallitzin (d. 1840), "Apostle to the Alleghenies," in the Hague, Netherlands. Born the son of a Russian nobleman, Gallitzin was converted to Catholicism in 1787. He arrived in America five years later, attended Baltimore Seminary, and was ordained into the priesthood in 1795. He devoted the remainder of his life to his work as a frontier missionary. Sometimes called "Father Smith," Gallitzin built up the Catholic church in the Alleghenies (parts of Pennsylvania, Maryland, Virginia and West Virginia), exhausting his personal fortune in the process. Gallitzin, Pennsylvania was named for him.

1804 Anglican missionary to Persia Henry Martyn commented in his journal: "I look forward to a day of prayer; for my soul hath great need of quickening and restoration, that it may act more in the view of eternity."

1833 Roman Catholic cardinal John Henry Newman stated in a letter: "All things one tries to do must be mixed with great imperfection, and it is part of one's trial to be obliged to attempt things which involve incidental error and give cause for blame. This is all very humbling, particularly when a person has foretold to himself his own difficulties and scrapes, and then is treated as if he was quite unconscious of them, and thought himself a very fine fellow."

1837 Mercer University was chartered in Penfield, Georgia, under Baptist support. In 1871 the college moved to Macon, Georgia.

1862 American revivalist Billy Sunday lost his father in the U.S. Civil War, five months after he had enlisted in the Union Army. William Ashley ("Billy") was only one month old.

1888 Death of Isaac Thomas Hecker (b.1819), American Catholic priest and founder of the Paulists. Baptized a Lutheran at birth, Hecker associated briefly with Methodism and later with transcendentalism. In 1844 he was baptized a Roman Catholic, and entered the Redemptorist order the following year. Completing his novitiate in Europe, he returned to the U.S., where he felt the need for an English-speaking order to evangelize American Protestants. In 1858 he formed the Missionary Society of St. Paul the Apostle (the Paulist Fathers or Paulists). Hecker was superior general of the society his remaining 30 years. He also founded *The Catholic World* in 1865, the chief Roman Catholic periodical in the U.S. today, and edited it until his death.

1899 Death of Dwight L. Moody (b.1837), American evangelist. Born in Northfield, Massachusetts, he went to Boston at 17 to work as a clerk in his uncle's shoe store. He was led to faith in Christ there through his Sunday-school teacher, Edward Kimball. In 1856 he moved to Chicago, and by 1860 was preaching there full time. With organist and Gospel singer Ira D. Sankey, Moody conducted revivals in the British Isles 5 times in 31 years (1860, 1870, 1873–75, 1881–84 and 1891). His Northfield, Massachusetts, conferences for college students led to the formation of the Student Volunteer Movement. Moody also founded the Chicago (now Moody) Bible Institute (1886). He married Emma C. Revell (sister of religious publisher Fleming H. Revell), who taught him social graces and bore him three children.

1921 The first radio station license for a religious broadcaster in the U.S. was granted to the National Presbyterian Church of Washington, D.C. Within the next 5 years there were more than 60 licensed religious stations, including KJS-Biola/Los Angeles in 1922, KFUO-Concordia/St. Louis in 1924, and WMBI-Moody Bible Institute/Chicago in 1926.

December 23

1569 St. Philip of Moscow, Primate of the Russian Orthodox Church, was martyred by Ivan the Terrible.

1648 Birth of Robert Barclay, Quaker theologian, at Gordonstown, Scotland. Interested briefly in Roman Catholicism while studying in Paris, Barclay returned to Scotland and followed his father into the Society of Friends in 1667. Barclay became an itinerant evangelist, traveling throughout Great Britain, Holland and Germany. In 1673 he published *A Catechism* and *Confession of Faith*, the nearest thing to a Quaker confession of faith ever written. In 1676 he published his most famous work: *An Apology for the True Christian Divinity*, a systematic presentation of the mystical spiritualism on which Quakerism is based. Barclay's writings made him the most prominent—indeed, the only—remarkable theologian of the early Quaker faith. Barclay spent his last seven years as Governor of East New Jersey (1683–90), even though he never traveled to the New World.

1652 Death of John Cotton (b.1584), Massachusetts Bay Colony pastor. Born in Derby, England, Cotton was ordained in 1610 in the Anglican Church. His increasing interest in Puritan ideas and in New England led him to Boston, where he arrived in 1633. A close friend of John Winthrop, he served as teaching pastor at the Boston Congregational Church until his death. Cotton was involved in the controversies with both Roger Williams and Anne Hutchinson. He stressed both the unconditional nature of election and the inner experience of the Holy Spirit in regeneration.

1790 Birth of Jean Francois Champollion, French Egyptologist, at Figeac, France. His mastery of ancient languages at a young age led to his first teaching appointment at Grenoble in 1809. Champollion succeeded in decoding the hieroglyphics of the Rosetta Stone in 1822 (discovered in 1799). In 1828 he conducted a scientific expedition to Egypt, and in 1831 was appointed to teach Egyptology at the College de France. Though some of his linguistic claims were disputed after his death, Champollion is, nevertheless, recognized as the founder of modern Egyptology.

1841 Birth of Handley C.G. (Carr Glyn) Moule, Anglican theologian, at Fordington, England. Ordained in 1867, he pastored at his father's church in Dorset from 1867–80. He began a teaching career at Trinity College (1873–77), and taught later at Cambridge (1881–1901). In 1901 he succeeded B.F. Westcott as Bishop of Durham. Moule supported the English Reformation. He believed in the authority of Scripture, and was associated with the Keswick Movement in his latter years. He was a profound scholar, but could speak and write for ordinary people. He published commentaries on nearly all the Pauline epistles.

1862 Birth of Amos R. Wells, American Christian educator. From 1891 until his death in 1933, he was editorial secretary of the newly organized United Society of Christian Endeavor, forerunner of the youth fellowship organizations in today's churches. Beginning in 1901, Wells also edited *Peloubet's Notes for the International Sunday School Lessons*.

1889 Birth of Emil Brunner, Swiss dialectical theologian, in Winterthur, Switzerland. After pastoring at Obstalden from 1916–24, he began teaching theology at Zurich (1924–53). One of the more influential theologians of the 1920s and 1930s, Brunner was a colleague of Karl Barth's, but broke with him in 1934 over Barth's denial of the efficacy of general revelation. An original thinker, Brunner's *The Mediator* (1927; English translation 1934) was the first neo-orthodox Christology. Brunner was deeply influenced by Soren Kierkegaard and Martin Buber, and he rejected both theological liberalism and evangelical orthodoxy. He also regarded communism as "an anti-religion without God" in which all the elements of Antichrist are present. His most comprehensive work was his three-volume *Dogmatics* (1946–60; English translation 1949–62).

December 24

1491 Birth of Ignatius Loyola, founder of the Jesuits, in Guipuzcoa, Spain. Crippled for life by a battle wound in 1521, Ignatius began reading books on the life of Christ by St. Dominic and Francis of Assisi. He dedicated his life to the service of Jesus Christ and entered a Dominican monastery at age 30. But, like Martin Luther, he found that mortification of the flesh does not bring peace to a troubled soul. However, Ignatius found peace by yielding himself with full abandon to the traditions of the church. In 1522 he wrote the *Spiritual Exercises*. In 1534 Ignatius and six companions adopted the demands of the *Spiritual Exercises*, took vows of poverty, chastity and obedience and formed the Society of Jesus. The new religious order was approved by Pope Paul III in 1540, and Loyola was made its first general. The Jesuits became a great power in the Catholic church, leading the Counter-Reformation. Loyola, who died in 1556, was canonized in 1622 by Pope Gregory XV.

1541 Death of Andreas Carlstadt (b.ca.1477), German Protestant reformer. In support of Martin Luther's 95 theses, he wrote, in 1518, 380 theses on the supremacy of Scripture and the fallibility of church councils. Therefore, the papal bull, *Exsurge Domine* which condemned Luther and other reformers, included Carlstadt. But there were differences between the theologies of Carlstadt and Luther. Carlstadt was more austere, mystical and more works-oriented. Luther supported his beliefs with Scripture, but Carlstadt claimed direct revelation from the Holy Spirit. In many ways, Carlstadt's variation on Luther's themes anticipated the German Pietism which sprang from stagnated Lutheranism during the 17th-18th centuries.

1784 Methodism was officially organized in the U.S., in Baltimore, Maryland. Francis Asbury was consecrated the first Methodist bishop in America a few days later. The Methodist church did not officially separate from the Church of England, however, until 1791.

1784 American statesman James Madison published his famous *Remonstrances Against Religious Assessments* in Virginia. This document advocated the separation of church and state, which became a growing ideal in the new American nation.

1813 Birth of Henry W. Greatorex, American sacred music organist, in Derbyshire, England. After receiving his music education in England, Greatorex emigrated to the U.S. in 1839. Between 1839 and his death in 1858, Greatorex served as the organist at Episcopal churches in Hartford, Connecticut, New York City and Charleston, South Carolina. He published several collections of traditional and original hymns. Of his own 37 original melodies, at least 2 remain popular: GLORIA PATRI ("Glory Be to the Father") and SEYMOUR ("Gentle Jesus, Meek and Mild").

1816 James Montgomery's new hymn, "Angels from the Realms of Glory," first appeared in print, being published in the *Iris*, a Sheffield, England newspaper edited by Montgomery himself.

1818 Austrian church organist Franz Gruber composed a guitar tune for pastor Joseph Mohr's poem "Stille Nacht, Heilige Nacht," and the congregation of St. Nicholas Church in Oberndorf sang "Silent Night" for the first time.

1866 Birth of Annie Johnson Flint, a crippled poet. She wrote the poem "Hands and Feet for Him," which says: "Christ has no hands but our hands/ To do His work today; He has no feet but our feet/ To lead men in His way. . . ."

1870 Death of Albert Barnes (b.1798), American Presbyterian clergyman and Bible expositor. He pastored at Morristown, New Jersey, from 1825–30 and at the First Presbyterian Church in Philadelphia from 1830–67. He was examined by the Second Presbytery of Philadelphia in 1835 for espousing an unlimited atonement. Although he was acquitted, his ideas became a catalyst for the 1837 split in the Presbyterian church in the U.S. Barnes was an active abolitionist and strong advocate of the Sunday school. His most famous work is the 11-volume *Notes on the New Testament* and *Notes on the Old Testament*, both still in print and widely used.

1871 The Northside Tabernacle in Chicago was dedicated by Dwight L. Moody. This tabernacle became the original structure of what is today the Moody Memorial Church.

1915 Death of William H. Doane (b.1832), American Baptist businessman and hymnwriter. Raised in Connecticut, he was converted at 17. After becoming a machinery manufacturer, he later moved to Cincinnati, Ohio (1860), where he lived the rest of his life. A beloved civic and church leader, Doane was superintendent of the Mt. Auburn Baptist Sunday School for over 25 years. In spite of his business commitments, he also composed many hymn tunes. His most successful songs were collaborations with Fanny J. Crosby, who frequently provided texts for tunes he had sent to her. Many of Doane's hymn tunes are still popular in Christian worship, including I AM THINE ("I Am Thine, O Lord"), MORE LOVE TO THEE ("More Love to Thee, O Christ"), NEAR THE CROSS ("Jesus, Keep Me Near the Cross"), OLD, OLD STORY ("Tell Me the Old, Old Story"), RESCUE ("Rescue the Perishing"), PRECIOUS NAME ("Take the Name of Jesus with You") and PASS ME NOT ("Pass Me Not, O Gentle Savior").

1922 Religious radio broadcasting began in the British Isles when the Rev. J.A. Mayo gave a 10-minute talk over "the wireless" just 40 days after its first commercial installation in England.

1933 The famous ancient Greek Bible manuscript Codex Sinaiticus first arrived in London. Discovered by C. Tischendorf in the monastery of St. Catherine on Mount Sinai, the New Testament manuscript was acquired by the Czar of Russia. The new communist Soviet government sold the 4th-century manuscript to the trustees of the British Museum for 100,000 pounds.

1943 German Lutheran theologian and Nazi martyr Dietrich Bonhoeffer observed in a letter from prison: "Gratitude changes the pangs of memory into a tranquil joy."

1949 Death of William C. Poole (b.1875), American Methodist clergyman and author of the Gospel song "Just When I Need Him Most." Born on a farm in Maryland, Poole was converted to Christ at age 11, ordained to the Methodist ministry at age 25 and served pastorates in the Wilmington Conference for the next 35 years. Through the motivation of Charles H. Gabriel, Poole began writing Gospel song texts.

1951 *Amahl and the Night Visitors*, a Christmas musical, had its TV debut. Written by Italian-American composer Gian Carlo Menotti, it was the first musical to be broadcast over television.

1968 The Apollo 8 astronauts became the first men to orbit the moon. In the midst of their ten orbits, they read the first ten verses of Genesis 1, the creation story, to listeners on earth.

December 25 — Christmas Day

800 Pope Leo III crowned Charlemagne (768–814) the first ruler of the Holy Roman Empire, an event which has sparked religious and political controversy ever since. The symbolic significance of the head of the Roman Catholic Church giving the crown of secular authority is still disputed.

1413 In a letter penned two years before he was martyred, Bohemian reformer John Huss declared: "Rejoice, that the immortal God is born, so that mortal men may live in eternity."

1537 German reformer Martin Luther was recorded as saying: "It is the most ungodly and dangerous business to abandon the certain and revealed will of God in order to search into the hidden mysteries of God."

1723 The German Baptists (the Dunkards) held their first immersion service in America at Germantown, Pennsylvania.

1766 Birth of Christmas Evans, Welsh Baptist preacher, near Cardigan, Wales. Converted at age 17, Evans was afterward beaten so badly by his former companions that he lost his sight in one eye. Ordained in 1789, he began an evangelistic ministry lasting 35 years (1791–1826) on the island of Anglesey off the Welsh coast. He moved to Caernarvon, Wales, in 1832 and remained there the rest of his life. Evans' great strength as a preacher lay in his oratorical imagination. Welsh tradition holds him up as one of its three greatest evangelists, alongside John Elias and William Williams of Wern.

1821 Birth of Clara (Clarissa Harlowe) Barton, American humanitarian and founder of the American Red Cross, in Oxford, Massachusetts. Her heroic services to American Civil War wounded brought her to a nervous collapse several years later. While recuperating in Europe, Barton worked with the International Red Cross in Geneva, Switzerland. She returned to the U.S. and helped organize the American chapter of the Red Cross in 1881. She was elected its first president, and served from 1881–1904. Barton, a universalist, was also an advocate of temperance, women's rights and improved social conditions.

1865 Birth of Evangeline Cory Booth, English social reformer and general of The Salvation Army, in London, England. Daughter of William Booth, the founder of The Salvation Army, she supervised field operations in Great Britain, Canada and Alaska. In 1904 she was promoted to commander of the American branch of the S.A., and in 1934 was elected General of the International Salvation Army. Before her retirement in 1939, she published several books and also authored many well-known Salvation Army hymns.

1918 Death of J. (John) Wilbur Chapman (b.1859), American Presbyterian evangelist. Ordained in 1882, Chapman held four pastorates in Ohio, Indiana, New York and Pennsylvania between 1884–1905. Nevertheless, he devoted more than half his ministry to evangelism. He worked at one time with D.L. Moody, and later, for ten years, with evangelistic songleader Charles M. Alexander. Chapman's evangelistic tours took him to many large American cities, as well as to a number of foreign countries. He was made the first director of the newly founded Winona Lake Bible Conference, and he did much to develop other such conferences. From 1903 until his death, Chapman was Executive Secretary of the Presbyterian General Assembly's committee on evangelistic work.

1931 Missionary radio station HCJB, located in Quito, Ecuador, under the World Radio Missionary Fellowship, Inc., first began broadcasting the Gospel to the nations of Eastern Asia.

December 26

1065 The first building of Westminster Abbey, in England, was dedicated. According to legend, the abbey was founded as early as 616, and was refounded by Edward the Confessor in 1050 as an abbey of Benedictine monks. From the 18th century on, the abbey has been the burial place for many famous Englishmen.

1356 Emperor Charles IV (1316–78) issued the famous *Golden Bull*. The document transformed the Holy Roman Empire from a monarchy into an aristocratic federation. Seven electors were named, each a virtual sovereign: the Archbishops of Mainz, Trier, and Cologne; the Count Palatine of the Rhine; the Duke of Saxony; the Margrave of Brandenburg; and the King of Bohemia. These electorates were to be indivisible, and were to be passed on by primogeniture. No mention of papal rights or claims was made in the document. The *Golden Bull* remained the constitution of the Holy Roman Empire for 450 years, until 1806.

1620 Plymouth Colony was settled by the *Mayflower* Colonists on the coast of present-day Plymouth, Massachusetts, five days after their sailing vessel weighed anchor in Plymouth Harbor. The following year a peace treaty was made with the neighboring Wampanoag Indians, which lasted for 50 years. In 1691 Plymouth joined other settlements in the area to form the royal colony of Massachusetts.

1822 Birth of Richard Francis Weymouth, English Baptist philologist, in Plymouth Dock, Devonshire, England. Having taught in France as well as at Surrey and Plymouth, England, Weymouth was appointed in 1869 to teach at London University, where he remained until 1886. He retired to devote himself to Bible study and to textual analysis of the Greek New Testament. The most noted of his subsequent writings was *The New Testament in Modern Speech*, based on his earlier *Resultant Greek Testament*, and published in 1903, the year after Weymouth's death.

1836 Death of Hans G. Nageli (b.1773), Swiss pioneer music educator and composer of the hymn tune for "Blest Be the Tie That Binds" (DENNIS). He established a music publishing firm at age 19, and went on to become founder and president of the Swiss Association for the Cultivation of Music. His innovative methods of teaching music influenced individuals such as Lowell Mason, who used Nageli's methods in the U.S.

1838 Wake Forest College was chartered in Wake Forest, North Carolina. It was founded under Baptist auspices in 1834.

1968 Death of Kenneth Scott Latourette (b.1884), American Baptist church historian. Educated at Yale University, Latourette began his teaching career in China in 1909, until ill health forced him home in 1912. After his recovery, he began teaching at Yale in 1921. He authored many books on church history and Christian missions. Latourette's greatest literary achievements are his *History of the Expansion of Christianity* (seven vols., 1937–45) and *Christianity in a Revolutionary Age* (five vols., 1958–62). Latourette never married, but continued to live on campus in his bachelor quarters at Yale, even after his retirement from full-time teaching in 1953.

1970 American Presbyterian apologist Francis Schaeffer admitted in a letter: "We can fail after we are truly Christians because becoming a Christian does not rob us of our true humanity."

December 27

1774 English founder of Methodism, John Wesley, explained in a letter: "Although there is much advantage in long experience, and we may trust an old soldier more than a novice: yet God is tied down to no rules; he frequently works a great work in a little time. He makes young men and women wiser than the aged, and gives to many, in a very short time, a closer and deeper communion with himself, than others attain in a long course of years."

1784 In Baltimore, Maryland, at the first general conference held in America, Francis Asbury was ordained the first American bishop of the Methodist Church.

1797 Birth of Charles Hodge, the leading American Reformed theologian of the 19th century, in Philadelphia, Pennsylvania. Having studied theology under Archibald Alexander, Hodge began teaching at Princeton Seminary in 1820. With the exception of two years (1826–28), he remained at Princeton the rest of his life, 58 years in all. During a half-century of teaching and writing, Hodge instructed over 3,000 students. He held a high view of verbal inspiration and biblical inerrancy. In 1825 he founded the *Biblical Repository*, later renamed the *Princeton Review*, and was editor for over 40 years. A voluminous writer, Hodge's most important work was his three-volume *Systematic Theology* (1872–73). Before his death in 1878, he was considered by some "the greatest American Calvinist theologian since Jonathan Edwards."

1893 Birth of Samuel ("Sam") Shoemaker, American Episcopal clergyman and writer, in Baltimore, Maryland. Ordained in 1921, he was rector of Calvary Episcopal Church in New York City from 1925. He gained his enthusiasm for evangelism from a brief association with Frank Buchman's Oxford (Moral Rearmament) group. Shoemaker became a popular lecturer, counselor and radio speaker. He helped Alcoholics Anonymous develop its "Twelve Steps" formula. Shoemaker's numerous publications include *Realizing Religion* (1921), *Religion That Works* (1928), and *Twice Born Ministers* (1929).

1899 American temperance leader Carry Nation raided and wrecked her first saloon in Medicine Lodge, Kansas. In 1901 she began wielding a hatchet, to help expedite her work, as she went on similar rampages in Wichita and Topeka, Kansas, and other cities in Iowa and Illinois.

1902 Death of Richard F. Weymouth (b.1822), English Baptist philologist and New Testament scholar. He taught in a private school in Surrey, and later founded a school for boys in Plymouth, England. In 1869 Weymouth was appointed to London University, where he taught until 1886. He retired to devote himself to biblical study and to textual criticism of the Greek New Testament. The most notable of his publications, *The New Testament in Modern Speech*, was based on his earlier *Resultant Greek Testament*, and was first published in 1903, a year after his death.

1908 Followers of the prophet Lee J. Spangler gathered on top of South Mountain, near Nyack, New York, to await the end of the world. They wore white robes for the occasion.

1931 Death of Peter C. Lutkin (b.1858), American Episcopal choral director and organist. He held his first position as church organist at age 14, in Chicago's St. James Cathedral. After serving in other positions as organist and music teacher, Lutkin became the first dean of the School of Music established by Northwestern University in 1896. He earned a reputation as an excellent choral conductor and lecturer on sacred music. He was one of the founders of the American Guild of Organists, and served as president of the Music Teacher's National Association (1911, 1920). He was on the editorial committee for both the *Methodist Hymnal* (1905) and the *Episcopal Hymnal* (1918). Among Lutkin's many compositions, one which remains in popular use is the hymn tune LANIER, to which we sing Sidney Lanier's "Into the Woods My Master Went."

1937 Death of Cyrus S. Nusbaum (b.1861), American Methodist clergyman. Ordained in 1886, Nusbaum served six pastoral appointments in Kansas. He was a chaplain during World War I, then traveled throughout the Midwest as a conference evangelist. During his ministry, Nusbaum wrote and composed many hymns, including "Would You Live for Jesus, and Be Always Pure and Good?" (a.k.a. "His Way with Thee").

December 28

1524 Death of Johann von Staupitz (b.ca.1469), German monastic educator. He was appointed professor at the University of Wittenberg in 1502, then vicar-general of his Augustinian order the following year. Staupitz advocated Bible study, moral reform in the church and the strengthening of his religious order. In 1508 he called 25-year-old Martin Luther to teach at Wittenberg. In 1512 Luther succeeded Staupitz as professor of theology. Through his example of piety, Staupitz occupies an important place in the early history of the Reformation. He became a positive influence on Martin Luther's life, much as Edward Kimball was to Dwight L. Moody.

1741 English revivalist George Whitefield advised in a letter: "Go to bed seasonably, and rise early. Redeem your precious time: pick up the fragments of it, that not one moment of it may be lost. Be much in secret prayer. Converse less with man, and more with God."

1832 St. Louis University was chartered under the Roman Catholic Church at St. Louis, Missouri. Founded in 1818 as St. Louis Academy, and known as a college since 1820, it was the first Roman Catholic university to be established in the U.S. west of the Allegheny Mountains.

1838 Greensborough Female College was chartered in Greensboro, North Carolina, under the Methodists. In 1913 the name of the school was changed to Greensboro College for Women, and was changed again in 1920 to Greensboro College.

1847 Birth of Samuel A. Ward, American music publisher, in Newark, New Jersey. Having received his early training in music in New York City, Ward returned to Newark and established a successful retail music store. He also took an active role in the music life of the city, playing organ at the Grace Episcopal Church of Newark for many years. Ward composed the tune MATERNA, the melody to which we sing "America, the Beautiful" ("O Beautiful for Spacious Skies").

1866 Birth of John M.P. Smith, American Baptist Bible scholar, in London, England. Educated in the U.S., Smith taught Semitic language and literature at the University of Chicago for 33 years (1899–1932). He also edited several religious and archeological journals in addition to writing many articles and books. Smith worked with E.J. Goodspeed on the 1931 *The Bible—An American Translation*.

December 29

1170 Martyrdom of Thomas a Becket (b.ca.1118), English Roman Catholic and Archbishop of Canterbury. A student of law during his earlier years, Thomas was raised to chancellor of England in 1155 by King Henry II, becoming one of the best chancellors in English history. In 1162 he was elected Archbishop of Canterbury, and Becket turned his full allegiance to the church. His entire manner changed from pomposity to asceticism. In 1164 Becket fell out of favor with Henry and was forced to flee to France for six years. In 1170 through the Pope's intervention, Becket was permitted to return safely to England. Again he raised the king's ire; and Henry, in a fit of rage, uttered words that inspired four of his knights to go to Canterbury and assassinate Becket in his cathedral. Becket's shrine in Canterbury became one of the chief attractions for pilgrims in Christendom.

1809 Birth of William E. Gladstone, British statesman, in Liverpool, England. Educated at Eton and Oxford, Gladstone would have entered the Anglican ministry had not his father planned a political career for him. Gladstone entered Parliament in 1832, and continued serving there until 1895. He was a devout Anglican and an evangelical Christian, a humanitarian, a student of the Bible and a man of prayer. Gladstone sought to base his decisions on moral and spiritual grounds. In 1869 he helped dissolve the Anglican Church in Ireland. His better-known religious writings include *The State in Its Relation with the Church* and *The Impregnable Rock of Holy Scripture*.

1841 Howard College was chartered in Marion, Alabama, under Baptist sponsorship. The campus relocated to Birmingham, Alabama, in 1887.

1849 Pastor Edmund H. Sears' Christmas hymn "It Came upon a Midnight Clear" was published. It first appeared in the Dec. 29 issue of *The Christian Register*. The hymn has been described as one of the first of the carol-like hymns that seem to have sprung from American poets. Hymns stressing the social message of Christmas—"peace on earth, good will toward men"—are distinctly American.

1851 The first Y.M.C.A. in the U.S. was organized in Boston, Massachusetts.

1876 Popular American hymnwriter Philip P. Bliss (b.1838) died in a tragic railroad accident near Astabula, Ohio. The train in which Bliss and his wife were riding plunged off a bridge into a ravine 60 feet below and burned. Bliss survived the fall, but returned to the wreckage to rescue his wife. He perished with her in the fire. Bliss was only 38 years old. He had written and composed many hymns, including "Almost Persuaded," "Hallelujah, What a Savior," "I Will Sing of My Redeemer," "The Light of the World Is Jesus," "Wonderful Words of Life," "I Gave My Life for Thee" and "Let the Lower Lights Be Burning."

1925 The Board of Trustees of Trinity College in Durham, North Carolina, changed the name of the school to Duke University in exchange for a $40 million trust fund from the estate of James B. Duke, recently deceased founder of the American Tobacco Company.

1980 Death of John R. Rice (b.1895), American Baptist evangelist and editor. Born and raised in Texas, Rice taught briefly, pastored for a short time and served in the U.S. Army briefly. He became an evangelist, holding many city-wide campaigns across the country. Rice later became a radio pastor, and editor and publisher of *The Sword of the Lord*, a fundamentalist monthly newspaper he founded in 1934. Rice published over 100 books and pamphlets.

December 30

39 Birth of Flavius Titus, early Roman Emperor (ruled A.D. 79–81). The son of Roman Emperor Vespasian (ruled A.D. 69–79), Titus was instrumental in suppressing the Jewish Revolt of 66–70. Sent to Jerusalem in the Spring of 70, his armies besieged the city for six months, until Sept. 8, when the last strongholds were broken. Josephus reported that over 1,000,000 perished in the city's destruction. Titus returned to Rome victorious, and was the actual ruler during his father's last nine years as emperor.

1678 Birth of William Croft, English sacred music organist and choir director, in Nether Eatington, Warwickshire, England. He composed the hymn tune for "O God, Our Help in Ages Past" (ST. ANNE). During his earlier years, Croft composed secular theater music, but later devoted himself entirely to sacred music. Croft has become one of the greatest names in English sacred music history, especially because of his psalm tunes. His are the earliest examples of the English psalm tune, distinguished from the Genevan (Swiss) or French psalm tunes.

1741 English revivalist George Whitefield lamented in a letter: "O how little do I for Jesus, who has done so much for me."

1823 American revivalist Charles G. Finney (1792–1875) was licensed to preach. A former lawyer, he had taken up preaching from his conversion. He became the most effective evangelist America has ever seen. Over half a million people were converted under his ministry.

1838 Hanover College was chartered by the Presbyterian General Assembly of Indiana. The school had been founded by Rev. John Finley Crowe the previous year as a seminary "in the wilderness" for training ministers.

1843 Cumberland University was chartered in Lebanon, Tennessee, under Presbyterian auspices. The school had been founded the previous year.

1892 Death of Andrew A. Bonar (b.1810), Scottish clergyman. The youngest brother of Horatius Bonar, Andrew began his ministry in 1838 and joined the Free Church, like his older brother, in 1843 when it began. From 1856 until his death, he pastored at the Finnieston Church in Glasgow. He was identified with the evangelical and revival movements of his day, and at different times, worked with both Dwight L. Moody and Robert Murray McCheyne. Like his brother Horatius, Andrew was also an ardent premillenialist.

1937 Birth of Noel Paul Stookey, American folk singer and music producer. Stookey first became a celebrity as "Paul" of the 1960s folk trio Peter, Paul and Mary. He is now a Christian recording artist, operating his own recording studio. He prefers his "born-again" name Noel.

1947 Death of Alfred North Whitehead (b.1861), English philosopher and theologian. Emigrating to the U.S. in 1924, he taught at Harvard until his retirement in 1938. Whitehead was instrumental in laying the foundations of process theology, which defines reality as time, process and "evolutionary becoming," rather than as unchanging substance. Process theology differs from Christian orthodoxy in that it views God as dependent on human decisions, evolving through history. Orthodoxy affirms a transcendent, unchanging God. Whitehead's philosophy was heavily influenced both by G.W.F. Hegel and Darwinian evolution. Whitehead, in turn, has influenced the theologies of Pierre Teilhard de Chardin, Charles Hartshorne and Norman Pittenger.

December 31

1384 Death of John Wycliffe (b.1328), English reformer and theologian. Though raised in the Catholic church, Wycliffe was repulsed by the "Babylonian Captivity" (1305–77) of the papacy in Avignon, France, and embarrassed at having two popes during the Great Schism (1378–1417). In his disdain, Wycliffe turned to the Scriptures and early church fathers for guidance. He eventually developed his own view of the true church. Wycliffe maintained that every person is a servant of God, and that the church does not provide the only access to grace nor possess the right to unquestioned secular sovereignty. Known as "the Morning Star of the Reformation," Wycliffe received support for his ideas among the aristocracy in England, especially after 1380. His writings also had a major influence on England's poorer clergy, such as the Lollards, and on others, such as Czech scholar John Huss. Wycliffe spent his last four years in retirement, devoting himself to a new translation of the Bible—the first translation of the Scriptures into English.

1530 The Schmalkald League was formed in Germany on the heels of the Diet of Augsburg. Purely a defensive alliance, it was a league of Protestant princes who opposed the efforts of Holy Roman Emperor Charles V to stamp out Lutheranism in Germany. The alliance survived until 1547, when the forces of Charles V defeated the Protestants in the Battle of Muhlberg, and the city of Wittenberg fell during the Schmalkaldic War.

1687 The first shipload of emigrating Huguenots (French Protestants) left France for South Africa.

1701 In Friesland, Holland, this date became Jan. 12, 1702, when this northern province of the Netherlands officially adopted the Gregorian calendar. The old Julian calendar had been prepared by Julius Caesar in 46 B.C., and had been the standard calendar of Christian nations from Roman times. Over 16 centuries, the Julian calendar had lost 10 days against the sun. The 1582 calendar by Pope Gregory XIII was designed to keep pace with the solar year. By 1950, the Gregorian calendar had been adopted worldwide.

1712 Birth of Peter Bohler, Moravian missionary, in Frankfort-on-Main, Germany. In 1737 he was appointed by Count Zinzendorf to travel to the American colonies, by way of London, to work among the blacks of South Carolina and Georgia. While in London, he met John Wesley, who had just returned from his mission in Georgia. Bohler taught Wesley the joy of personal conversion and self-surrendering faith and Wesley incorporated these spiritual emphases within the Methodist movement. Upon arrival in Georgia, Bohler found the mission in shambles. Abandoning the work, he migrated with the remaining members to a new settlement in Bethlehem, Pennsylvania. In 1747 Bohler was made superintendent of the Moravian Church in England. He returned to work in America (1753–64), and was appointed superintendent of the Moravian Church in America in 1756.

1823 Birth of William Orcutt Cushing, American Christian Church clergyman, in Hingham, Massachusetts. He served 5 different pastorates in the New York area for over 20 years. Following the death of his wife in 1870, ill health forced him to retire from the active ministry. He developed a deep interest in hymn-writing, and before his death in 1902, Cushing penned over 300 hymns. His most famous hymns are "When He Cometh," "Under His Wings," "Ring the Bells of Heaven" and "Hiding in Thee."

1837   Birth of John R. Sweney, American sacred music chorister, in Westchester, Pennsylvania. He taught music from age 22. Following the U.S. Civil War, he served 25 years as professor of music at the Pennsylvania Military Academy. Sweney was in great demand as a song leader at summer Christian assemblies, including Ocean Grove, New Jersey; Lake Bluff, Illinois; New Albany, Indiana; Old Orchard, Maine; Round Lake, New York; and many others. He composed more than 1,000 Gospel songs and published more than 60 collections of sacred music. His most enduring hymn melodies include I SHALL KNOW HIM ("When My Life-Work Is Ended, and I Cross the Swelling Tide"), STARS IN MY CROWN ("I Am Thinking Today of that Beautiful Land"), STORY OF JESUS ("Tell Me the Story of Jesus"), SUNSHINE ("There Is Sunshine in My Soul Today") and SWENEY ("More About Jesus I Would Know").

1900   Birth of Stephen C. (Charles) Neill, British Anglican clergyman and scholar, in Edinburgh, Scotland. Ordained in 1926, Neill has taught at such prestigious universities as Cambridge, Hamburg, Oxford and Union Seminary. In addition to preaching and teaching, Neill has served as a foreign missionary and has been an international ecumenical leader. A prolific writer, some of his better-known titles include *A History of Christian Missions* (1964), *The Interpretation of the New Testament, 1861–1961* (1964, 1966), and *The Modern Reader's Dictionary of the Bible* (1966).

Index

Booth, William: 1/19; 4/10; 7/5; 8/20; 9/3; 11/2; 12/25
Bora, Katherine von: 1/29; 6/13; 12/20
Bornkamm, Heinrich: 6/26
Borthwick, Jane L.: 4/9; 9/20, 7; 10/22
Borthwick, Sarah: 4/9
Bosco, St. John: 8/16
Bottome, Frank: 5/26; 6/29
Bourbon, Louis de: 5/7
Bowie, Walter Russell: 10/8
Bowman, Dr. Robert H.: 3/16; 4/26; 6/4
Bowring, John: 10/17; 11/23
Bradbury, William B.: 1/8; 8/17; 10/6, 7, 18
Bradford, William B.: 9/16
Brady, Nicholas: 7/30
Brahms, Johannes: 4/3; 5/7
Brainerd, David: 1/2, 17; 2/3, 8, 20, 23; 3/3, 20, 28; 4/1, 8, 15, 20, 26; 5/24; 6/12, 14, 21, 22; 10/5, 9; 11/25
Bratcher, Robert G.: 4/17; 9/15
Bray, Thomas: 2/15
Bray, William (Billy): 5/25; 6/1; 11/4
Breakspear, Nicholas: 9/1; 12/4
Breck, Carrie Ellis: 1/22; 3/27
Brenz, Johann: 8/5
Brewster, William: 9/16
Bridgers, Luther B.: 2/14; 5/27
Bridges, Matthew: 7/14; 10/6
Bridges, Robert S.: 4/21
Briggs, Charles Augustus: 1/15; 5/12; 6/1, 8; 9/6
Briggs, Emilie Grace: 3/17
Bright, Bill: 8/28; 10/19
Bright, Vonette: 8/28; 10/19
Broadus, John Albert: 1/24; 3/16
Brocar, Arnold Guillen de: 1/10
Brock, Blanche Kerr: 1/3; 2/3
Brock, Virgil P.: 1/3, 6
Broger, Dr. John: 6/4
Broger, John: 3/16; 4/26
Bromily, G.W.: 9/23
Bromily, Geoffrey: 3/7
Brooks, Phillips: 1/23; 5/2; 8/7; 10/14; 12/13
Brown, Charlie: 11/26
Brown, F.: 9/6
Bruce, A.B. (Alexander Balmain): 1/30; 8/7
Bruce, F.F. (Frederick Fyvie): 10/12
Brunner: 4/6
Brunner, Emil: 4/6; 12/23
Bryan, William Jennings: 7/10; 10/21
Buber, Martin: 2/8; 4/6; 6/13; 12/23
Bucer: 9/8; 12/12
Buchanan, President James: 9/11
Buchman, Frank N.: 6/4; 8/7; 11/17; 12/27
Buckoll, Henry J.: 6/6; 9/9
Buck, Pearl S.: 6/26

Budry, Edmond L.: 8/30; 11/12
Buell, Harriett Eugenia Peck: 2/6; 11/2
Buhl, F.: 9/6
Buksbazen, Victor: 9/1
Bullinger, Ethelbert William: 12/15
Bullinger, Heinrich: 3/27
Bullinger, Henry: 7/18; 9/17
Bultmann, Rudolf: 7/30; 9/14; 11/11
Bunyan, John: 2/18; 6/1; 8/18, 31; 11/30
Buonarroti, Michelangelo (see Michelangelo)
Burba, Alexander: 10/27
Buren, Abigail Van: 7/4
Burgess, John Melville: 12/8
Burnell, Elizabeth: 11/14
Burnet, Gilbert: 9/18
Burney, Charles Fox: 11/4
Burroughs, George: 8/19
Burrows, Millar: 10/26
Burton, Ernest DeWitt: 5/26
Burton, Spence: 11/1
Butler, Joseph: 5/18; 6/16
Buttrick, George Arthur: 3/23
Byron: 2/19

C

Cabrini, Mother Frances Xavier: 7/7
Caesar, Julius (see Julius Caesar)
Caesarius of Arles: 7/3; 9/11
Calixtus II: 3/18
Calixtus, George: 12/14
Calkin, John Baptiste: 3/16; 4/15
Callixtus II: 4/6
Calvin, John: 1/16, 31; 3/5, 14; 4/12; 5/15, 27; 7/4, 10, 18, 24; 8/1, 20; 9/17; 10/24; 11/24; 12/4, 9
Campbell, Alexander: 3/4; 9/12
Campbell, Thomas: 3/4; 8/17; 9/12
Campion, St. Edmund: 4/15
Canisius, Peter: 12/21
Canitz, Friedrich R.L.: 8/11; 11/27
Carey, William: 6/9; 8/17; 10/2
Carlson, Dr. Paul E.: 11/24
Carlstadt, Andreas: 5/27; 12/24
Carmichael, Amy Wilson: 12/16
Carmichael, Ralph: 5/27
Carrier, Martha: 8/19
Carroll, Father John: 1/23; 6/9
Carroll, John: 5/31; 8/15
Carter, President Jimmy: 10/6
Carter, Russell K.: 8/23; 11/18
Cartwright, Peter: 9/1, 25
Cary, Alice: 9/4
Cary, Phoebe: 9/4
Cash, Johnny: 2/26
Cassian, John: 7/3

Mather, Cotton: 2/12, 13; 8/23
Mather, Increase: 2/13; 6/21; 8/23; 9/5
Mather, Richard: 8/17
Matheson, George: 3/14, 27; 4/8; 6/6; 8/28
Mathews, Shailer: 5/26; 10/23
Matthews, Timothy R.: 1/5; 11/4
Maurice, F.D.: 7/30
Maurin, Peter: 5/1
Maxentius: 1/22, 28
Maximianus, Galerius Valerius: 2/24
Mayo, J.A.: 12/24
Mead, Frank S.: 1/15
Means, Jacqueline: 1/1; 9/16
Medici, Catherine de: 8/24
Medley, Samuel: 6/23; 7/19
Meineke, Charles: 5/1; 11/6
Melanchthon, Philip: 2/15, 20; 4/19, 25; 5/21; 9/17; 7/18; 10/1, 4
Mendel, Gregor Johann: 1/6; 7/22
Mendelssohn, Felix: 2/3; 8/22; 11/4
Mendozo Grajales, Father Don Martin Francisco Lopez de: 9/8
Menotti, Gian Carlo: 12/24
Mercer, W. Elmo: 2/15
Merrill, William P.: 1/10; 2/16; 6/19
Merton, Thomas: 1/31; 3/3; 7/28; 9/11, 19; 11/24; 12/10
Messenger-Harris, Beverly: 6/1
Messiter, Arthur H.: 4/1; 7/2
Metzger, Bruce M.: 2/9
Meyer, F.B. (Frederick Brotherton): 2/10; 3/28; 4/8
Meynell, Wilfred: 11/13; 12/16
Michelangelo: 2/18; 3/6; 5/21, 30; 8/26; 11/1
Migne, Jacques Paul: 10/24, 25
Miller, Dr. Basil William: 2/26; 3/26; 5/7, 19; 9/22; 10/1
Miller, Esther Kirk: 5/19; 6/9; 9/22; 10/1
Miller, Lewis: 8/4
Miller, William: 4/23; 10/22
Milligan, George: 4/2, 7; 10/11; 11/25
Millikan, Robert A.: 11/1
Mill, John Stuart: 7/30
Milman, Henry H.: 2/10; 9/24
Milton, John: 3/27; 4/27; 8/27; 11/8; 12/9
Minear, Paul S.: 2/17
Minor, George A.: 1/29; 12/7
Moffat, Mary: 3/19
Moffat, Robert: 3/19; 8/9; 12/21
Moffatt, James: 6/27; 7/4
Mohammed: 6/8
Mohr, Joseph: 6/7; 8/25; 10/30; 12/5, 11, 24
Molay, Jacques de: 3/11
Moltmann, Jurgen: 4/4
Monica, mother of St. Augustine: 11/13
Monk, W.H.: 12/15

Monk, William H.: 3/1, 16; 12/15
Monroe, Harry: 11/19
Monsell, John S.B.: 3/2
Montefiore, Moses: 11/9
Montessori, Maria: 8/31
Montgomery, James: 4/30; 11/4
Montini, Cardinal Giovanni Battista: 6/21, 30; 9/26
Moody, Betsy Holton: 5/28
Moody, Dwight L. (Lyman): 1/3, 28; 2/2, 5, 26, 28; 3/4, 5, 11, 28; 4/2, 19, 21; 5/28; 7/16; 8/13, 28, 30; 9/1, 5, 9; 10/3, 6, 10, 16, 20, 26; 11/8, 12, 21, 22; 12/5, 22, 24, 25, 28, 30
Moody, Edwin: 1/3; 5/28
Moody, Emma: 10/10
Moody, Joseph N.: 10/18
Moore, Clement C.: 7/10, 15
Moore, George Foote: 5/16; 10/15
Moore, John M.: 9/1
Moore, Thomas: 2/25; 5/28
More, Hannah: 9/7
More, Sir Thomas: 2/7; 7/6
Morgan, G. Campbell: 5/16; 8/20, 27; 12/9
Morgan, Nancy: 8/20
Moroni: 9/22
Morris, Lelia Naylor: 4/15
Morrison, Robert: 1/5; 8/1
Morse, Samuel F.B.: 5/24
Mote, Edward: 1/21; 11/13
Mott, John R.: 1/31; 5/25
Moule, C.F.D. (Charles Francis Digby): 12/3
Moule, Handley C.G. (Carr Glyn): 5/8; 12/23
Moulton, James Hope: 4/7, 2; 10/11; 11/25
Moulton, William F.: 2/5; 3/14; 10/11
Mountain, James: 6/27
Mowinckel, Sigmund O.P.: 8/4
Mozart, Wolfgang Amadeus: 1/27; 3/31; 12/5, 17
Mueller, George: 4/11; 9/27; 11/1
Muhlenberg, Henry Melchior: 9/6; 10/7
Muntzer, Thomas: 3/10; 5/15, 27; 12/20
Murray, Andrew: 1/18; 5/9
Murray, James R.: 3/10, 17

N

Nageli, Hans G.: 5/26; 12/26
Nakada, Juji: 9/24; 10/29
Nanzianzus, Gregory: 1/1
Nast, William: 6/15; 8/19
Nation, Carry A. (Amelia): 6/9; 11/25; 12/27
Nave, Orville J.: 4/30; 6/24
Neal, Daniel: 12/14
Neale, John Mason: 1/24; 8/6

Y

Yates, John Henry: 9/5; 11/21
Yeats, W.B.: 3/31
Youderian, Roger: 1/8; 10/29
Young, Brigham: 8/29; 9/11
Young, John F.: 10/30

Z

Zahn, Theodor: 10/10
Zinzendorf, Count Nickolaus Ludwig von:
    4/27; 5/9, 26; 12/31
Zundel, John: 12/10
Zwemer, Samuel M.: 3/23; 4/12, 29
Zwingli, Ulrich: 1/1; 2/7; 3/10, 31; 4/2; 7/18;
    9/5, 8, 17; 10/1, 4, 11, 27; 11/11; 12/4,
    12